Venture Capital

The International Library of Management
Series Editor: Keith Bradley

Titles in the Series:

Venture Capital

Edited by

Mike Wright

The Centre for Management Buy-out Research, School of Management and Finance, University of Nottingham

and

Ken Robbie

The Centre for Management Buy-out Research, School of Management and Finance, University of Nottingham

Dartmouth
Aldershot · Brookfield USA · Singapore · Sydney

Published by
Dartmouth Publishing Company Limited
Gower House
Croft Road
Aldershot
Hants GU11 3HR
England

Dartmouth Publishing Company
Old Post Road
Brookfield
Vermont 05036
USA

British Library Cataloguing in Publication Data
Venture capital. – (The international library of
    management)
    1. Venture capital
    I. Wright, Michael, 1952–   II. Robbie, Ken
    658.1′522

Library of Congress Cataloging-in-Publication Data
Venture capital / edited by Mike Wright and Ken Robbie.
        p.   cm. — (The international library of management)
    Includes bibliographical references.
    ISBN 1-85521-855-0
    1. Venture capital. I. Wright, Mike, 1952–   . II. Robbie, Ken.
III. Series.
HG4751.V458   1997
332′.0415—dc20   96-19708
                                                                                    CIP

ISBN 1 85521 855 0

Printed in Great Britain by Galliard (Printers) Ltd, Great Yarmouth

Contents

PART V ALTERNATIVE SOURCES OF VENTURE CAPITAL: INFORMAL VENTURE CAPITALISTS, CORPORATE VENTURE CAPITAL AND RELATIONSHIP BANKING

Acknowledgements

The editors and publishers wish to thank the following for permission to use copyright material.

American Finance Association for the essays: Paul A. Gompers (1995), 'Optimal Investment, Monitoring, and the Staging of Venture Capital', *Journal of Finance*, **L** (5), pp. 1461–89; Anat R. Admati and Paul Pfleiderer (1994), 'Robust Financial Contracting and the Role of Venture Capitalists', *Journal of Finance*, **XLIX**, pp. 371–402; Josh Lerner (1995), 'Venture Capitalists and the Oversight of Private Firms', *Journal of Finance*, **L** (1), pp. 301–18; William L. Megginson and Kathleen A. Weiss (1991), 'Venture Capitalist Certification in Initial Public Offerings', *Journal of Finance*, **XLVI**, pp. 879–903.

Baylor University for the essay: Mike Wright, Ken Robbie, Yves Romanet, Steve Thompson, Robert Joachimsson, Johan Bruining and Artur Herst (1993), 'Harvesting and the Longevity of Management Buy-outs and Buy-ins: A Four-Country Study', *Entrepreneurship: Theory and Practice*, **18**, Winter, pp. 90–109. Copyright © 1994 by Baylor University.

Blackwell Publishers for the essays: Gordon C. Murray (1995), 'Evolution and Change: An Analysis of the First Decade of the UK Venture Capital Industry', *Journal of Business Finance and Accounting*, **22**, pp. 1077–106. Copyright © 1995 Blackwell Publishers Ltd; James O. Fiet (1995), 'Risk Avoidance Strategies in Venture Capital Markets', *Journal of Management Studies*, **32**, pp. 551–74. Copyright © 1995 Blackwell Publishers Ltd; R.C. Sweeting (1991), 'UK Venture Capital Funds and the Funding of New Technology-Based Businesses: Process and Relationships', *Journal of Management Studies*, **28**, pp. 601–22.

Elsevier Science Inc. for the essays: Ian C. MacMillan, Lauriann Zemann and P.N. Subbanarasimha (1987), 'Criteria Distinguishing Successful from Unsuccessful Ventures in the Venture Screening Process', *Journal of Business Venturing*, **2**, pp. 123–37. Copyright © 1987 Elsevier Science Publishing Inc.; Ian C. MacMillan, David M. Kulow and Roubina Khoylian (1988), 'Venture Capitalists' Involvement in Their Investments: Extent and Performance', *Journal of Business Venturing*, **4**, pp. 27–47. Copyright © 1988 Elsevier Science Publishing Inc.; John C. Ruhnka, Howard D. Feldman and Thomas J. Dean (1992), 'The "Living Dead" Phenomenon in Venture Capital Investments', *Journal of Business Venturing*, **7**, pp. 137–55. Copyright © 1992 Elsevier Science Publishing Inc.; Sanford B. Ehrlich, Alex F. De Noble, Tracy Moore and Richard R. Weaver (1994), 'After the Cash Arrives: A Comparative Study of Venture Capital and Private Investor Involvement in Entrepreneurial Firms', *Journal of Business Venturing*, **9**, pp. 67–82. Copyright © 1994 Elsevier Science Publishing Inc.; Hollister B. Sykes (1990), 'Corporate Venture Capital: Strategies for Success', *Journal of Business Venturing*, **5**, pp. 37–47. Copyright © 1990 Elsevier Science Publishing Inc.

Series Preface

The International Library of Management brings together in one series the most significant and influential articles from across the whole range of management studies. In compiling the series, the editors have followed a selection policy that is both international and interdisciplinary. The articles that are included are not only of seminal importance today, but are expected to remain of key relevance and influence as management deals with the issues of the next millennium.

The Library was specifically designed to meet a great and growing need in the field of management studies. Few areas have grown as rapidly in recent years, in size, complexity, and importance. There has been an enormous increase in the number of important academic journals publishing in the field, in the amount published, in the diversity and complexity of theory and in the extent of cross-pollination from other disciplines. At the same time, managers themselves must deal with increasingly complex issues in a world growing ever more competitive and interdependent. These remarkable developments have presented all those working in the field, whether they be theorists or practitioners, with a serious challenge. In the absence of a core series bringing together this wide array of new knowledge and thought, it is becoming increasingly difficult to keep abreast of all new important developments and discoveries, while it is becoming ever-more vital to do so.

The International Library of Management aims to meet that need, by bringing the most important articles in management theory and practice together in one core, definitive series. The Library provides management researchers, professors, students, and managers themselves, with an extensive range of key articles which, together, provide a comprehensive basis for understanding the nature and importance of the major theoretical and substantive developments in management science. The Library is the definitive series in management studies.

In making their choice, the editors have drawn especially from the Anglo-American tradition, and have tended to exclude articles which have been widely reprinted and are generally available. Selection is particularly focused on issues most likely to be important to management thought and practice as we move into the next millennium. Editors have also prefaced each volume with a thought-provoking introduction, which provides a stimulating setting for the chosen articles.

The International Library of Management is an essential resource for all those engaged in management development in the future.

KEITH BRADLEY
Series Editor
The International Library of Management

Introduction[1]

In the last 15 years, venture capital has emerged as an important area of finance for academic researchers. This interest lags well behind the development of the industry both in the US and elsewhere. Venture capital can be defined broadly as the investment by professional investors of long-term, risk equity finance where the primary reward is an eventual capital gain, rather than interest income or dividend yield. Earlier reviews of the literature have covered the period up to 1981 (Tyebjee and Bruno, Chapter 4 in this volume), from 1981 to 1988 (Fried and Hisrich, 1988) and more recent research (although less exhaustively, by Barry (1994)). The emphasis in these earlier reviews has been on US studies which focus primarily on formal venture capital as early-stage finance, frequently with a high technology aspect. Yet the potential contribution of venture capital and venture capitalists goes far beyond this limited perspective.

Not only does venture capital have an input to the debate about so-called equity gaps in the provision of finance to new small firms, but it may also widen the emerging literature on corporate restructuring which has hitherto tended to focus on debt forms of finance (Jensen, 1993).[2] In addition, venture capitalists provide important insights into the wider corporate governance debate. Given that a particular feature of venture capitalists is their involvement in an investee company, their role can have implications for both performance and accountability simultaneously (Lorenz, 1989, p.5). Much of the recent corporate governance debate has tended to emphasize accountability to the detriment of the equally important issue of promoting enhanced performance;[3] that is, negative control rather than positive added value. The management of these two aspects is a crucial feature of the operation of venture capitalists. This review therefore encompasses the range of investment stage activities undertaken by venture capitalists, which includes development capital, management buy-outs and management buy-ins.

This book aims to draw together a set of readings which cover the principal issues raised in venture capital. Papers were selected on the basis that they had appeared in journals and represented significant contributions to the subject area. The *Journal of Business Venturing* provides a particularly rich source of material relating to venture capital; as such, the journal figures prominently in the set of papers presented here. However, there is a growing diversity of studies which reflects the broader scope of interesting research questions which are raised by the concept of venture capital. This in turn is evident in the range of journals from which we have drawn the papers contained in this volume.

The papers selected are grouped under five main headings: The Institutional Framework; The Venture Capital Process: Screening, Valuation and Contracting; Venture Capital Monitoring; Investment Realization and Performance; and Alternative Sources of Venture Capital: Informal Venture Capitalists, Corporate Venture Capital and Relationship Banking. This Introduction sets the readings in the context of the wider body of literature on venture capital and is structured in line with these themes. Part I outlines the nature of venture capitalists and their international diffusion. Part II reviews existing literature concerning the roles of venture capitalists in relation to their clients in the context of a model of the venture capital process. These issues concern pre-contracting problems, deal valuation and structuring. Part III examines post-transaction monitoring, restructuring and failure. Part IV deals with evidence on investment realization and the performance of venture capital firms. Part V compares the operation of venture capitalists to other, potentially competing, forms of finance, in particular informal venture capital, LBO associations, corporate venturing and banks. To conclude we present conclusions and suggestions for further research.

Institutional Framework

Two broad distinctions may be made between formal venture capitalists: firstly, the investment stages targeted by venture capitalists and, secondly, their main sources of capital. In terms of investment stages, it has been suggested that late-stage investors, especially those investing in smaller buy-outs, should not be considered venture capitalists (e.g. Bygrave and Timmons, 1992); however, given that many such venture-backed transactions can involve considerable product and organizational innovation, this argument seems debatable (Wright, Robbie and Ennew, 1995). There is growing recognition of the need to consider the portfolio mix of investment stages adopted by venture capitalists (see e.g. Elango et al., 1995), especially given evidence on the differing returns from the various investment stages, to which we return below. Moreover, industry statistics encompass in the term 'venture capitalists' all stages of investment (Table 1). While some venture capitalists do invest across the range of investment stages, others invest only in late-stage projects. As much of the activity of venture capitalists is focused on later-stage investments, the term 'private equity capitalists' may increasingly become a more appropriate descriptor.

The second distinction has traditionally concerned the sourcing of funds used by venture capitalists. 'Captive' venture capitalists, which are part of banks or insurance companies, do not have to raise capital from third parties (Abbott and Hay, 1995). In the UK they are often viewed as investing primarily in later-stage projects such as development capital and management buy-outs and buy-ins. 'Independent' firms tend to be seen as the more traditional type of venture capitalist. They are typically funded through limited-life closed-end funds and are more committed than captives to generating a return for investors through realizing a capital gain within a more clearly specified period of time; the latter are more likely to place a higher emphasis on the income stream from their investments. Recent developments, however, have meant that traditional captive institutions have become more hybrid as they source funds from outside to add to those provided by their parent bank or insurance company.

The governance of venture capital firms, and the monitoring by such firms of their investees, are crucial aspects of the phenomenon. A pioneering study by Sahlman (Chapter 1 in this volume) examines, in a principal-agent context, the relationship between funds providers and venture capitalists. In particular a contract between the two parties is established to provide incentives for mutual gain and the specific prohibition of certain acts on the part of the venture capitalist which would cause conflicts of interest, together with the expenditure of resources on monitoring the venture capitalist. Venture capitalists also agree to supply specific information to the funds providers on a regular basis. The terms of the

Table 1: Venture Capital Investment by Stage in Main European Markets (% of value invested in 1994)

Market (descending size order)	Early Stage %	Expansion %	Buy-out/Buy-in %
UK	2.5	32.5	65.0
France	2.3	68.6	29.1
Germany	10.2	54.2	35.6
Italy	15.6	48.6	36.8
Netherlands	13.0	67.0	20.0

Source: EVCA (1995).

contract both communicate the expectations of funds providers and filter out those venture capitalists who are unable to meet these requirements. Agreements in specialist funds typically have a limited life which exposes venture capitalists to possible non-renewal if they fail to perform. Venture capitalists' remuneration is typically based on a modest annual management fee plus some percentage of the realized profits from the fund. Mechanisms are also introduced to ensure that gains are distributed to the investors rather than kept inside the fund. Sahlman points out that good venture capitalists – by accepting a finite funding life and performance dependent compensation – are signalling their quality in relation to weak ones, but that the funds provider has to invest in intensive screening in order to guard against false signalling.

A significant agency problem may also arise in the valuation of investments for the purposes of reporting to providers of funds. It is venture capitalists as agents who are responsible for such valuations and on which their performance will be judged (Fried and Hisrich, 1994). However, since it may take many years for a venture capital investment to come to fruition, considerable subjectivity surrounds the valuation of investments in any particular year before the investment is realized. In the absence of clear and 'complete' rules, management may have the scope and incentive to report biased interim investment values. The adoption of different valuation practices also makes it difficult to compare the performance of individual venture capital firms. Moreover, in the case of syndicated transactions, such practice leads to a range of valuations for individual investee companies. In an attempt to produce a more consistent approach to valuation in the UK, the BVCA has introduced guidelines which recommend four appropriate valuation methods for its members (BVCA, 1993).

From major initial developments in the US, there has been a diffusion of venture capital market growth first to the UK and then throughout Europe and beyond.[4] Studies have examined the factors influencing such diffusion. Manigart (1994) finds support for a population ecology approach in identifying what drives the creation of a venture capital firm. Using data relating to the UK, France and the Netherlands, she finds that the major influence on the overall founding rate is the density of the industry – that is, the number of firms which already exist. Institutional changes, notably the establishment of a secondary tier stock market or favourable taxation regimes, were found not to influence the founding rate of venture capital firms. Tyebjee and Vickery (1988) note the variation in maturity of different venture capital markets in Europe. Ooghe et al. (1991) show that characteristics of mature markets in Europe are the presence of pension funds and insurance companies as investors, greater syndication of investments, the absence of the government as an investor and a high proportion of investments accounted for by management buy-outs (see Table 1 for indications in relation to the five largest markets in Europe). Wright et al. (1992), in focusing on management buy-out markets in Europe, also make the link with developed venture capital markets and refer to the need for favourable tax regimes and the presence of well-versed accounting intermediaries. In Chapter 2, Murray analyses the strategic issues confronting mature venture capital industries, notably that in the UK. His analysis shows that, in a maturing market, the impact of environmental factors on valuations and fund raising, together with intensifying inter-firm rivalry, have a marked influence on increasing the following: concentration, the importance of marketing and product differentiation, the emphasis both on later-stage investments and on performance.

The nature of the development and operation of venture capital markets may also be influenced by the objectives of venture capital firms. In Chapter 3, Hurry et al. compare Japanese and US venture capital firms and identify significantly different motivations. US firms were found to operate a 'project strategy' seeking direct gains, while Japanese firms generally operated an 'option strategy'. The latter involves the recognition that venture capital investment potentially offers the opportunity to obtain new technology for the investing firm; through an initial investment, the venture capital firm gains an implicit right, or option, which may be exercised by making further subsequent investment necessary to adopt the new technology.[5]

The Venture Capital Process: Screening, Valuation and Contracting

In appraising potential investments, venture capitalists as principals are faced both with uncertainty and an adverse selection problem. As agents, they are also faced with the risk that, if they do not perform satisfactorily, they will fail to attract further funding. Moral hazard problems faced by venture capitalists as principals arise in the post-investment monitoring of their investee companies as agents for their fund providers. Reid et al. (1995) show that venture capitalists attempt to manage the risks involved in their activities, firstly, through fine filters on proposals, high hurdle rates of return and being strongly resistant to downside risk exposure to address adverse selection and, secondly, through tight monitoring and an unwillingness to bear all the risk in order to address moral hazard issues.

Tyebjee and Bruno (in Chapter 4) made a major contribution to identifying the stages in the venture capital process, thus giving rise to a number of further studies (e.g. Bygrave and Timmons, 1992; Fried and Hisrich, 1994; MacMillan et al., 1985; Sweeting, Chapter 15). The following sub-sections review evidence relating to these venture capitalist-investee stages. Issues concerning the relationship between funds providers and venture capitalists are examined in the next section.

Deal Generation and Screening – Pre-contracting Problems

Whenever a venture capital investment is being considered, institutions are faced with a potential adverse selection problem in that they are unable to gauge the managers' performance in the enterprise prior to deal completion (see Amit et al. in Chapter 6). Adverse selection issues also raise crucial problems in the potential effectiveness of post-transaction monitoring by institutional investors (Stiglitz and Weiss, 1981). To the extent that these problems lead investors to misjudge the situation, a deal and accompanying financial structure may be agreed which are inappropriate and possibly unviable. As a result, the control mechanism introduced by the commitment to meet the cost of servicing external finance may lead to sub-optimal decisions.

Amit, Glosten and Muller point out in Chapter 6 that, while the entrepreneur's familiarity with the industry, personal characteristics and track record can provide some insight for the venture capitalist, these criteria are at best partial predictors of future success. Sweeting (1991) points out that UK venture capitalists have been particularly proactive in deal generation in an attempt to reduce adverse selection problems by becoming more involved with entrepreneurs at an earlier stage. Problems may, however, vary between types of investment.

In a management buy-out, investing institutions may be guided by incumbent managements' experience in post and their deep knowledge of the business, but may face the problem that management have an incentive not to reveal full information in an attempt to obtain the most favourable terms. In a buy-in, as the entrepreneur comes from outside, there may be problems of asymmetric information, both in relation to their true skills and because it has not been possible to observe the manager in post (Robbie and Wright, 1996). In replacement and development capital situations, it may be difficult to judge whether the entrepreneur's apparent previous performance will continue in the future when his/her equity stake is diluted by the introduction of venture capital. These different entrepreneurial situations suggest the need for studies to identify empirically the extent and nature of potential adverse selection problems.

Amit, Glosten and Muller also show that, where venture capitalists are unable to assess private information about an entrepreneur's capabilities, low-ability entrepreneurs will accept the venture capitalist's price offer while high-ability entrepreneurs will not.[6] However, the extent to which venture capitalists raise the price of their involvement or simply refuse to invest is debatable. The use of equity ratchets (i.e. performance contingent contracts) is one reflection of how venture capitalists may raise the price, though this is typically used where the venture capitalist is satisfied with the quality of management but there is disagreement about the level and timing of meeting forecast performance.

Studies, primarily US based, which examine venture capitalist investment criteria have evolved from descriptions of the variables taken into account by venture capitalists to attempts to identify the relative importance of various criteria using a variety of rating and ranking scales and principally focused on start-ups (e.g. Bruno and Tyebjee, 1985; MacMillan et al., 1985 and Chapter 5; Hall and Hofer, 1993; Rah et al., 1994). In Chapter 5, an important relatively early (1987) study, MacMillan et al. show that the most important criteria used by venture capitalists in screening investment proposals were entrepreneurial personality and experience, with lesser dependence being placed on market, product and strategy. In a replication study, Fried et al. (1993) show that, six years on, venture capitalists have become more concerned with market acceptance and less demanding of high potential rates of return and quick exit, which these authors interpret as a more realistic view of venture potential. Murray (1994) provides similar findings in a European context. However, while providing useful insights, these studies are open to a number of criticisms: they primarily focus on early-stage investments rather than later-stage; they primarily use rating scales where individual respondents may attach differing importance to a particular score; they generally use mail questionnaires which may fail to obtain the full essence of the screening process; and they generally fail to identify the trade-offs which venture capitalists need to make between different criteria.

More recent studies have attempted to address these issues. In a critique of the questionnaire-based methodology and early-stage focus of many previous studies, Fried and Hisrich (1994) use detailed analysis of the process adopted by venture capitalists in specific cases covering the full range of investment stages. They suggest that venture capitalists make use of three generic criteria for screening investment – the viability and novelty of the project; the integrity, track record and leadership skills of management; and the possibility for high returns and an exit – before proceeding to detailed evaluation. Muzyka et al. (1995) emphasize the important point that venture capitalists have to make trade-offs between various criteria in their screening of investments, and that previous approaches fail to take this into account. Using conjoint analysis, Muzyka et al. importantly conclude that venture capitalists would prefer to select an opportunity which offers a good management team and reasonable financial and product market characteristics, even if it does not meet overall fund and deal requirements.

These last results are consistent with a recent study by Wright and Robbie (Chapter 8) of UK venture capitalists which showed that they place considerable emphasis on the specific attributes of a potential investee company in relation to assessing both its value and the rate of return to be expected from it. While accounting information is an important element in deal screening and in arriving at a valuation and a target rate of return, venture capitalists place most emphasis on very detailed scrutiny of all aspects of a business, typically including sensitivity analysis of financial information, discussions with personnel and assessing considerably more information of an unpublished and subjective kind. This use of information is quite different from that found in studies of investment analysts dealing with quoted companies (e.g. Arnold and Moizer, 1984).

There is some debate in the US literature about the extent to which the use of non-accounting information varies between different stages of investment (Elango et al., 1995; Fried and Hisrich, 1994; Carter and Van Auken, 1994). There appears to be greater consensus that later-stage investors will be more interested in market acceptance of a product and liquidity. Early-stage investors emphasize a range of product strength and market growth characteristics, particularly as early-stage transactions are technology-based, with little available data on market acceptance, and are geared more to projects that require a change in management.

A variety of issues broadly categorized as time restrictions, cost constraints and situational factors may directly impact the level of due diligence during an acquisition process (Harvey and Lusch, 1995). Evidence from buy-ins (Robbie and Wright, 1996) identifies a major problem related to the ability to obtain adequate up-to-date information concerning the target company. While due diligence is expected to be undertaken in a thorough manner, its cost in relation to transaction value in smaller buy-ins and time constraints in negotiations means that this ideal is difficult to achieve. There are indications that venture capitalists have adapted to such asymmetric problems through recent developments involving hybrid inside and outside management and investor buy-outs where there is direct negotiation between vendors and venture capitalists.

An important exception to the dearth of empirical studies on the role of intermediaries in entrepreneurs' venture capital search is the work of Hustedd and Pulver (1992) which examined the role of different types of intermediary in securing venture funds for their entrepreneurial clients. Their results showed that entrepreneurs who failed to seek advice were likely to be less successful in acquiring equity finance. The chances of failure were increased if they used bankers, public agencies or universities as intermediaries. While providing interesting insights, Hustedde and Pulver primarily addressed start-up, early and expansion funding stages. In a similar study but focusing on management buy-outs and buy-ins, Murray and Wright (1996) show that intermediaries play a modest role in the search for venture capital in smaller transactions, but that this is not the case for larger deals. They find that management generally takes the dominant role in the venture capital identification process and, particularly, the final choice decision. Given the considerable uncertainty of the process and the acknowledged inexperience of most managers in respect of obtaining venture finance, it is surprising that, in smaller deals, they involve their key advisers only late in the process, if at all. This has clear implications for the nature of the contracting process since it suggests an asymmetry in bargaining to the advantage of the venture capitalist.[7]

Valuation, Target Returns and Deal Structuring

Evidence shows that venture capital projects will in essence be valued by applying one or more valuation techniques to the financial and accounting information relating to the potential investee typically contained in the business plan submitted by management to the venture capitalist (Wright and Robbie, Chapter 8). Forward looking information in the Business Plan may be subject to sensitivity analysis both by management and their advisers and by the venture capitalist according to the expected influence on future performance of other information. Most importance appears to be attached to price earnings multiples-based valuation methods (Wright and Robbie, Chapter 8), particularly among later-stage investors, but with greater emphasis on DCF-based methods than is the case for assessment of quoted companies by investment analysts (Arnold and Moizer, 1984). The process is likely to involve several iterations based on assumptions about the future trend in performance to test the robustness of the point at which the proposed venture meets an acceptable IRR, the most common measure of performance used in the industry (Murray, 1991). Using data relating to the buoyant economic conditions of the late 1980s, Dixon (1991) suggests that little scrutiny of information to assess risk and adjust target IRRs takes place. However, Wright and Robbie (this volume) indicate that, by the early-mid 1990s, venture capitalists were undertaking widespread assessment of risk. Moreover, Murray and Lott (1995) show that venture capitalists perceive technology-based projects to be more risky than alternative later-stage projects and use a higher target rate of return in assessing them, but also that the stage of financing is significantly more important in determining project risk than the state of technology involved.

Relatively little attention has been devoted to financial structuring issues, yet an appropriate financial structure has important implications for the ability of venture capitalists to earn their target rates of return, irrespective of the monitoring devices they introduce. Norton and Tenenbaum (1992) find that venture capitalists favoured the use of preference shares regardless of the presence or absence of deal specific influences, and that the use of debt was consequent on several expectations: that the investment would shortly generate taxable income, would have collateralizable assets, would have products resistant to the economic cycle and was more likely to be later stage. A follow-up study by the same authors (Chapter 7 in this volume) examines the link between financing structures, financing stages and venture capitalists' characteristics. They find that smaller, less diversified venture capitalists make greater use of ordinary equity instruments; however, the use of preference shares did not increase in higher risk (early) stage investments, nor did investors who were subject to greater amounts of unsystematic risk make greater use of preferred instruments.

A particular problem concerns the consequences of the venture capitalist and the entrepreneur failing to agree on the degree to which the venture will be profitable, with consequent implications for splitting the equity stake attributable to each. Such difficulties may arise because of differing views of an uncertain situation and because of the agency cost problem when entrepreneurs own less than all the equity (Jensen and Meckling, 1976). Chua and Woodward (1993) suggest that this problem can be addressed through the use of stock options in the financing structure; this provides entrepreneurs with an incentive to perform since it increases the cost to them of excessive consumption of perks. Similar devices (termed 'equity ratchets' in the UK) have been used extensively in practice. Available evidence suggests that they may pose major problems in terms of specifying (relatively) complete contracts concerning the definition of financial performance to be used, the manipulation of information by managers and the timing of their crystallization[8] (Thompson and Wright, 1991). These problems may lead to major relationship difficulties between the venture capitalist and the entrepreneur.

A second financing issue to have been examined concerns the widespread syndication of venture capital investments. Bygrave (1988) finds that an important reason for syndication is to share information to reduce uncertainty and that this may be as important, if not more important, than the spreading of financial risk. In Chapter 10, Lerner also finds support for this view, as well as for the argument that typical later-round syndication involves less experienced venture capitalists investing in a deal begun by established organizations. However, in terms of issues related to effecting post-contractual monitoring, to which we return below, the extent and nature of syndication may be dynamic. Venture capitalists may in effect search over time for a network of syndicate partners with whom they are able both to complete transactions and undertake effective monitoring. This aspect of syndication has received little research attention.

Venture Capital Monitoring

General

In order for investors to engage in effective post-transaction monitoring so as to reduce moral hazard problems, a key requirement is access to reliable information about the firm's activities. Whilst active investors may be faced with less severe moral hazard problems than arm's length shareholders, significant asymmetric information difficulties may remain. Theoretical work by Chan et al. (1990) provides a two-period agency model to explain the nature of venture capitalists' monitoring contracts. Empirical work by Sahlman (Chapter 1) indicates that venture capitalists use various mechanisms to encourage entrepreneurs both to perform and to reveal accurate information. These mechanisms include staging of the commitment of investment funds; convertible financial instruments ('equity ratchets') which may give financiers control under certain conditions; basing compensation on value created; preserving mechanisms to force agents to distribute capital and profits, and powers written into Articles of Association which require approval for certain actions (e.g. acquisitions, certain types of investment and divestment, etc.) to be sought from the investor(s). In Chapter 14, Gompers examines the role of the staging of venture capital investments in a sample of 794 venture-backed firms. He finds evidence to support the view that venture capitalists cut off new financing in the light of negative information about future returns and, conversely, provide more financing and a greater number of rounds of financing in the more successful transactions.

Sweeting (1991) specifically addresses the use of accounting information in the venture capital monitoring process, which the above studies tend to play down. Mitchell et al. (Chapter 16) show that venture capitalists' accounting information demands are designed to deal with moral hazard and information asymmetry problems as well as provide safeguards through bonding arrangements. Accounting information flows were typically required on a more regular and more detailed basis than are statutory requirements for quoted companies.

In addition to such structural mechanisms, the process of the relationship with the investee company is also an important aspect of the corporate governance framework. It has been pointed out that staging of investments can lead to myopia and overinvestment where (initially) entrepreneurs and (subsequently) first-round venture capitalists as insiders present misleading information to outsiders in an attempt to persuade them to invest. Admati and Pfleiderer show in Chapter 9 that a contract in which venture capitalists continue to maintain the same fraction of equity in the various rounds of financing a project can neutralize a venture capitalist's incentive to mislead. Gompers (Chapter 14) provides a further extension.

Sapienza, Amason and Manigart (1994) provide evidence that there is less involvement by venture capitalists in monitoring activities which are more developed and presumably less risky, such as buy-outs, buy-ins and development capital cases. MacMillan, Kulow and Khoylian (Chapter 12) show that differing levels of involvement in venture capital investments (e.g. hands-on/close trackers versus hands-off/laissez-faire approaches) were not related to the nature of the operating business, but to the choice exercised by the venture capital firm itself as to the general style it wished to adopt. There were, however, no significant differences in the performance of businesses subject to differing levels of involvement. Similarly, Elango et al. (1995) identify three levels of assistance by venture capitalists to their investees: inactives, active advice-givers and hands-on. Surprisingly, however, they find that this involvement is not primarily related to the stage of investment. There were major variations in the amount of time spent and severity of actions taken by different venture capitalists on problem investees. Barry (1994) cites evidence that venture capitalists intensify their monitoring activities as the need dictates. Venture capitalist representation on the board is found to increase around the time of chief executive turn-over, while the number of other outsiders remains constant, according to evidence from the biotechnology industry, i.e. an early-stage sector (Lerner in Chapter 13).

Rosenstein, Bruno, Bygrave and Taylor (1993) find that the value added by venture capitalists on the investee's board was not rated significantly higher by CEOs than that of other board members. There was some evidence that larger venture capitalists provided significantly more value added, but that in such cases the venture capitalist frequently controlled the board. Entrepreneurs were found to value venture capitalists on their board with operating experience more highly than those with purely financial expertise. Murray (1994) shows that finance was the only area where venture capitalists' skills were judged by entrepreneurs to be greater than those of other parties. Indications are that the general type of skills possessed by venture capital executives varies between types of venture capitalist, with those employed by captive funds (e.g. development capital subsidiaries of clearing banks) tending to have more financial skills, whilst those employed by independents having greater industrial skills (Beecroft, 1994). Flynn (1992), however, finds that venture capitalists are less involved in the administrative component of new ventures than is necessary for their survival and recommends the need for such involvement.

Sweeting (Chapter 15) and Hatherly et al. (1994) for the UK and Fried and Hisrich (1995) for the US provide evidence of the importance of flexibility in the governance of venture capital and buy-out investments through personal relationships and that, to be effective, formal power needs to be used sparingly and virtually only when things go wrong. However, this may be because of inertia rather than a deliberate policy. While venture capitalists may take control when things go seriously wrong, such action has to be exercised with care since, as Sweeting points out, to act precipitously may destroy carefully nurtured relationships and commit the venture capitalists to unknown amounts of time to put matters right. We return to these issues in dealing with problem investments below.

Similarities but also differences emerge in the operation of active investor governance in buy-outs and buy-ins. UK evidence in buy-outs and buy-ins shows that board representation is the most popular method of monitoring investee companies, with venture capitalists also requiring the regular provision of accounts (Robbie, Wright and Thompson, 1992). However, evidence shows that there appears to be a greater degree of control exercised by institutions over management buy-ins than over buy-outs or other forms of investment. A much higher requirement for regular financial reports is indicated than for venture capital investments generally (Robbie et al., 1992). Equity ratchets are also found to be more frequently used in buy-ins, reflecting the greater uncertainty about their future performance. Evidence from smaller buy-ins suggests that, even where they have non-executive directors, institutions may not be as active in responding to signals about adverse performance as might have been expected (Robbie and Wright, 1996), and that relationships between entrepreneurs and investors had not developed to the extent that potential crises could be identified and understood by the venture capitalist. These problems reflect the high cost of monitoring and control in relation to the value of investments. In larger buy-ins there is evidence of extensive and repeated active monitoring (see Wright et al., 1994). This difference illustrates the comparative cost-effort-reward trade-offs involved in the active monitoring of large and small investments.

Restructuring and Failure

Particular importance has been attached to the governance role of active investors in cases where buy-outs and other venture capital investments require restructuring. Ruhnka et al. (Chapter 17) find that living dead investments, generally later-stage investments which are economically viable but fail to achieve adequate growth and returns, usually arise because of deficiencies with management coupled with problems with markets. Ruhnka et al. find that successful turnround, which occurs in only 56 per cent of cases, is influenced by the nature of the problems and the ability of venture capitalists to control them.

Subsequent research (Wright et al., Chapter 21) has distinguished between 'living dead' and 'good rump' investments, where the former essentially involve enterprises where the business collapses with little prospect of turnaround whereas the latter are capable of being turned round, but the effects of restructuring are problematic. A difficulty of enforcing restructuring is that it may be difficult to obtain consensus with other parties, both entrepreneurs and co-investors, concerning the form this should take. In smaller investments, since management are usually important majority shareholders, great care is needed in taking action. If institutions are a controlling shareholder, as is usually the case in larger buy-outs and buy-ins, making changes is theoretically straightforward. However, in cases with large syndicates of financiers, restructuring may be delayed or take a particular direction because of differences in the attitudes of syndicate members.[9]

In the limit, problems in the screening and control of venture capital investments may be expected to be closely associated with business failure. The influences on likelihood of failure in buy-outs in the UK were examined using logit analysis by Wright, Wilson, Robbie and Ennew (1995) who found that, while positive managerial motives for both buy-outs and greater levels of restructuring undertaken expeditiously at buy-out are associated with survival, direct investor monitoring *per se* was found not to be significant.

Investment Realization and Performance

Investment Realization

Issues surrounding the exit or realization of venture capital investments concern the timing and nature of such actions. Realization may be through IPO, full or partial sale to a third party, secondary buy-out/buy-in or receivership. There is clear evidence that timing of investment realization is heterogeneous, that there is considerable variance around the mean period of investment in a venture capital project.[10]

An important point to emerge is that the timing and form of realization of venture capital investments require the objectives of all parties to be satisfied (Relander et al., 1994; Wright et al., 1994). Barry et al. (1990) indicate that venture capitalists have several mechanisms to ensure firms go public at times perceived to be optimal, including board seats and informal advice. Writing in the context of venture-backed management buy-outs, Wright et al. (1994) suggest that institutions' desire for realization in order to achieve their returns may influence the nature of corporate governance to achieve a timely exit. In order to achieve timely exit, institutions are more likely to engage in closer (hands-on) monitoring of their buy-out investments and to use exit-related equity ratchets on management's equity stakes (Wright, Thompson, Robbie and Wong, 1995). Both quantitative and case study evidence suggests that the greater the conflicts in the objectives of the parties, which had to be suppressed at the time of the transaction to enable it to be completed, the more important that the governance structure be able to respond in terms of flexibility. Even so, exit arrangements will largely be influenced by the relative bargaining power between venture capitalists and entrepreneurs.

In the context of venture capital investments generally, most attention has focused on exit through IPO. Barry et al. (1990) show that successful timing of a venture-backed IPO provides significant benefits to venture capitalists in that taking companies public when equity values are high minimizes the dilution of the venture investor's ownership stake. Barry (1994) cites evidence that venture capitalists' governance may be biased where they have incentives to offer bad advice to their investees in the matter of premature IPO timing. Such a potential reverse principal-agent conflict may arise where venture capitalists seek a premature IPO in order to gain profile and report prior performance in the raising of new funds.[11] Lerner (1994) shows that seasoned venture capitalists appear to be particularly good at taking companies public near market peaks, though of course this does not necessarily mean that such timing is appropriate from the point of view of the company itself (Wright et al., 1994).[12]

While there is evidence that unseasoned IPOs generally result in significant underpricing (see e.g. Ibbotson et al., 1988 for a review), Megginson and Weiss (Chapter 18) show that there is less underpricing in venture-backed IPOs than in those without such finance, a finding consistent with a recognized role for venture capitalists as monitors.[13] Moreover, whilst supporting this evidence, Jain and Kini (Chapter 19) go further and show that venture capitalist-backed IPO firms have superior post-issue operating performance compared to non-venture capital-backed IPO firms over a three-year post-issue period. Importantly, they also show that the extent of superior performance is positively associated with the quality of venture capitalists' monitoring.

The valuation of venture capital investments at the time of exit may be particularly problematic since, as Lam (1991) has shown, a venture capitalist may not be able fully to realize the value of an investment in a low information environment due to the existence of estimation risk – that is, the incremental variation in the predictive return distribution that is attributable to investors' ignorance of the parameters of its true return distribution.[14] Estimation risk may be expected to decline as more information becomes known about the firm's performance. Thus, if part of the estimation risk is transitory and can be dissipated in the aftermarket following IPO, then it is worthwhile for the venture capitalist to adopt a graduated policy towards the realization of cash gains.

Despite the academic emphasis on realization through IPO, there are clear indications that venture capitalists maintain a flexible approach to the timing and form of exit (Wright et al., Chapter 21; Relander et al., 1994). Sale to a third party is an important exit route in practice, and in some circumstances is the most commonly preferred and actual form of exit. Using European evidence, Relander et al. (1994) show that, although in principle IPOs may be the preferred realization route, in practice sale to a third party is the most common form used, principally if a threshold for an IPO is not reached or because an attractive but unforeseen acquisition proposal is received. Wright et al. show in Chapter 21 that venture capitalists' attitudes to exit are not homogeneous between European countries. Petty et al. (1993) examine trade sales as an exit route for US venture capitalists and find that, although this provides more immediate full liquidity of an investment than is possible in an IPO, the objectives of the entrepreneur may not be satisfied, particularly because of loss of control. In a study of exit possibilities from early-stage investments, Murray (Chapter 20) shows that venture capitalists rank trade sale as their preferred route, with IPO third. Exit to a next stage (i.e. development capital stage) was ranked only fourth, despite early-stage investors' expressed preference for such a form of finance. Murray expresses concern that young, growing firms may be faced with a second equity gap and suggests that such companies are still too small and too immature for development capitalists. Such companies may represent rather small acquisitions for trading groups seeking to obtain economies of scale and/or scope, though they may be attractive where purchasers are seeking to gain access to new technology or product innovations.

Serial Contracting

The existence of entrepreneurs who are exiting from venture capitalists' own portfolios adds a feedback loop to the source of deal generation and also raises issues concerning the extent to which venture capitalists assess entrepreneurs at the time of exit and subsequently monitor their progress. As venture capital markets mature, increasing realization of investments is likely to be followed by exits by entrepreneurs. While we have earlier touched upon recontracting at different stages of the same project, this section focuses on the issue of the attractiveness of recontracting with exiting entrepreneurs, especially given the importance accorded to entrepreneurs' track records in investment screening, as seen earlier.

Studies which have specifically examined cases of habitual entrepreneurship (e.g. Birley and Westhead (1994) and Kolvereid and Bullvag (1993)) generally find little difference in characteristics and performance between novice and experienced entrepreneurs. Starr and Bygrave (1991) suggest that, although there is a danger that experienced entrepreneurs may become fixated on repeating past behaviour, the positive experience of previous entrepreneurial ventures should make it easier to raise start-up financing *per se* and in larger amounts. At the initial investment stage, venture capitalists may see themselves as able to negotiate relatively advantageous terms compared to entrepreneurs who are inexperienced in dealing with such situations, using their screening expertise as discussed earlier.[15] In recontracting with entrepreneurs who have exited from their own portfolio, venture capitalists are potentially faced with a situation in which the entrepreneur is more aware of the effectiveness of the venture capitalist's monitoring and of how (dis)advantageous the initial contract was. This is essentially a multi-period game whereby serial entrepreneurs will seek to shift the distribution of expected gains in their favour. As a result, venture capitalists, believing they are able to assess entrepreneurs effectively, may have some preference for initiating negotiations with an entrepreneur who has exited from another venture capitalist's portfolio. Thus, though an experienced entrepreneur may find it easier to obtain finance the next time around, this may be from a different source. Hence, whilst in principle venture capitalists may prefer to fund entrepreneurs with a successful track record, they may be sceptical about investing again in those who have exited from their own portfolio.

Performance of Venture Capital Firms

Evidence of the target rates of return sought by venture capitalists *ex ante* (e.g. Dixon (1991), Murray and Lott (1995) and Wright and Robbie (Chapter 8)) indicate that, in the UK, the overall average internal rate of return sought on venture capital investments is around 29 per cent. This target return varies according to the stage of the investment, as well as the size of and the degree of technology risk involved in the project.

There is relatively little rigorous analysis of the performance of venture capital firms outside of the US. This is partly because of the relative newness of most markets, where venture capital portfolios have generally not reached maturity. A major problem also arises in respect of access to adequate data.

A review of the main US literature to 1987 by Bygrave (1994) concludes that 'contrary to the folklore figure of 30–50 per cent, actual venture capital returns have most often been in the teens, with occasional periods in the 20–30 per cent range and rare spikes above 30 per cent'. Bygrave's own study of the performance of funds formed in the period 1969–85 shows that the median IRR peaked in 1982 at 27 per cent and that early-stage funds had higher returns than later-stage ones.

Kleiman and Shulman (1992) examined the comparative performance of publicly-traded venture capital firms and government-sponsored small business investment companies and found that, for 1980–86, the latter demonstrated significantly greater total and unsystematic risk and greater returns on a risk-adjusted basis, but significantly less systematic risk, than the former. However, this difference disappeared for later years. An analysis of 33 quoted European venture capital firms during the period 1977–91 (Manigart et al., 1993) showed only eight of the sample with a return higher than the market return, although the systematic risk was lower than the market risk. Venture capital companies specializing in a specific investment stage had a higher return.

In Europe, the sensitivity of returns information has led to analyses being conducted by national venture capital associations, notably in the UK and the Netherlands. Though these studies provide some data, there is a lack of transparency in the process of analysis. Dutch evidence shows that, in the venture capital industry in that country, an average annual return on investment of 13 per cent was obtained for the period 1986–90. However, these figures are based on realizations only and ignore the value of portfolio companies which have not been realized (and which might be expected to lower these returns). It is also notable that, in contrast to US evidence, the Dutch analysis showed that early-stage finance was on average loss-making (-3 per cent annual return) compared with much less risky management buy-outs, which earned a high positive return of 25 per cent per year. Analysis of returns in the UK for a sample of funds launched between 1980 and 1990 showed an overall annual return to end December 1994 of 12.1 per cent, with the upper quartile earning 14.6 per cent; large MBO funds produced the highest returns at 23.1 per cent and early-stage 4 per cent (BVCA, 1995b). Funds raised in 1986 and 1987 were the worst performers, while the best ones were raised in 1985 and 1990, reflecting the effects of differing market conditions, notably the entry price/earnings ratios paid for investees. Unlike the Dutch study, but in line with US approaches, the UK analysis was based on all investments, not just exited ones, and related to the performance of funds not companies.

It is clear from these studies of performance that returns depend to a great extent on the stage of investment and the timing of the raising of the fund, and have generally fallen internationally since the market began to develop significantly from the early 1980s. Moreover, it is also the case that the bulk of returns are earned on the top decile or quartile. Huntsman and Hoban (1980) show that eliminating the top decile meant that the average return fell from 18.9 per cent to −0.28 per cent. In Bygrave's study, the top quartile funds peaked at 44 per cent. It is also notable, if not perverse, that funds involving the lowest-risk categories earned the highest returns.

Alternative Sources of Venture Capital

In addition to the comparisons between mutual funds and venture capitalists seen in the previous section, four other competing sources of finance are of particular interest: informal venture capitalists (or business angels), LBO associations, corporate venturing and banks.

Informal Venture Capitalists

Evidence by Landstrom (1993) shows that there are marked international differences between the involvement of informal investors in their investee companies. In terms of transaction screening, investors in the UK are found to devote little attention, whereas in the US this is moderately high and in Sweden high. Post-transaction, such investors in the UK are generally passive; in Sweden they are generally active but not involved in day-to-day operations, whilst in the US they are active and highly involved in day-to-day activities. US informal investors take the highest risk in their portfolio of investments. Contrary to views expressed that informal investors are not so constrained by the need to earn returns in a specified period, Landstrom finds that, in all three countries, they have relatively short exit horizons, usually less than five years. There is also some evidence that informal venture capital markets are inefficient in terms of the communications channels between investors and entrepreneurs seeking such funds (Harrison and Mason, 1992; Freear, Sohl and Wetzel, Chapter 23).[16]

An important issue concerns the extent to which agency theory applies as specifically to informal venture capitalists as the evidence (discussed above) suggests it does to formal venture capitalists. Finding little evidence to support his view that the involvement of business angels in monitoring their investments will vary according to the level of agency risk, Landstrom (1992) suggests that the agency framework is inappropriate in these circumstances. He argues that the assumptions applicable in agency theory – which concern rational economic maximizing behaviour, asymmetric information and conflicting objectives – are not valid in the case of informal investors. The reasons he adduces concern the motivation of informal investor behaviour by non-economic factors, the desire of the informal investor to make a value-added contribution, and the prior relationship and close involvement of the investor in the business which helps to mitigate asymmetric information.

However, it is necessary to understand the differing approaches of the two types of venture capitalists towards two types of risk. In Chapter 11, Fiet finds that, in comparison with informal venture capitalists, formal venture capitalists attach more importance to market risk than agency risk and vice versa. Fiet argues that formal venture capitalists are less concerned about agency risk because they have learnt how to protect themselves from it through stringent contracting which enables them to replace underperforming entrepreneurs. Informal venture capitalists, who screen very few deals per year, have access to comparatively limited information and place more emphasis on agency risk – that is, finding the 'right' entrepreneur who will be able to address market risk. Fiet (1995) also shows that formal venture capitalists make greater use of formal informant networks than do informal venture capitalists, and that the former prefer their own due diligence to reliance on informal networks.[17]

There is also evidence by Ehrlich et al. in Chapter 24 of significant differences between formal and informal venture capitalists in the nature of their monitoring of investees, with the former providing more difficult targets, greater feedback and involvement in monitoring and staff selection, especially when the firm is experiencing problems. These differences may arise because private investors neither have the time, expertise nor flexibility to engage in close monitoring. The implications are that formal venture capitalists may be more appropriate for entrepreneurs with high technical but low managerial skills, and vice versa for private investors. These arguments suggest that agency theory is also of importance for informal investors, but that greater emphasis is placed on *ex ante* rather than *ex post* issues. In order for the informal investor to arrive at a position of trusting the entrepreneur in whom he has invested to manage market risk, the informal investor will have had to develop skills for dealing with adverse selection problems. In the absence of these skills, business angels may react by not investing ('virgin angels') despite screening large numbers of potential investments.

LBO associations

There is some considerable degree of overlap between specialist providers of funds to buy-outs (LBO associations; Jensen, 1989) and venture capitalists (Sahlman, Chapter 1). Both invest funds on behalf of other institutions and, although there is a degree of heterogeneity in the forms they take, both are often, especially in the US, organized as limited partnerships. Both cases involve relationship investment with management, managerial compensation being oriented towards equity and probable severe penalties for underperformance. The principal differences concern the nature of the relationship between investor and investee; also, in investments by LBO associations, most of the funding required to finance an acquisition is through debt. In comparing LBO associations with venture capitalists, Sahlman notes that executives in the former may typically assume control of the board of directors, but are generally less likely than venture capitalists to assume operational control. Investments by venture capitalists, which may also involve buy-outs as well as start-ups and development capital, make greater use of equity and quasi-equity.[18] These differing relationships and financing instruments may be used to perform similar functions in different types of enterprise, so widening the applicability of the active investor concept within the Anglo-American system of corporate governance (Wright et al., 1994).

Corporate venturing

Corporate venturing may involve either direct investment in minority stakes (internally managed corporate venturing) or indirect investment through investment in venture capital funds (externally managed corporate venturing). Such investment can provide corporations with both a financial return and an opportunity to access new technologies and markets at a relatively early stage in their development (Block and MacMillan, 1993).[19] In Chapter 25, Sykes analyses the relative advantages of these two types of corporate venturing and concludes that they serve differing purposes which may be complementary, with an indirect approach providing contacts and access to deal flow, and the direct approach enhancing specific business relationships.

McNally (1994), who focuses on indirect corporate venturing, finds that corporations have played a relatively small role in providing funds for the formal venture capital industry; this he attributes both to an unwillingness on the part of corporations to invest and to a venture capital community that has been largely discouraged by previous experiences with such companies. His evidence shows that corporates may consider that they do not obtain sufficient direct contact with investees to meet their strategic objectives, nor have sufficient say in the evaluation and selection of investments. From the point of view of venture capitalists, corporate investors may develop unrealistic expectations about financial and strategic benefits, may have time horizons which are too short, may attempt to place too much pressure on investees (in effect trying to treat them as subsidiaries), and may have objectives which conflict with those of the venture capitalist.

Banks

Chan et al. (1990) raise the issue of the need to explore the conditions which lead to the simultaneous existence of banks and venture capitalists.[20] They suggest that venture capitalists may have advantages over banks in providing finance in settings where entrepreneurial skills are highly uncertain at the outset and where the role of close monitoring is potentially significant. As banks begin to develop close long-term relationships involving detailed information flows with their corporate customers (Ennew and Binks, 1995; Holland, 1994), there would appear to be increasing convergence with the approach adopted by venture capitalists. Moreover, the problems faced by venture capitalists in respect of adverse selection and their response in terms of increased price versus refusal to fund is analogous to issues concerning the so-called debt gap (De Meza and Webb, 1987). There is also evidence relating to the role and operation of debt covenants in management buy-out investments; that in the UK, at least, these are operated in a more flexible manner than might have been supposed (Citron, Robbie and Wright, 1995). These developments suggest a need to compare the investment selection and monitoring behaviour of banks and venture capitalists as the overlap in their activities increases.

Conclusions

One of the main thrusts of this review has been to emphasize the richer array of research issues which arise from taking an institutional rather than a financial-instrument view of venture capital. That is, rather than focusing on the narrow view that venture capital is about investment in new (innovative) start-ups, it is important to investigate the range of investment activities actually undertaken by venture capitalists. Not only does this approach key in more closely with what venture capital firms do, but it also permits greater application of important finance and accounting concepts and issues. Increasingly, at least in the UK and European contexts, it would seem important to view the issues as relating to the provision of private equity, within which venture capital is a subset.

There is growing evidence concerning the mechanisms and processes by which venture capitalists monitor their investee companies which has shed important light on principal-agent issues.[21] However, there has been relatively little research on the other crucial principal-agent relationship, that between venture capitalists and their funds providers. Though highly interesting, the Sahlman study provides only a starting point for research into this aspect of venture capital. The study examined only limited partnership venture capital funds and not captive funds where the monitoring relationship, investment stage and time horizon emphasis, and overall objectives may be different. In addition, while analysing in detail the nature of the contracts, the study did not examine their operation and effectiveness, either from the perspective of the venture capitalist or from that of the funds providers. There would thus appear to be scope for more detailed finance-based clinical studies of the processes involved in the operation of venture capital contracts. There is also an emerging issue concerning the appropriate conceptual underpinning to the relationships both between funds providers and venture capital firms and between the latter and their investees. Procedural justice theory, which focuses on the perceived fairness of monitoring relationships in which no one party has control over decisions, provides a potentially complementary approach to principal–agent theory (Sapienza and Korsgaard, 1996). Further research appears to be warranted in this area.

In respect of the realization of venture capital investments, the review of previous studies indicates the need for greater attention than hitherto to the trade sale route. In particular, such issues as the pricing of such sales, the determination of an acceptable price and the process of divestment of portfolios in this way (such as the search for buyers, the establishment or not of an auction and the use of contingent prices (earn-outs)) would seem to warrant further analysis. Further study of post-IPO performance issues also appears desirable, particularly in respect of the influence of information asymmetry on the timing of IPOs and the question of whether post-IPO venture capitalist involvement is positively associated with performance.

In the context of the growing extent of realizations from venture capitalists' portfolios, there has been little attempt to address the issues involved in the reinvestment of exiting entrepreneurs, either by the original venture capitalist or an alternative one. This area would appear to introduce important issues concerning the problems of recontracting with entrepreneurs who have learnt about the venture capital process, which may change the relative bargaining position of the two parties. A similar issue also arises in staged investments where an investee company is growing successfully, giving the entrepreneur greater bargaining power. There also remains a paucity of rigorous academic studies on the performance of venture capital investments and of venture capitalists themselves. In this context, a subset of important issues concerns the methods used in the valuation of initial venture capital proposals, the continuous revaluation of venture capital portfolios by both captive and independent funds, and the implications of valuation policies for the ultimate realization of investments.

A further research area concerns examination of the extent to which venture capitalists and venture capital-backed firms are different from other institutions and firms. This review has identified studies which have drawn attention to differences between venture capitalists and investment analysts in respect of information use; others have considered differences in the performance of venture capital funds and mutual funds, and in respect of differences in IPO performance between venture-backed and non-venture-backed firms. There has been some analysis of the difference between venture capitalists, LBO associations and banks, and also some limited discussion of the differences between formal and informal venture capitalists. However, much of this work has either been confined to US conditions, with an emphasis only on start-up investments, or has related to much earlier time periods when, as the discussion has suggested, conditions may have been significantly different from currently. There is also relatively little analysis of how firms select between competing sources of finance – banks and formal and informal venture capitalists.

Notes

1 Financial support for CMBOR from BZW Private Equity and Deloitte and Touche Corporate Finance is gratefully acknowledged.
2 The corporate restructuring literature, with its emphasis on enterprises in mature markets with limited investment opportunities and free cash flow, as in leveraged buy-outs (Jensen, 1993), has tended to focus on reducing agency cost problems rather than the stimulation of growth and entrepreneurial actions. Yet the larger number of management buy-out and buy-in transactions which take place, even in the US, make extensive use of venture capital and engage in significant R&D and investment expenditure (see e.g. Zahra, 1995; Malone, 1989; Wright et al., 1992).
3 This focus may in large part be because of the limitations placed on the terms of reference of the Cadbury Committee. See e.g. Keasey and Wright (1993) for a review and critique. Sykes (1994), for example, also draws attention to the contribution that active investors in MBOs may offer to the corporate governance debate.
4 Prior to this more recent substantial market growth, it needs to be borne in mind that the world's largest venture capital institution, 3i (based in the UK), has been investing since the mid-1940s (Coopey and Clarke, 1995), whilst Charterhouse and other banks provided venture capital at least a decade earlier.
5 The outcome of the first-stage decision is the purchase of a real call option and the outcome of the second is the exercise of this option.
6 Intermediaries may play an important role in securing venture capital funding irrespective of the entrepreneur's skills. Hustedde and Pulver (1992) examine the role of different types of intermediaries in securing venture capital funds for their clients and find that entrepreneurs who fail to seek advice and those who make use of bankers, public agencies or universities as intermediaries had a significantly low chance of success.
7 This can lead, for example, to an overemphasis on equity stake by entrepreneurs, with the venture capitalist making counter-balancing adjustments in other aspects of the contract that an inexperienced entrepreneur may not fully appreciate, as well as to insufficient search on the part of the entrepreneur for an appropriate venture capitalist. This is consistent with notions that, finding themselves in unfamiliar situations, entrepreneurs under-search for information as they fail to appreciate fully the issues involved or their complexity.
8 Performance may be in terms of profits over a given period, market value on flotation, etc. Flotation at a date prior to that expected in the ratchet contract may provoke disputes about the extra amount of equity to which management is entitled where a sliding scale operates.
9 For discussion of syndication of venture capital investments, see Chapter 10 by Lerner.

10 For the case of venture-backed management buy-outs, see Wright, Thompson, Robbie and Wong (1995).
11 This issue also raises further governance problems in relation to conflicts between venture capitalists and their investors.
12 Evidence from IPOs of buy-outs in the UK also indicates a marked increase in activity at times of market buoyancy (see Wright and Robbie, 1996).
13 Parallel evidence in a study of stock market flotations of LBOs (DeGeorge and Zeckhauser, 1993) shows that reverse LBOs outperform comparable firms in terms of operating profitability pre-flotation but not post; a finding consistent with the informational asymmetry view that managers and their institutional supporters wait for a good year before coming to market. However, evidence that, despite this change in relative performance, reverse LBOs do not underperform the share price of non-LBOs suggests that the market anticipates such a change.
14 Estimation risk has transitory and permanent components. The former may be eliminated as more information becomes available while the latter is due to the random nature of asset return parameters.
15 Although some entrepreneurs mitigate this problem with the use of intermediaries, there is evidence to suggest that intermediaries become involved at a late stage, especially in smaller transactions (Murray et al., 1995).
16 It is not clear, however, how representative these studies are of informal investors. For example, 'more informed' informal investors may utilize their links with banks to identify investment opportunities rather than using 'marriage bureaux'; such entrepreneurs may therefore not be fully represented in these studies.
17 Wright and Robbie (1996), who examined only formal venture capitalists, also find that a high degree of importance is attached to own due diligence.
18 Though the LBO industry in the US is typically seen to be distinct from the venture capital industry, venture capitalists are extensively involved in funding buy-outs, especially smaller ones (see e.g. Malone, 1989). In the UK, there is probably much greater overlap between venture capitalists and what may be seen as LBO associations (Wright, Thompson and Robbie, 1996).
19 The Japanese element of the paper by Hurry et al. (Chapter 3) may also be seen as reflecting a quasi-corporate venturing perspective in its emphasis on obtaining access to new technology.
20 For example, in the UK management buy-out market, venture capitalists are involved in funding around half of all smaller transactions, with banks fully funding the rest (Wright and Robbie, 1996).
21 There may also be wider corporate governance applications of the flexible active investor approach adopted by venture capitalists (Jensen, 1993; Thompson and Wright, 1995).

References

Abbott, S. and Hay, M. (1995), *Investing for the Future*, London: FT–Pitman.
Arnold, J. and Moizer, P. (1984), 'A survey of the methods used by UK investment analysts to appraise investments in ordinary shares', *Accounting and Business Research*, Summer, 195–207.
Barry, C. (1994), 'New directions in research on venture capital finance', *Financial Management*, 23 (3), 3–15.
Barry, C., Muscarella, C., Peavy, J. and Vetsuypens, M. (1990), 'The role of venture capitalists in the creation of public companies: Evidence from the going public process', *Journal of Financial Economics*, 27, 447–71.
Beecroft, A. (1994), 'The role of the venture capital industry in the UK' in N. Dimsdale and M. Prevezer (eds), *Capital Markets and Corporate Governance*, Oxford: OUP.
Birley, S. and Westhead, P. (1994), 'A comparison of new businesses established by "novice" and "habitual" founders in Great Britain', *International Small Business Journal*, 12 (1), 38–60.
Block, Z. and MacMillan, I. (1993), *Corporate Venturing*, Boston, Ma: Harvard Business School Press.

Brophy, D. and Gunther, M. (1988), 'Publicly traded venture capital funds: Implications for institutional "fund of funds" investors', *Journal of Business Venturing*, **3**, 187–206.

Bruno, A. and Tyebjee, T. (1985), 'The entrepreneur's search for capital', *Journal of Business Venturing*, **1**, 61–74.

BVCA (1995a), *Report on Investment Activity*, London: BVCA.

BVCA (1995b), *BVCA Performance Measurement Survey*, London: BVCA.

BVCA (1993), 'Guidelines for the Valuation and Disclosure of Venture Capital Portfolios', London: BVCA, November.

Bygrave, W. (1988), 'The structure of investment networks of venture capital firms', *Journal of Business Venturing*, **3**, 137–57.

Bygrave, W. (1994), 'Rates of return from venture capital', Ch. 1 in W. Bygrave, M. Hay and J. Peeters (eds), *Realizing Investment Value*, London: FT-Pitman.

Bygrave, W. and Timmons, J. (1992), *Venture Capital at the Crossroads*, Boston: Harvard Business School Press.

Carter, R. and Van Auken, H. (1994), 'Venture capital firms' preference for projects in particular stages of development', *Journal of Small Business Management*, **32** (1), 60–73.

Chan, Y., Siegel, D. and Thakor, A. (1990), 'Learning, corporate control and performance requirements in venture capital contracts', *International Economic Review*, **31** (2), 365–81.

Chua, J. and Woodward, R. (1993), 'Splitting the firm between the entrepreneur and the venture capitalist with the help of stock options', *Journal of Business Venturing*, **8** (1), 43–58.

Citron, D., Robbie, K. and Wright, M. (1995), 'Debt covenants in UK MBOs', *CMBOR Quarterly Review*, Summer, 9–33.

Coopey, R. and Clarke, D. (1995), *3i – Fifty Years Investing in Industry*, Oxford: Oxford University Press.

DeGeorge, F. and Zeckhauser, R. (1993), 'The reverse LBO decision and firm performance: Theory and evidence', *Journal of Finance*, **48** (4), 1323–49.

De Meza, D. and Webb, D. (1987), 'Too much investment: A problem of asymmetric information', *Quarterly Journal of Economics*, **102**, 281–92.

Dixon, R. (1991), 'Venture capitalists and the appraisal of investments', *Omega*, **19** (5), 333–44.

Elango, B., Fried, V., Hisrich, R. and Polonchek, A. (1995), 'How venture capital firms differ', *Journal of Business Venturing*, **10** (2), 157–79.

Ennew, C. and Binks, M. (1995), 'The provision of finance to small business: Does the banking relationship constrain performance', *Journal of Small Business Finance*, forthcoming.

EVCA (1995), *EVCA Yearbook 1995*, Zaventem: European Venture Capital Association.

Fiet, J. (1995), 'Reliance on informants in the venture capital industry', *Journal of Business Venturing*, **10** (3), 195–223.

Flynn, D. (1992), 'The critical relationship between venture capitalists and entrepreneurs: Planning, decision-making and control', *Small Business Economics*, **3** (3), 185–96.

Freear, J. and Wetzel, W. (1990), 'Who bankrolls high-tech entrepreneurs?', *Journal of Business Venturing*, **5**, 77–90.

Fried, V. and Hisrich, R. (1988), 'Venture capital research: Past, present and future', *Entrepreneurship: Theory and Practice*, Fall, 15–28.

Fried, V. and Hisrich, R. (1994), 'Towards a model of venture capital investment decision making', *Financial Management*, **23** (3), 28–37.

Fried, V. and Hisrich, R. (1995), 'The venture capitalist: A relationship investor', *California Management Review*, **37** (2), 101–13.

Fried, V., Hisrich, R. and Polonchek, A. (1993), 'Research note: Venture capitalists' investment criteria: A replication', *Journal of Small Business Finance*, **3** (1), 37–42.

Gorman, M. and Sahlman, W. (1989), 'What do venture capitalists do?', *Journal of Business Venturing*, **4**, 231–48.

Gupta, A. and Sapienza, H. (1992), 'Determinants of venture capital firms' preferences regarding the industry diversity and geographic scope of their investments', *Journal of Business Venturing*, **7**, 347–62.

Haar, N., Starr, J. and MacMillan, I. (1988), 'Informal risk capital investors: Investment patterns on the east coast of the USA', *Journal of Business Venturing*, **3**, 11–29.

Hall, J. and Hofer, C. (1993), 'Venture capitalists' decision criteria in new venture evaluation', *Journal of Business Venturing*, **8**, 25–42.

Harrison, R. and Mason, C. (1992), 'International perspectives on the supply of informal venture capital', *Journal of Business Venturing*, 7, 459–75.

Harvey, M. and Lusch, R. (1995), 'Expanding the nature and scope of due diligence', *Journal of Business Venturing*, **10**, 5–21.

Hatherly, D. et al. (1994), 'An exploration of the MBO-financier relationship', *Corporate Governance*, **2** (1), 20–29.

Hisrich, R. and Jankowicz, A. (1990), 'Intuition in venture capital decisions: An exploratory study using a new technique', *Journal of Business Venturing*, **5** (1), 49–62.

Holland, J. (1994), 'Bank lending relationships and the complex nature of bank-corporate relations', *Journal of Business Finance and Accounting*, **21** (3), 367–93.

Huntsman, B. and Hoban, J. (1980), 'Investment in new enterprise: Some empirical observations on risk, return and market structure', *Financial Management*, Summer, 44–51.

Hustedd, R. and Pulver, G. (1992), 'Factors affecting equity capital acquisition: The demand side', *Journal of Business Venturing*, 7 (5), 363–80.

Ibbotson, R., Sindelar, J. and Ritter, J. (1988), 'Initial public offerings', *Journal of Applied Corporate Finance*, Summer, 37–45.

Jensen, M.C. (1993), 'The modern industrial revolution: Exit, and the failure of internal control systems', *Journal of Finance*, **48**, 831–80.

Jensen, M.C. (1989), 'Eclipse of the public corporation', *Harvard Business Review*, **89**, Sept./Oct., 61–74.

Jensen, M.C. and Meckling, W. (1976), 'The theory of the firm: Managerial behavior, agency costs and ownership structure', *Journal of Financial Economics*, **3**, 305–60.

Kaplan, S.N. (1991), 'The staying power of leveraged buyouts', *Journal of Financial Economics*, **29**, 287–313.

Keasey, K. and Wright, M. (1993), 'Issues in corporate accountability and governance', *Accounting and Business Research*, **23** (91A), 291–303.

Kleiman, R. and Shulman, J. (1992), 'The risk-return attributes of publicly traded venture capital: Implications for investors and public policy', *Journal of Business Venturing*, 7 (3), 195–208.

Kolvereid, L. and Bullvag, E. (1993), 'Novices versus experienced founders: An exploratory investigation', in S. Birley and I. MacMillan (eds), *Entrepreneurship Research: Global Perspectives*, Elsevier Science Publishers, 275–85.

Lam, S. (1991), 'Venture capital financing: A conceptual framework', *Journal of Business Finance and Accounting*, **18** (2), 137–49.

Landstrom, H. (1992), 'The relationship between private individuals and small firms: An agency theory approach', *Entrepreneurship and Regional Development*, **4**, 199–223.

Landstrom, H. (1993), 'Informal risk capital in Sweden and some international comparisons', *Journal of Business Venturing*, **8**, 525–40.

Lerner, J. (1994), 'Venture capitalists and the decision to go public', *Journal of Financial Economics*, **35**, 293–316.

Lorenz, T. (1989), *Venture Capital Today*, 2nd edn, Cambridge: Woodhead-Faulkner.

MacMillan, I.C., Siegel, R. and Subbanarasimha, P.N.S. (1985), 'Criteria used by venture capitalists to evaluate new venture proposals', *Journal of Business Venturing*, **1** (1), 119–28.

Malone, S. (1989), 'Characteristics of smaller company leveraged buy-outs', *Journal of Business Venturing*, **4**, 349–59.

Manigart, S. (1994), 'What drives the creation of a venture capital firm?', *Journal of Business Venturing*, **9** (6), 525–41.

Manigart, S., Joos, P. and De Vos, D. (1993), 'The performance of publicly traded European venture capital companies', in N. Churchill et al. (eds), *Frontiers of Entrepreneurship Research 1992*, Wellesley, Ma: Babson College.

Martin, J. and Petty, J. (1983), 'An analysis of the performance of publicly traded venture capital companies', *Journal of Financial and Quantitative Analysis*, **18** (3), 401–10.

McNally, K. (1994), 'Sources of finance for UK venture capital funds: The role of corporate investors', *Entrepreneurship & Regional Development*, **6**, 275–97.

Murray, G. (1991), *Change and Maturity in the UK Venture Capital Industry 1991–95*, London: BVCA.

Murray, G. (1994), 'The European Union's support for new technology-based firms: An assessment of the first three years of the European seed capital fund', *European Planning Studies*, **2** (4), 435–61.

Murray, G. and Lott, J. (1995), 'Have venture capitalists a bias against investment in new technology firms?', *Research Policy*, **24**, 283–99.

Murray, G., Nixon, B., Robbie, K. and Wright, M. (1995), 'Managements' search for venture capital in smaller buy-outs and the role of intermediaries', Paper presented at 6th EFER Conference, Ghent (Belgium), November.

Murray, G. and Wright, M. (1996), 'The role of intermediaries in management buy-out and buy-in teams' search for venture capital', *International Journal of Bank Marketing*, **14** (2), 14–25.

Muzyka, D., Birley, S. and Leleux, B. (1995), 'Trade-offs in the investment decisions of European venture capitalists', *Journal of Business Venturing*, forthcoming.

Norton, E. and Tenenbaum, B. (1992), 'Factors affecting the structure of venture capital deals', *Journal of Small Business Management*, **30** (3), 20–29.

Norton, E. and Tenenbaum, B. (1993), 'Specialisation versus diversification as a venture capital investment strategy', *Journal of Business Venturing*, **8**, 431–42.

Ooghe, H. et al. (1991), 'Growth patterns in the European venture capital industry', *Journal of Business Venturing*, **6**, 381–404.

Petty, J., Bygrave, W. and Shulman, J. (1993), 'Harvesting the entrepreneurial venture: A time for creating value', *Journal of Applied Corporate Finance*, **7**, 48–58.

Rah, J., Jung, K. and Lee, J. (1994), 'Validation of the venture evaluation model in Korea', *Journal of Business Venturing*, **9**, 509–24.

Reid, G., Terry, N. and Smith, J. (1995), 'Risk management in venture capital investor-investee relations', Paper presented at ESRC Conference on Risk in Organisational Settings, University of York.

Relander, K-E., Syrjanen, A-P. and Miettinen, A. (1994), 'Analysis of the trade sale as a venture capital exit route', in W. Bygrave, M. Hay and J. Peeters (eds), *Realizing Investment Value*, London: FT-Pitman.

Robbie, K. and Wright, M. (1996), *Management Buy-ins: Entrepreneurship, Active Investors and Corporate Restructuring*, Manchester: Manchester University Press.

Robbie, K., Wright, M. and Thompson, S. (1992), 'Management buy-ins in the UK', *Omega*, **20**, 445–56.

Rosenstein, J., Bruno, A., Bygrave, W. and Taylor, N. (1993), 'The CEO, venture capitalists, and the board', *Journal of Business Venturing*, **8** (2), 99–113.

Ruhnka, J. and Young, J. (1991), 'Some hypotheses about the risk in venture capital investments', *Journal of Business Venturing*, **6** (2), 115–33.

Sapienza, H. (1992), 'When do venture capitalists add value?', *Journal of Business Venturing*, **7**, 9–27.

Sapienza, H., Amason, A. and Manigart, S. (1994), 'The level and nature of venture capitalist involvement in their portfolio companies: A study of three European countries', *Managerial Finance*, **20** (1), 3–18.

Sapienza, H. and Korsgaard, M.A. (1996), 'Procedural Justice in Entrepreneur-Investor Relations', *Academy of Management Journal*, **39** (3), 544–74.

Starr, J. and Bygrave, W. (1991), 'The assets and liabilities of prior start-up experience: An exploratory study of multiple venture entrepreneurs' in N. Churchill et al. (eds), *Frontiers of Entrepreneurship Research*, Wellesley, Ma: Babson College.

Stiglitz, J. and Weiss, A. (1981), 'Credit rationing in markets with imperfect information', *American Economic Review*, **71**, June, 393–410.

Sweeting, R. (1991), 'Early-stage new technology-based businesses: Interactions with venture capitalists and the development of accounting techniques and procedures', *British Accounting Review*, **23**, 3–21.

Sykes, A. (1994), 'Proposals for internationally competitive corporate governance in Britain and

America', *Corporate Governance*, **2** (4), 187–95.

Thompson, S. and Wright, M. (1991), 'UK management buy-outs: Debt, equity and agency cost implications', *Managerial and Decision Economics*, **12** (1), 15–26.

Thompson, S. and Wright, M. (1995), 'Corporate governance – The role of restructuring transactions', *Economic Journal*, **105**, May, 690–703.

Thompson, S., Wright, M. and Robbie, K. (1992), 'Management equity ownership, debt and performance: Some evidence from UK management buy-outs', *Scottish Journal of Political Economy*, **39** (4), 413–30.

Tyebjee, T. and Vickery, L. (1988), 'Venture capital in Western Europe', *Journal of Business Venturing*, **3**, 123–36.

Wright, M., Robbie, K. and Ennew, C. (1995), 'Venture capitalists and second time entrepreneurs', in W. Bygrave et al., *Frontiers of Entrepreneurship Research*, Boston: Wellesley.

Wright, M., Robbie, K., Thompson, S. and Starkey, K. (1994), 'Longevity and the life cycle of MBOs', *Strategic Management Journal*, **15**, 215–27.

Wright, M., Thompson, S. and Robbie, K. (1992), 'Venture capital and management-led leveraged buy-outs: A European perspective', *Journal of Business Venturing*, **7**, 47–71.

Wright, M., Thompson, S. and Robbie, K. (1996), 'Buy-ins, buy-outs, active investors and corporate governance', *Corporate Governance*, **4** (4), 222–34.

Wright, M., Thompson, S., Robbie, K. and Wong, P. (1995), 'Management buyouts in the short and long term', *Journal of Business Finance and Accounting*, **22** (4), 461–82.

Wright, M., Wilson, N., Robbie, K. and Ennew, C. (1995), 'An analysis of failure in UK buy-outs and buy-ins', *Managerial and Decision Economics*, forthcoming.

Zahra, S. (1995), 'Corporate entrepreneurship and financial performance: The case of management leveraged buy-outs', *Journal of Business Venturing*, **10** (3), 225–47.

Part I
The Institutional Framework

[1]

Journal of Financial Economics 27 (1990) 473–521. North-Holland

The structure and governance of venture-capital organizations

William A. Sahlman*

Harvard Business School, Boston, MA 02163, USA

Received August 1989, final version received December 1990

Venture-capital organizations raise money from individuals and institutions for investment in early-stage businesses that offer high potential but high risk. This paper describes and analyzes the structure of venture-capital organizations, focusing on the relationship between investors and venture capitalists and between venture-capital firms and the ventures in which they invest. The agency problems in these organizations and to the contracts and operating procedures that have evolved in response are emphasized. Venture-capital organizations are contrasted with large, publicly traded corporations and with leveraged buyout organizations.

1. Introduction

The venture-capital industry has evolved operating procedures and contracting practices that are well adapted to environments characterized by uncertainty and information asymmetries between principals and agents. By venture capital I mean a professionally managed pool of capital that is invested in equity-linked securities of private ventures at various stages in their development. Venture capitalists are actively involved in the management of the ventures they fund, typically becoming members of the board of directors and retaining important economic rights in addition to their ownership rights. The prevailing organizational form in the industry is the limited partnership, with the venture capitalists acting as general partners and the outside investors as limited partners.

Venture-capital partnerships enter into contracts with both the outside investors who supply their funds and the entrepreneurial ventures in which

*The author gratefully acknowledges the useful comments of Bruce Greenwald, Michael Jensen, Christopher Barry, Clifford Smith, Kenneth French, Richard Ruback, two anonymous referees, Geoff Barss, Howard Stevenson, Jeffry Timmons, Regina Herzlinger, Andre Perold, Peter Wendell, Tench Coxe, and Christina Darwall. All errors and omissions remain the responsibility of the author.

they invest. The contracts share certain characteristics, notably:

(1) staging the commitment of capital and preserving the option to abandon,
(2) using compensation systems directly linked to value creation,
(3) preserving ways to force management to distribute investment proceeds.

These elements of the contracts address three fundamental problems:

(1) the sorting problem: how to select the best venture capital organizations and the best entrepreneurial ventures,
(2) the agency problem:[1] how to minimize the present value of agency costs,
(3) the operating-cost problem: how to minimize the present value of operating costs, including taxes.

From one perspective, venture capital can be viewed as an alternative model for organizing capital investments. Like corporations, venture-capital firms raise money to invest in projects. Many projects funded by venture capitalists (for example, the development of a new computer hardware peripheral) are similar to projects funded within traditional corporations. But the governance systems used by venture-capital organizations and traditional corporations are very different. This paper addresses some of the differences.

The information and analysis in the paper comes from two basic sources. Most of the data cited come from Venture Economics, the leading information source on the venture-capital industry. Venture Economics publishes the *Venture Capital Journal* (VCJ), a monthly magazine on trends in the industry, as well a number of specialized studies. The second major source is extensive field research I have done over the past eight years. This effort has resulted in 20 Harvard Business School cases based on decisions in venture-capital firms or in the companies they fund [e.g., Sahlman (1986c), Knights and Sahlman (1986d)], four technical and industry notes [e.g., Sahlman and Scherlis (1988)], and several articles [e.g., Sahlman and Stevenson (1985)]. The field research embodied in the cases and notes has been supplemented with on-site interviews with 25 venture-capital-firm management teams, over 150 venture capitalists, and approximately 50 venture-capital-backed entrepreneurial management teams.

Section 2 provides background information on the venture-capital industry, emphasizing the great uncertainty about returns on individual venture-capital projects. Sections 3, 4, and 5 discuss the general structure of a venture-capital firm and the contracts between external investors and venture capitalists. Sections 6 and 7 examine the contractual relationship between the venture-

---

[1]See Jensen and Meckling (1976), Fama (1980), and Fama and Jensen (1985) for background on the theory of agency costs. See also Williamson (1975, 1988) for background on transaction-cost theory. For related articles using the same basic framework to analyze organizational forms, see Wolfson (1985) on oil and gas limited partnerships and Brickley and Dark (1987) on franchises. Smith and Warner (1979) provide a similar analysis of financial contracts.

capital firm and the companies in which it invests. Venture-capital organizations are compared with other organizational forms for corporate or project governance in section 8. Section 9 summarizes the paper.

2. General industry background

Table 1 presents historical data on the venture-capital industry from 1980 to 1988. In 1988 an estimated 658 venture-capital firms in the U.S. managed slightly over $31 billion in capital and employed 2,500 professionals (panel A, table 1).[2] Industry resources were concentrated: the largest 89 firms controlled approximately 58% of the total capital. The average amount controlled by these 89 firms was just under $200 million [VCJ April 1990, p. 13)].

In each of the last several years, venture capitalists disbursed approximately $3 billion to fewer than 2,000 companies, most in high-technology industries (panel C, table 1). Although a typical large venture-capital firm receives up to 1,000 proposals each year, it invests in only a dozen or so new companies.

Venture capitalists invest at reasonably well-defined stages (panel C, table 1). The seed stage typically precedes formation of a complete management team or completion of a product or service design. Each successive stage is generally tied to a significant development in the company, such as completion of design, pilot production, first profitability, introduction of a second product, or an initial public offering [Plummer (1987), Kozmetsky et al. (1985)]. The stages of investment are described more completely in table 2.

Approximately 15% of the capital disbursed in each of the last three years went to ventures in early stages, whereas 65% was invested in later-stage companies, typically still privately held. The remaining 20% was invested in leveraged buyout or acquisition deals. In recent years venture capitalists have channeled roughly two-thirds of the capital invested each year into companies already in their portfolios, and one-third into new investments. Venture capitalists often participate in several rounds of financing with the same portfolio company, as illustrated in table 3.

Venture-capital investing plays a small role in overall new-business formation. According to Dun & Bradstreet, approximately 600,000 to 700,000 new businesses are incorporated in the United States each year [Council of Economic Advisors (1990)]. The vast majority of those that seek external funding do so from sources other than venture capitalists. Some analysts

---

[2] Venture Economic's estimate of total industry capital is based on commitments of capital and is measured at cost rather than market value: thus, the $31.1 billion cited in table 1 consists of capital that has been committed to venture-capital funds but not yet invested, some cash, and portfolio investments in individual ventures by venture-capital funds. The market value of the assets under management in the industry probably exceeds book value.

Table 1

Selected data on the United States venture-capital industry, 1980–1988.[a]

	1980	1981	1982	1983	1984	1985	1986	1987	1988
Panel A: Aggregate venture-capital industry statistics									
1 Total venture-capital pool ($M)	$4,500	$5,800	$7,600	$12,100	$16,300	$19,600	$24,100	$29,000	$31,100
2 Number of venture-capital firms	NA	NA	331	448	509	532	587	627	658
3 Number of industry professionals	NA	NA	1,031	1,494	1,760	1,899	2,187	2,378	2,474
4 Net new commitments to the venture-capital industry ($M)	$700	$1,300	$1,800	$4,500	$4,200	$3,300	$4,500	$4,900	$2,900
Panel B: Data on the independent private sector (noncorporate and non-SBIC venture capital organizations)									
1 Net new commitments to the independent private sector ($M)	$661	$867	$1,400	$3,400	$3,200	$2,300	$3,300	$4,200	$2,100
Sectoral analysis (% of total capital)									
2 Independent private	40.0%	44.0%	58.0%	68.7%	72.0%	73.0%	75.0%	78.0%	80.0%
3 Corporate	31.1%	28.0%	25.0%	21.0%	18.0%	17.0%	16.0%	14.0%	13.0%
4 SBIC	28.9%	28.0%	17.0%	11.0%	10.0%	10.0%	9.0%	8.0%	7.0%
Sectoral analysis – Average capital per firm ($M)									
5 Independent private	NA	NA	$27	$36	$45	$52	$57	$65	$65
6 Corporate	NA	NA	$30	$37	$36	$37	$34	$32	$29
7 SBIC	NA	NA	$6	$5	$5	$5	$5	$6	$5
8 Median size of independent private firms ($M)	NA	NA	$22	$18	$21	$25	$30	$30	$30

Independent private-sector partnership formation

9 Total # of funds raising capital	22	37	54	89	101	77	77	110	84
10 Total capital raised ($M)	$661	$866	$1,423	$3,460	$3,300	$2,327	$3,320	$4,184	$2,810
11 # of follow-on funds	12	13	18	47	58	40	44	66	59
12 Capital raised by follow-on funds ($M)	$418	$477	$628	$2,383	$2,300	$1,396	$2,800	$3,347	$2,422
13 # of new funds	10	24	36	42	43	37	33	44	25
14 Capital raised by new funds ($M)	$243	$389	$795	$1,077	$1,000	$931	$520	$837	$388

Sources of capital to the independent private sector (%)

15 Corporations	19.0%	17.0%	12.0%	12.0%	14.0%	12.0%	11.0%	10.0%	12.0%
16 Individuals	16.0%	23.0%	21.0%	21.0%	15.0%	13.0%	12.0%	12.0%	8.0%
17 Pension funds	30.0%	23.0%	33.0%	31.0%	34.0%	33.0%	50.0%	39.0%	47.0%
18 Foreign	8.0%	10.0%	13.0%	16.0%	18.0%	23.0%	11.0%	14.0%	13.0%
19 Endowments	14.0%	12.0%	7.0%	8.0%	6.0%	8.0%	6.0%	10.0%	11.0%
20 Insurance companies	13.0%	15.0%	14.0%	12.0%	13.0%	11.0%	10.0%	15.0%	9.0%

Panel C: Investment activity of venture capitalists

Disbursements

1 Estimated value of disbursements ($M)	$610	$1,160	$1,450	$2,580	$2,760	$2,670	$3,230	$3,940	$3,650
2 Number of companies financed	504	797	918	1,320	1,469	1,377	1,504	1,729	1,474
3 Average investment per company	$1.21	$1.46	$1.58	$1.95	$1.88	$1.94	$2.15	$2.28	$2.48

Allocation of investments

4 New company commitments as a % of total	58.0%	55.0%	39.0%	34.0%	31.0%	23.0%	37.0%	39.0%	33.0%
5 Follow-on financings as a % of total	42.0%	45.0%	61.0%	66.0%	69.0%	77.0%	63.0%	61.0%	67.0%

Stages of financing

6 Seed and startup as a % of total	25.0%	22.6%	20.0%	17.2%	21.0%	15.0%	19.0%	13.0%	12.5%
7 Expansion and later-stage as a % of total	75.0%	77.4%	68.0%	70.8%	67.0%	69.0%	58.0%	69.0%	67.5%
8 Leveraged buyouts as a % of total	NA	NA	12.0%	12.0%	12.0%	16.0%	23.0%	18.0%	20.0%

Continued overleaf

Table 1 (continued)

	1980	1981	1982	1983	1984	1985	1986	1987	1988
Panel D: Exiting venture-capital investments									
1 # of venture-capital-backed companies that are acquired	28	32	40	49	86	101	120	147	106
Venture-capital-backed initial public offerings (IPOs)									
2 # of companies	27	68	27	121	53	46	97	81	35
3 Total amount raised ($M)	$420	$770	$549	$3,031	$743	$838	$2,118	$1,840	$756
4 Total market value of companies with IPO in each year ($M)	$2,626	$3,610	$2,374	$14,035	$3,495	$3,258	$8,434	$6,893	$3,122
All IPOs									
5 # of companies	95	227	100	504	213	195	417	259	96
6 Total amount raised ($M)	$1,089	$2,723	$1,213	$9,580	$2,545	$3,166	$8,190	$5,220	$2,392
7 Total market value of companies ($M)	$5,717	$10,922	$5,466	$40,473	$10,792	$11,618	$31,616	$23,813	$11,759
Venture capital backed IPOs as % of total IPOs									
8 # of companies	28.4%	30.0%	27.0%	24.0%	24.9%	23.6%	23.3%	31.3%	36.5%
9 Total amount raised	38.6%	28.3%	45.2%	31.6%	29.2%	26.5%	25.9%	35.2%	31.6%
10 Total market value of companies	45.9%	33.1%	43.4%	34.7%	32.4%	28.0%	26.7%	28.9%	26.5%

Source: Various publications of Venture Economics (Needham, MA).
NA: not available.
[a] Total capital (for example. panel A. row 1) is the book value of all commitments to professional venture-capital firms (net of fund liquidations). See also footnote 2 in text.
Data on initial public offerings in panel D, rows 5–7, come from Securities Data Corporation (see footnote 3 in the text).

Table 2

The stages of venture-capital investing.[a]

1. *Seed investments*
   Although the term is sometimes used more broadly, the strict meaning of 'seed investment' is a small amount of capital provided to an inventor or entrepreneur to determine whether an idea deserves of further consideration and further investment. The idea may involve a technology, or it may be an idea for a new marketing approach. If it is a technology, this stage may involve building a small prototype. This stage does not involve production for sale.

2. *Startup*
   Startup investments usually go to companies that are less than one year old. The company uses the money for product development, prototype testing, and test marketing (in experimental quantities to selected customers). This stage involves further study of market-penetration potential, bringing together a management team, and refining the business plan.

3. *First stage – early development*
   Investment proceeds through the first stage only if the prototypes look good enough that further technical risk is considered minimal. Likewise, the market studies must look good enough so that management is comfortable setting up a modest manufacturing process and shipping in commercial quantities. First-stage companies are unlikely to be profitable.

4. *Second stage – expansion*
   A company in the second stage has shipped enough product to enough customers so that it has real feedback from the market. It may not know quantitatively what speed of market penetration will occur later, or what the ultimate penetration will be, but it may know the qualitative factors that will determine the speed and limits of penetration. The company is probably still unprofitable, or only marginally profitable. It probably needs more capital for equipment purchases, inventory, and receivable financing.

5. *Third stage – profitable but cash poor*
   For third-stage companies, sales growth is probably fast, and positive profit margins have taken away most of the downside investment risk. But, the rapid expansion requires more working capital than can be generated from internal cash flow. New VC capital may be used for further expansion of manufacturing facilities, expanded marketing, or product enhancements. At this stage, banks may be willing to supply some credit if it can be secured by fixed assets or receivables.

6. *Fourth stage – rapid growth toward liquidity point*
   Companies at the fourth stage of development may still need outside cash to sustain growth, but they are successful and stable enough so that the risk to outside investors is much reduced. The company may prefer to use more debt financing to limit equity dilution. Commercial bank credit can play a more important role. Although the cash-out point for VC investors is thought to be within a couple of years, the form (IPO, acquisition, or LBO) and timing of cash-out are still uncertain.

7. *Bridge stage – mezzanine investment*
   In bridge or mezzanine investment situations, the company may have some idea which form of exit is most likely, and even know the approximate timing, but it still needs more capital to sustain rapid growth in the interim. Depending on how the general stock market is doing, and how given types of high tech stocks are doing within the stock market, 'IPO windows' can open and close in very unpredictable ways. Likewise, the level of interest rates and the availability of commercial credit can influence the timing and feasibility of acquisitions or leveraged buyouts. A bridge financing may also correspond to a limited cash-out of early investors or management, or a restructuring of positions among VC investors.

8. *Liquidity stage – cash-out or exit*
   A literal interpretation of 'cash-out' would seem to imply trading the VC-held shares in a portfolio company for cash. In practice, it has come to mean the point at which the VC investors can gain liquidity for a substantial portion of their holdings in a company. The liquidity may come in the form of an initial public offering. If it does, liquidity is still restricted by the holding periods and other restrictions that are part of SEC Rule 144, or by 'stand-off' commitments made to the IPO underwriter, in which the insiders agree not to sell their shares for some period of time after the offering (for example, 90 or 180 days). If acquisition is the form of cash-out, the liquidity may be in the form of cash, shares in a publicly traded company, or short-term debt. If the acquisition is paid for in shares of a nonpublic company, such shares may be no more liquid than the shares in the original company. Likewise, if the sellers take back debt in a leveraged buyout, they may wind up in a less liquid position than before, depending on the liquidity features of the debt.

[a] This table is drawn from Plummer (1987, pp. I-11 to I-13).

Table 3

Participation in multiple financing rounds by a venture-capital fund.[a,b]

Company/Date of purchase	Security purchased	Price per share	Number of shares	Total cost
Company 1				
5/1/85	Convertible preferred series B	$0.68	525,145	$354,473
8/1/85	Convertible preferred series B	$0.68	972,531	$656,458
3/1/86	Convertible preferred series C	$2.25	444,445	$1,000,001
4/1/87	Convertible preferred series D	$4.50	66,667	$300,002
Totals (average price per share)		$1.15	2,008,788	$2,310,934
7/24/90	Estimated value	$23.00		$46,202,124
Company 2				
6/1/85	Convertible preferred series A	$15.00	20,833	$312,500
11/1/85	Convertible preferred series A	$15.00	20,833	$312,495
4/1/86	Convertible preferred series A	$15.00	25,000	$375,000
5/2/88	Convertible preferred series B	$8.60	28,588	$245,857
Totals (average price per share)		$13.08	95,254	$1,245,852
Note: Loans totalling $206,500 were made in 1987 and these were converted to series B preferred on 5/2/88				
7/24/90	Estimated value	$3.27		$311,463
Company 3				
2/1/87	Convertible preferred series B	$1.15	347,827	$400,001
7/1/87	Convertible preferred series C	$1.90	131,579	$250,000
3/16/88	Convertible preferred series D	$1.60	283,326	$453,322
Totals (average price per share)		$1.45	762,732	$1,103,323
Note: Loans totalling $200,000 were made in 1987 and these were converted to series D preferred on 3/16/88				
7/24/90	Estimated total value	$1.45		$1,103,323

Company 4

2/1/86	Convertible preferred series B	$0.95	1,473,684	$1,400,000
12/1/86	Convertible preferred series D	$1.85	461,808	$854,345
7/22/87	Convertible preferred series D	$1.85	141,829	$262,384
	Totals (average price per share)	$1.21	2,077,321	$2,516,728
7/24/90	Estimated value	$4.34		$9,005,259

Company 5

11/1/85	Convertible preferred series A	$0.34	1,470,588	$500,000
3/1/86	Convertible preferred series B	$0.45	2,083,333	$937,500
3/1/87	Convertible preferred series C	$0.75	1,333,333	$1,000,000
	Totals (average price per share)	$0.50	4,887,254	$2,437,500
7/24/90	Estimated value	$0.00		$0

Total cost for 5 companies	$9,614,336
Total estimated value for 5 companies	$56,622,169
Total gain for 5 companies	$47,007,832

[a] *Source:* An interim report to the limited partners of a venture-capital fund with more than $20 million in capital.
[b] The amounts listed do not include investments made by others at the same time or at other times.

estimate that the amount invested by so-called angels is an order of magnitude larger than the amount invested by professional venture capitalists [see, for example, Wetzel (1983) and Freear and Wetzel (1990)].

Venture-capital investing is also modest in comparison with the level of capital investment in the domestic corporate sector: total capital expenditures in 1988 by the nonfinancial, nonfarm sector exceeded $380 billion [Economic Report of the President (1990)]. Total expenditures on research and development in the U.S. each year are estimated to top $150 billion, of which $74 billion is invested by private industrial concerns [Studt (1990)]. Finally, the $3 billion disbursed by all professional venture capitalists in 1988 was only slightly less than one-third the amount invested by IBM in capital expenditures and R & D in the same year, and 25% of the amount invested by General Motors.

Despite its modest scope, the industry has helped create many successful enterprises, including Apple Computer, Intel, Federal Express, People Express, Businessland, Lotus Development, Microsoft, Sun Microsystems, Digital Equipment, Compaq Computer, Teledyne, Tandem, Tandon, Hybritech, and Genentech. Each of these companies received venture capital early in its development and later went public. In aggregate, 579 venture-capital-backed companies went public during the 11 years ending in 1988. Their total market value exceeded 30% of the total market value of all comparable companies going public during the same period (panel D, table 1).[3]

The payoff to venture capitalists has been handsome in some cases. During 1978 and 1979, for example, slightly more than $3.5 million in venture capital was invested in Apple Computer. When Apple went public in December 1980, the approximate value of the venture capitalists' investment was $271 million, and the total market capitalization of Apple's equity exceeded $1.4 billion. Similarly, several venture capitalists invested slightly over $4.7 million in Lotus Development Corporation in two rounds of financing in 1982: their equity was assigned a market value of almost $130 million in October 1983. The lead venture capitalist, Ben Rosen of Sevin-Rosen Partners, played a very important role in the formation and evolution of the company [see Sahlman (1985e) for background on the Sevin-Rosen investment in Lotus].

The industry has also been involved in some spectacular failures. Well-known examples include Ovation Technologies, Osborne Computer, Ztel, and Gavilan. In each case, venture capitalists lost their entire investment. In late 1983 Ovation Technologies raised almost $6 million in venture capital to compete with Lotus Development in microcomputer software. The product proved far more difficult and costly to complete than anticipated, however,

---

[3]Venture Economics provides the data on the venture-capital-backed companies. Data on all initial public offerings (IPOs) during the period come from Securities Data Corporation. The specific comparison sample excludes all closed-end investment companies, savings and loan conversions, and companies with an offering price under $5.00 per share.

and the venture-capital firms chose to liquidate the company rather than continue funding development. Ovation closed its doors in late 1984 without having generated one dollar of revenues. [For further information on Ovation, see Knights and Sahlman (1986a).]

Although comprehensive data are difficult to obtain, the overall rate of return on venture capital seems to have been high from the mid-1960s through the mid-1980s, the only period for which reliable data are currently available. Between 1965 and 1984, for example, the median realized compound rate of return on 29 venture-capital partnerships over the life of each partnership (an average of 8.6 years) exceeded 26% per year [Venture Economics (1985, p. 69)]. The minimum compound annual rate of return for the 29 funds was 6%.[4]

A more recent and comprehensive study [Venture Economics (1988c)] suggests that funds started before 1981 experienced generally positive returns through 1987. For example, the average annual rate of return (weighted by initial investment) on the 13 funds started in 1980 was 20.6% for the period ending December 31, 1987, compared with 16% for the Standard & Poor's 500 and 16% for smaller capitalization stocks during the same period [Ibbotson Associates (1988)]. These 13 funds represented 50% of the total funds raising money in 1980 and 66% of the capital raised that year. This study also reveals that rates of return have declined since 1983, particularly for funds started later in the period. It is extremely difficult to estimate the extent to which returns have declined, however, because accounting practices in the industry typically reflect a downward bias. [See also VCJ (August 1989) and Sahlman (1989).]

Returns on individual investments in a venture-capital portfolio vary widely. According to Huntsman and Homan (1980), slightly more than half of the 110 investments made by three venture-capital firms from 1960 to 1975 resulted in a realized rate of return of less than 10%; over one-quarter resulted in an absolute loss. According to Venture Economics (1988c), more than one-third of 383 investments made by 13 firms between 1969 and 1985 resulted in an absolute loss. More than two-thirds of the individual investments made by these same firms resulted in capital returns of less than double the original cost.

Nevertheless, the returns on a few investments have more than offset these disappointments. Venture Economics (1988c) reports, for example, that 6.8% of the investments resulted in payoffs greater than ten times cost and yielded 49.4% of the ending value of the aggregate portfolio (61.4% of the profits).

---

[4]The findings reported in Venture Economics (1985) are supported by Huntsman and Homan (1980), Chiampou and Kellet (1989), Bygrave et al. (1987), Horsley Keogh (1988), and analysis of the returns reported by 20 venture-capital funds in offering memoranda used to raise new capital. No attempt was made in these studies to adjust for the systematic risk incurred in venture-capital investing.

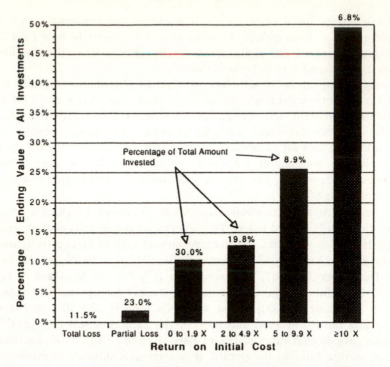

Fig. 1. Payoffs from venture-capital investing.

This graph shows the distribution of gains and losses on a group of investments made by venture-capital firms. The data are taken from Venture Economics (1988c) and cover investments by 13 venture-capital partnerships in 383 companies from 1969 to 1985. In total, $245 million was invested, which resulted in total value of $1.049 billion (4.3 times cost). The vertical axis shows the percentage of total ending value (that is, the $1.049 billion) resulting from six groups of investments, comprising investments with differing returns on capital invested (from total loss to more than 10 times capital invested). At the top of each bar the percentage of total cost represented by each group is shown. Thus, 6.8% of the capital invested resulted in payoffs of more than 10 to 1 and contributed almost 50% of the total ending value. Similarly, 11.5% of the cost was invested in companies that experienced a total loss.

Fig. 1 shows the distribution of outcomes analyzed in Venture Economics (1988c). An earlier Venture Economics report (1985) reached similar conclusions: investments in 22 of 216 companies yielded more than ten times cost, and the profits realized were more than 40 times larger than the losses incurred on the 70 companies that failed to return the amount invested. The same basic patterns are found by Keeley (1986) and Horsley Keogh (1988). See also Stevenson et al. (1987) and Sahlman and Soussou (1985a).

Even companies that are successful in the long run sometimes flirt with failure. For example, an analysis of various documents filed with the Securities and Exchange Commission (SEC) reveals that Federal Express raised

Table 4

Multiple financing rounds for selected venture-capital-backed firms.[a]

Company (business)	Investor[b]	Date	Amount raised ($000)	Cumulative funding ($000)	Stock received (000)	Total shares outstanding (000)	% ownership acquired	Fully diluted valuation ($000)	Price per share ($)	Estimated ending ownership %[c]
Apple Computer (computer)	Founders	Mar-77	1	1	16,640	16,640	100.0%	1	0.00	30.7%
	Founders	Nov-77	115	116	10,480	27,120	38.6%	298	0.01	19.3%
	Venture 1	Jan-78	518	634	5,520	32,640	16.9%	3,063	0.09	10.2%
	Founders	Jul-78	426	1,060	4,736	37,376	12.7%	3,362	0.09	8.7%
	Venture 2	Sep-78	704	1,764	2,503	39,879	6.3%	11,216	0.28	4.6%
	Venture 3	Dec-80	2,331	4,095	2,400	43,306	5.5%	42,061	0.97	4.4%
	IPO	Dec-80	101,200	105,295	4,600	54,215	8.5%	1,192,730	22.00	8.5%
Cray Research (computer)	Founders	Aug-72	2,550	2,550	2,869	2,794	102.7%	2,483	0.89	24.3%
	Venture 1	Jan-74	2,675	5,225	2,006	4,875	41.1%	6,501	1.33	17.0%
	Venture 2	Jan-75	642	5,867	387	5,302	7.3%	8,796	1.66	3.3%
	Venture 3	Apr-75	2,720	8,587	1,530	6,832	22.4%	12,146	1.78	13.0%
	IPO	Mar-76	10,890	19,477	4,950	11,783	42.0%	25,923	2.20	42.0%
Federal Express (transportation)	Founders	Jan-72	4,745	4,745	100	100	100.0%	4,745	47.45	0.7%
	Venture 1	Sep-73	12,250	16,995	60	160	37.5%	32,667	204.17	0.4%
	Venture 2	Mar-74	6,400	23,395	872	1,032	84.5%	7,574	7.34	6.4%
	Venture 3	Sep-74	3,876	27,271	6,200	7,232	85.7%	4,521	0.63	45.8%
	IPO	Apr-78	25,800	53,071	4,300	13,535	31.8%	81,210	6.00	31.8%
Genentech (biotechnology)	Founders	Jan-76	126	126	3,200	3,200	100.0%	126	0.04	41.4%
	Venture 1	Apr-76	850	976	1,180	4,280	27.6%	3,083	0.72	15.3%
	Venture 2	May-78	950	1,926	475	4,945	9.6%	9,890	2.00	6.1%
	Corporate	Sep-79	10,000	11,926	1,000	6,348	15.8%	63,480	10.00	12.9%
	IPO	Oct-80	38,500	50,426	1,100	7,724	14.2%	270,340	35.00	14.2%

Continued overleaf

Table 4 (continued)

Company (business)	Investor[b]	Date	Amount raised ($000)	Cumulative funding ($000)	Stock received (000)	Total shares outstanding (000)	% ownership acquired	Fully diluted valuation ($000)	Price per share ($)	Estimated ending ownership %[c]
Lotus Development (software)	Founders	Apr-82	13	13	4,410	4,410	100.0%	13	0.00	30.9%
	Venture 1	Apr-82	1,000	1,013	3,500	7,910	44.2%	2,260	0.29	24.5%
	Venture 2	Dec-82	3,755	4,768	3,767	11,677	32.3%	12,044	1.03	26.4%
	IPO	Oct-83	46,800	51,568	2,600	14,277	18.2%	256,988	18.00	18.2%
Midway Airlines (transportation)	Founders	Jun-76	7	7	700	700	100.0%	7	0.01	19.2%
	Venture 1	Jul-79	5,739	5,746	1,380	2,080	66.3%	8,650	4.16	37.9%
	Venture 2	Sep-80	6,000	11,746	789	2,789	28.3%	23,620	7.60	21.7%
	IPO	Dec-80	11,475	23,221	850	3,639	23.4%	53,433	13.50	23.4%
Seagate (disk drives)	Founders	Oct-79	161	161	11,723	11,723	100.0%	161	0.01	64.1%
	Venture 1	Jun-80	1,000	1,161	3,125	14,848	21.0%	4,751	0.32	17.1%
	IPO	Sep-81	25,000	26,161	2,500	18,277	13.7%	182,770	10.00	13.7%
Staples (retailing)	Founders/ Venture 1	Jan-86	4,425	4,425	1,844	1,844	100.0%	4,425	2.40	20.2%
	Venture 2	Jan-87	13,927	18,352	2,211	4,054	54.5%	25,543	6.30	24.2%
	Venture 3	Dec-87	13,597	31,950	1,563	5,617	27.8%	48,871	8.70	17.1%
	Venture 4	Sep-88	2,800	34,750	267	5,884	4.5%	61,782	10.50	2.9%
	IPO	Apr-89	61,750	96,500	3,250	9,134	35.6%	173,546	19.00	35.6%

[a]Sources: Annual reports, prospectuses.

[b]Venture 1, etc., represent rounds of financing from venture capitalists; IPO = Initial Public Offering.

[c]Ending ownership is based on final total shares outstanding. The figures do not always add exactly to 100%, which reflects stock options issued and other capital structure changes, including share repurchases, warrants issued, and debt conversions.

three rounds of venture capital in 1973 and 1974. With the company behind plan and over budget, the price paid per share in the third round was $0.63, compared with the adjusted price of more than $200 in the first round and just over $7 per share in the second round. By 1976, when the company made its first public offering of shares, the adjusted price per share was $6; by 1981, it was $47.45. Table 4 shows the prices paid and capital raised in Federal Express and seven other ventures.

Conversely, companies that give venture capitalists and their investors high rates of return do not always succeed in the long run. Priam Corporation, a disk-drive manufacturer, received five rounds of venture capital before it went public. In the initial round of financing in 1978 the price per share was less than $1, whereas the per-share value assigned soon after the company went public in 1983 was $23. Every intervening round had taken place at a higher price per share, but although it raised more than $70 million in its IPO, Priam filed for bankruptcy in 1989. [See Sahlman (1984), Knights and Sahlman (1986c, 1986d), and Sahlman and Stevenson (1985) for details on Priam and other disk-drive manufacturers.]

An important variable in venture-capital investments is the time that elapses between the initial investment and the return of capital. According to Venture Economics (1988c), the average holding period for an investment is 4.9 years. Roughly one-third of the individual investments studied are held for more than six years. Investments with payoffs greater than five times the invested capital are held significantly longer than investments that fail completely. The average investment in companies with high payoffs is approximately $1 million, versus $366,000 for the losers.

3. The most common structure of venture-capital firms[5]

By 1988 the typical venture-capital firm was organized as a limited partnership, with the venture capitalists serving as general partners and the investors as limited partners. According to Venture Economics (1987), 500 firms with $20 billion in capital in 1987 were structured as limited partnerships. The remaining one-third of industry capital was invested in independent private venture-capital firms not organized as limited partnerships (for example, incorporated venture-capital companies and publicly traded closed-end funds) (9% in 1987); in venture-capital subsidiaries of industrial and financial corporations (14%); and in independent small-business investment companies (SBICs) (8%), which had access to government-guaranteed debt to

---

[5]For background information on the venture-capital industry and the structure of venture-capital firms, see Gorman and Sahlman (1989), Sahlman and Stevenson (1985), Sahlman (1988, 1989), Wilson (1985), Morris (1988a), Bartlett (1988), and Venture Economics (1985, 1987, 1988a, 1988b, 1988c).

leverage their equity capital (panel B, table 1). The share of total industry capital managed by the independent private sector, which comprises mostly limited partnerships, increased dramatically over the nine years ending in 1988.

Table 1 (panel B) also reveals that in 1988 12% of the new capital committed to the private independent sector (i.e., noncorporate subsidiaries and non-SBICs) came from individuals, whereas 64% came from pension funds, endowments, and insurance companies. Typically, the general partners provide only a small proportion (about 1%) of the capital raised by a given fund. Most venture-capital firms are structured as management companies responsible for managing several pools of capital, each representing a legally separate limited partnership.

In each new fund, the capital is invested in new ventures during the first three to five years of the fund. Thereafter few if any investments are made in companies not already in the portfolio, and the goal is to begin converting existing investments to cash. As investments yield cash or marketable securities, distributions are made to the partners rather than reinvested in new ventures.

Typically, well before all of the capital from a venture-capital pool is distributed to the partners, a new fund is raised and invested in new ventures. For example, Institutional Venture Partners (IVP), a California-based venture-capital firm, raised $16.5 million in 1980, the year it was formed. In 1982 the IVP management company raised $40 million in a fund called IVP II. The group raised $96 million in 1985, launching IVP III, which was followed in 1988 by IVP IV, a $115 million fund [VCJ (May 1989, pp. 26–29)]. Thus investment and distribution periods overlap. Approximately 72% of the increase in capital controlled by the private independent sector from 1977 to 1988 was attributable to so-called follow-on funds, new venture-capital pools raised by existing firms.

The average firm in 1988 had $65 million in committed capital (measured at cost rather than market value). The largest 89 firms, as noted earlier, had average committed capital of almost $200 million and controlled almost 60% of the industry's assets. A fund with $200 million in committed capital is typically managed by a professional staff of between 6 and 12, who invest approximately $15 to $35 million each year in new companies and companies already in the portfolio.

Most venture-capital firms have several general partners and a staff of associates and administrative support personnel. Associates function as apprentices to the general partners and often become general partners themselves in later funds. In 1988, the average capital managed per professional (partner or associate) was $12.6 million. For the independent private sector, the figure was $15 million per professional [Venture Economics (1989)]. The capital managed by each professional is a function of total capital under management. For independent private firms with total committed capital of more than $200 million, each professional was responsible for managing $34 million.

Institutional Venture Partners, for example, had six general partners and two associates responsible for managing the various active funds. In 1988 IVP invested $11.2 million in 11 new companies not already in one of the fund portfolios and $19.2 million in 27 follow-on deals.

By 1988 roughly one-third of all venture-capital firms had at least one partner with more than 10 years of experience, and these firms managed almost 60% of total industry capital. In the independent private sector, which was characterized by more experience, roughly 68% of the firms (managing 89% of the capital) had one partner with at least five years of experience in the industry [Venture Economics (1989)].

Venture-capital firms tend to specialize by industry or stage of investment. Some firms focus on computer-related companies, others on biotechnology or specialty retailers. Some will invest only in early-stage deals, whereas others concentrate on later-stage financings. Many firms also limit their geographic scope.

4. The contract between the investors and the venture-capital firm

The relationship between investors and managers of the venture funds is governed by a partnership agreement that spells out the rights and obligations of each group. Key elements of the contract are described in this section, and an economic analysis follows in section 5. The description of the legal structure of a venture-capital firm is based primarily on Venture Economics (1987), which studied contracts for 76 funds raised between January 1986 and August 1987. These funds represented 76% of all venture-capital funds raised during this period. Of the 76, 40 were initial funds and 36 were follow-on funds started by firms already managing other pools. The findings in that report were checked against primary-source documents from 25 venture capital firms. See also Bartlett (1988).

4.1. Legal structure

The limited-partnership organizational form has important tax and legal considerations. Limited-partnership income is not subject to corporate taxation; instead income is taxable to the individual partners. Also, partnerships can distribute securities without triggering immediate recognition of taxable income: the gain or loss on the underlying asset is recognized only when the asset is sold. To qualify for this form of tax treatment, partnerships must meet several conditions:[6]

(1) A fund's life must have an agreed-upon date of termination, which is established before the partnership agreement is signed.
(2) The transfer of limited partnership units is restricted; unlike most registered securities, they cannot be easily bought and sold.
(3) Withdrawal from the partnership before the termination date is prohibited.
(4) Limited partners cannot participate in the active management of a fund if their liability is to be limited to the amount of their commitment.

General partners, in contrast, bear unlimited liability, so they can conceivably lose much more than they commit in capital. The consequences of unlimited liability are minor, however, because venture-capital partnerships typically do not borrow, nor are they exposed to the risk of having liabilities in excess of assets.

Despite restrictions on their managerial rights, limited partners are almost always permitted to vote on key issues such as amendment of the limited-partnership agreement, dissolution of the partnership before the termination date, extension of the fund's life, removal of any general partner, and valuation of the portfolio. Contracts vary, but typically a two-thirds majority of limited-partnership votes is required to effect change.

4.2. General-partner contribution

Of the 76 partnerships surveyed in Venture Economics (1987), 61% report general-partner contributions of exactly 1% of committed capital. This contribution can be, and often is, in the form of a promissory note rather than cash. Some tax advisors counsel those forming venture-capital partnerships to have the general partners contribute at least 1% in order to be assured of favorable tax treatment.

4.3. Economic life

For the Venture Economics (1987) sample, the economic life of 72% of the funds is set at ten years. All of the partnerships include provisions to extend the life of the funds, with 52% requiring some level of consent by the limited partners and 48% leaving the decision up to the general partners. The most frequent extension period is three years maximum in one-year increments. At the end of a fund's legal existence, all cash and securities are distributed and a final accounting is rendered.

[6]The list below is replicated from Venture Economics (1987, p. 7). See also Wolfson (1985), who describes the use of the limited-partnership organization form in the oil and gas industry, which is driven primarily by tax considerations.

4.4. Takedown schedules

In the survey sample the limited partners typically are required to invest a certain amount at the outset, but can phase in the remainder of their investment over time. Most fund agreements call for a cash commitment of between 25% and 33% at the close, with additional capital to be invested at some future date or dates (for example, 25% each year). The venture capitalists exercise considerable control over the timing of capital infusions by the limited partners.

If limited partners renege on a funding commitment, severe penalties are imposed on the ownership percentages associated with the partners' earlier investments and their ability to withdraw already invested funds. The kinds of penalties imposed vary considerably, though a common clause calls for the limited partner to forfeit one-half of the partner's capital account in the partnership and therefore one-half of the profits to which the partner would have been entitled.

4.5. Compensation

Venture-capital management companies typically receive compensation from two sources for managing the investments in each limited partnership. They are entitled to a management fee, and they receive some percentage of the profits over the life of each fund. More than 50% of the contracts surveyed by Venture Economics call for an annual management fee equal to 2.5% of committed capital through the life of the fund. Most of the remaining partnerships base the management fee on capital committed, though the formula varies. Only seven of the funds base the fee directly on the estimated value of the portfolio. Typically the base management fee increases annually by the rate of consumer price inflation. The survey finds little evidence that the percentage fee declines with the amount of capital under management.

In 88% of the funds surveyed, venture capitalists are entitled to 20% of the realized gains on the fund. In the remaining partnerships, the general partner's share of realized gains ranges from 15% to 30%. Given the diversity of fund organizers and their differing stated purposes, this seems remarkably consistent, in sharp contrast to the widely varying contract terms found in oil and gas partnerships [Wolfson (1985)].

4.6. Distributions

Half of the partnership agreements studied by Venture Economics require annual distributions from realized profits. In 18% of the agreements, the general partners state their intentions to make annual distributions, whereas the remaining partnerships leave the issue of distribution to the discretion of the general partners.

In 29% of the contracts studied, the general partners are entitled to take their profit participation (called the 'carried interest') – in income or gains without restriction. In the other partnerships the general partners are not entitled to take the carried interest until the limited partners have received an amount at least equal to their cumulative capital contribution.

General partners generally have the option to make distributions in the form of securities, cash, or both. Often when a portfolio company becomes successful, its shares are registered with the SEC and a public offering takes place [see Barry et al. (1990)]. Typically, the venture-capital firm does not or cannot liquidate its shareholdings on the offering. The shares can be distributed to the limited partners in proportion to their ownership of the fund, or the fund can continue to hold the shares, taking responsibility for distributing them at some future date, or converting them to cash through a transaction such as a secondary offering. If the shares are distributed to the limited partners, the value assigned is the last price in the stock market before the distribution.

4.7. Reporting and accounting policies

All venture-capital firms surveyed agree to provide the limited partners with periodic reports on the value and progress of portfolio companies, including an annual meeting with the general partners and selected portfolio-company management teams. Because most investments are made in private companies with highly uncertain prospects, assigning values is very difficult. Often the partners agree to recognize losses quickly and to write up the value of an investment only if there is a significant arms-length transaction at a higher value. If no such transactions have occurred and no loss seems likely, cost is used as a basis for reporting. As a result of these policies, most venture-capital firms report negative rates of return during the first few years of the fund [see also Venture Economics (1988c)].

4.8. Specific conflicts of interest

Most contracts specify the percentage of time the venture capitalists propose to devote to the management of the fund being raised. A small number of partnership agreements restrict the ability of general partners to coinvest or receive securities from portfolio companies. Some partnerships restrict follow-on funds from investing in securities held by a previous fund managed by the same venture capitalists. Other fund agreements prevent the general partner from raising a new fund until some percentage (for example,

50%) of the capital raised in the existing fund has been invested in portfolio companies.

4.9. Special advisory committees

Of the 76 funds studied by Venture Economics (1987), 41 establish formal advisory boards; another 17 create informal advisory boards. Of those with formal advisory boards, 19 require limited-partner representation. An additional 18 funds establish boards composed solely of representatives of the limited partners; these boards are separate and distinct from the advisory board.

Advisory boards and boards composed of limited partners are often designed to provide access to deals or technical expertise. Some boards are structured like traditional boards of directors, providing guidance and oversight for the operation of the venture-capital fund. Still other advisory committees are assigned specific responsibilities, the most important of which is determining the value of the portfolio.

5. Analyzing the relationship between external investors and venture capitalists

Venture capitalists act as agents for the limited partners, who choose to invest in entrepreneurial ventures through an intermediary rather than directly. In such situations, conflicts arise between the agent and the principal, which must be addressed in the contracts and other mechanisms that govern their relationship.

In the venture-capital industry, the agency problem is likely to be particularly difficult. There is inevitably a high degree of information asymmetry between the venture capitalists, who play an active role in the portfolio companies, and the limited partners, who cannot monitor the prospects of each individual investment as closely.

The contractual provisions outlined in section 4 can be explained as attempts to resolve the agency problem, the operating cost problem, and the sorting problem simultaneously.

5.1. Agency costs

Venture capitalists have many opportunities to take advantage of the people who invest with them. To a degree, the agency problem is exacerbated by the legal structure of limited partnerships, which prevents limited partners from playing a role in the management of the venture-capital partnership.

Contracts are designed with several key provisions to protect the limited partners from the possibility that the venture capitalists will make decisions against their interests. First, the life of a venture-capital fund is limited; the venture capitalist cannot keep the money forever. Organizational models like mutual funds or corporations, in contrast, have indefinite life spans. Implicitly, the investors also preserve the right not to invest in any later fund managed by the same venture capitalists.

Second, the limited partners preserve the right to withdraw from funding the partnership by reneging on their commitments to invest beyond the initial capital infusion as described in section 4.4. Third, the compensation system is structured to give the venture capitalists the appropriate incentives. The fund managers are typically entitled to receive 20% of the profits generated by the fund. For reasons which will be explored more fully below, the profit participation and other aspects of the contract encourage the venture capitalist to allocate the management fee to activities that will increase the total value of the portfolio.

Fourth, the mandatory distribution policy defuses potential differences of opinion about what to do with the proceeds from the sale of assets in the portfolio. The general partners cannot choose to invest in securities that serve their own private interests at the expense of the limited partners.

Finally, the contract addresses obvious areas of conflict between the venture capitalist and the limited partner. Thus, the venture capitalist is often explicitly prohibited from self-dealing (for example, being able to buy stock in the portfolio on preferential terms or receiving distributions different from those given to the limited partner). Also, the venture capitalists are contractually required to commit a certain percentage of their effort to the activities of the fund. Although this requirement is difficult to monitor, egregious violations can be the subject of litigation if fund performance is poor.

5.2. Further analysis of the compensation system

The compensation system plays a critical role in aligning the interests of the venture capitalists and the limited partners. To understand the implicit incentives, consider a $200 million fund with eight general partners that receives a management fee of 2.5% of total capital committed. Annual revenues are $5 million and revenues per partner are $625,000. Various expenses must be subtracted, including partner base salaries, office expenses, travel, insurance, and support staff. A reasonable estimate of the partners' base pay is $250,000 per year per partner, equivalent to 40% of total revenues. An informal survey of five venture-capital firms with this amount of capital under management revealed that the firm can be expected to clear a profit each year. If total expenses are 2.1% of the capital committed (the average reported in the informal survey), the annual operating profit is $800,000, or $100,000 per partner. Such profits are typically distributed to partners at the end of the year as a bonus.

If this hypothetical $200 million fund is successful and achieves a 20% rate of return on committed capital over its five-year duration (before consideration of the profit participation but after taking into account the management fee), the ending value will be approximately $498 million. The general partners will be entitled to 20% of the $298 million profit, or $59 million, equivalent to $7.4 million per partner. This figure translates to a $4.2 million present value per partner, assuming payment at the end of the last year and a 10% discount rate, or roughly $1.2 million per year per partner on a comparable annuity basis (also assuming a 10% discount rate). This figure far outweighs each general partner's combined base salary and annual bonus, estimated at $350,000 per year. An extra 1% in compound rate of return increases the present value of the carried interest from $4.2 million to $4.5 million, based on the assumptions used earlier. As long as the compound annual rate of return on the fund is positive, the percentage increase in the venture capitalists' share exceeds the percentage increase in the total value of the portfolio.[7]

Gathering hard data on venture-capital compensation is very difficult: many firms do not reveal key statistics about their business. According to a survey of 63 private independent venture-capital firms with over $5 billion in total committed capital in 1988 [Hay Management Consultants (1988)], however, the average 1987 base pay of a managing partner of a private, independent venture-capital firm was $223,000. The annual operating bonus was $51,000 and the average realized profits distribution was $163,000, resulting in total compensation of $437,000. These figures are not as dramatic as the simple numerical calculation used above, which accurately reflects the data provided by the four venture firms interviewed specifically about compensation. Also, the Hay Management Consultants data are difficult to interpret in light of the poor overall returns for most venture-capital funds in 1987 and the tendency for general partners to defer as long as possible the recognition of income for tax purposes. Nevertheless, the carried interest component of compensation is large in relation to the other components.[8] The implication is that the venture capitalists have incentives to engage in activities that increase the value of the carried interest, which is precisely what benefits the limited partners.

---

[7]These calculations ignore the return the venture capitalists receive on their direct investments in the partnership (for example, on the 1% investment described in section 4.2).

[8]The informal survey cited earlier also revealed that a number of successful venture-capital firms operate on an annual budget, which is negotiated each year with the limited partners. Examples include Greylock, Sutter Hill, and Charles River Partners. In these firms, the partners receive modest cash salaries and the venture-capital management company does not realize an annual profit. The partners are dependent on the carried interest to supplement current salaries. It is difficult to find evidence of a correlation between compensation structures and performance, however. For example, one highly regarded firm, Kleiner Perkins, receives a management fee of 3% and a carried interest percentage of 30%.

Although the compensation system seems to provide appropriate incentives, there are some difficult issues. One area of potential conflict between the limited and general partners relates to risk. The venture capitalist's equity participation may be thought of as an option that entitles the venture-capital management firm to 20% of the increase in value of the underlying fund. The exercise price of the option is the cost basis of the fund, and the life of the option equals the life of the fund.

Numerical analyses, based on a simple Black–Scholes model, suggest that the ex ante value of the venture-capital contract might be as high as 10% of the initial total capital of the fund. Thus the value of the contract on a $100 million fund might be $10 million at the time of signing. Table 5 presents estimates of the value of the contract (as a fraction of the original cost of the fund assets) based on different assumptions about the volatility of returns, current fund value, the carried interest percentage, and the life of the fund.

The fact that the management contract can be viewed as an option suggests the inherent agency problem: if one party has a contingent claim on value, there is an implicit incentive to increase risk [Myers (1986)]. The value of the contingent claim increases as risk increases. In the example above, the value of the contract would rise from approximately $13.2 million to $16 million if the assumed annual volatility were increased from 50% to 80%. In some situations, it will pay a venture capitalist to make negative-net-present-value investments because doing so increases the value of the option by more than the loss in value on his portion of the equity claim.

Partnership agreements respond in several ways to the possibility that the venture capitalist will take undue risks. Since the contract can be cancelled by the limited partners at any point in the life of the fund, the venture capitalist's incentive to incur such uncompensated risks is reduced. Although this solution helps resolve the agency problem from the limited partners' perspective, however, it can be abused. In one situation [Sahlman (1988c)], for example, a contract was cancelled by the sole limited partner after three years of a ten-year term. At the time of cancellation, the estimated value of the fund's underlying assets was close to the cost of those assets. The contract stipulated that the only payment due the venture-capital management company by the limited partner upon cancellation was the 20% share of estimated realized and unrealized gains on the portfolio. The limited partner was not contractually required to pay anything to the venture-capital management company for canceling the contract per se, even though from an option-valuation perspective the contract was clearly valuable. Most contracts, however, make cancellation more difficult than this (for example, by defining a narrow set of circumstances – such as fraud – under which the general partner can be fired).

Other mechanisms are also used to manage the perverse incentives of the contract. For example, the partnership agreement usually limits the amount

Table 5

Sensitivity of the present value of the carried interest of a venture-capital fund (as a fraction of original cost) to changes in volatility, current market value of fund assets, carried interest percentage, and life of the fund.

Assumptions:

Total original capital of the fund (cost)	$100,000,000
Current market value of fund assets	$100,000,000
Profit participation % – Carried interest	20%
Time to maturity – Economic life in years	7
Risk-free interest rate	10.0%
Volatility – Standard deviation of annual returns	50.0%

Results:

Estimated present value of carried interest	13,212,516
Estimated value of carried interest as a % of original capital (cost)	13.2%

Present value of the carried interest as a fraction of the original capital of the fund as a function of volatility and the current market value of the fund assets

Volatility	Current market value of fund (millions)						
	$70.00	$80.00	$90.00	$100.00	$110.00	$120.00	$130.00
10.0%	4.2%	6.1%	8.1%	10.1%	12.1%	14.1%	16.1%
20.0%	5.0%	6.7%	8.5%	10.4%	12.3%	14.2%	16.2%
30.0%	6.0%	7.7%	9.4%	11.2%	13.0%	14.9%	16.7%
40.0%	7.1%	8.7%	10.4%	12.2%	14.0%	15.8%	17.6%
50.0%	8.1%	9.8%	11.5%	13.2%	15.0%	16.8%	18.6%
60.0%	9.0%	10.7%	12.5%	14.2%	16.0%	17.8%	19.7%
70.0%	9.9%	11.6%	13.4%	15.2%	17.0%	18.8%	20.7%
80.0%	10.6%	12.4%	14.2%	16.0%	17.9%	19.7%	21.6%
90.0%	11.3%	13.1%	14.9%	16.8%	18.7%	20.5%	22.4%

Continued overleaf

Table 5 (continued)

Present value of the carried interest as a fraction of the original capital of the fund as a function of volatility and the profit participation – Carried interest (%)

Volatility	Profit participation – Carried interest (%)						
	5.0%	10.0%	15.0%	20.0%	25.0%	30.0%	35.0%
10.0%	2.5%	5.0%	7.6%	10.1%	12.6%	15.1%	17.6%
20.0%	2.6%	5.2%	7.8%	10.4%	13.0%	15.6%	18.2%
30.0%	2.8%	5.6%	8.4%	11.2%	14.0%	16.8%	19.5%
40.0%	3.0%	6.1%	9.1%	12.2%	15.2%	18.3%	21.3%
50.0%	3.3%	6.6%	9.9%	13.2%	16.5%	19.8%	23.1%
60.0%	3.6%	7.1%	10.7%	14.2%	17.8%	21.3%	24.9%
70.0%	3.8%	7.6%	11.4%	15.2%	19.0%	22.8%	26.6%
80.0%	4.0%	8.0%	12.0%	16.0%	20.0%	24.0%	28.1%
90.0%	4.2%	8.4%	12.6%	16.8%	21.0%	25.2%	29.4%

Present value of the carried interest as a fraction of the original capital of the fund as a function of volatility and the time to maturity (life) of the fund

Volatility	Time to maturity – Life (years)						
	2.5	4.0	5.5	7.0	8.5	10.0	11.5
10.0%	4.5%	6.6%	8.5%	10.1%	11.5%	12.6%	13.7%
20.0%	5.1%	7.1%	8.9%	10.4%	11.7%	12.8%	13.8%
30.0%	6.0%	8.0%	9.7%	11.2%	12.4%	13.4%	14.3%
40.0%	7.0%	9.1%	10.8%	12.2%	13.3%	14.3%	15.1%
50.0%	7.9%	10.1%	11.8%	13.2%	14.3%	15.2%	16.0%
60.0%	8.9%	11.2%	12.9%	14.2%	15.3%	16.1%	16.8%
70.0%	9.9%	12.2%	13.9%	15.2%	16.2%	16.9%	17.5%
80.0%	10.8%	13.2%	14.8%	16.0%	16.9%	17.6%	18.1%
90.0%	11.6%	14.0%	15.7%	16.8%	17.6%	18.2%	18.6%

of capital that can be invested in a single venture, which prevents excessive investments in high-risk ventures with inadequate rewards. As mentioned earlier, many contracts call for mandatory distributions of realized gains. If venture capitalists were allowed to invest realized gains in new ventures, they might increase the risk to the fund without a commensurate increase in return. Mandatory distributions also protect the principals against activities not consistent with the goals of the fund.

One final contractual response to the problem of risk is to force the general partner to invest more in the fund than the customary small amounts mentioned earlier. Then the venture capitalists bear a greater share of the costs of investing in ventures that perform poorly. On the other hand, the risk problem will be intensified if the venture capitalist is required to pay a fee up front for the right to manage the funds of the limited partners.[9] This has the effect of making the excise price on the option higher. The same basic problem arises if there is a rate-of-return hurdle that has to be exceeded before the venture capitalist is entitled to a carried interest. In this case, the exercise price of the option rises each year, which means that an increase in risk has a significant payoff to the option holder.

One other area of concern in the compensation system used in the venture-capital organization relates to incentives to increase the amount of capital under management and/or to manage multiple pools of capital over time. The basic issues are discussed in the next section.

5.3. Operating costs

Two kinds of operating costs deserve analysis when discussing venture capital, taxes, and continuing operating costs. With respect to taxes, partner-ship gains are not subject to partnership-level taxation. The limited and general partners report the realized gains and losses on their individual tax returns. Second, securities can be distributed without triggering immediate taxable income for the recipient. Thus a limited partner who receives stock in a portfolio company can defer recognizing the gain (or loss) until that security is sold. Third, the venture capitalists do not incur taxable income when they receive their carried interest in the partnership: they report taxable income only as gains and losses are realized· on the underlying securities.

Finally, the partnership's compensation scheme can be structured to allo-cate losses to those who can make best use of them. This feature of partnerships has been used widely in structuring oil-and-gas partnerships [Wolfson (1985)] and research-and-development limited partnerships. Tax

---

[9]In a number of cases, venture-capital management firms have been purchased. Examples include Ampersand Ventures, TA Associates, and Brinson Partners.

incentives in venture capital are less important, however, because many of the investors in venture funds are tax-exempt. More importantly, there are no significant tax losses to be allocated because a fund's unrealized losses are not recognized by the IRS for tax purposes unless the underlying securities are transferred to another party in an arms-length transaction. Often partnerships do allocate these losses to the limited partners, but the economic impact is minimal.

With respect to operating costs, scale economies, scope economies, and learning-curve effects are often very significant to a venture-capital management company that manages one or more funds. Scale economies exist if the unit cost of production and distribution of a product or service declines as volume increases. In the venture-capital organization, production and distribution encompass raising capital, finding and structuring deals, monitoring the investments, and distributing the proceeds. Scope economies exist if unit costs decline if multiple products or services are produced simultaneously (for example, if more than one fund is managed at a time). Learning-curve effects exist if the unit cost of a process declines over time with accumulated volume.

With respect to scale economies, it seems likely that unit costs decline with the absolute size of the venture-capital pool under management because there are a number of fixed (or near-fixed) costs, including items in the overhead budget such as rent, information acquisition, accounting, and certain legal costs. Economies of scope are also likely because the cost of managing multiple pools of capital does not rise linearly with the number of such pools.

Finally, with respect to learning-curve effects, venture-capital firms become repositories of useful institutional knowledge. Venture capitalists and their support staffs benefit from learning-curve effects as they become adept in dealing with each other and with other resource suppliers, such as law firms, accounting firms, investment bankers, and management recruiting firms. They cultivate a deal flow based on networks of contacts and relationships. The venture-capital organization develops a reputation that has economic value. The ultimate effect is to make the firm more efficient as time passes and experience accumulates.

Compensation practices give evidence of scale and/or scope economies as well as experience effects. According to the Hay Management Consultants (1988) survey, the total compensation for the managing partner of a venture-capital fund with less than $25 million in capital averages $163,000. The comparable figure for a managing partner of a fund with more than $200 million under management is $581,000. The annual bonus, which is based on the operating profit of the management company rather than the investment performance of the fund, constitutes 28% of total compensation in the larger funds, compared with 17% in the small funds. These differences suggest that venture capitalists have an incentive to increase the size of the firm. One driving factor in this regard is the fact that the percentage fee charged to manage a venture-capital fund does not appear to decline with the size of the fund [see Venture Economics (1987)].

There can also be incentives to create multiple funds over time, all managed by the same venture capitalists. Doing so accomplishes two goals. First, keeping the venture-capital management company in existence preserves the learning that has taken place. Second, managing multiple funds takes advantage of any scale or scope economies. From 1977 to 1988, new funds averaged less than one-half the size of follow-on funds (panel B, table 1).

Even though unit costs decline as the size of the venture-capital management firm (or number of funds under management) increases, the limited partners and general partners will not necessarily agree about the optimal size and structure of the firm. This is because the unit costs and risk-adjusted rates of return to the limited partners may be negatively correlated, and because the limited and general partners do not have equal stakes in all the income streams generated by the fund. There could easily be situations in which the venture capitalists find it more profitable to have a large firm, one effect of which is lower returns to the limited partners. This would be true if there were diseconomies of scale or scope in the investment-return-generating process.

The possibility that the interests of the general and limited partners will diverge over time is addressed directly by limiting the lifespan of the venture-capital partnership. If the venture capitalists make decisions that aren't in the best interests of the limited partners, they can be denied access to capital. Any learning, scale, or scope economies will then go to waste. The ability to withdraw funding support is the ultimate tool for aligning the interests of the agent and principal in this organizational form, and is reinforced by the existence of the scale or scope economies and learning-curve effects.

5.4. The sorting problem

The final component of this analysis of the economic relationship between the limited partners and the venture capitalists is an examination of how limited partners decide which venture capitalists to back. For obvious reasons, filtering out the 'good' from the 'bad' venture capitalists is extremely important. 'Good' venture capitalists have the skill and intention to generate high risk-adjusted rates of return for the limited partners. Actual rates of return will also depend, of course, on such factors as the capital markets, competition among venture capitalists, and the market for innovation.

Limited partners in venture-capital firms typically invest at least $1 million in each fund. Before committing this amount of capital, the investors spend resources on due diligence. They read the offering memoranda prepared by the venture capitalists in accordance with SEC regulations, and they often check the venture capitalists' credentials. This investigation acts as a preliminary screen on potential investments.

The governance structure also helps potential investors distinguish between good venture capitalists and weak ones. The basic argument is simple: good venture capitalists are more likely than weak venture capitalists to accept a finite life for each new partnership and a compensation system heavily dependent on investment returns. By doing so, they agree explicitly to have their performance reviewed at least every few years: if they engage in opportunistic acts or are incompetent, they will be denied access to funds. In addition, most of their expected compensation comes from a share in the fund's profits. If they perform well, they will participate handsomely in the fund's success. They will also be rewarded by being able to raise additional capital and, most likely, benefit from the various economies characteristic of the business. If they are not confident of performing well, or if they intend to neglect the interests of the limited partners, they will probably not agree to the basic terms of the contract.[10]

5.5. The overall incentives

In sum, the relationship between the limited and general partners in a venture-capital fund is fraught with agency problems. The limited partners structure a contract that creates incentives for mutual gain, and they specifically forbid certain obvious acts of self-interest like buying stock in portfolio companies at prices less than those paid by the fund. The limited partners then expend resources to monitor the fund's progress, often through special committees. At the same time the venture capitalists agree to forego certain self-interested acts and to supply information to the limited partners. The venture capitalists willingly enter into an agreement with a finite life, exposing the contract to renewal. In effect, the limited partners stage the commitment of capital to the venture capitalists while preserving mechanisms to ensure that the profits will be distributed rather than kept inside the venture-capital fund. And the terms of the contract both communicate the

---

[10]This description of the incentives of the venture capitalists is drawn from the signaling literature [Spence (1973), Ross (1977), Leland and Pyle (1977), and Bhattacharya (1979)]. The implicit condition for the sorting process to work is that the short-term payoff (in present-value terms) to the venture capitalist must be less than the opportunity cost for a 'bad' venture capitalist. Note also that each limited partner spends time and resources researching venture capitalists seeking to raise funds, which helps guard against false signaling. From another perspective, accepting these terms may be viewed as a bonding commitment by the venture capitalist, who implicitly agrees not to divert money from the fund.

expectations of the limited partners to the venture capitalists, and filter out those who are unable or unwilling to meet those expectations.

The contracts and operating procedures that have evolved in the venture-capital industry address three issues simultaneously: sorting good from bad venture capitalists, minimizing the present value of agency costs, and minimizing the present value of operating costs. The same basic issues confront the venture capitalists when they invest in entrepreneurial ventures. In this case, the venture capitalists become the principals and the entrepreneurs the agents. Analogous contractual and operating responses to these issues are made by the venture-capital fund.

6. The venture-capital investment process

Once a venture-capital fund is raised, the venture capitalists must identify investment opportunities, structure and execute deals with entrepreneurial teams, monitor investments, and ultimately achieve some return on their capital. For the purposes of this paper, I focus on structuring deals.

Just as venture-capital partnerships have many elements in common, the contracts between the venture capitalists and the companies they invest in are similar in many ways. The basic document that governs the relationship between the venture-capital firm and the venture is the stock-purchase agreement, which is described below.[11] The economic rationale for the terms and conditions of this document and other aspects of the venture-capital process are explored in section 7.

6.1. Amount and timing

Each stock-purchase agreement fixes the amount and timing of the investment. Venture capitalists typically invest more than once during the life of a company, and the amount invested often increases with each round (see tables 3 and 4). They expect the capital invested at each point to be sufficient to take the company to the next stage of development, when it will require additional capital to make further progress.

---

[11]This account of stock-purchase agreements is drawn from a number of sources. First, I have gathered approximately 40 such agreements from a broad range of venture-capital partnerships. Venture capitalists tend to use the same deal structure in all of their deals so that knowing how one deal is structured sheds light on many investments made by the same fund. Some of these materials have formed the basis for case studies used at Harvard Business School, including Knights and Sahlman (1986a, 1986b, 1986c, 1986d), Sahlman (1983a, 1983b, 1984, 1985a, 1985b, 1985c, 1985d, 1985e, 1986a, 1986b, 1986c, 1986d, 1988c, 1989b), Sahlman and Knights (1986), Sahlman and Scherlis (1988), Sahlman and Soussou (1985a, 1985b), and Soussou and Sahlman (1986). See also Sahlman (1988). A broad survey of the characteristics of deals struck by venture-capital firms is included in Plummer (1987). Finally, a number of texts describe standard operating procedures in the industry, including Bartlett (1988) and Morris (1988a).

6.2. Form and terms of investment

Many venture-capital investments are made as purchases of convertible preferred stock. Specific terms concern:

(1) conversion price, which can vary according to the performance of the company;
(2) liquidation preference, including a description of the events that trigger liquidation (for example, a merger or reorganization with a total value less than some predetermined amount);
(3) dividend rate, payment terms, and voting rights (typically on an as-if-converted basis).

Typically, the convertible preferred stock does not pay a dividend on a current basis, but at the discretion of the board of directors. Some preferreds have provisions that call for accruing dividends but deferring the payment of cash. The liquidation preference amount is equal in most cases to the face amount of the convertible preferred issue and all accrued but unpaid dividends.

6.3. Puts and calls

Agreements typically give the venture capitalists the right to put the security by calling for redemption of the preferred stock. Less frequently, contracts give portfolio-company management the right to call the security away from the venture capitalists at some point.

6.4. Registration rights

Most agreements give the venture capitalists the right to register their shares at some point or points in the future. This enables the venture capitalists to demand registration at any two dates in the future, with the expenses of registration paid by the company. Venture capitalists also insist on piggyback registration rights that entitle them to register shares at the same time as the company, subject to limitations imposed by the SEC and the underwriters.

6.5. Go-along rights

Many agreements specify that the venture capitalists can sell shares after conversion at the same time and on the same terms as the key employees.

6.6. Preemptive rights and rights of first refusal

Many agreements entitle the venture-capital investors to participate in new financings by buying newly issued shares from the company, often in proportion to their common-stock-equivalent holdings before the issuance of new equity-equivalent shares. The terms of such financing rounds are not typically negotiated in advance; they reflect the then-current conditions in the capital markets and the performance and prospects of the firm.

6.7. Option pool

Most agreements fix the number of shares outstanding and the size of the pool of shares that can be granted or sold to current and future employees. Provisions for modifying the option pool are also included in the stock-purchase agreement.

6.8. Employment contracts

Most agreements require that key employees execute employment contracts and agree to noncompete clauses. Such contracts usually specify compensation, benefits, and, most important, the conditions under which the contract can be terminated and the consequences of termination.

6.9. Vesting schedules and buy-back provisions

Employees of venture-capital-backed companies often accept modest cash salaries in return for equity ownership. Many agreements set explicit vesting schedules for management shares and also grant the company being financed the right to repurchase shares in the event of an employee's voluntary or involuntary departure. When shares are repurchased under these agreements, the price paid by the company to the departing entrepreneur is often based on book value, which may be below market value.

6.10. Information rights

Most agreements call for regular transmission of information, including financial statements and budgets, and permit the venture capitalists to inspect the company's financial accounts at will. Venture capitalists insist on timely access to such information. They typically receive detailed monthly financial statements and more frequent operating statements. They evaluate this information to anticipate problems and respond expeditiously when performance falls short.

6.11. Board structure

Most agreements call for venture capitalist representation on the company's board of directors [see Barry et al. (1990) for information on venture-capitalist board representation of companies going public]. Often, the agreement calls for other mutually acceptable people to be elected to the board. The venture capitalists typically receive no cash compensation for board duties; if any cash is received for board membership, it is paid into the partnership. Outside members recruited to join the board usually receive inexpensive common stock or warrants to acquire shares, and little or no cash compensation.

7. The relationship between the venture capitalists and the entrepreneurial ventures

Each year venture capitalists screen hundreds of investment proposals before deciding which ideas and teams to support. The success or failure of any given venture depends on the effort and skill of the people involved as well as on certain factors outside their control (for example, the economy), but the capabilities of the individuals involved are difficult to gauge up front.

Once investment decisions are made and deals consummated, it is difficult to monitor progress. The probability of failure is high (see fig. 1, which shows that 34.5% of the capital invested in the survey resulted in a loss). The venture capitalist and the entrepreneur are also likely to have different information. Even with the same information, they are likely to disagree on certain issues, including if and when to abandon a venture and how and when to cash in on investments.

Venture capitalists attack these problems in several ways. First, they structure their investments so they can keep firm control. The most important mechanism for controlling the venture is staging the infusion of capital. Second, they devise compensation schemes that provide venture managers with appropriate incentives. Third, they become actively involved in managing the companies they fund, in effect functioning as consultants. Finally, venture capitalists preserve mechanisms to make their investments liquid.

7.1. Staging the commitment of capital and other control mechanisms

Venture capitalists rarely, if ever, invest all the external capital that a company will require to accomplish its business plan: instead, they invest in companies at distinct stages in their development. As a result, each company begins life knowing that it has only enough capital to reach the next stage. By staging capital the venture capitalists preserve the right to abandon a project whose prospects look dim. The right to abandon is essential because an entrepreneur will almost never stop investing in a failing project as long as others are providing capital.

Staging the capital also provides incentives to the entrepreneurial team. Capital is a scarce and expensive resource for individual ventures. Misuse of capital is very costly to venture capitalists but not necessarily to management. To encourage managers to conserve capital, venture-capital firms apply strong sanctions if it is misused. These sanctions ordinarily take two basic forms. First, increased capital requirements invariably dilute management's equity share at an increasingly punitive rate. (This was the case with Federal Express). Second, the staged investment process enables venture-capital firms to shut down operations completely. The credible threat to abandon a venture, even when the firm might be economically viable, is the key to the relationship between the entrepreneur and the venture capitalist [see also Stiglitz and Weiss (1983) for a similar argument in the banking industry].[12] By denying capital, the venture capitalist also signals other capital suppliers that the company in question is a bad investment risk.

Short of denying the company capital, venture capitalists can discipline wayward managers by firing or demoting them. Other elements of the stock-purchase agreement then come into play. For example, the company typically has the right to repurchase shares from departing managers, often at prices below market value (for example, at book value). The use of vesting schedules limits the number of shares employees are entitled to if they leave prematurely. Finally, noncompete clauses can impose strong penalties on those who leave, particularly if their human capital is closely linked to the industry in which the venture is active.

Entrepreneurs accept the staged capital process because they usually have great confidence in their own abilities to meet targets. They understand that if they meet those goals, they will end up owning a significantly larger share of the company than if they had insisted on receiving all of the capital up front. As discussed below, entrepreneurs also must make conscious choices about who provides capital and what value they can add in addition to capital.

Finally, whereas venture capitalists insist on retaining the option to abandon a particular venture, they also want to be able to invest more if the company requires and warrants additional capital. This option is preserved by insisting on rights of first refusal or pre-emptive rights.

---

[12]The seemingly irrational act of shutting down an economically viable entity is rational when viewed from the perspective of the venture capitalist confronted with allocating time and capital among various projects. Although the individual company may be economically viable, the return on time and capital to the individual venture capitalist is less than the opportunity cost, which is why the venture is terminated.

7.2. The compensation scheme

Entrepreneurs who accept venture capital typically take smaller cash salaries than they could earn in the labor market. The shortfall in current income is offset by stock ownership in the ventures they start. Common stock and any subsequent stock options received will not pay off, however, unless the company creates value and affords an opportunity to convert illiquid holdings to cash. In this regard, the interests of the venture-capital investor and entrepreneur are aligned.

This compensation system penalizes poor performance by an employee. If the employee is terminated, all unvested shares or options are returned to the company. In almost all cases, the company retains the right to repurchase shares from the employee at predetermined prices.

Without sanctions, entrepreneurs might sometimes have an incentive to increase risk without an adequate increase in return. An entrepreneur's compensation package can be viewed as a contingent claim, whose value increases with volatility. The sanctions, combined with the venture capitalists' active role in the management of the venture, helps to mitigate the incentive to increase risk.

7.3. Active involvement of venture capitalists in portfolio companies

No contract between an entrepreneur and venture capitalist can anticipate every possible disagreement or conflict. Partly for this reason, the venture capitalist typically plays a role in the operation of the company.

Venture capitalists sit on boards of directors, help recruit and compensate key individuals, work with suppliers and customers, help establish tactics and strategy, play a major role in raising capital, and help structure transactions such as mergers and acquisitions. They often assume more direct control by changing management and are sometimes willing to take over day-to-day operations themselves. All of these activities are designed to increase the likelihood of success and improve return on investment: they also protect the interests of the venture capitalist and ameliorate the information asymmetry.

According to one survey [Gorman and Sahlman (1989)], lead venture investors visit each portfolio company an average of 19 times per year, and spend 100 hours in direct contact (on site or by phone) with the company. Since each venture capitalist in the survey is responsible for almost nine investments and sits on five boards of directors, the allocation of time to each portfolio company is considerable [see also MacMillan et al. (1989) and Timmons (1987)]. In addition to devoting time to companies already in the portfolio, a venture capitalist must allocate time to raising capital for the venture-capital firm, finding new deals, managing the venture-capital firm, and meeting with various resource suppliers, such as bankers and accountants.

Successful venture capitalists bring instant credibility associated with their capital, their contacts, and their range of projects. A venture-capital-backed company can often gain access to more capital from the fund itself, and the venture capitalist's contacts in the financial community can make it easier to raise new capital from other sources. In addition, resource suppliers form implicit and explicit relationships with venture capitalists in an attempt to piggyback on the data-gathering and monitoring process [see the HBS cases Sahlman (1986d, 1985e) and Knights and Sahlman (1986b)]. Venture capitalists have incentives not to exploit a resource supplier on any individual deal, since the repercussions can affect other deals. At the same time, the resource suppliers have incentives to preserve their relationship with venture-capital firms by avoiding opportunistic behavior on individual deals.

Finally, venture capitalists maintain close ties to investment bankers who can assist companies going public or merging with other companies [Barry et al. (1990)]. Venture capitalists also often have contacts in large companies to which entrepreneurial ventures might be sold.

7.4. Mechanisms related to liquidity

Both venture capitalists and entrepreneurs want eventually to convert their illiquid holdings into cash or cash equivalents, but they can disagree on the timing or the method. The standard stock-purchase agreement has a number of features that control the process by which the venture capitalists and the entrepreneurs achieve their goals. Chief among these is the decision to invest in the form of a convertible preferred.

Using preferred stock with a dividend creates a mechanism for deriving some income from an investment if the company is only marginally successful. Most deals defer payment of the dividend until the board allows it, but because venture capitalists often control the board, they can make the decision. Since the dividends are not tax-deductible, the burden of paying dividends is often onerous, which often leads the entrepreneurs to try to buy out the preferred.

Many agreements also give the venture capitalists the right to force redemption of a preferred stock or the right to put the stock to the company, to achieve liquidity. This option may be exercised if the company is financially viable but too small to go public. Some contracts give entrepreneurs the right to sell stock back to the venture capitalist, as might happen if the venture capitalists terminate the entrepreneur's employment without cause.

Finally, venture capitalists are concerned about situations where the entrepreneurs have an opportunity to sell their shares before the venture capitalists sell theirs. Therefore, the contract typically specifies that the venture capitalists can sell their shares at the same time and on the same terms as the entrepreneur.

7.5. Additional implications of using convertible preferred stock

Using a convertible preferred also provides flexibility in setting the conversion terms. The venture capitalist often can base the conversion ratio for the preferred stock on the company's performance. If the company does well, the conversion price might be higher, with lower dilution for the management team. A similar tool is the 'ratchet', which ensures that the effective price per share paid by the venture capitalist is at least as low as any price paid in the future.

Flexible conversion terms alter the risk-and-reward-sharing scheme. One intent is to discourage entrepreneurs from overstating their projections to increase the initial valuation, and to encourage them to build value. Incorporating these provisions into contracts also serves as a negotiating tool to account for differences of opinion about future prospects.[13]

One final consequence of having preferred stock in the capital structure relates to taxation: using a preferred creates two kinds of securities, one with superior rights. A security that is senior in rights to common stock in effect lowers the economic value of the common. Members of the management team can therefore buy the common stock at low prices without incurring taxable income. Common-stock value is frequently set at 10% of the conversion price of the preferred. If the common stock had the same rights as the preferred, the managers would have to report taxable income on the difference between the price they paid and the price paid by the venture capitalists. There is no immediate tax disadvantage to using preferred stock, however, because the dividend is deferred and many of the ultimate recipients are tax exempt.

7.6. Using the contract to sort out entrepreneurs

A key feature of the contracts and operating procedures is that risk is shifted from the venture capitalists to the entrepreneur. The entrepreneur's response to these terms enables the venture capitalist to make informed evaluations and judgments. It would be foolish for entrepreneurs to accept such contract terms if they were not truly confident of their own abilities and deeply committed to the venture.

For example, by substituting stock ownership for higher current income, the contract shifts the risks of poor performance to the entrepreneur. Similarly, the convertible preferred security shifts some of the costs of poor performance to the entrepreneurial team. Given the liquidation preference

---

[13]See Knights and Sahlman (1986b) for a description of a conditional conversion price. In that situation, the venture capitalists agreed to increase the conversion price (from $0.45 to $0.67) if the company met its business-plan sales-and-profit targets.

Table 6[a]

Stage	Discount rate range (%)
Startup	50 to 70
First stage	40 to 60
Second stage	35 to 50
Third stage	35 to 50
Fourth stage	30 to 40
IPO	25 to 35

[a]*Source:* Plummer (1987, p. I-18).

embodied in the security, the venture capitalists will be entitled to a larger share of total value if total value is low.

Moreover, the entrepreneurs typically hold undiversified portfolios. Much of their wealth is invested in the securities of the company they manage. The entrepreneur's willingness to bear diversifiable risk also conveys useful information to the venture capitalists.

7.7. Evaluation techniques

The methods venture capitalists use to judge the prospects of individual projects are also used to sort out entrepreneurs. In screening potential ventures, venture capitalists use certain standard evaluation techniques, including this simple method for determining the value of the companies[14]:

(a) A forecast is made reflecting successful attainment of achievable long-term goals.

(b) The venture capitalist estimates a possible terminal value that would obtain if the investment in the company were harvested at that point.

(c) The terminal value is converted to a present value by applying a high discount rate, usually between 40% and 60%.

(d) The proportion of company stock to be owned by the venture-capital firm is then calculated by dividing the required investment by the total present value.

The most important element of this process is determining the discount rate. According to Plummer (1987), the discount rates used by venture capitalists vary by the company's stage of development. The results of that study are summarized in table 6 (the stages are defined in table 2):

These discount rates seem high compared with other rates of return in the economy [for example, the returns on publicly traded stocks and bonds as reported in Ibbotson (1988)] or even the actual returns reported by profes-

---

[14]See Plummer (1987), Morris (1988b), and Sahlman and Scherlis (1988) for more detailed descriptions of the method.

sional venture-capital funds [Venture Economics (1985, 1988c)]. In theory the required rate of return on an entrepreneurial investment reflects the risk-free interest rates in the economy, the systematic risk of the particular asset and the market risk premium, the liquidity of the asset,[15] and compensation for the value added by the supplier of capital (including favored access to other resources). This last adjustment is required to compensate venture capitalists for monitoring the company and playing an active role in management, while leaving the limited partner with the appropriate rate of return after taking into account the venture-capital fund's management fees and profit participation.

In practice, the use of high discount rates also reflects a well-known bias in financial projections made by entrepreneurs. Because few companies ever do as well as their founders believe they will, the numerator used in the calculation described above is typically higher than the expected value, though it may be an unbiased estimate conditional on success. To adjust for the bias, projections can be lowered or a higher discount rate can be used. The latter mechanism seems to dominate in the venture-capital industry [Keeley (1986)].

The use of high discount rates, however, means that few projects are feasible. Suppose a venture requires a $2 million capital infusion (the average invested in recent years in each venture) and that in five years the company will be worth $12 million. If the required rate of return is 50% per year, the $2 million investment must be worth approximately $15.2 million by the end of the fifth year, an amount exceeding the likely value of the entire company. Accordingly, venture capitalists are reluctant to back any company that cannot reasonably be expected to generate at least $25 to $50 million in total value in five years [MacMillan et al. (1985)]. The entrepreneurs' willingness to accept high discount rates indicates belief in the prospects of the company.

The use of high discount rates in venture-capital investing seems to fly in the face of conventional wisdom. One often reads that high discount rates discourage investments in highly uncertain, long-term projects [Hayes and Garvin (1982)], but in venture capital high discount rates are part of a more complex process of investing and managing the agency problem.

7.8. Adverse selection

Using very high discount rates might have the unintended effect of driving the most competent entrepreneurs to seek alternative sources of capital, leaving only those with no other financing options.

---

[15]Venture-capital investments are illiquid for a number of reasons, including the existence of information asymmetries and restrictions imposed by regulatory authorities on transfers of unregistered securities.

The adverse-selection problem is a difficult one in venture capital. Venture capitalists argue that by playing a positive role in the venture, they can increase total value by enough to offset the high cost of the capital they provide. To the extent that venture capitalists make good on this claim, the adverse-selection issue is effectively mitigated. In addition, the due diligence conducted before an investment is made is intended partly to make sure the entrepreneurs are qualified.

Although it seems that venture capitalists retain much of the power in the relationship with entrepreneurial ventures, there are checks and balances in the system. Venture capitalists who abuse their power will find it hard to attract the best entrepreneurs, who have the option of approaching other venture capitalists or sources other than venture capital. In this regard, the decision to accept money from a venture capitalist can be seen as a conscious present-value-maximizing choice by the entrepreneur.

7.9. Comparing the venture-capital fund – limited partner and venture capitalist – entrepreneur relationships

The relationship between the limited partners and the venture capitalists shares several elements with that between the venture capitalists and the entrepreneurs. First, each relationship entails staging the commitment of capital and preserving the option to abandon. The limited partners insist on a limited life for the fund, and the venture capitalists invest in stages related to the attainment of specific goals by the venture.

The compensation schemes are similar as well. The venture capitalists have strong incentives to create value because they share in the profits of the fund. The entrepreneurs receive a significant share of the value they help create (see table 4 for evidence about the share held by founders).

Also, in both cases, there are defined mechanisms in place to achieve liquidity. The limited partners insist on distributions of investment returns. The venture capitalists build into their stock-purchase agreements a number of mechanisms for achieving liquidity, such as the right to demand redemption of their convertible preferred stock.

Finally, the venture capitalist and entrepreneur alike face serious consequences if they fail. Entrepreneurs will be denied access to capital, their equity participation will be retracted, and their reputations damaged. Similarly, venture capitalists will find capital more difficult and costly to raise and their reputations will suffer as well, though their penalties are modest in comparison with those confronting entrepreneurs. In both cases, however, the multiperiod nature of the game creates strong incentives to perform well and to forego opportunistic behavior.

These common elements reinforce each other. For example, because venture capitalists capture 20% of their funds' profits, they structure incentives for the entrepreneurs that reward value creation. Similarly, because venture capitalists are legally required to liquidate the fund in ten years or so, they build mechanisms into their contracts with the entrepreneurs to make that feasible.

8. Other organizational forms

The venture-capital organization has evolved in response to the demanding investment environment in which new businesses are built. But, sorting, agency, and transactions cost problems are present in other settings as well.

A venture-capital firm performs economic functions similar to those of a corporation. Both raise capital from outsiders and invest in projects on behalf of the outside investors. The outside investors in both cases create a governance structure for monitoring the decisions made by the agents. When investments are made in individual projects, the managers within the venture-capital fund or within the corporation must monitor performance. Ultimately, the outside investors insist that they receive some return on their capital.

A venture-capital firm is also similar to a leveraged buyout fund. Each organization raises capital to invest in individual projects. In the venture-capital example, the projects tend to be early-stage ventures: in the leveraged-buyout example, the projects are more mature businesses with substantial debt capacity. The following sections compare the venture-capital organization, the corporate organization, and the leveraged-buyout-fund organization.

8.1. Capital budgeting

Corporate managers confront issues similar to those facing venture capitalists, yet their responses are very different. For example, consider an opportunity to invest in a new computer technology that could be funded inside a large company or as a separate business by venture capitalists.

If the project is funded within a corporation, the project initiation and management team probably will not receive a significant share of the value it creates. More likely, if the project is successful, their rank in the company and current compensation will increase [see Baker (1987)]. Team members often own or receive some stock options in the company, but the value of these options does not necessarily reflect the success of the project they undertook.[16] If the project is not successful, on the other hand, team members probably will find other tasks within the corporation, provided they

---

[16]See Jensen and Murphy (1990) for information on the relationship between compensation and value changes for American managers.

were not guilty of gross incompetence or malfeasance. Though the pecuniary rewards for success are modest, so too are the consequences of failure.

During development of the technology, the in-house team receives assistance from other members of company management, who monitor performance and try to increase the chances that the project will succeed. The specific team generally does not need to compensate these advisors. To the extent that the project is charged with the costs of monitoring, the costs reflect standard overhead-absorption charges rather than the amount of assistance provided or its perceived value, and the compensation of the advisors will probably not be dramatically affected by the project's outcome.

In contrast, if the project is financed by a venture-capital fund, the initiators and key members of the team own part of the venture, and they probably receive lower salaries than an in-house management team. If the project succeeds, management participates directly in the value it helped create. The team is not broken up as often occurs in large companies when individual managers in a team are promoted or transferred after a successful venture.[17] If the project fails, management suffers the consequences directly. If the project falters in midstream, entrepreneurial managers stand a good chance of being fired, often losing equity shares because of the vesting schedules used by venture capitalists. Further, the compensation of the venture capitalists (and the other outside directors) mirrors that of the entrepreneurial team: they will benefit only if the company succeeds, and they will suffer the consequences if the venture fails.

There is often one other substantive difference between the two approaches. In the corporate setting, projects are often funded all at once. In the venture-capital situation, the capital is meted out according to perceived performance at each successive project stage. Although in either situation managers will not purposefully pour good money after bad, team managers inside the company feel more secure about access to future capital than managers do in the venture-capital scenario.

If the typical American corporation were organized like a venture-capital fund, its discrete business units would be separated into individual business entities, equity shares in those entities would be awarded to their managers, capital would be meted out according to the attainment of specific business goals, a separate board of directors would be constituted for each business entity, and each board would be compensated according to the value created in each unit. The board would have the right to demand that funds be returned from the operating units to the holding company, and the ultimate

---

[17]The venture capitalists ultimately do leave the team, often when the company goes public, and always when the company is sold. In these instances, however, new directors are recruited who bring skills and resources appropriate to the issues confronting the company as it matures. Also, in many instances (for example, Teradyne, Thermo Electron, New England Business Services, Apple Computer), the venture capitalists remain on the board long after the limited partners have received distributions of shares in the company.

owners of the holding company would also have the right to demand distribution of the rewards of investing (for example, by imposing a finite life on the organization). In contrast to a traditional corporation, the new organization would be structured as a limited partnership, which would eliminate the possibility of adverse tax consequences in distributing the rewards of investing to the ultimate owners. In effect, the entire incentive system for directors and unit managers would be radically altered, as would the process of allocating capital. This model is similar to the leveraged-buyout fund, described in the following section.

8.2. Leveraged-buyout funds

Separation of ownership and management has become a pressing problem in American business [Jensen and Ruback (1983), Jensen (1986, 1988)]. Evidence from the capital markets suggests that corporate managers do not always make value-maximizing decisions. One response to this problem has been the leveraged buyout (LBO). In an LBO, a company or business unit is acquired by a group of managers and financiers who end up owning the equity in the new organization. Most of the capital required to finance the acquisition is raised as debt rather than equity.

The reallocation of equity to management and the imposition of heavy debt burdens (interest and amortization) can be interpreted as a direct response to the agency problems inherent in corporations [Jensen (1989)]. After an LBO, managers have greater incentives to create value than they did when they had little or no equity stake in the outcome. Because of the substantial debt burdens, there is little or no discretionary cash flow that can be dissipated on negative-net-present-value investments, including perquisites.

In LBO organizations the relationships among the company, its management, and financiers are similar to the deal struck between venture capitalists and management teams in entrepreneurial ventures. The compensation scheme is oriented toward equity, whose value depends on the efforts and skills of the managers involved. There are severe penalties for underperformance: for example, managers' equity shares are often vested over time so that, if they are fired before full vesting has occurred, they lose the unvested portion of their claim. The debt used in LBOs is similar in function to the staged-capital-commitment process used in venture-capital deals; in neither is there much discretionary cash flow. The critical characteristic of the debt is really the contractual right to take control of the project by denying access to new funds or changing the terms of that access if the company's performance falters.[18]

---

[18]See Hart and Moore (1989) for a discussion of the nature of control in a firm and the somewhat arbitrary distinction between debt and equity.

Venture-capital funds and LBO funds are also similar in structure; indeed, many venture-capital firms also invest in leveraged buyouts. LBO funds are typically organized as private limited partnerships with the LBO fund managers acting as general partners: each partnership has a finite life, typically ten years. These funds raise capital from larger financial institutions such as pension funds and endowments, and they invest in diversified portfolios of companies. LBO fund managers also raise multiple funds over time; as investment activities wind down in one fund, a new one is raised, often from the same investors. LBO fund managers are active in the operation of the companies in which they invest, typically assuming control of the board of directors, but they are generally less likely than venture capitalists to assume operational control. They bring a great deal of process knowledge to bear, particularly in the area of financing, and they have close contacts with financial institutions and investment bankers. Their compensation is highly sensitive to value creation; like general partners in venture-capital deals, general partners of LBO funds typically receive a 20% share of the value created in addition to a periodic management fee. Most importantly, LBO fund managers are skilled and active monitors of the decisions being made by the company managers. They are the antithesis of the passive institutional investors who have come to dominate ownership of American companies.

Both the venture-capital fund and the LBO fund invest capital on behalf of institutions that could conceivably invest directly rather than through intermediaries. The LBO-fund model is interesting because the same institutions that invest in publicly traded residual claims also choose to participate through the LBO limited partnership in the new structure. Investing through the LBO fund addresses some of the inherent agency problems in publicly traded securities while also minimizing the present value of tax burdens.

There are also some significant differences between the venture-capital model and the leveraged-buyout firm. First, leveraged buyouts are typically restricted to companies that have modest growth rates and stable cash flows, firms in which management would otherwise have significant control over discretionary cash flows. After the LBO, management has an incentive to use its cash flow to pay down debt, thus increasing the value of its equity. In the traditional venture-capital model, there is little discretionary cash flow to begin with. Value is created by building the company to gain access to more resources, which in turn facilitates more growth. A final distinction to be drawn is that leveraged-buyout funds often charge up-front investment banking fees and continuing management fees to the companies in which they invest: venture capitalists rarely if ever charge fees to portfolio companies.

9. Conclusions

The venture-capital industry is a productive place to study organizational responses to agency and other problems. The environment is characterized by substantial uncertainty about payoffs on individual investments and a high degree of information asymmetry between principals and agents. To cope with the challenges posed by such an environment, certain standard operating procedures and contracts have evolved, including staging the commitment of capital, basing compensation on value created, and preserving mechanisms to force agents to distribute capital and profits. These procedures and contracts help sort out the skills and intentions of the participants while simultaneously addressing cost and taxation issues.

The venture-capital organizational form may be applicable in other settings, particularly corporate and project governance. At the corporate level, adopting some aspects of the venture-capital organization, such as the compensation system and the finite-life form of organization, might solve some of the problems that lead to leveraged-buyout transactions in the first place. Then the goals of shareholders, monitors, and managers would be better aligned [see Sahlman (1990) for a description of the specific issue of compensating corporate boards of directors].

At the project level, there are also important insights from studying the organization of venture-capital firms. For example, establishing project boards of directors, with skills and resources specifically tailored to the project, seems to make sense. Also, implementing value-sensitive compensation systems and staging the commitment of capital has potential advantages, particularly for projects designed to exploit new business opportunities.

Much research remains to be done on the venture-capital organization. Though the economic resources under management are modest, the model seems to have been effective. Understanding why it works is in the interests of academics and practitioners alike.

References

Baker, George P., 1987, Incentives in hierarchies: Promotions, bonuses and monitoring, Working paper no. 88-023 (Harvard Business School, Boston, MA).

Barry, Christopher B., Chris J. Muscarella, John W. Peavy III, and Michael R. Vetsuypens, 1990, The role of venture capital in the creation of public companies: Evidence from the going-public process, Journal of Financial Economics, this volume.

Bartlett, Joseph W., 1988, Venture capital law, business strategies, and investment planning (Wiley, New York, NY).

Bhattacharya, Sudipto, 1979, Imperfect information, dividend policy and the 'bird in the hand' fallacy, Bell Journal of Economics 10, 259–270.

Brickley, James A. and Frederick H. Dark, 1987, The choice of organizational form: The case of franchising, Journal of Financial Economics 18, 401–420.

Bygrave, William, Norman Fast, Roubina Khoylian, Linda Vincent, and William Yue, 1987, Early rates of return of 131 venture capital funds started 1978–1984, Journal of Business Venturing 4, 93–106.

Chiampou, Gregory F. and Joel J. Kellet, 1989, Risk/return profile of venture capital, Journal of Business Venturing 4, 1–10.

Council of Economic Advisors, 1990, Economic report of the President (U.S. Government Printing Office, Washington, DC).

Fama, Eugene F., 1980, Agency problems and the theory of the firm, Journal of Political Economy 88, 288–307.

Fama, Eugene F. and Michael C. Jensen, 1985, Organization forms and investment decisions, Journal of Financial Economics 14, 101–119.

Freear, John and William E. Wetzel, Jr., 1990, Who bankrolls high-tech entrepreneurs?, Journal of Business Venturing 5, 77–90.

Gorman, Michael and William A. Sahlman, 1989, What do venture capitalists do?, Journal of Business Venturing 4, 231–248.

Hart, Oliver and John Moore, 1989, Default and renegotiation: A dynamic model of debt, Working paper no. 89-069 (Harvard Business School, Boston, MA).

Hay Management Consultants, 1988, Survey of compensation among venture capital/leveraged buy-out firms (Hay Group, New York, NY).

Hayes, Robert H. and David Garvin, 1982, Managing as if tomorrow mattered, Harvard Business Review, May–June, 70–79.

Horsley Keogh & Associates, 1988, Horsley Keogh venture study (Horsley Keogh & Associates, Pittsford, NY).

Huntsman, Blaine and James P. Homan, Jr., 1980, Investment in new enterprise: Some empirical observations on risk, return, and market structure, Financial Management 9, 44–51.

Ibbotson Associates, 1988, Stocks, bonds, bills, and inflation, 1988 yearbook (Ibbotson Associates, Chicago, IL).

Jensen, Michael C., 1986, The agency costs of free cash flow: Corporate finance and takeovers, American Economic Review 76, 323–329.

Jensen, Michael C., 1988, Takeovers: Their causes and consequences, Journal of Economic Perspectives 2, 21–38.

Jensen, Michael C., 1989, Active investors, LBOs, and the privatization of bankruptcy, Journal of Applied Corporate Finance 2, 35–49.

Jensen, Michael C. and William H. Meckling, 1976, Theory of the firm: Managerial behavior, agency costs and ownership structure, Journal of Financial Economics 3, 305–360.

Jensen, Michael C. and Kevin J. Murphy, 1990, Performance pay and top management incentives, Journal of Political Economy 98, 225–264.

Jensen, Michael C. and R. Ruback, 1983, The market for corporate control: The scientific evidence, Journal of Financial Economics 11, 5–50.

Keeley, Robert, 1986, Risk (over)adjusted discount rates: The venture capitalist's method, Unpublished working paper.

Knights, David H. and William A. Sahlman, 1986a, Horizon Group, 286-058 Rev. 9/86 (Publishing Division, Harvard Business School, Boston, MA).

Knights, David H. and William A. Sahlman, 1986b, Centex Telemanagement, Inc., 286-059 Rev. 9/88 (Publishing Division, Harvard Business School, Boston, MA).

Knights, David H. and William A. Sahlman, 1986c, Vertex Peripherals, 286-069 Rev. 12/87 (Publishing Division, Harvard Business School, Boston, MA).

Knights, David H. and William A. Sahlman, 1986d, Priam Corporation – Vertex Peripherals, 286-103 Rev. 9/86 (Publishing Division, Harvard Business School, Boston, MA).

Kozmetsky, George, Michael D. Gill, Jr., and Raymond W. Smilor, 1985, Financing and managing fast-growth companies: The venture capital process (Lexington Books, Lexington, MA).

Leland, Hayne and David Pyle, 1977, Information asymmetries, financial structure and financial intermediation, Journal of Finance 32, 371–387.

MacMillan, Ian C., David M. Kulow, and Roubina Khoylian, 1989, Venture capitalists' involvement in their investments: Extent and performance, Journal of Business Venturing 4, 27–34.

MacMillan, Ian C., Robin Siegel, and P.N. Subba Narisimha, 1985, Criteria used by venture capitalists to evaluate new venture proposals, Journal of Business Venturing 1, 119–128.

Morris, Jane K., ed., 1988a, Pratt's guide to venture capital sources, 12th ed. (Venture Economics, Inc., Needham, MA).

Morris, Jane K., 1988b, The pricing of a venture capital investment, in: Pratt's guide to venture capital sources, 12th ed. (Venture Economics, Inc., Needham, MA) 55–61.

Myers, Stewart C., 1977, Determinants of corporate borrowing, Journal of Financial Economics 5, 147–176.

Plummer, James L., 1987, QED report on venture capital financial analysis (QED Research, Inc., Palo Alto, CA).

Ross, Stephen, 1977, The determination of financial structure: The incentive signalling approach, Bell Journal of Economics 8, 23–40.

Sahlman, William A., 1983a, Technical Data Corporation, 283-072 Rev. 12/87 (Publishing Division, Harvard Business School, Boston, MA).

Sahlman, William A., 1983b, Technical Data Corporation Business Plan, 283-073 Rev. 11/87 (Publishing Division, Harvard Business School, Boston, MA).

Sahlman, William A., 1984, Priam Corporation, 284-043 Rev. 9/84 (Publishing Division, Harvard Business School, Boston, MA).

Sahlman, William A., 1985a, CML Group, Inc. – Going public (A), 285-003 Rev. 9/86 (Publishing Division, Harvard Business School, Boston, MA).

Sahlman, William A., 1985b, Business Research Corporation (A), 285-089 (Publishing Division, Harvard Business School, Boston, MA).

Sahlman, William A., 1985c, Business Research Corporation (B), 285-090 (Publishing Division, Harvard Business School, Boston, MA).

Sahlman, William A., 1985d, CML Group, Inc. – Going public (B), 285-092 Rev. 9/86 (Publishing Division, Harvard Business School, Boston, MA).

Sahlman, William A., 1985e, Lotus Development Corporation, 285-094 Rev. 11/87 (Publishing Division, Harvard Business School, Boston, MA).

Sahlman, William A., 1986a, CML Group, Inc. – Going public (C), 286-009 (Publishing Division, Harvard Business School, Boston, MA).

Sahlman, William A., 1986b, Note on the venture capital industry – update (1985), 286-060 (Publishing Division, Harvard Business School, Boston, MA).

Sahlman, William A., 1986c, Palladian Software, 286-065 Rev. 11/87 (Publishing Division, Harvard Business School, Boston, MA).

Sahlman, William A., 1986d, Bank of Boston New Ventures Group, 286-070 Rev. 9/86 (Publishing Division, Harvard Business School, Boston, MA).

Sahlman, William A., 1988a, Aspects of financial contracting in venture capital, Journal of Applied Corporate Finance 1, 23–36.

Sahlman, William A., 1988b, Note on financial contracting: 'Deals', 288-014 Rev. 6/89 (Publishing Division, Harvard Business School, Boston, MA).

Sahlman, William A., 1988c, Sarah Jenks-Daly, 288-008 Rev. 9/88 (Publishing Division, Harvard Business School, Boston, MA).

Sahlman, William A., 1989a, Report on the Harvard Business School venture capital conference: September 23–24, 1988, Unpublished manuscript (Harvard Business School, Boston, MA).

Sahlman, William A., 1989b, Tom Volpe, 289-025 Rev. 2/89 (Publishing Division, Harvard Business School, Boston, MA).

Sahlman, William A., 1990, Why sane people shouldn't serve on public boards, Harvard Business Review 90-3, 28–37.

Sahlman, William A. and Howard H. Stevenson, 1985, Capital market myopia, Journal of Business Venturing 1, 7–30.

Sahlman, William A. and David H. Knights, 1986, Analog Devices – Bipolar Integrated Technology, 286-117 Rev. 12/88 (Publishing Division, Harvard Business School, Boston, MA).

Sahlman, William A. and Dan Scherlis, 1988, A method for valuing high-risk long-term investments, 288-006 Rev. 6/89 (Publishing Division, Harvard Business School, Boston, MA).

Sahlman, William A. and Helen Soussou, 1985a, Note on the venture capital industry (1981), 285-096 Rev. 11/85 (Publishing Division, Harvard Business School, Boston, MA).

Sahlman, William A. and Helen Soussou, 1985b, Precision Parts, Inc. (A), 285-131 (Publishing Division, Harvard Business School, Boston, MA).

Smith, Clifford W., Jr. and Jerold B. Warner, 1979, On financial contracting: An analysis of bond convenants, Journal of Financial Economics 7, 117–161.

Soussou, Helen and William A. Sahlman, 1986, Peter Wendell, 286-008 Rev. 1/86 (Publishing Division, Harvard Business School, Boston, MA).

Spence, A. Michael, 1973, Job market signalling, Quarterly Journal of Economics 3, 355–379.

Stevenson, Howard H., Daniel F. Muzyka, and Jeffry A. Timmons, 1987, Venture capital in transition: A Monte Carlo simulation of changes in investment patterns, Journal of Business Venturing 2, 103–122.

Stiglitz, Joseph E. and Andrew Weiss, 1983, Incentive effects of terminations: Applications to the credit and labor markets, American Economic Review 73, 912–927.

Studt, Tim A., 1990, There's no joy in this year's $150 billion for R & D, Research & Development, Jan., 41–44.

Testa, Richard J., 1988, The legal process of venture capital investment, in: Pratt's guide to venture capital sources, 12th ed. (Venture Economics, Inc., Needham, MA).

Timmons, Jeffry A., 1987, Venture capital: More than money, in: Pratt's guide to venture capital sources, 12th ed. (Venture Economics, Inc., Needham, MA).

Venture Economics, 1985, The venture capital industry: Opportunities and considerations for investors (Venture Economics, Inc., Needham, MA).

Venture Economics, 1987, Terms and conditions of venture capital partnerships (Venture Economics, Inc., Needham, MA).

Venture Economics, 1988a, Exiting venture capital investments (Venture Economics, Inc., Needham, MA).

Venture Economics, 1988b, Trends in venture capital – 1988 edition (Venture Economics, Inc., Needham, MA).

Venture Economics, 1988c, Venture capital performance: Review of the financial performance of venture capital partnerships (Venture Economics, Inc., Needham, MA).

Venture Economics, 1989, Venture capital yearbook 1989 (Venture Economics, Inc., Needham, MA).

Wetzel, William E., 1983, Angels and informal risk capital, Sloan Management Review 24, 23–34.

Williamson, Oliver E., 1975, Markets and hierarchies (Free Press, New York, NY).

Williamson, Oliver E., 1988, Corporate finance and corporate governance, Journal of Finance XLII, 567–591.

Wilson, John, 1985, The new venturers: Inside the high stakes world of venture capital (Addison-Wesley, Reading, MA).

Wolfson, Mark A., 1985, Empirical evidence of incentive problems and their mitigation in oil and gas tax shelter programs, in: John W. Pratt and Richard J. Zeckhauser, eds., Principals and agents; The structure of business, (Harvard Business School Press, Boston, MA) 101–126.

[2]

Journal of Business Finance & Accounting, 22(8), December 1995, 0306-686X

EVOLUTION AND CHANGE: AN ANALYSIS OF THE FIRST DECADE OF THE UK VENTURE CAPITAL INDUSTRY

GORDON C. MURRAY*

INTRODUCTION

After almost ten years of uninterrupted growth, the UK venture capital industry has entered its second decade of activity in a more competitive and hostile environment than most of its participants can remember. Venture capital, a part of the burgeoning financial services sector, was one of the most vigorous growth areas of the British economy in the 1980s. In 1981, some thirty venture capital organisations committed £66 million of investments to 163 investee companies (Lorenz, 1989). Eleven years later, in 1992, the UK industry invested a total of £1,326 million in 1,297 enterprises world wide, primarily small and medium sized, unquoted companies (British Venture Capital Association 1993). This represented, in real terms, an annualised growth rate over the period of 27%. The number of venture capitalist companies peaked in 1989 at 124 full members of the British Venture Capital Association (BVCA).[1] The industry, between 1985 and 1992, had invested a cumulative £8.8 billion in approximately ten thousand companies.

The UK has become, after the United States and Japan (Bannock, 1991), the largest venture capital centre in the world. While venture capital has grown significantly in continental Europe since the mid 1980s (Tyebjee and Lister, 1988), the UK industry continues to dominate European activity taking 39% of the total of Ecu 4,701 million in new European investment in 1992 (European Venture Capital Association, 1993[2]). The UK is an active exporter of venture capital investment and expertise to other European Community countries as well as being a significant importer and exporter of venture finance from/to the US.

Since 1989, the year in which new funds into the industry and venture capital investments peaked, confidence in UK venture capital has been tested by a number of very public casualties, particularly among some of the largest management buy-outs and buy-ins (MBOs/MBIs). The MBO of Lowndes

*The author is from the University of Warwick. (Paper received February 1994, revised and accepted June 1994)

Address for correspondence: Gordon C. Murray, Warwick Business School, University of Warwick, Coventry CV4 7AL, UK.

1078   MURRAY

Queensway (£460 million) was subsequently put into liquidation and, also in the recession-hit, domestic furnishing retail market, the MBOs of MFI/Hygena (£718 million) and Magnet (£667 million) each needed substantial refinancing in 1990. In 1993, the troubled MBI of Isosceles/Gateway (£2,375 million) was still subject to the repeated renegotiation of finance with its bankers four years after its genesis.[3] This loss of confidence, reflecting wider concerns as the UK economy slid into recession, was also corroborated in reports from several independent venture capitalists noting the increasing difficulties of raising substantial new funds from 1989 onwards.

This paper seeks to examine the nature of the environmental factors which have driven the growth of UK venture capital activity, and to determine how these factors are likely to influence both the future size and the structure, conduct and performance of the industry. The factors which have influenced the provision of investment capital to venture capital firms are particularly explored, including the implications on the industry's future of a dearth of new finance.

Given the industry's role in financing both the genesis of what Story et al. (1989) term 'fast track' firms (via seed and start-up capital) and the restructuring of existing, established firms (via management buy-out/buy-in, expansion, and secondary purchase investments), it is suggested that the industry's future size and activity have an important bearing on issues of both small firm financing and the market for corporate control in the UK. It is further argued that a financial service sector which has developed and changed so rapidly within its relatively short life span is a subject worthy of greater academic attention. However, with few notable exceptions (Pratt, 1990; Dixon, 1991; Sweeting, 1991; and Wright et al., 1994), the interest among UK finance and accountancy researchers remains remarkably muted. This is in stark contrast to the established corpus of research on the US venture capital industry by American academics.

Despite the British Government's support in the November 1993 Budget for third party equity financing of unquoted businesses, there remains little empirical evidence on the performance of UK venture capital funds or the nature of risk/reward trade-offs between different types of venture capital activity including issues of fund specialisation or diversification. The absence of rigorous cross country comparisons in Europe and between Europe and the US is a particular omission. The apparent inability for venture capitalists to create successful funds for early stage and/or technology based businesses is of special concern for policy makers (Murray, 1993). As Dixon (1991) has observed, the venture capital industry appears to embrace few of the portfolio management instruments widely available to other financial service sectors. (This is a view supported by Tyebjee and Bruno, 1984; and Ruhnka and Young, 1991, in their US studies.) It is thus argued that the established UK industry represents a fruitful, but as yet poorly exploited, source of enquiry for finance-based academics.

CHANGE AND THE UK VENTURE CAPITAL INDUSTRY   1079

METHODOLOGY

The data presented in this paper on the nature of change within the UK (and its comparison to the US) venture capital industry are primarily derived from industry statistics published by the two national associations: the British Venture Capital Association (BVCA) and the National Venture Capital Association (NVCA), respectively. Findings are further supported with reference to the increasing body of empirical research conducted in the UK and USA. (Where BVCA data are used, UK trend figures can only be given up to and including 1991, with the exception of 1992 UK investment value. In 1992, the BVCA materially changed the basis on which statistics from members were collected. For the first time both secured and unsecured debt has been aggregated with equity investment. As the BVCA notes in its Report on Investment Activity 1992, direct comparisons cannot be made between figures in 1992 and prior years).

The paper also uses extensively, analyses based on the findings of a survey of the UK venture capital industry undertaken in 1990 by the author at the request of the BVCA (Murray, 1991). Commitment to this study was assisted by a widespread concern among the BVCA's members that the industry was not likely to sustain the remarkable growth rate of the previous decade. This data is employed to fit secondary sources of industry statistics into an analytical framework of structural and operational change over the period.

The 1990 BVCA Survey

In order to investigate the contemporary process of change in the UK industry, the CEOs of twenty venture capital organisations were approached with the active co-operation of the British Venture Capital Association (BVCA). In addition, two further participants, deemed by the BVCA to have expert knowledge of the UK industry, were also interviewed. The respondents were questioned on their opinions as to:

(i) the key successes and failures of the industry's performance over the decade 1980–90,
(ii) the genesis, nature and effect of major changes in the competitive environment impacting on the industry over this period,
(iii) the major competitive changes, including both opportunities and threats, likely to face the industry over the next five years 1991–95,
(iv) those factors which would be material to the future success of the industry, and to individual venture capital firms.

The process of the twenty-two interviews was based on an extended, semi-structured discussion with the CEO respondents. In seeking their views, the respondents were not prompted with pre-defined lists. Other than setting the

1080   MURRAY

subject areas for the interview, the respondents were encouraged to articulate
their own perceptions of the key factors influencing present and future changes
within the UK venture capital industry.

Sample Selection

All twenty venture capital organisations contacted agreed to participate in the
survey. The sampling procedure was not random. The criteria used to select
the research respondents were that they were:

  (i)   seen by their peers as leading participants in the UK venture capital
        industry,
  (ii) controlled large and successful[4] venture capital organisations,
  (iii) had been active participants in the industry throughout the majority
        of the 1980s.

The purpose of the survey was to ascertain the opinions of a sample of venture
capitalists reckoned by their peers to be *leaders* in their industry in both the
quality of their experience and the size of funds under their control. Given
that the sample concentrated on a number of the largest and, arguably, most
influential firms in the industry, the research method was not designed to obtain
a statistically representative view of *all* sectors of the UK venture capital
community.

   The average size of the funds managed by the 19 venture capital firms (i.e.
excluding 3i plc) was £223.5 million with a standard deviation of £201.4 million
(primarily because one small fund specialising in high technology start-ups with
funds under management of £9 million was included in the sample). Only two
other venture capital firms in the sample had funds under management of less
than £100 million. The sample included 3i plc, the largest venture capital firm
in the world with funds under management of over £2.5 billion. In total, the
sample represented 65% of the 29 UK venture capital firms with funds under
management of over £100 million in 1990.

                        INDUSTRY TRENDS IN THE 1980s

The UK venture capital industry, as it is presently recognised, had its genesis
in the late 1970s/early 1980s. While equity investments in unquoted companies
were regularly undertaken by a number of banks and finance houses before
the last decade, they were generally seen as a specialist and largely peripheral
element of a wider corporate finance activity (Hannah, 1992). With the notable
exception of 3i plc (formerly ICFC), there were few organisations of any
significant size with a predominant interest in small unquoted investments.
This situation was to change markedly in the 1980s with the renaissance of
governmental and corporate financiers' interest in entrepreneurial and small
firm activity.

CHANGE AND THE UK VENTURE CAPITAL INDUSTRY   1081

Decline in Rate of Industry Growth: Funds Invested

Actual and potential industry growth may be measured, respectively, in terms of the annual total investment committed by venture capitalists to investee companies and by reference to the amounts of external finance raised for future investment activity by the industry. In 1992, the UK venture capital industry invested £1,326 million of equity in 1,297 companies world wide (BVCA, 1993). In 1991, the last year of comparable UK trend information published by the BVCA, £989 m. was invested in 1,196 UK companies. Investment activity had declined by 30% in nominal terms for two successive years against the peak year of 1989 when £1,647 m. was invested world-wide and £1,420 m. in the UK.

Some six months before the 1990 annual UK statistics were released, only two of the twenty-two BVCA survey respondents believed that investments would continue to grow for the next three years, including 1990/91. Seventeen respondents (77%) estimated that the growth of new funds invested would decline, in nominal terms, for the next three years from the peak of the 1989 figure by an average of 26%. In reality, the decline in the total value of nominal investment between 1989−92 was 19.5%.

The period, 1980−91, saw the UK economy move from one recession through a period of significant economic growth and into the start of a second recession. In order to show the real underlying growth in UK venture capital activity, the annual investment data, i.e. domestic investments made by UK venture capitalists, were deflated to real (1985 = 100) figures, using an 'investment goods' deflator, and then adjusted for economic cyclicality using an index of GDP at constant factor cost (see Figure 1). The trend in UK venture capital

Figure 1

Annual UK Investment by BVCA Members 1981−91

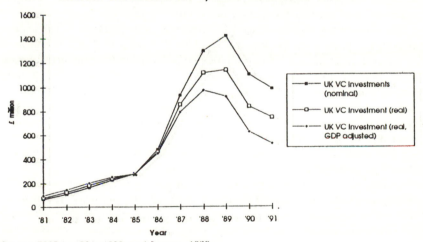

Source: BVCA, 1984−1993; and Lorenz, 1989.

1082   MURRAY

Figure 2

UK Venture Capital Activity and FTA Index 1981−91

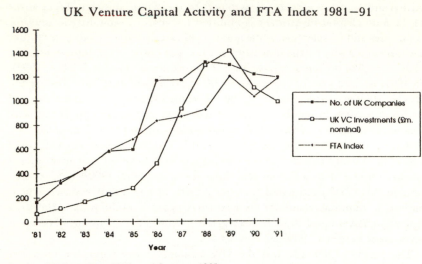

Source: BVCA, 1984−1993; and Lorenz, 1989.

activity over time shows a pronounced sigmoid curve reflecting a distinct period of growth followed by a marked decline in investment activity.[5] It is to be expected that an industry based on future growth expectations of investee companies is highly sensitive to underlying change in the macro-economy. However, this paper argues that the influence of the wider economic environment has also served to engender a process of major changes to the structure, conduct and performance of the industry, which will continue irrespective of the UK economy's move out of recession.

The US venture capital industry has shown a marked pattern of cyclicality, since its inception in the early post Second World War period, in both the level of annual funds raised and the profitability of subsequent investments (Bygrave et al., 1989). Similar extensive time series data is not available for the younger UK industry. However, as Figure 2 shows, the growth of UK venture capital industry activity appears to be closely associated with traded stock movements over time.[6] Given long run, cyclical trends in the price movement of stocks, it is plausible that the decline from 1989 to 1991 in UK venture capital activity was the result of adverse economic and stock market conditions on investors' short run confidence.

However, the sensitivity of venture capital activity to the movement in UK stock prices does not confound the assertion of industry maturity. It is feasible that the consequences of lower stock prices on the potential profitability of venture capital firms' portfolios became a catalyst for the necessary restructuring of a young and unstable industry where the number of investing firms and

CHANGE AND THE UK VENTURE CAPITAL INDUSTRY   **1083**

the supply of funds to invest had grown too large to support the present and likely future deal flow. The nature of the industry which responds to contemporary incentives post the 1989—1992 recession will be markedly different from the industry in the mid to late 1980s. It is likely to be characterised by a smaller number of larger, and more product/market focused, surviving firms (Murray, 1992). All BVCA survey respondents believed that the number of venture capitalist firms in the UK industry would decline over the next five years.

Funds Raised by the Venture Capital Industry

The likelihood of a decline in the future rate of venture capital investments is also supported by the annual figures for the value of new, institutional funds raised by independent UK venture capital firms.[7] However, it should be noted that the investment into independent funds is only one part of the industry's total resources. Captives organisations, which are owned by a financial services parent including banks, insurance companies and pension funds, undertook 25% of the value of total equity investment in 1991. On the revised BVCA reporting basis of 1992, captives and semi-captive organisations (i.e. a captive organisation also managing an independent fund) invested 50% of the equity and debt provided by the industry.

The funding of independent venture capital organisations grew rapidly through the 1980s, peaking in 1989 at £1,684 million. The level of funding, post 1989, has reflected the anxieties felt by many institutional investors as to the potential for attrative future returns from UK venture capital activity (see *Financial Times* Annual Venture Capital Surveys 1990—1992). The nominal figure for 1992, at £347 million, was 79% lower than the 1989 funds raised. In real terms, 1992 represented the lowest sum raised by the UK industry since 1984. There is a two or three year lag between creating a new fund and making substantial new investments in a portfolio of client companies. Unless there

Table 1

Capital Commitments to UK Independent Funds, Nominal and Real
(1985 values)

	1983	1984	1985	1986	1987	1988
Nominal £m	112	195	278	239	684	612
Real £m	123	206	278	229	626	528

	1989	1990	1991	1992	1993
Nominal £m	1684	830	368	347	479
Real £m	1354	630	279	272	375

Source: Venture Economics Ltd., 1992, and BVCA, 1992—1994.

is a sustained reversal in the downward trend in new inward investment in independent venture capital firms, it is likely that this will be reflected directly in the reduced value of annual investments from 1993/94 onwards once the UK industry's estimated £1 billion of uninvested funds (BVCA, 1993) is used up.

Increase in Market Information

In 1993, there were 119 'full' (i.e. investor) members of the BVCA. Including non BVCA members, there are likely to be less than 150 UK organisations with a primarily economic purpose of venture capital investment. This statistic excludes 'informal investors' (aka 'business angels') which invest in unquoted companies from their own personal resources (Harrison and Mason, 1992). Thus, the UK venture capital industry is small when measured by the number of firms within the industry. The firms themselves may also be characterised as 'small firms' if defined by the number of executive staff. The median size of the UK venture capital firm in 1991 was 7 investment professionals (Venture Economics, 1992). This small scale, with most firms spatially concentrated in a few major cities (Mason and Harrison, 1991), facilitates the level of inter-firm communication. Several BVCA survey respondents referred to the industry as a 'club' in which everyone knows everyone else.

The incidence of deal sharing ('syndication') between venture capitalists; communications via the BVCA; the regular reporting of deals through the statistics of Venture Economics and the trade press; and the physical concentration of many of the larger organisations within the City of London has meant that the level of inter-firm communication is high. However, for both the institutional providers of venture capital funds and the potential, investee firm clients, access to information has been more problematic. Both parties incur significant monitoring or search costs, respectively. BVCA survey respondents noted that, in the present competitive climate, venture capitalists would have to put materially more resources into both marketing to institutions and subsequently keeping them better informed on the state of investments undertaken in the funds to which they have subscribed, if they are to retain investors' confidence. A recent survey of institutional investors cited small firms' stock performance and venture capital as UK fund managers' two greatest concerns in late 1991 (Alexander, 1991).

Arguably, the most critical need to facilitate an efficient market for venture capital is for reliable figures on the performance of the funds of individual venture capital organisations to become widely available to institutions wishing to choose between competing new funds. The relatively early stage of the development of the UK venture capital industry and the fact that most funds have been raised since 1987 as 'closed end' funds for ten year periods has meant that, with few exceptions, detailed, terminal performance information does not yet exist. The 1992 Chairman of the BVCA announced that the provision of

CHANGE AND THE UK VENTURE CAPITAL INDUSTRY   1085

comparative performance data would be a major responsibility of his year's tenure. This announcement reflected the BVCA's concern at the growing unease felt by many institutional investors in venture capital as to the likely net terminal performance of their investments (Brakell, 1988).

Institutional investors' fears have been exacerbated by the highly ambivalent performance data of the US venture capital industry where fund returns post the vintage 1982/83 year have been disappointing (Bygrave et al., 1989). This has been directly reflected in a decline of 59% in nominal, new capital commitments to independent, private US venture capital firms from 1983 to 1991 (NVCA, 1993). The paucity of information available to institutional investors in venture capital is not purely due to issues of timing. In the US, Bygrave (op cit., p. 93) noted that 'published information on rates of return was skimpy and not very reliable', despite the organised venture capital industry in the US being over 40 years old. Chiampou and Kallett (1989, p. 2) also similarly observed in their American study of the risk/return profile of venture capital that 'the lack of even working studies on this topic is remarkable'.

For the potential investee recipient of venture capital funds, the accountant is the primary and most important source of information and access to venture capitalists (Llanwarne, 1990; Murray et al., 1995; see also Hustedd and Pulver, 1992). As an intermediary between the potential client and venture capitalist investor, the accountancy firms perform an important market allocation role. The power of major accountancy firms as a conduit for future deal flow reached its apogee with the practice of 'beauty parades' whereby accountants and their investee firm clients required a shortlist of several interested venture capitalists to make competitive presentations from which a subsequent investor was selected.

This practice has subsequently moderated, post 1990, as venture capitalists reacted strongly against a practice which they viewed as giving excessive power to the accountant at the cost of the venture capital firm. The BVCA survey respondents acknowledged that the more professional management teams, particularly those from the larger MBOs, were increasingly well informed of the competitive offerings from individual venture capitalists and had increased their relative negotiating power. However, 58% of respondents still believed that potential clients did not have an accurate understanding of the uses of venture capital. The inability of the majority of financial intermediaries to redress this information asymmetry was supported by a 1991 study of accountants and bank managers which identified their limited understanding of venture capital; 85% of accountants and 92% of bank managers surveyed 'never or rarely' had experienced any personal contact with venture capitalists (Hovgaard, 1991).

Contemporary research on the UK MBO/MBI market by Murray et al. (1995) supports Hovgaard's findings as to the variable role of financial advisers in the investee applicants' search for venture capital finance. A 1993 survey of seventy CEOs having undertaken a UK management buy-out or buy-in of between £2—10 million deal value in the last three years indicated that only 25% of the respondents rated their financial advisers as 'highly influential' in the *identification* of appropriate sources of venture capital. Only 9% of managers similarly rated their advisers as highly influential in the final venture capital *selection* decision. Forty percent of the managers interviewed had chosen a venture capitalist *before* commissioning a financial adviser to assist the management team in the deal process.

Increase in Buyer Power

Porter's (1979) popular 'competitive forces model', which is based on managerial economics antecedents, seeks to determine the ability of a firm or industry to sustain long term, supra-normal profits by reference to the degree of existing inter-firm rivalry and to the power balance between four interest sets — customers, suppliers, new entrants, and providers of substitute products/services. In using this model, it is therefore of fundamental importance both to define who are buyers from and who are suppliers to the venture capital industry. Sahlman (1989) in the US and Lloyd (1989) in the UK have each used this model to analyse the changing competitive environment facing venture capital firms. Using Porter's terminology, these authors see institutional providers of capital as the *suppliers* and investee companies as the *customers* for the venture capital firms.

It is argued that this analysis is incorrect (Murray, 1991b). Rather, it is suggested that the providers of finance, be they external sources for independent firms or internal sources for captive organisations, are the 'primary customer'[8] of the venture capitalist. It is to these providers that the venture capitalists have to justify the performance of their investment activities, and ultimately to reward by the provision of rates of return commensurate with the peculiar risks and illiquidity of investment in venture capital funds. When venture capital firms seek contributions for the financing of a new fund, it is the institutions which control the purchase decision, and select the recipient of their funds between an increasing number of venture capital firms competitively seeking new capital. The power of the institutional funders is also evidenced by their ability to set increasingly tight constraints on the rewards of the venture capital fund's general partners (Gregory, 1991).

The investee company clients should more properly be seen as the 'raw material' or 'firm stock' from which the investors' value added and capital gain is derived. In Porter's terms, the applicant firms seeking venture capital finance are suppliers. Their limited bargaining power, which is in part a function of their inexperience of the finance raising process, is reflected in the stark statistic that approximately 95% of applicants for finance are rejected by the venture capitalists (Bannock, 1991; and Dixon, 1991).

This changing balance of power is also a consequence of the supply and demand conditions pertaining at the time of the transaction. The reduction

CHANGE AND THE UK VENTURE CAPITAL INDUSTRY   1087

in new capital available from institutions, post 1989, has occurred at a time when several independent venture capitalists firms have fully invested their earlier funds. The recent recession exacerbated funding issues by increasing the finances required to support vulnerable investee companies within the venture capitalists' existing portfolios. The husbanding of power by institutional investors may also be a consequence of the excessive investment expectations created by the venture capital industry. A remarkable 74% of the BVCA survey respondents agreed with the statement that 'UK venture capitalists had oversold the potential returns of their industry to institutional funders'.

One prescriptive response by major UK institutional investors to imperfect information has been the creation of an informal 'Venture Investors' Circle' at which issues of common interest are discussed. This forum, which embraces some twenty major investors, thus provides funders with the opportunity to discuss the nature of the relationship between the institutions and venture capitalists. It is unlikely that the existence of a better informed and powerful caucus of institutional investors will do other than increase the bargaining power of the investors *vis à vis* the venture capital suppliants for their funds during a period of capital scarcity. The extent of their potential power can be evidenced by Initiative Europe's (1994) estimate that independent venture capital firms are currently attempting to raise £1.25 billion of new funds. This figure is approximately four times the size of funds raised in either 1992 or 1993.

Increase in Inward International Competition

Financial services are becoming increasingly global in scope (Bryan, 1993). As a market grows, it can become attractive to international companies provided the revenue and cost structures of product and service provision enable profitable market entry and development (Kay, 1990). With the exception of approximately ten (primarily American) organisations, the UK venture capital industry has remained determinedly domestic in ownership. International investors have largely preferred to enter the UK market by participating in a UK originated fund managed by a British venture capital firm. In the peak year of 1989, new capital commitments by overseas investors to independently managed funds grew nearly five fold to represent 42.3% of the total funds raised that year. Foreign investment was to decline by over half (53%) in 1990, and by 1992 represented 36% of the £347 million of new funds raised (Venture Economics Ltd., 1991/92).

The twenty-two BVCA survey respondents were asked their views on the likelihood of foreign companies either creating new venture capital firms in the UK or, conversely, acquiring existing UK firms. While it was agreed that an increased foreign presence in the UK could occur, 86% of respondents did not see it as a significant future trend. When asked to estimate the number of such transactions over the next five years (1991–95) the median category was 6–10 deals. Firms from the United States were seen as the most likely acquirers (12 respondents) followed by continental Europe (8) and Japan (7). Survey respondents were also asked to estimate the number of total new entrants into the UK venture capital industry over the period 1991–95. An average response of sixteen firms was given. When asked to describe the types of new entrants only three respondents (13.6%) mentioned overseas companies.

The reason cited for this lack of international threat was the high level of development of the mature and competitive UK market in comparison to other European markets. This maturity, and the consequent limitation on supernormal profits, was seen as the most significant barrier to entry. Respondents believed that mainland Europe presented more attractive opportunities for non-UK venture capitalists. They also noted that contemporary problems (in 1990) of loan defaults and capital adequacy in US and Japanese banking would reduce the likelihood of new entrants from either country becoming a serious threat in the UK in the short term. These opinions appear to have been correct. No major (i.e. > £100 million fund) foreign-owned venture capital operation has been established in the UK since 1990.

Decline in Industry Profitability

For the management company of an independent venture capital fund, the sources of income are primarily two-fold. An annual management fee is paid by the institutional investors as a proportion of the total funds invested. At the end of the investment period, the general partners in the venture capital company normally participates in any capital gain of the fund, i.e. the 'carried interest', subject to a prior agreed 'hurdle rate' which is designed to ensure a minimum real return to investors before the management company is rewarded. As Sahlman (1991, p. 11) has noted, if the fund is successful, the capital gain accruing to the partners is likely to be significantly greater than their combined base salaries and bonuses. The managers of captive funds, who are essentially employees of the parent company, do not have the opportunity of a carry on internally raised funds but are usually rewarded by bonus schemes.[9]

It was noted by all BVCA survey respondents that the incomes paid to venture capitalists as management fees by the limited partner investors in their funds were coming under increased pressure as bargaining power moved to the advantage of the institutional customers. Gregory (1991) also notes the increasing conditions put on the release ('draw down') of funds and the repatriation of capital gains to investors. The industry standard is for the venture capitalist to be paid a fee of between two and two and a half percent per annum in order to cover the costs associated with managing the fund and the ensuing portfolio of investments. These percentage costs are largely consistent with US funds (Sahlman, 1991; and Bygrave and Timmons, 1992). Respondents observed that, in a period of capital scarcity, venture capitalists were under increasing pressures to accept lower incomes. One-off commissioning fees

CHANGE AND THE UK VENTURE CAPITAL INDUSTRY   1089

Figure 3

Comparison of Private and Quoted UK Company Price-Earnings Ratios
1987−93

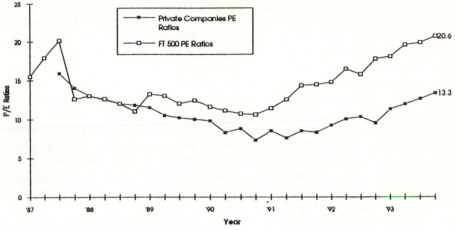

Source: Stoy Hayward/Acquisitions Monthly 1994.

charged by the venture capitalist when raising a new fund, which were common
in the early and mid 1980s, have disappeared. However, there have not been
similar pressures to reduce the venture capitalist's carried interest. Investors
appear to wish to maintain a key management incentive for fund performance.
The recent innovation in the UK since the late 1980s of a US practice whereby
consultants, termed 'gatekeepers', act on behalf of the funding institutions in
their identification and selection of high performing venture capitalist firms
is a possible further means by which pressures to reduce operating costs will
be applied to the industry.

As noted, the primary means by which a venture capital firm accrues capital
gain, as opposed to operating income, is through its share of the aggregate,
appreciation in value of its successful investments when they are sold. The selling
price at which an investment exits from the venture capitalist's portfolio and
the timing of the exit are the two most important external determinants on
fund profitability (Bygrave et al., 1989). From 1980 to 1987, the market value
of firms, as measured by the price-earning ratio of the *Financial Times 500 Index*,
rose from six to twenty. It has taken the six succeeding years for this ratio to
return to 1987 levels. Over the same period, post black Monday in October
1987, the price earnings ratios of UK private companies have performed
relatively less well. At the end of 1992, the Private Company Index stood at
a 43% discount to the price earnings ratios of the FT 500 companies — the
widest gap for several years (*Financial Times*, 25 January, 1993, p. 16). Twelve
months later, in December 1993, private company price earnings ratios, at
13.3, were still only 84% of their 1987 high point.

1090   MURRAY

From 1989 until the latter half of 1992, the use of public stock markets as an exit channel through which venture capital portfolio companies could be sold had become extremely difficult. Exceptionally, no private companies raised funds by joining the Unlisted Securities Market in the first quarter of 1991.[9] Only two MBOs exited by stock market flotation in the whole of 1991 compared to 132 in the period 1985–1988 (Centre for Management Buy-Out Research, 1992). Trade sales, which represent the dominant exit route, were similarly depressed reflecting cash flow and profitability constraints facing would-be acquiring firms in an international recession. However, the substantial increase in the value of UK equities in 1992/93 was also mirrored in a spate of Initial Public Offerings (IPOs) of venture backed companies in the four quarters July 1992 to June 1993. Excluding non-commercial, company stock market listings (mainly investment trusts) venture backed company flotations represented 48% of the total of the 75 IPOs floated during these four quarters. MBOs represented 50% of the 36 venture-backed flotations (BVCA, 1993b). This fickle interest by the London Stock Market in venture backed issues appears to parallel the similarly erratic pattern seen towards the attraction of IPOs to US investors over recent years (Bygrave and Timmons, 1992).

Thus, firms which invested substantial portfolio funds in the high price period from 1985 to 1987 have found subsequently their ability to realise investments (typically, over an approximate five year cycle, Bannock, 1991) at an attractive capital gain difficult for other than their most attractive investee companies. In effect, they have bought high and have had to sell low in a period of depressed firm prices as measured by stock market indicators or trade sale statistics. While the upward trend of small firm stock prices might appear to give some cause for optimism, it is necesary to remember that venture backed flotations barely reach double figures each year. UK venture capital firms have regularly invested in over 1,000 investee companies annually since 1987. Given the difficulties of obtaining attractive exit values during the recent recession, the stock of investee firms in the collective portfolio of the UK venture capital industry, which investors would wish to exit via an IPO, is likely to be very substantially greater than the praticable opportunity this channel represents. It is salutary to observe that, for MBOs, which remain the most popular investment activity of the UK venture capital industry, the CMBOR only recorded 12 flotations for the three years 1990–92, compared to 34 in both 1987 and 1988 (CMBOR, 1993).

All twenty-two BVCA survey respondents agreed that the difficulties of realising attractive exit prices would produce casualties in the UK venture capital industry as well as making institutional investors increasingly nervous of making unquoted investments in smaller companies via venture capital funds. Smaller, independent venture capital firms, i.e. with < £50 million of funds under management, were seen as particularly vulnerable. However, respondents believed that the dearth of new funds would extend to all firms which cannot demonstrate an attractive investment performance to potential funders.

CHANGE AND THE UK VENTURE CAPITAL INDUSTRY 1091

The computed return to the venture capitalist's investment, the annualised Internal Rate of Return (IRR), at which the deal is struck can be used as a surrogate for the price of its finance (Dixon, 1991). While individual firm data were not requested, several BVCA survey respondents noted that the IRRs at which deals were concluded had diminished over the 1980s. In 1991, an attractive MBO deal was likely to be accepted with a projected IRR in the low thirties (Murray and Lott, 1995). The same deal in 1985 would have been negotiated at an IRR around ten percentage points higher. Given the systematic risk associated with start-ups or early stage deals and their relative unpopularity to the majority of venture capital firms (Lorenz, 1989; and Bannock, 1991), price pressures have here remained less in evidence. Respondents stated that they would still expect IRRs of at least sixty percent per annum for such deals to be considered seriously.

Increase in Industry Leavers

Until 1989, the barriers to entry were low and approximately one hundred new venture capital firms entered the UK industry over the decade. This growth phase ended in 1989 and the industry was subsequently characterised by leavers rather than new firm entrants. However, a number of primarily regional funds have recently been created which confound, in the short term, forecasts of a shake-out. That the industry has not contracted more rapidly (see Figure 4) is a function of the high barriers to exit. Once a venture capital firm has raised a fund and is fully invested in a number of client companies, it is committed to running the fund for its allotted period. In the event of making unattractive investments, the fund still has to nurture its remaining investee companies until an exit can be arranged. The alternatives are allocating shares of the unquoted portfolio company to the private investors or organising a 'fire sale' in an attempt to regain some liquidity. Both alternatives are likely to be commercially unattractive to the institutional investors. This combination of low entry and high exit barriers is likely to increase competition between industry incumbents for both deal flow and new capital funding.

Over half the BVCA survey respondents shared a common belief that a number of existing venture capitalists with indifferent investment records would face the prospect of a 'funds famine' in the coming five years, 1991–95. This was seen as the single biggest threat to the future of the industry and was mentioned, unprompted, by 59% of the sample. If additional funds are not forthcoming, these organisations, on winding down and realising the 'rump' of their portfolios, will be obliged to exit from the industry. Seventy seven percent of respondents saw this as the most common reason for a firm leaving the venture capital industry. They suggested that only a minority of these firms will be attractive as merger of acquisition targets to either financial institutions or other, more successful, venture capital firms. However, present uncertainties do present the potential for arbitrage activity and structural changes might encourage 'portfolio brokers' (or, more accurately, 'breakers'). While there

Figure 4

Actual and Projected Growth of BVCA Full Membership 1983−95

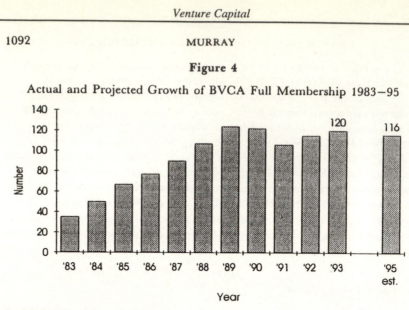

Source: BVCA, 1993.

is some evidence of limited activity, Initiative Europe (1994) only identified five transactions by 1993 in which UK funds have been terminated through acquisition by larger or more successful organisations.

In 1990, the BVCA survey respondents forecast that, on average, 24 firms would exit from the UK industry in the next five years. With an average of 16 new entrants also forecast, the stock of firms in 1994 was projected to decline marginally to around 116 i.e. very nearly the number of BVCA full members in 1993.[11] Since 1991, eleven new firms have entered the industry. The majority of these are smaller regional based funds or captives. Similarly, seven firms have unequivocally left the industry rather than remaining dormant, i.e. not investing or unable to invest. Six of the seven exiting companies were captives with only a peripheral interest in venture capital finance.

Thus, it would be more correct to describe this restructuring as a 'fade-out' rather than a precipitant process of 'shake-out'. In practice, the change in BVCA membership has been occasioned almost entirely by a smaller number of industry leavers than the greater flows forecast. This is likely to reflect the noted high exit costs. Performance pressures were seen as becoming particularly acute for poorly performing independents (noted by 59% of respondents) without the support of a powerful parent organisation, and small venture capital firms not enjoying a strong 'niche' position nor significant scale or scope economies (noted by 45% of respondents).

Concentration of Market Share

The number of firms in a market takes no cognisance of the market power

CHANGE AND THE UK VENTURE CAPITAL INDUSTRY   1093

Table 2

Annual Funds Raised by Independent UK Venture Capital Firms
(excluding BES Funds) for the Period 1985 to 1991[13]

Year	Top Four Funds £m	Average Top Four Funds £m	Total Funds Raised £m	Top Four Funds % Total Raised
1985	83.3	20.8	133.3	62.4
1986	93.5	23.4	212.9	43.9
1987	353.0	88.3	685.1	51.5
1988	356.6	89.2	667.5	53.4
1989	1084.0	273.5	1695.9	64.5
1990	427.0	106.8	852.1	50.1
1991	151.5	37.9	275.9	54.9

Source: Venture Economics Ltd., 1993.

of individual organisations. The importance of industry structure was explicitly recognised by several BVCA survey respondents who commented that there were only about twenty to thirty 'real' players in the UK venture capital market. From the period 1986 to 1989 inclusive, the four largest fund raisers have represented an increasing proportion of the total funds raised each year. With the exception of 1986, in the period 1985–91, the top four fund raisers, which are not the same firms every year, have accounted for over 50% of the total value of institutional investment raised.

This process of concentration is corroborated by reference to the Venture Economics Ltd.'s Special Reports 'Resources of the UK Venture Capital Industry', published for the years 1987–91. (The figures for 3i plc have been excluded from these survey results.) In 1987, in a sample of 107 firms, 27 venture capitalists had funds under management exceeding £50 million. By 1991, the number of firms with funds above £50 million had increased to 41 (44%) of the sample of 93 venture capital firms. At the lower end of the scale, the number of firms with funds under £5 million had dropped from 22 in 1987 to 13 in 1991.

Figure 5 shows graphically the degree of concentration existing in the UK industry by 1992. If 3i plc is excluded, twenty-eight firms each managed funds in excess of £100 million. Collectively, their resources represented 77% of the total funds controlled by the full membership of the BVCA. The driving forces towards concentration in the industry are three-fold. As institutional funders, with the assistance of gatekeepers, become more able to discriminate between successful and unsuccessful firms, the market moves to reward disproportionately the successful firms with additional capital. Similarly, firms with poorer performances experience a dearth of new funds. Secondly, there are, as Sahlman (op. cit.) notes, economies of both scale and scope operating to the advantage of a management company or partnership which operates simultaneously more than one fund. Larger funds with a commensurately larger

1094   MURRAY

Figure 5

Concentration of UK Investments by Fund Size, 1991/92

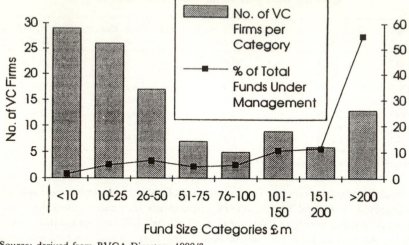

Source: derived from BVCA Directory 1992/3.

deal flow may also have the benefit of 'learning curve effects' if the cost of the investment process declines over time with accumulated volume.

The third factor encouraging the growth in fund size is the compensation benefits captured by the managers of a large fund. The percentage fee charged by the venture capital company to manage the fund on behalf of the limited partners, at 2—2.5%, does not appear to decline with the size of fund. This 'stickiness' of the management fee has appeared to operate both in the UK and the US. Thus, managers have a direct incentive to increase the size of the funds under their management, irrespective of the performance implications on portfolio management, given that a number of the operating costs do not rise proportionately to the additional funds managed. The issue of divergent interests, or 'agency costs' (Jensen and Meckling, 1976), between the managing and private partners of a fund has come to the fore as institutions have downgraded their expectations on net returns from a number of their investments. Initiative Europe (1994), reflecting on the substantial fee-based remuneration of the management in a number of poorly performing funds, suggested contentiously that on occasions the institutions have been 'mugged'. The economic attraction of managing a large level of aggregate funds is supported in a survey conducted by Hays Management Consultants (1988) on US venture capitalists' remuneration. The total compensation of a managing partner of a venture capital firm controlling funds of over $200 million was, at $581,000 per annum, over three times the size of his/her opposite number managing a fund of $25 million.

CHANGE AND THE UK VENTURE CAPITAL INDUSTRY 1095

The outcome of these factors was that, throughout the 1980s, the UK industry had become increasingly polarised into a small number of large, and increasingly international, venture capital firms with combined funds in excess of £100 million. By 1991, there were 29 such funds. The remainder of the industry included a large concentration (55 firms) of small players each controlling funds of less than £25 million.

The Importance of Management Buy-Outs

The single biggest product for the UK venture capital industry throughout the 1980s and early 1990s has been the Management Buy-Out (MBO). The need to restructure over-diversified, multi-enterprise businesses in an increasingly competitive environment resulted in a substantial supply of new businesses which required external equity to complement the management team's limited personal resources. The substantial growth of acquisition activity in the mid 1980s also increased the supply of MBOs as the acquiring companies resold parts of the purchased company not required in the enlarged business.[12]

In 1992 MBOs/MBIs accounted for 35% and 57% of the number and value, respectively, of the combined activity of the UK market for corporate control. Over the period 1979−92, 3,952 MBOs with an aggregate value of £21.7 billion were financed. Over the same period, there were a further 829 Management Buy-Ins (MBIs) created with an aggregate value of £7.9 billion. Although 1990

Figure 6

Growth of Management Buy-Outs and Buy-Ins 1980−92

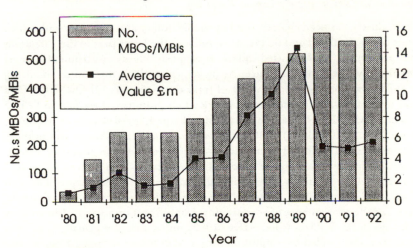

Source: CMBOR 1993.

was a record year for the number of total transactions, with 484 new MBOs recorded (a growth in number of 29.8% over 1989), the average value of individual deals dropped sharply to £5.1 million from the exceptional figure of £10.4 million in 1989 (CMBOR, 1994). MBO/MBI activity was broadly sustained in 1992 with 445 MBOs and 134 MBIs representing aggregate investment of £3.26 million, the highest annual value of total deals since the record year of 1989 when transactions worth £7.5 billion were completed.

The importance of MBOs/MBIs can be evidenced if their value is removed from UK annual investment statistics. When excluded, venture capital investment has declined in nominal value terms over the last four years from £565 million in 1988 to £445 million in 1991. In the latter year, MBOs/MBIs represented 55% of total UK investment by the industry.

The BVCA survey respondents estimated that MBOs would continue to be the single most important product in the UK venture capital industry, still representing 51% of the value of annual transactions in 1995. Respondents also believed that a greater proportion of annual investment (1995 estimate 36%, 1991 actual 34%) would be applied to later stage financing including development capital, secondary finance and, reflecting the problems of recession, rescue-type, refinancing deals. The ability to provide capital for firms that remain basically sound but are financially constrained as traditional sources of borrowing and new equity become less available during a recession was seen as the single biggest contemporary opportunity in late 1990, being mentioned by 59% of respondents. In this context, UK venture capitalists have become increasingly interested in the novel activity of investing in smaller, quoted companies (see *UK Venture Capital Journal*, March/April 1991).

The Role of Debt in Venture Capital Financing

The industry has been characterised by the flexibility and creativity with which deals can be initiated and financed. Notable in the latter part of the 1980s was the growth in sophisticated quasi debt/quasi equity instruments, most importantly 'mezzanine' finance. At its zenith in 1989, mezzanine financing at £933.3 million represented 16% of total deal value in MBOs/MBIs. One year later, the value of mezzanine finance had plummeted six fold to £155.5 million (CMBOR, 1992) as the risk to subordinated, quasi-debt in over-geared, larger (i.e. >£10 million) MBO deals became apparent. The growth in these instruments had allowed increasingly larger deals to be financed with a corresponding increase in the indebtedness of the deal. The well publicised problems of corporations which have funded expansion and acquisition with a heavy reliance on debt, both within and outside the venture capital arena, have had the consequence of encouraging a significant trend away from highly indebted deals. KPMG (Oct. – Dec. 1992) noted that the gearing (i.e. debt + mezzanine divided by equity) on larger MBOs had dropped from a ratio of 5.9:1 in the last six months of 1989 to a more conservative ratio of 1.7:1 two years later.

Twenty-one of the twenty-two BVCA survey respondents believed that there would be a significant and conservative move to a greater proportion of equity in the financing of future venture capital deals. This trend was also a recognition (noted by 10 respondents) that the clearing banks were increasingly refusing to provide senior debt financing without investors providing significantly higher contributions of equity to around 40–50% of deal value. There was a greater divorce of opinions about the future use of mezzanine funding. Nine respondents (41%) believed that it would increase in importance over the next five years. Five of these respondents also saw venture capitalist firms becoming a more important source of mezzanine finance as specialist providers withdrew from this activity, at least in the shorter term. Recent statistics support the trend to more conservative financing of larger (>£10 million) MBOs/MBIs. The role of mezzanine has continued to reduce, declining from 15% of total funding in 1990 to 7% in 1991. This shortfall has been made up by equity providers who in 1991 provided 34% of total funding of £2,620 million with the remaining 57% being supplied by debt providers (KPMG, 1991).

The latter half of the 1980s saw an increase in the size of venture capital backed deals culminating in the Reedpack MBO in 1988 of £805 million and the Gateway/Isosceles MBI in 1989 of £2,375 million. While the average value for an MBO over the 1980s was £5.9 million, between 1987–92 inclusive there were 14 MBO/MBIs of over £250 million and 290 MBO/MBIs of between £10–250 million (KPMG, April/June 1993). Venture capital over the decade grew from a useful form of specialist finance for start-ups and refinancing non-core enterprises out of the corporate parent to a major financial instrument within the wider market for corporate control. The attraction of MBOs was such that a number of funds were created in the late 1980s specifically for the financing of large MBOs (and to a lesser extent MBIs) of deal sizes of £50 million and above. Current analyses from CMBOR and KPMG suggest that, while the economic attraction of size remains, a more cautious approach by investors to larger deals is likely to exist for the foreseeable future or, at least, until a sustained upturn in economic activity in the UK is unequivocally demonstrated.

Search for New Markets/Internationalisation

The UK industry has placed increased emphasis in establishing continental European operations, either as wholly owned subsidiaries or as alliances and joint ventures with domestic partners in the new country markets (CMBOR, 1991). With few exceptions, the only other market of interest to UK venture capitalists outside continental Europe has been the United States.

The substantial 1990 increase in investments by UK venture capitalists into continental Europe from £47 million in 1988 indicated the relative attraction of these emerging markets, despite the considerable legal and fiscal barriers to unquoted equity investments in several European countries (CMBOR, 1991). KPMG estimated that the annual value of continental European MBOs had by the end of 1990 reached parity with the value of UK MBOs at £2.8 billion

1098   MURRAY

Table 3

National and International Investment by UK Venture Capitalists
1989−91

| | Number of Financings | | | Amount Invested £ million | | |
	1989	1990	1991	1989	1990	1991
UK	1,302	1,221	1,196	1,420	1,106	989
US	156	178	92	127	62	70
Contin. Europe	94	150	94	97	223	92
Overseas	17	10	4	3	3	2
Total	1,569	1,559	1,386	1,647	1,394	1,153

Source: BVCA 1992.

each. They forecast that continental activity would, in 1991, exceed for the first time UK values (KPMG, January 1991). However, EVCA figures for 1992 indicate that the UK has re-established its dominance representing 61% of European MBO/MBI activity by value (EVCA, 1993).

As the deadline for full harmonisation of the EC by the end of 1992 approached, Europe has replaced the US as the second most important investment focus of UK venture capitalists. This geographic expansion of the contemporary venture capital model from its US origins to the UK, subsequently to Western Europe and, more recently, to the Pacific Rim and Eastern Europe is an apposite illustration of the 'international product life-cycle' (Murray, 1990).

The BVCA survey respondents were asked if they saw continental Europe as a major opportunity for the UK venture capital industry. Seventeen respondents (77%) agreed that it was. However, five respondents challenged this view arguing that the opportunities had either been over estimated or that, while opportunities did exist, they would only be available to a limited number of well resourced organisations that had effectively nurtured cross-border linkages. In terms of the most likely areas of attractive deal flow, the growing European MBO market was seen as the area of highest potential, (45% of respondents) followed by the opportunities from arranging the succession in family firms (41% of respondents). Figures from CMBOR show a total of 1,548 MBOs/MBIs valued at $25.07 billion were undertaken in 14 continental European countries over the period 1989−92 inclusive (CMBOR, 1993). These figures give the UK a four year average, total European market share by value of 53%, albeit almost entirely derived from domestic investment in UK firms.

Rationalisation of Existing Products and Services

A frequent criticism repeatedly made of the UK venture capital industry is the modest amounts of money which it allocates both to start-up/early stage

CHANGE AND THE UK VENTURE CAPITAL INDUSTRY 1099

Table 4

Start-Up and Early Stage UK Venture Capital Investments 1987–91

	1987	*1988*	*1989*	*1990*	*1991*
Start-Ups:					
Number	191	202	177	199	158
Value (£m)	75	70	86	76	35
% Total Invested	8	5	6	7	4
Early Stage:					
Number	133	182	344	141	115
Value (£m)	45	60	129	52	23
% Total Invested	5	5	9	5	2

Source: BVCA, 1992.

companies and to high technology related investments (for example, see Confederation of British Industry criticisms reported in the *Financial Times*, 6th May, 1993).

Seventy seven percent of the BVCS survey respondents observed that this paucity of what Bygrave and Timmons term as 'classic venture capital' represented the single most important failing of the industry to date. Over the decade of the 1980s, the UK industry had become increasingly focused on large MBO deals, particularly in the retail sector. In 1991, 158 start-up and 115 other early stage financings were allocated 4% and 2%, respectively, of the total funds invested by BVCA members that year compared to £544 million (55% of annual investment) on 288 MBOs and MBIs.

BVCA survey respondents estimated that start-ups and early stage deals would take on average 14% of total investments in 1995. There is little evidence to support the size of this estimate as, with the exception of 1989, the value of investment into early stage deals has declined since 1985. The availability of pre-start up funds, i.e. 'seed capital', is even more difficult with the UK figure for 1991 being estimated at less than 0.035% of total funds invested (EVCA, 1992; Murray and Francis, 1993; and Murray, 1995).

The BVCA survey respondents gave no optimism for expecting an increase in new technology investments (i.e. computer related, electronics, medical and biological, and communications). By 1995, 40% of the respondents believed this area of investment would be a lower proportion of total investment than the 1989 figure of 12%. One third of respondents (35%) believed that technology investment would increase as a proportion of the total while 25% of respondents thought that it would remain at the 1989 level. The recently released figures of the BVCA (1993) support the pessimists with technology investment declining to 9% of total UK investment value (including debt provided by venture capitalists) in 1992.

A 1991 survey of 40 UK venture capitalists, which were prepared to consider

1100   MURRAY

Table 5

Technology Related Investments as a Percentage of the Value of Total
UK Venture Capital Investments 1987—91

	1987	*1988*	*1989*	*1990*	*1991*
% Technology	15.9	8.5	12.0	14.0	13.0

Source: BVCA, 1992.

technology-related investment, indicated that venture capitalists imposed higher
rates of return in the evaluation process when compared to non technology
proposals. Technology related proposals also had to be more international in
market scope in order to gain funding (Murray and Lott, 1994). Table 5 shows
clearly the increasing disillusionment with technology projects from 1987 which
was occasioned by the commercial difficulties of a number of funds which had
specialised in technology investments. These figures contrast dramatically with
the US where 80% of the annual investment of $1,358 million by NVCA
members was directed to technology-related enterprises in 1991. Software
investment alone took 25% of all disbursements (Venture Economics Inc.,
1992). Even after removing the influence of MBOs/MBIs and Leverage Buy-
Outs on UK and US investment figures respectively, the US invests *pro rata*
nearly three times (29% *v* 83%) as much of its annual venture capital
disbursements in technology-related investments in 1991 (Murray, 1993).

It is a reflection of the UK reality that, until recently, 'replacement equity'
in later stage deals, primarily buy-outs, have produced better risk/return yields
than the more speculative areas of true venturing or 'new equity' within the
UK market. Classic venture capital activity, both in start-up and early stage
deals, needs specialist skills from the venture capital provider (Roberts, 1991a;
and Sweeting, 1991). The costs associated with selecting and subsequently
supporting such activities allow few economies of scale or scope and have
increasingly become the focus of smaller, more specialist venture capital firms.
However, a small number of larger, portfolio based, UK firms still undertake
both types of deal albeit as a minority activity.

Increased Emphasis on Costs and Services

The largest operational cost for venture capital firms is their specialist workforce.
There are no public data on whether or not the increased competitive climate
has produced a decline in management incomes and only anecdotal evidence
which suggests that the industry is starting to slim down its labour force.[13] The
unpopularity of start-up/early stage deal, as indicated above, is in part due
to the staff cost implications of monitoring and supporting a large number of

CHANGE AND THE UK VENTURE CAPITAL INDUSTRY   1101

small entrepreneurial investments (Murray, 1991a; and Bannock, 1991).

Ironically, cost pressures generated from the institutions' greater negotiating power over fee incomes and the carry (Gregory, 1991) have grown at a time when investee companies may well expect a greater level of service and support from their investors. The effects of recession have increased the need to support existing portfolio companies. A 1990 press article on the industry suggested that up to one third of portfolio companies 'were now on the sick list' (Gant, 1990).

Twenty (91%) of the BVCA survey respondents believed that investee companies would in future want a closer relationship with their venture capitalist or would expect greater involvement from them. However, only 62% of the sample believed that the industry would actually become more 'hands on'. The support available to the client may become a more important selling point in differentiating a firm from its competitors in seeking new dealflow. The efficacy of closer venture capital involvement on the performance of the investee company has been questioned by some authors (Macmillan et al., 1989; and Fredriksen et al., 1990) although seen as more positive by others (Sweeting, 1991). For several of the smaller but non-specialist venture capitalists with scarce executive resources and limited funds to contract in specialist skills, such a trend could be problematic. The disproportionate cost of client support was cited as one of the major problems associated with making small, seed capital funds commercially viable (Murray and Francis, 1992).

UNITED STATES' PARALLELS AND EUROPEAN IMPLICATIONS

The BVCA survey was completed in the last months of 1990 and concentrated exclusively on the experiences of UK venture capital firms. However, parallels since the early 1980s between the UK venture capital industry and its more established American counterpart are impressive. The increasing difficulties in the investment climate for venture capital noted in the annual reports of the National Venture Capital Association from 1989 onwards and Swartz's (1991) contemporary evaluation of short term problems (i.e. poor returns; unrealistic investor expectations; decline in venture capital firm numbers; excessive numbers of undifferentiated late entrants; and concentration in fund suppliers) could as easily have been written about the UK industry post 1988.

The UK experience is starting to mirror the cyclicality evidenced in the US industry with the latter's current decline from the historically high activity levels of 1986/7 after a sustained period of growth since 1980. The US industry experienced an erratic fall in the number of venture-backed 'Initial Public Offerings' (IPOs) from the 1983 peak (121 at $3031 million) to the 1988 nadir (36 at $789 million). 1992 saw a strong recovery in this market with a record 151 companies generating a total amount offered of $4,420 million (NVCA,

1102   MURRAY

1992) mirroring the recent activity in the UK IPO market in 1992/93. The annual level of investment has also seen an upturn in the US. In 1991, $1,358 million was invested — the lowest annual figure since 1981. One year later, this figure had doubled to $2,543 million, although, excluding years 1990 and 1991, this was still the lowest level of nominal investment activity since 1982.

The confidence of institutional investors in private venture capital firms has also appeared to have increased. After a ten year low point in 1988 ($1,388 million), new capital commitments in 1992 grew 84% to $2,550 million. Irrespective of the 9% (i.e. 53 firms) of industry leavers over the period 1989—92, the industry has continued to concentrate. By 1992, seventy firms, representing 11% of the NVCA membership, controlled $17.84 billion of managed funds, or 57% of the total pool of funds committed to the US industry.

This paper's primary concentration on the UK venture capital industry is purposive. The UK in 1992 accounts for nearly two-fifths (39%) of total European annual investment (EVCA, 1993). The UK experience continues to cast a long shadow over the rest of Europe just as the US experience has influenced UK venture capital firms. Through the integrating work of the EVCA and the increasing number of international alliances between UK and other European venture capital firms, the lessons of the UK industry have been rapidly absorbed and adapted on the mainland of Europe.

Continental European countries have not invested heavily in technology based, new investments which overall took only 12% of total annual disbursements in 1992. Similarly, unlike the UK in the early 1980s, continental European venture capital firms did not start by investing significantly in start-up activity before developing into secondary financing activities. With the exception of Finland (39%), Spain (23%), and to a lesser extent Portugal (14%) and Italy (11%), the majority of European countries invest under 10% of annual funds at the seed capital or start-up stages. The continental industry has, *ab initio*, developed largely as a source of expansion and replacement capital. In 1992, these two categories took 46% and 9%, respectively, of total investment. MBOs/MBIs accounted for a further 40% of annual investment (EVCA, 1993).

Just as the continental European industries have developed rapidly to assume a similar investment pattern to the UK, they will more quickly have to face the strategic issues currently concerning the UK industry. As Europe becomes more integrated, the dominance of country based, venture capital markets will be challenged. For the larger deals, syndication may become more transnational in scope. Over time, investors, including banks and insurance companies, will wish to see acceptable, risk adjusted returns on this novel asset class from their venture capital intermediaries or specialist, equity providing subsidiaries. Changing market and environmental parameters will require individual firms to make decisions regarding their product/market choices. Like their UK counterparts, strategic competence will become a necessary precursor of success. In making these decisions, the recent history of the UK venture capital industry may offer informative parallels.

CHANGE AND THE UK VENTURE CAPITAL INDUSTRY   1103

Table 6

Porter's Model of Industry Maturity

Environmental Changes:	Occurrence in UK VC Industry by 1993
Decline in Rate of Industry Growth	yes
Increase in Market Information	yes
Increase in Buyer/Supplier Power	yes
Increase in International Competition	no
Consequences and/or Firm Responses:	
Decline in Industry Profitability	yes
Increase in Industry Leavers	yes (but limited)
Concentration of Market Share	yes
Search for New Products and Services	yes
Search for New Markets/Internationalisation	yes
Rationalisation of Existing Products and Services	yes
Increase in Emphasis on Costs and Services	yes

Source: Porter, 1980.

CONCLUSIONS

The responses from the BVCA survey respondents, supported by industry statistics, suggest that the present dynamics of the UK venture capital industry closely fit Porter's (1980) model of industry maturity. Since 1989, there have occurred clear signs of the onset of maturity after allowing for the influence of external economic trends. The recent recessionary climate has negatively affected the value of current investments in client firms while making the institutional funders, or primary customers, more circumspect about the long term performance of venture capital investment. Their caution is seen in the contemporary difficulties experienced by UK venture capitalists in raising new funds.

Changing UK demand/supply conditions for venture capital in the last decade of the 20th Century is likely to result in a significant increase in inter-firm rivalry which will similarly encourage the trend for greater concentration in the industry. The ability to market effectively their financial products and services to prospective investee clients will become a key element of future success for UK venture capitalists. Similarly, the need to demonstrate performance in terms of risk adjusted, return on capital to institutional or parent funders will become imperative. Over the current decade, funders will increasingly be able to see the terminal performance details of existing venture capital, fixed term funds. The poor performance of some funds will oblige unsuccessful venture capitalists to leave the industry as their ability to attract future funds disappears.

Increased competitive pressure on the domestic market will likely produce

1104   MURRAY

more specialist product offerings (e.g. greater client advice/support or sector specialisms) by individual firms. The industry is, at present, remarkable for the near absence of product/service differentiation between the majority of competing firms. The maturity of the UK market has also prompted several larger UK venture capital firms to set up new offices in continental Europe. However, given the relative ease of the international transferability of specialist skills in financial services, the continued specificity of country markets and the dominance of local providers, particularly banks, the opportunity for UK firms to profit from the internationalisation of their markets remains, as yet, unproven. None the less, the opportunity for continental venture capital firms to profit from UK and US experiences in crafting their own strategic responses does exist.

NOTES

1 While the BVCA does not represent all UK venture capital firms within its membership, the larger firms are almost universally full members.
2 EVCA annual statistics in 1993 covered 18 European countries.
3 In July 1992, the 70 + institutions involved in financing Isosceles were involved in urgent refinancing of the MBI. The £400 million equity contribution in the original deal structure was likely to be rendered worthless (*Financial Times*, 9th July, 1991 p. 24). MFI was subsequently floated on the UK main market in 1993.
4 This was a subjective assessment made by the Council of the BVCA.
5 A liner regression of annual, nominal investment values between 1981 and 1991 against an average GDP index, as the independent variable, indicates a high level of association (correlation coefficient = 0.96, F ratio = 114).
6 A regression of annual, nominal investment activity against the *Financial Times All Shares Index*, 1981–91 as the independent variable, also shows a strong association (correlation coefficient = 0.908, F ratio = 42).
7 These figures do not include the funds raised internally by captive organisations such as bank owned venture capitalists. The finances raised by 3i are also excluded.
8 Edwin Goodman, President of Hambro America Inc., also suggests that US venture capitalists have ignored their real 'customers' (*Pension World*, July 1989, pp. 35–36).
9 This may help to explain the increase, post 1987, in semi-captive organisations establishing independent funds in tandem with existing, parental funding.
10 Given the continuing decline in the number and value of companies quoted on the USM, the planned closing of the USM in 1996 has been widely reported (*Financial Times*, 30 November, 1992, p. 16).
11 Contemporary industry opinion in 1993 was that the number of leavers will be substantially higher in the medium term than that forecast in 1990. However, a number of smaller venture capital firms have recently joined the BVCA taking its current full membership at the start of 1994 to 120.
12 If the annual value of MBOs/MBIs is regressed against the annual value of UK M&A activity from 1979–92, a correlation coefficient of 0.898 is obtained (F value 50.2).
13 Since 1990, 3i plc has undertaken a major cost reduction programme involving the closure of five UK regional offices in addition to a number of overseas offices, and a significant reduction in professional staff numbers.

REFERENCES

Anon. (1991), *Pension Fund Investment Survey — the Performance Challenge* (Alexander Consulting Group).
Bannock, G. (1991), *Venture Capital and the Equity Gap* (National Westminster Bank).
Brakell, J.R. (1988), 'Institutional Investor Expectations from Investment in Venture Captial', *1988 Guide to European Venture Capital Sources* (Venture Economics Ltd).

CHANGE AND THE UK VENTURE CAPITAL INDUSTRY   1105

British Venture Capital Association (1992/93), *Report on Investment Activity 1991/2* (BVCA).
_____ (1993a), *Directory 1993/4* (BVCA)
_____ (1993b), *High Proportion of New Flotations are Venture Backed*, Press Release: 19th Occtober (BVCA).
Bryan, L.L., M. Muth, P.S. Wufflie and D. Hunt (1993), 'The New World of Financial Services' *The McKinsey Quarterly*, Vol. 2, pp. 59−106.
Bygrave, W., N. Fast, R. Kholyian, L. Vincent and W. Yue (1989), 'Early Rates of Return of 131 Venture Capital Funds Started 1978−1984', *Journal of Business Venturing*, Vol. 4, pp. 93−105.
_____ and J. Timmons (1992), *Venture Capital at the Crossroads* (Harvard Business School Press).
Centre for Management Buy-Out Research (eds.) (1991), *The Economist's Guide to European Buy-Outs* (Economist Publications).
_____ (1992), *Management Buy-Outs of Companies From Receivership* (University of Nottingham).
_____ (1993), *UK Management Buy-Outs 1992/3* (University of Nottingham).
Dixon, R. (1991), 'Venture Capital and the Appraisal of Investments', *Omega*, Vol. 4, NO. 19, pp. 333−44.
European Venture Capital Association (1993), *1992 EVCA Yearbook* (KPMG).
Fredriksen, O., C. Olofsson and C. Wahlbin (1990), 'The Role of Venture Capital in the Development of Portfolio Companies', Paper for the Strategic Management Society's Strategic Bridging Conference, Stockholm (September).
Gant, J. (1990), 'Portfolios, Provisions, and Above All, Pragmatism', *Acquisitions Monthly* (November), pp. 4−8.
Gorman, M. and W.A. Sahlman (1989), 'What Do Venture Capitalists Do?', *Journal of Business Venturing*, Vol. 4, No. 4, pp. 231−248.
Gregory, R. (1991), *An Examination of the Fund Raising Environment for UK Venture Capitalists 1989−91*, unpublished MBA dissertation (Warwick Business School, University of Warwick).
Hannah, L. (1992), *The Financing of Innovation 1880−1980* (Economic & Social Research Council).
Harrison, R.T. and C.M. Mason (1992), 'International Perspectives on the Supply of Informal Venture Capital', *Journal of Business Venturing*, Vol. 7, pp. 459−475.
Hovgaard, S. (1991), *London Business School/British Venture Capital Association Survey on Venture Capital in the UK* (BVCA).
Hustedd, R. and G. Pulver (1992), 'Factors Affecting Equity Capital Acquisition: the Demand Side', *Journal of Business Venturing*, Vol. 7, No. 4, pp. 363−374.
Jensen, M. and W. Meckling (1976), 'Theory of the Firm: Managerial Behaviour, Agency Costs and Ownership Structure', *Journal of Financial Economics*, Vol. 3, pp. 305−360.
Kay, J.A. (1990), 'Identifying the Strategic Market', *Business Strategy Review* (Spring), pp. 2−24.
KPMG Peat Marwick McLintock (1991−1993), *Management Buy-Out Statistics* (KPMG).
Llanwarne, P.A. (1990), *Survey of the Attitudes of Small, High Growth Companies Towards Venture Capital*, unpublished BMA Dissertation (Warwick Business School, University of Warwick).
Lloyd, S. (1989), 'Special Report: An Industry on the Brink of the 1990s', *UK Venture Capital Journal* (November), pp. 10−15.
Lorenz, T. (1989), *Venture Capital Today*, 2nd Edn (Woodhead Faulkner).
Macmillan, I.C., D.M. Kulow and R. Khoylain (1989), 'Venture Capitalists' Involvement in Their Investments: Extent and Performance', *Journal of Business Venturing*. Vol. 4, No. 1, pp. 27−47.
Mason, C.M. and R.T. Harrison (1991), 'Venture Capital, the Equity Gap and the "North-South Divide" in the United Kingdom', in M.B. Green (ed.) *Venture Capital International Comparisons* (Routledge), pp. 202−247.
Murray, G.C. (1989), 'The Birth of a Pan-European Industry', *The European Buy-Out Directory 1990−91* (Venture Corp/Pitman), pp. 13−29.
_____ (1991a), *Change and Maturity in the UK Venture Capital Industry 1991−95* (BVCA).
_____ (1991b), 'The Changing Nature of Competition in the UK Venture Capital Industry', *National Westminster Bank Quarterly Review* (November), pp. 65−80.
_____ (1992), 'A Challenging Market Place for Venture Capital', *Long Range Planning*, Vol. 25, No. 6, pp. 79−86.
_____ (1993), *Third Party Equity Support for New Technology Based Firms in the UK and Continental Europe*, Paper presented at the Six Countries Programme workshop, Montreal.
_____ (1995), 'An Assessment of the First Three Years of the European Seed Capital Fund Scheme', *European Planning Studies*, Vol. 2, No. 4, pp. 435−461..

1106   MURRAY

Murray, G.C. and D. Francis (1992), *The European Seed Capital Fund Scheme: A Review of the First Three Years* (Commission of the European Communities, DGXXIII).

———— and J. Lott (1995), 'Have Venture Capital Firms a Bias Against Investment in High Technology Companies?', *Research Policy*, Vol. 24, pp. 283–299.

————, B. Nixon, P. Pounsford and M. Wright (1995), 'The Role and Effectiveness of UK Professional Intermediaries in the Selection of a Venture Capital Partner', *International Journal of Bank Marketing* (forthcoming).

Porter, M.E. (1979), 'How Competitive Forces Shape Strategy', *Harvard Business Review* (March/April), pp. 137–145.

———— (1980), *The Competitive Strategy: Techniques for Analysing Industries and Competitors* (The Free Press, Macmillan Inc.).

Pratt, G. (1990), 'Venture Capital in the United Kingdom', *Bank of England Quarterly Bulletin* (February).

Roberts, E.B. (1991a), 'High Stakes of High Tech Entrepreneurs: Understanding Venture Capital Decision Making', *Sloan Management Review* (Winter), pp. 9–20.

———— (1991b), *Entrepreneurs in High Technology* (Oxford University Press).

Robinson, R.R. (1987), 'Emerging Strategies in the Venture Capital Industry', *Journal of Business Venturing*, Vol. 2, No. 1, pp. 53–77.

Ruhnka, J. and J. Young (1991), 'Some Hypotheses About Risk in Venture Capital Investing', *Journal of Business Venturing*, Vol. 6, pp. 115–133.

Sahlman, W.A. (1989), *The Changing Structure of the American Venture Capital Industry* (National Venture Capital Association Annual Conference).

———— (1991), 'Insights from the American Venture Capital Organisation', Working Paper (Harvard Business School, Division of Research).

Storey, D., R. Watson and P. Wynarczyk (1989), *Fast Growth Businesses Case Studies of 40 Small Firms in the North East of England*, Paper No. 67 (Department of Employment).

Swartz, J. (1991), 'The Future of the Venture Capital Industry', *Journal of Business Venturing*, Vol. 6, pp. 89–92.

Sweeting, R.C. (1991), 'Early Stage New Technology Based Businesses: Interactions with Venture Capitalists and the Development of Accounting Techniques and Procedures', *The British Accounting Review*, Vol. 23, No. 1, pp. 3–21.

Thornton, S. (1994), *UK Venture Industry Review* (Initiative Europe).

Tyebjee, T. and A. Bruno (1984), 'A Model of Venture Capital Activity', *Management Science*, Vol. 30, No. 9, pp. 1051–1066.

———— and L. Vickery (1988), 'Venture Capital in Western Europe', *Journal of Business Venturing*, Vol. 3, pp. 123–136.

Venture Economics Inc. (1990–1993), *National Venture Capital Association 1989–92 Annual Reports* (NVCA).

———— (1990), *Current State of US Venture Capital*.

Venture Economics Ltd. (1988), 'Special Report: Resources in the Venture Capital Industry', *UK Venture Capital Journal* (July/August), pp. 8–14.

———— (1989), 'Focus on Fund Raising in 1989', *European Venture Capital Journal* (May/June), pp. 6–12.

———— (1990), 'Special Report: Resources of the UK Venture Capital Industry', *UK Venture Capital Journal* (July/August), pp. 8–14.

———— (1991a), 'Special Report: Capital Commitments to UK Funds in 1990', *UK Venture Capital Journal* (January/February), pp. 12–20.

———— (1991b), 'Special Report: Venture Capital Investment in Quoted Companies', *UK Venture Capital Journal* (March/April), pp. 8–13.

Wright, M., K. Robbie, S. Thompson and K. Starkey (1994), 'Longevity and the Life-Cycle of Management Buy-Outs', *Strategic Management Journal*, Vol. 15, pp. 215–227.

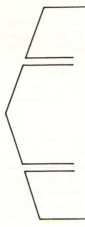

[3]

Strategic Management Journal, Vol. 13, 85–101 (1992)

CALLS ON HIGH-TECHNOLOGY: JAPANESE EXPLORATION OF VENTURE CAPITAL INVESTMENTS IN THE UNITED STATES

DILEEP HURRY
Cox School of Business, Southern Methodist University, Dallas, Texas U.S.A.

ADAM T. MILLER
Harvard Business School, Boston, Massachusetts, U.S.A.

E. H. BOWMAN
The Wharton School, University of Pennsylvania, Philadelphia, Pennsylvania, U.S.A.

The strategic logic of Japanese high-technology venture capital investment reveals the existence of an implicit call option, or 'shadow option', on new technology. This option is exercised by further investment in product development, manufacturing and distribution. The process is described with reference to a comparative study of Japanese and U.S. venture capital firms. Similarities and differences between the two groups are reported, and a conceptual model of Japanese option strategy is formulated. The implications for our understanding of Japanese strategy and for strategic management theory are discussed.

INTRODUCTION

Japanese corporations are well-known for their recent commercial successes in the United States in the form of a growing market share in major industries (e.g. Toyota and Honda) or through highly visible acquisitions such as Sony's purchase of Columbia Pictures and Matsushita's takeover of MCA Entertainment. These successes, however, are largely a mature consequence of a basic thrust which has characterized Japanese business from its beginnings: the development of technology first obtained from external sources. Though less visible than the more publicized successes, this thrust still continues through a sustained emphasis on improving and refining products and processes initially developed in the West (Jauch and Osborn, 1981; Zimmerman, 1985; Osborn and Baughn, 1987; Johnson, 1988).

A strategy of technology acquisition might take several forms, including out-sourcing of product design, licensing of new technologies, strategic alliances such as joint ventures and research programs, and venture capital investments in high-technology enterprises. This paper studies one of these forms viz. venture capital investment in high-technology companies. The objective is to describe the Japanese process of investment and to examine how the Japanese strategy differs from that used by U.S. firms. Twenty Japanese venture capital companies with investments in the United States and twenty U.S. venture capital firms with similar investments form the sample for this study.

Key words: Option, venture capital, Japanese strategy.

0143-2095/92/020085-17$08.50

Received 3 July 1991
Final revision received 7 October 1991

86   *D. Hurry* et al.

HIGH-TECHNOLOGY VENTURES AND VENTURE CAPITAL

A new high-technology venture start-up is a risky proposition for most stock market investors and hence is usually financed partly by the entrepreneur and largely by venture capital firms. These firms are often limited partnerships of investors who are willing to provide risk capital and who can afford to wait for 5 to 7 years before earning returns. Once the venture has succeeeded in introducing new products and earning revenues, it will make its initial public offer of stock. At this point, the venture capital firms are in a position to reap their rewards.

Venture capital investment in its basic form is similar to a long-term project in which investment is made in year 1 and positive cash flow is earned in say, year 7, often in the form of a lump sum.

However, a new high-technology venture also offers a potential source for new technology for the investing firm. A firm interested in exploring new technologies might invest in a new high-technology venture in order to participate in the development of the new technology and to share in its profits. This is similar to the practice of large companies (e.g. Apple Computer) to 'spin-off' new firms in which the parent firm retains an interest. External ventures may be preferred over internal corporate ventures since they avoid problems of structural incompatibility between the parent firm and the entrepreneurial new venture.[1]

A firm's technology plays a central role in developing and sustaining its competitive advantage (Schumpeter, 1934; Ansoff, 1965; Andrews, 1971; Kantrow, 1980; Porter, 1983; Venkatraman and Camillus, 1984; Frohman, 1985; Grinyer, Al-Bazzaz and Yasai-Ardekani 1986). The rapid rate of diffusion of technology (Mansfield, 1985; Ghemawat, 1986) exerts a pressure on the firm to retain competitive vitality through innovation. Outside sources of knowledge are critical to the innovation process (Cohen and Levinthal, 1990). In fact, innovation mainly arises from external sources (March and Simon, 1958; Mueller, 1962; Hamberg, 1963; von Hippel, 1988). Hence, it is reasonable to expect

high-technology outside ventures to form vehicles for technological revitalization.

If venture capital investment is aimed at gaining new technology, the investment pattern goes beyond a simple project. Investment will be motivated less by the new venture's profit potential and more by the opportunity for gaining a new technology. This will entail further in-house investments in product design, development, manufacturing and marketing. Two investments are required: first there is the basic 'external' investment in the venture, and next there is the further 'internal' investment needed to acquire the new technology. The return from the second investment cannot be forseen at the first stage, even its timing cannot usually be known in advance, because the second investment will depend on the successful development of the new technology by the venture in the first place. The initial investment yields more than a simple project return, for it enables the firm to position itself to capture the future technological opportunity.

The first investment thus gives the firm an implicit right, or option, to acquire the new technology at a future point in time. This option will be exercised by making the further investment necessary to adopt the new technology. The outcome of the first-stage decision is the purchase of a real call option (Myers, 1984) while the outcome of the second is the exercise of this option. A real call option works analogously to a stock call option in conferring a right to take future discretionary action towards capturing an underlying economic opportunity (Bowman and Hurry, 1987). In the same way that a stock call option gives the holder the right to purchase the underlying stock at a later date, the real call option gives the investor the right to make a subsequent investment to capture the underlying opportunity. Several studies have confirmed that corporate investments in operating assets and ventures behave like stock options (Paddock, Seigel and Smith, 1983; Majd and Pindyck, 1987; Mitchell and Hamilton, 1987; Kogut, 1983, 1988, 1991; Kester, 1984; Hurry, 1991).

Venture capital investment, therefore, in its broader form, is similar to the purchase of a call option in year 1. This option may or may not pay dividends during its holding period and is exercisable at the holder's discretion any time after say, year 7 upon payment of a 'strike price' in the form of the investment needed to acquire the technology.

---

[1] This problem has been identified as a cause of failed internal ventures by several authors (e.g. Weiss, 1981; Block, 1982; MacMillan, Block, and Subbanarasimha, 1986).

Thus a firm can have one of two strategic alternatives: a 'project strategy' of seeking direct venture gains, or an 'option strategy' of seeking new technology. While not mutually exclusive, the two strategies reflect different perceptions of the available opportunity set. A project strategy implies that the new technology opportunity was not recognized (or positively evaluated, if recognized) by the investing firm. On the other hand, an option strategy (or a combined project-cum-option strategy) suggests recognition and positive evaluation of this opportunity.

At the outset a new high-technology venture, therefore, can be said to offer a 'shadow option' or latent option to the investing firm. The positive value of this shadow option may or may not be recognized, thus yielding the two different investment patterns.

VENTURE CAPITAL INDUSTRIES IN THE UNITED STATES AND JAPAN

Venture capital investment by U.S. firms has existed for approximately 25 years, with a peak around the mid-to-late 1980s when over 75 major corporations had formal venture capital investment programs while three times that number were in the market through limited partnerships (Winters and Murfin, 1988). A firm typically began by investing in a venture capital fund as a limited partner, and would then progress to direct investments in venture companies, sometimes eventually establishing its own venture capital subsidiary. Venture capital investments in the U.S. were enormously lucrative to investors in the early to mid-1980s, when venture capital funds recorded an average return of 25% per year compounded since 1965 (ibid.).

Venture capital investment by Japanese firms is a more recent phenomenon which became noticeable in 1982 when the Japan Associated Finance Company (JAFCO—a consortium of banking, industrial and securities' firms) established the country's first venture capital fund. Prior to this event, several large, cash-rich corporations had begun to invest in high-technology ventures in the United States. JAFCO began formal U.S. operations in 1987 by which time many companies had set up their own venture capital subsidiaries in the United States.

It appears that Japanese corporations have adopted a theme originating in the U.S. and, as seen on several occasions in the past, have enlarged its scope. This has led to basic structural differences in the two industries. In the U.S. there is a preponderance of limited partnerships in the form of multiple investor venture capital funds while in Japan the industry appears to be dominated by large cash-rich firms with multinational operations. The U.S. business press has generally reported on venture investments by U.S. firms in terms of the return on investment earned by the investing company upon disposal of its holdings following the venture's initial public stock offering. The Japanese press, on the other hand, has tended towards a strategic description of Japanese venture investments. For example, Japan's leading business news journal, *Nihon Kezai Shimbun*, reported in 1986 that Sumitomo Corporation had invested in Grace Venture Partnership and Hambro International Venture Fund in order 'to obtain new technologies and new business opportunities'. This view is consistent with studies of other Japanese foreign direct investments such as joint ventures and acquisitions which reflect similar strategic motivations and contrast the Japanese long-term approach with the U.S. short-term, returns-driven stance (Yoshino, 1975; Tsurumi, 1976; Osborn and Baughn, 1987; Jubak, 1988; Rapoport, 1988; Reich and Mankin, 1986; Kester, 1991).

The usefulness of venture capital investments in the process of technological and competitive revitalization is a function of the firm's 'absorptive capacity' for new technology (Cohen and Levinthal, 1990). Japanese and U.S. firms differ in their ability to exploit external knowledge, U.S. firms being 'poor imitators' while the opposite is true of Japanese firms (Westney and Sakakibara, 1986; Mansfield, 1988; Rosenberg and Steinmueller, 1988). The institutional context in the U.S. and Japan reinforces this difference by encouraging technological isolationism in the U.S. firm and technological eclecticism in the Japanese firm. In the U.S., patent protection is sought in order to obtain a temporary first-mover advantage against competition (Scherer, 1977). On the other hand in Japan, the Ministry for International Trade and Industry (MITI) encourages the diffusion of technology and import of technology to support continuous innovation (Baba, 1989).

88   *D. Hurry* et al.

THE STUDY

Most academic studies of new ventures have presumed that investments are made for the strategic aim of developing new products, processes and technologies (Kazanjian, 1988). On the assumption that technology and commercial development occur largely in the venture itself and not in the investing firm, these studies have looked at the determinants of venture performance (Van de Ven, Hudson and Schroeder, 1984; Roure and Maidique, 1986; Stuart and Abetti, 1987; Sandberg and Hofer, 1984; MacMillan and Day, 1987). This view is appropriate from the standpoint of studying simple project strategies. If investment in the investing firm is also required at a later point in time, this view may ignore the existence of option strategies. The success of a firm's option strategy need not always be identical with the venture's performance because the two phenomena are not necessarily congruent. If the new venture is designed to serve as a transition mechanism to carry the investing firm to a new technology, the success of the transition will take precedence over the success of the venture itself.

It is therefore necessary to study venture investments from the viewpoint of the investing firm and to consider the possible existence of an option strategy.

Japanese venture capital firms

Based on published sources in Japan and discussions with venture capital fund managers in the U.S. and Japan, we estimated that the total population of Japanese venture capital investors with U.S. investments was around 50 companies. Of these we were able to clearly identify 35 companies. We were able to obtain positive responses from 20 companies (40% of the estimated population) upon guaranteeing complete confidentiality of information. The sample of investing organizations was distributed over the following broad industries: banking, chemicals, communications, electronics, food and beverages, light manufacture, securities, steel and trading. Five of the firms surveyed were venture capital partnerships of two or more investing firms, while the remainder were venture capital subsidiaries of major corporations.

The sample was surveyed through structured telephone interviews which were immediately documented in a written questionnaire administered by fax. The primary respondent to the survey was a member of senior management (in most cases the Chief Executive Officer of the firm). In some cases the questionnaire was actually completed by a mid-level manager. Given the short time lag between interview and questionnaire (a few hours in most cases), it is not surprising that agreement between the two reports was virtually perfect (minor details conflicted in one case, which we were able to resolve quickly).

The sample firms were reluctant to divulge sensitive or specific detailed information, but we were able to collect categorical data covering a variety of topics including the firm's venturing history, its stated venture policy, method of evaluation of potential ventures, venture management, venture portfolio performance, external relationships with venture firms outside the basic funding arrangement, venture divestiture and disposal, a brief conclusion regarding the firm's underlying motivation for venture capital investment, and summarized descriptions of typical actual ventures.

The questionnaire was pretested using the U.S. and Tokyo office executives of a major U.S. consulting firm with experience in the venture capital industry. Several key items of data (e.g. strategic motivation for venturing) were confirmed by multiple questions distributed over different sections of the instrument. All questions offered a list of response categories but were left open-ended, a facility which was extensively used by the responding organizations. These residual responses have been included in the analysis upon placement in additional categories or in summarized category groups. This classification was performed independently by two members of the research team. Since the responses were straightforward and succinct in all cases, it was possible to obtain complete agreement between the researchers.

U.S. venture capital firms

We contacted 60 comparable U.S. venture capital firms, of which 20 responded to our survey. We were able to match investing firm industries completely across the two groups, but we were not able to match investing firms in terms of their constitution. The Japanese group comprised 15 venture capital subsidiaries and 5 partnership funds, while the U.S. group consisted of 4 venture capital subsidiaries and 16 partnership funds. It is our belief that the sample reflects structural differences in the two industries. We were able to control for this population effect during hypothesis testing. Since both groups had investments in identical target high-technology industries in the United States, we felt that a comparison was valid and would yield valuable insights.

Research hypothesis

Based on the prior studies reviewed earlier, it seems that U.S. firms are poor imitators of outside technology who take a short-term view towards their investments. Japanese firms, on the other hand, are excellent imitators with high absorptive capacity and a long-term strategic view of their investments. Moreover, the venture capital industry yielded high returns to U.S. investors prior to Japanese large scale entry. Given these observations, our research hypothesis is as follows:

U.S. venture capital investing firms will follow a project strategy while Japanese venture capital investing firms will follow an option strategy.

This in turn yields several testable hypotheses.

Venture portfolio hypotheses

Call options are small, limited-risk investments which position the investor to make the full-scale exercise investments at some later point in time. The investor's downside risk is limited to the investment in the option.

In comparison to a project investor, a venture capital investor following an option strategy would therefore: (a) make smaller individual investments, (b) make a larger number of investments so as to be better positioned to capture a wide range of future technology opportunities, and (c) be less concerned about the possibility of loss-making investments, since downside risk has been fixed in advance at an acceptable level. Accordingly, we have the following hypotheses:

Hypothesis 1: Japanese firms will have a larger portfolio of ventures than U.S. firms.

This is because Japanese firms, being option players, will seek to explore several technologies simultaneously.

Hypothesis 2: Japanese firms will make smaller individual investments than U.S. firms.

As option investors, there will exist a pressure to limit risk to small, manageable amounts of capital.

Hypothesis 3: Japanese firms will have a higher percentage of loss-making ventures than U.S. firms.

Given a downside risk that is held constant at a small possible capital loss in each venture, option players are likely to reflect a high level of 'overall' loss tolerance.

Venturing strategy hypotheses

The option investor has a different perception of the available opportunity set than the project investor, since an option strategy presumes recognition of the shadow option contained in the external venture. While a project strategy will include a clear perception of a time horizon in which the project must earn returns, an option strategy is more fluid since recognition of the shadow option implies an awareness that this opportunity may become realizable at some currently unforseeable point in time.

Hypothesis 4: Japanese firms will describe their venturing objectives in terms of long-term, indirect strategic gains while U.S. firms will state their venturing goals in terms of short-term, direct gains.

The above strategic objective will motivate both industry and venture selection by Japanese firms.

Hypothesis 5: Japanese firms will choose indirect strategic reasons over direct venture-related and financial reasons to explain their choice of target industries, while U.S. firms will choose the latter type of reasoning.

Hypothesis 6: Japanese firms will choose ventures based on strategic considerations such

90   *D. Hurry* et al.

as future technology possibilities while U.S. firms will choose ventures based on the possibility of direct venture gains.

Venture management hypotheses

Project investments yield returns 'when the project is ready' while real option investments yield returns 'when the investor is ready'.

In other words, a firm following a project strategy will monitor its ventures frequently to check whether the venture is ready to produce returns, while a firm following an option strategy will monitor its own readiness for the new technology and will hence evaluate the venture infrequently.

Hypothesis 7: Japanese firms will monitor venture performance less frequently than U.S. firms.

A firm following a project strategy will, further, seek to gauge project readiness through external measures such as ROI or sales, while the option player will seek to gauge compatibility of the venture with its own technology and organization. Thus:

Hypothesis 8: Japanese firms will evaluate venture performance using measures related to the investing firm, while U.S. firms will use measures related to the venture.

Finally, a firm following a project strategy will gain from attempts to actively make the venture ready for profit-taking. On the other hand, an option player will tend to allow the venture to develop without assistance.

Hypothesis 9: Japanese firms will manage their ventures at arms' length compared to U.S. firms which will offer their ventures more administrative and managerial support.

Venture culmination hypothesis

The venture capital investors role comes to an end when the new high-technology venture makes its initial public stock offering (IPO). An investing firm following a project strategy may now conclude its investment by profit-taking through disposal of its stock, thus earning a return on its investment. A firm following an option strategy, however, has to make a second, and larger, investment before earning its final return. The latter firm might choose to retain its option on the new technology, by not selling off its stock, or it might choose to commence exercising its option, by forming contractual arrangements to acquire and use the new technology (e.g. upgrading the investment to a joint venture or forming other business arrangements with the venture). This leads to our final hypothesis:

Hypothesis 10: Japanese firms will culminate their venture investment by either retaining their stock or by entering into a contractual business relationship with the venture, while U.S. firms will dispose of their shares following the venture's initial public stock offering.

Method of analysis

Given the categorical nature of the available data, we were able to make some inferences by simply inspecting the relevant frequency distribution. One obvious limitation of the small sample size (coupled with the reluctance of the surveyed firms to divulge sensitive information) is that controlling for confounding variables such as size of the investing firms and constitution of the venture capital fund was not possible. However, we were able to control for age effects in testing hypotheses where this variable might have a confounding influence. Another limitation of this study is that our data gave us general information rather than specific information in the sense that we were given ranges of values rather than the values themselves, or a list of important criteria rather than a precise ranking of items.

Despite these limitations, we were able to obtain a fairly coherent picture of the process of Japanese venture capital investment and to make a comparison with the U.S. group. We were also able to confirm inferences by using the Del method (Hildebrand, Laing, and Rosenthal, 1974, 1977).

The Del method is suitable for small sample sizes and permits evaluation of relationships between categorical variables based on specific *a priori* predictions (Auster, 1990; Drazin and Kazanjian, 1990). The statistic is based on the proportionate reduction of error under the prediction rule being tested. Another possible approach might have been the chi-square method which, however, suffers from the limitation of being sensitive to small or zero cell sizes. This limitation does not apply to the Del method, since it tests the entire distribution of observations rather than cell-wise frequencies. Further, the Del statistic is analogous to the coefficient of determination (R squared) and hence permits inferences to be drawn in a manner similar to correlation analysis. The significance of Del was tested as a Z value since it follows the normal distribution for the number of observations available in this study.

Two Del values were computed for each hypothesis. In the first place the data were retained as pure observations drawn from the two groups, while in the second instance the data were adjusted to control for population effects. Both Del values were taken together in forming inferences. The adjusted Del values permit conservative inferences to be made to confirm the results of the primary unadjusted Del analysis. The unadjusted Del values point to differences in venture capital activity that suggest that Japanese and U.S. firms take inherently different approaches to strategic investment. These approaches have produced the divergent industry structures reflected in the composition of the two groups in our sample.

FINDINGS

Venture portfolios

The venture investment portfolios of the Japanese firms in our sample were found to be larger than those of the U.S. firms. While 11 U.S. firms had invested in 25 ventures or less, only 1 Japanese firm had a portfolio containing so few ventures. On the contrary as many as 12 Japanese firms reported between 100 and 400 venture investments, whereas only one U.S. firm had invested in more than 100 ventures. After controlling for age of the venture capital investment program, and after adjusting for the population effect (i.e. the difference in composition of the two groups) Hypothesis 1 received strong support.

Hypothesis 2, that Japanese firms typically make smaller venture capital investments than U.S. firms was tested by comparing responses to

questions about the size of the firm's typical contribution to the total cost of a venture and its typical investment in a single venture over time (see Table 1). Del values of 0.85 and 0.75 (adusted) show support for this hypothesis at the 0.1% level.

Responses to other questions confirmed this finding. 18 Japanese firms reported that their smallest investment was between $100,000 and $300,000, while only 9 U.S. firms reported comparably small investments. While 12 U.S. firms reported their largest individual investment in the $5–20 million range, for 16 Japanese firms the largest single investment did not exceed $5 million.

Our prediction that Japanese portfolios will hold a higher proportion of loss-making ventures than U.S. firms (Hypothesis 3) was tested through two sets of questions in order to obtain internally consistent responses. One set asked for the proportion of loss-making and negative cash flow ventures in the portfolio while the other asked for the proportion of ventures at break-even point and in the profit and positive cash flow region. This hypothesis was not supported by the unadjusted Del statistic which, though in the right direction, did not have a significant value. The adjusted Del statistic, however, was significant at the 5% level (see Table 1).

Venturing strategy

Our *a priori* expectation was that the goals stated by Japanese firms would reflect recognition of the technology shadow option while the goals stated by U.S. firms would not show such recognition (or positive evaluation). Fourteen U.S. firms reported 'ROI' as their venturing objective while 17 Japanese firms reported 'technology'. This part of the fourth hypothesis received strong support (see Table 1).

An option strategy would also imply a longer time horizon than a project strategy. The time horizon of venture capital investment was not, however, significantly different for the two groups of firms (see Table 1). This finding is somewhat counter-intuitive given the widespread general belief that Japanese firms have a longer time frame in their business activities than U.S. firms.

We found no significant differences across the two groups in terms of their reasons for choosing their target industries (Hypothesis 5). Both

92   D. *Hurry* et al.

Table 1.   Observations and Del statistics

Category	JAPAN			US			Adj. Total[1]
	Corp.	Funds	Total	Corp.	Funds	Total	
HYPOTHESIS 1: Venture portfolio size[2]							
Small/Young	–	2	2	1	3	4	5
Large/Young	14	1	15	–	2	2	1
Small/Old	1	1	2	3	11	14	14
Large/Old	–	1	1	–	–	–	–
Total	15	5	20	4	16	20	20

Del[3] = 0.70 ($p < 0.01$) Adjusted Del[4] = 0.74 ($p < 0.001$)

HYPOTHESIS 2: Individual venture investment size

(a) Contribution to total cost of venture

Category	Corp.	Funds	Total	Corp.	Funds	Total	Adj. Total
Low (1–20%)	15	3	18	–	10	10	3
High (> 20%)	–	2	2	4	6	10	17
Total	15	5	20	4	16	20	20

Del = 0.85 ($p < 0.001$) Adjusted Del = 0.75 ($p < 0.001$)

(b) Typical investment in a venture over time

Category	Corp.	Funds	Total	Corp.	Funds	Total	Adj. Total
Low ($.1m–0.5m)	3	2	5	–	2	2	1
(>$.5m–1m)	12	1	13	–	4	4	2
High (>$1m–5m)	–	2	2	4	10	14	17
Total	15	5	20	4	16	20	20

Del = 0.60 ($p < 0.001$) Adjusted Del = 0.75 ($p < 0.001$)

HYPOTHESIS 3: Percentage of loss/−ve cash flow ventures

Category	Corp.	Funds	Total	Corp.	Funds	Total	Adj. Total
0– 25%	3	–	3	1	3	4	5
26– 50%	3	2	5	2	4	6	9
51– 75%	5	3	8	1	6	7	5
76–100%	4	–	4	–	3	3	1
Total	15	5	20	4	16	20	20

Del = 0.10 ($p < 0.25$) Adjusted Del = 0.30 ($p < 0.05$)

HYPOTHESIS 4: Venturing strategy

(a) Objective

Category	Corp.	Funds	Total	Corp.	Funds	Total	Adj. Total
ROI	1	2	3	2	12	14	11
Technology	14	3	17	2	4	6	9
Total	15	5	20	4	16	20	20

Del = 0.55 ($p < 0.001$) Adjusted Del = 0.40 ($p < 0.01$)

(b) Time horizon

Category	Corp.	Funds	Total	Corp.	Funds	Total	Adj. Total
1–5 yrs	–	–	–	–	5	5	2
5–10 yrs	13	5	18	4	11	15	18
> 10 yrs	2	–	2	–	–	–	–
Total	15	5	20	4	16	20	20

Del = − 0.09 ($p < 0.63$) Adjusted Del = 0 ($p < 1$)

Table 1. Continued

Category	JAPAN			US			Adj. Total[1]
	Corp.	Funds	Total	Corp.	Funds	Total	
HYPOTHESIS 5: Choice of target industry[5]							
Strategic directives	10	2	12	3	6	9	13
To diversify	15	2	17	4	9	13	18
Fit	5	1	6	4	10	14	18
Business relations	8	3	12	–	5	5	2
Marketing forecasts	5	5	10	4	16	20	20
Venture tech/ Managerial skills	2	7	9	–	13	13	5

Del = 0.14 ($p < 0.08$) Adjusted Del = – 0.04 ($p < 0.61$)

Category	JAPAN			US			Adj. Total[1]
	Corp.	Funds	Total	Corp.	Funds	Total	
HYPOTHESIS 6: Choice of target venture[5]							
Option strategy							
Past relations							
– Always	9	–	9	–	–	–	–
– Sometimes	8	2	10	–	3	3	1
Present relations	11	3	14	–	5	5	2
Future relations	13	2	15	–	–	–	–
Project strategy							
Profit	–	2	2	4	16	20	20
Sales	1	3	4	4	10	14	18
Technical ability	–	4	4	1	16	17	9
Managerial skills	–	5	5	3	16	19	16

Del = 0.63 ($p < 0.001$) Adjusted Del = 0.73 ($p < 0.001$)

Category	JAPAN			US			Adj. Total[1]
	Corp.	Funds	Total	Corp.	Funds	Total	
HYPOTHESIS 7: Frequency of performance reviews							
Quarterly	–	–	–	3	13	16	15
Six-month	15	5	20	1	3	4	5
Total	15	5	20	4	16	20	20

Del = 0.67 ($p < 0.001$) Adjusted Del = 0.60 ($p < 0.001$)

groups reported similar reasons such as: strategic directives, diversification, strategic fit, the search for future business relations, financial and market forecasts, venture management's technical ability and managerial skills (see Table 1).

Significant differences were seen in the two groups' reasons for selecting target ventures, however, in strong support of Hypothesis 6 (see Table 1). Most U.S. firms used sales and profit forecasts and assessments of the venture management's technical and managerial abilities to select target ventures. Most Japanese firms, on the other hand, chose ventures based on the existence of past or present business relations with the venture (outside of the current arrangement) and the possibility of future relations with the venture.

Venture management

Hypothesis 7 predicted that the Japanese group would monitor their ventures less frequently than the U.S. firms. This prediction was supported by the data (see Table 1).

Our prediction, in Hypothesis 8, that Japanese firms would evaluate venture performance using

94   *D. Hurry* et al.

Table 1. Continued

Category	JAPAN			US			
	Corp.	Funds	Total	Corp.	Funds	Total	Adj. Total[1]
HYPOTHESIS 8: Venture evaluation measures[5]							
Option strategy							
Tech. fit	3	1	4	2	4	6	9
Tech. access	3	2	5	1	–	1	–
Project strategy							
ROI	13	5	18	4	16	20	20
Sales growth	11	2	13	4	7	11	17
Del = 0.01 (*p* < 0.94) Adjusted Del = 0.03 (*p* < 0.79)							
HYPOTHESIS 9: Method of venture management							
Board	8	2	10	3	9	12	14
Staff	3	1	4	1	4	5	5
Other admn.	4	2	6	–	3	3	1
Total	15	5	20	4	16	20	20
Del = 0.10 (*p* < 0.92) Adjusted Del = 0.2 (*p* < 0.18)							
HYPOTHESIS 10: Venture culmination[5]							
Option strategy							
Retain	15	2	17	1	3	4	5
Internal sale	8	–	8	–	–	–	–
Upgrade	13	–	13	2	–	2	1
Other relations	15	4	19	1	6	6	6
Project strategy							
Private sale	–	–	–	3	13	16	15
Sale to mgmt.	–	–	–	2	9	11	10
Public sale	–	–	–	2	14	16	12
Del = 0.76 (*p* < 0.001) Adjusted Del = 0.63 (*p* < 0.001)							

[1]Adjusted totals were obtained by weighting the U.S. group's observations to match the composition of the Japanese group. (U.S. Corporate figures were given a weightage of 15/4 and U.S. Fund figures were given a weightage of 5/16).
[2]Portfolio size: Small: < 50 Large: > 50 ventures Age: Young = started in 1981 or later, Old = pre 1981.
[3]Computation of Del statistics shown in the Appendix.
[4]Del statistic computed using adjusted U.S. total figures.
[5]Since multiple measures were reported, the Total columns will not add to 20.

measures related to the investing firm (viz. fit with existing technology, or transferability of the new technology), while U.S. firms would use venture-related measures (viz. ROI, or market growth) was not supported (see Table 1). Both groups showed a strong preference for venture-related measures, notably return on investment, in venture performance evaluation.

We also predicted that the Japanese group would manage ventures at arms length relative to the U.S. group, with fewer firms reporting supportive measures (e.g. appointing executives to the venture's board of directors, transfer of managerial staff to the venture, and other administrative support). The data did not support this hypothesis, since the Del statistics did not take significant values, although they were in the right direction (see Table 1).

Venture culmination

Our final hypothesis was that the Japanese firms would culminate their venture investment by either retaining or exercising their technology option, while we expected the U.S. firms to complete their project by profit-taking. We found that the Japanese group responded to our open-ended question on venture culmination to report that: (a) stock in the venture was either retained by the firm or transferred to a sister firm in the keiretsu (corporate group), or (b) a variety of business relations, including joint ventures, were commenced. While a few responses from the U.S. group were similar, the majority reported the following actions: (a) negotiated sale of stock to private investors, (b) sale of stock to venture management and employees, and (c) public sale of stock. Our hypothesis thus received strong support (see Table 1).

Japanese venturing as a strategic process

Most of the Japanese firms in our sample had invested in ventures with whom they had prior business relations or with whom they hoped to have future relations. Firms often reported as follows: 'we have had good dealings with this management in the past', or 'investment was made because the venture company had a special relationship with a Japanese firm which had a good relationship with our company'. The intention of future relations was apparent in comments such as 'possibility of future relationship with the venture', 'potential business relationship', and 'any type of future relationship or joint venture with the company'.

A clear recognition of the new technology shadow option was evident. While most of the U.S. firms stated objectives such as '25% to 50% ROI in 5 years', most of the Japanese firms reported: 'we are looking for technology', 'we are looking to buy more viable businesses', 'new technology and business development', 'a strategic move to new areas', 'proprietary technology or unique marketing potential with market opportunities in Japan', 'diversification of our company's business is the most important factor', and 'the possibility to develop a market in Japan'. Only one U.S. firm reported seeking a 'window on technology for parent company'.

Both groups reported the following target industry choices: biotechnology, computer hardware, electronics, medical equipment and health care technology, plastics and synthetic materials, semiconductors and computer software. The Japanese firms also reported seeking technology for automotive component manufacture and investment management (i.e. quantitative 'black box' securities trading methods).

Despite the fact that the Japanese investing firms were typically multinationals with multi-billion dollar assets and cash reserves, their typical investment per venture was in the region of three to five hundred thousand dollars and rarely exceeded one million dollars prior to the IPO stage. This suggests that venture investments are merely preliminary in nature and are intended to precede the full-scale investments needed to develop and commercialize new technology. Only four Japanese firms reported that over 25% of their portfolios contained newly started ventures, compared to eight for the U.S. group, the preference being for ventures which had proved themselves by earning revenues. Over the years, venture investments accumulated to form a portfolio of between 50 and 400 wide-ranging exploratory investments.

Although the Japanese firms' venture investment was motivated by past and current business relations with the venture, subsequent evaluations were made along strictly financial and market-driven lines (e.g. ROI) similar to the U.S. firms in the sample.

While most of the U.S. firms in the sample eventually divested their venture stock, this practice was rare among the Japanese firms. Two Japanese firms reported instead that divestment was 'rarely an issue' and 'not usually considered'.

After a venture had shown itself to be successful (i.e. in terms of ROI and the initial public stock offering) the Japanese firms sought to establish contractual arrangements with the venture to begin the large-scale commercial use of the new technology. It is possible that these arrangements were provided for in the initial financing contract with the venture. While the U.S. firms reported business relations mainly in the form of debt-financing arrangements with their ventures, the Japanese firms reported the following:

1. Joint research programs.
2. Licensing agreement for the venture's new technology.

96   *D. Hurry* et al.

3. Product technology development arrangements.
4. Manufacture (usually in Japan) of the venture's
   products.
5. Distribution of the venture's products in
   Japan.
6. Marketing and after sales service of the
   venture's exports to Japan.

These arrangements suggest that the Japanese
firms acquired the new technology and continued
development through further research and the
provision of manufacturing and distribution
capacity.

In some instances, the venture was upgraded
to a joint venture or was acquired. *Nihon Kezai
Shimbun*, a Japanese business journal, reported
one such case on April 15, 1987. In 1985, JAFCO,
Japan's largest venture capital investment firm,
had invested in Japan Fellow Fluidex Corporation, a subsidiary of Fellow Fluidex Corporation,
a U.S. firm in the field of magnetic fluid
technology. JAFCO had stipulated that the
venture develop certain viable technologies. In
1986, Japan Fellow Fluidex Corporation recorded
revenues of Yen 2.2 billion. In 1987, JAFCO
and Kubota Limited (a Japanese manufacturer
and partner in JAFCO) acquired the venture.
This step was said 'to reflect an acceleration of
Kubota and JAFCO's high-technology strategy'.

An instance of venture option abandonment
was reported, however, on December 6, 1988 by
the *Asian. Wall Street Journal*. Mitsui and
Company had invested more than $20 million
over 3½ years in Gain Electronics Corporation,
a U.S. high-technology venture which sought to
develop gallium arsenide computer chips. The
venture failed to yield a net positive cash flow,
and Mitsui reported that 'it became clear that a
market for gallium arsenide was unlikely to
develop soon . . . it was a really promising
technology when we went in, but the timing just
wasn't right'. The Japanese firm consequently
announced its withdrawal of investment from the
venture.

The strategic process of Japanese venture
investment and technology acquisition forms an
example of a real call option which is purchased
and exercised in two stages as shown in Figure
1. The process unfolds as follows:

1. **Shadow Option:** High technology venture

investments provide a latent option on technology acquisition. Prior relations with the
venture firm encourage the possibility of
investing in the heretofore unproven technology by creating a working base of contacts,
shared experience and familiarity with the
venture.

2. **Recognition of Option Value:** At some point,
   this latent opportunity is recognized by the
   investing firm, possibly on being approached
   by the venture for capital and other resources.

3. **Call Option Purchase:** A decision is made to
   invest in the venture with the clear objective
   of acquiring a new technology at some
   currently unforseeable point in the future. In
   keeping with the risk-limiting property of
   option investments, only a small sum is kept
   at risk in this first-stage investment in the new
   venture.

4. **Holding the Option:** Venture investments
   take around 5–7 years to produce commercial
   successes in most instances. During this period,
   the investing firm seeks to maintain its option
   by infusing capital in small doses if needed.
   The venture portfolio meanwhile continues to
   grow.

5. **The Strike Signal:** During the option holding
   period, the investing firm evaluates performance through stringent ROI and market
   criteria. This is very different from the
   relative disregard for such considerations at
   the exploratory option purchase stage.[2] The
   venture's initial public stock offer signals the
   successful attainment of performance that
   satisfies the investing firm's evaluation criteria.
   This signal triggers the investing firm's exercise
   or 'strike' of its option to acquire the now
   proven technology.

6. **Call Option Exercise:** The investing firm,
   accordingly, exercises its 'call' on the technology upon payment of a strike price in the
   form of a larger investment. The investment
   usually takes the form of joint programs
   for product development, manufacture and
   distribution in Japan, but sometimes might
   occur as the acquisition of the venture.

---

[2] Though somewhat counter-intuitive, this behavior admits a
straightforward explanation. At the purchase stage, the main
objective was to gain access to a potential future source of
technology. At the option holding stage, the objective is to
evaluate this technology for the larger exercise investment
to follow.

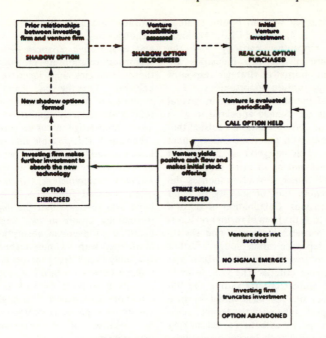

Figure 1. Venture Investment: The option strategy process

7. **Option Abandonment:** During the holding period, if it seems likely that a strike signal might never emerge from the venture the investing firm may divest the venture, thus abandoning its option.[3] This is, however, a rare occurrence.

8. **Formation of new Shadow Options:** As a consequence of its venture involvement, the investing firm has acquired more business contacts and shared experiences with a U.S. firm or management team, thereby forming the background for new venture investments.

Thus, by commiting a small amount of risk capital, the Japanese firm is able to purchase the right to acquire a new technology at a later date. When the benefits of this new technology appear realizable, and not before, the firm will make a full scale investment.

DISCUSSION AND CONCLUSION

Our findings suggest that Japanese and U.S. venture capital investment have different motivations.[4] Even though the U.S. firms in our sample were probably aware of the new technology window open through venturing (cf. Winters and Murfin, 1988) and invested in generally the same industries as the Japanese group, a significant number seemed to follow a project strategy. They did not recognize (or positively value) the technology shadow option (Hypothesis 4) nor did they conclude venturing with technology transfer (Hypothesis 10). The strategic nature of venture investment is clearly visible in Japanese venturing, which appears to

---

[3] It is precisely the choice of walking away from a venture that gives meaning to the term 'option', incidentally.

[4] DeSarbo, MacMillan, and Day (1986) reported that U.S. venture capitalists judged the following variables to be important in their choice of ventures: low initial investment, fit with existing businesses, proprietary technology, low competitive threat, experienced venture champions in the investing firm and, above all, return on investment. Only the first three of these variables appear to be important to the Japanese corporation.

98   *D. Hurry* et al.

proceed in accordance with an option strategy (Hypotheses 1, 2, 4, 7 and 10). National differences in absorptive capacity and the resulting structure of the two industries are reflected in these alternative strategic responses to high-technology venture opportunities.

Recognition of the shadow option in several Japanese firms in our sample appeared to arise out of the prior or current relations (outside that particular venture) with the same management (Hypothesis 4). This suggests a process of retrospective sense-making of prior investments (cf. Weick, 1979) which possibly underlies the well-known Japanese trait of seeking to build long-term relationships. Culmination of venture investments also took the form of further relations with the same parties.[5] However, one should note that the Japanese firms sought further relations with ventures only in cases which met rigorous performance criteria. The U.S. firms in the sample used similar criteria during the life of the project but did not base initial venture investments on prior relationships. Hence, since they appeared to operate without a sense-making apparatus that favored such business relations, these firms were not inclined to seek continued involvement with their ventures past the initial public stock offering stage.

At first glance, one might be persuaded to believe that the Japanese management's preference for long-term business relations supports the commonly held opinion that they take the 'long-term view' of strategy. In contrast, it is often said that U.S. managements are myopic to the point of rarely seeing beyond the next quarter's earnings. Our findings do not reveal a significant difference between the stated time horizons of the two groups. This suggests that the Japanese long-term view might be best understood instead in the form of a sequence of medium-term investments.

Our findings contain two sets of implications for strategic management theory. The first set enhances our understanding of Japanese strategy specifically, while the second applies more generally to descriptions of strategy at the organizational level. The Japanese economic

'miracle' has been attributed in part to business strategies based on knowledge-intensive products and cooperative alliances (Smothers, 1990). A reciprocal relationship probably exists between these strategies and Japanese venture capital behavior. On the one hand, the deliberate exploration of new technologies and business relationships clearly supports a strategy of cooperative, knowledge-intensive production. On the other hand, it is possible that this strategy could have evolved from the retrospective sense-making of exploratory behavior in the early days of Japanese manufacture, when technology was often licensed from U.S. firms. Our findings have also revealed that the exploration of new technology occurs in two stages, which might facilitate its eventual absorption by permitting familiarity with the new technology to develop gradually over a few years. It is possible that the linkage between a firm's strategy of exploration and its absorptive capacity is in the opposite direction. A Japanese firm might exhibit a high absorptive capacity as a consequence, rather than as a cause, of its incremental strategy of exploration.

Though similar in spirit to the notions of building on past activities (Nelson and Winter, 1982) and incremental trial-and-error strategic processes (e.g. Mintzberg, 1977; Pondy, 1983; Quinn, 1980; Johnson, 1988), Japanese venture exploration implies a modification of the picture supplied by the currently prevalent incrementalist view of strategy. Under this view, a strategy is described as a sequence of decisions (and hence, as the sequential investment of organizational resources). Each decision is a step taken under the constraints of environmental uncertainty and bounded rationality to provide the best course of action possible at the time. This description, however, is silent on the question of whether investment occurs as a project or an option.

Our findings imply that descriptions of strategy at the organizational level require a distinction between project and option investments. It is generally thought that the objective of a decision is to earn the best possible returns from the investment under review. However, in many business situations the best possible returns may be obtained instead by sacrificing gains from the investment on hand in favor of the next investment. The current decision may seek little more than a foothold in preparation for the next

---

[5] This accords well with the finding that high-technology ventures predominantly form cooperative arrangements to commercialize their new products in foreign markets (Shan, 1990).

decision. Some decisions, therefore, seek gains from the current investment, while others seek to defer gains till a later stage when higher returns may be possible from future investments. As our study shows, firms behave differently based on whether the initial decision to invest is made as a project or as an option. In our sample, the firms which followed the former course (i.e. the U.S. firms) did not eventually acquire the technology, while those which followed the latter course (i.e. the Japanese firms) did acquire the new technology.

A theoretical description of strategy, therefore, needs to reflect an appreciation of the linkage across successive strategic decisions. Over time, this linkage has two aspects: an 'economic' linkage and a 'cognitive' linkage. The economic linkage is in the form of the 'positioning value' which a decision or investment gives an organization. This is comprised of the value of 'waiting to invest' under uncertainty (cf. Cukierman, 1980; Bernanke, 1983) and the value of 'accumulating prior investments'. The first investment yields the right, or option, to make the second investment and thus holds the window of opportunity open for the organization. In this way the organization is allowed to gather sufficient information before commiting itself to a course of action. When it makes the next investment, the organization benefits from the effect of the 'critical mass' of investment and effort which has now been achieved.

The cognitive linkage across decisions occurs through a cumulative sense-making process involving both retrospective and prospective rationality. Several Japanese firms in our sample reported both types of motivations for their venture investment. Responses such as 'prior relations' indicating retrospective reasoning and the more usual prospective ones such as 'diversification' and 'new technology' were reported simultaneously. At the outset, the Japanese corporation is probably no more able to foretell the future than its U.S. counterpart. However, its cognitive and strategic processes structure the investment in two stages such that its shadow or implicit option value is recognized, realized through investment, and finally exercised through further investment upon receiving the strike signal. The resulting description takes the form of a decision-dyad sequentially linked over time by both strategic sense-making and economic value.

APPENDIX: COMPUTATION OF DEL STATISTIC

The general procedure for computation of Del statistic is as follows (Hildebrand et al. 1974, 1977):

Observations are arranged in a matrix designed to show the *a priori* categories for analysis. Under each hypothesis a prediction rule is established. This prediction rule will classify the observations in some cells as 'errors'. These are given a weight = 1. The other cells are given a weight = 0. The cell probabilities and marginal probabilities are computed by dividing cell values and row and column totals by the number of observations in the matrix.

$$\text{Del}(\nabla) = 1 - \frac{K}{U}$$

where

$$K = \Sigma_i \Sigma_j (\omega_{ij} P_{ij})$$

and

$$U = \Sigma_i \Sigma_j (\omega_{ij} P_{i\cdot} P_{\cdot j})$$

where ω_{ij} are cell weights, P_{ij} are cell probabilities, and $P_{i\cdot}$ and $P_{\cdot j}$ are row and column marginal probabilities.

The hypothesis $\nabla > 0$ is tested against normal tables using the following statistic:

$$Z = \frac{\nabla}{\sqrt{v}}$$

where v = variance of Del =

$$\frac{\Sigma_i \Sigma_j (\omega_{ij} P_{ij}) - (\Sigma_i \Sigma_j \omega_{ij} P_{ij})^2}{n[\Sigma_i \Sigma_j (\omega_{ij} P_{i\cdot} P_{\cdot j})]^2}$$

For each test, the adequacy of the sample size was checked using the following rule of thumb:

$$\frac{5}{n} \leq u(1 - \nabla) \leq 1 - \frac{5}{n}$$

ACKNOWLEDGEMENTS

The authors are grateful to Professors Richard Bettis and John Mears of Southern Methodist University, and to Dean Hiroki Funamoto and

100   *D. Hurry* et al.

Dr. Yuji Hirai of Kwansei Gakuin University, Nishinomiya, Japan for assistance in contacting Japanese firms for this survey. Valuable review comments were provided by Andrew Chen, William F. Hamilton, Rita Gunther McGrath and two anonymous SMJ reviewers. This project was supported by the Reginald Jones Center for Management Policy, Strategy and Organization in the Wharton School, University of Pennsylvania, and by the Business Policy Department of the Cox School of Business, Southern Methodist University.

REFERENCES

Andrews, K. R. *The Concept of Corporate Strategy*, Dow Jones-Irwin, Homewood, IL, 1971.

Ansoff, H. I. *Corporate Strategy*, McGraw–Hill, New York, 1965.

Asian Wall Street Journal, 'Mitsui abandons high-tech U.S. venture', U. Gupta (reporter), Tokyo, December 6, 1988, p. 1 (col 3)–p. 8 (col 3).

Auster, E. R. 'The relationship of industry evolution to patterns of technological linkages, joint ventures and direct investment between U.S. and Japan', *Academy of Management Proceedings*, 1990, pp. 96–100.

Baba, Y. 'The dynamics of continuous innovation in scale-intensive industries', *Strategic Management Journal*, 10, 1989, pp. 89–100.

Bernanke, B. S. 'Irreversibility, uncertainty and cyclical investment', *Quarterly Journal of Economics*, 98, 1983, pp. 85–106.

Block, Z. 'Can corporate venturing succeed?' *Journal of Business Strategy*, 3(2), 1982, pp. 21–33.

Bowman, E. H. and D. Hurry. 'Strategic options', Working Paper 87–20, Reginald Jones Center, Wharton School, 1987.

Cohen, W. M. and D. A. Levinthal. 'Absorptive capacity: A new perspective on learning and innovation', *Administrative Science Quarterly*, 35, 1990, pp. 128–152.

Cukierman, A. 'The effects of uncertainty on investments under risk neutrality with endogenous information', *Journal of Political Economy*, 88, 1980, pp. 462–475.

DeSarbo, W., I. C. MacMillan and D. Day. 'Criteria for corporate venturing: Importance assigned by managers', Working Paper, Wharton School, 1986.

Drazin, R. and R. Kazanjian. 'A re-analysis of Miller and Friesen's life cycle data', *Strategic Management Journal*, 11, 1990, pp. 319–325.

Frohman, A. L. 'Putting technology into strategic planning', *California Management Review*, 27, 1985, pp. 48–59.

Ghemawat, P. 'Sustainable advantage', *Harvard Business Review*, 64, 1986, pp. 53–58.

Grinyer, P., S. Al-Bazzaz and M. Yasai-Ardekani. 'Toward a contingency theory of corporate planning: Findings in 48 U.K. companies', *Strategic Management Journal*, 7, 1986, pp. 3–28.

Hamberg, D. 'Invention in the industrial research laboratory', *Journal of Political Economy*, 71, 1963, pp. 95–115.

Hamel, G. and C. K. Prahalad. 'Strategic intent', *Harvard Business Review*, 67(3), 1989, pp. 63–76.

Hildebrand, D., J. Laing and H. Rosenthal. 'Prediction logic: A method for empirical evaluation of formal theory', *Journal of Mathematical Sociology*, 3, 1974, pp. 163–185.

Hildebrand, D., J. Laing and H. Rosenthal. *Prediction Analysis of Cross-Classification*, John Wiley, New York, 1977.

Hurry, D. 'Option-like properties of organizational claims: Tracing the process of multinational exploration', Working Paper 91–011, Cox School of Business, Southern Methodist University, 1991.

Jauch, L. R. and R. N. Osborn. 'Toward an integrated theory of strategy', *Academy of Management Review*, 6, 1981, pp. 391–398.

Johnson, G. 'Rethinking Incrementalism', *Strategic Management Journal*, 9, 1988, pp. 75–91.

Jubak, J. 1988: 'I have a yen for you', *Venture*, July 1988, pp. 27–35.

Kantrow, A. M. 'The strategy-technology connection', *Harvard Business Review*, 58, July–August 1980, pp. 6–21.

Kazanjian, R. K. 'Relation of dominant problems to stages of growth in technology-based new ventures', *Academy of Management Journal*, 31(2), 1988, pp. 257–279.

Kester, W. C. 'Today's options for tomorrow's growth', *Harvard Business Review*, March–April 1984, pp. 153–160.

Kester, W. C. *Japanese Takeovers: The Global Quest for Corporate Control*, Harvard Business School Press, Boston, MA, 1991.

Kogut, B. 'Foreign direct investment as a sequential process'. In C. P. Kindleberger and D. B. Audretsch (eds), *The Multinational Corporation in the 1980s*, pp. 62–75, M.I.T. Press, Boston. 1983.

Kogut, B. 'Multinational flexibility and the theory of foreign direct investment', Working Paper 88–10, Reginald Jones Center, Wharton School, 1988.

Kogut, B. 'Joint ventures and the option to expand and acquire', *Management Science*, 37(1), 1991, pp. 19–33.

MacMillan, I. C., Z. Block and P. N. Subbanarasimha. 'Corporate venturing: Alternatives, obstacles and experience effects', *Journal of Business Venturing*, 1(2), 1986, pp. 177–192.

MacMillan, I. C. and D. L. Day. 'Corporate ventures into industrial markets: Dynamics of aggressive entry', *Journal of Business Venturing*, 2(1), 1987, pp. 29–39.

Majd, S. and R. S. Pindyck. 'Time to build, option value and investment decisions', *Journal of Financial Economics*, 18, 1987, pp. 7–27.

Mansfield, E. 'How rapidly does new technology leak out', *Journal of Industrial Economics*, December 1985, p. 217–223.

Mansfield, E. 'The speed and cost of industrial innovation in Japan and the United States: External vs. internal technology', *Management Science*, 34(10), 1988, pp. 1157–1168.

March, J. G. and H. A. Simon. *Organizations*, Wiley, New York, 1958.

Mintzberg, H. 'Strategy formulation as a historical process', *International Studies of Management and Organization*, VII(2), 1977, pp. 28–40.

Mitchell, G. R. and W. F. Hamilton. 'Managing R&D as a strategic option', *Research Management*, 31, 1987, pp. 15–22.

Mueller, W. F. 'The origins of the basic inventions underlying DuPont's major product and process innovations', In R. R. Nelson (ed.) *The Rate and Direction of Inventive Activity*, Princeton University Press, Princeton, NJ, 1962, pp. 323–358.

Myers, S. C. 'Finance theory and financial strategy', *Interfaces*, 14(1), 1984, pp. 126–137.

Nelson, R. R. and S. G. Winter. *An Evolutionary Theory of Economic Change*, Belknap Press, Boston, MA, 1982.

Nihon Kezai Shimbun. 'JAFCO and Kubota expand Fellow-Fluidex Company', Tokyo, April 15, 1987, p. 1 (col. 4).

Osborn, R. N. and C. C. Baughn. 'New patterns in the formation of US/Japanese cooperative ventures: The role of technology', *Columbia Journal of World Business*, Summer 1987, pp. 57–65.

Paddock, J. L., D. R. Seigel and J. L. Smith. 'Option valuation of claims on physical assets: The case of offshore petroleum leases', M.I.T. Energy Laboratory Working Paper, 1983.

Pondy, L. R. 'Union of rationality and intuition in management action'. In S. Srivastva (ed.), *The Executive Mind*, Jossey Bass, San Francisco, CA, 1983, pp. 97–108.

Porter, M. E. 'The technological dimension of competitive strategy'. In R. S. Rosenbloom, (ed.), *Research on Technological Innovation, Management and Policy*, pp. 1–33, vol. 1, JAI Press, Greenwich, CT, 1983.

Quinn, J. B. *Strategies for Change: Logical Incrementalism*, Dow Jones-Irwin, Homewood, IL, 1980.

Rapoport, C. 'How Japan will spend its cash', *Fortune*, November 1988, pp. 195–201.

Reich, R. B. and R. D. Mankin. 'Joint ventures with Japan give away our future', *Harvard Business Review*, March–April 1986, p. 78–86.

Rosenberg, N. and W. E. Steinmueller. 'Why are Americans such poor imitators?' *American Economic Review*, 78(2), 1988, pp. 229–234.

Roure, J. B. and M. A. Maidique. 'Linking prefunding factors and high-technology venture success: An

exploratory study', *Journal of Business Venturing*, 1(3), 1986, pp. 295–306.

Sandberg, W. A. and C. W. Hofer. 'Improving new venture performance: The role of strategy, industry structure and the entrepreneur', *Journal of Business Venturing*, 2(1), 1984, pp. 5–28.

Scherer, F. M. *The Economic Effects of Compulsory Licensing*, New York University Press, New York, 1977.

Schumpeter, J. A. *The Theory of Economic Development*, Harvard University Press, Cambridge, MA, 1934.

Shan, W. 'An empirical analysis of organizational strategies by entrepreneurial high-technology firms', *Strategic Management Journal*, 11, 1990, pp. 129–139.

Smothers, N. P. 'Patterns of Japanese strategy: Strategic combinations of strategies', *Strategic Management Journal*, 11, 1990, pp. 521–533.

Stuart, R. and P. A. Abetti. 'Start-up ventures: Towards the prediction of initial success', *Journal of Business Venturing*, 2(3), 1987, pp. 215–229.

Tsurumi, Y. 'The multinational spread of Japanese firms and Asian neighbors' reactions'. In D. E. Apter and L. W. Goodman (eds), *The Multinational Corporation and Social Change*, pp. 118–147, Praeger, New York, 1976.

Van de ven, A. H., R. Hudson and D. Schroeder. 'Designing new business start-ups: Entrepreneurial, organizational and ecological considerations', *Journal of Management*, 10(1), 1984, pp. 87–108.

Venkatraman, N. and J. C. Camillus. 'Exploring the concept of "Fit" in Strategic Management', *Academy of Management Review*, 9, 1984, pp. 513–525.

von Hippel, E. *The Sources of Innovation*, Oxford University Press, New York, 1988.

Weick, K. E. *The Social Psychology of Organizing*, Addison-Wesley, Reading, MA, 1979.

Weiss, L. E. 'Start-up businesses: A comparison of performance', *Sloan Management Review*, 23(1), Fall 1981, pp. 37–53.

Westney D. E. and K. Sakakibara. 'The role of Japan-based R&D in global technology strategy'. In M. Hurowitch (ed.), *Technology in the Modern Corporation*, Pergamon Press, London, 1986, pp. 217–232.

Winters, T. E. and D. L. Murfin. 'Venture capital investing for corporate development objectives', *Journal of Business Venturing*, 3, 1988, pp. 207–222.

Yoshino, M. Y. 'Japanese foreign direct investment'. In I. Frank (ed.), *The Japanese Economy in International Perspective*, pp. 248–272, Johns Hopkins University Press, Baltimore, MD, 1975.

Zimmerman, M. *How to do Business with the Japanese*, Random House, New York, 1985.

Part II
The Venture Capital Process:
Screening, Valuation and Contracting

[4]

MANAGEMENT SCIENCE
Vol. 30, No. 9, September 1984

A MODEL OF VENTURE CAPITALIST
INVESTMENT ACTIVITY*

TYZOON T. TYEBJEE AND ALBERT V. BRUNO

School of Business, University of Santa Clara, Santa Clara, California 95053

The paper describes the activities of venture capitalists as an orderly process involving five sequential steps. These are (1) Deal Origination: The processes by which deals enter into consideration as investment prospects, (2) Deal Screening: A delineation of key policy variables which delimit investment prospects to a manageable few for in-depth evaluation, (3) Deal Evaluation: The assessment of perceived risk and expected return on the basis of a weighting of several characteristics of the prospective venture and the decision whether or not to invest as determined by the relative levels of perceived risk and expected return, (4) Deal Structuring: The negotiation of the price of the deal, namely the equity relinquished to the investor, and the covenants which limit the risk of the investor, (5) Post-Investment Activities: The assistance to the venture in the areas of recruiting key executives, strategic planning, locating expansion financing, and orchestrating a merger, acquisition or public offering. 41 venture capitalists provided data on a total of 90 deals which had received serious consideration in their firms. The questionnaire measured the mechanism of initial contact between venture capitalist and entrepreneur, the venture's industry, the stage of financing and product development, ratings of the venture on 23 characteristics, an assessment of the potential return and perceived risk, and the decision vis-à-vis whether to invest. The modal venture represented in the database was a start-up in the electronics industry with a production capability in place and seeking $1 million (median) in outside financing. There is a high degree of cross-referrals between venture capitalists, particularly for the purposes of locating co-investors. Factor analysis reduced the 23 characteristics of the deal to five underlying dimensions namely (1) Market Attractiveness (size, growth, and access to customers), (2) Product Differentiation (uniqueness, patents, technical edge, profit margin), (3) Managerial Capabilities (skills in marketing, management, finance and the references of the entrepreneur), (4) Environmental Threat Resistance (technology life cycle, barriers to competitive entry, insensitivity to business cycles and down-side risk protection), (5) Cash-Out Potential (future opportunities to realize capital gains by merger, acquisition or public offering). The results of regression analyses showed expected return to be determined by Market Attractiveness and Product Differentiation ($R2 = 0.22$). Perceived risk is determined by Managerial Capabilities and Environmental Threat Resistance ($R2 = 0.33$). Finally, a discriminant analysis correctly predicted, in 89.4% of the cases, whether or not a venture capitalist was willing to commit funds to the deal on the basis of the expected return and perceived risk. The reactions of seven venture capitalists who reviewed the model's specification were used to test its validity.
(FINANCE—INVESTMENT CRITERIA; FINANCIAL INSTITUTIONS—INVESTMENT; RESEARCH AND DEVELOPMENT—PROJECT SELECTION; STATISTICS—REGRESSION—VENTURE CAPITAL)

Introduction

Venture capital has become an increasingly important source of financing for new companies, particularly when such companies are operating on the frontier of emerging technologies and markets. It plays an essential role in the entrepreneurial process. The purpose of this paper is to model the deal flow in a venture capital firm, namely the stages in the consideration, scrutiny and disposition of venture investment deals. The theory of equity markets is well developed in finance; it will not be reviewed here. These theories are typically oriented toward equity financing in publicly traded companies. Venture capital investments, however, differ in several important aspects (Poindexter 1976). First, venture capital is usually invested in new firms which have very little performance history. As a result, the investor cannot rely on historical performance data, as in the case of the stock market. Second, the investment is typically in small firms and the nature of the investor and investee relationship involves a higher degree of direct involvement as

* Accepted by Burton V. Dean; received June 13, 1983. This paper has been with the authors 1 month for 1 revision.

compared to the relatively inactive role of investors in publicly traded companies. Third, venture capital investments are illiquid in the short term because of the lack of efficient capital markets for equity shares of privately held companies. Long horizons of product and market development make valuation difficult. Moreover, the legal restrictions that apply to the resale of such investments lock the investor in for a certain period. Fourth, when a venture capitalist invests in a new startup, it is usually with the implicit realization that future rounds of capital infusion may have to be financed before the initial investment can bear fruit (Cooper and Carleton 1979).

The lack of capital markets for the financial instruments of small, new companies introduces considerable problems in studying venture capital investments within the paradigm of the capital asset pricing model. The absence of a clearing price determined by the market makes the valuation of an investment vulnerable to the subjective assessment procedures of the analyst. One study of 29 SBIC funds found that venture capital funds enjoy a rate of return 63% higher than Standard & Poor's market index returns. This premium, however, is offset by a higher risk; the variability of the firm's returns were higher than that of the market index return (Poindexter 1976). Poindexter concludes that venture capital markets are efficient since higher returns are offset by higher risk. Using a considerably different methodology, Charles River Associates (1976) reached the same conclusion.

The efficiency of venture capital markets is a central public policy concern because of the latter's goal of stimulating the flow of funds to new, small companies. However, the efficiency proposition provides little insight into the decision process of venture capitalists, other than the implication that they select investments with potential returns high enough to offset the higher risk. In the next section we develop a descriptive model of the activities or processes involved in managing a venture capital fund. Portions of the model are empirically tested on the basis of interviews with venture capitalists, and analyses of the characteristics and disposition of deals which they had recently considered. This methodology is not without its problems. In the experience of the authors, venture capitalists are reluctant to violate the confidentiality of their investees. Also they are not receptive to highly structured measurement instruments, which are perceived to be time consuming to complete. They view every deal and every venture capital fund to be peculiar to itself, and resist the generalizations which behavioral scientists wish to impose upon them. For this reason, research methodology which relies on the cooperation of venture capitalists in divulging data on their activities is likely to suffer from a high nonresponse bias and criticisms regarding the generalizability of small sample research. It is with this backdrop that we seek to model the activities of venture capitalists.

Model of the Venture Capitalist's Investment Activity

The investment activity of a venture capitalist is modeled as a sequential process involving five steps (see Figure 1). The first step is one of *deal origination* which describes how venture capitalists become cognizant of potential investment activities. The second step is a *screening* process by which venture capitalists seek to concentrate only on a manageable set of potential deals. The *evaluation* step involves an assessment of the potential return and risk of a particular deal. If the outcome of the evaluation process is a favorable one, the venture capitalist enters into a negotiating process with the potential investee so as to *structure the deal* in terms of the amount, form and price of the investment. Once a deal is consummated, the venture capitalist typically has close contact with the venture. These *post-investment activities* include setting up controls to protect the investment, providing consultation to the fledgling management of the venture, and, finally, helping orchestrate the merger, acquisition, or public offering which would create a public market for the investment.

On the basis of several previous studies (Dorsey 1977; Hoffman 1972; Poindexter 1976; Timmons and Gumpert 1982; Wells 1974) we can describe the salient features of each of these steps as follows:

Step 1—Deal Origination. The venture capitalist faces a very poorly defined environment within which to find prospective deals. The typical investment prospect is too small a company to be readily identifiable as a potential candidate. For this reason, we could expect that various intermediaries play an important role in matching venture capital investors with fledgling ventures with cash needs.

Step 2—Screening. Venture capital firms typically have small staffs. As a result, these firms must screen the relatively large number of potential deals available and consequently invest in only a fraction of the deals which come to their attention. Their screening criteria reflect a tendency to limit investments to areas with which the

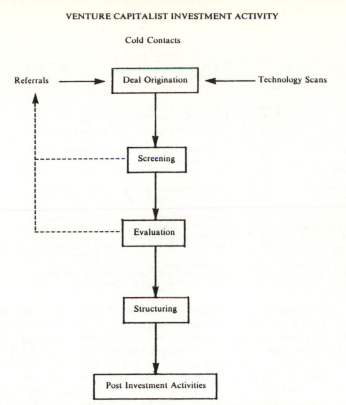

FIGURE 1. Decision Process Model of Venture Capitalist Investment Activity.

venture capitalist is familiar, particularly in terms of the technology, product and market scope of the venture.

Step 3—Evaluation. As noted before, most ventures in search of capital have very little, if any, operating history. The venture capitalist has to rely on a subjective assessment procedure based upon the business plan presented by the venture's management. Venture capitalists do weigh risk and return in their decision whether or not to invest in a particular deal, but few formalize this assessment into a computation of an expected rate of return or determine its sensitivity to future uncertainties. Instead, the evaluation procedure seeks to subjectively assess the venture on a multidimensional set of characteristics. Table 1 shows the characteristics found to be important in previous studies. Not surprisingly, these criteria are similar to those found in several new product evaluation models (Montgomery and Urban 1969; O'Meara 1961; Pessemier 1982). It is interesting to note, however, that none of these criteria reflects how a prospective deal may correlate with one already in the venture capitalist's investment portfolio.

Step 4—Deal Structuring. Once the venture capitalist has decided that a deal is acceptable, the deal will be consummated only if the venture capitalist and the entrepreneur are able to structure a mutually acceptable venture capital investment agreement. From the perspective of the venture capitalist, the agreement serves several purposes. First, it establishes the price of the deal, that is the equity share the entrepreneur will give up in exchange for the venture capital (Golden 1981). Second, it establishes protective covenants which limit capital expenditures and management

1054   TYZOON T. TYEBJEE AND ALBERT V. BRUNO

TABLE 1

Venture Evaluation Criteria

WELLS (1974) Sample: Eight Venture Capital Firms (Personally interviewed)		POINDEXTER(1976) Sample: 97 Venture Capital Firms (Mailed questionnaires)	TYEBJEE & BRUNO (Study I) Sample: 46 Venture Capitalists (Telephone survey, open-ended questions)	
Factor	Average Weight	Investment Criteria by Rank Order Of Importance	Factor	% of Respondents Mentioning
Management Commitment	10.0	1. Quality of Management	1. Management Skills & History	89
Product	8.8	2. Expected Rate of Return	2. Market Size/Growth	50
Market	8.3	3. Expected Risk	3. Rate of Return	46
Marketing Skill	8.2	4. Percentage Equity Share of Venture	4. Market Niche/Position	20
Engineering Skill	7.4	5. Management Stake in Firm	5. Financial History	11
Marketing Plan	7.2	6. Financial Provisions for Investor Rights	6. Venture Location	11
Financial Skill	6.4	7. Venture Development Stage	7. Growth Potential	11
Manufacturing Skill	6.2	8. Restrictive Covenants	8. Barriers to Entry	11
References	5.9	9. Interest or Dividend Rate	9. Size of Investment	9
Other Participants in Deal	5.0	10. Present Capitalization	10. Market/Industry Expertise	7
Industry/Technology	4.2	11. Investor Control	11. Venture Stage	4
Cash-Out Method	2.3	12. Tax Shelter Consideration	12. Stake of Entrepreneur	4

salaries. Covenants also establish the basis under which the venture capitalist can take control of the board, force a change in management or liquidate the investment by forcing a buy-back, a merger, acquisition or public offering even though the venture capitalist holds a minority position. The covenants may also restrict the power of the venture management to dilute the equity of the original investors by raising additional capital elsewhere (Cooper and Carleton 1979; Glassmeyer 1981). Third, through a mechanism known as the earn-out arrangement, where the entrepreneur's equity share is determined by meeting agreed upon performance objectives, the venture capitalist is able to assess the entrepreneur's expectations for the venture (Leland and Pyle 1977; Ross 1977).

Step 5—Post-Investment Activities. Once the deal has been consummated, the role of the venture capitalist expands from investor to collaborator. This new role may be via a formal representation on the board of directors or via informal influence in market, supplier and creditor networks. The intensity of involvement in the venture's operations differs from one venture capitalist to another. However, most of those interviewed agree that it is undesirable for a venture capital company to exert control over the day-to-day operations of the venture. If a financial or managerial crisis occurs, the venture capitalist may intervene and even install a new management team.

Finally, venture capitalists typically want to cash-out their gains five to ten years after initial investments. To this end, they play an active role in directing the company towards merger, acquisition or a public offering. Bruno and Cooper (1982) followed up on 250 startups of the sixties. They found that over half of these had either gone public, or had been merged or acquired.

The post-investment activities of venture capitalists vis-à-vis their portfolio companies have been ignored by the bulk of research on venture capital. In particular, the venture capitalist's decision-making process for second and subsequent rounds of financing for ventures already in his portfolio remains a fertile area of research.

Method

The results of two databases, referred to as Study I and Study II, are presented in the next section. These databases are described briefly below.

Study I

A telephone survey of 46 venture capitalists in California, Massachusetts and Texas. Of these, half were SBIC's. The telephone survey used a structured questionnaire which asked about how ventures are evaluated. The responses were open-ended and their analysis is based upon a post-hoc categorization of responses.

Study II

Venture capital firms listed in Pratt's directory (1981) of venture capital were contacted by mail to solicit their participation in a study of investment decision criteria. The mailing was restricted to the 156 venture capital firms in the states of California, Massachusetts, and Texas as these states account for a major portion of the venture capital industry, particularly as it applies to high technology startups. Forty-one venture capital firms agreed to participate in the study. For nonparticipants, the dominant reason for refusing to participate was the sensitivity of the information we requested. A second reason was the busy schedule of the venture capitalists. Finally, several firms disqualified themselves as participants in the survey as they were either inactive in new investments or only invested in deals put together by others. The 41 cooperating venture capital firms were mailed a structured questionnaire on which to evaluate deals under consideration. We asked that they indicate their decision vis-à-vis investing in that deal. Ninety completed evaluations were returned by the 41 participants, an average of 2.2 deals per participating venture capitalist. The industries represented in the 90 deals in our sample were computers, semiconductors and telecommunications (59.6%), energy (13.5%), consumer goods (10.1%) and miscellaneous industries including transportation, construction and biomedical (16.8%).

A major problem with the methodology used in this study for describing the evaluation step is that it may be biased in favor of the results obtained. In particular, the statistical relationships between subjectively assessed characteristics of deals and the venture capitalist's decision regarding them may reflect a post-hoc rationalization of the decision. To mitigate this problem, the methodology includes a validation component in which the key results described in the next section were presented to 7 venture capitalists and their reactions recorded. The validation component was administered by mail and its outcome is discussed following the next section.

Results

In this section, the results from Studies I and II are discussed within the context of the five-step model developed earlier. While the data and results are largely focused on the deal evaluation step of the model, results for the first two steps are also presented. The last two steps, namely deal structuring and post-investment activities, are not considered in this section, but will be discussed in the validation section which follows.

Step 1—*Deal Origination*

Potential deals are brought to the attention of venture capitalists from three sources. In Study II, 25.6% of the 90 deals in the sample originated as unsolicited cold calls from entrepreneurs. The typical response of the venture capitalist is to request the inquirer to send in a business plan. The second source is through a referral process. Sixty-five percent of the deals were referred to the venture capitalist. A third of the referrals came from within the venture capital community, 40% were referred by prior investees and personal acquaintances, 10% were referred by banks and the remainder involved an investment broker.

Of those deals referred by other venture capitalists, a substantial number represent the case of the referring venture capitalist acting as a lead investor and seeking the participation of other venture capital funds. This practice, known as a syndication, is becoming more prevalent as venture capital firms seek to diversify their portfolios over a larger number of deals. Syndication offers the capability of adding investments to the portfolio without adding to the administrative burden, the bulk of which is borne by the lead investor.

The third mechanism of deal origination is the active search for deals by the venture capitalist. The venture capitalist sometimes played an active role in pursuing companies at the startup stage or those at the critical point of needing expansion financing. The venture capitalist monitors the environment for such potential candidates through an informal network and attendance at conventions, trade shows and special conferences by groups such as the American Electronics Association. An extreme variant of this active role occurs when the venture capitalist first decides which technology markets he would like to add to his portfolio and uses executive search agencies to locate the management team for the venture. In such cases, the roles of venture capitalist and entrepreneur overlap considerably.

Step 2—Screening

The venture capital firm receives a large number of proposals; far more than they can possibly fund with the size of the staff and portfolio of the typical venture fund. Wells (1974) reports that in seven venture capital funds, the annual number of proposals received ranged between 120 and 1,000, with an average of about 450 per year. Broad screening criteria are used to reduce this set to a more manageable number for more indepth evaluation. The initial screening is based upon four criteria:

(1) *The size of the investment and the investment policy of the venture fund.* The lower limit of this policy is determined by the fact that a venture capital company is run with a lean staff and it cannot afford to spread its portfolio over too many small deals because the subsequent control and consultation demands placed on the venture capitalists are essentially the same regardless of the size of the investment. Brophy (1981) reports that of 73 venture capitalists surveyed in 1979 the average number of deals invested in was 5.6 and the average portfolio size was ten ventures. The upper boundary of the investment policy is determined by the capitalization of the portfolio and the desire to maintain an investment base which is diversified across several ventures. However, the upper limit to the investment policy is relatively flexible because a venture capitalist may consider larger deals with the intent of soliciting the participation of other venture capital funds. In fact, in our research we found that the venture capital community is highly inbred with a substantial amount of participation across funds, leading many entrepreneurs to conclude that the venture capital market involves substantially less competition between suppliers than is indicated by the mere count of number of funds in existence. Brophy (1981) estimates that approximately 80% of the venture capital deals struck in 1980 involved the participation of more than one venture capital fund and about a third of the deals involved five or more participants. Fifty-six percent of the deals analyzed in Study II involved the participation of more than one venture capital fund. In the case of two-thirds of the deals which were given a positive evaluation, the venture capitalist was himself willing to commit less than 75% of the amount requested, with the balance to be raised by inviting the participation of other venture capital funds.

The investment policy, in terms of the maximum and minimum amounts which will be considered, is quite heterogeneous across venture capital firms (Timmons and Gumpert 1982). The dollar amount requested in the 90 deals examined in Study II reflects this diversity. The amounts range from $30,000 to $7,500,000, with the median amount being $1,000,000. About a third of the deals were for less than $500,000 and another third were for amounts in excess of $1,500,000.

(2) *The technology and market sector of the venture.* Of 46 venture capitalists interviewed in Study I, 29 used this screening criterion. The venture capitalist is investing in more than a company. Implicitly, he/she is investing in the future of a particular technology or market. For this reason, the venture capitalist must have some familiarity with the technology or the market of the proposed venture. This leads to an implicit specialization in a few technology markets because of the inability of the venture capital fund's manager to be well-versed across a large number of technologies or markets. Also, venture capitalists tend to favor nascent technology industries over mature technologies, the industrial market over the consumer market, and products over services.

The 90 deals in Study II, which presumably had passed initial screening, demonstrated these preferences. More than three out of four were in technology-intensive industries, only a tenth were in the consumer goods sector, and over 90% were manufacturing companies. Sixty-four percent of the deals were described by the venture capitalist as involving either a new technology or a new application of an existing technology, 18% were described as improvements on current products, and the remaining 18% were described as me-too products.

(3) *Geographic location of the venture.* Of 46 venture capitalists interviewed in Study I, 9 used this screening criterion. When a venture capitalist invests in a company, he expects to meet regularly with the management of the new venture. To maintain travel time and expense at manageable levels, some venture capitalists limit their investment activity to major metropolitan areas with easy access. Sometimes, this screening criterion will be ignored if the venture capitalist can involve the participation of another venture capital fund which is close to the venture's location and which can oversee the venture with greater ease. Though most venture capital companies do not actively pursue a policy of restricting their investment activity to a specific geographic boundary, their portfolios often exhibit this specialization because of a tendency of entrepreneurs to search for capital close to their venture's home where their banking, legal and accountancy contacts are strongest.

(4) *Stage of financing.* Of 46 venture capitalists interviewed in Study I, 22 used this screening criterion. Venture capital infusions into a company occur at several points in the life cycle of the venture. Seed capital refers to funds invested before the venture exists as a formal entity. Venture capitalists rarely invest seed capital and entrepreneurs typically turn to informal sources for this money (Wetzel 1981). Startup capital refers to financing for establishing the operation; subsequent rounds of financing are used for expanding operations. Brophy (1981) reports that of 196 venture investments in 1978, 34.2% were for startups, 40.3% were for first round expansion and 19.4% were for second round expansion (6.1% were unclassified).

In Study II, the 90 deals showed a very similar profile to Brophy's data: 45.6% were startups, 22.2% were first round expansion deals and 21.1% were second round expansion deals. Described in another manner, in the case of 23% of the deals the product was still at the design stage, in the case of another 23% a working prototype had been developed and in the case of the remaining 54% the product was already in production.

These aggregate statistics, however, hide the fact that the risk preferences of venture capital funds differ. As a result, some funds will commit capital to later stage rounds only. Others will not commit to later stage rounds unless they have already invested in the venture in the prior rounds.

Step 3—Evaluation

We asked cooperating venture capitalists to rate several deals which had passed their initial screen and were under serious consideration. The deals were rated on 23 criteria

1058   TYZOON T. TYEBJEE AND ALBERT V. BRUNO

TABLE 2

Factor Structure of Evaluation Criteria

Evaluation Criteria	Factor 1	Factor 2	Factor 3	Factor 4	Factor 5
Management Skills (6.6%)*	0.15	− 0.07	0.85	0.16	0.10
Marketing Skills (8.9%)	0.31	− 0.06	0.80	− 0.07	− 0.03
Financial Skills (6.6%)	− 0.23	− 0.01	0.74	0.16	0.12
References of Entrepreneur (16.7%)	0.24	0.09	0.48	0.16	0.33
Technical Skills (7.8%)	0.11	0.72	0.01	− 0.12	0.27
Profit Margins (13.4%)	0.19	0.62	0.25	− 0.02	−- 0.04
Uniqueness of Product (11.1%)	0.14	0.87	− 0.02	0.03	0.06
Patentability of Product (30.0%)	− 0.02	0.67	− 0.31	0.27	0.01
Raw Material Availability (31.1%)	0.12	0.18	− 0.07	0.05	− 0.07
Production Capabilities (30.0%)	0.11	0.11	0.06	0.04	− 0.03
Access to Market (12.3%)	0.66	0.07	0.14	0.13	0.24
Market Need for Product (12.2%)	0.79	0.07	0.00	0.12	0.04
Size of Market (10.0%)	0.84	0.03	0.00	0.10	0.07
Growth Potential of Market (13.3%)	0.66	0.35	0.06	− 0.20	0.20
Freedom from Regulation (16.7%)	0.09	− 0.09	− 0.20	0.07	0.41
Protection from Competitive Entry (12.3%)	− 0.01	0.36	− 0.12	0.77	0.24
Resistance to Economic Cycles (12.2%)	0.28	0.32	0.27	0.59	− 0.38
Protection from Obsolescence (17.8%)	0.10	− 0.19	0.12	0.75	0.17
Protection against Down-side Risk (13.4%)	0.02	− 0.13	0.09	0.70	0.18
Opportunities for Exit (15.6%)	0.28	0.15	0.12	0.24	0.76
Merger/Acquisition Potential (17.8%)	0.12	0.20	0.25	0.12	0.80
Hedge Against Current Investments (53.3%)	—	—	—	—	—
Tax Benefits (34.4%)	—	—	—	—	—
% Variance Explained	22.5	12.9	9.6	8.2	7.2

*Percentage of deals for which evaluation was not reported.

(see Table 2) using a four-point rating scale (Poor = 1, Adequate = 2, Good = 3, Excellent = 4). In addition to rating the venture on the 23 criteria, the participant also rated the venture on overall expected return and risk, respectively. A straightforward measure of expected return proved intractable because in 42% of the cases the venture capitalist was unable to assign a numerical estimate of the expected rate of return. For this reason, expected return was measured on a four-point scale (Low = 1, Moderate = 2, High = 3, Very High = 4). The perceived riskiness of the deal was measured by asking the venture capitalist to assign a subjective probability to the venture being a commercial failure. Finally, the venture capitalists indicated their decision regarding the deal. Of the 90 deals in the sample, 25 were rejected, 43 were found to be acceptable and thus fundable, 18 were pending further investigation, and in the case of 4 deals, the decision was not specified.

Table 2 lists the 23 items which served as the basis for evaluating deals under consideration. The number in parentheses next to each item reports the frequency with which deals received no evaluation at all on each of these criteria. A deal would not be evaluated on a particular criterion if it did not enter the decision-making process. The frequency of missing responses was particularly high in the case of five of the evaluation criteria. The patentability of the product was not evaluated in 30% of the cases. Manufacturing aspects such as raw material availability and production capabilities were not evaluated in almost one-third of the cases. The tax benefits of the investment were not evaluated in 34.4% of the deals. Finally, the extent to which the investment offset or hedged the risk of the existing portfolio was not evaluated in 53.3% of the cases.

Why do these five items sustain such a high nonresponse rate? Though the data themselves do not answer these questions, it is possible to speculate why this occurs. There is a disillusionment with the patent process and many entrepreneurs and venture capitalists feel that the public disclosure of the product design in the patent application leads to more competitive entry rather than less. Venture capitalists generally do not worry about raw material and production capabilities as these are technical problems easily solved if the product and its marketing are viable. Tax benefits are not relevant in evaluating many deals because venture capitalists see their mission as reaping capital gains rather than providing tax shelters for the investors in their fund. Finally, the fact that a deal's relationship to the existing portfolio is not evaluated in more than half the cases is consistent with the results of Study I. Of the 46 venture capitalists interviewed, 28 claimed that they evaluated each deal on its own individual merit. Only one of the interviewees claimed that impact on portfolio risk was formally analyzed.

All the scales, with the exception of the two which had the highest rate of missing data, namely the tax benefits and hedge against current portfolio, were factor analyzed.

The varimax factor loadings are given in Table 2. A five-factor solution explains 60.4% of the variation in the 21 rating items. Adding a sixth factor would have added an incremental 6.3% of the variance explained; however the interpretability of this sixth factor was poor (each factor was interpreted on the basis of the items which load most heavily on it).

Based upon the factor structure in Table 2, we conclude that venture capitalists evaluate potential deals in terms of five basic characteristics. The first characteristic which we labeled *Market Attractiveness* depends upon the size, growth and accessibility of the market and on the existence of a market need. The second characteristic reflects *Product Differentiation* which is determined by the ability of the entrepreneur to apply his technical skills in creating a product which is unique can deter competition through patents and enjoy a high profit margin. The third characteristic reflects the *Managerial Capabilities* of the venture's founders. This capability results from skills in managing several business functional areas and is associated with favorable references given to the entrepreneurs. The fourth factor represents the extent to which the venture is resistant to uncontrollable pressures from the environment. These pressures may result from obsolescence due to changing technology, from sensitivity to economic conditions or from low barriers to entry by competition. This factor was labeled *Environmental Threat Resistance*. The final factor represents the extent to which the venture capitalist feels that the investment can be liquidated or "cashed out" at the appropriate time. This is labeled as *Cash-Out Potential*.

The next step was to profile each deal in terms of the five dimensions. A score was computed for each deal on each factor as an average of the ratings of the items which loaded heavily on the factor.[1] For each factor, a Cronbach alpha was computed as an indication of the reliability of that factor. The Cronbach alpha values are reported on the diagonal of the matrix in Table 3. These range from 0.71 to 0.79. Table 3 also reports the intercorrelation of the factors.

A linear regression model was used to relate each deal's scores on the five dimensions to subjective estimates of its level of expected return and perceived risk, respectively. The expected return was estimated on a four-point scale. Risk was

---

[1]The items used in computing each factor score are those blocked in Table 1, with the exception of "Reference of Entrepreneur" and "Patentability of Product" which were excluded as they lowered the Cronbach alpha reliability.

TYZOON T. TYEBJEE AND ALBERT V. BRUNO

TABLE 3

Cronbach Reliability and Intercorrelation of Evaluation Factors[1]

	Market Attractiveness	Product Differentiation	Managerial Capabilities	Environmental Threat Resistance	Cash-Out Potential
Market Attractiveness	0.79*	0.35*	0.20*	0.48*	0.39*
Product Differentiation		0.76	0.12	0.33*	0.25*
Managerial Capabilities			0.77	0.18	0.18
Environmental Threat Resistance				0.71	0.26
Cash-Out Potential					0.77[2]

[1] Cronbach alpha reliability is reported on the diagonal. The off-diagonal elements are Pearson correlation coefficients between the factors.

[2] The Cronbach alpha when only two items are used in constructing a scale is equivalent to the Pearson correlation between the two items.

* $p < 0.05$.

estimated in terms of the probability of commercial failure: the higher the probability of failure, the greater the riskiness of the venture.[2] Table 4 reports the results of the two regressions.

The evaluation scores are able to explain 33% of the variance in perceived risk and 22% of the variance in estimated rate of return. The R^2 values associated with the two regressions are significant at the 0.01 level.

Two aspects of the deal's evaluation have a significant impact on the risk associated with the deal. A lack of managerial capabilities significantly increases the perceived risk ($p < 0.05$). The relative magnitudes of the beta coefficients show that managerial capabilities have the strongest effect on reducing the riskiness of the deal and resistance to environmental threats has the next highest effect. Other characteristics of the deal do not influence the perceived risk at a significant level.

Two different aspects of the deal's evaluation influence the expected rate of return. Attractive market conditions have the strongest effect ($p < 0.01$) and a highly differentiated product has the next highest effect ($p < 0.05$). Other characteristics of the deal do not significantly influence the expected return.

Interestingly, the cash-out potential of a venture does not seem to influence either perceived risk or return. This is particularly surprising because without a merger, acquisition or public offering, the investor is severely constrained in realizing any gains.

TABLE 4

Determinants of Risk and Return Assessment

Dependent Variable	Market Attractiveness	Product Differentiation	Managerial Capabilities	Environmental Threat Resistance	Cashout Potential	Adjusted R^2
Risk	− 0.05	− 0.12	− 0.46[a]	− 0.23[b]	0.01	0.33[a]
Return	0.40[a]	0.26[b]	0.03	0.02	− 0.13	0.22[a]

[a] Significant at the 0.01 level.
[b] Significant at the 0.05 level.

[2] The correlation between expected risk and return was −0.13. This relationship is not statistically significant.

In our sample of 90 deals, 43 were endorsed as acceptable investments, 25 were denied funds and the balance were either pending a decision or no decision was specified. Discriminant analysis was used to examine the ability of the perceived risk and return to distinguish between rejected and accepted deals. For this purpose, we analyzed only the 68 deals for which a definite decision was made.

The standardized discrimination function coefficients of the two predictor variables, expected return and perceived risk, are 0.52 and −0.87, respectively. The signs are as expected; namely, a high expected return increases the likelihood that the deal is accepted and a high perceived risk increases its likelihood of being rejected. The fact that the signs of the discriminant coefficients are different, i.e., one is positive whereas the other negative, indicates a trade-off relationship between risk and return, a lower expected return is acceptable if offset by a lower risk.

The predictive ability of the discriminant function can be evaluated in terms of the accuracy with which it can classify deals as accepted or rejected. 68.4% of the deals actually rejected were classified as such and 95.2% of the deals actually accepted were classified as such. Together, this represents 86.9% of the deals being correctly classified. The predictive ability of a discriminant function can be evaluated by comparing the percentage of cases correctly classified against two criteria (Morrison 1969).

Proportional Chance Criterion: $C_{pro} = \alpha^2 + (1 - \alpha)^2$,

Maximum Chance Criterion: $C_{max} = \max(\alpha, 1 - \alpha)$,

where α and $1 - \alpha$ are the proportions in each group.

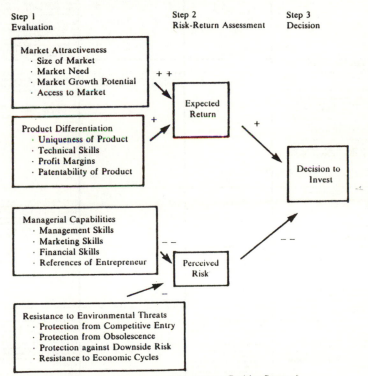

FIGURE 2. Venture Capital Investment Decision Process.*

*The + +, +, −, − − symbols indicate the direction and magnitude of the parameters describing the relationships of variables.

1062   TYZOON T. TYEBJEE AND ALBERT V. BRUNO

TABLE 5
Validation of the Model

	Venture Capitalist No. 1	Venture Capitalist No. 2	Venture Capitalist No. 3
DEAL ORIGINATION			
Most deals are referred to the venture capitalist rather than being cold contacts.	Agrees, but do get many cold contact deals. They tend to be considerably lower quality on average than "referred" deals.	Agrees.	Agrees.
A little less than half of the deals referred to the venture capitalist are referred by a former investee or a personal acquaintance; about a third are referred by other venture capitalists.	Agrees.	Agrees. In this case, "personal acquaintance" includes lawyers, auditors, and investment bankers that are well known to the venture capitalist.	Substantially true. A large number of deals come from personal or professional acquaintances. Number from other venture capitalists seems to be of less overall importance particularly for early stage deals.
Referrals by other venture capitalists are often in the form of an invitation to participate in a deal.	Agrees.	Agrees.	Not true in our experience. Often other venture capitalists invite us to examine a deal in conjunction with themselves. Their hope is to leverage our expertise and perspective in analyzing the deal. Quite often this may lead to a negative investment decision.
Sometimes a venture capitalist may select an industry and set up a venture by searching out a management team. Such cases are rare. The more typical approach is when the venture capitalist lets the deal come to him.	Agrees.	Agrees.	Substantially true. Just as often as selecting an industry, however, we have more typically selected a management team and built a company around them.
DEAL SCREENING			
The most commonly used screening criteria are the size of investment, the technology and/or market, the stage of financing, and the geographic proximity	Interesting management team may be most important screening criterion.	Size of investment is not critical in the investment decision. Experience level of management group is the most important criterion.	The size of investment is often used as an excuse for turning a deal down but rarely would stand in the way of our participation if everything else seemed good. Technology and/or market are of interest but more particularly relate to barriers of entry achievable or ultimate size of the company achievable. Stage of financing has been a criteria for us in the past, i.e., we focus on first or second round deals. Geographic location has not been a concern. However, it is often used as an excuse to turn a deal down.
DEAL EVALUATION			
The decision to invest is based upon the expected return relative to the risk level.		The capabilities of the management team is a better indication of expected return than risk level.	Overall, I believe your conclusions are correct. Factored into this, however, are issues such as portfolio diversification, other investors and the size of capitalization required.
The best indicators of return prospect are			
(a) Market Attractiveness (size & growth potential, market used and ability of the venture to access the market).	Agrees.		Ability to develop a particular technology and bring it to market at a particular time represents a substantial risk in many deals.
(b) Product Differentiation (uniqueness of product, technical skills, profit margins/value added, patents).	Agrees.		
The best indicators of the risk level are:			Overall, it is very difficult to be comprehensive and succinct at the same time in stating all of the factors entering into a deal evaluation.
(a) Managerial Capabilities (management, marketing, financial skills, entrepreneur's background).	Agrees.		
(b) Protection from Uncontrollables (competition, obsolescence, economic cycles).	Agrees.		
DEAL STRUCTURING			
Convertible preferred stock is the typical form of financing.		Agrees.	With rare exceptions, all of our financing involve convertible preferred stock. Debt is used only in very rare instances for our partnership. A distinction should be made here between SBIC style financings versus more traditional mainstream venture capital financing; SBIC's are more prone to finance with debt instruments.
Equity share required is determined by pay-out expectations relative to rate of return objectives.			
The entrepreneur's equity is determined by earn-out conditions.	In our experience, earn-out agreements are quite rare and counter productive for both the management team and venture capitalists.		Price is determined largely by the quality of the opportunity as well as comparable opportunities which have recently been financed. In general we receive liquidity either through merger or public stock offering.
The negotiations regarding the earn-out agreement give insight into the entrepreneur's expectations for the venture.			
POST INVESTMENT ACTIVITIES			
The venture capitalist provides the venture with management guidance and business contacts. A representative of the venture capital firm generally sits on the board. The venture capitalist plays a significant role in orchestrating a merger, acquisition on public offering.	"Management guidance" can cover a lot of sins. Critical input most often comes in the areas of: (1) Recruiting key executives or managers to fill out the team. (2) Acting as a sounding board to CEO on self-evaluation and evaluation of other top management (3) Strategy development.	Agrees.	Management guidance and business contacts vary widely depending on the particular investment and our level of involvement. This level of involvement is tied directly to our participation on the deal. However, we sit on the board in less than one-third of our portfolio companies, and typically only those deals in which we are lead investors. I would view our role in orchestrating a merger acquisition or public offering as relatively minor compared to our role as a management sounding board.

VENTURE CAPITALIST INVESTMENT ACTIVITY

TABLE 5 *(continued)*

Venture Capitalist No. 4	Venture Capitalist No. 5	Venture Capitalist No. 6	Venture Capitalist No. 7
Agrees.	Founders have become very sophisticated. They develop relationship with lawyer and apprise bank contact of their intentions to start company.	Agrees.	Agrees.
Agrees.	They also use their network, especially banks, lawyers and former associates who have started companies. This helps the targeting of vc potentials as well as providing introductions.	More than 1/2, 1/2 by other v.c.'s. Also past & present investees, corporate contacts & personal accounts	Agrees.
Agrees.			Agrees.
Agrees.			Agrees.
For us, I would rank in priority: (1) Management team (2) Technology/market (3) Stage of financing (4) Size (5) Location (only re being lead investor).	Missing is the most important... the people! I check the founders out before I will have first meeting.	We use potential return on capital as an early screening criterion.	Agrees.
Agrees. Agrees.	We don't actually use separate determinants of risk & return. Rather we use 3 evaluation criteria, weighted as follows: 40% - management quality/experience 40% - market (big wave can carry many surf boards) 20% - product niche, i.e., segmentation (performance/competition and many other implications)	Quality of management reflects return potential rather than the risk.	Managerial capabilities are an indicator of return prospects relative to the risk level.
Convertible preferred stock is typical for us; note that we discourage dividends.	One way to handle the question of per-formance is through a buy-back provision where the stock position of the entrepreneur is vested over a period of time. This allows for the replacement of poor/marginal performers and the ability to use repurchased (non-vested) stock to attract replacement in the management team. Past experiences in the realized valuation of comparable ventures which we have backed help determine the equity split between entrepreneur & us in future deals. For example, if we expect a company to have an upside potential of $10 million, we might put in $4 million and expect 40% equity in the venture.	Equity share is determined by the total equity valuation process; earn-out conditions are not used by our firm.	Converts were used more in the mid-seventies. They're still used by SBIC's but typically not by conventional VC partnerships. There hasn't been a convert in our last 40-50 investments. Equity share is determined by pay-out required expectations and by an assessment of the value currently represented by the business. Most VC's I know won't get involved in an earn-out. I haven't done one in 14 years in the business. You strike a deal with the management at the outset. Hopefully more equity is provided over time to successful management, but there's no way to take it away from them unless they leave or are fired. If you replace "earn-out" with "equity split," the statement would more accurately describe our reality.
For us, board seats for at least some venture investors. At least some of the venture capital investors, & especially the lead investor, should have representation on the board.	We agree. We especially contribute as follows: Help in recruiting key people Serve as sounding board to first time CEO Security check on strategy (OEM or direct sales, etc.)	We always serve on the board of our portfolio companies. We provide our portfolio companies with assistance in such areas as identifying legal counsel, performing compensation audits, focusing the product or service, recruiting management, locating additional capital and guiding acquisition/merger decisions.	Agree, but only one VC may be on the board even if there are 2-3 VC's in the deal, i.e., all of the investors don't go on the Board.

In our study, 43 of 68 deals were accepted ($\alpha = 0.63$) and 25 of 68 deals were rejected ($1 - \alpha = 0.37$). Thus $C_{pro} = 0.53$ and $C_{max} = 0.63$. Since the discriminant function classified 86.9% of the cases correctly, it performs considerably better than both the proportional chance criterion and the maximum chance criterion.

Figure 2 is a schematic representation of how evaluation criteria have an impact on the venture capitalist's decision to invest, as inferred by Study II. In summary, the attractiveness of the market and the product's differentiation are related to the expected return. A capable management team and resistance to environmental threats indicate a lower risk of commercial failure. Finally, the decision to invest is determined by the risk vs. return expectations vis-à-vis a venture. As expected, venture capitalists are risk-averse and profit-oriented in their decision and, moreover, they are willing to invest in risky deals if offset by the profit potential.

Neither Study I nor II collected any data relevant to the deal structuring (Step 4) or post-investment activities (Step 5) aspects of the model in Figure 1. These were addressed in a more general fashion in the validation component described in the next section.

Validation of the Model

Seven cooperating venture capitalists agreed to participate in a follow-up study to validate the model. The participants were selected to provide representation from the viewpoint of the various types of venture capital investors. Included in the set of cooperating venture capitalists were: a large venture capital firm which also participates in underwriting new equity issues; a small venture capital partnership composed of successful entrepreneurs who have sold their companies; a venture capital partnership with several generations of funds ranked in the top five in terms of number of deals made and dollars invested for 1982; a well-known venture capital firm which specializes in a narrow high technology industry segment; an SBIC; an individual venture capitalist investor; and a venture capital partnership substantially owned by a major banking institution. Each of the participating venture capitalists was asked to review the specification of the components of our model. These are summarized in the left-hand column of Table 5. Also the venture capitalists were asked to elaborate upon their reaction to the validity of the model. These responses are also shown in Table 5.

In general, there is agreement with the model's specification. Some of the comments elaborate upon the model specifications; others take exception with selected components of the model. The major departures from the model's specification are as follows:

(1) The model may have under-represented the extent to which venture capitalist's stress the quality of the management team as an early screening criterion. Also, the size of investment is not a screening criterion for several respondents.

(2) There was considerable disagreement with our statistical result that the quality of the management team influences risk but not expected return. Three of the seven respondents feel that management capabilities are an indicator of potential return rather than risk. A more fundamental issue is raised by VC5. This respondent does not formally distinguish between risk and return, as was implicitly assumed in our formulation.

(3) Earn-out arrangements are not extensively used in structuring deals. VC5 offers insight into a different type of deal structure which tries to achieve the same objective as an earn-out. In an earn-out arrangement, the share of the entrepreneur is determined by the venture's performance, thereby giving the investor control if the performance is poor. Instead, VC5 achieves much the same effect by the use of a "vesting" arrangement. Since the share of the entrepreneur vests over time, this gives the investor control in the early development of the venture even though his ultimate share may be a minority position.

Though the responses in Table 5 are in general agreement with our model's specification, there is a disturbing lack of common structure to the way the 7 venture capitalists reacted to the model. The diversity of the responses, both in content and style, demonstrates the heterogeneity in the practices of different venture capital firms. This heterogeneity cautions against too rigid a specification in any model describing venture capital management.

Conclusions

The purpose of this paper is two-fold. The first is to stimulate an interest in modeling the management of venture capital funds. The second is to provide entrepreneurs with insights which can help in their dealings with venture capitalists.

With respect to the first objective, the value of the study may perhaps be as much in what it did not achieve as in what it did achieve. A five-step model of the activities of venture capitalists has been developed. The model, however, is highly descriptive and lacks a theoretical basis. Moreover, the model is admittedly simplistic. A more rigorously specified model, however, could not capture the heterogeneity of practices across the many venture capital firms. Wells (1974) achieved a higher level of specificity in his modeling of venture capital fund management, but only at the expense of a unique model for each of the firms in his relatively small sample. Finally, the empirical portion of this paper has focused on the first three steps, and especially the third step, of the model. Most of the previous research on this topic share the same focus. In contrast, the fourth and fifth steps, namely deal structuring and post-investment activities, have not received much attention. In particular, the pricing of venture capital investments, in terms of the equity relinquished has not been modeled. Also, since most ventures involve several rounds of financing, the implications of future capital needs on investment decisions in earlier rounds of financing need to be explored. These limitations of the model presented in this paper are, hopefully, the stimuli for a continued interest in modeling venture capital investments.

The second objective of this paper is to provide potential entrepreneurs with insight into the way venture capitalists manage their funds. These insights are also valuable to managers in large companies who wish to improve their allocation of resources to internal ventures competing for new business development funds. First, professional relationships with CPAs, lawyers, bankers and successful entrepreneurs who have a high degree of credibility with the venture capital community is a help in locating capital. Second, the venture capital community is often smaller than it seems due to the high incidence of syndication whereby several venture capitalists co-invest in a venture. Third, venture capitalists differ in the screening criteria used to guide their investments. Most deals would have to match the investor's industry and geographic preferences, risk preferences for different financing stages, and investment policy in terms of the amount they will invest in a single deal. Finally, four aspects of the business plan are used to evaluate the riskiness and potential profit associated with a particular deal. These are (1) the marketing factors and the venture's ability to manage them effectively, (2) product's competitive advantages and uniqueness, (3) quality of the management team, particularly in its balance of skills, (4) exposure to risk factors beyond the venture's control, e.g., technological obsolescence, competitive entry, cyclical sales fluctuations. In presenting a deal to a venture capitalist, these four aspects should be used to favorably position the venture.[3]

[3] This research was funded by a National Science Foundation Grant NSF PRA-8006620-A01.

References

BROPHY, D. J., "Flow of Venture Capital 1977-1980," in *Frontiers of Entrepreneurship Research*, K. H. Vesper (Ed.), Babson College, Wellesley, Mass., 1981, 246–280.

BRUNO, A. V. AND A. C. COOPER, "Patterns of Development and Acquisitions for Silicon Valley Startups," *Technovation*, Elsevier Scientific Publishing Company, Amsterdam, Netherlands, 1982, 275–290.

CHARLES RIVER ASSOCIATES, "An Analysis of Venture Capital Market Imperfections," NTIS Report PB-254996, National Bureau of Standards, Washington D.C., 1976.

COOPER, I. A. AND W. T. CARLETON, "Dynamics of Borrower-Lender Interaction: Partitioning Final Payoff in Venture Capital Finance," *J. Finance*, 34 (1979), 517–529.

DORSEY, T. K., "The Measurement and Assessment of Capital Requirements, Investment Liquidity and Risk for the Management of Venture Capital Funds," unpublished doctoral dissertation, University of Texas, Austin, 1977.

GLASSMEYER, E. F., "Venture Financing Techniques," in S. E. Pratt (Ed.), *Guide to Venture Capital Sources*, Capital Publishing Corp., Wellesley, Mass., 1981, 64–66.

GOLDEN, S. C., "Structuring and Pricing the Financing," in S. E. Pratt (Ed.), *Guide to Venture Capital Sources*, Capital Publishing Corp., Wellesley, Mass., 1981, 67–76.

1066   TYZOON T. TYEBJEE AND ALBERT V. BRUNO

HOFFMAN, C. A., "The Venture Capital Investment Process: A Particular Aspect of Regional Economic
    Development," unpublished doctoral dissertation, University of Texas, Austin, 1972.
LELAND, H. E. AND D. H. PYLE, "Informational Asymmetries, Financial Structure, and Financial Intermedi-
    ation," *J. Finance*, 32 (1977).
MONTGOMERY, D. B. AND G. L. URBAN, *Management Science in Marketing*, Prentice-Hall, Englewood Cliffs,
    N.J., 1969, 303–312.
MORRISON, D. G., "On the Interpretation of Discriminant Analysis," *J. Marketing Res.*, 6 (May 1969),
    156–163.
O'MEARA, J. O., "Selecting Profitable Products," *Harvard Business Rev.*, 39 (1961), 84–85.
PESSEMIER, E. A., *Product Management: Strategy and Organization*, John Wiley, New York, 1982, 347–351.
POINDEXTER, J. B., "The Efficiency of Financial Markets: The Venture Capital Case," unpublished doctoral
    dissertation, New York University, New York, 1976.
PRATT, S. E. (Ed.), *Guide to Venture Capital Sources*, Capital Publishing Corp., Wellesley, Mass., 1981.
ROSS, S. A., "The Determination of Financial Structure: The Incentive Signalling Approach," *Bell J
    Econom.*, 8 (1977), 23–40.
TIMMONS, J. AND D. GUMPERT, "Discard Many Old Rules About Getting Venture Capital," *Harvard
    Business Rev.*, 60 (1) (1982).
TYEBJEE, T. T. AND A. V. BRUNO, "Venture Capital Decision Making" in *Frontiers of Entrepreneurship
    Research*, K. H. Vesper (Ed.), Babson College, Wellesley, Mass., 1981, 281–320.
WELLS, W. A., "Venture Capital Decision Making," unpublished doctoral dissertation, Carnegie-Mellon
    University, 1974.
WETZEL, W. E., JR, "Informal Risk Capital in New England," in *Frontiers of Entrepreneurship Research*,
    K. H. Vesper (Ed.), Babson College, Wellesley, Mass., 1981, 217–245.

[5]

CRITERIA DISTINGUISHING

SUCCESSFUL FROM

UNSUCCESSFUL VENTURES

IN THE VENTURE

SCREENING PROCESS

IAN C. MACMILLAN
The Wharton School

LAURIANN ZEMANN
Citibank

P. N. SUBBANARASIMHA
New York University

EXECUTIVE SUMMARY

Venture Capitalists responded to a questionnaire in which they rated a highly successful and a highly unsuccessful venture on 25 screening criteria and on several performance criteria. In all, 150 ventures were rated by 67 venture capital firms.

Cluster analysis revealed three broad classes of unsuccessful ventures. The first type is the bane of all venture capitalists—the venture in which the venture team is lacking in experience or staying power, the product has no prototype, and there is no clear market demand for the product, yet the venture somehow slips through the screens and gets funded. The second type is one in which the venture team is very well credentialed, but the venture faces early competition and the team has no staying power and runs out of steam. The third major class of venture is one in which the team has exceptional staying power, so much so that by perserverance it demonstrates that a market exists, only to lose that market to competition because of a lack of protection for the product.

Cluster analysis also showed that there are four broad classes of successful ventures. First is the high-tech venture with a well-qualified venture team that has the staying power needed to face competitive attack. Second is the class of venture where the venture team does not have much in the way of credentials, but the product has a very high level of protection and turns out to be highly successful. Third is a class of "market makers"—a venture team with exceptional perseverance that demonstrates that there is in fact a market for the product, but also has some form of product protection once that market has been demonstrated.

It can be seen that each of these classes of successes has a look-alike class of failures that is very similar except for some flaw in the venture team.

A final class of successful venture is a small group of low-tech products in which distribution skills are critical. We suspect that these ventures tend to be for consumer goods.

Address correspondence to Prof. Ian C. MacMillan, Snider Entrepreneurial Center, The Wharton School, University of Pennsylvania, 3200 Steinberg Dietrich Hall, Philadelphia, Pennsylvania 19104.

The authors wish to thank the Center for Entrepreneurial Studies at New York University for support.

124 MACMILLAN, ZEMANN, AND SUBBANARASIMHA

An important finding is the identification of two major criteria that are predictors of venture success. These are 1) the extent to which the venture is initially insulated from competition and 2) the degree to which there is demonstrated market acceptance of the product. Regression analyses indicate that only these two screening criteria correlate pervasively across several performance criteria. Interestingly, neither of these criteria were rated as essential in an earlier study. Much more importance needs to be attached to these criteria in screening venture proposals.

The final analysis was a factor analysis, which indicates that the 150 ventures were screened according to five major classes of criteria, each class corresponding to some facet of risk management of the venture. These were as follows:

1. *Criteria that screen out ventures where there is a risk of failure due to unqualified management;*
2. *Criteria that screen out management that may well be qualified but lack experience;*
3. *Criteria that screen out ventures where basic viability of the project is in doubt;*
4. *Criteria that screen out ventures where there is high exposure to competitive attack and profit erosion before the investment can be recouped;*
5. *Finally, criteria that avoid ventures that lock up the investment so that it cannot be cashed out for long periods of time.*

INTRODUCTION

Several studies have been undertaken to determine which criteria are used by venture capitalists to evaluate venture proposals (Wells 1974; Poindexter 1976; Tyebjee and Bruno 1981, 1984; MacMillan, Siegel, and SubbaNarasimha 1985; and Knight 1986). However, none of these studies addressed whether these criteria are actually helpful in distinguishing successful from unsuccessful ventures. Given the venture capital community's traditional argument that it is by and large "gut feel" that determines which ventures to back, it seemed a useful exercise to determine whether there are any criteria at all that consistently predict performance. The purpose of this study was to determine the extent to which criteria identified in past studies are useful predictors of performance.

METHODOLOGY

This study was conducted as the follow-up to a project by MacMillan, Siegel, and SubbaNarasimha (1985), which identified the most common selection criteria currently used by the venture capital community, in addition to how each criterion was weighted. The sample of venture capital firms used in the preliminary study was supplemented by questionnaires sent to the venture capitalists from the directories of National Venture Capital Association and of Venture Magazine, as well as the Venture Capital Funds list in *Who's Who in Venture Capital* (Silver 1984).

The questionnaire designed from a previous study formed the basis for a new questionnaire. This was developed via structured personal interviews and then pretested with six venture capitalists from the New York metropolitan area. The final survey form is depicted in the Appendix. This basically consists of two sets of survey questions, identical except for their instructions—the first asked the respondent to rate one of the most successful ventures they had funded. The second asked for a rating of one of the least successful ventures they had funded. It should be noted here that the responding venture capitalists decided what a successful or unsuccessful venture was, according to their own definitions.

As can be seen from the questionnaire, the survey asked for ratings of several groups of criteria: 1) characteristics of the venture team, 2) characteristics of the proposed product or service, 3) characteristics of the target market, and 4) forecast financial characteristics. Note that what was requested were a posteriori ratings, not a priori ratings. In addition to rating the venture according to the above characteristics, the participants were asked to rate the venture's performance. Seven performance variables were chosen: sales, market share, marketing costs, production costs, general and administrative expenses, profits, and return on investment. The reason why several measures were chosen was to avoid the perennial argument as to which is the most appropriate measure in the early stages of a firm's existence—revenues or profits. Accordingly, two measures of volume, Sales and Market share, and two measures of profitability, Absolute profits and ROI, were selected. In addition, since costs are so important early in the life of the venture, we decided to also have the ventures assessed on their performance in three broad classes of costs: costs associated with start-up and development (G&A costs), costs associated with manufacturing (Production costs), and costs associated with selling and distribution (Marketing costs).

The questionnaire was mailed to 220 venture capitalists throughout the U.S., to which there were 67 responses. The 30% response rate indicates a significant level of interest by venture capitalists in the study. Sixty-two of the respondents each evaluated two ventures—a success and a failure. Five of the 67 respondents agreed to rate six ventures—three successful and three unsuccessful. A total of 150 responses were usable in the study.

RESULTS

The means and standard deviations of the participants' responses regarding the successful and unsuccessful ventures are listed in Table 1. As can be seen from the very high differences in ratings for successes and failures, these results should be interpreted with some circumspection. We were concerned that respondents would tend to overrate successful ventures, whereas the unsuccessful ventures tend to be consistently underrated. It was felt that such upward and downward biases would "force" the results of a discriminant analysis. (In fact, when a discriminant analysis was run the "hit rates" were 95%, causing us to suspect bias in the responses.) This meant that any analysis that compared successful with unsuccessful ventures would be suspect. This problem is addressed formally below.

There is another problem that plagues studies of the venture capital community, and that is the fact that there is so much heterogeneity in the ventures that are supported. Ventures range in scope from microelectronics to genetics to specialty retailing to publishing. The first analysis that was conducted was therefore a cluster analysis to see if there were any broad subpatterns of successes and failures.

CLUSTER ANALYSIS

For the cluster analysis the two groups of venture types—unsuccessful and successful—were analyzed separately. The problem of bias is not present when separately clustering samples in which *all* criteria were either overrated or underrated. The results of the analyses are listed in Tables 2 and 3. For the successful ventures, the analysis for which the cubic clustering appeared to change in slope occurred between four and five clusters, so the four-cluster solution was chosen. Similarly four clusters were also chosen for the analysis of unsuccessful ventures, but the size of the fourth cluster was so small (3 ventures) that it was eliminated from further consideration.

TABLE 1   Means and Standard Deviations for Successful and Unsuccessful Ventures

	Successful		Unsuccessful	
	Mean	S.D.	Mean	S.D.
Entrepreneurial team characteristics				
1. Capacity for sustained and intense effort.	4.40	0.85	3.19	1.29
2. Ability to evaluate and react to risk well.	4.01	0.77	2.01	0.81
3. Ability to articulate well when discussing venture.	4.17	0.83	3.19	1.02
4. Attention to detail.	3.87	0.85	2.36	1.06
5. Personal compatibility with me.	1.90	0.34	1.63	0.57
6. Familiarity with the market targeted by the venture.	4.37	0.81	3.00	1.21
7. Degree of leadership ability demonstrated in the past.	3.87	0.97	2.86	0.91
8. Track record relevant to the venture.	3.76	0.98	2.96	1.04
9. Familiarity with the venture team's reputation.	1.42	0.50	1.29	0.49
10. Venture team referred by a trustworthy source.	1.57	0.64	1.51	0.69
Product/service characteristics				
11. Protection of product.	3.27	1.20	2.88	1.29
12. The product enjoyed demonstrated market acceptance.	3.58	1.39	2.32	1.08
13. Product developed to the point of functioning prototype.	3.67	1.29	3.07	1.36
14. The product was "high tech".	4.07	1.29	3.75	1.14
Market characteristics				
15. Well-established distribution channel.	1.44	0.64	1.35	0.56
15. b. If "yes" to #15, did venture team have access to it?	1.65	0.72	1.53	0.84
16. Target market enjoying a significant growth rate.	1.75	0.52	1.59	0.58
17. An existing market would be stimulated.	1.65	0.56	1.67	0.56
18. Venture in an industry with which we are familiar.	1.61	0.52	1.60	0.49
19. Competition present or anticipated in first two years.	1.95	0.28	1.79	0.45
20. The venture could create a new market.	1.38	0.49	1.33	0.50
Financial characteristics				
21. Investment could easily be made liquid.	1.38	0.51	1.30	0.46
22. Return 10 times in five years.	1.83	0.38	1.72	0.48
23. Would not be expected to make subsequent investments.	1.28	0.45	1.35	0.51
24. It was the first round of investment.	1.70	0.84	1.79	0.44
Performance				
1. Sales.	4.81	1.57	1.60	0.78
2. Market share.	4.84	1.33	1.91	1.03
3. Marketing costs.	4.36	0.91	3.37	1.73
4. Production costs.	4.27	0.93	3.20	1.59
5. General and administrative costs.	4.25	0.82	3.30	1.59
6. Profits.	4.61	1.59	1.31	1.58
7. ROI.	4.94	1.58	1.19	0.44

TABLE 2 Cluster Analysis for Unsuccessful Ventures

	Cluster 1 T value	Cluster 2 T value	Cluster 3 T value
Entrepreneurial team characteristics			
Capacity for sustained effort.	-2.42^a	6.60^c	-2.72^b
Evaluates and reacts to risk well.	-0.58	2.53^a	1.35
Articulate when discussing venture.	-0.84	3.61^c	-2.19^a
Attention to detail.	0.49	1.59	-1.66
Personal compatibility with me.	0.03	0.60	-0.59
Familiarity with the market.	3.15^b	1.36	-3.67^c
Leadership ability demonstrated.	1.40	0.88	-1.66
Relevant track record.	5.33^c	1.72	-3.65^c
Familiarity with team's reputation.	0.14	1.23	-0.96
Referred by a trustworthy source.	1.17	0.71	-1.16
Product/service characteristics			
Protection of product.	1.59	-2.02^a	0.06
Demonstrated market acceptance.	0.39	0.16	-0.72
Functioning prototype.	-0.29	1.82	-1.40
"High-tech" product.	1.51	-0.44	-0.87
Market characteristics			
Established distribution channel.	0.07	-0.62	0.55
Target market has high growth rate.	0.02	-0.36	-0.52
Existing market would be stimulated.	1.10	-1.30	-0.31
Familiar with industry.	2.37^a	0.54	-1.28
Competition anticipated in two years.	2.43^a	-0.51	-1.11
Venture could create a new market.	-1.64	1.59	-0.41
Financial charcteristics			
Investment easily made liquid.	0.93	-0.29	-0.28
Return 10 times in five years.	-0.37	0.14	-0.71
No subsequent investments.	-2.09^a	-1.48	0.90
First round of investment.	1.67	0.02	0.38
Sample size	14	23	35

$^a p < 0.05.$
$^b p < 0.01.$
$^c p < 0.001.$

Unsuccessful Ventures

In Cluster 1 (19% of failures) the team was highly familiar with the targeted market and had a well-established relevant track record. Because the venture capitalists knew the market well they were fully prepared to make subsequent investments, despite anticipated competition. However, the fundamental flaw was that when push came to shove these teams were just not capable of sustained intense effort against competition—a characteristic that earned them the title of "well-qualified dropouts." It is precisely this type of venture team—highly qualified, with all the credentials but with no endurance, that justifies the venture capitalists' insistence on staying power as an essential criterion, as was found in earlier studies. It is

128 MACMILLAN, ZEMANN, AND SUBBANARASIMHA

TABLE 3 Cluster Analysis for Successful Ventures

	Cluster 1 T values	Cluster 2 T values	Cluster 3 T values	Cluster 4 T values
Entrepreneurial team characteristics				
Capacity for sustained effort.	1.82	0.40	3.33[b]	−4.02[a]
Evaluates and react to risk well.	1.04	−0.57	1.89	−3.98[c]
Articulate when discussing venture.	0.24	1.79	2.44[a]	−3.76[c]
Attention to detail.	1.67	−3.15[a]	1.09	−2.30[a]
Personal compatibility with me.	0.47	2.36[a]	−0.54	−0.82
Familiarity with the market.	1.54	−0.52	−0.09	−2.01[a]
Leadership ability demonstrated.	2.29[a]	−0.71	−4.13[c]	−1.71
Relevant track record.	1.01	1.93	−1.23	−1.65
Familiarity with team's reputation.	0.24	0.48	0.09	−1.01
Referred by a trustworthy source.	−0.53	−1.20	1.59	0.84
Product/service characteristics				
Protection of product.	−0.13	−6.05[c]	2.10[a]	2.99[b]
Demonstrated market acceptance.	5.55[c]	−0.87	−4.38[c]	−3.61[c]
Functioning prototype.	3.07[b]	−1.53	1.76	−3.74[c]
"High-tech" product.	2.30[a]	−11.00[c]	0.52	0.29
Market characteristics				
Established distribution channel.	1.15	2.36[a]	−0.56	−2.79[b]
Target market has high growth rate.	0.07	0.34	0.28	−0.57
Existing market would be stimulated.	1.16	−1.93	−1.18	1.87
Familiar with industry.	−0.72	−0.62	1.38	0.74
Competition anticipated in two years.	0.38	−0.51	1.66	−0.88
Venture could create a new market.	−0.24	−0.47	−0.14	0.94
Financial characteristics				
Investment easily made liquid.	0.05	−0.47	0.35	−0.09
Return 10 times in five years.	−0.82	−0.81	3.93[c]	0.96
No subsequent investments.	0.19	1.60	−2.33[a]	−0.14
First round of investment.	−0.86	−0.49	1.13	1.58
Sample Size	34	10	14	19

[a] $p < 0.05$.
[b] $p < 0.01$.
[c] $p < 0.001$.

clear from the large proportion of such failures that venture capitalists still experience difficulty in judging the team's capacity for sustained effort prior to funding the venture.

In Cluster 2 (32% of unsuccessful ventures) we find the opposite of cluster 1. By dint of exceptional effort and perseverance they demonstrate that there is in fact a market for the product. They are capable of this sustained effort, know the risks, and are highly articulate in discussing the venture. The problem here lies not with the characteristics of the venture team but with the absence of protection of the product. Once a market is demonstrated, other companies invade it with impunity. These venturers are reminiscent of the frontiersmen that often lost their lives opening up new territory for the settlers who later occupied the territory. Hence the term "arrow-catchers" is applied to this group of entrepreneurs.

Cluster 3 represents a venture team lacking in terms of all the desirable criteria. They are not capable of sustained effort, they are not articulate in discussing the venture, they are not familiar with the targeted market, and finally they have no track record. These "hapless amateurs" fail in droves—a high proportion (almost 50% of the unsuccessful ventures) belong to this cluster. What is surprising is that so many of them slip through the venture capitalists' screens and actually get funded.

In summary, if we look at the clusters of failures they collectively justify the weightings assigned in earlier studies to the venture team characteristics. Most of the reasons for failure lie in specific flaws in the venture team. This also explains why, in the analyses below, team characteristics do not predict success when analyzing the whole sample. When analyzing the ventures in the aggregate the fatal flaws in one cluster are compensated by the absence of these flaws in the rest of the sample—thus averaging out the effect.

Successful Ventures

Cluster 1 (52% of successes) involves "high-tech" products. Much like the "well-qualified dropouts" in the unsuccessful ventures, these start-ups had strong initial credentials: venture teams which had demonstrated high leadership abilities, teams that had developed a functioning prototype of a product that had demonstrated acceptance by the market. The big difference is that these venture teams were not lacking in capacity for sustained and intense effort. We called these ventures the "high-tech sure bets"—firms that justify the sustained attractiveness of high-tech products to the venture capital community in the past decade.

Cluster 2 (13% of successes) is a small group of ventures, which involve distinctly "low-tech" products—presumably consumer goods that have low product protection but have well-established distribution channels. As a result they were labeled "distribution players"—ventures in which distribution expertise is the name of the game.

Cluster 3 (18% of successes) are similar in almost every way to the "arrow catchers" found in the unsuccessful ventures with the singularly important exception that these teams *have* product protection (even though the product does not have market acceptance). Hence these "market makers" employ their articulateness and their perseverance to forcibly create a market, which is subsequently protectable from competitive attack.

Cluster 4 ventures are almost the same as the "hapless amateurs" in the unsuccessful cluster. The venture team is not articulate in discussing the venture; they are neither hard-working nor adroit risk managers. They have not completed a functioning prototype nor has the product been accepted by the market. Their only redeeming feature is high product protection. This type of venture is probably one where the venture team patents an invention that proves extremely successful, or comes up with some other barrier to competitive attack of a product that turns out to be surprisingly easy to develop and market. We called this class of winners the "lucky dilettantes." Their frequency of occurrence (nearly 25% of all successes) perhaps explains why so many venture capitalists are prepared to take a chance on their siblings—the "hapless amateurs."

In summary we can appreciate the difficulty that venture capitalists face as they evaluate ventures. Each class of failures has a look-alike class of successful ventures: "market maker" versus "arrow catcher"; "lucky dilettante" versus "hapless amateur"; and "sure bet" versus "well-qualified dropout." In each case the major difference between a winner and loser cluster is some difficult-to-define venture team characteristic, which is probably much easier to identify post hoc than a priori. Thus it is not surprising that venture evaluation remains an art, a long way from becoming a science.

130   MACMILLAN, ZEMANN, AND SUBBANARASIMHA

This made us particularly interested in identifying any criterion that generally predicted performance across the entire sample.

REGRESSION ANALYSIS

As discussed above, we obtained very high hit rates in the initial discriminant analysis of the results. This caused us to be suspicious of the data and led us to the conclusion that the results had an overrate/underrate bias. However, if one takes the mean values of the ratings for each pair of ventures (successful and unsuccessful) and assumes that the upward bias for successes is approximately equal to the downward biases for failure, it can be shown that these means are unbiased estimates of the actual means. Unfortunately this averaging process collapses the two samples into a single composite sample, precluding any discriminant analysis. On the other hand, regression analysis is feasible. Several regression analyses were run to determine those criteria that had significant betas for each of the performance variables in the study. This process yielded the results reported in Table 4, which will now be discussed.

Overall Explanation of Variance

The relatively low (but highly significant) R-square values obtained from the regression should not be surprising. After all, the entire, relatively sophisticated, venture capital community encounters enormous difficulty "picking winners" out of the huge array of very

TABLE 4   Regression Results

Criterion with significant beta	Performance variables						
	Sales	Market share	Production costs	Marketing costs	G&A costs	Profits	ROI
Evaluates, reacts to risk well.			-0.23^a		-0.38^c		
Personal compatibility with me.	-0.22^a				0.25^a		
Team's familiarity with the market.			0.23^a		0.22^a		
Demonstrated leadership ability.		0.22^a					
Familiarity with team's reputation.							0.24^a
Demonstrated market acceptance for product.	0.28^b	0.26^b	0.32^b	0.22^a	0.25^a		
Access to established distribution channel.			0.21^a				
Existence of a prototype.					0.34^c		
Competition present or anticipated in first two years.	-0.25^b	-0.31^b	-0.26^b		-0.24^a	-0.27^a	-0.23^a
Venture creating a new market.							0.23^a
First round of investment.					0.41^c		
R-square	0.13	0.13	0.24	0.04	0.30	0.06	0.15
F	4.96	4.92	5.66	3.96	5.86	6.09	5.44
Significance of F	c	c	c	a	c	a	c

$^a p < 0.05$.
$^b p < 0.01$.
$^c p < 0.005$.

diverse investments that are proffered **annually**. Given the high variety of products, entrepreneurs, markets, and services it would be surprising indeed to attain very high values of
R-squared.

The results obtained tend to pan out much as the conventional wisdom (which emerged
in earlier interviews with venture capitalists) would predict: Easiest to predict are cost-related
performance measures, then revenue-related, and most difficult are profit-related performance
measures and market share. Furthermore, as could be expected, the order of predictability
of costs is: general and administrative, then production, and finally marketing costs. All
these results fit well with the qualitative predictions of the venture capitalists themselves,
and in our opinion add to the validity of the study.

Given the relatively low expectations one *could* have regarding the ability of specific
criteria to predict performance over so heterogeneous a set of ventures, any criterion that
predicts across several performance variables is of special significance. This is why we are
particularly interested in a) competitive threat and b) market acceptance of product, both of
which correlate with success on virtually every performance variable. It appears that for all
the 150 ventures that dozens of venture capitalists backed, these two criteria were the *only*
ones that consistently and pervasively predicted performance. No other criterion did—none.
So, of all the criteria that have been identified in past studies it would seem that these two
are the most critical. What is particularly interesting is that *neither* of these was weighted
particularly heavily by venture capitalists in the earlier study.

The question that arises is why those criteria that relate to the venture team's characteristics and which are so popular with venture capitalists (Wells 1974; Poindexter 1976;
Tybjee and Bruno 1981, 1984; MacMillan et al. 1985) did not have pervasively significant
betas. In the previous study factors such as "capacity for sustained effort," "demonstrating
leadership," and "track record in past ventures" were rated as essential for receiving venture
capitalists' support. To us, the issue is clearly a case of the distinction between necessary
conditions for success versus sufficient conditions for success. No venture capitalist will
back a venture where the entrepreneur or venture team is clearly faint hearted, obviously
cannot lead, or has an uninspiring track record. Such teams would *naturally* fail to get
funding—which is not the issue here. Here we are not concerned with whether the venture
gets funded but with what happens to those that *are* funded. It is obvious that ventures can
still fail no matter how hard the entrepreneurs work, or how meticulous they are, or what
their past record looks like—such team characteristics may be necessary for success but they
are just not sufficient.

Therefore the two criteria that did prove pervasive as predictors of success are particularly important. What is especially encouraging from the point of view of validity is that
both these criteria are market related rather than product or entrepreneur related. Thus the
ultimate arbiter of what will succeed is the market, and the results suggest that at the most
generic level the most desirable ventures are those for which there is a market that de-
monstrably wants the product and for which there is some insulation from early competitive
attack. These results are supported by the small sample study of Roure and Maidique (1986).
A key predictor of success for the high-technology start-ups in their research was the ability
of the entrepreneurs to find segments in an established market that were uninhabited by
strong competitors or where direct head-on competition could be avoided.

We are not suggesting that such ventures *will* succeed (after all, no R-squares are
higher than 0.30) nor that other ventures *cannot* succeed. However, these are the only
variables that were significant across several performance measures, for the many ventures

132 MACMILLAN, ZEMANN, AND SUBBANARASIMHA

in the study, and the many venture capitalists who backed these ventures, and therefore seem to be particularly important indicators of future potential.

FACTOR ANALYSIS

The final analysis conducted on the responses from the study was one that was concerned with the issue of validity development. In the study by Tyebjee and Bruno (1984) and the study by MacMillan et al. (1985) the responses were factor-analyzed to determine what major groupings of criteria occurred among criteria. Both these studies factor analyzed a priori weightings assigned to various criteria by venture capitalists when evaluating proposals prior to funding. There was some interstudy correspondence of factors. *This* study was concerned with the ratings used a posteriori by venture capitalists on proposals that had actually *received* funding. We felt that it would considerably enhance the confidence in previous results as well as current results if we could demonstrate that there was further correspondence between the factor analyses of this study and the factor analyses of previous studies.

Obviously it is ludicrous to expect perfect correspondence, but if there is a good correspondence between results of this factor analysis and those from the previous studies, this is an encouraging indicator of an emerging validity of the series of studies.

The SPSS Varimax rotation procedure was used on the venture sample on the assumption that upward and downward biases (for successful and unsuccessful ventures, respectively) would be approximately the same for all criteria, and thus the correlations

TABLE 5 Varimax Rotated Factor Analysis (Same Selection Criteria as Previous Study)

	Factor 1 management risk	Factor 2 Competitive exposure	Factor 3 Inexperience risk	Factor 4 Viability risk	Factor 5 Cash-out risk
Capable of sustained intense effort.	82	−09	−06	−03	−09
Evaluates and reacts to risk well.	78	−01	27	13	20
Articulate in discussing venture.	73	13	05	−20	−12
Familiarity with targeted market.	69	21	25	−16	25
Attention to detail.	57	−11	27	01	18
High growth rate target market.	00	77	−03	−09	08
10 times return in 10 years or less.	10	74	04	−29	03
Present or anticipated competition.	11	67	01	28	−22
Venture stimulates existing market.	−17	65	−02	20	18
Demonstrated leadership in past.	35	−10	79	04	−06
Demonstrated track record.	29	06	67	13	09
Protection of product.	05	−03	21	80	03
Industry familiar to venture capital.	28	12	−43	46	34
Developed prototype.	22	−04	25	45	43
Highly liquid investment.	02	02	−05	08	78
Demonstrated market acceptance.	14	34	47	−20	51
Eigenvalues	3.88	2.25	1.45	1.11	1.22
Percent variance explained	24.3	14.1	9.1	7.0	7.7

among the criteria would not be affected. To permit comparison across studies, we used the same venture evaluation criteria that had been used in the factor analysis of the previous study.

The results of the factor analysis are reported in Table 5. In interpreting the factors we draw once again on the concept proposed by Driscoll (1974), who asserted that the role of the venture capitalist goes beyond mere provision of funds to the venture. He argued that the real challenge to the venture capitalist lies in managing the risk of the venture. Using Driscoll's concept, one could argue that each factor reflects a specific facet of the risk management problem facing the venture capitalist.

Factor 1 loads on several attributes of the entrepreneurial team and reflects a grouping of criteria round the *management risk*—the danger that the team will not have the capabilities required to succeed. In order to facilitate the understanding of how these factors compare with the factor analysis in the earlier study, Table 6 was developed. The crosses indicate which criteria in this study correspond to factors in the prior study. Note that this factor closely parallels the "management risk" factor found in the first study—all of the three criteria in the original study recurred (capacity for sustained effort, risk evaluation skill, and familiarity with market) and have now been supplemented with two other characteristics

TABLE 6 Correspondence among Factor Items in Current and Prior Studies

Factors and items in this study	Factor 1 management risk	Factor 2 Investment risk	Factor 3 Competitive risk	Factor 4 Leadership risk	Factor 5 Bail-out risk	Factor 6 Implementation risk
	Factors and items among factor study					
Factor 1: Management risk						
Capable of sustained intense effort.	×					
Evaluates and reacts to risk well.	×					
Articulate in discussing venture.						×
Familiarity with targeted market.	×					
Attention to detail.		×				
Factor 2: Competitive exposure						
High growth rate target market.		×				
10 times return in 10 years or less.		×				
Present or anticipated competition.			×			
Venture stimulates existing market.			×			
Factor 3: Inexperience risk						
Demonstrated leadership in past.				×		
Demonstrated track record.		×				
Factor 4: Viability risk						
Protection of product.			×			
Industry familiar to venture capital.					×	
Developed prototype.						×
Factor 5: Cash out risk						
Highly liquid investment.					×	
Product has market acceptance.						×

that *also* reflect venture team attributes: articulateness in discussing ventures and attention to detail.

Factor 2 we conceive as capturing "competitive exposure"—it contains two of the three "Competitive Risk" factors in the earlier studies: low threat of early competition and a product that stimulates an existing market. It also includes two other criteria previously associated with the factor called "investment risk" in the previous study: rapid, high return and high market growth rates. To us, ventures with the combination of rapid payback potential, low competitive threat, and stimulation of a high growth market suggests very low exposure to the risk of losing the entire investment as a result of early competitive attacks. This factor also corresponds rather well Tyebjee and Bruno's "uncontrollable risk" factor.

Factor 3 we called the "Inexperience Risk" factor. In the previous study this was a single item factor (leadership), which has now been associated with another attribute (track record). Combined, these two venture team attributes capture the risk of supporting venture teams who may well have high credentials but have no proven record of leading or managing an enterprise.

The fourth factor and fifth factors were not clearly related to the earlier study by MacMillan et al., but did relate to the study of Tyebjee and Bruno.

To us factor 4 reflects the "viability" factor of the study by Tyebjee and Bruno—to the extent that a proposed business has no protection for a product which has yet to be prototyped, in an industry which is unfamiliar to the venture capitalist, the basic viability of the whole venture is in serious doubt.

Factor 5 parallels the "cash out" factor of Tyebjee and Bruno: A product and service with low market acceptance and requiring a highly illiquid investment cannot easily be "cashed out" and thus exposes the venture capitalist to being locked in to the investment until the market has been proven.

In summary the factor analysis shows a moderate but encouraging convergence among the three studies—there appears to be some validity to the "risk management" construct articulated by Driscoll. In the evaluation of venture proposals there appear to be a few important classes of risks to be managed—management risk, investment risk, inexperience risk, cash out risk, and viability risk.

SUMMARY AND CONCLUSIONS

Despite the obvious self-report limitations of this study and the problems of bias introduced by the survey methodology itself, there are several notable results from this study.

First the cluster analysis yielded several major classes of successful and unsuccessful ventures. The major finding of interest was that each class of unsuccessful venture had a look-alike class of successful venture that differed only in one major flaw—and it was this flaw that led to failure rather than success.

Second the regression analysis identified two criteria that were not heavily weighted by venture capitalists in a previous study but which were the only consistent predictors across several performance criteria. These were degree of competitive threat and degree of market acceptance of product. Those critiera, which were highly weighted in the earlier study, were not good predictors—not because they were of no value but because the venture capitalists had already applied them to weed out undesirable ventures.

Finally, the factor analysis evidenced a modest level of convergence between this and other studies.

APPENDIX: Questionnaire

Venture 1: One of the Most Successful Ventures. Rate the venture on the following characteristics:

	0 Did not apply to venture	1 Extremely poor	2 Poor	3 Satisfactory	4 Highly satisfactory	5 Outstanding
I. *Characteristics of venture team*						
Capability of sustained intense effort.	0	1	2	3	4	5
Ability to evaluate and react to risk well.	0	1	2	3	4	5
Ability to articulate when discussing venture.	0	1	2	3	4	5
Attention to detail.	0	1	2	3	4	5
Personal compatability with me.	0	No		Yes		
Familiarity with the market targeted by the venture.	0	1	2	3	4	5
Degree of leadership ability demonstrated in the past.	0	1	2	3	4	5
Track record that was relevant to venture.	0	1	2	3	4	5
We were already familiar with the venture team's reputation.	0	No		Yes		
The venture was referred to us by a trustworthy source.	0	No		Yes		
II. *Characteristics of product or service*						
Protection of product.	0	1	2	3	4	5
The product enjoyed demonstrated market acceptance.	0	1	2	3	4	5
The product had been developed to the point of a functioning prototype.	0	1	2	3	4	5
The product was "high tech."	0	1	2	3	4	5
III. *Characteristics of the market*						
There was a well-established distribution channel.	0	No		Yes		
If "Yes" to #15, did the venture team have access to it?	0	No		Yes		
The target market was enjoying a significant growth rate.	0	No		Yes		
An existing market would be stimulated.	0	No		Yes		
The venture was in an industry with which we were familiar.	0	No		Yes		

(Continued)

136   MACMILLAN, ZEMANN, AND SUBBANARASIMHA

Venture 1: One of the Most Successful Ventures. Rate the venture on the following characteristics:

	0 Did not apply to venture	1 Extremely poor	2 Poor	3 Satisfactory	4 Highly satisfactory	5 Outstanding
Appendix (Continued)						
Competition was present or anticipated in the first two years.	0		No		Yes	
The venture would create a new market.	0		No		Yes	
IV. *Financial considerations*						
The investment could be easily made liquid.	0		No		Yes	
Expected return equal to at least 10 times our investment within at five years.	0		No		Yes	
Would not be expected to make subsequent investments.	0		No		Yes	
It was the first round of investment.	0		No		Yes	

What is the age of the venture? _____ years.
Please rate the venture on its performance in each of the following categories:
("Achieved Expectations" meeting projections stated in plan.)

	Extremely poor	Significantly worse than expectations	Worse than expectations	Achieved expectations	Better than expectations	Significantly better than expectations	Outstanding performance
1. Sales	1	2	3	4	5	6	7
2. Market Share (of served market)	1	2	3	4	5	6	7
3. Costs							
a. Marketing	1	2	3	4	5	6	7
b. Production	1	2	3	4	5	6	7
c. General and administrative	1	2	3	4	5	6	7
4. Profits	1	2	3	4	5	6	7
5. ROI	1	2	3	4	5	6	7

The questionnaire was then repeated for "one of the least successful ventures."

REFERENCES

Driscoll, F.R. March 1974. Venture capital: The risk-reward business. IEEE International Convention.

Knight, R.M. 1986. Criteria used by venture capitalists. ASAC Conference, Vancouver.

MacMillan, I.C., Siegel, R., and SubbaNarasimha, P.N. Winter, 1985. Criteria used by venture capitalists to evaluate new venture proposals. *Journal of Business Venturing*, 1(1), 119–128.

Poindexter, E.A. 1976. The efficiency of financial markets: The venture capital case, Unpublished doctoral dissertation, New York University, New York.

Roure, J.B., and Maidique, M.A. Fall 1986. Linking prefunding factors and high-technology venture success. *Journal of Business Strategy.* 3(1). 295–306.

Silver, A.D. 1984. *Who's Who in Venture Capital.* New York: Wiley.

Tyebjee, T.T., and Bruno. A.V. 1981. Venture capital decision-making: Preliminary results from three empirical studies. *Frontiers of Entrepreneurship Research.* Wellesley, Mass.: Babson College.

Tyebjee, T.T., and Bruno, A.V. September, 1984. A model of venture capitalist investment activity. *Management Science,* 30(9). 1051–1066.

Wells, W.A. 1974. Venture capital decision-making. Unpublished doctoral dissertation, Carnegie-Mellon University, Pittsburgh.

[6]

MANAGEMENT SCIENCE
Vol. 36, No. 10, October 1990
Printed in U.S.A.

ENTREPRENEURIAL ABILITY, VENTURE INVESTMENTS, AND RISK SHARING*

RAPHAEL AMIT, LAWRENCE GLOSTEN AND EITAN MULLER

Faculty of Commerce and Business Administration, University of British Columbia, Vancouver, B.C., V6T 1Y8 Canada

Graduate School of Business, Columbia University, New York, New York 10027

Recanati Graduate School of Business Administration, Tel-Aviv University, Tel-Aviv, Israel 69978

A number of issues that relate to the desirability and implications of new venture financing are examined within a principal-agent framework that captures the essence of the relationship between entrepreneurs and venture capitalists. The model suggests: (1) As long as the skill levels of entrepreneurs are common knowledge, all will choose to involve venture capital investors, since the risk sharing provided by outside participation dominates the agency relationship that is created. (2) The less able entrepreneurs will choose to involve venture capitalists, whereas the more profitable ventures will be developed without external participation because of the adverse selection problem associated with asymmetric information. (3) If a costly signal is available that conveys the entrepreneur's ability, some entrepreneurs will invest in such a signal and then sell to investors; these entrepreneurs, however, need not be the more able ones. The implications for new venture financing of these and other findings are discussed and illustrated by example.
(ENTREPRENEURSHIP; VENTURE CAPITAL; ADVERSE SELECTION; MORAL HAZARD; RISK REDUCTION)

1. Introduction

Numerous studies in the management and economics literature address qualitatively important and fundamental issues about entrepreneurs, their activities and behaviors, and the process of new venture formation. Baumol (1968), Drucker (1985), Kirzner (1985), Leibenstein (1968), MacMillan, Siegel and Narasimha (1985), MacMillan, Zemann and Narasimha (1987), Rumelt (1987), Schumpeter (1942), Teece (1987), Tyebjee and Bruno (1984) and others elaborate on the roles of entrepreneurs, their main characteristics, how they differ from managers, and the market functions of entrepreneurship. Relatedly, this literature also explores the essential elements of new venture formation, how value is created through the entrepreneurial process, and how venture investments are made by venture capital firms.

In addition, there are many descriptive field and empirical studies of the same issues that provide insights about entrepreneurs, their ventures in both independent and corporate settings, and the activities of venture capital firms. (See, for example, Tyebjee and Bruno 1984; Van de Ven, Hudson and Schroeder 1984; Timmons 1985; Brophy 1986; MacMillan and Day 1987; Cooper and Bruno 1987; Day 1988; and a comprehensive literature review by Low and MacMillan 1988.) Supplementing the descriptive and qualitative body of literature are manuscripts that provide rules-of-thumb and common wisdom criteria for developing new ventures (e.g., Brandt 1982), but which have no theoretical foundations.

However instructive, the received literature offers neither a predictive theory of the behavior of entrepreneurs nor much in the way of guidance for practice. That it is important to fill both of these gaps is evidenced by the great increases in entrepreneurial activity over the past two decades, accompanied by the high failure rate of new ventures.

* Accepted by Diana L. Day, John U. Farley, and Jerry Wind.

ENTREPRENEURIAL ABILITY, VENTURE INVESTMENTS, AND RISK SHARING   1233

In fact, a recent study (Bygrave, Fast, Khoylian, Vincent and Yue 1988) documents the alarmingly low rates of return for venture capital funds. (The mean IRR was less than 10% by the end of 1985.) As investors may seek compound annual rates of returns in excess of 70% for early stage financing, the reported low average return reflects the high failure rate of entrepreneurial ventures. Among the intuitive explanations for this phenomenon are poor risk management by entrepreneurs, the availability to investors of inherently less profitable ventures, bad luck, or the inability of the venture capitalists to evaluate adequately the abilities of entrepreneurs to turn their ideas into viable enterprises.

The purpose of this study is to investigate analytically these and other issues that relate to the behavior of entrepreneurs, focusing on the decisions of entrepreneurs to develop their ventures independently or with venture capitalists. Within a principal-agent framework that captures the essence of the venture capital/entrepreneur relationship, we examine a number of unanswered theoretical questions including: who decides to enter into an agreement with outsiders? Why? How is this decision related to the unobservable ability of the entrepreneur, the desire to share risk, or the need for capital? Would it be worthwhile for the entrepreneur to expend resources to convey his ability to outside investors before involving them in the venture?

2. Entrepreneurs and Entrepreneurial Ventures

No clear definition prevails as to what constitutes the creation of an entrepreneurial venture; however, the act of innovation that involves endowing existing resources with new wealth-producing capacity (Drucker 1985) is central to the conceptualization. The innovation that lies at the heart of the entrepreneurial activity is not restricted to a technological invention which results from R&D or to an innovative cost-reducing process. It may simply involve a new application of existing technologies, a product or a service innovation, or a new way or place of doing business. Whatever form it takes, however, there is a substantial amount of ex-ante uncertainty about the wealth-producing capacity of the newly created capital. This uncertainty has two main sources. The feasibility and market acceptance (or the production and demand functions) of the innovation and the pace at which imitation will erode the extraordinary profit from the innovation are unknown ex-ante (see Kamien and Schwartz 1982; Teece 1987, Chapter 9). If the imitation is instantaneous, then no surplus entrepreneurial profits will result. The source of the entrepreneurial rents that may be inherent in the innovation is the rareness, limited imitability and tradeability and importance to customers of the bundle of firm-specific assets that are created by the entrepreneur.

Our conceptualization of an entrepreneurial activity suggests that it centers on the entrepreneur's *ability* (talent, skill, experience, ingenuity, leadership, etc.) to combine tangible and intangible assets in new ways and to deploy them to meet customer needs in a manner that could not easily be imitated. This ability may be known to the entrepreneur but unknown to outsiders, such as venture capitalists. The inability of outsiders to assess the venture founders' core attributes, namely their entrepreneurial skills and abilities, may affect both the decisions of entrepreneurs to involve outsiders and the prices venture capital firms may be willing to pay for new ventures. Indeed, our discussion explicitly considers this asymmetry of information.

3. Related Literature and Model Overview

Surprisingly little theoretical, quantitative, and rigorous literature focuses on decisions of entrepreneurs to develop their ventures and the bases for entrepreneurial investment decisions. In fact, the issue of involving venture investors does not typically arise because research begins with the assumption that outside financing is required to develop the venture (Chan, Siegel, and Thakor 1987; Hirao 1988). Presumably, at some cost to the venture's future profits, an able entrepreneur might be willing either to forgo outside investment or to borrow funds personally.

Kihlstrom and Laffont (1979) consider a related issue. In a general equilibrium framework under uncertainty, they focus on risk aversion as the determinant that explains which individuals become entrepreneurs and which work as laborers. They implicitly assume that all potential entrepreneurs are equally able, and find that, at equilibrium, the less risk-averse individuals become entrepreneurs, while the more risk-averse choose to become laborers. As not all potential entrepreneurs may be equally able or equally industrious in the development of their venture, it seems useful to consider these attributes along with the risk-bearing aspects of new venture formation in a formal analysis.

In our model, the entrepreneur is characterized as having some given level of ability. He chooses the level of effort he is willing to expend and the level of capital investment required to form the venture and to realize an uncertain payoff. Thus, the size of the expected state-contingent ultimate payoff is a function of the ability of the entrepreneur, the level of effort expended, and the capital invested.

In order to analyze whether the entrepreneur should develop the venture independently or with outside equity investors, we posit that a distinguishing feature of the entrepreneur's reward system is the relationship between the ultimate profits from the venture and his share. The independent entrepreneur is rewarded by the entire profits, whereas the entrepreneur who involves outsiders may only be rewarded by some fraction of future profits. When equity investors are involved, we allow the form of the sharing agreement of the ultimate payoff to be chosen by them. Indeed, the sharing of ultimate payoff between the entrepreneur-manager and the venture capitalist, who both face risk, is consistent with stylized facts about venture capital contracts. (See Chan, Siegel, and Thakor 1987 for details.) Our model considers the risk bearing aspects as well as the ability and efforts of the entrepreneur in determining the sharing arrangement.

Admittedly, we take an extreme view in that we consider the decision to involve investors as an "all or nothing" decision. Once the decision is made, the entrepreneur is assumed to turn over to the investors the right to determine the sharing arrangement. The investors, in turn, maximize their profits by determining the entrepreneur's share of ultimate payoff, the size of their new investment, and the entrepreneur's level of effort, a point to which we shall return.

Our model is designed to predict which entrepreneurs will decide to enter into an agreement with venture capitalists. We note here that our first result, using a model in which investors are risk neutral and the entrepreneur is risk averse, predicts that every entrepreneur will wish to involve outsiders. We find that as long as there is no private information about the skill of the entrepreneur, entrepreneurs will sell out to investors. This occurs because the risk sharing provided by outside participation dominates the agency relationship that is created.

The prediction is strong, and armchair empiricism would suggest that such action is not consistent with observed behavior, since some entrepreneurs do not sell out. Presumably they do not do so because they do not expect to get full value for their ideas, either because of noncompetitive aspects in the capital markets or because the entrepreneur and outsiders have different information about the venture's potential. Our focus is on the latter explanation. The conclusions of the analysis of the model with asymmetric information are that: (1) As long as the pool of projects is good enough and the entrepreneur is slightly risk averse or his need for new funds is not trivial, there will always be some entrepreneurs who will sell out; (2) If only a proportion of entrepreneurs sell out, it is the less profitable ventures—those started by less capable entrepreneurs—that are sold, whereas the more profitable ventures are retained by the more skillful entrepreneurs; and (3) Under certain circumstances, it becomes worthwhile for the entrepreneur to expend resources to convey his ability to outsiders before settling on a contract.

ENTREPRENEURIAL ABILITY, VENTURE INVESTMENTS, AND RISK SHARING   1235

For the purposes of this study, we focus on the behavior of a risk-averse entrepreneur in an independent setting who seeks to maximize expected utility of terminal wealth.

4. The Model

We follow the methodology of a principal-agent problem (Harris and Raviv 1978; Holmstrom 1979), and let X denote the random profits from the venture, gross of any new investment. The density of X depends upon the endowed skill level of the entrepreneur, denoted by γ; his chosen level of activity (or effort), denoted by a; and the magnitude of investment in the venture, denoted by I. Formally, let $f(x; \gamma, a, I)$ denote the density of the profits evaluated at the realization x, for an entrepreneur with skill level γ, when activity a and a new investment I are chosen. We assume that larger values of γ, a, and I lead to a first order stochastic dominance relation. Thus, letting $f_i(x; \gamma, a, I)$ denote the derivative of the density with respect to the ith parameter, $\int h(x) f_i(x; \gamma, a, I) > 0$ for any increasing function $h(\cdot)$ and for $i = \gamma, a, I$.

First we formulate the problem of an unfettered entrepreneur. He has a utility function U (increasing and concave) defined over future wealth. Furthermore, there is disutility associated with choosing larger levels of activity a. We assume that the utility of wealth and the disutility of the activity are separable. Thus, the utility of payoff x when activity a is chosen is $U(x) - V(a)$, where $V(\cdot)$ is normalized so that it is zero when there is no activity.

The entrepreneur who develops the venture on his own has the option of using his own assets, or he may borrow fully collateralized funds (i.e., the lender is not making a risky loan) to develop the venture. Let $B(I)$ be the cost of raising I where $B(I) \geq I$. A strict inequality may hold when borrowing occurs. This entrepreneur therefore chooses a and I in order to maximize expected utility given by

$$\underset{a,I}{\text{Maximize}} \int U(x - B(I)) f(x; \gamma, a, I) - V(a). \tag{1}$$

Let $u^*(\gamma)$ denote the maximum utility in (1), and let a_c and I_c be respectively the optimal activity level and the investment chosen by the entrepreneur.

Should the entrepreneur choose to involve outside investors, we presume that the following sequence of events occurs. The entrepreneur solicits bids for the company, and takes the maximum bid w. This bid is a fixed amount of capital which is independent of the entrepreneur's demonstrated skill and eventual profits from the venture. It is paid to the entrepreneur in case he decides not to continue with the venture after the sale to investors or in case the investors decide to relieve the entrepreneur from productive control. If the entrepreneur stops managing, he is enjoined from pursuing the activity. This amount w is commonly referred to as the buyout option in venture capital contracts (Chan, Siegel, and Thakor 1987).

After accepting the bid w, the entrepreneur cedes the right of determining his share of the ultimate payoff to the venture capital investors. As the entrepreneur's skill level γ will eventually be revealed, we assume that when the sharing agreement is made γ can be contracted on directly.[1] The risk neutral investors therefore determine their investment level I, the entrepreneur's activity level a, and the entrepreneur's share of ultimate profits $s(x)$, so as to maximize their profits. This maximization is subject to the entrepreneur's willingness to manage the venture after he sells out to investors and to an incentive compatibility constraint on the activity choice. Consistent with the principal-agent lit-

---

[1] If the ability of the entrepreneur is not known when the sharing agreement is determined, then a revelation contract (or sorting condition) that will induce the entrepreneur to report his true ability is required. It is, however, beyond the scope of this study to consider a setting that includes the revelation game.

erature (Holmstrom 1979), the actual actions chosen cannot be observed. Specifically the investors' problem is to maximize profits (the support of x does not depend on the activity level a):

$$\text{Maximize} \int (x - s(x)) f(x; \gamma, a, I) - I \qquad (2)$$

s.t.

$$\int U(s(x)) f(x; \gamma, a, I) - V(a) \geq U(w), \qquad (3)$$

$$a \text{ maximizes} \int U(s(x)) f(x; \gamma, a, I) - V(a). \qquad (4)$$

Assuming a solution exists, let $\text{NPV}(w, \gamma)$ denote the maximized value of the objective function (2). Inequality (3) states that the entrepreneur is at least as well off after he expended the effort a to develop the venture as he would have been had he walked away from it with the buyout payment w. Constraint (4) insures incentive compatibility; that is, it assures the investors that the entrepreneur will choose their profit maximizing level of effort.

If, during the bidding, the skill level of the entrepreneur is known to the outside investors, then competition among potential investors will determine the bid $w(\gamma)$ which, as long as the set is nonempty, satisfies

$$w(\gamma) = \max \{ w: \text{NPV}(w, \gamma) \geq 0 \}. \qquad (5)$$

It can be verified that $\text{NPV}(w, \gamma)$—the maximized value of the objective function—is continuous in w.

If the skill level of the entrepreneur is not known during the bidding, then competition among investors will lead to a bid so that investors expect a zero NPV investment. This expectation is taken over the skill level the investors expect to face.

5. Bidding with Common Knowledge

We first analyze the case in which the skill level is common knowledge during the bidding for the venture. Our first result concerns the consistency of the model. We prove that as long as the project is worthwhile to the entrepreneur—that is, $u^*(\gamma) \geq U(0)$—there is a $w(\gamma)$ which makes the investment a zero net present value one. The existence of such a price is shown by arguing that if the investors pay zero for the venture, then it is a nonnegative NPV investment. Furthermore, if they pay a very high price it will be a negative NPV investment. By continuity, there is a w that makes the venture a zero NPV investment.

PROPOSITION 1. *Assume that for a skill level γ, the entrepreneur finds the venture attractive; that is, $u^*(\gamma) \geq U(0)$. Then there exists a nonnegative $w(\gamma)$ satisfying* $\text{NPV}(w(\gamma), \gamma) = 0.$

PROOF. See the Appendix.

Having established the consistency of the relationship between the investors and the entrepreneur, we now address the issue of the entrepreneur's decision to sell out. Before presenting the result, we note the intuitively appealing observation that $\text{NPV}(w, \gamma)$ is nonincreasing in w, because increasing w increases the minimum utility that the entrepreneur must enjoy. This imposes a direct cost on the investors.

LEMMA 1. *The function $\text{NPV}(w, \gamma)$, the present value of the investment to the investors, is decreasing in the payment w.*

ENTREPRENEURIAL ABILITY, VENTURE INVESTMENTS, AND RISK SHARING   1237

PROOF. Consider $w_1 > w_2$ with associated optimal solutions (s_1, a_1, I_1) and (s_2, a_2, I_2). Note that

$$\int U(s_1(x))f(x; \gamma, a_1, I_1) - V(a_1) \geq U(w_1) > U(w_2).$$

Thus, s_1, a_1, I_1 is feasible for the problem with w_2. Hence,

$$NPV(w_1, \gamma) = \int (x - s_1(x))f(x; \gamma, a_1, I_1) - I_1$$

$$\leq \int (x - s_2(x))f(x; \gamma, a_2, I_2) - I_2 = NPV(w_2, \gamma). \quad Q.E.D.$$

We next show that every entrepreneur facing competitive investors will choose to sell out. The result is derived by showing that a *feasible* strategy for the investors is to offer a compensation contract which mimics the payoffs the entrepreneur could expect on his own. However, the investors can construct a better contract by absorbing some of the risk. Thus, if the investors could offer an amount which would lead to the entrepreneur's indifference between selling out and developing the venture alone, the investment would be a nonnegative NPV investment. Since the competitive bidding insures that the investment will be a zero NPV investment, the investors in equilibrium will offer more than the amount needed to make the entrepreneur indifferent between retaining the venture and selling.

PROPOSITION 2. *Assuming that ability level is common knowledge at the time of the bidding, every entrepreneur will find it optimal to sell off the firm. That is,*

$$u^*(\gamma) \leq U(w(\gamma)) = \int U(s^*(x))f(x; \gamma, a^*, I^*) - V(a^*),$$

where $s^*(\cdot)$, a^* *and* I^* *are the optimizers for the principal-agent problem in* (2)–(4).

PROOF. We need to prove that $w(\gamma) \geq U^{-1}(u^*(\gamma))$, which can be established by showing that

$$NPV(U^{-1}(u^*(\gamma)), \gamma) \geq 0$$

and by using the above lemma.

$$NPV(U^{-1}(u^*(\gamma)), \gamma) = \underset{s(\cdot), a, I}{\text{Maximize}} \int (x - s(x))f(x; \gamma, a, I) - I$$

s.t.

$$\int U(s(x))f(x; \gamma, a, I) - V(a) \geq U^*(\gamma),$$

a maximizes $\int U(s(x))f(x; \gamma, a, I) - V(a).$

A feasible contract, action, and investment triple is $s(x) = x - B(I_e)$, a_e, I_e. So

$$NPV(U^{-1}(u^*(\gamma)), \gamma) \geq \int (x - x + B(I_e))f(x; \gamma, a_e, I_e) - I_e$$

$$= B(I_e) - I_e \geq 0. \quad Q.E.D.$$

We note several aspects of this result. First, the need for new investment is not critical to the results; it makes them stronger. The incentive to share risk is large enough to make the proposition true even if the density of the profits does not depend upon the new investment I. Strict preference does depend upon risk aversion. If the entrepreneur is risk neutral, then we know that the first best can be obtained in the principal-agent problem as well as when the entrepreneur works alone. Thus, if the entrepreneur is risk neutral, he is indifferent between retaining the firm or selling out. Of course, if the entrepreneur is risk neutral but faces difficulty in raising new investment (i.e., $B(I) > I$), then he will prefer to sell out. In such a way, the first best is obtained with the optimal amount of new investment, which is better than developing the venture without external participation.

Furthermore, it can be verified that the utility achieved by the entrepreneur who involves outside investors in the venture is equal to the utility achieved if competition among investors solves the following problem:[2]

$$\underset{s(\cdot),a,I}{\text{Maximize}} \int (U(s(x))f(x; \gamma, a, I) - V(a) \tag{6}$$

s.t.

$$\int (x - s(x))f(x; \gamma, a, I) - I \geq 0, \tag{6a}$$

$$a \text{ maximizes} \int U(s(x))f(x; \gamma, a, I) - V(a). \tag{6b}$$

It should be noted that the entrepreneur need not enjoy limited liability; that is, $s(x)$ is not restricted to being nonnegative. Certainly, the entrepreneur has no interest, ex ante, in insisting upon limited liability. This can be seen by noting the equality of the utility achieved in our modeling of the relationship and that of Chan, Siegel and Thakor. Restricting $s(x)$ to be nonnegative in the second formulation (problem (6)–(6b)) will lead to no greater expected utility, and if the nonnegativity constraint is binding there will be lower expected utility. On the other hand, our failure to restrict $s(x)$ may be inconsistent with bankruptcy law. That is, the contract may not be enforceable in states in which $s(x)$ is negative. The results above will go through if we restrict $s(x)$ to be greater than or equal to $[\underline{x} - B(I_e)]$, where $\underline{x}$ is the smallest possible realization of X. That is, if the entrepreneur's problem, as we have formulated it, is consistent with bankruptcy law, then $s(x)$, so restricted, is consistent with bankruptcy law (and hence enforceable) and our results remain intact.

6. Bidding with Asymmetric Information

Since entrepreneurs do not always sell out, another explanation must be sought. We suspect that it lies in private information about the skill level. The problem can be seen by considering an extreme case. Suppose the entrepreneur is risk neutral and there is no need for new investment. If the investors price the firm based on the average skill level, then only those entrepreneurs with ability below the average will sell out. The investment will then be a poor one. No matter what price is set during the bidding, only those whose ability is worse than the investor-perceived expected ability of the entrepreneur will sell out. Consequently, the adverse selection problem is so severe that there will never be any selling out. If the entrepreneur is risk averse, then the market may not break down completely. In this case, some entrepreneurs may sell out while others may develop the venture on their own.

We show that, as long as the entrepreneurs are somewhat risk averse and the minimum skill level is not too low, some or all entrepreneurs will sell out. If only some sell out,

---

[2] This is the formulation adopted by Chan, Siegel and Thakor (1987).

ENTREPRENEURIAL ABILITY, VENTURE INVESTMENTS, AND RISK SHARING   1239

they will be those with lower skill levels. The investors will still find that, on average, the purchase of the ventures is a zero NPV investment, but the price will be relatively low and the ventures will not be outstanding performers.

To describe the environment with informational asymmetry, we need some further assumptions and notations. Assume that from the perspective of the investors, γ is distributed on some interval $[\underline{\gamma}, \bar{\gamma}]$. Further, assume that $u^*(\underline{\gamma}) \geq U(0)$. Finally,[3] we assume that $NPV(w, \gamma)$ is increasing in γ.

Define $\bar{w}$ by $U(\bar{w}) = u^*(\bar{\gamma})$; that is, $\bar{w} \geq 0$ is the amount needed to get the most skillful entrepreneur to sell out. Further, define $\underline{w}$ by $U(\underline{w}) = u^*(\underline{\gamma})$; that is, $\underline{w} \geq 0$ is the amount needed to get the least skillful entrepreneur to sell out. Note that $u^*(\gamma)$ is strictly increasing in γ, so that the entrepreneur with skill level γ will sell out for w if $\gamma \leq u^{*-1}(U(w))$. Let $e(w)$ denote the investor's expectation function:

$$e(w) = E[NPV(w, \gamma)|\text{entrepreneur sells for } w].$$

No entrepreneur will sell out for less than $\underline{w}$, so the investors' expectation function $e(w)$ for $w \geq \underline{w}$ is given by

$$e(w) = \begin{cases} NPV(w, \underline{\gamma}), & w = \underline{w}, \\ E[NPV(w, \gamma)|\gamma \leq u^{*-1}(U(w))], & \underline{w} < w < \bar{w}, \\ E[NPV(w, \gamma)], & w \geq \bar{w}. \end{cases} \quad (7)$$

Equilibrium in the asymmetric information case is[4]

$$w^* = \text{Max}(w: e(w) = 0). \quad (8)$$

Define γ^* to be such that $u^*(\gamma^*) = U(w^*)$. If $\gamma > \gamma^*$ the entrepreneur will not sell, while if $\gamma < \gamma^*$ the entrepreneur will sell.

PROPOSITION 3.   *If the expectation function $e(w)$ is continuous in w, then there exists a bid w^* such that $e(w^*) = 0$, and it is larger than the bid that will yield a zero NPV for the venture with the least skillful entrepreneur, which is larger than the bid needed to get the least skillful entrepreneur to sell out, i.e., $w^* \geq w(\underline{\gamma}) \geq \underline{w}$.*

PROOF.   Note that

$$e(w^*(\underline{\gamma})) = E[NPV(w(\underline{\gamma}), \gamma)|u^*(\gamma) \leq U(w(\underline{\gamma}))] \geq NPV(w(\underline{\gamma}), \underline{\gamma}) = 0.$$

Furthermore, if w is very large, $e(w)$ is $E[NPV(w, \gamma)]$, which can be made negative (see Proposition 1). Hence, by continuity of $e(w)$ there exists w^* satisfying $e(w^*) = 0$. Furthermore, $w^* \geq w(\underline{\gamma}) \geq \underline{w}$ (by Proposition 2).   Q.E.D.

If $NPV(\underline{w}, \underline{\gamma})$ is strictly positive, as will be the case if the entrepreneur is risk averse or if he faces additional costs of obtaining new financing, then w^* will be strictly greater than $\underline{w}$, and hence γ^* will be strictly greater than $\underline{\gamma}$. That is, the venture capital market does not break down completely in that there will be some interval of entrepreneurs (indexed by their skill level) who will sell out to investors.

The intuitive explanation of why there is not a complete breakdown of the market is as follows. Suppose the investors start out anticipating the worst and bid $w(\underline{\gamma})$. Then they know they will attract entrepreneurs with the lowest skill level, but they also know they will attract risk-averse entrepreneurs with a higher skill level. Thus, they expect positive profits at $w(\underline{\gamma})$ and hence w^* will be set higher in equilibrium.

---

[3] It can be shown that $NPV(w, \gamma)$ is increasing in γ if $f(x; \gamma, a, I) = h(x; g(\gamma, a, I))$ where $g_{aa} \leq 0$ and $g_{a\gamma} \geq 0$.

[4] There may be several bids w satisfying $E(w) = 0$. We assume that competition will lead to the largest being chosen.

The assumption that the venture is worthwhile even for the least skillful entrepreneur is an important one for showing that some entrepreneurs will sell out. If this is not the case, then (following the formalism above) $\underline{w}$ could be negative as could be w^*. But in this case, entrepreneurs will either quit or continue the venture on their own.

It is logically possible for there to be no market breakdown whatsoever, i.e. $w^* \geq \bar{w}$. This will occur if there is relatively little uncertainty about γ, or if entrepreneurs are very risk averse, or if personal borrowing is very costly for the entrepreneur.

7. Information about Entrepreneurial Ability

In the asymmetric information case we observed that an entrepreneur with ability γ will not sell out if $\gamma > \gamma^*$. Recall that γ^* corresponds to the equilibrium bid w^*. Note that w^* was established in an informational setting in which investors were not able to assess the entrepreneur's unique ability. The entrepreneur may find it worthwhile to invest in accurate and verifiable information about his skill level if the technology for generating such a signal is available and affordable. We now turn to the question of who will generate a perfectly revealing signal that eliminates information asymmetries and then sell to investors.

We assume that the perfectly revealing signal can be generated at a cost C. It is obvious that an entrepreneur will not plan to generate a signal and then develop the venture alone. Consequently, there are three possibilities: sell without a signal for some amount w^{**}, generate a signal and sell for the resulting competitive bid (which is a function of γ), and develop the venture alone without generating a signal.

If an entrepreneur invests in a signal and sells the venture, he will get utility $U(\hat{w}(\gamma, C))$, where $\hat{w}(\gamma, C)$ is derived below. After seeing the signal, investors know that if they obtain rights to the venture they will solve

$$\text{Maximize} \int (x - s(x)) f(x; \gamma, a, I) - I$$

s.t. $$\int U(s(x) - C) f(x; \gamma, a, I) - V(a) \geq U(w - C),$$

$$a \text{ maximizes} \int U(s(x) - C) f(x; \gamma, a, I) - V(a).$$

Define $\hat{w}$ by $\hat{w} = w - C$ and $\hat{s}(x) = s(x) - C$. Then the equivalent problem is

$$\text{Maximize} \int (x - \hat{s}(x)) f(x; \gamma, a, I) - I - C$$

s.t. $$\int U(\hat{s}(x)) f(x; \gamma, a, I) - V(a) \geq U(\hat{w}),$$

$$a \text{ maximizes} \int U(\hat{s}(x)) f(x; \gamma, a, I) - V(a).$$

The maximized net present value is $\text{NPV}(\hat{w}, \gamma) - C$. In equilibrium, $\hat{w}$ will be set so that

$$\hat{w}(\gamma, C) = \max (w: \text{NPV}(w, \gamma) \geq C).$$

Note that $\hat{w}(\gamma, C)$ is increasing in γ.

If an entrepreneur does not generate a signal, but sells out at w^{**}, he will realize utility $U(w^{**})$. The competitive bid, w^{**}, is determined by

$$w^{**} = \text{MAX} \{ w: E[\text{NPV}(w, \gamma) | \text{entrepreneur sells for } w \text{ with no signal}] = 0 \}. \quad (9)$$

Proof of the existence of $w^{**} \geq w(\underline{\gamma})$ is identical to the proof of the existence of w^*.

ENTREPRENEURIAL ABILITY, VENTURE INVESTMENTS, AND RISK SHARING   1241

We first investigate the relation between w^* and w^{**}. Intuitively, if the signal is feasible, then the investors face an additional adverse selection problem. The case of an entrepreneur wishing to sell without a signal may be worse for investors than that of an entrepreneur wishing to sell when a signal is not an option. The proof is in the following proposition.

PROPOSITION 4.   *The bid when a signal is not an option, w^*, is not smaller than the bid when a signal is an option, w^{**}; i.e. $w^* \geq w^{**}$.*

PROOF.   Define $M(\gamma) = \text{Max}\ [U(\hat{w}(\gamma, C)), u^*(\gamma)]$. If an entrepreneur chooses to sell at some w without a signal, it must be that $U(w) \geq M(\gamma)$. Note that for any w the set $\{\gamma: U(w) \geq M(\gamma)\}$ is contained in the set $\{\gamma: U(w) \geq u^*(\gamma)\}$. Since $M(\gamma)$ is increasing in γ, we have that

$$E[\text{NPV}(w, \gamma) | U(w) \geq M(\gamma)] \leq e(w),$$

where $e(w)$ is defined by (7). Since w^* is the largest w such that $e(w)$ is zero, and since if w is very large, $e(w) < 0$, we have that

$$E[\text{NPV}(w, \gamma) | U(w) \geq M(\gamma)] \leq e(w) < 0 \qquad \text{for} \qquad w > w^*.$$

Thus, $w^{**} \leq w^*$.   Q.E.D.

The equilibrium bid w^{**} made when a signal is possible but not offered (as in (9)) can, however, be equal to w^*, the equilibrium bid made when no signal is possible (as in (8)). If an entrepreneur with ability γ^* (recall that we defined γ^* to be such that $u^*(\gamma^*) = U(w^*)$) weakly prefers developing the venture alone to generating the signal and selling, w^* and w^{**} will be equal. Intuitively, if this condition is satisfied, then at w^*, the entrepreneur is indifferent between selling without an entrepreneurial ability signal and developing the venture alone. But this is precisely the condition that determines w^*, and hence w^{**} will equal w^*. Thus we have

COROLLARY 1.   *If $u^*(\gamma^*) \geq U(\hat{w}(\gamma^*, C))$, then $w^* = w^{**}$.*

PROOF.   From Proposition 4, $w^{**} \leq w^*$. However, under the condition of the corollary,

$$E[\text{NPV}(w^*, \gamma) | U(w^*) \geq M(\gamma)] = E[\text{NPV}(w^*, \gamma) | \gamma \leq M^{-1}(U(w^*))]$$
$$= E[\text{NPV}(w^*, \gamma) | \gamma \leq u^{*-1}(U(w^*))] = 0,$$

since $M(\gamma^*) = u^*(\gamma^*) = U(w^*)$.   Q.E.D.

In the setting of Corollary 1, the two bids are the same. However, they are not in general equal. In particular, suppose that the signal is costless. Failure to provide a costless signal tells the investors that the entrepreneur is worse than the average. That is, if a bid is offered so that the entrepreneurs who sell are the ones whose ability is low, then the investors lose money. Thus, the only way they can protect themselves is to make a bid based on the profitability of the least skillful entrepreneur. But if this is the case, then all but the least skillful entrepreneurs will choose to generate a signal.

PROPOSITION 5.   *If the cost of the signal is zero, then all entrepreneurs will prefer to generate the signal. That is, $w^{**} = w(\gamma)$.*

PROOF.   If $C = 0$, then $U(\hat{w}(\gamma, C)) = U(w(\gamma)) \geq u^*(\gamma)$. Thus, if $w > w(\gamma)$,

$$E[\text{NPV}(w, \gamma) | U(w) \geq M(\gamma)] = E[\text{NPV}(w, \gamma) | U(w) \geq U(w(\gamma))]$$
$$= E[\text{NPV}(w, \gamma) | w \geq w(\gamma)]$$
$$< E[\text{NPV}(w(\gamma), \gamma) | w \geq w(\gamma)] = 0,$$

by the definition of $w(\gamma)$. Thus, w^{**} must be equal to $w(\gamma)$.   Q.E.D.

1242   RAPHAEL AMIT, LAWRENCE GLOSTEN AND EITAN MULLER

Figure 1 presents various possibilities for the relation between the entrepreneur's utility when a report is generated at some positive cost (i.e., $U(\hat{w}(\gamma, C))$) and the entrepreneur's utility derived from developing the venture alone ($u^*(\gamma)$). The figures illustrate several intuitively appealing results. First, if the signal is very inexpensive, then we would expect the situation to be as depicted in a_1. In this case, all entrepreneurs sell, but lower skill entrepreneurs do so without signalling their ability. Recall from the above proposition that if the cost is in fact zero, all entrepreneurs will generate the signal. The opposite situation is depicted in b_1, a case in which the signal is very expensive. This situation is identical to the situation in which generating the signal is impossible.

The remaining illustrations in Figure 1 describe intermediate cases. Note that it is not a general result that high-ability entrepreneurs necessarily generate the signal nor necessarily develop the project alone (compare the cases in a_2 and b_2). In all cases, there is an interval of low-ability entrepreneurs who choose to sell without the signal. The intuitive explanation for this result is the same as that which accounts for the interval of low-ability entrepreneurs who choose to sell out when no ability signal is possible. That is, given the equilibrium price, the utility of such low-ability entrepreneurs exceeds their utility had they chosen to develop the venture alone.[5]

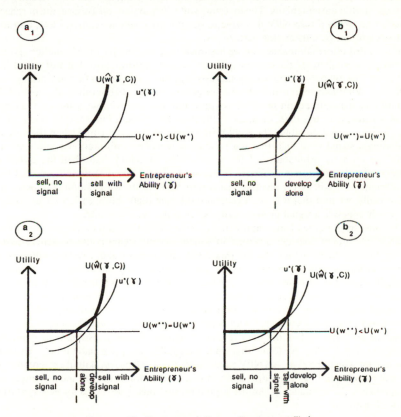

FIGURE 1. The Entrepreneur's Venture Development Choices.

[5] A detailed example of the asymmetric information case, which illustrates both analytically and graphically the implications of our general results, is available from the authors.

8. Conclusions and Implications

In the analytical model an uncertain payoff from an entrepreneurial venture is assumed to depend on the ability of the entrepreneur, the efforts devoted to developing the venture, and the amount of capital that is invested. In considering the desirability of financing, entrepreneurs—who are assumed to know their abilities—seek to share risk and raise capital. While the entrepreneurs' abilities are a critical determinant of the ultimate payoff from the venture investment, the venture capitalists may be unable to assess accurately this ability when pricing the deal. This raises both moral hazard and adverse selection problems which we addressed by considering three informational settings.

First, we assumed that the entrepreneur's abilities are common knowledge. We found that all risk-averse entrepreneurs choose to involve risk-neutral venture capital investors, since the risk sharing provided by such outside participation dominates the agency relationship that is created. In the second setting we assumed asymmetry of information with respect to the entrepreneur's ability. That is, the entrepreneur knows his skill level while the venture capitalist does not. In this setting we found that because of the adverse selection problem that is created, it is the less profitable ventures—those started by less capable entrepreneurs—that are sold, whereas the more profitable ones are retained by the more skillful entrepreneurs. The investors will still find that, on average, the purchase of such ventures is a zero NPV investment, but the price will be relatively low, and the ventures will not be outstanding performers.

In the third informational setting we assumed that asymmetry of information exists, but that it is possible for the entrepreneur to invest in information that will reveal his skill level. The analysis of this setting suggests that there will always be some selling out by the less skillful entrepreneurs who do not generate a signal about their abilities. Also, we find that the equilibrium price for ventures that are sold without using an available signal will always be less than, or equal to, the price for ventures that are sold to investors when a signal is not possible. The equilibrium prices will be just equal when the cost of generating a signal is so high that not producing it has no informational implications about the ultimate profitability of the venture. We also find that when the signal is costless, all entrepreneurs will choose to produce a signal about their abilities, and the equilibrium price will be the one that yields zero NPV for the least skillful entrepreneur. Additionally, we find that it is not a general result that high-ability entrepreneurs either necessarily generate a signal or necessarily develop the venture alone.

The analysis presented leaves many unanswered theoretical and empirical issues. For instance, one might consider a setting in which a costly signal could be generated to reduce, but not to eliminate, the informational asymmetries about the entrepreneur's abilities. A model with incomplete signals may be particularly interesting in a dynamic setting in which the venture capitalist gradually learns about the entrepreneur's ability. Other theoretical extensions include the formulation and analysis of models that capture additional aspects of the adverse selection problem such as the revelation game, as well as the bargaining issues associated with negotiating the venture capital contract.

Our model helps explain the poor return of venture capital investments as reported by Bygrave et al. (1988). We found that while the equilibrium price paid for new ventures is the one for which the expected NPV equals zero, there will be less skillful entrepreneurs that will receive funding. The implication of this observation is that, to the detriment of entrepreneurs, the resistance of venture capital firms to raise prices paid for new ventures is indeed justified.[6]

[6] The authors thank Debra Aron, Ravi Jagannathan, Cynthia Montgomery, Don Siegel, Birger Wernerfelt, and seminar participants at the Universities of British Columbia, Chicago, Illinois, Indiana, Michigan, and Pennsylvania, as well as Northwestern, Purdue, Rice, Southern Methodist and Tel-Aviv Universities for helpful suggestions.

1244   RAPHAEL AMIT, LAWRENCE GLOSTEN AND EITAN MULLER

Appendix

PROOF OF PROPOSITION 1.   Consider NPV$(0, \gamma)$. A feasible contract, investment, and action triple is $s(x)$ $= x - B(I_e)$, I_e, a_e (recall that I_e and a_e are the solutions to the entrepreneur's problem). This triple is feasible since it satisfies the constraints of the investors' problem (3)–(4), respectively:

$$\int U(s(x))f(x; \gamma, a_e, I_e) - V(a_e) = \int U(x - B(I_e))f(x; \gamma, a_e, I_e) - V(a_e) = u^*(\gamma) \geq U(0),$$

and by definition a_e maximizes $\int U(x - B(I_e))f(x; \gamma, a, I_e) - V(a)$. Then,

$$\text{NPV}(0, \gamma) \geq \int [x - (x - B(I_e))]f(x; \gamma, a_e, I_e) - I_e = B(I_e) - I_e \geq 0.$$

Let s^0, a^0, I^0 be the first best solution when w is paid, and let $G(w, \gamma)$ be the maximized net present value of the first best problem:

$$\text{Maximize} \int (x - s(x))f(x; \gamma, a, I) - I$$

s.t.

$$\int U(s(x))f(x; \gamma, a, I) - V(a) \geq U(w),$$

Pointwise maximization implies that $s^0(x)$ must satisfy $\lambda = 1/U'(s^0(x))$ and hence s^0 is constant and positive. Note that from the constrained maximization we obtain

$$G_w(w, \gamma) = \frac{-U'(w)}{U'(s^0)}.$$

In order to satisfy the constraint of the first best problem, $s^0 > w$, and hence, $U'(s^0) < U'(w)$. This, in turn, implies that $G_w(w, \gamma) < -1$. Therefore, when w is large enough, $G(w, \gamma)$ is negative. Since $\text{NPV}(w, \gamma) \leq G(w, \gamma)$, $\text{NPV}(w, \gamma)$ must be negative for a sufficiently large w. Continuity proves the existence of $w^*(\gamma)$, for which $\text{NPV}(w(\gamma), \gamma) = 0$.   Q.E.D.

References

BAUMOL, W. J., "Entrepreneurship in Economic Theory," *Amer. Economic Rev.*, 38, 2 (1968), 64–71.

BRANDT, S. C., *Entrepreneuring: The Ten Commandments for Building a Growth Company*, Addison-Wesley, Reading, MA, 1982.

BROPHY, D. J., "Venture Capital Research," in D. L. Sexton and R. W. Smilor (Eds.), *The Art and Science of Entrepreneurship*, Ballinger, Cambridge, MA, 1986, 119–143.

BYGRAVE, W., N. FAST, R. KHOYLIAN, L. VINCENT, AND W. YUE, "Rates of Return on Venture Capital Investing: A Study of 131 Funds," in B. A. Kirchhoff, W. A. Long, K. H. Vesper and W. E. Wetzel, Jr. (Eds.), *Frontiers of Entrepreneurship Research*, Babson College, Babson Park, MA, 1988, 275–289.

CHAN, Y. S., D. SIEGEL AND A. V. THAKOR, "Learning, Corporate Control and Performance Requirements in Venture Capital Contracts," Finance Dept. Working Paper No. 36, J. L. Kellogg Graduate School of Management, Northwestern Univ., Evanston, IL, 1987.

COOPER, A. C. AND A. V. BRUNO, "Success among High-Technology Firms," *Business Horizons*, (April 1987), 16–23.

DAY, D. L., "An Empirical Test of Main and Contingent Effects of Relatedness in Corporate Venturing," in B. A. Kirchhoff, W. A. Long, K. H. Vesper and W. E. Wetzel, Jr. (Eds.), *Frontiers of Entrepreneurship Research*, Babson College, Babson Park, MA, 1988, 538–541.

DRUCKER, P. F., *Innovation and Entrepreneurship*, Harper and Row, New York, 1985.

HARRIS, M. AND A. RAVIV, "Some Results on Incentive Contracts with Applications to Education and Employment, Health Insurance, and Law Enforcement," *Amer. Economic Rev.*, 68 (1978), 20–30.

HIRAO, Y., "Learning and Incentive Problems in Repeated Partnerships: An Application to Venture Capital Finance," Dept. of Economics Working Paper, Univ. of Pennsylvania, Philadelphia, PA, 1988.

HOLMSTROM, B., "Moral Hazard and Observability," *Bell J. Economics*, 10, 1 (1979), 74–91.

KAMIEN, M. I. AND N. L. SCHWARTZ, *Market Structure and Innovation*, Cambridge Univ. Press, Cambridge, MA, 1982.

KIHLSTROM, R. E. AND J. J. LAFFONT, "A General Equilibrium Entrepreneurship Theory of Firm Formation Based on Risk Aversion," *J. Political Economy*, 87, 4 (1979), 719–748.

KIRZNER, I. M., *Discovery and the Capitalist Process*, Univ. of Chicago Press, Chicago, 1985.

LEIBENSTEIN, H., "Entrepreneurship and Development," *Amer. Economic Rev.*, 38, 2 (1968), 72–83.

ENTREPRENEURIAL ABILITY, VENTURE INVESTMENTS, AND RISK SHARING   1245

Low, M. B. AND I. C. MacMILLAN, "Entrepreneurship: Past Research and Future Challenges," *J. Management*, 14, 2 (1988), 139–161.

MacMILLAN, I. C. AND D. L. DAY, "Corporate Venturing into Industrial Markets: Dynamics of Aggressive Entry," *J. Business Venturing*, 2, 1 (1987), 29–40.

———, R. SIEGEL AND P. N. S. NARASIMHA, "Criteria Used by Venture Capitalists to Evaluate New Venture Proposals," *J. Business Venturing*, 1, 1 (1985), 119–128.

MacMILLIAN, I. C., L. ZEMANN AND P. N. S. NARASIMHA, "Criteria Distinguishing Successful from Unsuccessful Ventures in the Venture Screening Process," *J. Business Venturing*, 2, 2 (1987), 123–137.

RUMELT, R. P., "Theory, Strategy, and Entrepreneurship," in D. J. Teece (Ed.), *The Competitive Challenge: Strategies for Industrial Innovation and Renewal*, Ballinger, Cambridge, MA, 1987, 137–158.

SCHUMPETER, J. A., *Capitalism, Socialism, and Democracy*, First Ed., Harper and Brothers, New York, 1942.

TEECE, D. J., *The Competitive Challenge: Strategies for Industrial Innovation and Renewal*, Ballinger, Cambridge, MA, 1987.

TIMMONS, J. A., *New Venture Creation*, Second Ed., Richard D. Irwin, Homewood, IL, 1985.

TYEBJEE, T. T. AND A. V. BRUNO, "A Model of Venture Capitalist Investment Activity," *Management Sci.*, 30, 9 (1984), 1051–1066.

VAN DE VEN, A. H., R. HUDSON AND D. M. SCHROEDER, "Designing New Business Start Ups: Entrepreneurial, Organizational and Ecological Considerations," *J. Management*, 10, 1 (1984), 87–107.

[7]

THE EFFECTS OF VENTURE CAPITALISTS' CHARACTERISTICS ON THE STRUCTURE OF THE VENTURE CAPITAL DEAL*

by Edgar Norton and Bernard H. Tenenbaum

Previous research has found that venture capitalists seek to specialize. Such specialization occurs by way of geographical, industry, and investment stage preferences (Bygrave 1987, 1988; Gupta and Sapienza 1988; Tankersley 1989; Timmons 1990). Rosenstein, Bruno, Bygrave, and Taylor (1990) discovered the perceived contribution of the lead venture capital investor is greater if the lead investor is one of the top 20 venture capital firms that specialize in high-tech investment. Cluster analysis of survey data by MacMillan, Kulow, and Khoylian (1989) finds differences among venture capitalists with respect to their philosophy toward managing their portfolio firms; they detect three distinct philosophies which they label as "laissez faire," "moderate," and "close tracker."

If venture capitalists possess different specializations and management philosophies, the same may be true regarding preferences for investment vehicles. Unlike the typical capital structure decision addressed in the finance literature,

casual empiricism implies the venture capital investor, rather than the firm, plays the major role in determining the pricing and type of security to be purchased by investors. Thus, an analysis of venture capitalists' use of different investment vehicles is warranted.

Venture capitalists face three basic investment vehicles: common equity, preferred equity, and debt. While it is true that many provisions and covenants can be attached to any investment vehicle, the research discussed in this article, as part of an initial empirical study, focuses solely on these three deal structures. The analysis in this article will extend the study of deal structure influences contained in Norton and Tenenbaum (1992).

PRIOR EMPIRICAL RESEARCH

The main thrust of Norton and Tenenbaum (1992) was to gather and examine quantitative evidence on influences affecting the choice of deal structure by venture capital investors. By examining mean responses from 98 venture capitalists on 26 survey items, Norton and Tenenbaum provide empirical evidence on the positive and negative impacts of external and internal deal specific factors on the choice of common equity, preferred equity, and debt as financing structures. Norton and Tenenbaum

Dr. Norton is an associate professor of finance at Fairleigh Dickinson University, Madison, N.J.

Professor Tenenbaum is director of the George Rothman Institute of Entrepreneurial Studies and clinical professor at Fairleigh Dickinson University.

*The authors acknowledge financial support from a Fairleigh Dickinson University Research Grant-In-Aid. Assistance from Glenn Cates and the staff of the George Rothman Institute of Entrepreneurial Studies is also gratefully acknowledged.

found that survey respondents favored the use of preferred stock as a financing vehicle regardless of the presence or absence of various deal specific influences. They found that items encouraging the use of debt investments by venture capitalists included expectations that the portfolio firm would soon generate taxable income; the presence of collateralizable assets; production of a good or service that is resistant to economic cycles; and an investment involving a latter financing stage. Positive influences for common equity investments were expectations of a strong initial public offering market at cashout; expectations of a capital gains tax cut; a strong economy; venture capitalist control of a majority of the investee's voting stock; and a firm producing a recession resistant good or service.

Whereas this earlier work focused on deal specific influences affecting deal structure, the contribution of this present study is to examine the impact of venture capitalists' characteristics on deal structure. Driscoll (1974) and Mac-Millan, Siegel, and SubbaNarasimha (1985) state that a goal of venture capitalists is to control and manage risk. This article develops and tests hypotheses regarding the potential use of preferred equity and common equity investments as a means to do so.

DOES THE FORM OF INVESTMENT VEHICLE MATTER?

It is a fair question to ask if choice of an investment vehicle has any practical importance to the venture capitalist. If, by selecting various structures and covenants, the cash flow, security provisions, and voting rights are identical between two investment vehicles, the name given the investment contract is irrelevant; all investment structures are merely benign mutations of a standard contract. Thus, a zero coupon debt investment with a provision for voting

rights can be considered identical to a voting preferred or common equity issue that is not expected to pay dividends until the firm is ready to go public.

However, "costly contracting" (see Malitz 1986) will lead to cases where the form of vehicle and covenants are relevant as they can affect firm value and management incentives. The entrepreneurial team and venture capitalist(s) agree on a price, provisions, and covenants as that specific set of terms leads to an optimum tradeoff between costs and benefits, and risks and returns so that overall firm value is maximized.

Below we discuss several influences which may affect the choice of investment structure in line with the costly contracting perspective.

Factors Favoring the Use of Common Stock

As mentioned in Driscoll (1974), Mac-Millan, Siegel, SubbaNarasimha (1985), and Ruhnka and Young (1991), the major task facing venture capitalists is to manage risk and to seek downside protection. Equity is an appropriate investment if flexibility (both financial flexibility and flexibility with regard to meeting covenants) is needed to guide the firm in its formative stages or in difficult economic periods (Williamson 1988, Cornell and Shapiro 1988).

As a means to manage risk, evidence exists that venture capitalists seek to specialize in certain industries and products (Tankersley 1989). Venture capitalists, with their technical, marketing, and/or management expertise, seek to add more than just money to their portfolio firms; they also seek to add value (Sapienza and Timmons 1989; Rosenstein, Bruno, Bygrave, and Taylor 1990). The specialized knowledge possessed by venture capitalists helps them enter networks and gain access to information that flows between networking investors (Bygrave 1987, 1988). Bygrave found that the level of networking and deal syndication increases as the level of uncertainty regarding the investment rises. Bygrave also forecasts that smaller venture capital investors, with only a few partners and limited financial resources, will become more like "boutiques" in their desire to specialize in certain deals.

Therefore smaller, more specialized (and hence less diversified) venture capitalists, with their limited financial and personnel resources, may view themselves as co-partners with the entrepreneurial team seeking the success of the firm in early stage (i.e., high risk) investments. These venture investors may seek to manage their unsystematic risk exposure by playing an active role in working closely with the management team. An investment in common stock places investors on the same level as the management team and thus will emphasize the partnership relationship between the venture capitalist and entrepreneurial team.

Factors Opposing the Use of Common Stock

A concern of investors is if the invested capital will be used to help achieve venture success. Profits or positive cash flow may be appropriated by the management team rather than properly returned to the investors or reinvested to meet the firm's goals (Jensen and Meckling 1976, Jensen 1986).[1] Monitoring and opportunity costs which arise from restrictions placed on management via investment covenants are known as agency costs. A goal of investing is to minimize agency costs by structuring management incentives so management will make decisions that benefit investors.

Common stock, by placing investors on the same level as the management team, is not attractive as an investment mode if investors have concerns about control of the firm's cash flows and other potential agency problems. Such may be the case with a larger, more generalized venture capital firm, or with a venture capital firm falling into MacMillan, Kulow, and Khoylian's (1989) "laissez faire" or "moderate" categories.

Factors Favoring the Use of Debt

Debt places the investor in the position of lender, not owner. As discussed by Williamson (1988), debt is an appropriate financing tool when rules are an appropriate governance structure. Debt financing may protect the investors' claim on firm assets and cash flow (to protect the investors' downside) to the detriment of the firm's future viability. Given both the high degree of risk prevalent in most venture capital deals and the potential for agency problems, debt may be perceived to be an attractive mode of financing by the venture capitalist.

Factors Opposing the Use of Debt

In the typical venture capital deal, most assets are intangible growth opportunities. In addition, operating risk is typically high, arising from technical risk and from lack of a sales track record for the new product or service. This is especially true for seed and other early stage deals.

Moreover, the characteristics of debt which give investors extra safety and protection will make it unpalatable in many venture capital deals. Debt may not be appropriate if investors and managers want flexibility to deal with intermittent cash flow and other crises. Debt also robs the growing entrepreneurial firm of precious cash flow, whereas deals involving common and preferred equity issues are typically structured so that dividends are not paid, nor do they

[1]For example, cash may be used to increase staff, perks, or salaries above optimal levels; or the team may seek to direct money to their own pet projects rather than focus on producing a marketable product which will give investors the largest return possible.

accumulate. Tax-deductible interest payments are usually unimportant to venture capital-backed firms with little, if any, operating profit. Additionally, the use of debt financing may (a) preclude additional debt issues in the future and (b) make future equity issues more difficult to sell as debtholders will have a senior claim on firm cash flow and assets. Thus, even an investment structure such as zero coupon debt may not generally be attractive in a venture capital setting.

The Case for Preferred Equity Investments

The features of preferred equity allow investors to preserve the advantages of debt and common equity while retaining few of their drawbacks. By investing in preferred stock that has voting rights, investors can exercise some control over the firm and have a priority claim over the management team with respect to cash flow in case of success and with respect to asset liquidation in the case of venture failure.

Like debt, preferred equity gives investors protection against selfish managers, but without causing the firm to lose financial flexibility or cash flow. Like common equity, preferred stock allows flexibility to handle crises or meet covenants and has much of the upside return potential of common equity. Unlike common equity, preferred equity places the investors in a senior position, thereby reducing some agency concerns inherent with straight common equity. As it provides a means to control risk while maintaining the potential for large returns, preferred equity financing may be especially favored in early stage deals.

Conclusions on the Choice of Financing Structure

All financing vehicles are not alike in their ability to enhance firm value. From this section, it appears many ven-

ture capitalists will use preferred equity as an investment tool. Debt may only be appropriate for venture capital firms requiring steady cash flows from their portfolio firms or for venture capitalists investing in deals with characteristics conducive to debt finance (e.g., latter stage deals). Common equity may be used by investors seeking to control risk by forging a "team" relationship with the entrepreneur.

HYPOTHESIS BUILDING

In this section we develop hypotheses involving several investment strategies that may be used by venture capitalists. As debt is inappropriate as a vehicle for many venture capital investments, our tests focus on the choice of equity investment.

Risk Management

As discussed above and by Sahlman (1988), preferred stock has many attractive characteristics for managing risk in venture capital deals. As it helps to facilitate risk management and agency cost reduction, preferred stock should be the primary investment vehicle for venture capital deals, especially those involving high risk:

H_i: *Preferred stock will be the most frequently used financing structure in venture capital deals.*

Corollary: The use of preferred stock as a venture capitalist investment vehicle will increase in high risk situations such as:
(a) venture capitalists with large relative commitments to seed-round investments;
(b) venture capitalists with large relative commitments to first-round investments;
(c) venture capitalists that have investments in a small number of industries;
(d) venture capitalists that have investments in a small number of companies;
(e) venture capitalists with smaller amounts of funds to invest.

Items (a) and (b) obviously involve an investment philosophy containing a great deal of risk and uncertainty. Items (c), (d), and (e) of the corollary involve situations in which the venture capitalist may not be widely diversified. To help control unsystematic risk, such firms may rely more heavily on preferred equity financing.

Risk Management and Specialized Investors

As discussed previously, some early stage investors may manage and assist their portfolio firms with more of a "team-oriented" approach toward management. Because this approach involves staying close to and working with the entrepreneurial team, this strategy may also help to mitigate agency problems and to manage risk.

Common stock places investors on the same level as the management team and thus emphasizes the partnership relationship between the venture capitalist and entrepreneurial team. The team and investors will share in the rewards of a successful relationship. Of course, common equity deals still can be structured in such a way that venture capitalists possess majority control or other provisions to protect their investment.

Based upon this perspective, we propose a second hypothesis:

H_2: Venture capitalists that are smaller or more specialized (i.e., less diversified) will rely more heavily on a "team-oriented" investment philosophy. As a result, they will use relatively more common equity financing than larger or more diversified venture capitalists.

To empirically test these hypotheses, a survey instrument was developed to collect the necessary information from venture capitalists.

THE SURVEY INSTRUMENT

A survey instrument to examine venture capital investment structure was designed and pretested among eight venture capitalists. Their comments and suggestions were incorporated into the final survey format, and these venture capitalists were not included in the final mailings. Surveys were mailed in February and March 1990 to 300 members of the National Venture Capital Association; a second mailing to non-respondents occurred in May and June 1990. A total of 98 responses were received for a response rate of 32.7 percent. The cover letter promised the responses would be held in confidence. After comparing the mean responses from the first and second mailings, no statistical evidence of response bias existed.

Except for Norton and Tenenbaum (1992), prior empirical work in venture capital finance has not examined financing structure influences. Due to the proprietary nature of the deals, data bases do not exist to provide "hard" data for a study of deal structure. The responses to this survey project comprise a data base, albeit limited, for the study of venture capital financing preferences and influences. The survey instrument requested information on various items, including the characteristics of the respondent's venture capital firm, the percentage of financing done at different financing stages, and the use of different financing structures.

The typical responding venture capital firm is a private limited partnership (table 1A). Most are larger funds, with more than $50 million of total funds managed. Their portfolios are also fairly diversified; over half the respondents' portfolios have investments in more than seven industries and more than 30 companies.

Table 1A
PROFILE OF RESPONDENTS
FIRM TYPE AND
PORTFOLIO CHARACTERISTICS

Type of venture capital firm	N
Public	6
Private	89
Missing	3
Limited partnership	74
SBIC/MESBIC	10
Corporate Subsidiary	10
Other	7

(Some respondents checked more than one category.)

Number of industries represented in firm's portfolio (DIFINDS)

	N
1-3 industries:	10
4-6 industries:	25
7-9 industries:	28
10 or more:	33
Missing:	2

Number of companies in firm's portfolio (COMPS)

	N
1-9:	16
10-19:	20
20-29:	13
30 or more:	48
Missing:	1

Total funds managed within the venture capital firm (TOTFUNDS)

	N
< $10 million:	9
$11-20 million:	8
$21-30 million:	9
$31-40 million:	8
$41-50 million:	3
> $50 million:	59
Missing:	2

The individual numerical responses on the percentage of financing done at each financing stage are summarized in the four categories presented in table 1B. The financing stages listed are commonly used in the venture capital literature and are in standard use by practitioners (Sahlman 1990). The reported means are based upon the actual numerical responses.

Table 1B also reports the categorical responses and the mean categorical response for the percentage of venture

capitalists' investments that involve common stock, preferred stock, and debt financing. The most popular financing mode is preferred equity; the least used is debt. There is a wide range of responses for each financing choice, including venture capitalist firms that always use a particular financing mode (100 percent) or never use a particular financing mode (0 percent).

HYPOTHESIS TESTING

The hypotheses H_1 and H_2 can be tested using the venture capitalists' responses to the survey items. Table 1B has already provided evidence in favor of H_1, namely that preferred equity is the most popular financing structure among the respondents. Calculation of appropriate t-statistics indicates that the use of preferred equity is significantly greater than the use of common equity and debt.

Table 2 indicates the hypothesized relationships predicted by items (a) through (e) of the corollary. The corollary items are tested by computing the correlation coefficients between the venture capitalist's percentage of investments that use preferred equity financing, PSFIN, (from table 1B) and the variables of interest for corollary items (a) through (e). The correlations indicate uncertain support for the components of the corollary. The correlation between the percentage of seed stage financing and PSFIN has the correct sign but is statistically insignificant; the correlation between the percentage of first stage financing and PSFIN has the correct sign and is significant. The correlation between industry diversification and use of preferred equity (item c) has the incorrect sign and is not statistically significant. The hypotheses represented by (d) and (e) are not supported, as the statistically significant correlations have the wrong sign. Counter to the hypothesis, the empirical results imply that the

Table 1B
PROFILE OF RESPONDENTS
STAGES AND TYPE OF FINANCING

Percentage of financing done at each stage and number of firms

STAGE	0-9%	10-20%	21-49%	50% or more	Average	Number of firms
Start-up or seed	33	23	22	17	23.8%	95
First	25	27	32	10	22.1%	94
Second	29	28	30	7	18.3%	94
Third	46	24	18	6	13.1%	94
Bridge	72	16	4	2	5.6%	94
Other	60	9	11	14	17.1%	94

Percentage of current investments, by category, and number of firms

CATEGORY	1 0%	2 1-20%	3 21-40%	4 41-60%	5 61-80%	6 81-99%	7 100%	Number of firms
Common equity (CSFIN)	5	41	14	6	2	8	22	98
Preferred equity (PSFIN)	6	6	3	13	15	37	18	98
Debt	7	39	19	17	2	2	6	92

	Mean Categorical Response	Standard Deviation of Categorical Responses
Common equity:	3.708	2.137
Preferred equity:	5.146	1.692
Debt:	2.956	1.497

use of preferred equity as an investment tool rises as the venture capitalist is more diversified.

H_1 is supported in our sample; preferred stock is the most popular form of financing. However, the belief that preferred stock is popular as it is an effective means to control risk is questioned. Little evidence (item b) supports the corollary to H_1 and much evidence (items a, c, d, e) does not support it. Venture capitalists who have smaller amounts of funds to invest or who are undiversified must have other means of managing their exposure to unsystematic risk.

Table 3 presents evidence regarding H_2, which relates the use of common stock financing to investment philosophy. This table gives three means tests comparing the level of common stock financing between venture capitalists classified by size and diversification. Venture capitalists were placed into different categories based upon the number of industries (DIFINDS), companies (COMPS), and total funds managed (TOTFUNDS) in their portfolios. Venture capitalists which identified themselves as being in one of the first two categories for DIFINDS (i.e., six industries or fewer are represented in their portfolio) had no significant difference with regard to use of common equity financing than venture capitalists diversified across seven or more industries.

In support of H_2, the t-tests indicate that the low COMPS (less than 20 firms in the portfolio) investors use significantly more common equity financing than the high COMPS group. Additional support for H_2 is indicated in the TOTFUNDS analysis. The t-statistic indicates that smaller firms (i.e., TOTFUNDS of

Table 2
THE RELATIONSHIP BETWEEN PREFERRED STOCK FINANCING,
VENTURE CAPITALIST CHARACTERISTICS, AND STAGE OF FINANCING

Hypothesized and actual signs of the relationships between the use of preferred stock financing and (i) involvement in early stage financing (sub-hypotheses a and b); (ii) venture capitalist characteristics (sub-hypotheses c, d, and e). Tests reported below use correlation coefficients; probability values are reported for each in parenthesis.

Corollary hypothesis	Hypothesized sign	Correlation coefficient
a) Seed stage (Relative use of preferred equity should rise, the greater the percentage of seed stage financing done by the investor)	+	.0270 (.397)
b) First stage (Relative use of preferred equity should rise, the greater the percentage of first stage financing done by the investor)	+	.2448 (.009)
c) DIFINDS (Relative use of preferred equity should rise, the less diversified the investor is across different industries)	−	.0679 (.255)
d) COMPS (Relative use of preferred equity should rise, the less diversified the investor is across different companies)	−	.3811 (.000)
e) TOTFUNDS (Relative use of preferred equity should rise, the less funds the venture capitalist has for investment purposes)	−	.4671 (.000)

$30 million or less) use significantly more common equity as an investment vehicle than larger firms.

With the exception of industry diversification, it appears that venture capitalists which are smaller (TOTFUNDS) and diversified across fewer companies (COMPS) invest a higher percentage of common equity in their portfolio firms than larger, more diversified venture capitalists. These findings support H_2 and the use of the team approach to manage venture capital risk.[2]

CONCLUSION

This article reviews responses to a survey completed by 98 venture capitalists and seeks to determine if financing strategies differ across deals in different

[2]Further analysis shows that the relative involvement in seed stage investing is significantly greater for the smaller, less diversified venture capitalists. Correlations between the size/diversification measures and the percentage of funds invested in seed stage deals are all negative and significant at the 10 percent level. Analysis of the venture capitalists who reported that 50 percent or more of their funds are invested in seed stage deals shows that they are significantly smaller and less diversified than venture capitalists that are less heavily involved in seed stage deals.

financing stages and venture capitalists of different characteristics. We examine how strategies to manage risk can affect the choice of investment vehicle (common, preferred, and debt) and investment strategy. Due to its inappropriateness for early stage investments, debt is only cursorily examined in this research.

The most frequently used financing choice is preferred stock. However, contrary to expectations, the use of preferred equity as an investment tool did not increase in perceived high risk situations, such as early stage investments; neither did investors who are subject to greater amounts of unsystematic risk use relatively larger amounts of preferred equity. Rather, the evidence supported the hypothesis that smaller, less diversified investors in the sample made greater use of common equity investments.

A range of other research possibilities exist to further examine the role of fi-

Table 3
COMPARING VENTURE CAPITALIST USE OF COMMON EQUITY FINANCING

The analysis compares the use of common stock investments (CSFIN) by venture capitalists based on size and diversification characteristics. "Low DIFINDS" venture capitalists are invested in six or fewer industries; "low COMPS" investors have stakes in fewer than 20 different companies; "low TOTFUNDS" venture capitalists have $30 million or less in managed funds. Reported results include the average categorical response of venture capitalists in the "low" and "high" groups, the *t*-ratio from a test of the difference between two means, and a one-tailed probability value (in parenthesis).

	Low DIFINDS average CSFIN ranking:	High DIFINDS average CSFIN ranking:	*t*-ratio (*p*-value)
CSFIN:	3.8000	3.6721	0.28 (0.389)
Number of firms:	35	61	
	Low COMPS average CSFIN ranking:	High COMPS average CSFIN ranking:	*t*-ratio (*p*-value)
CSFIN:	4.3056	3.4098	2.01 (0.023)
Number of firms:	36	61	
	Low TOTFUNDS average CSFIN ranking:	High TOTFUNDS average CSFIN ranking:	*t*-ratio (*p*-value)
CSFIN:	4.1923	3.5143	1.38 (0.085)
Number of firms:	26	70	

nance in venture capital deals. Such research can provide insight to the venture capital community, entrepreneurs, as well as academic researchers and teachers in the area of entrepreneurial studies. Deal pricing, financing structure, covenants, and the degree of control exercised over the portfolio firm by the venture capitalist are areas in which casual empirical evidence presently dominates empirical research, hypothesis testing, and careful case study analysis. Also unresearched is the impact of these factors on the success or failure of the entrepreneurial firm and on the returns earned by venture capital investors. Theoretical or conceptual studies are also needed in order to best determine when one particular deal structure or set of covenants should be preferred to other possibilities.

REFERENCES

Bygrave, W. (1987), "Syndicated Investments by Venture Capital Firms: A Networking Perspective," *Journal of Business Venturing* 2 (Spring), 139-154.

Bygrave, W. (1988), "The Structure of the Investment Networks of Venture Capital Firms," *Journal of Business Venturing* 3 (Spring), 137-157.

Cornell, B., and A. Shapiro (1988), "Financing Corporate Growth," *Journal of Applied Corporate Finance* 1 (Summer), 6-22.

Driscoll, F. (1974), "Venture Capital: The Risk-Reward Business," *IEEE International Convention* (March).

Gupta, A., and H. Sapienza (1988), "The Pursuit of Diversity of Venture Capital Firms: Antecedents and Implications," in *Frontiers of Entrepre-*

neurship Research 8, ed. B. Kirchhoff, W. Long, W. McMullan, K. Vesper, W. Wetzel, Jr., Wellesley, Mass.: Babson College, 290-302.

Jensen, M. (1986), "Agency Costs of Free Cash Flow, Corporate Finance, and Takeovers," *American Economic Review* 76 (May), 323-329.

Jensen, M., and W. Meckling (1976), "Theory of the Firm: Managerial Behavior, Agency Costs, and Ownership Structure," *Journal of Financial Economics* 3 (October), 305-360.

MacMillan, I., D. Kulow, and R. Khoylian (1989), "Venture Capitalists' Involvement in Their Investments: Extent and Performance," *Journal of Business Venturing* 4 (January), 27-47.

MacMillan, I., R. Siegel, and P. SubbaNarasimha (1985), "Criteria Used by Venture Capitalists to Evaluate New Venture Proposals," *Journal of Business Venturing* 1 (Winter), 119-128.

Malitz, I. (1986), "On Financial Contracting: The Determinants of Bond Covenants," *Financial Management* 15 (Summer), 18-25.

Norton, E., and B. Tenenbaum (1992), "Factors Affecting the Structure of Venture Capital Deals," *Journal of Small Business Management* (July), 20-29.

Rosenstein, J., A. Bruno, W. Bygrave, and N. Taylor (1990), "How Much Do CEOs Value the Advice of Venture Capitalists on Their Boards?" unpublished working paper, Center for Entrepreneurial Studies, Babson College.

Ruhnka, J., and J. Young (1991), "Some Hypotheses About Risk in Venture Capital Investing," *Journal of Business Venturing* 6 (March), 115-133.

Sahlman, W. (1988), "Aspects of Financial Contracting in Venture Capital," *Journal of Applied Corporate Finance* 1 (Summer), 23-36.

——— (1990), "The Structure and Governance of Venture-Capital Organizations," *Journal of Financial Economics* 27 (October), 473-521.

Sapienza, H., and J. Timmons (1989), "Launching and Building Entrepreneurial Companies: Do the Venture Capitalists Add Value?" presentation at 1989 Babson Entrepreneurship Research Conference.

Tankersley, G. J. (1989), "How to Choose and Approach a Venture Capitalist," in *Pratt's Guide to Venture Capital Sources,* 13th edition, ed. J. Morris and S. Isenstein, Needham, Mass.: Venture Economics, Inc., 264-265.

Timmons, J. (1990), *New Venture Creation,* third edition. Homewood, Ill.: Irwin.

Williamson, O. (1988), "Corporate Finance and Corporate Governance," *Journal of Finance* 43 (July), 567-591.

[8]

Accounting and Business Research. Vol. 26, No. 2, pp. 153–168, 1996

Venture Capitalists, Unquoted Equity Investment Appraisal and the Role of Accounting Information

Mike Wright and Ken Robbie*

Abstract—This paper aims to add to the understanding of venture capitalists' investment decision-making behaviour by providing evidence relating to the general policies they adopt in their approaches to due diligence, valuation methods, benchmark rates of return and adjustments for risk. The evidence shows that in order to address potential adverse selection problems, venture capitalists use a wide range of accounting and non-accounting information and techniques relating to the specific factors concerning a particular investment. Unpublished accounting information and subjective information are important. Significant differences emerge in the approaches to valuation and use of accounting information for valuation purposes between types of venture capitalist, according both to their stage of investment focus and whether they were captive or independent.

Introduction

In two seminal papers, extending the work of Lee and Tweedie (1981), Arnold and Moizer (1984) and Moizer and Arnold (1984) provide important evidence on the behaviour of investment analysts in appraising investments in ordinary shares. Subsequent research has updated these findings for the UK and extended them to cover comparisons with Germany (Pike, Meerjanssen and Chadwick, 1993) and the use of annual reports by investment analysts (Day, 1986). The focus of attention has very much been on analysts' behaviour with respect to recommendations regarding buy/hold/sell decisions. The emphasis in these studies has also been on equity investments in quoted companies. A parallel set of issues relates to the appraisal of investments in unquoted shares and in particular the behaviour of venture capitalists in this regard.

Several studies examine the relative importance of a wide range of factors taken into account by venture capitalists in the screening process for new venture investment (for example, Bruno and Tyebjee, 1985; MacMillan et al., 1987; Fried and Hisrich, 1994). MacMillan et al. (1987) show that the most important criteria venture capitalists use in

screening investment proposals were entrepreneurial personality and experience, with lesser dependence being placed on market, product and strategy. For the UK, smaller sample studies provide a broad overview of the appraisal process among larger venture capitalists (Dixon, 1991) and address the use of accounting information in the venture capital monitoring process (Sweeting, 1991).

None of the above studies addresses important issues concerning venture capitalists' use of information in adopting the returns they seek and in the valuation methods used. Yet such issues are important. Venture capital firms' investment decisions are highly influenced by the extent to which they can identify appropriate investment candidates. In addition, they are also influenced by the extent to which they can invest on the basis of initial valuations, which enables target rates of return to be achieved and satisfactory returns made for the providers of funds to the venture capitalist. An important aspect of investment decision-making behaviour is the extent to which valuations and target rates of return hurdles are adjusted in the light of general and specific conditions. Pre-investment appraisal issues raise crucial problems in the potential effectiveness of institutional investors' subsequent post-transaction monitoring (Stiglitz and Weiss, 1981). To the extent that these problems lead investors to misjudge the situation, an agreed deal and accompanying financial structure may turn out to be inappropriate and possibly unviable. As a result, the control mechanism introduced by the commitment to meet the cost of servicing external finance may lead to sub-optimal

*The authors are at the Centre for Management Buyout Research, University of Nottingham. They gratefully acknowledge financial support for CMBOR from BZW Private Equity Limited and Touche Ross Corporate Finance. Thanks also go to David Citron, Peter Moizer, Richard Pike and two anonymous referees for comments on an earlier draft. Correspondence should be addressed to Professor Wright, School of Management and Finance, Portland Building, University of Nottingham, University Park, Nottingham NG7 2RD.

Venture Capital

decisions.[1] Alternatively, a deal that would have been viable may be rejected.

Given the importance of these issues, this paper aims to add to the understanding of venture capitalists' investment decision-making behaviour. By taking account of these issues, venture capitalists may further reduce potential adverse selection problems at stages in the appraisal process beyond the more general analysis of information, as in the studies referred to above. The paper provides evidence relating to the general policies adopted by venture capitalists in respect of approaches to due diligence, valuation methods, benchmark rates of return and adjustments for risk. It investigates the types of accounting and non-accounting information used in effecting policies relating to valuation and adjusting expected rates of return for risk. The existence of a potential adverse selection problem leads to the expectation that venture capitalists will use a wide range of information and techniques relating to the specific factors concerning a particular investment. Unpublished accounting information and subjective information may be expected to be important, but its use may vary between different types of venture capitalist, particularly depending on their emphases on stages of investment and on whether they are independent or captive. The paper seeks to identify the extent to which venture capitalists take account of specific factors, and the nature of the accounting and non-accounting information used in so doing.

The study relates only to the pre-investment, that is the 'buy' or invest decision, aspect of venture capitalists' work and not to the 'hold/sell' decisions examined as part of the studies of investment analysts referred to above,[2] and proceeds as follows. The first section discusses the stages in the venture capitalist investment decision process, and highlights expected information needs and problems in obtaining such information. Section two outlines the data and methodology used in the study. In section three, the results are presented in relation to valuation methods and the information used in valuations, the setting and adjustment of target rate of return hurdles, and the reporting of the investments' subsequent performance to the venture capitalist's provider's funds. The final section discusses the results and draws some conclusions.

---

[1] Investee remuneration schemes and the size and nature of investee stakeholding in venture-backed companies can to some extent address these issues, but the venture capitalist still requires a flow of accounting information in order to be able to monitor performance. However, this is likely to be subject to asymmetric information problems, and if adverse selection problems are present, then incentive systems may be set at inappropriate levels (for discussion see Mitchell et al., 1995, p. 188).

[2] For recent discussion of venture capitalists' post-investment demand for accounting information, see Mitchell et al. (1995).

Framework and theoretical perspectives

In appraising potential investments, venture capitalists as principals are faced both with uncertainty and an adverse selection problem (Sahlman, 1990). As agents of funds providers, they are also faced with the risk that if they do not perform satisfactorily they will fail to attract further funding, which in turn may place pressure on the venture capitalist to make appropriate use of accounting and non-accounting information in reducing exposure to this problem.

Uncertainty arises in relation to problems in forecasting future performance. Adverse selection arises, as venture capitalists have to rely greatly on information about the enterprise's state of affairs supplied by the entrepreneur. Amit, Glosten and Muller (1993) point out that while the entrepreneur's familiarity with the industry, personal characteristics and track record can provide some insight for the venture capitalist, these criteria are at best partial predictors of future success and may not be conveyed to the venture capitalist in an unbiased manner. It may be expected that venture capitalists seek ways of both reducing the adverse selection problem and of taking risk and uncertainty into account. They may aim both to enhance the robustness of available information and use such information in ways that allow for these problems. Venture capitalists may exercise considerable efforts in due diligence to verify the robustness of accounting information, particularly profit and cash flow forecasts. In addition, they may make use of a variety of valuation techniques and adjustments to expected rates of return from potential investments in order to identify the scope of adverse selection problems. Schematically, the elements of this process may be identified as follows.

Our review of the existing academic and practitioner literature suggests that the stages in the venture capitalists' appraisal process can be portrayed as in Figure 1. Bruno and Tyebjee (1985), Bygrave and Timmons (1992) and Fried and Hisrich (1994) in particular have sought to identify the stages in the venture capitalists' appraisal process, and the stages presented in Figure 1 are derived from these authors' findings. Recent work by Fried and Hisrich (1994), which extends earlier studies, elaborates the screening stage to include consideration of whether a proposal meets firms' general investment criteria, whether a proposal is prima facie viable and the gathering of further information to enable a second stage screening to occur.

This implied iterative approach is supported by Steier and Greenwood (1995) who, using a single case study, emphasise its occurrence in the deal-structuring phase within the context of the need to conform to individual venture capitalists' bureau-

Figure 1
Schematic Outline of Venture Capital Appraisal Stages, Policies and Information Requirements

Venture capital stage	*Venture capitalist's policy*	*Information*
1.Deal generation	General investment criteria	Broad indicators
2.Initial screening	General investment criteria	Business plan
3.Second/detailed screening	Due diligence policy	Business plan
	Valuation methods	Other accounting and non-accounting information
	Benchmark rates of return	
	Policy on assessing investees' rates of return, including effects of gearing levels	Specific and general information considered to affect rate of return and risk
	Policy on adjusting for risk	
4.Deal approval	Specific investment criteria	Investment executive/partner recommendation report based on prior stages

Source: Derived from Bruno and Tyebjee (1985), Bygrave and Timmons (1992), Fried and Hisrich (1994) and discussions with venture capitalists

cratic requirements. In terms of general investment criteria, Fried and Hisrich (1994) focus on venture capitalists' policies in respect of investment stage and industry preferences. As such, many proposals may not be formally valued, as they are deemed unacceptable at this early stage, either because they do not meet the criteria regarding the kind of proposals in which a particular venture capitalist invests or because, on the basis of initial information, the proposal is clearly not viable.

This paper's focus is on the stage in the appraisal process after a proposal has passed through initial screens, and has reached a more advanced stage where detailed valuation and assessment of potential returns takes place. This is stage 3 in Figure 1. Initial discussions with a small group of venture capitalists, intended to help frame the survey instrument, suggested that during this more detailed screening stage there is a need for firm-wide policies as well as detailed accounting and financial information. As seen in Figure 1, these policies involve the establishment of general firm-wide policies relating to due diligence methods, valuation methods, benchmark target returns, approaches to the assessment of returns from a potential investee and to the assessment of project riskiness. Figure 1 also indicates the broad nature of the information expected to be taken into account in this process. The results of the survey reported below show without exception the existence of at least one and an average of two formal organisational decision-making layers. As such, while venture capital executives may apply their individual skills and judgment to each particular case, our discussions suggest that they are likely to operate within the framework of an organisational policy. The interpretation and use of information

in preparing a case to be presented to an investment committee will draw heavily on individual executives' skills. However, the need to be consistent about investment decisions, at least in part to guide the venture capitalist in making the returns indicated to their funds providers, emphasises the importance of organisation-wide criteria. As explained in the Methodology section, the focus of this paper is on these overall policies of the venture capital firm.

Following Fried and Hisrich (1994), information will be subject to extensive scrutiny and due diligence by the venture capitalist to ascertain its robustness before making a valuation. This scrutiny will include analysis of both financial and non-financial information provided by the entrepreneur and typically contained in the business plan, as well as information initiated by the venture capitalists and gathered from elsewhere. Forward-looking information, an essential element, is likely to be subject to sensitivity analysis by the venture capitalist according to the expected influence on future performance of other information. The first requirement, then, is for a policy on approaches to due diligence.

DeAngelo (1990) shows that for fair valuation assessments of management buy-out candidates, investment banks may use both a variety of information and techniques to produce a range of values within which an acceptable investment price can be negotiated. Indications from our initial discussions with venture capitalists are that a venture will in essence also be valued by applying one or more valuation techniques to the financial and accounting information relating to the potential investee. The second and third requirements concern the establishment of a policy on valuation techniques and the kind of information to be used in effecting such valuations. The existence of a potential adverse selection problem leads to the expectation that in making a valuation, venture capitalists will use a wide range of information and techniques relating to the specific factors concerning a particular investment. Unpublished accounting information and subjective information may be expected to be particularly important in providing a current, detailed assessment of the potential investee.

As may be seen from practitioner texts (for example, Sharp, 1993; Walker, 1990), valuations of potential investees will be used as a basis for determining the most appropriate financing structure and thence for calculating the expected internal rate of return (IRR), the performance measure most commonly used in practice by the venture capital industry (Lorenz, 1989). Where there is no clear-cut accept/reject decision, attempts may be made to reassess the variables in the decision-making process, renegotiation of the purchase price, and/or changes to the proposed gearing ratio in the financing structure.

In assessing rates of return there is an initial requirement for a general benchmark against which projects are to be judged. However, given the wide variety of possible types of investment candidates, venture capitalists may or may not apply a fixed benchmark to all of them. Hence, the second aspect of rates of return to be investigated is the extent to which venture capitalists have a varying target rate of return policy. To the extent that they do, interest then focuses on the relative importance of the factors taken into account in adjusting target rates of return. Besides the stage of investment (see below) these factors may be related to a range of general and/or specific factors including industry sector, expected length of investment horizon, and so on. In investigating the nature of these factors, the expectation is that general market factors will have some influence on expected returns in general. However, for a particular investment, venture capitalists are expected to place more emphasis on information relating to specific issues. Finance theory also suggests that expected returns need to be adjusted for the riskiness of a project, and again there is expected to be more emphasis on specific attributes.

Differences may arise between venture capitalists in respect of these issues and be associated with variations in the rates of return that are sought and the factors influencing those returns. In particular, two broad distinctions may have important implications for the demand for and use made of information. The first concerns those venture capitalists, important in the UK, who only target investments that are later stage (i.e., do not invest at all in seed or start-up projects), and those

investing across all stages (Elango et al., 1995).[3] In 1994 later stage financings represented 94% of the total value of investments and 81% of the total number of financings made in that year by members of the British Venture Capital Association (BVCA, 1995). Given the established trading record of later stage investments, venture capitalists focusing on such projects may be expected to place greater emphasis on valuation methods that utilise historic information and to place greater emphasis on financial and accounting sources of information in preparing valuations. There is some debate in the US literature about the extent to which the use of non-accounting information varies between stages of investment, especially in respect of the greater emphasis placed by later stage investors on management characteristics and market acceptance of a product (Elango et al., 1995).

The second distinction concerns captive and independent venture capitalists. Captive venture capitalists—part of banks or insurance companies—do not have to raise capital (though increasingly they may) from third parties (Abbott and Hay, 1995). They are often viewed as investing primarily in later stage projects such as development capital and management buy-outs and buy-ins. Independents tend to be seen as the more traditional type of venture capitalist, are typically funded through limited-life closed-end funds, and may be more committed than captives to generating a return for investors through realising a capital gain within a more clearly specified period of time, while the latter tend to focus more on the income stream from their investments. In 1994, independent venture capitalists accounted for 54% of new funds invested (BVCA, 1995).

Data and methodology

It is important to note that, as indicated earlier, this paper is concerned with the general policies adopted by venture capitalists in their assessment of all types of investment. As such, an organisation-wide response was sought, with the questionnaires being sent to chief executives of the venture capital firms or senior colleagues with whom the Centre for Management Buyout Research has regular contact through its buyout and buy-in surveys. The covering letter to the questionnaire spe-

[3]Some would go so far as to argue that late-stage investors, especially investing in smaller buy-outs, should not be considered venture capitalists (e.g., Bygrave and Timmons, 1992), though given that many such venture-backed transactions can involve considerable product and organisational innovation, this argument seems debatable (Wright, Robbie and Ennew, 1995). Moreover, from the point of view of the industry itself, all stages are encompassed in the term venture capitalists and reported in BVCA statistics.

Table 1
Due Diligence

Source of due diligence information	Mean score+	Std. dev.
Carry out own market evaluation	4.14	0.89
Place great reliance on personal references	3.94	0.86
Always have independent accountant's report	3.69	1.44
Never use same reporting accountant as management's accounting adviser	3.14	1.35
Always obtain independent market reports	3.09	1.17

Note: + where 5 = essential through to 1 = irrelevant

cifically asked repondents to report institutions' perceptions,[4] rather than individuals' approaches.

The survey was carried out in early 1994. A draft questionnaire designed to help the researchers understand the nature of the evaluation process was developed following initial discussions of up to an hour with a small group of venture capitalists and related practitioners. The questionnaire was then piloted with venture capitalists, advisers and academics. Following analysis of the replies, modifications were made to its content and structure.[5] The questionnaire was mailed to the 114 institutions listed as full members of the BVCA. Mailing of the questionnaires took place in March 1994. A follow-up reminder was sent to non-respondents in April 1994.

A total of 66 completed and usable replies were received, representing a response rate of 57.9%. A further 16 replies were received. Of these, eight had ceased investing in the UK, or their funds were now being managed by another venture capital institution. Reasons for non-completion among the remainder generally related to the size of transactions undertaken by the venture capital firm, or reflected a deliberate policy not to answer questionnaires.

Analysis of the respondents showed they covered a substantial proportion of the UK venture capital industry. Virtually all the principal and longest established venture capitalists in the UK had participated in the study. The respondents had on average been in existence for 13 years (median = 10.5 years) and employed on average 9.6 (median = 6) investment executives. Within the total sample, some 31 venture capitalists stated that they would invest only in later stage transactions, and 35 would consider projects at all stages. There

were equal numbers of captive (include affiliate) and independent venture capitalists in the sample.

Results

The analysis of results is divided into four broad sections. The first examines due diligence, valuation methods and sources of information used in valuations. The second considers evidence relating to the target rates of return sought by venture capitalists. The third tests for differences between venture capitalists according to their stage of investment preferences and whether they are captives or independent, while the fourth relates to information used to value portfolios post investment.

Valuation

Due diligence reports. The importance of due diligence reports in preparing valuations was indicated earlier. The evidence in Table 1 reinforces the prime importance of venture capitalists' own reports, and the low standard deviation indicates generally high consensus on this source. Although all sources shown have at least moderate importance on average, personal references score higher than independent accountants' reports or other independent market reports. Both of those have higher standard deviations, indicating the existence of marked differences between venture capitalists.

Our discussions with venture captialists suggest that accountants' reports tend to be used more where verification of information relating to later stage investments such as buyouts is required. Moreover, because of the level of expertise required, it is generally the Big Six accounting firms that are employed where accountants' reports are used. Such reports may be more likely to be commissioned by the lead investor in cases where funding is to be syndicated between several venture capitalists, with the use of Big Six accountants playing a signalling role about the quality of the investigation to other syndicate members.

---

[4]The letter said '. . .In order to obtain an overall view of the appraisal and valuation process...we are currently surveying these issues in depth. The enclosed questionnaire asks for institutions' perceptions on key elements of their equity investment appraisal process. . .'.

[5]A copy of the final questionnaire is available from the authors.

Table 2
Methods Used in Valuing Potential Investments

	Mean score+	Std. dev.
Historic cost book value	2.42	1.26
Replacement cost asset value	1.98	1.10
Liquidation value of assets (orderly sale)	2.05	1.14
Liquidation value of assets (forced sale)	1.97	1.06
Discounted future cash flows	3.23	1.37
Dividend yield basis	2.22	1.11
Capitalised maintainable earning (price/earning multiple)(historic basis)	4.27	0.86
Capitalised maintainable earning (price/earning multiple)(prospective basis)	4.31	0.87
Capitalised maintainable earning (EBIT multiple)	3.91	1.23
Recent PE ratio of the parent company's shares	1.97	1.00
Recent transaction prices for acquisitions in the sector	3.63	1.18
Responses to attempts to solicit bids for the potential investee	2.74	1.20
Industry's special 'rule of thumb' pricing ratios (e.g. turnover ratios)	2.97	1.13

Note: + where 5 = almost always used through to 1 = almost never used

Table 3
Selection of Final/Benchmark Valuation

	Mean score+	Std. dev
Place greatest weight on one particular method and use others as a check	4.15	1.13
Use the average valuation	2.61	1.25
Use the lowest valuation	2.33	1.11
Use the median valuation	2.29	1.08
Use the highest valuation	1.65	0.77

Note: + where 5 = almost always used through to 1 = almost never used

Valuation Methods. Various standard methods of valuing potential investments are used by venture capitalists, with more than one method frequently being employed.[6] Although methods may be grouped into three main types—asset value, price earnings multiple and discounted future cash flow basis—there is considerable variation around these basic methods of valuation, including identifying prices paid for transactions of a similar nature. Venture capitalists were asked to rate their use of each method on a scale ranging from 5 = 'almost always' to 1 'almost never' (Table 2).[7]

The most commonly used valuation methods employed were variations of price earnings ratio multiples. Overall, the technique with the best score was capitalised maintainable earnings (price earnings ratio) on a prospective basis, over half the respondents using this 'almost always'. A historic basis valuation was only marginally less frequently used, while capitalised maintainable earnings (EBIT multiple) was the third most common. In

[6]The scale used was limited to a range from 'almost always' to 'almost never', and on the basis of a review of the literature and the pilot study, respondents were presented with the closed list shown in Table 2. While this might present some limitations to the results, it is unlikely to affect the rankings of the techniques, and our piloting suggested that the absence of the absolute extremities to the scale would be more acceptable to respondents. Respondents were not presented with the formal option to record a different method from those listed, but for purposes of the study all major known techniques were included.

[7]Of course, it needs to be borne in mind that not all the possibilities listed in Table 2 will be available in each case, which may introduce some element that the results reflect information availability rather than information usefulness. However, it is observable that some forms of readily accessible information such as historic cost asset values are in fact used relatively infrequently, while certain more difficult to obtain ones such as discounted cash flows are used relatively frequently.

Table 4
Sources of Information in Preparing a Valuation

	Mean score+	Std. dev.
Financial press	3.03	1.19
Trade journals	2.69	1.09
Interviews with entrepreneurs	3.65	1.14
Interviews with other company personnel	3.17	1.30
Government industry statistics	2.27	1.00
Statistical and information services	2.77	1.04
Other venture capitalists	2.82	1.05
Own due diligence report	4.47	0.75
Due diligence by accounting/consulting firms	3.75	1.17
Business plan: Balance sheet	4.00	1.05
Business plan: Profit and loss account	4.36	0.92
Business plan: Unqualified audit report	3.46	1.22
Business plan: Qualified audit report	3.70	1.25
Business plan: Unaudited management projections (1 year ahead)	4.03	0.91
Business plan: Unaudited management projections (more than 1 year ahead)	3.63	1.02
Business plan: Unaudited 'latest period' financial statements	4.00	0.99
Business plan: Overall coherence of business plan	4.06	1.06
Proposed exit timing and method	3.70	1.08
Sales and marketing information	3.80	0.88
Product information	3.47	0.99
Production capacity/technical information	3.42	0.95
Curriculum vitae of management	3.91	1.0

Note: + where 5 = vital influence through to 1 = no influence

contrast, reference to the recent PE ratio of the parent company's shares was reported to be used relatively rarely. This measure may, however, only be relevant in the case of buyout and buy-in proposals relating to divestments from quoted groups.

A further possibility is to obtain details of transaction prices for similar types of deal. Almost three-fifths of respondents usually or almost always used recent transaction prices in the same sector as a further yardstick. In over a third of cases, venture capitalists frequently attempted to solicit bids for potential investee companies as another means of establishing a valuation guide.[8] Discounted cash flows emerged as much more frequently used than asset value bases and was the fifth most common method. Although asset value methods may be common for bank debt analysis, over two-fifths of respondents almost never used replacement cost asset value or liquidation value asset methods, and a third did not use historic

book value methods. Dividend yield bases were also less likely to be used.

There was generally greater consensus, as indicated by the standard deviations reported in Table 2, surrounding the use of the two methods receiving the highest average scores, while there was generally less consensus in respect of other methods, notably those based on discounted cash flow and asset valuations. It is notable, however, that the methods receiving the third and fourth highest average scores (EBIT multiples and recent transaction prices for acquisitions in the same sector) had relatively high standard deviations.

The evidence above implies that several valuation methods are regularly used by venture capitalists. Over four-fifths of respondents usually or almost always place greatest weight on one particular method but use others as a check. None appeared to make frequent use of the method that produced the highest valuation (Table 3).

These results provide some interesting contrasts with the studies by Arnold and Moizer (1984), and that by Pike et al. (1993). Venture capitalists, while also most frequently using forms of price earnings multiples, make more frequent use of discounted

[8]Such an approach may involve contacting other venture capitalists (potential syndicate partners) on the basis of 'what if?', or eliciting information concerning the broad level of alternative bids for the company where the vendor is selling the company in an auction.

Table 5
Required Rate of Return on Equity

Rate of return	Investment type			
	Later stage	MBO	MBI	Early stage
Below 20% p.a.	5.9	1.9	0.0	2.4
21 to 25% p.a.	19.6	15.4	7.7	0.0
26 to 30% p.a.	25.5	19.2	15.4	4.8
31 to 35% p.a.	31.4	46.2	28.8	7.1
36 to 45% p.a.	15.7	13.5	40.4	19.0
46 to 55% p.a.	0.0	1.9	5.8	40.5
Above 55% p.a.	2.0	1.9	1.9	26.2
Total	100.0	100.0	100.0	100.0
Sample size	51	52	52	42

Table 6
Target Rates of Return

	Mean score+	Std. dev.
We require the investment to meet a standard required rate of return on equity (internal rate of return, IRR), regardless of the investee company's risk profile	2.27	1.13
We require the investment to meet a standard required rate of return on equity (IRR), according to the risk band of the investment	3.29	1.25
We require the investment to meet a specific required rate of return on equity (IRR), according to the characteristics of each investment	3.64	1.22
We require the funding structure to meet standard gearing ratios	2.06	0.98
We require the funding structure to meet standard gearing ratio according to the risk band of the investment	2.41	1.07
We require the funding structure to meet gearing ratios appropriate to each investment	3.94	0.98
We require a rate of return which yields a total cash return commensurate with amount invested	3.38	1.32

Note: + where 5 = essential through to 1 = irrelevent

cash flow approaches than asset-based methods. Their frequency of use reflects the use of this method in the calculation by venture capitalists of internal rates of return. Although there are theoretical problems with IRR, this technique is commonly used as a principal indicator of investment performance.

Sources of information in preparing a valuation. In preparing a valuation of the business, the venture capitalist may rely on a variety of information generated either by the entrepreneurs, or internally within the venture capital firm, or by obtaining external information, which either already exists or is obtainable on a specially commissioned basis. Our search of the literature and discussions with venture capitalists yielded 22 potential sources of

information that could be of influence in preparing a valuation, each of which respondents were asked to rate out of 5, where 5 represented a 'vital influence' and 1 'no influence' (Table 4).

The critical source of information was rated to be the venture capitalist's own due diligence report, almost three-fifths of the sample seeing this as a vital influence. While due diligence was requested from accounting and consulting firms, relatively little emphasis was placed upon it (only just over a quarter of the sample scored it as having a vital influence). The overall coherence of the business plan was also important.

Accounting statements contained in the entrepreneur's business plan was the next most influential set of information, especially the profit and

Table 7
Targeted Return Variations

	Mean score+	Std. dev.
The expected length of investment in a particular proposal	3.52	1.00
The actual cash amount invested in a particular proposal (i.e. size of proposal)	2.81	1.08
Market conditions relating to a particular proposal	3.34	0.97
General economic conditions	3.16	0.88
Changes in returns for quoted equities	2.48	1.00
Changes in returns for long-term gilts	2.14	0.96
Changes in base rates	2.52	0.98
The actual cash amount you seek to receive from an investment	2.88	1.16
The industrial/product sector of the investment	3.11	1.01
The geographical region of the investment	2.06	1.11
The expected gearing ratio when the finance is structured	2.94	1.02
Whether you (and the institutional syndicate where appropriate) have a majority of the equity	2.40	0.87

Note: + where 5 = amost always through to 1 = never

loss account. However, considerable influence was assigned to unaudited latest period financial statements and management projections for one year ahead. Some influence was assigned to qualified audit reports and longer term management projections, but these were scored no higher than a number of non-financial pieces of information. The curricula vitae of management, sales and marketing information, interviews with management and proposed exit timing and method were especially influential.

Publicly available sources of information such as the financial press, trade journals and external statistical and information services were poorly rated, with government industry statistics having the lowest ratings of all. There was also a low level of influence of other venture capitalists.

In general, there was greater consensus concerning the most important factors, as indicated by the size of the standard deviations reported in Table 4. For the factors of less than average importance, there were slightly higher standard deviations, indicating that some venture capitalists did see these factors as being important, even though others did not.

These findings provide both similarities and marked contrasts with those of Arnold and Moizer (1984) and Pike et al. (1993). Pike et al. note the increasing emphasis placed on personal company contacts. However, venture capitalists require access to considerably more information of an unpublished and subjective kind than investment analysts appraising quoted companies can realistically hope to obtain, especially unaudited detailed management projections. Further evidence of the influence of this extra information is reflected in the wide range of factors covered in the business plan and due diligence procedures. These factors essentially provide the means by which the venture capitalist can test the robustness of the accounting and financial projections presented in the business plan, rather than simply taking such information that is presented at face value, and provide a means of addressing asymmetric information problems.

As with the scrutiny of extra information uncovered by investment analysts noted by Arnold and Moizer, the subjective judgment of individual venture capitalists is also likely to be important. Space precludes full elaboration of these results, but, in summary, the most important may be categorised as follows. The most notable factors relating to the entrepreneur's personality and characteristics were, in order of importance: evidence of ability to evaluate and react to risk well (mean 4.41); being capable of sustained intense effort (4.25); a clear desire to be wealthy (4) and being articulate in discussing the venture (2.82); attention to detail (3.5); and seeking independence (3). The two most important features concerning the entrepreneur's experience were that the entrepreneur had demonstrated leadership/managerial ability in the past (4.54), and was thoroughly familiar with the market targeted by the venture (4.54).

High rankings were also given to the entrepreneur with a track record relevant to the venture (4.24) and the ability to provide good references (4.2). In respect of product characteristics, the need for a product to have a strong market niche

Table 8
Assessment of the Riskiness of Investment

	Mean score+	Std. dev.
Nature of company's product market	4.29	0.80
Nature of the capital market	2.57	1.07
Contribution by management in terms of their managerial skills	4.76	0.53
Management's financial contribution	3.29	1.09
Expected time horizon to company's exit (stock market/trade sale)	3.52	0.93
Expected time horizon to redemption of preference shares	2.97	1.02
Expected participating dividend yield	2.49	1.04

Note: + where 5 = extremely important through to 1 = irrelevant

had the highest mean score (4), followed by the need for the product to have been developed to the point of a functioning prototype (3.71), the product enjoying market acceptance (3.82), perceived product quality and company reputation (3.88), and the experience and skills of the salesforce (3.62).

The most important market characteristic was that the target market enjoyed a significant growth rate (3.61). The two highest rated operational qualities were employee experience and skills (3.91) and organisational control systems (3.79). In respect of financial factors, the most important feature emerged as the presentation of a coherent and thorough business plan (4.2), closely followed by the state of financial control systems (4.14).

Targeted Rates of Return and Degree of Risk

According to our sample, the benchmark IRR used to evaluate expected after-tax returns was a mean of 29.2% (median 30%), a finding similar to that of Dixon (1991), though the time periods covered are different. Venture capitalists may use a standard benchmark IRR for investments, regardless of the investee company's profile, or may vary the required IRR according to the type of deal and its individual circumstances.

It may be expected that important differences in targeted rates of return will be reflected in the stage of investment, given the variation in risk factors between established and new firms (Lorenz, 1989). The survey shows that in moving from later stage to buyout to buy-in and finally early stage, the current required rates of return on equity, in terms of after-tax return, become progressively higher (Table 5). Although buyouts and buy-ins share the same median, the buy-in mean is considerably higher. Two-thirds of early stage investments look for rates of return of at least 46%.

Venture capitalists also adjust their targeted rates of return for smaller sized investments or where it is considered that there will be above av-

erage requirements for post-deal reorganisation, thus increasing risk. On average, the target return was 3.9% greater for small size investments (sample = 30), and 7.6% greater in cases where there was above-average requirement for post-deal reorganisation.

It is also possible that venture capital firms vary their required IRR according to whether they manage both closed-end funds as well as other sources of finance (e.g. own resources). Only 14.3% of the relevant respondents employed different target rates of return, depending on which funds were being managed.

Assessment of targeted rates of return. In terms of the required rate of return on equity, a flexible policy is generally adopted, involving the basing of targeted rates of return on the particular circumstances of each deal, rather than relying on deals meeting a standard benchmark rate (Table 6). More than two-thirds of respondents felt it was important or essential that the proposed investment met a specific rate of return on equity according to the individual characteristics of each investment, though the size of the standard deviation indicates that a substantial minority of venture capitalists do not share this view.

However, less than a quarter of venture capitalists attached the same degree of importance to the investment meeting a standard required rate of return regardless of the investee company's risk profile. Over half of the respondents felt it important or essential that the investment met a standard required rate of return according to the risk band of the investment, but this approach has a high standard deviation. A further feature was the importance attached to a deal being able to earn a rate of return that yielded a total cash return commensurate with the amount invested, but with the highest standard deviation. This appears to be important to only some venture capitalists.

Variation of targeted rates of return. The above analysis indicated that venture capitalists vary

Table 9
Significant Differences in Financial and Accounting Factors According to Investment Stage Preferences

Financial and accounting Factors	*Later stage only*	*All stage*
Valuation methods:		
Discounted cash flow	2.94	3.50+
Capitalised maintainable earnings (historic basis)	4.55	4.00**
Transactions prices for acquisitions in the sector	3.90	3.38+
Information used:		
Financial press	3.32	2.77*
Trade journals	3.00	2.43*
Business plan/balance sheet	4.26	3.77*
Business plan/profit & loss account	4.65	4.11*
Business plan/unqualified audit report	3.77	3.17*
Business plan/qualified audit report	4.19	3.25**
Business plan/unaudited 1yr projections	4.42	3.69**
Business plan/unaudited > 1yr projections	3.90	3.38*
Business plan/unaudited latest	4.26	3.77+
Due diligence:		
Always use independent accountants' report	4.26	3.19**
Terminate if inadequate current information	3.83	3.20*
Target IRR variations:		
Length of investment	3.27	3.74+
Cash amount invested	2.60	3.00+
Change in returns for quoted equity	2.76	2.24*
Change in base rates	2.73	2.32+
Risk assessment:		
Expected time to preference share redemption	3.35	2.63**

Note: significance levels for Mann-Whitney U test of differences between the two groups:
** 1%; * 5%; + 10%

their standard targeted rates of return to take account of deal-specific factors. The relative frequency with which each of a set of factors would cause the targeted return to vary was scored on the basis of 5 = 'almost always', through to 1 = 'never' (Table 7). The most frequently occurring factor, which would cause targeted returns to vary, emerged as the expected length of investment in a particular proposal followed by market conditions relating to the particular proposal, general economic conditions, the industrial or product sector of the investment and the expected gearing ratio when the finance was structured.

It was notable that changes in general financial variables, which would have an immediate influence on the quoted equity markets, had low scores. This finding is indeed surprising, given the need for the suppliers of funds to venture capitalists to ensure that the differential between the returns earned by venture capital firms and other types of financial instrument is maintained. Changes in re-

turns for quoted equities, changes in returns for long-term gilts and changes in base rates were infrequently seen to respondents to be of influence.

Size of investment was only moderately important, although smaller size is associated with venture capitalists seeking higher returns, as noted above. In over two-fifths of cases, the geographical region of investment never caused targeted returns to vary. Given the need to control the investment, it was surprising that rates of return did not vary according to whether the venture capital firm (or syndicate) had a majority of the equity. There was generally greater consensus about the most and least important factors, as indicated by the size of the standard deviations. However, the high standard deviations around the relatively low average scores for geographical region, and in respect of the amounts of cash investments and returns sought, suggests that for some venture capitalists these are important influences on target returns.

170

Venture Capital

164

ACCOUNTING AND BUSINESS RESEARCH

Table 10
Non-financial Factor Differences Between Investment Stages (Mean Scores)

	Later stage only	All stage
Meets minimum funding levels	4.23	2.86**
Company is profitable	3.45	2.50**
Positive cash flow history	3.48	2.40**
Three to five-year exit horizon	3.90	3.31*
Entrepreneur handles risk well	4.62	4.23*
Entrepreneur seeks security	1.58	1.97+
Entrepreneur demonstrated leadership	4.71	4.40+
Familiarity with entrepreneur	2.06	2.51+
Proprietary product	3.00	3.49+
Market acceptance of product	4.19	3.49**
High technical product	1.42	2.17**
Experienced sales force	3.81	3.46+
Product will stimulate market	2.55	3.26**
Little competitive threat	2.58	3.03+
Product will create new market	1.52	2.49**
Familiar region	2.81	3.51*
Overseas market potential	2.65	3.43**
Number	31	35

Note: significance levels for Mann-Whitney U test of differences between the two groups:
** 1%; * 5%; + 10%

Assessment of a project's riskiness. Venture capital firms assess the riskiness of an investment through various factors. Based on scores ranging from 5 'extremely important' to 1 'irrelevant', the dominant influence was management's contribution to the venture in terms of their managerial skills. Over two-fifths of respondents rated this as extremely important, and the very low standard deviation indicates considerable agreement between venture capitalists (Table 8). The second influence was the nature of the company's product market, with there also being a relatively low standard deviation. The actual financial contribution being made by the management was, however, considerably less important, although still the fourth most important factor overall and with the highest standard deviation. A further key factor in assessing the riskiness of the project was the expected time horizon to exit. Dividend and preference share redemption issues were relatively lowly rated on average and had higher standard deviations, as did the nature of the capital market. These findings indicate a greater degree of scrutiny of available information in assessing risk and adjusting target IRRs than suggested by Dixon (1991).

Different Types of Venture Capital Firm

In what follows, the focus of attention is on areas where there are significant differences between venture capitalists according to their investment stage preferences and whether they are captive or independent.

Investment stage preferences. Given the importance of later stage investments in the UK venture capital industry, as noted earlier, respondents were divided for purposes of the following analysis into those who would only consider such projects and those who would consider projects across the full stage range. Venture capitalists focusing solely on later stage investments placed significantly greater emphasis on valuation methods, which made use of past performance information, and sale prices of similar enterprises, than did those also prepared to fund early stage projects (Table 9). The latter placed greater emphasis than the former on DCF valuation methods.

As expected, venture capitalists focusing on later stage investments to the exclusion of early stage projects believe that financial information is of significantly greater influence in preparing a valuation than other venture capitalists, reflecting the greater reliability of such information in enter-

Table 11
Financial Factor Differences Between Types of Venture Capital Firm (Mean Scores)

Variable	Mean score independent	Mean score captives etc.
Stage preferences		
Must be an MBO	2.91	3.76**
Must be an MBI	2.69	3.45**
Valuation methods		
Replacement cost asset	1.69	2.12+
Capitalised maintainable earning		
-historic p/e	3.90	4.61**
-EBIT multiple	3.60	4.18*
Information used		
Statistical information service	2.48	3.06*
Other venture capitalists	3.06	2.58+
Overall coherence of business plan	4.31	3.81*
Proposed exit timing	3.94	3.45+
Due diligence		
Always independent accountant report	2.88	3.30**
Own market evaluation	4.39	3.88*
Target IRR assessment		
Funding structure to standard gearing	2.28	2.55+
Target IRR variations		
Effect of marketing conditions	3.48	3.19+
Change in long-term gilts	1.91	2.39*
Change in base rates	2.33	2.71+
Risk assessment		
Expected time to exit	3.73	3.30+
Expected participating dividend yield	2.21	2.76*

Note: significance levels for Mann-Whitney U test of differences between the two groups:
** 1%; * 5%; + 10%

prises with an established trading record. No significant differences were found in the influence placed on sales and marketing information, product and production information, and management's curriculum vitae.

Significant differences between venture capitalists with varying investment stage preferences were identified in the use of non-financial information (Table 10). Later stage venture capitalists place significantly greater importance on large-sized investments, profitability and cash flow, and relatively short exit horizons. Also, as expected, later stage investors placed greater emphasis on products with strong market acceptance, while venture capitalists also willing to consider early stage projects place significantly greater importance on a wider range of product and market-related characteristics. In contrast to some recent US findings (e.g. Elango et al., 1995), this study shows that

later stage investors were significantly more likely to seek entrepreneurs experienced in leadership and able to handle risk.

Independents and captives. The earlier discussion suggested that there may be variations between different types of venture capitalist according to the nature of their fund and associated investment time horizons. In particular, there may be differences between independent and the group of 'non-independents', which includes captive, affiliate and public sector venture capital firms.

From the discussion in section two, general preferences for different types of investment may be expected to arise between different types of venture capitalist. This perception is strongly borne out by the survey, which shows that captives are significantly more likely than independents to prefer to invest in management buyouts and buy-ins (Table 11).

Table 12
Non-financial Factor Differences Between Type of Venture Capitalist (Mean Scores)

	Mean score independent	Mean score captive
Return > 10 times investment within at least five years	3.18	2.43*
Target is profitable	2.63	3.27*
Positive cash flow	2.67	3.15+
Entrepreneurial compatible personality	3.03	2.39*
Entrepreneurial demonstrated leadership	4.36	4.73+
Entrepreneurial track record	4.09	4.39+
Functioning prototype development	3.39	4.03+
High tech product	2.09	1.55+
Production creates new market	2.30	1.76+
Market is mature	2.12	2.63**
Overseas market potential	3.36	2.76**
State of production facilities	3.39	3.88*
Organisational control systems	3.58	4.00*
Employee attitudes	3.82	3.45+

Note: significance levels for Mann-Whitney U test of differences between the two groups:
** 1%; * 5%; + 10%

Although both types of venture capitalist use a range of valuation methods, captives placed significantly more emphasis on historic P/E and EBIT multiples than independents, perhaps reflecting the greater interest by the former in enterprises with more established and stable performance records such as classic management buyouts and buy-ins (Jensen, 1986).

Independents place significantly greater emphasis than captives on more detailed specific sources of information, both in the potential investee's business plan and in respect of their own evaluations. Although both groups of venture capitalist score their own market evaluations higher on average than reports by independent accountants, captives place relatively more emphasis on such due diligence than independents. In particular, independent accountants' reports were found to play a significantly more important role in due diligence for captive venture capitalists. Over four-fifths of captives felt it was important or essential to have an independent accountant's report, compared to just over half of other venture capital firms. There may be little a priori reason why different types of venture capitalist seek different IRRs from the various categories of venture capital investment in general, and indeed the survey identified no significant differences between the two sub-samples in this respect.

Independent firms were more likely to vary targeted rates of return according to changes in market conditions relating to a proposal, and to pay significantly less attention to changes in interest rates than non-independents. Attitudes to both changes in base rates and changes in returns for long-term gilts saw most independents considering these as irrelevant or only slightly important (75.8% and 60.6%, respectively), with significantly more emphasis being placed on these by the group of captives and other venture capital firms (41.9% and 32.3%, respectively, seeing them as irrelevant or only slightly important).

Some venture capitalists place considerable emphasis on participating dividends, that is, significantly increased dividends linked to the level of profits, rather than exit in obtaining their required rate of return. In particular, captive and other venture capital firms that may have less pressure to exit than the independents, who are financed by closed-end funds, may be expected to pay closer attention to participating dividends. There were significant differences between the independent and other venture capital firms in the sample in this respect. Correspondingly, the different emphasis placed on exit timing by the two types of venture capitalist was weakly significant.

Independents place significantly more emphasis on the ability of a prospective investment to earn a high overall rate of return (Table 12). Examination of desire to exit in three to five years showed weak significance and that independents placed greater emphasis on this issue than captives and others. Independents were less likely than the group of captives and other venture capital firms to attach importance to backing profitable companies or those with a history of positive cash flow. Significantly greater importance is placed by captives on the entrepreneur's track and leadership records, the state of production facilities and organisational control systems, and the maturity of markets.

Discussion and conclusions

This paper has examined the role of accounting and non-accounting information in the valuation and assessment of potential investments and the setting of target rates of return. The study showed that in attempting to deal with potential adverse selection problems, venture capitalists place considerable emphasis on the specific attributes of a potential investee company both in relation to assessment of its value and the rate of return to be expected from it. While accounting information is an important element in arriving at a valuation and a target rate of return, it appears neither to be taken at face value nor to be the only kind of information used.

Significant differences emerged in the approaches to valuation and use of accounting information for valuation purposes between types of venture capitalist, according both to their stage of investment focus and whether they were captive or independent, reflecting the differing nature of the adverse selection problem in these cases. Significant differences in assessment and information usage were identified for a number of variables, such as expectations about timescales to investment realisation and the importance attached to carrying out own diligence. These differences may reflect independents' greater emphasis on earlier stage investments where there may be relatively little historic accounting information. There may also be considerable uncertainty about future prospects, which can only be assessed to the venture capitalists' satisfaction by their own expertise, which may be more specifically skilled and/or more attuned to the venture capitalists' perspectives on risk and uncertainty than it may be feasible to obtain through the employment of external advisers. As captives focus more attention on later stage investments, there is likely to be a more established market, organisation and set of historical financial information which renders due diligence more amenable to standard procedures and the use of historic P/E and EBIT multiple-based valuation techniques more reliable.

This study's findings show both similarities to and differences from those relating to investment analysts' assessments of quoted companies. First, in common with other findings, venture capitalists were found to use several techniques for estimating company valuations. In contrast with investment analysts, however, venture capitalists make greater use of discounted cash flow approaches and less use of asset-based methods, reflecting the use of IRRs as an important indicator of investment performance in this sector.

Second, in respect of the type of information used in assessments and valuations, venture capitalists are found to place most emphasis on very detailed scrutiny of all aspects of a business,

typically including discussions with personnel and accessing considerably more information of an unpublished and subjective kind than investment analysts appraising quoted companies can realistically hope to obtain. Venture capitalists were found to place considerable emphasis on unaudited management projections. As with investment analysts, but to a considerably greater depth, venture capitalists use wider non-financial information to test the robustness of the accounting and financial projections presented in the business plan. This process provides a means of addressing asymmetric information problems.

The results and limitations of the study suggest areas for further research. In particular, while the approach used here has focused on the use of accounting and non-financial information in pre-investment analysis by venture capitalists, further research may usefully focus on attempts to discriminate between the relative importance of information used in assessing differing stages of investment by venture capitalists, and in assessing investments that were subsequently successful and unsuccessful. Further study may also be useful with respect to the rationales different types of venture capitalists (i.e., captives versus independents and all stages versus late stage only) allow to influence their preferences for different valuation methods, and sources of information. In the light of initial discussions with venture capitalists, the study was limited to an assessment of organisations' general policy approaches. Further research may be directed at assessing the approaches of individual executives within venture capitalists, particularly in respect of the processes by which accounting and non-accounting information is used in the assessment process, and in relation to the behaviour they adopt in interpreting general policy guidelines.

References

Abbott, S. and Hay, M. (1995), *Investing for the Future* (London: FT-Pitman)

Amit, R., Glosten, L. and Muller, E. (1993), 'Challenges to Theory Development in Entrepreneurship Research', *Journal of Management Studies*, 30(5), pp. 815–834.

Arnold, J. and Moizer, P. (1984), 'A Survey of the Methods Used by UK Investment Analysts to Appraise Investments in Ordinary Shares', *Accounting and Business Research*, Summer, pp. 195–207.

British Venture Capital Association (1995), *Report on Investment Activity 1994* (London: BVCA).

Bruno, A. and Tyebjee, T. (1985), 'The Entrepreneur's Search for Capital', *Journal of Business Venturing*, 1, pp. 61–74.

Bygrave, W. and Timmons, J. (1992), *Venture Capital at the Crossroads* (Boston, Harvard: Business School Press).

Day, J. (1986), 'The Use of Annual Reports by UK Investment Analysts', *Accounting and Business Research*, Autumn.

DeAngelo, L. (1990), 'Equity Valuation and Corporate Control', *Accounting Review*, Vol. 65, No. 1, pp. 93–112.

Dixon, R. (1991) 'Venture Capitalists and the Appraisal of Investments', *Omega*, 19(5), pp. 333–44.

Elango, B., Fried, V., Hisrich, R. and Polonchek, A. (1995), 'How Venture Capital Firms Differ', *Journal of Business Venturing*, 10, pp. 157–179.

Fried, V. and Hisrich, R. (1994), 'Toward a Model of Venture Capital Investment Decision Making' *Financial Management*, 23(3), pp. 28–37.

Jensen, M.C. (1986), 'Agency Costs of Free Cash Flow, Corporate Finance and Takeovers', *American Economic Review*, May, pp. 326–9.

Lee, T.A. and Tweedie, D.P. (1981), *The Institutional Investor and Financial Information* (London: ICAEW).

Lorenz, T. (1989), *Venture Capital Today*, 2nd edition (Cambridge: Woodhead-Faulkner).

MacMillan, I.C., Zemann, L. and Subbanarasimha, P.N.S. (1987), 'Criteria Distinguishing Successful from Unsuccessful Ventures in the Venture Screening Process', *Journal of Business Venturing*, 3, pp. 123–137.

Mitchell, F., Reid, G. and Terry, N. (1995), 'Post Investment Demand for Accounting Information by Venture Capitalists', *Accounting and Business Research*, Vol. 25, No. 99, pp. 186–196.

Moizer, P. and Arnold, J. (1984), 'Share Appraisal by Investment Analysts—A Comparison of the Techniques Used by Portfolio and Non-portfolio Managers', *Accounting and Business Research*, Vol.14 No.56, pp. 341–348

Pike, R., Meerjanssen, J. and Chadwick, L. (1993), 'The Appraisal of Ordinary Shares by Investment Analysts in the UK and Germany', *Accounting and Business Research*, Vol. 23, No. 92, pp. 489–499.

Sahlman, W. (1990), 'The Structure and Governance of Venture Capital Organisations', *Journal of Financial Economics*, 27(2), pp. 473–524.

Sharp, G. (1993), *The Management Buy-out Manual*, Euromoney Books, London.

Steier, L. and Greenwood, R. (1995), 'Venture Capitalist Relationships in the Deal Structuring and Post-investment Stages of New Firm Creation', *Journal of Management Studies*, 32(3), pp. 337–357.

Stiglitz, J. and Weiss, A. (1981), 'Credit Rationing in Markets with Imperfect Information', *American Economic Review*, 71, June, pp. 393–410.

Sweeting, R. (1991) 'Early-stage New Technology-based Business: Interactions with Venture Capitalists and the Development of Accounting Techniques and Procedures', *British Accounting Review*, 23, pp. 3–21.

Walker, A. (1990), 'Types of Finance Available and How They Can Be Used', Ch.5 in de Caires (ed), *Corporate Restructuring*, (London: Euromoney Books).

Wright, M., Robbie, K. and Ennew, C. (1995), 'Venture Capitalists and Second Time Entrepreneurs', in Bygrave, W. et al., *Frontiers of Entrepreneurship Research* (Boston: Wellesley).

[9]

THE JOURNAL OF FINANCE • VOL. XLIX, NO. 2 • JUNE 1994

Robust Financial Contracting and the Role of Venture Capitalists

ANAT R. ADMATI and PAUL PFLEIDERER*

ABSTRACT

We derive a role for inside investors, such as venture capitalists, in resolving various agency problems that arise in a multistage financial contracting problem. Absent an inside investor, the choice of securities is unlikely to reveal all private information, and overinvestment may occur. An inside investor, however, always makes optimal investment decisions if and only if he holds a fixed-fraction contract, where he always receives a fixed fraction of the project's payoff and finances that same fraction of future investments. This contract also eliminates any incentives of the venture capitalist to misprice securities issued in later financing rounds.

IN THIS ARTICLE WE develop a model of financial contracting with multiple investment decisions and show how conflicts of interest and informational asymmetries can be effectively resolved by an inside investor, i.e., an investor who not only provides capital but also works closely with the firm, monitors it frequently, and is generally very well informed about the firm's prospects and investment opportunities. Venture capitalists are obvious examples of inside investors, and their function has been an important motivation for this article. Banks, especially in Japan and Germany, are also involved in monitoring and can be viewed as playing the role of inside investors. In this article we examine the potential benefits of inside investors in a context where there are no restrictions beyond limited liability on the type of financial contracts that can be written.

We address a basic financial contracting problem involving an entrepreneur who has an idea for a project but does not have sufficient capital to fund it. An important assumption is that there are several stages in the project's development and that a decision must be made at each stage whether the project should be continued or abandoned. If the project is continued, the amount of additional capital to be invested must also be determined. We assume that the entrepreneur, as an insider, observes private information about the project's profitability at each stage. This information is not

*We would like to thank Bob Dammon, Bob Keeley, Alan Kraus, David Kreps, Eitan Müller, Roni Ofer, Motty Perry, Art Raviv, René Stulz, Jim Van Horne, Peter Wendell, Ingrid Werner, Mark Wolfson, Josef Zechner, an anonymous referee, and seminar participants at University of Chicago, Northwestern University, and the University of British Columbia for helpful comments. Support from the Robert M. and Anne T. Bass Fellowship, the Sloan Foundation, the National Science Foundation (through grant #SBR-9308238), and the Financial Services Initiative at Stanford Graduate School of Business is gratefully acknowledged.

observed by outside investors and is not verifiable at any point in time so contracts cannot be written contingent on its realization.

If capital for the project is provided by outside investors, but the continuation decision is made by the better informed entrepreneur, then it is easy to see that the entrepreneur has an incentive to continue projects even when it is optimal to abandon them. This occurs because the entrepreneur is not putting up the money for the continuation but does stand to gain if the option to continue pays off. Since the entrepreneur has the incentive to overinvest, she cannot be expected to report her private information truthfully.[1]

It seems that the overinvestment problem described above might be solved if capital is obtained from an inside investor who establishes close ties with the firm, observes the private information about the project's profitability, and becomes involved in making the subsequent investment decisions. However, in general the involvement of an inside investor can create problems as well as solve them. First, assuming that he is not the sole owner of the firm, the inside investor may also make suboptimal investment decisions. For example, and analogous to Myers (1977), if the inside investor must finance in full any future investment but only receives a fraction of the payoffs, he will be inclined to underinvest. Second, the project-specific information that the inside investor acquires in his monitoring activities can give him significant bargaining power in subsequent rounds of financing.[2] If the inside investor is able to use this bargaining power to appropriate much of the firm's value, the entrepreneur may find it too expensive to use the inside investor as a source of capital. Third, if outside investors are also involved in providing capital to the firm, then they would be at an informational disadvantage relative to the entrepreneur and the inside investor, and this can again lead to suboptimal investment decisions.

Our objective in this article is to find the type of financial contracts that the entrepreneur and the inside investor can use to realize the advantages of inside financing and mitigate the disadvantages. Our main focus is on the problem of making optimal continuation and investment decisions, but we will also look at some other agency problems. In examining these issues we believe that it is important to consider the effects of the massive uncertainty that typically accompanies new ventures. This uncertainty makes it very difficult for agents to construct precise probabilistic models, especially if they are "boundedly rational," i.e., have limited processing powers. As a

---

[1] This tendency to overinvest is in many ways the mirror image of the Myers (1977) underinvestment problem. Myers argues that shareholders in a firm will tend to underinvest in situations where risky debt holders in the firm would benefit. In Myers the shareholders put up the money but do not realize all of the gains, while in our model outside investors put up the money, but some of the gains accrue to the entrepreneur.

[2] This bargaining power may come about, since outside investors observe the inside investor's behavior. If the latter refuses to finance new investments, the entrepreneur is likely to have difficulty raising funds from outside investors, since these investors are likely to conclude that the project is not worth financing. Sharpe (1990) and Rajan (1992) consider the effects of this bargaining problem in the context of banking contracts. (See below for a more detailed discussion of these papers.)

Robust Financial Contracting and Venture Capitalists   373

consequence, agents are unsure that any particular probabilistic model of the world is correct and complete. This leads us to seek contracts that are "robust." Roughly speaking, a contract is robust with respect to some property if it is not critical that some specific probabilistic model of the world be correct for the contract to have that property. We capture this notion of robustness by allowing the state space in our model to be extremely large, so that effectively "nothing can be ruled out," and by requiring that contracts have certain properties no matter what distributions are assessed.

Before considering the role played by an inside investor, we examine what the entrepreneur can achieve by dealing directly with outside investors at each stage of the investment process. We call this *entrepreneur-led financing*. It has been suggested, for example in Heinkel (1982), Brennan and Kraus (1987), Constantinides and Grundy (1989), and Thakor (1989), that private information held by entrepreneurs (or managers) can be communicated to outside investors through the set of securities they issue. We show, however, that fully revealing signaling equilibria are not robust in the sense described above, and, in particular, do not exist in those cases where firms' types are distinguished by the probability that the project will fail. Thus, we cannot generally expect signaling equilibria to resolve information asymmetries in the environment we seek to model. Unresolved information asymmetries are then shown to be costly to the entrepreneur, since they can lead to suboptimal investment decisions, lowering the initial value of the firm.

We proceed to introduce an inside investor who makes the continuation and investment decisions. *For concreteness we will refer to the inside investor as a venture capitalist for the remainder of the paper*. We assume that the venture capitalist observes the same information about the project's viability observed by the entrepreneur in the later stage, which means that no informational asymmetries exist between the entrepreneur and the venture capitalist. However, outside investors who might also be involved in financing the project do not observe this information. We show that there is a unique contract, which we call a *fixed-fraction contract*, that can be written between the entrepreneur and the venture capitalist that is robust with respect to optimal continuation. In other words, under this contract the venture capitalist will make the optimal investment decision in any contingency, and no other contract has this property. The fixed-fraction contract gives the venture capitalist an equity-like position in the firm, so that he is paid a fraction of the total payoffs and finances that same fraction of any future investment. In a sense, the venture capitalist becomes the sole owner of a fixed portion of the project and he provides all the capital needed for this portion. If the entrepreneur retains a financial stake in the firm, this contract requires that outside investors are involved in later financing stages. In the context of venture capital contracting, this explains why, even in a risk-neutral setting without capital constraints, later stages are not fully financed by the lead venture capitalist.

An important feature of the fixed-fraction contract is that although the venture capitalist purchases new securities in later financing rounds, his payoff is independent of the pricing of any newly issued securities. The pricing of new securities only affects the division of surplus between the entrepreneur and outside investors, where the entrepreneur gains if new securities are overpriced and outside investors gain if they are underpriced relative to their value given all available information. Intuitively, the venture capitalist's incentives as a "new shareholder" to underprice new securities (and thereby take value away from the entrepreneur) are exactly offset by his incentives as an "old shareholder" to overprice them (and thereby take away value from outside investors). Since he cannot gain by mispricing the new securities, the venture capitalist can be given the responsibility of pricing those securities and revealing the information he knows.[3]

Our model and the specific results we obtain are generally consistent with the stylized facts about the venture capital industry. First, many authors, including Sahlman (1990), Lerner (1992b), Macmillan, Kulow, and Khoylian (1988), and Gorman and Sahlman (1989), document the many ways in which venture capitalists are involved with their portfolio firms. For example, venture capitalists often serve on boards of directors, provide help in recruiting and compensating key individuals, work with suppliers and customers, get involved in establishing strategies, and play a major role in raising capital. In some situations, in fact, venture capitalists take complete control over the firm and dismiss the original entrepreneur.[4] This evidence supports our assumption that the venture capitalist is likely to be significantly better informed than other capital providers and that he effectively makes continuation decisions.

As is key in our model, the staging of commitment of capital is common in the venture capital industry. Sahlman (1988, 1990) argues that this is intended to give venture capitalists a role in making continuation decisions.[5] As our results suggest, venture capitalists typically hold equity-linked claims, and many initial agreements give them "preemptive rights and rights of first refusal" in future financing rounds.[6] Also consistent with our results, a number of papers suggest that venture capitalists are typically very involved in obtaining capital from outside investors, especially in later stages of the

---

[3] We also show that the fixed-fraction contract resolves the bargaining problem that potentially exists between the entrepreneur and the venture capitalist. Under the terms of the contract the venture capitalist has no ability to extract surplus from the entrepreneur. Surplus can only be extracted if the contract is violated or renegotiated. In Section IV we discuss how the contract can be written so that renegotiation does not occur.

[4] For models that address the issue of control in the context of venture capital contracting see Chan, Siegel, and Thakor (1990) and Berglöf (1992). For a model in which the venture capitalist is able to change the probability distribution of the outcome, see Amit, Glosten, and Müller (1991).

[5] Gompers (1992b) suggests that staging mitigates various agency problems that arise when there are intangible assets, and his empirical results generally confirm this proposition.

[6] Specifically, venture capitalists are often entitled to participate in later financing rounds "by buying newly issued shares from the company, often in proportion to their common-share equivalent holdings before the issuance of new equity-equivalent shares" (Sahlman (1990, p. 505)).

project (see Sahlman (1990), Macmillan, Kulow, and Khoylian (1988), Sapienza and Timmons (1989), and especially Gorman and Sahlman (1989)). Moreover, the literature on the role of venture capitalists in initial public offerings (IPOs) also supports our model's conclusions and especially the "certification" role of venture capitalists.[7]

We are aware of two papers in the literature on venture capital contracting that examine specifically the issue of optimal continuation decisions in a multistage investment problem. In Cooper and Carleton (1979), the venture capitalist is the sole provider of funds throughout the life of the project. Both the venture capitalist and the entrepreneur make decisions in each stage whether to continue investing (capital and effort respectively) in the project to get to the next stage. There is no asymmetric information, and the potential role of the venture capitalist as an intermediary between the entrepreneur and outside investors is not considered. Hansen (1991) analyzes a model of two-stage financing of start-up firms where the entrepreneur obtains private information after the first stage of the project and makes the continuation decision. Since there is asymmetric information between the entrepreneur and the venture capitalist in the second stage of the project, the venture capitalist in Hansen's model is completely analogous to the uninformed, outside investors in our model of entrepreneur-led financing (see Section II).

As mentioned earlier, banks may also serve as inside investors, and so our work is related to some articles in the banking literature.[8] The most closely related papers to our work in this literature are Sharpe (1990) and Rajan (1992). In these models banks learn information about their borrowers that other lenders do not observe. In Sharpe (1990) this allows the inside bank to capture some surplus in later period loans, but investment distortions arise because competition drives banks to write loans in the first period at lower than break-even rates. Rajan argues that borrowing from an inside bank reduces effort-incentives, since the bank is able to extract surplus from the firm in the second stage. On the other hand, he shows that borrowing from the bank leads to better liquidation decisions in the second stage.

There are a number of important differences between our model and those of Sharpe (1990) and Rajan (1992). First, the contracting environment in these models is different from the one we consider. Sharpe focuses mainly on situations in which banks cannot make multiperiod binding commitments. In

---

[7]Lim and Saunders (1990), Megginson and Weiss (1991), Barry, Muscarella, Peavey, and Vetsuypens (1991), Lerner (1992a), and Gompers (1992a) discuss the certification role, as well as other roles venture capitalists play in later financings, specifically in initial public offerings (IPOs). Note, however, that if capital constraints exist, an IPO may be the main way for the venture capitalist to liquidate at least some of his position in the firm. Also, because of the size of the company at this stage, risk aversion may become important. Thus, the venture capitalist may not keep his fixed fraction at the IPO stage. This may not be a problem since, in an IPO, investment bankers typically take the role of financial intermediaries and use their reputations to resolve informational asymmetries.

[8]For a comprehensive survey of this very large literature see Bhattacharya and Thakor (1994).

the second stage of his model all banks make unobservable loan contract offers both to the firms they lent to in the first period and to firms that received loans from other banks in the first period. Banks capture surplus from the high quality firms they lent to in the first period by making slightly more attractive offers than uninformed banks. Rajan assumes that an informed bank engages in negotiation with the entrepreneur at the second stage, with an exogenous specification of the bargaining outcome. By contrast, we allow initial financing agreements to be written in which a restricted menu of continuation options is available to the venture capitalist in the second stage. Also, both Sharpe and Rajan make specific parametric assumptions, while our main focus is on the choice of robust contracts.[9]

A crucial distinction between the banking literature, including the articles discussed above, and this article is that the banking literature has focused almost exclusively on debt contracts. This is consistent with banking regulations in the U.S. and can also be justified by assuming costly payoff observation. By contrast, we assume here that the securities held by the inside investor can have any form as long as they are measurable functions of final payoffs. Our results suggest that the fixed-fraction contract, which is essentially a linear, equity-like contract, is the best contract to give an inside investor when there are no regulatory restrictions and payoffs are verifiable. It should be noted that banks in Japan and Germany, which are not restricted to holding debt and are generally more involved in monitoring than banks in the U.S., do hold equity.[10] The debate on whether banks should be allowed to own equity involves a number of issues not addressed above and is beyond the scope of this paper. Nevertheless, our analysis suggests that a move towards "universal banking" might allow banks to be more effective in their role as inside investors. For further discussion and additional references on this issue see Berlin, John, and Saunders (1993).

Several authors have shown that even when one is restricted to debt-like contracts, there are ways to alleviate information asymmetries and at least partially solve the over- and underinvestment problems discussed earlier. For example, Bester (1985) and Chan and Thakor (1987) examine the role of collateral in signaling private information; Berkovitch and Greenbaum (1991) explore the use of loan commitments; Berkovitch and Kim (1990) study the effectiveness of seniority rules and dividend covenants in controlling investment incentives; and Stulz and Johnson (1985) suggest that secured debt can be used to reduce distortions.[11] The use of many of these mechanisms may be

---

[9] Also, in Section V we show that the additional information used by the venture capitalist for pricing securities under the fixed-fraction contract partly alleviates the agency problems that arise when entrepreneurial effort is not observed. In Rajan's model, by contrast, the effort problem is aggravated in the presence of the inside bank because of the extraction of surplus in the second stage.

[10] Hoshi, Kashyap, and Scharfstein (1990, 1991) document some of the effects of having close ties with banks on investment decisions and the possibility of financial distress for Japanese firms.

[11] For a survey of these issues in the context of firms' capital structure decisions, see Harris and Raviv (1991).

quite limited in the context of start-up companies and new ventures. For example, the use of secured debt and collateral is not likely to be very effective, since in most cases the assets of start-up companies are intangible, and the initial funding is used mostly to purchase supplies, meet a payroll, rent space, etc. Also, these approaches do not typically lead to robust contracts, since the properties of the contracts depend on specific distributional assumptions.

The robustness of the fixed-fraction contract is due to the fact that it is linearly related to both payoffs and capital input requirements. The special features of linear contracts have been recognized in several papers. For example, Dybvig and Zender (1991) consider the suboptimal investment problems identified in Myers and Majluf (1984). These occur when a manager makes investment decisions and the market is imperfectly informed about the value of the firm's existing assets and new investment opportunities. Dybvig and Zender argue that the source of the suboptimal decisions in the Myers-Majluf model is the manager's suboptimal contract. They suggest that a contract similar to our fixed-fraction contract will create the proper incentives for the manager to make the optimal investment decisions. They also observe that capital structure is irrelevant under the optimal contract, which is related to our observation that, with a fixed-fraction contract, the venture capitalist's payoff is independent of the payoff of outside investors.

Another related article that points to the special properties of linear contracts is Ravid and Spiegel (1992). This article considers a contracting problem with a one-period payoff and assumes that there is a limited supply of positive net present value (NPV) projects but a potentially infinite supply of nonpositive NPV projects. It shows that contracts that screen bad projects essentially must be linear, since deviations from linearity can be exploited by entrepreneurs creating bad projects. Although the setting is somewhat different, this result is complementary to ours, since it applies to the first period screening problem while we are considering conditions for optimal investment in later periods.

The article is organized as follows. The basic model is presented in Section I. In Section II we analyze entrepreneur-led financing. Section III introduces the notion of venture capital financing and shows that the fixed-fraction contract is the only contract that always induces optimal continuation. In Section IV we discuss issues related to enforcement and renegotiation of the contract. Section V illustrates by an example how the presence of a venture capitalist can partly alleviate the agency problem that arises when effort is unobservable. In Section VI we discuss briefly the effects of risk aversion on our results. Concluding remarks are found in Section VII.

I. The Model

There are three periods. Initially, the entrepreneur has access to a project that requires an immediate investment of K and, if the project is not subsequently abandoned, some additional investment in the second period.

The entrepreneur has no capital in either period. We assume that the entrepreneur will sell securities in the first period sufficient to raise capital K, but will not raise more than K.[12] If financing of the first stage is successful, the project proceeds to the next period, when a decision concerning the level of additional funding for the project must be made. (This includes the possibility that no further investment is made, i.e., the project is abandoned.) This decision is made in light of the realization of the state of the world s.[13] The state is unknown in the initial period, but it is observed by the entrepreneur and, if he is involved, by the venture capitalist before the continuation decision must be made.

If the project is abandoned, the value that can be recovered is a nonnegative random variable $\tilde{\psi}$, whose value is completely determined by the state—in state s it is given by ψ_s.[14] If the project is continued in state s and an investment of I is made in the second stage, then the total payoff realized in the final period is a nonnegative random variable $\tilde{\theta}$, whose distribution function is parameterized by I and s and is denoted by $F(\cdot | I, s)$. We assume that the level of investment I is a choice variable that can be determined in the second period after the state is observed. The only restriction we impose on the distributions of $\tilde{\psi}$ and $\tilde{\theta}$ is that both conditionally and unconditionally they have finite expected values.

We will consider two possibilities for the entrepreneur to obtain financing for the project. In an *entrepreneur-led financing* the entrepreneur approaches outside investors in each of the two stages. To obtain financing in the first stage the entrepreneur issues claims on the project's payoffs with the following general structure. If the project is abandoned in state s, then the initial investors receive $M(\psi_s)$ and the entrepreneur receives $\psi_s - M(\psi_s)$. If the project is financed at a level I in the second stage, then the initial investors receive $N_I(\tilde{\theta})$, and the providers of the second stage capital receive $R_I(\tilde{\theta})$ when the total final period payoff of the project is $\tilde{\theta}$. More generally, $R_I(\tilde{\theta})$ represents any refinancing of the outside investors' claims on the firm that is done in the second period, so that the total net claims held by security holders in the final period is $N_I(\tilde{\theta}) + R_I(\tilde{\theta})$ if an investment of I is made and the total payoff is $\tilde{\theta}$.

---

[12] This means that the entrepreneur does not sell out completely in the first stage. Obviously, if an inside investor such as a venture capitalist buys out the entrepreneur, then the problem of optimal continuation becomes trivial. In practice venture capitalists do not buy out entrepreneurs entirely in the initial stages of a new project. Outside investors may lack the knowledge and ability to run the project and, more generally, it is likely that for a variety of reasons (in particular, those related to effort incentives) the project cannot be carried out if the entrepreneur is bought out. On this issue see also our discussion in Section III following Proposition 2.

[13] The state can represent any information that becomes known in the second period about the viability and marketability of the product being developed and about the technical and managerial ability of the entrepreneur.

[14] This abandonment value could be the liquidation value of the project's assets or it could be the value of running the project with no further investment.

Another way for the entrepreneur to finance the project is to involve a venture capitalist. In this case the venture capitalist provides all of the capital needed for the first stage and possibly some of the capital needed in the second stage. In the first period, the entrepreneur and the venture capitalist enter into an *initial financing agreement*. This agreement is represented by a pair $\{A(\cdot), Z\}$. The function $A(\cdot)$ is similar to $M(\cdot)$ above and describes how the payoffs of the project are divided between the entrepreneur and the venture capitalist, if the project is abandoned in the second period. If the project is abandoned in state s, the venture capitalist receives $A(\psi_s)$, and the entrepreneur receives $\psi_s - A(\psi_s)$. The set Z specifies the financing arrangements that are permissible for financing the second stage. An element z of Z is a triple $\{I_z, \beta_z, B_z(\cdot)\}$ with the following interpretation. If the financing arrangement z is implemented, then a total of I_z will be raised, of which the venture capitalist will provide $\beta_z I_z$, and outside parties will provide $(1 - \beta_z)I_z$. The venture capitalist will then receive $B_z(\bar\theta)$, if the final value of the project is $\bar\theta$. The initial financing agreement itself, including the venture capitalist's choice from the set Z, is assumed to be enforceable. (Section IV discusses this in more detail.) Table I summarizes the notation that will be used throughout the article.

We assume that in the case of entrepreneur-led financing, outside investors do not observe the state s. However, the venture capitalist does observe s when it becomes observable to the entrepreneur. This distinction arises from

Table I

Summary of Notation

K Amount of capital needed in the first stage.

I Amount of capital invested in the second stage, a choice variable.

s The state of the world, realized after the first stage.

ψ_s The total payoff of the project if it is abandoned after the first stage and the state is s.

$\bar\theta$ The total payoff of the project if further investments are made in the second stage.

$F(\cdot|I, s)$ The distribution of $\bar\theta$ if a level of investment I is chosen and the state is s.

$M(\psi_s)$ The payoffs to providers of first-stage capital (in an entrepreneur-led financing) if the project is abandoned in state s.

$N_I(\bar\theta)$ The payoffs to providers of first-stage capital (in an entrepreneur-led financing) if the project is continued with an investment of I and its total payoff is $\bar\theta$.

$R_I(\bar\theta)$ The payoffs to providers of second-stage capital (in an entrepreneur-led financing) if the project is continued with an investment of I and its total payoff is $\bar\theta$.

$A(\psi_s)$ The payoff to the venture capitalist if the project is abandoned in state s.

Z The set of financing arrangements for the second stage investment that the venture capitalist can choose from.

I_z The level of second-stage investment if z is the chosen financing arrangement for the second stage.

β_z The fraction of I_z which will be financed by the lead venture capitalist if z is the chosen financing arrangement for the second stage.

$B_z(\bar\theta)$ The payoff to the venture capitalist if z is the chosen financing arrangement for the second stage and the total payoff of the project is $\bar\theta$.

our assumption that, unlike other investors, the venture capitalist works closely with the entrepreneur and hence is able to monitor the project and observe the state.[15] Based on his information, the venture capitalist makes the decision whether to continue the project or abandon it, and, if the project is continued, he chooses an element from the set Z to maximize his expected payoff given s.[16] As we will see, it is possible to construct the set Z so that the continuation decision made by the venture capitalist is the one that maximizes the expected payoffs of the project net of the investment given the state. This also implies that if the entrepreneur cannot commit to following the optimal continuation strategy, she would prefer to have the venture capitalist make the continuation decision, since this would maximize the ex ante surplus earned by the entrepreneur.

We make the following additional assumptions:

ASSUMPTION 1: (*Risk neutrality and no discounting*). *All capital providers as well as the entrepreneur are risk neutral. The rate at which future cash flows are discounted is zero.*

ASSUMPTION 2: (*Limited liability*). *The contracts under both financing regimes are consistent with limited liability. Specifically, each of $A(\bar{\psi})$ and $M(\bar{\psi})$ is nonnegative and not larger than $\bar{\psi}$; each of $N_l(\bar{\theta})$, $R_l(\bar{\theta})$ and $B_z(\bar{\theta})$ is nonnegative and not larger than $\bar{\theta}$.*

ASSUMPTION 3: (*Competitive capital market*). *All capital providers obtain expected payoffs equal to their investment.*

ASSUMPTION 4: (*Asymmetric Information*). *If financing is entrepreneur led, the state of the world is observed only by the entrepreneur, but not by any provider of capital. If financing is done via a venture capitalist, then both the entrepreneur and the venture capitalist observe the state. Other providers of capital in the second stage do not observe the state.*

The risk neutrality assumption is relaxed in Section VI, where we discuss the effects of risk aversion. The assumption of no discounting is made purely for convenience and without loss of generality. The limited liability assumption is very important for our results. It simply says that no money other than that generated by the project can be paid out. If there were true unlimited liability, the entrepreneur could issue riskless debt and there would, of course, be no financing problems created by the asymmetric information. This, however, is inconsistent with the assumption that the

---

[15] We are not including in the analysis a cost for monitoring the project, i.e., a cost incurred by the venture capitalist in order to observe the state. See the concluding remarks for a discussion of this issue.

[16] Note that the formal statement of the initial financing agreement only addresses the role the venture capitalist plays in making continuation and investment decisions, but does not say anything about who makes other managerial decisions. In practice the entrepreneur and the venture capitalist are both actively involved in these other decisions, but we do not explicitly model how these other responsibilities are divided between them. See the concluding remarks for more discussion on the other roles the venture capitalist plays.

entrepreneur has no outside financial resources to draw upon. It also tends to distinguish the situation in a start-up company from the financing problem of an established firm that might have financial slack.[17] Assumption 3, that the capital market is competitive, however, is not important for much of our analysis. The basic results would not change much if, for example, the venture capitalist shares the ex ante surplus with the entrepreneur. As for Assumption 4 on the information structure, note that asymmetric information is assumed to exist in the second stage but not in the first stage. This allows us to focus on the second stage financing and investment decision. (See the concluding remarks for a discussion of asymmetric information at the first stage.) Note also that the fundamental distinction between entrepreneur-led financing and venture capital financing is that the venture capitalist is an inside investor who observes the state of the world, while investors in entrepreneur-led financing do not.

II. Entrepreneur-led Financing

We first consider the case where financing is led by the entrepreneur and involves only outside investors in each stage. In seeking capital for the second stage of the project, the entrepreneur has private information, since she observes the state s while investors do not. Heinkel (1982) and Brennan and Kraus (1987) have suggested that this type of asymmetric information can sometimes be overcome costlessly. This occurs in a signaling equilibrium in which the set of securities issued by the entrepreneur fully reveals her private information. Brennan and Kraus (1987) derive necessary and sufficient conditions on the type of private information held by the entrepreneur (or manager) and on the set of possible securities that can be issued for the existence of such a fully revealing signaling equilibrium.

We consider the following simple signaling game. First, nature chooses the state s, and the state is revealed to the entrepreneur. Then the entrepreneur chooses a set of securities to issue, where each security specifies the payoff to the claimholder as a function of the final payoff $\tilde{\theta}$. She also specifies the price for the securities. Investors then choose which claims to purchase given the price and their beliefs concerning the final payoff distribution. Investors face no capital constraints and are competitive, and the equilibrium concept we use is Bayesian Nash.

The next result shows that there is a sense in which fully revealing signaling equilibria are not robust. Specifically, whenever such an equilibrium exists, it is always possible to upset the equilibrium with the addition of one new state, and the equilibrium cannot be restored even if the entrepreneur is allowed to change the set of securities she issues. Moreover, the proposition and its proof imply that the conditions identified, in Brennan and

---

[17] Hansen (1991) analyzes a model in which the degree of liability for the entrepreneur is endogenous. In his model the entrepreneur may be liable for paying back wages earned during the life of the project.

Kraus (1987) and others for the existence of a fully revealing signaling equilibrium are quite severe; such equilibria do not exist for a large class of situations, including essentially all the realistic situations arising in the context of start-up firms. For example, new ventures tend to be very risky and typically have a positive probability of resulting in "total loss."[18] Some information about the likelihood of failure is often uncovered following the first few stages of the project. However, in the proof of the proposition below, we show that a fully revealing signaling equilibrium never exists if there are two states under which payoffs have the same distribution conditional on being positive but which imply different probabilities of zero payoffs. Two such states cannot be separated, because the worse type will always want to imitate the actions of the better type. Thus, in the context of entrepreneurial projects, we cannot expect asymmetric information to be completely resolved through costless signaling. The proof of this and subsequent results is in the appendix.

PROPOSITION 1: *Suppose financing is entrepreneur-led. Assume that there is a state $s \in S$ in which the optimal continuation level is I and, at this level of investment, $\Pr(\bar{\theta} - N_I(\bar{\theta}) < I | I, s) > 0$. Assume there exists a signaling equilibrium in which the set of contracts offered by the entrepreneur fully separates the states in S. Then it is possible to augment S by adding one other state s' so that with the augmented set of possible states there does not exist a fully revealing signaling equilibrium even if the set of possible contracts is allowed to change as well. In this sense the fully revealing signaling equilibrium is not robust to small changes in the model.*

The logic of the proof is straightforward: the new state s' is constructed so that it will be impossible to separate s from s' through financial contracts. State s' differs from state s, in that under s' some probability mass has been moved to an unfavorable outcome in which the firm does not cover the second stage investment in full given its initial commitments. It is easy to see that type s' will always want to imitate type s, breaking any potential separating signaling equilibrium. *This argument holds for any conjectured set of securities and refinancing possibilities.* There is no way that s and s' can be distinguished in equilibrium through the entrepreneur's choice of securities.[19]

We have established that if we rely on the communication of information through financial contracts, then asymmetric information between the

---

[18] Data on venture capital performance shows, for example, that of 383 investments made by 13 firms between 1969 and 1985, more than one-third resulted in an absolute loss (see Venture Economics (1988)).

[19] Note that the proposition requires that for some state there is a positive probability that the firm cannot cover the investment of I (after paying the initial security holders). In requiring this we eliminate cases in which the entrepreneur can finance the optimal second-stage investment with riskless debt in every state. If riskless debt can always be issued, then asymmetric information does not lead to any inefficiency. This does not seem to be a realistic situation—start-up firms are rarely in a position to finance their investment through riskless debt.

Robust Financial Contracting and Venture Capitalists   383

entrepreneur and capital providers is likely to persist in equilibrium. The main issue, however, is whether this information asymmetry can lead to suboptimal investment decisions by the entrepreneur. We now show by an example that in our setting the entrepreneur may indeed overinvest if her private information is not revealed to outside investors.

Assume that, in all possible states, $\tilde{\theta}$ can take on only two values, ten and zero. Also assume that the initial investment level is $K = 1$, that the second stage investment level is fixed at $I = 3$ and that the abandonment value ψ_s is 1 for all possible states. Finally, let the probability that $\tilde{\theta} = 10$ in state s be s. Assume that ex ante (in the initial period) s is distributed uniformly on [0,1]. In this example it is easy to see that the optimal continuation decision (in terms of the net expected payoff of the project) is to continue if and only if $s > (\psi + I)/10 = 0.4$. It is also straightforward to show that there is no signaling equilibrium that can fully reveal s through the entrepreneur's choice of contracts. We now show that in fact there is no equilibrium in which the entrepreneur makes the optimal continuation decision in all states of the world.

Let M be the payment made to the initial investors if the project is abandoned, let N be the payment made to initial investors if the project is continued and $\tilde{\theta} = 10$, and let R be the payment made to the providers of the second stage capital when $\tilde{\theta} = 10$. From our assumptions we must have $0 \le M \le \psi = 1$, both N and R must be nonnegative and $N + R \le 10$. If the entrepreneur invests precisely in states s, where $s > 0.4$, then M, N, and R must solve the following equations

$$0.4M + 0.6(0.7)N = K = 1, \tag{1}$$
$$0.4(10 - N - R) = \Psi - M = 1 - M, \tag{2}$$

and

$$0.7R = I = 3. \tag{3}$$

Equation (1) states that the securities given to the initial investors must be worth K. With probability 0.4 the project will be abandoned, in which case the initial investors will receive M, and with probability 0.6 the project will be continued, in which case the probability of receiving N is 0.7 since, conditional on continuation, s is uniformly distributed on the interval [0.4, 1]. The next condition, equation (2), guarantees that when $s = 0.4$, the entrepreneur is indifferent between continuing and not continuing. The final equation guarantees that the providers of second-stage capital have an expected payoff equal to I. The unique solution to these three equations is

$$M = -0.2414, \quad N = 2.6108, \quad R = 4.2857. \tag{4}$$

Obviously, since M is negative, this solution violates limited liability.

In this example, the best payoff for the entrepreneur is defined when

$$M = 0.0, \quad N = 2.2149, \quad R = 4.5749, \tag{5}$$

which leads the entrepreneur to choose to continue whenever $s > 0.3115$. Thus, for $0.3115 \le s < 0.4$, the entrepreneur continues the project, although in the first best world (where, for example, the entrepreneur has enough wealth to finance the project herself or s is directly observed by all parties) it is optimal to abandon it. This inefficiency is reflected in the ex ante value of the project—the project's ex ante value to the entrepreneur is reduced from 1.8 to 1.7608 as a consequence of the suboptimal continuation policy.

III. Financing with a Venture Capitalist

In this section we analyze the case where the financing of the first stage of the project, as well as possibly some of the second stage, is done by an inside investor such as a venture capitalist. Recall that in our model, after observing the state, the venture capitalist chooses a continuation course among the set of possible scenarios agreed upon initially. In order to maximize the net surplus from the project, the entrepreneur will wish to set up the initial financing agreement so that the venture capitalist has incentives to choose an investment level that maximizes the ex ante value of the project.

Below, we identify a particularly simple type of contract for the venture capitalist, in which, after the first investment of capital, the venture capitalist always obtains a fixed fraction of the *net* payoffs of the project. It is easy to see that this type of contract induces optimal continuation. We show, however, that this is the *only* robust contract with this property. Any other contract that might induce optimal continuation for a particular environment is not robust to small changes in the model such as adding another possible state of the world.

We first define precisely the notion that the initial financing agreement induces optimal continuation. Let S^N be the set of states for which it is optimal to abandon the project. That is, $s \in S^N$ iff

$$\sup_I (\mathrm{E}(\bar{\theta}|I, s) - I) < \psi_s.$$

Definition: An initial financing agreement $\{A(\cdot), Z\}$ induces optimal continuation if and only if for any possible state of the world, i.e., for every ψ_s and any family of distributions $F(\cdot|I, s)$, the following holds:

(a) if $s \in S^N$, then

$$\sup_z \left(\mathrm{E}\left(B_z(\bar{\theta})|I_z, s\right) - \beta_z I_z \right) \leq A(\psi_s).$$

and
(b) if $s \notin S^N$, then there exists $z \in Z$ such that

(i) $I_z \in \arg\max_I (\mathrm{E}(\bar{\theta}|I, s) - I)$,

(ii) $\mathrm{E}(B_z(\bar{\theta})|I_z, s) - \beta_z I_z \geq A(\psi_s)$,

(iii) for all $z' \in Z$

$$\mathrm{E}\left(B_z(\bar{\theta})|I_z, s\right) - \beta_z I_z \geq \mathrm{E}\left(B_{z'}(\bar{\theta})|I_{z'}, s\right) - \beta_{z'} I_{z'}$$

In words, an initial financing agreement induces optimal continuation if it always gives the venture capitalist incentives to make the optimal continuation decision in the second period. Such a contract will be robust with respect to optimal continuation. Condition (a) says that if $s \in S^N$, so that not continuing is the optimal strategy, then for every possible contract in the set Z, the venture capitalist (at least weakly) prefers that no continuation takes place. This ensures that no projects are continued that should be abandoned. Condition (b) says that if $s \notin S^N$, so that continuation is optimal at some level, then there exists a permitted financing arrangement $z = \{I_z, \beta_z, B_z(\cdot)\}$ that involves the optimal level of investment in the second stage and that leads to the highest payoffs to the venture capitalist among all possible financing arrangements.

The following result provides necessary and sufficient conditions for the set of initial financing agreements to induce optimal continuation.

PROPOSITION 2: *The initial financing agreement* $\{A(\cdot), Z\}$ *induces optimal continuation if and only if there exists* $\alpha \in (0, 1]$ *such that*

(a) $A(\psi) = \alpha\psi$;

(b) *for all* $I > 0$, *there exists* $z \in Z$ *such that*

  (i) $I_z = I$
  (ii) $\beta_z = \alpha$
  (iii) $B_z(\theta) = \alpha\theta$

(c) *for all* $z \in Z$ *and all* s, $E(B_z(\bar{\theta})|I_z, s) - \beta_z I_z \leq \alpha(E(\bar{\theta}|I_z, s) - I_z)$.

This result identifies a special type of financing agreement involving an equity-like contract with the following feature: the venture capitalist obtains a fraction α of the total payoffs of the project no matter what the continuation strategy is. If the project is continued and an investment of I is needed in the second stage, then the venture capitalist puts up αI and the rest, $(1 - \alpha)I$, is financed by third parties. Thus, the fraction of the second stage investment that is put up by the original venture capitalist is equal to the fraction of the total payoffs that he would obtain if no continuation takes place, and this is the same fraction of the total payoffs that he obtains for any positive second stage investment level that is chosen. We will call the contracts identified in Proposition 2 *fixed-fraction contracts*. Note that these contracts are similar to equity in that they give the venture capitalist a fixed fraction of the payoff. However, *unlike common equity, the venture capitalist does not own a residual claim, since his shares have priority over all other claims issued by the firm.*[20]

It is easy to see why fixed-fraction contracts induce optimal continuation. After the initial investment, the venture capitalist simply owns under all circumstances a fixed fraction of the project, for which he is also the sole provider of capital. Dybvig and Zender (1991) have observed in another

---

[20] The fixed-fraction contract bears similarity to the notion of "strip financing," where certain agents receive the same fraction of all the securities issued by the firm.

context that linear contracts of this type given to managers induce optimal choice of projects.[21] Proposition 2 is stronger, however, since it asserts that not only does the fixed-fraction contract always induce optimal continuation, but this is the only type of contract which has this property. Part (c) says that if there are any other contracts in the set Z that are not fixed-fraction contracts, then these contracts are redundant. The entrepreneur is at best indifferent between choosing these alternative contracts and the fixed-fraction contract. Thus, the fixed-fraction contract must be in any set Z that induces optimal continuation and anything else is superfluous.

To obtain some intuition for the result, let us restrict the possible contracts for the venture capitalist to be linear in the total payoff. If, for example, the fraction of the new investment that the venture capitalist had to put up were higher than the fraction of the final payoffs he was promised, then it is easy to see that in some situations the venture capitalist would abandon projects that should be continued. On the other hand, if the venture capitalist obtained a higher fraction of the payoff than the fraction of the investment he puts up, then there would be projects that he would choose to continue, although it would be optimal to abandon them. Thus, with linear contracts optimal continuation necessarily entails the perfect alignment of the fraction of the investment put up by the venture capitalist and the fraction of the payoffs he obtains. This, of course, does not rule out the possibility that there are other nonlinear schemes that can achieve the same results. The demonstration that nonlinear contracts are not robust is more complicated, and the interested reader is referred to the proof.

It is important to note that *any* fixed-fraction contract, i.e., any positive level of α, will induce optimal continuation. How α is actually determined depends on the relative bargaining power of the entrepreneur and the venture capitalist in the initial period. Under the assumption of a competitive capital market (Assumption 3), the value of α is determined in the first period to give the venture capitalist an overall expected payoff equal to the initial investment K, taking into account that he will receive α of the net payoffs no matter which continuation decision is made. This also requires, as we have assumed, that the venture capitalist does not completely buy out the entrepreneur, which would effectively correspond to the entrepreneur "raising" more than K in capital (assuming that the project has a positive NPV overall). If we allow the venture capitalist to buy the entrepreneur out, then the resulting contract is also a fixed-fraction contract, with $\alpha = 1$, and where the entrepreneur obtains the expected value of her idea given initial information. In this case the venture capitalist is the sole owner and capital provider of the project. This of course is a trivial solution to the investment problem. Proposition 2 asserts that it is possible to obtain optimal continuation under all circumstances, even without having the venture capitalist become the sole

---

[21] The contract suggested in Dybvig and Zender (1991) involves a constant payment as well. This is due to the reservation utility assumed for the manager. In our model the reservation utility for the venture capitalist is zero. In fact, in our model if the investment might result in a total loss then it is not possible to pay a fixed positive payment because of limited liability.

owner and capital provider of the entire project. This is important, since for a variety of reasons, such as effort incentives, it may be preferable that the entrepreneur has a stake in the firm rather than being paid a fixed amount. (See footnote 2.)

If $\alpha < 1$, which, as argued above, is the typical case, then the venture capitalist only finances a fraction $\alpha < 1$ of the investment in the second stage. Outside investors must therefore be called for to put up some capital. This provides a rationale, even in our risk-neutral setting with no capital constraints, for the fact that new investors are typically recruited in later stages of financing for start-up companies.

When outside investors are involved in financing the second stage of the project, we have to confront the problem that arises because the entrepreneur and the venture capitalist have an informational advantage over outside investors at that stage. The asymmetric information problem here is similar to that in entrepreneur-led financing. However, the presence of a venture capitalist who holds a fixed-fraction contract makes it possible to resolve the problem. This follows because it turns out that with fixed-fraction contracts, the venture capitalist's payoff is independent of the pricing of any securities issued in the second stage. The pricing of these securities simply determines how the surplus from the project is divided between the entrepreneur and outside investors; the venture capitalist obtains a fixed fraction of the net surplus in all cases. The venture capitalist's incentives to overprice new securities, being an old shareholder like the entrepreneur, are exactly offset by his incentives to underprice new securities, being a capital provider in the second stage. This is another attractive feature of fixed-fraction contracts.

Given the above, it is reasonable to allow the venture capitalist to play a certification role in the issuance of new securities. In effect, the venture capitalist can be assumed to reveal the state information truthfully, since he has no incentives to misrepresent it. If any reputational assets are at stake either with outside investors or with the entrepreneur, the venture capitalist will clearly reveal the information truthfully, thereby resolving the informational asymmetry. Dybvig and Zender (1991) also observe that if a contract similar to the one we focus on is given to risk-neutral managers, they become indifferent to the pricing of new securities. As they show, this can lead to irrelevancy of capital structure even with asymmetric information. Similarly, our model so far does not predict the type of securities issued in the second stage. In Sections V and VI we will introduce considerations such as effort incentives and risk aversion that will bear on this issue, since the types of securities issued to capital providers determine the payoff structure to the entrepreneur who holds the residual claim on the firm.

IV. Enforcement and Renegotiation

A maintained assumption in our analysis has been that initial financing agreements are enforceable. Note that in our formulation, enforcement of the contract does not require that the state of the world be verifiable by the courts. That is, the contract does not call for specific actions to be taken in specific states of the world.[22] It only places state-independent restrictions on what the venture capitalist can do in financing the project. The actions taken by the venture capitalist (e.g., his choice for the second stage financing arrangement from the menu Z) are observable by third parties such as a court. Thus, it is reasonable to assume that the entrepreneur can use the courts to prevent a deviation from the contract that hurts her interests.

Despite the enforceability of the contract, a deviation from the initial agreement might still occur if *both* the entrepreneur and the venture capitalist find that they can gain by renegotiating the contract after the observation of the state. This leads us to examine the "renegotiation-proofness" of the contract, i.e., whether there exists a state of the world in which both parties can be made better off by renegotiating the contract's terms. In the context of our model, it is easy to see that the fixed-fraction contract is in fact renegotiation-proof as long as the outside investors can observe deviations from the financing arrangements allowed by the fixed-fraction contract.[23] First, note that the outcome of the fixed-fraction contract is Pareto optimal—since the optimal continuation decision is made in all states of the world, there is no way a deviation from the contract can increase the total expected net payoff from the project. The entrepreneur and the venture capitalist can only gain by splitting the surplus among themselves and the outside investors in a different way. However, any joint gain to the venture capitalist and the entrepreneur must come at the expense of the outside investors. Thus, upon observing a deviation, outsiders would realize that the securities offered to them are likely to be overpriced and would refuse to buy them.[24]

An additional issue concerning renegotiation is related to the bargaining problem raised in Rajan (1992). We have already observed that since he is informed, the venture capitalist might have some bargaining power in the second stage that would allow him to extract some surplus from the entrepreneur. Can this occur under the fixed-fraction contract? We have shown that under the fixed-fraction contract there is no way for the venture capitalist to extract value from the entrepreneur by mispricing securities. The only way the venture capitalist can gain is by bargaining with the entrepreneur to change the terms of the contract. For example, the venture capitalist might threaten to withhold new funding unless the entrepreneur agrees to

---

[22] We do, however, assume that the final payoff θ and the abandonment value ψ_s are verifiable so that payoff-contingent financial contracts such as $B_z(\theta)$ are enforceable.

[23] A deviation from the fixed-fraction contract occurs, for example, if the venture capitalist puts up a different fraction of the investment than is called for or acquires securities that do not have the proportional payoff. It is reasonable to assume, however, that outsiders can observe such deviation, since the fraction of new capital put up by the venture capitalist as well as the type of financial claim he ends up holding are easily observable.

[24] It is, of course, possible that the entrepreneur and venture capitalist might conspire to overprice new securities but agree to deviate from the contract after the securities have been issued, not before. This potential problem can be solved if the outsiders demand that a covenant be included in the securities they buy that prevents deviations from the financing agreement.

renegotiate and replace the original fixed-fraction contract with one that gives the venture capitalist a higher fraction of the firm. It is important to note that if the venture capitalist does not put up funds for continuation, he is not violating the initial contract. In other words, if the venture capitalist carries out his threat, the entrepreneur cannot take him to court.[25] The possibility therefore exists that the venture capitalist can use his bargaining power to force the entrepreneur to renegotiate. This potential problem can be at least partially resolved if the venture capitalist posts a bond up front, which would be forfeited to the entrepreneur if the contract were renegotiated. As long as the value of the bond is greater than the surplus the venture capitalist can extract, "forced" renegotiation will not occur.[26]

Finally we should note that, in a different but related context, Persons (1994) argues that the contract proposed by Dybvig and Zender (1991) as a solution to the suboptimal investment problem in Myers-Majluf (1984) does not survive renegotiation. Specifically, he shows that there are states of the world in which the old shareholders and the manager will all benefit by renegotiating the manager's compensation contract. He goes on to argue that no contract that induces the manager to invest optimally is renegotiation proof.

Given the similarities between the fixed-fraction contract and the one proposed by Dybvig and Zender, it is instructive to discuss the differences between our setting and Persons' that give rise to these seemingly contradictory results. The key difference lies in the observability of renegotiation. Persons assumes that outsiders do not observe renegotiation when it occurs. In the context of a managerial contract this may be a reasonable assumption, since the manager is an employee of the shareholders and it may be possible for the board of directors to alter the manager's total compensation in ways that are not directly observable by outsiders. By contrast, the venture capitalist and the entrepreneur are independent parties (neither is an employee of the other), and their financial relationship is defined by the securities they hold. Outsiders can observe the financial stakes each has at the time new securities are issued and changes in the structure of financial claims can readily be identified. As mentioned above, these considerations lead us to

---

[25] As in Rajan (1992), we have not explicitly modeled the bargaining game that might take place. Whether the venture capitalist's threats are credible depends on the exact form of the game.

[26] Note that if the entrepreneur has a crucial input into the project, she may have incentives to use her bargaining power in the second stage to extract more of the surplus from the venture capitalist or to pressure the venture capitalist into overpricing the new securities. The first problem is analogous to that alluded to in the text with respect to the venture capitalist, and a way to solve it is for the entrepreneur to sign a contract stating that if the financing agreement is renegotiated then she is penalized, e.g., she cannot start any business for a fixed period of time. This is analogous to the bond posted by the venture capitalist and does not require that the entrepreneur have capital of her own. As to the second problem, it may be resolved if the venture capitalist has sufficient reputational assets that would be affected if he consistently misprices securities. A full model of this is beyond the scope of this paper.

assume that deviations from the fixed-fraction contract will be observable by outside parties.

The nonobservability of renegotiation in Persons' setting gives rise to a second and related difference between our results and his. This concerns information asymmetries between outsiders and insiders. We have allowed the venture capitalist to price securities based on the information he knows, and we have shown that under the fixed-fraction contract he has no incentive to misprice. Persons assumes that the information asymmetries persist under the linear contract. This is because the market only observes the investment decision the manager makes, i.e., whether he invests or not. The manager does not reveal to the outside market what he knows about the value of the assets in place or the new investment project. The key question is whether reports made by the manager in Persons' setting would be credible. It is easy to see that they would not be if the manager and shareholders were in a position to renegotiate the linear contract in an unobservable way, since then the manager and the shareholders could collude to overprice the new share-holders' shares and the manager's compensation could be altered to allow him to share in the gain. With observable renegotiation this cannot occur.

V. Incentives for the Entrepreneur

So far we have focused on the agency problem of ensuring optimal continuation decisions. Clearly, other agency problems might be important in start-up firms. For example, the success of the project may depend on the amount of effort put into the project by the entrepreneur. If this is the case and if certain payoff-relevant actions by the entrepreneur are unobservable or cannot be contracted upon, then the contract between the entrepreneur and capital providers can have an affect beyond the continuation decision discussed in our analysis above. We will argue that an inside investor can partly alleviate this agency problem even if he cannot directly observe the effort.[27] Intuitively, if contracts in the second period can be made contingent on the state, the entrepreneur's payoff becomes more sensitive to the effort she puts into the project and this improves incentives.

We now present a simple example to illustrate this. Assume that there are two possible states of the world. The final payoff of the project in either state is either ten or zero. In state s_1 the payoff is ten with probability 0.9, while in state s_2 the payoff is ten with probability 0.6. An investment of $K = 1$ is required in the initial period and an investment of $I = 3$ is required in the second period. Finally, in both states the abandonment value of the project is zero. Thus, it is always optimal to continue the project.

Now assume that the entrepreneur can affect the likelihood of the two states by the amount of effort she puts into the project. The effort level is unobservable to all investors, including the venture capitalist. If the

---

[27] In Rajan (1992) the inside bank observes the entrepreneur's effort, but because the bank extracts surplus in the second stage, its presence actually leads to worse effort incentives.

Robust Financial Contracting and Venture Capitalists 391

entrepreneur does not expend effort, state s_1 occurs with probability 0.25, and state s_2 occurs with probability 0.75. If effort is expended, then states s_1 and s_2 are equally likely to occur. Thus, the investment of effort increases the probability that the final payoff is ten from $(0.25)(0.9) + (0.75)(0.6) = 0.6875$ to $(0.5)(0.9) + (0.5)(0.6) = 0.75$, and therefore increases the value of the project by $(10)(0.075) = 0.75$. Assume that the cost (in monetary terms) to the entrepreneur of expending effort is 0.5. Then the efficient solution is clearly that the entrepreneur expends effort.

Consider first entrepreneur-led financing. Using arguments similar to those used to prove Proposition 1, it can be shown that there is no equilibrium in which the choice of securities issued in the second period reveals the state. Note that, because of limited liability, the securities issued to capital providers will promise an amount $0 \leq g \leq 10$ if the project's payoff is ten and will promise zero otherwise. If the market assumes that the entrepreneur will expend effort, then $g = 4.0/0.75 = 5\frac{1}{3}$. If it is assumed that the entrepreneur does not put in the effort, then $g = 4.0/0.675 = 5.926$. Table II gives the payoff to the entrepreneur when she expends and does not expend effort under the two possible assumptions the market can make. Clearly, the only rational expectations equilibrium involves the entrepreneur not expending effort and receiving a payoff of 2.75.

Now suppose financing involves a venture capitalist. In this case the pricing of securities issued in the second period can be done by the venture capitalist and can, therefore, depend on the state. We assume that the venture capitalist obtains a fixed-fraction contract, which implies, as noted above, that he has no incentives to misrepresent the state. Prices of securities are then constructed so investors break even in each state. Note that we assume that the venture capitalist observes the state but not the effort. The state, however, is a noisy signal of whether or not effort was expended. Table III shows that the only rational expectations equilibrium now involves the entrepreneur expending effort. This follows from noticing in the last two rows

Table II

The Entrepreneur's Payoffs in the Example when Financing is Entrepreneur-led

Payoffs are calculated for the cases in which the entrepreneur expends effort or does not expend effort and for each of two possible market expectations regarding effort. The table shows that the only rational expectations equilibrium in this case is that no effort is expended.

	Market Assumes that Entrepreneur Expends Effort	Market Assumes that Entrepreneur Does Not Expend Effort
Entrepreneur expends effort	3.000	2.556
Entrepreneur does not expend effort	3.150	2.750

392 *The Journal of Finance*

Table III
The Example with Venture Capital Financing

The first row gives the predicted value of the firm under the assumption that the initial investment of $K = 1$ is made. In calculating the next row, we assume that the total number of shares issued in the first stage is 1 so that this fraction represents the number of shares held by the venture capitalist. For example, if it is assumed that effort is expended, the initial value of the firm is 4.5 and since the venture capitalist is putting up 1, he retains $1/4.5 = 0.222$ shares. The next row gives the value of the firm in the second period if state s_1 is realized and the additional financing of $I = 3$ is raised. This is 9, which means that an additional 0.5 shares must be issued to obtain the needed investment, i.e., $(0.5/(1 + 0.5)) \times 9 = 3$. If the venture capitalist had an initial stake of 0.222 shares in the firm, then he will acquire $0.222 \times 0.5 = 0.1111$ of these new shares and the rest will be sold to outsiders. When the venture capitalist retains 0.222 in the initial financing, the expected payoff to the entrepreneur from the project if state s_1 occurs is $(0.778/1.5) \times 9 = 4.667$. The expected payoff to the entrepreneur if state s_2 occurs is calculated similarly. The last two rows give the ex ante payoff to the entrepreneur when she does and when she does not expend effort. For example, if she expends effort and it is assumed ex ante that she expends effort, then her ex ante payoff is $0.5(4.667) + 0.5(2.333) - 0.5 = 3.000$, since the states are equally likely, the expected payoff in state s_1 (resp. s_2) is 4.667 (resp. 2.333), and the cost of effort is 0.5.

	Initial Financing Based on Assumption That Effort Will Be Expended	Initial Financing Based on Assumption That Effort Will Not Be Expended
Period 1 value	4.500	3.750
Fraction of initial share retained by venture capitalist	0.222	0.267
Period 2 value if state s_1 is realized	9.000	9.000
Number of shares issued in period 2 in state s_1	0.500	0.500
Expected payoff to entrepreneur from project if state s_1 is realized	4.667	4.400
Period 2 value if state s_2 is realized	6.000	6.000
Number of shares issued in period 2 in state s_2	1.000	1.000
Expected payoff to entrepreneur from project if state s_2 is realized	2.333	2.200
Ex ante expected payoff to entrepreneur if effort is expended	3.000	2.800
Ex ante expected payoff to entreprenuer if effort is not expended	2.917	2.750

of the table that the entrepreneur's expected payoffs are higher if she expends effort both if the market believes that she expends effort or the market believes that she does not.

In this example the total unconditional expected payoff to the entrepreneur if financing is entrepreneur-led is 2.75, while her expected payoff if a venture capitalist is involved is 3.00. The gain is due to the fact that when the venture capitalist is involved, the prices of securities issued in period two depend directly on the state and therefore indirectly on the effort expended by the entrepreneur. The presence of the venture capitalist thus makes the entrepreneur's payoff more sensitive to her effort choice, and this sharpens incentives.

Although this example is very simple, it does capture an important aspect of the incentive problem in start-up firms. Much of the early effort expended by the entrepreneur probably serves to increase the chance of the ultimate success of the enterprise. At intermediate stages of investment the effects of entrepreneurial effort are probably not directly observable by outside parties who are not monitoring the firm, since these effects take the form of an increased probability of success that is hard to measure. The venture capitalist is more knowledgeable about these probabilities, and by making the prices of securities issued depend on the venture capitalist's knowledge, the incentive problem is at least partially solved.

Note that this example considers entrepreneurial effort only in the first stage. and it abstracts from the issue of optimal continuation, since it is never optimal to abandon the project. The optimal continuation problem generally becomes more complex when entrepreneurial effort is a significant input in the second stage. Let e be the level of effort (measured in monetary terms) contributed by the entrepreneur in the second stage, and let $E(\bar{\theta}|I, e, s)$ be the expectation of the final payoff if the state is s and I and e are, respectively, the levels of capital and entrepreneurial effort invested. Then in state s it is optimal to abandon if $\sup_{I,e}(E(\bar{\theta}|I, e, s) - I - e) < \Psi_s$. Otherwise I and e should be set at the level that maximizes $E(\bar{\theta}|I, e, s) - I - e$. The fixed-fraction contract leads the venture capitalist to trade off optimally the costs and benefits of investing *capital*, but it does not directly lead him to internalize the cost and benefits of entrepreneurial effort. This follows since the venture capitalist's payoff is $\alpha(E(\bar{\theta}|I, e, s) - I)$ and not $\alpha(E(\bar{\theta}|I, e, s) - I - e)$. If exactly I dollars of capital are raised, then in certain states it may be optimal to continue, but the entrepreneur's expected payoff net of her effort is negative. In these circumstances the venture capitalist might call for more than I to be raised and use the surplus to compensate the entrepreneur. It can be shown that in some cases the first best outcome can be achieved using this type of mechanism, but this cannot always be done. A full analysis is beyond the scope of this paper.

VI. Risk Aversion

Our results so far have been derived under the assumption that all parties are risk neutral. In this section we briefly explore how risk sharing concerns might affect our conclusions. First note that the fixed-fraction contract can still induce optimal continuation in a world where assets are priced based on risk characteristics. If the venture capitalist calculates values using the equilibrium state prices, then under the fixed-fraction contract he will still make the optimal continuation decision, where now optimal continuation involves maximizing the market value of the firm. (A similar observation is made for managerial contracts in Dybvig and Zender (1991).) Of course it is not clear whether the venture capitalist will value future cash flows according to the market's state pricing operator. However, the venture capitalists' financial backers (the limited partners), who tend to be wealthy investors, universities, and other institutional investors, are likely to hold well diversified portfolios and will possibly motivate this type of valuation.

Despite the notion that entrepreneurs tend to be risk-taking individuals, it seems likely that the venture capitalist and outside investors have a greater capacity to bear risk than the entrepreneur. In this case the contract design also needs to address risk-sharing considerations. The venture capitalist's fixed-fraction contract leaves little room for risk sharing to occur between the entrepreneur and the venture capitalist. However, there is no restriction on how payoffs are divided between the entrepreneur and outside investors who put up capital in the second stage. It would be possible, for example, to give the outside investors warrants, and this would tend to reduce the risk of the entrepreneur. In good states (high payoff realizations) the outside investors exercise their warrants and get a larger chunk of the firm, but in bad states (low payoff realizations) the outside investors get less than they would have gotten if they had simple equity. This makes the entrepreneur's payoff (the residual) less risky.

Risk sharing in the first stage of the project can be enhanced without affecting the continuation decisions if, instead of obtaining capital only from one venture capitalist, other investors participate in financing the first stage of the project as well as later stages. The "lead" venture capitalist, being an inside investor, would then be given the fixed-fraction contract and would make all of the continuation decisions. Other investors could be given securities that reduce the risk of the entrepreneur. Thus, the basic results of the previous sections may not be greatly affected when risk-sharing considerations are present. This is consistent with the notion that venture capitalists often form syndicates, with different types of contracts (and different responsibilities with respect to monitoring) for different capital providers.

VII. Concluding Remarks

This article has shown that with the appropriate financial contracts it is possible for inside investors such as venture capitalists to resolve agency problems related to investment decisions as well as informational asymmetries between outside investors and entrepreneurs. More specifically, our main results are the following:

(i) Fully revealing signaling equilibria in entrepreneur-led financing, where the entrepreneur interacts directly with less informed outside investors at each stage of the project, are not robust in the sense that the addition of one possible state of the world can upset the equilib-

Robust Financial Contracting and Venture Capitalists   395

rium, even if the entrepreneur is allowed to alter the set of securities she issues.

(ii) If informational asymmetries between the entrepreneur and outside investors persist in equilibrium, then suboptimal investment decisions may be made in later stages of a project.

(iii) The *only* contract for the venture capitalist that induces optimal continuation in all circumstances is a fixed-fraction contract, in which the venture capitalist owns the same fraction of the payoff independent of the continuation decision, and also finances that same fraction of any future investment. This implies that outside investors will necessarily be involved in later financing stages.

(iv) With the fixed-fraction contract the venture capitalist's payoff is independent of the pricing of any securities issued in later stages of the project. Thus, the venture capitalist has no incentives to misprice these securities given the information he has. This provides a rationale for the venture capitalist to be involved in arranging financing from outside investors in later stages of the project.

(v) The presence of an inside investor such as a venture capitalist can reduce some of the agency costs that arise if the entrepreneur's effort level is unobservable.

It is important to note that our results pertain to the potential *benefits* of financing by inside investors such as venture capitalists, while ignoring any potential *cost* that might be incurred in monitoring the company. Obviously, if monitoring is costly then the benefits we have identified must be balanced against these costs. Venture capitalists, however, are often not passive monitors—while they do not typically get involved in day-to-day operations, they do offer a variety of services to portfolio companies, including advice on strategic planning, management recruitment, and introduction to potential customers and suppliers. The information that the venture capitalist obtains can come as a by-product of other productive activities. This means that the effective cost of monitoring may be relatively low.

We have assumed that there is no asymmetric information between the entrepreneur and capital providers *in the first stage of the project*. It is quite possible, however, that the entrepreneur has superior information about her project or about her own ability in the first stage. The fixed-fraction contract cannot be used to solve the informational problems in the first stage, since at that stage the venture capitalist is not yet involved (and so he is not an insider). Moreover, the contract is not in force at that stage, because it is just negotiated at that point. A number of papers have examined how the entrepreneur might signal her private information through contract choice or other actions. In addition to costless signaling models such as Heinkel (1982) and Brennan and Kraus (1987), there are also costly signaling models such as Leland and Pyle (1977) and Amit, Glosten, and Müller (1990), which are based on the entrepreneur giving up some risk-sharing gains to signal her type. Note that the fixed-fraction contract we have identified can be modified to accommodate signaling in the first stage in ways similar to those discussed in Section VI in the context of risk aversion. That is, if additional investors are involved in financing in the first stage, then the inside investor can still obtain a fixed-fraction contract, while signaling or risk sharing can be accomplished through contracting between the entrepreneur and other investors. Signaling mechanisms, however, may not resolve all the asymmetry of information and, as shown in Section II, are not necessarily robust. If signaling is ineffective or too costly, then capital providers such as venture capitalists might engage in costly information acquisition, which would at least partly resolve the asymmetries. As compensation for his information-gathering activities, the venture capitalist might obtain a higher fraction of the firm in the fixed-fraction contract, but this would otherwise not affect our results.[28] Note also that it is possible that venture capitalists or other investors, especially those with extensive experience in the particular industry, might have better knowledge than the entrepreneur of the market conditions and the marketability of the product. How asymmetric information of this nature would affect the analysis remains open for future research.

Finally, the notion of robustness of contracts should be useful in a variety of contexts. It is often the case that contracts derived in specific models seem to depend crucially on (common) knowledge of probability distributions. Absent such knowledge, and especially if, as in our case, robust contracts have a particularly simple form and are not costly to write, it is reasonable to predict that robust contracts will be used whenever they are available.

Appendix

Proof of Proposition 1: Let $G(I, s) = \mathrm{E}(N_I(\bar{\theta})|I, s)$ be the expected payoff to the original security holders in state s if I is invested in the second stage. In any refinancing that takes place in a fully revealing equilibrium the original security holders will receive securities that are worth $G(I, s)$. At the same time the assumption of competitive, risk-neutral capital markets implies that the securities issued to the new investors will be worth I.

Let $R_I^*(\cdot)$ be the optimal refinancing for the entrepreneur in state s. Since by definition $N_I(\theta) + R_I^*(\theta)$ is the total amount paid out to all security holders after the refinancing takes place and when the final value of the firm is θ, it follows that

$$\mathrm{E}\big(N_I(\bar{\theta}) + R_I^*(\bar{\theta})|I, s\big) = G(I, s) + I. \tag{A1}$$

From this we see that

$$\mathrm{E}\big(R_I^*(\bar{\theta})|I, s\big) = I. \tag{A2}$$

---

[28] There is, of course, a bargaining problem that arises when the venture capitalist becomes more informed than other investors in the first stage. This problem is not addressed by our analysis and specifically by the fixed-fraction contract we have identified, since there is no contract in existence at this point.

Now let θ_0 be such that $\theta_0 - N_I(\theta_0) < I$. Since limited liability is imposed on $N_I(\cdot)$, any $\theta < I$ satisfies this restriction. Also, since the entrepreneur also has limited liability it follows that $R_I^*(\theta_0) < I$.

Consider now state s' in which $\bar{\theta}$ has the following probability distribution: with probability $\pi > 0$, $\bar{\theta} = \theta_0$ and with probability $(1 - \pi)$, $\bar{\theta}$ has the distribution $F(\cdot|I, s)$. Note first that

$$G(I, s') = (1 - \pi)G(I, s) + \pi N_I(\theta_0). \tag{A3}$$

If the state is s' and the entrepreneur refinances with $R_I^*(\theta)$, then the aggregate value of the outstanding claims on the firm is

$$
\begin{aligned}
(1 - \pi)&\mathrm{E}\big(N_I(\bar{\theta}) + R_I^*(\bar{\theta})|I, s\big) + \pi N_I(\theta_0) + \pi R_I^*(\theta_0) \\
&= G(I, s') + \pi I + \pi R_I^*(\theta_0) \\
&< G(I, s') + I
\end{aligned} \tag{A4}
$$

where the last inequality holds because $R_I^*(\theta_0) < I$. Thus, the entrepreneur can refinance the investment in state s' with overvalued securities if she uses those securities which would lead investors to believe the state is s. This means that there is no fully revealing signaling equilibrium. ∎

Proof of Proposition 2: To prove this result we will need the following lemma:

LEMMA 1: *Assume that $\{A(\cdot), Z\}$ induces optimal continuation. Let $\bar{\theta}^*$ be distributed so that $\mathrm{E}(\bar{\theta}^*) = x + I_o$ for some positive x and I_o. Then*

(i) $\forall z \in Z$ for which $I_z = I_o$,

$$\mathrm{E}\big(B_z(\bar{\theta}^*)\big) - \beta_z I_z \le A(x). \tag{A5}$$

(ii) $\exists z \in Z$ such that $I_z = I_o$ and

$$\mathrm{E}\big(B_z(\bar{\theta}^*)\big) - \beta_z I_z = A(x). \tag{A6}$$

Proof: To prove part (i) of Lemma 1 assume that there exists $\hat{z} \in Z$ such that $I_{\hat{z}} = I_o$ and

$$\mathrm{E}\big(B_{\hat{z}}(\bar{\theta}^*)\big) = (1 + \delta)(A(x) + \beta_{\hat{z}} I_{\hat{z}}), \tag{A7}$$

where $\delta > 0$. Now consider a state s' in which an investment of I_o produces $\bar{\theta}$, where $\bar{\theta}$ has the same distribution as $\bar{\theta}^*$ with probability $(1 + \frac{1}{2}\delta)/(1 + \delta)$ and $\bar{\theta}$ is equal to zero with probability $\frac{1}{2}\delta/(1 + \delta)$. Also assume that $\psi_{s'} = x$ and $I_o \in \arg\max_{I > 0}(\mathrm{E}(\bar{\theta}|I, s') - I)$. Then in state s' it is optimal to abandon since

$$\mathrm{E}\big(\bar{\theta}|I_o, s'\big) = \left(\frac{1 + \frac{1}{2}\delta}{1 + \delta}\right)\mathrm{E}(\bar{\theta}^*) = \left(\frac{1 + \frac{1}{2}\delta}{1 + \delta}\right)(x + I_o) < x + I_o. \tag{A8}$$

However, the venture capitalist will want to continue since

$$E\big(B_{\tilde{z}}(\tilde{\theta})|I_o, s'\big) = \left(\frac{1 + \frac{1}{2}\delta}{1 + \delta}\right)E\big(B_{\tilde{z}}(\tilde{\theta}^*)\big) = (1 + \tfrac{1}{2}\delta)(A(x) + \beta_{\tilde{z}}I_{\tilde{z}}), \quad (A9)$$

which implies that

$$E\big(B_{\tilde{z}}(\tilde{\theta})|I_o, s'\big) - \beta_{\tilde{z}}I_{\tilde{z}} = (1 + \tfrac{1}{2}\delta)A(x) + \tfrac{1}{2}\delta\beta_{\tilde{z}}I_{\tilde{z}} > A(x). \quad (A10)$$

Thus equation (A7) with $\delta > 0$ is inconsistent with optimal continuation.

To prove part (ii) assume that

$$\max_{\{z:\, I_z = I_o\}}\big(E\big(B_z(\tilde{\theta}^*)\big) - \beta_z I_z\big) = A(x) - \delta, \quad (A11)$$

where $\delta > 0$. Let $\bar{\theta} > x + I_o$ and assume that in state s'' an investment of I_o produces $\tilde{\theta}$, where $\tilde{\theta}$ has the same distribution as $\tilde{\theta}^*$ with probability $1 - \epsilon$ and $\tilde{\theta} = \bar{\theta}$ with probability ϵ. Assume that $0 < \epsilon < \delta/(\bar{\theta} + \delta - A(x))$. (Note that by assumption $\bar{\theta} > x$ and by limited liability $x \geq A(x)$ so that $\bar{\theta} > A(x)$.) Finally, assume that $\psi_{s''} = x$ and that $E(\tilde{\theta}|I_{o_2} s'') - I_o > E(\tilde{\theta}|I, s'') - I$ for all $I \neq I_o$. Since $E(\tilde{\theta}|I_o, s'') = (1 - \epsilon)(x + I_o) + \epsilon\bar{\theta} > x + I_o$, under these assumptions the project should be continued and I_o is the optimal investment. However, the venture capitalist will not wish to continue at this optimal investment level since

$$\max_{\{z:\, I_z = I_o\}}\big(E\big(B_z(\tilde{\theta})|I_z, s''\big) - \beta_z I_z\big)$$

$$= \max_{\{z:\, I_z = I_o\}}\big((1 - \epsilon)E\big(B_z(\tilde{\theta}^*)\big) + \epsilon B_z(\bar{\theta}) - \beta_z I_z\big)$$

$$\leq \max_{\{z:\, I_z = I_o\}}\big((1 - \epsilon)E\big(B_z(\tilde{\theta}^*)\big) + \epsilon\bar{\theta} - \beta_z I_z\big) \quad (A12)$$

$$< \max_{\{z:\, I_z = I_o\}}\big((1 - \epsilon)\big(E\big(B_z(\tilde{\theta}^*)\big) - \beta_z I_z\big) + \epsilon\bar{\theta}\big)$$

$$= (1 - \epsilon)(A(x) - \delta) + \epsilon\bar{\theta}$$

$$< A(x).$$

The first (weak) inequality follows from the limited liability of $B(\cdot)$, which implies that $B_z(\bar{\theta}) \leq \bar{\theta}$. The last inequality follows from ϵ being sufficiently small, i.e., less than $\delta/(\bar{\theta} + \delta - A(x))$. We therefore conclude that equation (A11) is inconsistent with optimal continuation and this proves part (ii). ∎

We now prove the proposition. Sufficiency is straightforward, and has been observed in another context by Dybvig and Zender (1991). To prove necessity we begin by showing that $A(\cdot)$ must be linear. Assume that $E(\tilde{\theta}_1) = x + I_o$. By part (ii) of Lemma 1 there exists z_1 such that $I_{z_1} = I_o$ and

$$E\big(B_{z_1}(\tilde{\theta}_1)\big) = A(x) + \beta_{z_1}I_{z_1}. \quad (A13)$$

Now assume that $\tilde{\theta}_2$ has the following distribution: for $\gamma \in (0, 1)$, $\tilde{\theta}_2$ has the same distribution as $\tilde{\theta}_1$ with probability $(\gamma x + I_o)/(x + I_o)$ and $\tilde{\theta}$ takes the value zero with probability $(1 - \gamma)x/(x + I_o)$. Then $E(\tilde{\theta}_2) = \gamma x + I_o$, and by part (i) of Lemma 1 it follows that

$$E\left(B_{z_1}(\tilde{\theta}_2)\right) = \left(\frac{\gamma x + I_o}{x + I_o}\right) E\left(B_{z_1}(\tilde{\theta}_1)\right) \le A(\gamma x) + \beta_{z_1} I_{z_1}, \qquad (A14)$$

or, using equation (A13),

$$\left(\frac{\gamma x + I_o}{x + I_o}\right)\left(A(x) + \beta_{z_1} I_{z_1}\right) \le A(\gamma x) + \beta_{z_1} I_{z_1}. \qquad (A15)$$

Rearranging equation (A15) we have

$$\frac{A(x) + \beta_{z_1} I_{z_1}}{x + I_o} \le \frac{A(\gamma x) + \beta_{z_1} I_{z_1}}{\gamma x + I_o}. \qquad (A16)$$

Since the argument leading to equation (A16) holds for all I_o it follows that

$$\frac{A(x)}{x} \le \frac{A(\gamma x)}{\gamma x}. \qquad (A17)$$

Now by part (ii) of Lemma 1 there exists z_2 such that $I_{z_2} = I_o$ and

$$E\left(B_{z_2}(\tilde{\theta}_2)\right) = \left(\frac{\gamma x + I_o}{x + I_o}\right) E\left(B_{z_2}(\tilde{\theta}_1)\right) = A(\gamma x) + \beta_{z_2} I_{z_2}. \qquad (A18)$$

By part (i) we know that

$$E\left(B_{z_2}(\tilde{\theta}_1)\right) \le A(x) + \beta_{z_2} I_{z_2}. \qquad (A19)$$

Combining equations (A18) and (A19) we obtain

$$\frac{A(\gamma x) + \beta_{z_1} I_{z_1}}{\gamma x + I_o} \le \frac{A(x) + \beta_{z_1} I_{z_1}}{x + I_o}. \qquad (A20)$$

Again, this must hold for all I_o so that

$$\frac{A(\gamma x)}{\gamma x} \le \frac{A(x)}{x}. \qquad (A21)$$

Combining equations (A17) and (A21), we have

$$\frac{A(x)}{x} = \frac{A(\gamma x)}{\gamma x} \qquad (A22)$$

Since this must hold for all x and for all $\gamma \in (0, 1)$, it follows that $A(\cdot)$ is linear and this establishes part (a).

To establish part (b) assume that $\tilde{\theta}$ is continuously distributed with cumulative distribution function $F(\cdot)$ and assume that $0 < F(\tau) < 1$ all $\tau > 0$. (For example, $\tilde{\theta}$ could be distributed exponentially.) Let $E(\tilde{\theta}) = \bar{\theta}$. By part (a) we know that for some $0 < \alpha < 1$, $A(\psi) = \alpha\psi$ and by part (ii) of Lemma 1 we know that there exists $\hat{z} \in Z$ such that $I_{\hat{z}} = I_o$ and

$$E\left(B_{\hat{z}}(\bar{\theta})\right) - \beta_{\hat{z}} I_{\hat{z}} = \alpha\left(\bar{\theta} - I_o\right). \tag{A23}$$

Now define $h_z(\theta) \equiv B_{\hat{z}}(\theta) - \alpha\theta + (\alpha - \beta_z)I_o$. Note that equation (A23) implies that $E(h_z(\bar{\theta})) = 0$. Now assume that over some interval $[0, \tau]$ where $\tau > 0$,

$$\int_0^\tau h_z(\theta) dF(\theta) = \gamma \neq 0. \tag{A24}$$

It then follows that

$$\int_\tau^\infty h_z(\theta) dF(\theta) = -\gamma. \tag{A25}$$

Now consider $\bar{\theta}'$, where $\bar{\theta}'$ has the following distribution: with probability $F(\tau) + \delta$ it is given by $\min\left(F(\theta)/F(\tau), 1\right)$, and with probability $1 - F(\tau) - \delta$ it is given by $\max\left((F(\theta) - F(\tau))/(1 - F(\tau)), 0\right)$. We assume that $|\delta|$ is sufficiently small so that both $F(\tau) + \delta$ and $1 - F(\tau) - \delta$ are probabilities.

Now let $\bar{\theta}_0^\tau \equiv E(\bar{\theta}'|\bar{\theta}' \leq \tau)$ and let $\bar{\theta}_\tau^\infty \equiv E(\bar{\theta}'|\bar{\theta}' > \tau)$. Then it is easily verified that $E(\bar{\theta}') = \bar{\theta} + \delta(\bar{\theta}_0^\tau - \bar{\theta}_\tau^\infty)$. By part (i) of Lemma 1 we must have

$$E\left(B_{\hat{z}}(\bar{\theta}')\right) - \beta_{\hat{z}} I_{\hat{z}} \leq \alpha\left(\bar{\theta} + \delta\left(\bar{\theta}_0^\tau - \bar{\theta}_\tau^\infty\right) - I_o\right). \tag{A26}$$

Using the definition of $h_z(\cdot)$ we have

$$\begin{aligned}
E\left(B_{\hat{z}}(\bar{\theta}')\right) - \beta_{\hat{z}} I_{\hat{z}} &= E(\alpha\theta' - \alpha I_o + \beta_{\hat{z}} I_{\hat{z}} + h_z(\theta')) - \beta_{\hat{z}} I_{\hat{z}} \\
&= \alpha\left(\bar{\theta} + \delta\left(\bar{\theta}_0^\tau - \bar{\theta}_\tau^\infty\right) - I_o\right) + (F(\tau) + \delta)E(h(\bar{\theta}')|\bar{\theta}' \leq \tau) \\
&\quad + (1 - F(\tau) - \delta)E(h(\bar{\theta}')|\bar{\theta}' > \tau) \\
&= \alpha\left(\bar{\theta} + \delta\left(\bar{\theta}_0^\tau - \bar{\theta}_\tau^\infty\right) - I_o\right) + (F(\tau) + \delta)\left(\frac{\gamma}{F(\tau)}\right) \tag{A27} \\
&\quad + (1 - F(\tau) - \delta)\left(\frac{-\gamma}{1 - F(\tau)}\right) \\
&= \alpha\left(\bar{\theta} + \delta\left(\bar{\theta}_0^\tau - \bar{\theta}_\tau^\infty\right) - I_o\right) + \delta\gamma\left(\frac{1}{F(\tau)} + \frac{1}{1 - F(\tau)}\right).
\end{aligned}$$

Together equations (A26) and (A27) imply that

$$\delta\gamma\left(\frac{1}{F(\tau)} + \frac{1}{1 - F(\tau)}\right) \leq 0. \tag{A28}$$

Since this must hold for both positive and negative δ, γ must be zero. Thus $\int_0^\tau h_z(\theta) dF(\theta) = 0$ for all τ. This implies that $h_z(\theta) = 0$ for all θ and therefore $B_z(\cdot)$ is equal to $\alpha\theta + (\beta_z - \alpha)I_o$. By limited liability, $0 \leq B_z(\theta) \leq \theta$ for all $\theta > 0$. This can only be true if $\beta_z = \alpha$. This proves part (b). Part (c) follows directly from part (i) of Lemma 1. ∎

Robust Financial Contracting and Venture Capitalists 401

REFERENCES

Amit, R., L. Glosten, and E. Müller, 1989, Venture capital regimes and entrepreneurial activity, Working paper, University of British Columbia School of Commerce and Business Administration.

————, 1990, Entrepreneurial ability, venture investments, and risk sharing, *Management Science* 36, 1232–1245.

Barry, C, C. J. Muscarella, J. W. Peavy III, and M. R. Vetsuypens, 1990, The role of venture capital in the creation of public companies, *Journal of Financial Economics* 27, 447–471.

Berglöf, E., 1992, A control theory of venture capital finance, Doctoral dissertation, European Centre for Advanced Research in Economics (ECARE), Université Libre de Bruxelles, and Stockholm School of Economics.

Berkovitch, E., and E. H. Kim, 1990, Financial contracting and leverage induced over- and under-investment incentives, *Journal of Finance* 45, 765–794.

————, and S. I. Greenbaum, 1991, The loan commitment as an optimal financing contract, *Journal of Financial and Quantitative Analysis* 25, 83–95.

Berlin, M., K. John, and A. Saunders, 1993, Should banks hold equity in borrowing firms? Working paper, Stern School of Business, New York University.

Bester, H., 1985, Screening vs. rationing in credit markets with imperfect information, *American Economic Review* 75, 850–855.

Bhattacharya, S., and A. Thakor, 1993, Contemporary banking theory, *Journal of Financial Intermediation*, Forthcoming.

Brennan, M., and A. Kraus, 1987, Efficient financing under asymmetric information, *Journal of Finance* 42, 1225–1243.

Chan, Y. S., and A. V. Thakor, 1987, Collateral and competitive equilibria with moral hazard and private information, *Journal of Finance* 42, 345–363.

————, D. Siegel, and A. V. Thakor, 1990, Learning, corporate control and performance requirements in venture capital contracts, *International Economic Review* 31, 365–381.

Constantinides, G. M., and B. D. Grundy, 1989, Optimal investment with stock repurchase and financing as signals, *Review of Financial Studies* 2, 445–465.

Cooper, I. A., and W. T. Carleton, 1979, Dynamics of borrower-lender interaction: Partitioning final payoff in venture capital finance, *Journal of Finance* 34, 517–533.

Dybvig, P. H., and J. F. Zender, 1991, Capital structure and dividend irrelevance with asymmetric information, *Review of Financial Studies* 4, 201–219.

Gompers, P. A., 1992a, Grandstanding in the venture capital industry, Working paper, Graduate School of Business Administration, Harvard University.

————, 1992b, The structure of venture capital investment, Working paper, Graduate School of Business Administration, Harvard University.

Gorman, M., and W. A. Sahlman, 1989, What do venture capitalists do? *Journal of Business Venturing* 4, 231–248.

Hansen, E., 1991, Venture capital finance with temporary asymmetric learning, Working paper, London School of Economics Financial Markets Group.

Harris, M., and A. Raviv, 1991, The theory of capital structure, *Journal of Finance* 46, 297–355.

Heinkel, R., 1982, A theory of capital structure relevance under imperfect information, *Journal of Finance* 37, 1141–1150.

Hoshi, T., A. Kashyap, and D. Scharfstein, 1990, The role of banks in reducing the costs of financial distress in Japan, *Journal of Financial Economics* 45, 33–60.

————, 1991, Corporate structure, liquidity, and investment: Evidence from Japanese industrial firms, *Quarterly Journal of Economics* 27, 67–88.

Leland, H. E., and D. H. Pyle, 1977, Informational asymmetries, financial structure, and financial intermediation, *Journal of Finance* 33, 371–387.

Lerner, J., 1992a, Venture capitalists and the decision to go public, Working paper, Graduate School of Business Administration, Harvard University.

————, 1992b, Venture capitalists and the oversight of privately-held firms, Working paper, Graduate School of Business Administration, Harvard University.

Lim, J., and A. Saunders, 1990, Initial public offerings: The role of venture capitalists, The Research Foundation of the Institute of Chartered Financial Analysts.

MacMillan, I. C., D. M. Kulow, and R. Khoylian, 1989, Venture capitalists' involvement in their investments: Extent and performance, *Journal of Business Venturing* 4, 27–34.

Megginson, W. L., and K. A. Weiss, 1991, Venture capitalist certification in initial public offerings, *Journal of Finance* 46, 879–903.

Myers, S. C., 1977, Determinants of corporate borrowing, *Journal of Financial Economics* 5, 147–175.

Myers, S. C., and N. Majluf, 1984, Corporate financing decisions when firms have information that investors do not have, *Journal of Financial Economics* 13, 187–221.

Persons, J. C., 1994, Renegotiation and the impossibility of optimal investment, *Review of Financial Studies*, Forthcoming.

Ravid, S. A., and M. Spiegel, 1992, Linear securities as optimal contracts in environments with an infinite number of bad projects, Working paper, New Jersey Center for Research in Financial Services.

Rajan, R. G., 1992, Insiders and outsiders: The choice between informed and arm's-length debt, *Journal of Finance* 47, 1367–1399.

Sahlman, W. A., 1988, Aspects of financial contracting in venture capital, *Journal of Applied Corporate Finance* 1, 23–36.

———, 1990, The structure and governance of venture-capital organizations, *Journal of Financial Economics* 27, 473–521.

Sapienza, H. J., and J. A. Timmons, 1989, The roles of venture capitalists in new ventures: What determines their importance? Best Papers Proceedings, Academy of Management.

Sharpe, S. A., 1990, Asymmetric information, bank lending, and implicit contracts: A stylized model of customer relationships, *Journal of Finance* 45, 1069–1087.

Stulz, R. M., and H. Johnson, 1985, An analysis of secured debt, *Journal of Financial Economics* 14, 501–522.

Thakor, A. V., 1989, Competitive equilibrium with type convergence in an asymmetrically informed market, *Review of Financial Studies* 2, 49–71.

Venture Economics, 1988, Venture capital performance: Review of the financial performance of venture capital partnerships, Venture Economics, Needham, MA.

[10]

The Syndication of Venture Capital Investments

Joshua Lerner

Joshua Lerner is Assistant Professor of Business Administration at Harvard Business School, Boston, Massachusetts.

Abstract: This paper examines three rationales for the syndication of venture capital investments, using a sample of 271 private biotechnology firms. Syndication is commonplace, even in the first-round investments. Experienced venture capitalists primarily syndicate first-round investments to venture investors with similar levels of experience. In later rounds, established venture capitalists syndicate investments to both their peers and to less experienced capital providers. When experienced venture capitalists invest for the first time in later rounds, the firm is usually doing well. Syndication also often insures that the ownership stake of the venture capitalist stays constant in later venture rounds. I argue that the results are consistent with the proposed explanations.

■ Cooperation among financial institutions is an enduring feature of the equity issuance process. Syndicated underwritings in the U.S. date back at least as far as an 1870 offering by Pennsylvania Railroad. By the 1920s, separate syndicates in many cases handled intricate arrangements for the purchase, inventory, and sale of securities (Galston (1925)). Co-managed offerings and selling syndicates continue to be prominent in equity issues to this day.

Despite its persistence, syndication has been little scrutinized in the corporate finance literature. The reason may lie in the difficulty of analyzing syndication patterns empirically and the complexity of motives behind syndication.

The syndication of venture capital investments in privately held firms differs in two ways from public sale of registered securities. First, the process through which private firms sell securities is little regulated by the Securities and Exchange Commission. Thus, financial intermediaries are bound by few constraints against working together.

Second, privately issued securities are purchased directly by the venture capital fund and must be held for at least a two-year period (Blumenthal (1993)). By contrast, underwriters take on relatively limited risks in a public

security issue; they ascertain the demand schedule for the security before the price is determined.

These differences suggest that securities sales by private firms provide an attractive arena in which to study the economics of syndication. I explore three hypotheses. The first two suggest that syndication may be a mechanism through which venture capitalists resolve informational uncertainties about potential investments:

1. Syndicating first-round venture investments may lead to better decisions about whether to invest in firms. Sah and Stiglitz (1986) show that hierarchical organizations, in which investments are made only if several independent observers agree, may be superior to ones where projects are funded after one affirmative decision. Another venture capitalist's willingness to invest in a potentially promising firm may be an important factor in the lead venture capitalist's decision to invest.

2. Admati and Pfleiderer (1994) develop a rationale for syndication in later venture rounds that is based on informational asymmetries between the initial venture investor and other potential investors. A venture capitalist who is involved in the firm's daily operations may exploit this informational advantage, overstating the proper price for the securities in the next financing round. The only way to avoid this opportunistic behavior is if the lead venture capitalist maintains a constant share of the firm's equity. This implies that later-round financings must be syndicated.

The author thanks for their suggestions Chris Barry, Joetta Forsyth, Ken Froot, Paul Gompers, Lisa Meulbroek, William Sahlman, Peter Tufano, several practitioners, and two anonymous referees. Assistance in obtaining data was provided by Jesse Reyes of Venture Economics and Mark Edwards of Recombinant Capital, and is gratefully acknowledged. Financial support was provided by the Division of Research, Harvard Business School. All errors and omissions are the author's.

Financial Management, Vol. 23, No. 3, Autumn 1994, pages 16-27.

The third hypothesis is different in emphasis. Syndication may also be a mechanism through which venture capitalists exploit informational asymmetries and collude to overstate their performance to potential investors:

3. Lakonishok, Shleifer, Thaler, and Vishny (1991) suggest that pension funds "window dress." Because institutional investors may examine not only quarterly returns but also end-of-period holdings, money managers may adjust their portfolios at the end of the quarter by buying firms whose shares have appreciated and selling "mistakes." Venture capitalists may similarly make investments in the late rounds of promising firms, even if the financial returns are low. This strategy allows them to represent themselves in marketing documents as investors in these firms.

While these three hypotheses do not exhaust the rationales for syndication, they lend themselves to empirical examination.

I examine these concepts using a sample of 651 investment rounds prior to going public at 271 biotechnology firms. I find that syndication is commonplace even in the first-round investments. Experienced venture capitalists primarily syndicate first-round investments to venture investors with similar levels of experience. In later rounds, established venture capitalists syndicate investments both to their peers and to less experienced capital providers. When experienced venture capitalists invest for the first time in later rounds, the firm is usually doing well (i.e., its valuation has increased since the prior venture round). Finally, the ownership stake of venture capitalists frequently stays constant in later venture rounds. I interpret these results as supporting the three hypotheses.

While industrial organization has long focused on incumbent-entrant relationships, corporate finance has devoted little attention to such interactions. Yet with its ability to measure interactions and returns, finance is a natural testing ground. This paper joins the relatively few studies of the relationship between incumbent and entrant financial institutions.[1]

I. Rationales for Syndication

I focus my analysis on three hypotheses. First, syndication may lead to a superior selection of investments. Sah and Stiglitz (1986) contrast decision-making in hierarchies and polyarchies: that is, settings in which projects are undertaken

only if two reviewers agree that the project is worthy and those in which the approval of either is sufficient. The authors show that it may be more efficient to undertake only those projects approved by two reviewers.

Venture capitalists, upon finding a promising firm, typically do not make a binding commitment to provide financing. Rather, they send the proposal to other investors for their review. Another venture capitalist's willingness to invest in the firm may be an important factor in the lead venture investor's decision to invest (Pence (1982)).

This motivation for syndication is often emphasized by practitioners:

> Venture capitalists prefer syndicating most deals for a simple reason—it means that they have a chance to check out their own thinking against other knowledgeable sources. If two or three other funds whose thinking you respect agree to go along, that is a double check to your own thinking. (George Middlemas of Inco Securities in Perez (1986))

> Most financing involves a syndicate of two or more venture groups, providing more capital availability for current and follow-on cash needs. Syndication also spreads the risk and brings together more expertise and support. These benefits pertain only to start-up financing requiring the venture capitalist's first investment decision. There are different strategies and motivations for syndication in follow-on financing. (Robert J. Kunze of Hambrecht and Quist (1990))

If opinions of others are an important motivation for syndication, venture organizations should be careful in their choice of first-round syndication partners. Established firms are unlikely to involve either new funds or small, unsuccessful organizations as co-investors. The choice of syndication partners should be less critical in later rounds.

Having decided to provide capital to a firm, venture capitalists should be much less concerned about confirming their judgment. This suggests that *(i)* experienced venture capitalists are likely to invest with one another in the first round and *(ii)* seasoned venture capitalists should invest with both experienced and inexperienced investors in later rounds.[2]

Admati and Pfleiderer (1994) argue that syndication in later rounds should occur even when venture capitalists are

---

[1]Examples are Beatty and Ritter (1986), Hayes, Spence, and Marks (1983), Lakonishok, Shleifer, and Vishny (1992), and Sirri and Tufano (1992).

[2]Another hypothesis that would generate a similar empirical pattern is Welch's (1992) model of "cascades" in equity sales. While Welch focuses on the sale of equity in initial public offerings (IPOs), the same pattern could appear in private financings: upon observing the decision of early venture capitalists to invest in the firm, less sophisticated venture investors rush in to invest in later rounds.

risk-neutral and under no capital constraints. Suppose informed entrepreneurs raise funds from outside investors directly. In keeping with Brennan and Kraus (1987), entrepreneurs can communicate all their private information with a set of contingent claims. If an unforeseen state of the world can occur, however, the signaling equilibrium breaks down. As a result, the entrepreneur may be unable to raise the full amount needed.

Lead venture capitalists who become involved in the firm's operations can solve this information problem. Other less well-informed investors will invest if this lead one does. Venture capitalists, however, may exploit their informational advantage and overstate the proper price for the securities in the firm's financings. Under the assumptions of the Admati and Pfleiderer model, the only way to insure optimal behavior in this circumstance is for lead venture capitalists to maintain a constant equity stake.

Suppose a lead venture capitalist obtains one-half of a company's two million shares in the first round. (The entrepreneur retains the other 50%.) If the second round involves the issuance of another million shares, the venture capitalist should buy only one-half of these. The remaining half-million shares should be purchased by other venture capitalists. This model provides a rationale for syndication in later rounds and suggests that venture capitalists will hold a constant equity stake across rounds.

Lakonishok, Shleifer, Thaler, and Vishny's (1991) discussion of money manager "window dressing" suggests a third rationale for venture syndication. Pension funds, which typically evaluate money managers once a quarter, examine performance in several ways. Because market-adjusted performance is a noisy indicator of a money manager's skill, plan sponsors also examine the portfolio of securities held at the end of the quarter. Anticipating this, money managers may adjust their portfolios just before the quarter's end. They may buy firms that have performed particularly well in that quarter or sell "mistakes" that incurred losses.

Venture capital funds may behave the same way. In their private placement memoranda for new funds, venture organizations discuss the performance of their previous funds. The performance data are often difficult for outsiders to confirm. In computing historical returns, venture capitalists may make generous assumptions about the valuation of securities.[3] Thus, potential investors may also examine venture organizations' prior investments. Offering documents also discuss successful past investments, often not clarifying whether the venture organization was an early or late investor.

Investment in a promising firm shortly before it goes public may consequently benefit a venture organization, even if the financial return is low. Early venture investors may curry favor with their colleagues by permitting them to invest in later-round financings of promising firms. The early-round investors may do so in the hope that the syndication partners will in turn offer them opportunities to invest in later rounds of their deals.

This hypothesis suggests that venture capitalists should offer shares in the best deals to those firms most able to reciprocate: well-established venture firms. Venture capitalists should be less likely to offer such opportunities to less established venture organizations.

A final rationale for syndication that I do not examine is risk avoidance through risk sharing (Wilson (1968)). Venture capitalists have much at stake in the performance of their funds. First, they typically receive as compensation between 20% and 30% of fund profits. Fund performance also affects the ability to raise new funds. Venture capitalists may consequently diversify their holdings to insure that they do not conspicuously underperform their peers. Many contracts establishing venture capital partnerships explicitly prohibit investing in other venture funds (Gompers and Lerner (1994)). By investing in many syndicated investments, however, a venture fund can achieve much the same effect.

It is unclear whether risk aversion will lead to a greater tendency to syndicate by less or more established funds. A new venture organization may believe that a follow-on fund is difficult to raise unless it performs very well (Gompers (1993a)). The fund may make high-risk solo investments. Alternatively, an established venture organization may believe that its reputation will allow it to raise a later fund even after a disastrous performance. Its fund may thus be willing to invest alone in risky but promising projects. To analyze empirically the relationship between risk aversion and syndication, we would need to know about the utility functions of the venture capitalists, the status of their current funds, and their future fund-raising plans.[4]

---

[3] Venture funds frequently do not sell shares of firms that have gone public, but rather, they distribute them to their limited partners. (Limited partners usually include tax-exempt and tax-paying entities, which may different preferences regarding the timing of sales.) The transfer of the securities from the venture capitalist to the limited partners may take several weeks. During this period, the firm's share price may fall sharply, either because the venture capitalists themselves sell their shares of the thinly traded security or because the market anticipates forthcoming sales by the limited partners. In calculating returns, venture funds may employ not the price on the date that the shares reached the limited partners, but rather the price on the date that the distribution was announced ("Stock Distributions—Fact, Opinion and Comment" (1987)).

[4] One test is to examine funds that specialize in start-ups, traditionally the most risky of venture investments. These venture capitalists, it might be anticipated, have relatively little risk aversion. Using a *t*-test, I compare the number of syndication partners (by round of investment) for these funds and

II. The Data

I examine financings between 1978 and 1989 by privately held biotechnology firms that received venture capital before going public. Here I summarize the construction of the data set and examine the implications of using an industry sample. (For a fuller description of the data, see Lerner (1994a, 1994b).)

I base the analysis on the records of the consulting firm, Venture Economics. Its Venture Intelligence database records the size of and participants in each funding round. Venture Economics obtains these data from individual and institutional investors in venture funds. The Venture Economics data are very comprehensive but have a significant bias (see Lerner (1994a)). Single venture rounds, particularly in more mature firms, are often recorded as several observations.

This may happen for three reasons. First, a contract between a company and its venture financiers may call for the staged distribution of the funds in a single venture round, which may then appear in the database as several distinct venture rounds.

Second, staggered disbursements arise without design. Venture capital funds typically do not keep large cash balances but, rather, draw down funds from their limited partners as needed. Limited partners will have between two weeks and several months to provide the funds. As several venture funds normally participate in a financing round, investments may be received over the course of several months and thus be recorded in the database as several rounds.

Finally, Venture Economics aggregates information about venture investments from reports by pension fund managers, individual investors, and investment managers. If the date of the investment differs in these records, a single investment round may be recorded as two or more events. While data accuracy has increased over time and Venture Economics has recently improved its data collection methodology to limit such problems in the future, the over-reporting of rounds is a significant factor in the historical Venture Economics data.

Thus, I confirm (and, if necessary, combine and correct) the observations. I use the data of a second consulting firm, Recombinant Capital (*Valuation Histories for Private Biotechnology Companies* (1992) and *Valuation Histories for Public and Acquired Biotechnology Companies* (1993)).

This firm gathers its information from public documents and company and venture capital contacts.

For firms not tracked by Recombinant Capital that had gone public, I corroborate the Venture Economics data using the "Certain Transactions" and "Financial Statements" sections of the IPO prospectuses. If these are ambiguous, I use the "Recent Sales of Non-Registered Securities" section of the S-1 or S-18 statements. (I also use these statements for companies that withdrew proposed IPOs.) I find financial statements of acquired private firms in the acquirers' proxy statements, 10-K, 10-Q, or registration statements. I attempt to corroborate the remaining cases through telephone contacts with companies and venture capitalists.

In all, I identify 651 financing rounds at 271 firms.[5] I determine the age and size of venture organizations using the publications of Venture Economics and other organizations, including these reports: *Pratt's Guide to Venture Capital Sources* (1991), *The Venture Capital Report Guide to Venture Capital in the U.K.* (Clay (1987)), *Corporate Finance Sourcebook* (1991), *Guide to European Venture Capital Sources* (1988, 1991).

While the use of an industry sample allows me to use other data sources to verify and correct the data set, it raises the concern that the investment patterns here are not representative of venture capital as a whole. In other work (Lerner (1994a,1994b)), I show that the IPOs of firms in this sample closely resemble the 433 venture-backed IPOs examined by Barry, Muscarella, Peavy, and Vetsuypens (1990) in several critical respects. These include the inflation-adjusted IPO size, the length of venture capitalist involvement with the firm, and the number of venture capitalists serving as directors of the firm.

Moreover, in the cross-sectional sample of venture-backed firms developed by Gompers (1993b), the cumulative venture funding that biotechnology firms receive is near the mean. The average funding for these firms is more than for computer software and medical device companies but considerably less than for computer and electronic component manufacturers.

III. The Syndication of Venture Investments

Table 1 describes the sample. Even in the first round, there is extensive syndication. In each later venture round, two or

---

[5] I employ in my sample all rounds in which external financiers provided a significant amount of capital ($100,000 or above) in exchange for equity (almost universally preferred stock) or convertible debt. The practical effect of my definition is to eliminate (i) company formations, where founders contributed a small amount of funds (typically under $20,000) in exchange for a considerable amount of common stock and (ii) bridge loans by venture capital providers in the months prior to an initial public offering and due immediately after the IPO.

---

all others. I identify the specialist funds using a database assembled by Venture Economics (described in Gompers and Lerner (1994)). I find that, while these funds have slightly fewer syndication partners, the differences are not statistically significant.

Table 1. Description of the Sample

The sample consists of 651 financing rounds of privately held biotechnology firms between 1978 and 1989. The table indicates the number of observations, the mean number of venture and non-venture investors, and the mean number of such investors investing in the firm for the first time. The table also reports the mean amount invested by venture and non-venture investors, in millions of nominal dollars.

	Round of External Financing		
	#1	**#2**	**#3+**
Number of Observations	269	184	198
Mean Number of Investors in Each Round			
Venture Investors	2.2	3.3	4.2
Non-Venture Investors	0.5	0.9	1.1
Mean Number of New Investors in Each Round			
Venture Investors	2.2	1.5	1.3
Non-Venture Investors	0.5	0.7	0.7
Amount Invested per Investor ($ mil)			
Venture Investors	0.5	0.6	0.6
Non-Venture Investors	0.9	0.9	1.3

Because some early-round investors do not invest in subsequent rounds, the number of investors in a given round is often less than the sum of the investors in the previous round and the new investors.

more new investors typically invest in the firm. The mean number of investors rises from 2.7 (including non-venture investors) to 5.3.[6] Because some early-round investors do not invest in subsequent rounds, the number of investors in a given round is often less than the sum of the number of investors in the previous round and the number of new investors.

The amount invested per venture and non-venture investor is quite stable. Consistent with Sahlman (1990), the size of each financing round increases (on an absolute and per investor basis) as the firm matures. This reflects the growing number of investors and the increasing representation of non-venture investors.

A. Syndication Partners in First and Later Rounds

I examine the choice of syndication partners in the sample. I expect that established venture capitalists will disproportionately syndicate first-round investments with other established firms. In later rounds, they should be much

more willing to syndicate investments with less seasoned firms.[7]

There is not an obvious way, however, to distinguish between established and marginal venture capital organizations. While many influential venture capital organizations, such as Greylock and TA Associates, date back to the 1960s, others of today's leading venture capitalists did not close their first fund until the 1980s, including Technology Venture Investors and Burr, Egan, Deleage. Furthermore, a substantial number of venture organizations have operated for some time without ever becoming major factors in the industry. I thus do not characterize venture capitalists simply by age, but also by the relative size of the organization's fund.

More established venture organizations should be able to access capital from investors for larger and more frequent funds. Venture capitalists generally prefer larger funds because of the substantial economies of scale in operating a large venture fund (or several large funds). I express the organization's size as a percentage of the total venture capital pool because venture capital expanded dramatically between

[6] I define venture investors as either *(i)* traditional limited partnerships where general partners invest the limited partners' capital and oversee these investments or *(ii)* corporate venture capital programs that are established enough to be listed in *Pratt's Guide to Venture Capital Sources* (1991). I include as non-venture investments private placements by other corporations or financial institutions, as well as by partnerships established solely to invest in a single firm. Investments that are made by an agent and marketed to retail investors are also designated as non-venture investments.

[7] One question suggested by this analysis is which firms do not syndicate at all. I compare the age and size of venture organizations investing alone to those organizations investing jointly. I find that larger and older venture organizations are only slightly more likely to invest alone than others. The *t*-tests comparing syndicating and solo investors are statistically insignificant and not reported in the tables.

1978 and 1989; it is relative rather than absolute size that measures relative experience.[8]

Table 2 divides all venture capitalists into quintiles based on size. I compute the ratio of a venture organization's committed capital (the total amount provided by investors) to the total venture pool in the year of investment. Venture organizations typically operate several funds (i.e., partnerships) at any given time. All funds sponsored by a venture capital organization are aggregated for the purpose of the analysis. I use the committed capital rather than the value of assets because venture capitalists follow divergent practices as to when they write up or write off their investments.

I examine the syndication partners in each size quintile of venture organizations, considering first-, second-, and later-round investments separately. If funds were equally likely to syndicate with a venture organization of any size, each cell would be equal: 20% of the syndications would be with the largest quintile of organizations, 20% with the middle quintile, and so on.

I present the analysis in Figure 1 and Table 2. There are uneven numbers of observations for each quintile, so the tabulations are not symmetric around the diagonal axis. For instance, there are 44 syndicated first-round investments between venture capitalists in the largest quintile and those in the middle quintile. The number of syndicated investments

involving the largest quintile of organizations is slightly larger than the number involving the middle quintile. Thus, co-investments with middle-quintile firms make up 20% of the joint investments by the largest quintile of organizations. These 44 transactions with the largest quintile comprise 22% of the co-investments by middle-quintile venture capitalists.

Venture capitalists in the smallest quintile are disproportionately likely to undertake early-round transactions with each other. The bottom quintile of venture organizations syndicate 43% of their first-round investments with other bottom-quintile venture capitalists. With each subsequent round, this pattern becomes less pronounced. In second and later rounds, the percentages are 32% and 24%.

Some patterns, however, are less clear. It is not obvious, for instance, why top-tier firms syndicate first-round investments more frequently with second-quintile organizations (35%) than with other top-quintile firms (14%).

Table 3 examines the statistical significance of these patterns. I test the null hypothesis that the probability of each cell is 20%, using a Pearson χ^2-test. For the size analysis reported in Table 2, I reject the null hypothesis at the 0.01 level of confidence in the first round. In the other rounds, I cannot reject the null hypothesis at conventional confidence levels.

Similar results appear when venture organizations are

Figure 1. Syndication Partners in Venture Financings of Privately Held Biotechnology Firms

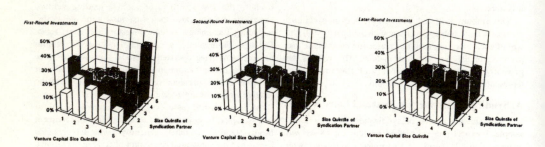

The sample consists of 651 financing rounds between 1978 and 1989. Venture organizations are divided into quintiles on the basis of committed capital, relative to all venture organizations active in biotechnology in the year of the investment. The quintile of the largest venture capital firms is denoted as 1; the smallest as 5. First-, second-, and later-round investments are considered separately. The vertical axis indicates, for each size quintile, the percentage of syndication partners in each of the five quintiles.

---

[8]Neither age nor relative size provides an indication of industry expertise. One might expect certain venture capitalists to develop special expertise in a complex industry such as biotechnology. If early-round investments involve specialists, it is not obvious that such specialists will be particularly likely to co-invest with each other. In many cases, early-round syndications between two established venture organizations will pair one group with industry-specific experience and another without such experience, which is expected to contribute general management and financial expertise. Established venture organizations can be expected to be involved as syndication partners, even when they do not have specialized industry expertise (Kunze (1990)).

22   FINANCIAL MANAGEMENT / AUTUMN 1994

Table 2. Syndication Partners in Venture Financings of Privately Held Biotechnology Firms

The sample consists of 651 financing rounds between 1978 and 1989. Venture organizations are divided into quintiles on the basis of committed capital, relative to all venture organizations active in biotechnology in the year of the investment. Each row of the table indicates, for one size quintile, the distribution of syndication partners (i.e., the percentage of syndication partners in each size quintile). First-, second-, and later-round investments are considered separately.

First-Round Financings

	Size Quintile of Syndication Partner				
Venture Capital Size Quintiles	**Largest (%)**	**2nd (%)**	**Middle (%)**	**4th (%)**	**Smallest (%)**
Largest Quintile	14	35	20	17	14
2nd Quintile	27	25	14	19	16
Middle Quintile	22	20	20	23	16
4th Quintile	18	25	21	16	20
Smallest Quintile	12	17	12	16	43

Second-Round Financings

	Size Quintile of Syndication Partner				
Venture Capital Size Quintiles	**Largest (%)**	**2nd (%)**	**Middle (%)**	**4th (%)**	**Smallest (%)**
Largest Quintile	21	22	24	18	15
2nd Quintile	25	22	20	15	17
Middle Quintile	26	19	21	21	13
4th Quintile	22	18	23	21	18
Smallest Quintile	18	18	14	18	32

Later-Round Financings

	Size Quintile of Syndication Partner				
Venture Capital Size Quintiles	**Largest (%)**	**2nd (%)**	**Middle (%)**	**4th (%)**	**Smallest (%)**
Largest Quintile	19	23	26	18	14
2nd Quintile	20	20	25	21	17
Middle Quintile	19	21	24	21	15
4th Quintile	17	21	25	20	17
Smallest Quintile	15	18	22	20	24

Rows may not add to 100%, due to rounding. Because certain size quintiles undertook more or fewer syndicated investments, the tables are not symmetric along the diagonal axis.

segmented by age. Of the first-round syndication partners of the quintile of youngest firms, 36% are also in the youngest quintile. Although I do not report the full results for age as I do for size in Table 2, the pattern is similar. I test for deviations from the equally likely distribution in Table 3. I again reject the null hypothesis of equal probabilities (at the 0.05 level of confidence) in the first round. In later rounds, I cannot reject the null hypothesis.

The analyses reported in Tables 2 and 3 using the age and size proxies suggest sharp divisions between more and less established venture capitalists. If the unwillingness of experienced venture capitalists to invest with smaller and younger organizations in the first round stems from a mistrust of inexperienced investors' judgment, then a second pattern should appear as well. Experienced venture capitalists should be reluctant to invest in the later rounds of deals begun by their less-seasoned counterparts. Inexperienced venture investors should be brought into

Table 3. Tests of the Randomness of the Distribution of Syndication Partners in Venture Financings of Privately Held Biotechnology Firms

The sample consists of 651 financing rounds between 1978 and 1989. Venture organizations are divided into quintiles on the basis of committed capital and age, relative to all venture organizations active in biotechnology in the year of the investment. The table indicates the test statistic and significance level for a Pearson χ^2-test, whose null hypothesis is that 20% of the observations are in each cell. Separate tests are performed for the first-, second-, and later-investment rounds.

| | Firms Divided into Quintiles by Venture Organization: | |
	Size	Age
First-Round Financings		
Pearson χ^2-statistic	48.08	26.87
p-value	0.000	0.043
Second-Round Financings		
Pearson χ^2-statistic	18.93	7.83
p-value	0.273	0.954
Later-Round Financings		
Pearson χ^2-statistic	6.44	16.07
p-value	0.983	0.448

later-round financings by experienced organizations, but not *vice versa*.

To assess this possibility, I examine venture organizations investing for the first time in the second or later venture rounds. I contrast the characteristics of the new investors with those of the venture organizations that invested previously in the firm. I compare funds along three dimensions of experience: size of the venture capital organization (committed capital in the year of the investment as a percentage of the total committed capital in the venture pool), age of the venture organization (in years), and number of biotechnology firms in which the organization had invested before this transaction.

I expect that the later-round venture investors would be less experienced than the previous investors. Table 4 compares the characteristics of the new investors to those of the previous venture financiers and presents the *p*-values from *t*-tests comparing these firms. The results are consistent with the hypothesis and are significant at the 0.01 confidence level. The typical later-round syndication involves less-experienced venture capitalists investing in a deal begun by established organizations.

Table 4. The Experience of Venture Capitalists Investing in the Second and Later Rounds

The sample consists of 651 financing rounds between 1978 and 1989. For each venture organization investing in a firm for the first time in the second or later round, I compare its experience level to the experience level of previous venture investors in the firm. Venture organizations are compared on the basis of size (committed capital in the year of the investment as a percentage of the total pool of venture capital), age (in years), and the number of biotechnology firms in which the organization had previously invested. The differences are expressed as the experience level of the new investor minus that of the previous investor.

Measures of Venture Experience	Average Difference, Experience of New Investor and Previous Investor	p-value, t-test of No Difference
Venture Organization Size as Percentage of Total Pool	-0.12%	0.008
Age of Venture Organization (years)	-1.42	0.006
Prior Biotech Investments by Venture Organization	-0.76	0.001

B. Changes in Equity Holdings Across Venture Rounds

I next examine an empirical prediction of Admati and Pfleiderer's model—that the stakes held by venture capitalists will be relatively constant across venture rounds.

Table 5 examines investors' aggregate equity holdings and their equity purchases in financing rounds. In the second round, first-round investors purchase 30% of the shares sold. New investors buy the remaining shares. The existing investors' purchase corresponds quite closely to their previous ownership position of 34% prior to the round. In the third round, when previous investors hold 51% of the equity, existing shareholders purchase about half the shares. In later rounds, current shareholders purchase over half the shares. These results confirm the prediction of Admati and Pfleiderer that venture shareholders strive to maintain a constant equity share.

Similarly, the equity ownership of individual venture organizations shows relatively little variation. Table 6 shows the change in equity held by each venture investor before and after each venture round. I compute:

$$\frac{(Stake\ After\ Round - Stake\ Before\ Round)}{Stake\ Before\ Round} \tag{1}$$

In 21% of the cases, the share of the firm held by the

Table 5. Equity Stakes in Privately Held Venture-backed Biotechnology Firms

The sample consists of 332 financing rounds between 1978 and 1989 where the size of the ownership stake for each investor can be determined. The table indicates the mean percentage of the firm's equity held by outside investors after each venture round, as well as the percentage of the equity sold in the round purchased by previous investors in the firm.

	Round of External Financing		
	#1 (%)	#2 (%)	#3+ (%)
Total Stake Held by Outside Investors after Investment Round	33.9	51.1	57.0
Share of Equity Sold in Round Purchased by Previous Investors		30.0	52.7

In computing the equity stake, all preferred shares are converted to common shares at the conversion ratios then in force. (These are typically stipulated in the amended bylaws prepared after each venture round.) Outstanding warrants and options are counted only if their exercise price is below the per-share price of the venture round.

venture capitalist changes by less than 5% after the venture round. In 70.5% of the cases, the change is less than 25%. [9]

C. Later-Round Syndications of Investments in Promising Firms

I finally examine suggestions of "window dressing" in the syndication of venture investments. An empirical implication of the hypothesis is that experienced venture capitalists will invest in the later rounds of deals particularly likely to go public.

I use as observations each second- and later-round venture investment. I run a pair of probit regressions using the same independent variables, but different dependent variables:

$$(INVEST?)_{ij} = \alpha_{0j} + (\Delta VALUE)_i \, \alpha_{1j}$$
$$+ \, (VCSIZE)_i \alpha_{2j} + \varepsilon_{ij} \qquad (2)$$

The dependent variables are dummy variables indicating whether *(i)* one or more experienced venture capitalists invested in the firm for the first time in the round and *(ii)* one or more inexperienced venture capitalists invested for the first time. In both cases, I code the dependent variable as 1.0 when a new investor is present. I define experienced and inexperienced firms as those above and below the median size of those venture organizations investing in

Table 6. Changes in Venture Equity Stakes in Privately Held Biotechnology Firms

The sample consists of 188 second or later financing rounds between 1978 and 1989 where the size of the ownership stake of each venture capitalist before and after the venture round can be determined. The table indicates the change in the equity ownership of each venture organization around each financing round: the difference between the new and old stakes divided by the old stake (a total of 871 observations). All funds of a given venture organization are considered together.

Change in Ownership (%)	Number of Observations	Percentage (%)
<-25	72	8.3
<-5 and >-25	298	34.2
<5 and >-5	183	21.0
<25 and >5	134	15.3
<50 and >25	94	11.1
<75 and >50	23	2.6
<100 and >75	27	3.1
>100	40	4.6

In computing the equity stake, all preferred shares are converted to common shares at the conversion ratios then in force. (These are typically stipulated in the amended bylaws prepared after each venture round.) Outstanding warrants and options are counted only if their exercise price is below the per-share price of the venture round.

biotechnology in that year, using the amount of capital committed to the venture organization as a measure of size.

I use two independent variables. To identify the most promising deals, I examine the change in the per share valuation of the firm between the current and previous venture rounds. I anticipate that the firms whose valuations increase sharply are superior performers and those most likely subsequently to go public (Sahlman (1990)). I include the size of the largest previous venture investor as an independent variable. In this way, I control for the reluctance of established firms to invest in deals begun by less established firms.

My partition of venture capitalists into experienced and inexperienced is crude; I here disregard much of the information about their characteristics. In unreported regressions, I repeat the analysis, using specifications that capture more detail. First, I run four separate regressions, examining whether venture capitalists in each of four size quartiles invested for the first time in the transaction. Then, I employ a Poisson specification, where my dependent variable is the number of new venture capitalists in each size

---

[9] That is, in 70.5% of the cases, a venture capitalist with a 10% stake in a company before a venture round would have an equity stake of between 7.5% and 12.5% thereafter.

quartile who invested in the firm. The results are robust to these changes.

I also examine the robustness of the analysis to the use of venture organization age rather than relative size. I regress:

$$(INVEST?)_{ij} = \beta_{0j} + (\Delta VALUE)_i \beta_{1j} + (VCAGE)_i \beta_{2j} + \varepsilon_{ij} \quad (3)$$

As before, I use two dependent variables, indicating whether an experienced or an inexperienced venture capitalist joined as a new investor. I now define experienced and inexperienced firms as those above or below the median age of those venture organizations investing in biotechnology in that year. Instead of size, I use the age of the oldest previous investor as an independent variable.

The results in Table 7 support suggestions of "window dressing." The coefficients 0.14 and 0.15 in the first and third regressions show that established venture capitalists are significantly more likely to invest for the first time in later rounds when valuations have increased sharply.[10] Valuation changes are insignificant (and actually negative) in explaining the probability of investments by less established firms.

IV. Discussion

In my sample of private investments in the biotechnology industry, I show that in the first round, established venture capitalists tend to syndicate with one another. Later rounds involve less established venture organizations. These results are consistent with the view that syndication allows

Table 7. The Probability of Venture Capitalists Investing for the First Time in a Second or Later Financing Round

The sample consists of 199 second or later financings of privately-held biotechnology companies between 1978 and 1989 in which the valuations of the firm in the current and previous rounds are available. The dependent variable is a dummy variable indicating if one or more venture investors above or below the median size or age of venture organizations active in biotechnology in that year were first-time investors in this round. (Rounds with new investors are coded as 1.0.) The independent variables are the percentage change in the valuation of the firm from the previous to the current venture round, the age (or size) of the most experienced venture organization that had previously invested in the firm, and a constant. A probit regression is employed (absolute t-statistics in parentheses).

	Dependent Variable			
	Organization Above Median Size Invested	Organization Below Median Size Invested	Organization Above Median Age Invested	Organization Below Median Age Invested
Percentage Change in Valuation between Previous and Current Round	0.14 (2.21)	-0.04 (0.83)	0.15 (2.67)	-0.03 (0.57)
Size of Oldest Previous Investor (percentage of total venture pool)	21.86 (2.12)	12.33 (1.50)		
Age of Oldest Previous Investor (years)			0.03 (2.15)	0.02 (2.66)
Constant	0.33 (1.85)	-0.49 (3.15)	0.41 (1.12)	-0.62 (3.58)
Log Likelihood	-101.9	-128.2	-110.6	-128.4
χ^2-statistic	8.86	2.86	6.99	7.79
p-value	0.01	0.24	0.03	0.02
Number of Observations	199	199	199	199

The change in the firm value is computed using the price per share in the previous venture round and the price per share in the current round. I correct for any stock splits, reverse splits, or stock dividends.

---

[10]While it could be argued that the price per share increases because other experienced venture capitalists invested in the firm, there are strong arguments to the contrary. Venture capital partnership agreements frequently specify that new venture investors be involved in situations where venture capitalists may be tempted to price investments at too high a valuation. An example is when a venture fund makes a later-round investment in a company already held by the venture capitalist's earlier fund (*1992 Terms and Conditions of Venture Capital Partnerships* (1992)). The venture capitalist may be tempted to undertake a follow-on financing at a high valuation. This is because the value of the first fund's investment can then be written up in the hopes of impressing potential investors in a third fund. (The potential investors will find it difficult to assess the value of the privately held firm.) The investors in the second fund demand a co-investment by another venture capitalist who does not stand to benefit from the write-up of current holdings because they expect that this investor will demand a lower valuation.

established venture capitalists to obtain information in order to decide whether to invest in risky firms. When established funds join as new investors in later rounds, the firm's valuation has often increased sharply prior to the investment. This pattern supports suggestions of "window dressing" in the syndication of later-round investments. I also present evidence consistent with Admati and Pfleiderer's constant equity share hypothesis.

Results of this study of syndication in one particular environment may be more broadly applicable. We see many of these behaviors in public security issuances. For instance, decisions regarding IPOs of firms specializing in complex technologies are often taken in consultation with co-lead investment bankers. Decision-sharing is an important motivation in many of these co-managed offerings. (See, for instance, the description of Microsoft's IPO in Wallace and Erickson (1992).)

This analysis does not exhaust the important questions concerning syndication. One issue that I have acknowledged but not addressed is how reputation affects the risk aversion

of venture capitalists and their consequent willingness to syndicate. For instance, more established venture organizations may be willing to accept lower returns as long as the variance is lower. They may thus participate in many syndicated deals.

A second research question, suggested by the industrial organization literature, is the response to entrants. The 1980s saw the entry of many new firms into venture capital, just as in the leveraged buy-out business. While a few entrants participated in many syndicated first-round transactions, many more were relegated to later-round syndications. The process through which some of the entrants joined the core of established venture organizations remains unclear. Nor is it clear whether the syndication of later-round investments by established venture capitalists helped establish the stature of the new organizations. (One of the empirical examinations of entry in the finance literature is Beatty and Ritter (1986).) Thus, several aspects of the syndication of both public and private securities would reward further scrutiny. ■

References

Admati, A.R. and P. Pfleiderer, 1994, "Robust Financial Contracting and the Role of Venture Capitalists," *Journal of Finance* (June), 371-402.

Barry, C.B., C.J. Muscarella, J.W. Peavy III, and M.R. Vetsuypens, 1990, "The Role of Venture Capital in the Creation of Public Companies: Evidence from the Going Public Process," *Journal of Financial Economics* (October), 447-471.

Beatty, R.P. and J.R. Ritter, 1986, "Investment Banking, Reputation, and the Underpricing of Initial Public Offerings," *Journal of Financial Economics* (January/February), 213-232.

Blumenthal, H.S., 1993, *Going Public and the Public Corporation*, New York, Clark Boardman Callaghan.

Brennan, M.J. and A. Kraus, 1987, "Efficient Financing Under Asymmetric Information," *Journal of Finance* (December), 1225-1243.

Clay, L., 1987 and earlier years, *The Venture Capital Report Guide to Venture Capital in the U.K.*, Bristol, U.K, Venture Capital Report.

Corporate Finance Sourcebook, 1991 and earlier years, Wilmette, IL, National Register Publishing Co.

Galston, A., 1925, *Security Syndicate Operations: Organization, Management and Accounting*, New York, Roland Press.

Gompers, P.A., 1993a, "Grandstanding in the Venture Capital Industry," University of Chicago Working Paper.

Gompers, P.A., 1993b, "The Structure of Venture Capital Investment," University of Chicago Working Paper.

Gompers, P.A. and J. Lerner, 1994, "The Use of Covenants: An Empirical Analysis of Venture Partnership Agreements," University of Chicago and Harvard University Working Paper.

Guide to European Venture Capital Sources, 1988 and earlier years, London, Venture Economics, Ltd.

Hayes, S.L., A.M. Spence, and D. Van Praag Marks, 1983, *Competition in the Investment Banking Industry*, Cambridge, MA, Harvard University Press.

Kunze, R.J., 1990, *Nothing Ventured: The Perils and Payoffs of the Great American Venture Capital Game*, New York, HarperCollins.

Lakonishok, J., A. Shleifer, R. Thaler, and R. Vishny, 1991, "Window Dressing by Pension Fund Managers," *American Economic Review: Papers and Proceedings* (May), 227-231.

Lakonishok, J., A. Shleifer, and R. Vishny, 1992, "The Structure and Performance of the Tax-Exempt Money Management Industry," *Brookings Papers on Economic Activity: Microeconomics*, 331-391.

Lerner, J., 1994a, "Venture Capitalists and the Oversight of Private Firms," *Journal of Finance* (forthcoming).

Lerner, J., 1994b, "Venture Capitalists and the Decision to Go Public," *Journal of Financial Economics* (June), 293-316.

1992 Terms and Conditions of Venture Capital Partnerships, 1992, Boston, Venture Economics.

Pence, C.C., 1982, *How Venture Capitalists Make Investment Decisions*, Ann Arbor, MI, UMI Research Press.

Perez, R.C., 1986, *Inside Venture Capital: Past, Present, and Future*, New York, Praeger.

Pratt's Guide to Venture Capital Sources, 1991 and earlier years, Boston, Venture Economics.

Sah, R.K., and J.E. Stiglitz, 1986, "The Architecture of Economic Systems: Hierarchies and Polyarchies," *American Economic Review* (September), 716-727.

Sahlman, W.A., 1990, "The Structure and Governance of Venture Capital Organizations," *Journal of Financial Economics* (October), 473-521.

Sirri, E.R., and P. Tufano, 1992, "Competition in the Mutual Fund Industry," Harvard University Working Paper.

"Stock Distributions—Fact, Opinion and Comment," 1987, *Venture Capital Journal* (August), 8-14.

Valuation Histories for Private Biotechnology Companies, 1992, San Francisco, Recombinant Capital.

Valuation Histories for Public and Acquired Biotechnology Companies, 1993, San Francisco, Recombinant Capital.

Wallace, J. and J. Erickson, 1992, *Hard Drive: Bill Gates and the Making of the Microsoft Empire*, New York, John Wiley & Sons.

Welch, I., 1992, "Sequential Sales, Learning, and Cascades," *Journal of Finance* (June), 695-732.

Wilson, R., 1968, "The Theory of Syndicates," *Econometrica* (January), 119-132.

[11]

Journal of Management Studies 32:4 July 1995
0022-2380

RISK AVOIDANCE STRATEGIES IN VENTURE CAPITAL MARKETS

JAMES O. FIET

Clemson University

ABSTRACT

This research compares risk avoidance strategies employed by business angels and venture capital firm investors. It finds that differences in their approaches to evaluating risk lead them to hold predictably different views of the dangers of market and agency risk. The former tend to rely upon the entrepreneur to protect them from losses due to market risk. Consequently, they are more concerned with agency risk than market risk. The latter are more concerned with market risk because they have learned to protect themselves contractually from agency risk using boilerplate contractual terms and conditions. A likely result of their different approaches to avoiding risk is a segmentation of venture capital markets, which has important implications for both entrepreneurs and future research.

INTRODUCTION

The two most active US providers of capital to new and growing businesses are venture capital firms and business angels. The former are professionally managed, private, independent organizations that invest between $2.4 billion (Gaston, 1989) and $4.18 billion in capital annually (Timmons and Sapienza, 1992). The latter are private individuals who invest non-institutional funds, often their own, in amounts that are estimated to range annually between $5.0 billion (Wetzel, 1983) and $56 billion (Gaston, 1989). Each of these groups has a significant impact upon the supply of new venture capital. Together, their combined annual investments constitute the majority of external funding that is available to entrepreneurs (Fiet, 1991a).

Because it is possible that entrepreneurs could contact either of these investors (or venture capitalists) as they search for funding, it is important that they understand the types of deals that each prefers, if they are successfully to target their search. This is quite a different issue from the one investigated by researchers who have examined the stages in the venture capitalist's deal evaluation process (Hall, 1989; Hall and Hofer, 1993; Silver, 1985; Tyebjee and Bruno, 1984; Wells, 1974). While these studies have clarified what venture capital investors actually do to evaluate a deal, they do not address the question of whether there are any underlying factors that tilt the funding decision toward one type of a

Address for reprints: James O. Fiet, Fletcher Jones Professor of Entrepreneurship, Eberhardt School of Business, University of the Pacific, 3601 Pacific Avenue, Stockton, CA 95211, USA.

552   JAMES O. FIET

deal. Also, because they do not examine what Dubin (1978, p. 29) refers to as 'broad relationships', they tend to be exploratory and not easily utilized for theory building and testing.

This research examined one aspect of a deal – its riskiness – and the possibility that venture capitalists prefer to avoid investing in deals affected by a particular type of risk. This research was based upon the informational economics assumption that information to reduce the riskiness of a deal can be acquired at a cost (Hayek, 1945). Thus, the acquisition of risk-reducing information can be viewed as an investment decision affecting the cost of the evaluation process. One way to minimize the cost of investing in information is to specialize in assessing particular types of deals – in this case, deals affected by a particular form of risk. An examination of all forms of venture capital risk was beyond the scope of the present research. Hence, it limited itself to market and agency risk.

Market risk is due to unforeseen competitive conditions. It depends upon the size, growth and accessibility of the market, and on the existence of a market need.

Agency risk is the degree of uncertainty that either the entrepreneur or the venture capitalist will pursue his or her own interests rather than comply with the requirements of the contract for venture capital. Agency risk is caused by the difficulty in monitoring the separate and possibly divergent interests of investors and entrepreneurs. However, in this research, agency risk refers to the venture capitalist's risk that the entrepreneur will pursue his or her own interests at the expense of those of the venture capitalist.

The importance that venture capital investors attach to a particular type of risk could be inversely related to the kind of risk they believe they are most competent to control. It is also possible that the type of risk that they assess the most is the risk that they most want to avoid affecting their deals. For example, if they believed that they were especially qualified to monitor the entrepreneur, they would not need to worry as much about making agency mistakes because they would be confident that they make fewer of them and would be able to structure the deal so that they would be protected. What they would need to avoid is committing themselves to a deal where the market was unattractive, a factor which they would be less adept at controlling. Thus, we would expect them to specialize in assessing market risk factors and to avoid deals where there was any doubt about their attractiveness. They would not be as confident they could avoid market losses as they were that they could avoid losses due to agency risk. On the other hand, they might be less confident they could avoid agency losses and, as a consequence, view it as more threatening than market risk.

THE SPECIFIC NATURE OF RISK-REDUCING INFORMATION

If information is to be useful in reducing a deal's riskiness, it must pertain specifically to the deal under consideration. In fact, risk-reducing information is characteristically specific information (Hayek, 1945). The most specific form of information has little or no value for reducing risk in more than one deal (Barney and Ouchi, 1986, pp. 21, 22; Klein et al., 1978). The degree of informational specificity is a critical dimension because it can vary between being only relevant to a particular deal and being so general in nature that the signals that it sends would be meaningless to an investor.

Hayek (1945, pp. 321, 322) noted that it is often specific information about the particular circumstances of time and place that are most likely to affect a deal. It may consist of knowledge of people, of local conditions and special circumstances. Examples of such information for venture capitalists are assessments of the character and integrity of the entrepreneur, market studies to evaluate the potential for a new product, and evaluations of potential sites to determine traffic counts and development costs. In contrast, college educations, courses required for state licences, and information about macro-economic trends fall into the category of general information, rather than specific information, and provide little if any risk-reducing information for a particular deal.

Because of the specificity of risk-reducing information, it is likely that business angels and venture capital firms place more importance on one type of risk than another. That is, they selectively acquire information about different types of risk because it is 'not given to anyone in its totality' (Hayek, 1945, p. 320). If they saw themselves as more qualified to manage a particular type of risk, they would worry less about it and would acquire information about the specific aspects of the deal in which they had less confidence. To advance this study it was necessary to consider how venture capitalists might evaluate specific information about market and agency risk.

MARKET RISK

Market risk has been described in the strategy literature as the degree of uncertainty associated with gaining a competitive advantage due to environmental factors (Barney et al., 1989; Fiet, 1991b; Porter, 1980). Although market risk has been described in the literature, it cannot be directly observed. We can only make inferences about it based upon how it affects indicator variables that are observable. The following potential indicators of market risk were thought to be among the most promising of those found in previous conceptual research:

1. *Technical obsolescence* can cause losses when entrepreneurs invest in specialized assets. Once these specialized assets become obsolete, they have a lower value when used for purposes other than those for which they were previously purchased (Klein et al., 1978; Williamson, 1985).

2. *Many competitors* (Mcgee, 1988; Scherer, 1980) increase the difficulty of colluding to increase the level of joint profits (Rumelt, 1988; Stigler, 1961). When they cannot collude they are forced to compete for a share of a market that is presumed to be finite, even if it is growing. Competition increases inter-firm rivalry and lowers the level of prices that can be charged. Increased competition forces down the level of industry profits and increases an entrepreneur's risk of market losses.

3. *Many potential, new competitors* (Bain, 1956; Porter, 1980) increase the prospects that additional new firms will be bidding to provide more products/ services at lower, more competitive prices. Lower prices increase the level of competitive rivalry which increases the risk of market losses.

554   JAMES O. FIET

4. *Many substitute products/services* (Porter, 1980; Scherer, 1980) blur any distinctions in output held by suppliers. When the cross-elasticities of substitutes are positive, lowering the price of one substitute lowers the demand for the other (Mcgee, 1988). Substitutes also increase the power of buyers to set prices. This transfer of competitive power occurs when products can no longer be differentiated by buyers as distinctive. The result is an increase in competitive rivalry and an increased risk of market losses.

5. *Weak customer demand for a product or service* (Porter, 1980) causes sellers to offer concessions that increase the risk of market losses.

6. *Market attractiveness* (Day, 1986; Porter, 1980; Tyebjee and Bruno, 1984; Williamson, 1975) is a qualitative variable that summarizes those structural characteristics of an industry that are peculiar and slow to change. It is a function of its size, growth and accessibility and on the existence of a market need. The more attractive a market, the lower will be the level of competitive rivalry within it, the higher will be the profitability of its firms, and the lower will be the level of risk to its firms due to market losses.

AGENCY RISK

The concept of agency risk has been described by financial economists, but only a couple of known studies have attempted to apply it in the venture capital arena (Barney, Busenitz, Fiet and Moesel, 1989; Fiet, 1991b). The following potential indicators are extensions of those found in the mainstream literature and were selected for further study:

1. *Potentially dishonest entrepreneurs* (Alchian and Demsetz, 1972; Jensen and Meckling, 1978) increase the risk that they will deliberately withhold information that is critical to equitable contract negotiation. Dishonesty could result in agency losses due to opportunism.

2. *Entrepreneurs knowing more than venture capitalists* about the enterprise (Alchian and Demsetz, 1972; Eisenhardt, 1989) constitutes a form of information asymmetry that creates an agency risk when entrepreneurs are opportunistic.

3. *Great distance* to be travelled between the venture capitalist and the entrepreneur's enterprise (Alchian and Demsetz, 1972; Gupta and Sapienza, 1992) increases the' likelihood that less frequent monitoring will permit losses due to agency risk.

4. *Short-term self interest seeking* by the entrepreneur inhibits joint profit maximization for both the venture capitalist and the entrepreneur (Alchian and Demsetz, 1972).

5. *Numerous entrepreneurs to be monitored* (Eisenhardt, 1989) increase a venture capitalist's span of control and decrease the time that can be spent monitoring each venture.

6. *Not performing as agreed* may result from either unforeseen circumstances or from self-interest seeking with guile (Williamson, 1975).

7. *Game playing* is a form of intentional self-interest seeking (Williamson, 1975).

RISK AVOIDANCE STRATEGIES 555

INVESTOR SPECIALIZATION

The acquisition of specific information about either market or agency risk sends a clearer, more relevant signal than general risk-reducing information (Hayek, 1945; Hirschleifer, 1970). Because venture capital investors and business angels cannot costlessly acquire specific information, they are guided in its selection by the type of risk that they are most interested in avoiding. Moreover, their tendency to concentrate on a particular type of risk would enable them to avoid starting over from the beginning each time they consider a new deal. On average, we would expect they would acquire information specifically related to the type of risk that they perceived to be the most threatening to them.

Venture Capital Firm Investors and Their Views of Market Risk

There is substantial evidence to indicate that venture capital firm investors view market risk as more threatening than agency risk. They may worry less about agency risk because they are able to protect themselves through the use of boilerplate contractual terms and conditions that they append to each venture capital agreement. Boilerplate reduces the cost of protecting themselves against agency risk by generating economies of scale in the writing of contracts. These economies of scale can then be used to offset the cost of investigating market risk, which according to Driscoll (1974), has become their most important function. It has become their most important function, in all probability, because they see themselves as most vulnerable to it.

On average, venture capital firms spend about half of their time monitoring nine investments for factors that could affect a new venture's competitive position (Gorman and Sahlman, 1989). Even after they commit themselves financially to a deal, they spend about eight hours on-site, and about 30 hours on the telephone evaluating the competitive position of each company in their portfolio (Gorman and Sahlman, 1989).

Tyebjee and Bruno (1984) examined how venture capital firm investors evaluate the riskiness of a deal. They found that the venture capital firm investor's evaluation consisted of five assessment stages: market attractiveness, product differentiation, managerial capabilities, resistance to environmental threats, and anticipated cashout potential. Each of these stages evaluated market risk with the exception of managerial capabilities, which is an agency issue. In general, however, venture capital firms seem to be assessing market factors more than agency factors.

New businesses are subject to more market risk than established businesses because they are often exploring markets where competitive equilibriums among buyers, suppliers, potential entrants, current competitors, and product/service substitutes have not been established (Porter, 1980). A new firm's own competitive actions may even be the source of some unexpected shifts in equilibrium (Schumpeter, 1936). Assuming that venture capital firm investors specialize in evaluating market factors, we would expect to find them avoiding start-up deals that are fraught with the most market risk. In fact, previous researchers have reported that venture capital firms do avoid start-up deals (Rea, 1989; Wetzel, 1986).

556   JAMES O. FIET

Small businesses that are growing too fast to finance their own growth could also be expected to be subject to greater market risk. As we would expect, Wetzel (1986) also reported that venture capital firms avoid providing equity capital for small firms that are growing too fast to finance their own growth, but that are not yet large enough to gain access to public equity markets. They prefer instead to invest after the first few rounds of equity funding have already been put in place (Bygrave and Timmons, 1992).

Venture capital firms often screen as many as a thousand deals a year looking for opportunities that pose the least amount of market risk (Fiet, 1991a). They focus comparatively less on an individual entrepreneur's character, integrity, reputation, and intentions. Not only may they feel that agency problems can be regulated more effectively through contract provisions, but they may simply not have time to evaluate agency issues during the early part of their screening process. They know that most deals will be rejected and that it would not be prudent to investigate each entrepreneur's habits at this stage of the due diligence process. Also, they may think that agency issues are better evaluated through face-to-face contacts in which the evaluator can consider richer forms of more subjective data (Daft and Lengel, 1986; Wetzel, 1986).

For the foregoing reasons, venture capital firm investors view market risk as more important than agency risk, which is the first hypothesis.

Hypothesis 1: Venture capital firm investors view market risk as more important than agency risk.

Business Angels and Their Views of Agency Risk

In contrast, there is substantial evidence to indicate that business angels view agency risk as more threatening than market risk. Although Wetzel (1981, p. 217) reported that they are 'financially sophisticated individuals of means, often with previous investment or managerial experience with entrepreneurial ventures', Haar et al. (1988) reported that they rely more upon their hunches and upon recommendations from other angels to learn about the entrepreneurs (agents) in the deal. Because of their previous experience, they may feel that their understanding of the market aspects of a deal is adequate. However, unless the entrepreneur is well known to them, they may feel that a deal will succeed only if they have the right entrepreneur.

Why would reportedly sophisticated individuals rely upon hunches to guide their investment decisions? Although not much is known about how they invest, it may be that the venture capital markets in which business angels operate are comparatively inefficient disseminators of information about deals, as suggested by Gaston and Bell (1985) and Wetzel (1987). This suspected informational inefficiency should not be interpreted to imply that business angels would not consider all available investment information, whether it was public or private, as suggested by Fama (1970). The problem appears to be that what is available to them is quite scant. Under these circumstances, investment information often finds its way to business angels through friends and business associates. In fact, friends and business associates were the most frequent and reliable sources of information for business angels (Gaston and Bell, 1985; Wetzel, 1981, 1983, 1986, 1987).

Their reliance upon friends and business associates may be an indication that they are precluded from gaining access to the same deal channels employed by venture capital firms that commonly seek out co-investors among other venture capital firms (Bygrave, 1988; Fiet, 1991b). Compared to venture capital firms, business angels do not consider as many deals a year, simply because they do not have access to them. Gaston and Bell (1985) reported from their study of Sunbelt investors that business angels are frustrated and dissatisfied with the amount of information that they receive about potential deals. One third of the investors in their study reported that they were dissatisfied. The average investor wanted to invest 83 per cent more than he or she did, but could not find sufficiently attractive deals.

Unlike many venture capital firms, business angels usually do not have analysts on staff, nor offices dedicated to investigating deals. As a result, they often lack competency with sophisticated analytical tools to evaluate market risk (Fiet, 1991a). According to Wetzel (1986), it is not surprising that they often do not require formal business plans from entrepreneurs because they normally would not be qualified to evaluate them. However, there may be another explanation of their not requiring them – they may feel that they do not see enough deals so that they can properly compare and analyse them. Not having more opportunities to screen deals may result from their having a comparatively less visible market presence.

Nevertheless, business angels do consult with other business angels, friends and business associates about deals, particularly about the character, track record, and intentions of the entrepreneur. However, they simply do not have access to as many deals as they would like to consider. Because they seem to be rather frustrated in obtaining market risk information themselves, they may substitute agency information for it. That is, business angels may rely upon the entrepreneur to evaluate market risk for them. Making such a substitution would allow a business angel to specialize in evaluating whether or not the entrepreneur understands the deal, and whether or not the entrepreneur can be relied upon as a venture manager, even if they as investors do not have enough market information to understand it completely. That is, business angels can specialize in evaluating agency risk, while relying upon the entrepreneur to manage market risk. Thus:

Hypothesis 2: Business angels view agency risks as more important than market risk.

Based on the previous arguments it is likely that business angels and venture capital investors have their own views of which risk is more important to them. Their differing access to information about risk leads to the last two hypotheses.

Hypothesis 3: Market risk is viewed as more important by venture capital firm investors than business angels.

Hypothesis 4: Agency risk is viewed as more important by business angels than by venture capital firm investors.

558   JAMES O. FIET

METHODS

Testing these hypotheses involved: (1) specifying the research design, (2) data collection, (3) developing the survey instrument, and (4) data analysis.

Research Design

The research design was a cross-sectional sampling of two separate and distinct populations of venture capitalists: venture capital firms and business angels. Data were collected using mailed surveys, personal solicitations to investor groups, anonymous third-party referrals, and anonymous mailings to participants in investor networks. Data were analysed using the following applications of Bentler–Weeks covariance structure modelling: confirmatory factor analysis, a null model to check for multicollinearity, and discriminant analysis. Combining these separate applications in one Bentler–Weeks covariance structure model facilitated the determination of measurement error and provided tests of statistical significance for each hypothesis. Finally, a subset of both venture capital firm investors and business angels was interviewed in face-to-face interviews to confirm the interpretation of the statistical results and to avoid common method variance.

Data Collection[1]

There are approximately 700 venture capital firms in the United States (Bygrave and Timmons, 1992, p. 52). These are professionally managed organizations usually investing other people's money. A deliberate attempt was made to include both firms with large and small portfolios of investments. Representatives of firms with larger portfolios were selected from a census of the 216 members of the National Venture Capital Association (NVCA). Representatives of firms with smaller portfolios were selected from a census of the 29 members of the Houston Venture Capital Association (HVCA). No attempt was made to completely separate these two sub-populations, however, because four HVCA firms were also NVCA firms and a few had portfolios that were as large as medium sized NVCA firms.

After four rounds of mailed surveys, 141 usable responses were obtained from a total of 245 subjects, for a response rate of 57 per cent. The four rounds of surveys were mailed according to Dillman's (1978) recommendations. The first round consisted of a letter and a survey instrument. The second round consisted of a postcard reminder that was sent one week later. The third round included a replacement survey, along with a letter, all of which was mailed only to non-respondents three weeks after the postcard. The fourth round was a certified letter that was mailed four weeks later to all remaining non-respondents. This last mailing included a final plea to respond along with another replacement survey. Refer to Table I for a more detailed analysis of how usable data were obtained from venture capital firm investors.

Gaston (1989) estimated that there are as many as 490,000 US business angels. They are an elusive group to study because they have a preference for anonymity. Furthermore, sometimes they are in the market for deals and at other times they are inactive. There are no comprehensive lists of business angels. They have been studied in the past using survey and referral techniques. The average response rate from these studies has been less than 5 per cent. All

RISK AVOIDANCE STRATEGIES   559

Table I. Analysis of data collection

Respondents	Number of surveys	Number of responses	Number of usable responses	Percentage of usable responses %	Number of follow-up interviews	Percentage of follow-up interviews %
Venture capital firms:						
NVCA[1]	216	122	122	57	4	3
HVCA[2]	29	19	19	66	19	100
Total	245	141	141	58	23	16
Business angels:						
Longview[3]	207	74	19	9	0	0
Opera[4]	500	193	61	12	21	34
Networks[5]	80	24	2	3	0	0
3rd Party[6]	27	21	1	4	0	0
Presentation[7]	35	3	0	0	0	0
Total	849	315	83	10	21	25

Notes:
1. National Venture Capital Association.
2. Houston Venture Capital Association.
3. Survey referrals from the Director of Economic Development for the City of Longview, Texas.
4. Contributors to Greater Houston Opera.
5. Responses anonymously received from two Texas networks of business angels.
6. Anonymous referrals from other business angels.
7. Responses received from participants in venture capital clubs in Dallas and Waco, Texas.

previous efforts to collect representative data on business angels have been inconclusive because it is mathematically impossible to demonstrate that a sample is representative without being able to identify the population from which it comes. Because the population of business angels is unknown, and probably unknowable, the conclusions of all previous studies, as well as those of the present study, must be limited in their generalizability to the sample that they represent.

To be counted as a business angel, a respondent had to have acted as an individual, normally investing his or her own money, not a firm's, and had to have been active during the last three years. Earlier researchers used a cutoff that varied between three years (Haar et al., 1988) and five years (Sullivan, 1990). Because respondents were being asked to report how they evaluated risk, and because they would probably find it useful to remember how it had affected them in previous decisions, the more restrictive criteria was selected. An individual who had invested his own money, but had done it through a firm, was viewed as a quasi-angel. Eighteen per cent of otherwise qualified respondents were eliminated because they were quasi-angels and their responses could obscure the discriminant validity of the statistical tests.

Dillman's (1978) procedure for mailing surveys was modified by omitting the final certified letter. The marginal benefit of sending it to an unknown population appeared to be less than contacting new, potential investors. (It was more than twice as expensive to send the final certified mailing as it was to send the

560   JAMES O. FIET

first three rounds.) Also, for venture capital firms, it only increased the overall response rate by approximately 7 per cent.

Data from business angels were collected through a variety of contacts. Surveys were mailed to 207 potential business angels, based on the recommendation of the Director for Economic Development for the City of Longview, Texas. He suspected that the subjects were investors because they had previously indicated to him an interest in supporting any new businesses that could be attracted to the community. After three rounds of surveys, 74 completed surveys were received, 55 of which were disqualified for not having made an investment during the last three years. In total, these efforts resulted in a usable response rate of 9 per cent.

Five hundred contributors to the Greater Houston Opera were mailed three rounds of surveys. They were selected solely based on a hunch that they might occasionally be business angels. Of these, 193 surveys were completed and returned. After eliminating non-qualifying respondents, 61 remained, resulting in a usable response rate of 12 per cent.

In addition to mailed surveys, three other methods were utilized to collect data. First, there are two known Texas networks of business angels whose purpose is to anonymously review deals. Approximately 80 surveys were mailed through their network offices. Second, the investigator made presentations to, and distributed, surveys to potential business angels at venture capital forums in Houston, Waco and Dallas, Texas. Third, some business angels became enthusiastic supporters and volunteered to personally deliver surveys, or to mail them at their own expense. The results of these last three methods, together with the previous efforts to contact business angels, are summarized in Table I.

Development of the Survey Instrument
There were three constructs to be measured: investor type, market risk, and agency risk. The investor type construct was dichotomously coded so that it could be used to categorize business angels and venture capital firms. If a respondent was a venture capital firm investor, he or she was coded as a one. If it was a business angel, he or she was coded as a zero.

The market risk and agency risk constructs were measured indirectly. A preliminary survey instrument was constructed using the previously discussed indicators that were found in the literature. Informal feedback on the survey instrument was obtained from 22 academic colleagues representing such institutions as Aarhus University, Denmark, Babson College, Harvard University, Texas A&M University, the University of Tennessee, and the University of Texas, Austin. Next, these indicators were pre-tested in 38 face-to-face interviews with venture capital firm investors, business angels, academic scholars, and public policy makers. This pre-testing was conducted in accordance with Dillman's (1978, pp. 155–9) recommendations. The purpose of these pre-test interviews was to ensure that the questions were tapping on to the intended constructs and that the questions were correctly interpreted.

As the respondents filled out the survey instrument, they were watched for signs that they did not understand a question. Contemporaneous probing of respondents concerning any apparently misunderstood questions resulted in the redesign of a few questions, the elimination of a few others, and the substitution of completely new questions in a few instances. For example, with regard to market risk, the wording of several questions was altered by pre-testers and one item, 'Few buyers' was added by pre-testers as an additional indicator of market risk. With regard to agency risk, only one of the seven original indicators survived unchanged after pre-testing. In most cases, changes to agency risk indicators were clarifications of wording. In other cases, they involved eliminating an indicator, such as 'game playing' and replacing it with 'contractual ambiguities'. Appendices I and II describe the changes that were made in the indicators as a result of pre-testing. It is important to note that these indicators are substantially different from those that were derived from the original literature review. However, no changes were made unless they were initiated by the pre-testers, support could be found for them in the literature, and they were approved by the 22 academic colleagues who had previously provided feedback. Appendices III and IV contain the actual questions that were used to collect data on market risk and agency risk.

A more parsimonious set of construct indicators was identified through use of a factor analytic application of covariance structure modelling. Thus, some of the questions in Appendices III and IV were not used in the final analysis as construct indicators. The results of these data reduction procedures are also found in Appendices I and II. The factor models for market risk and agency risk are contained in Appendices V and VI.

Data Analysis
Table II contains a correlation matrix of the final indicator variables for the market risk and agency risk constructs. These variables were multiplied by their standard deviations to generate a covariance matrix that was later decomposed to model the relationships among the constructs.

Table II. Correlation matrix of indicators of market risk and agency risk

	1	2	3	4	5	6	7	8	9	10
1. Venture capital firm/business angel	1.00									
2. Many current competitors	0.02	1.00								
3. Many potential new competitors	−0.01	0.58	1.00							
4. Competitive products/services that are ready substitutes	0.07	0.49	0.48	1.00						
5. Weak customer demand for product/service	0.11	0.27	0.26	0.49	1.00					
6. Entrepreneurs and venture capitalist having different cash flow objectives	−0.03	0.05	0.05	0.17	0.13	1.00				
7. entrepreneurs and venture capitalist having different profit objectives	−0.13	0.16	0.15	0.15	0.07	0.72	1.00			
8. Manipulation of profitability	−0.06	−0.04	0.07	0.09	0.19	0.46	0.49	1.00		
9. Short-term self-interest seeking by entrepreneur	−0.03	0.06	0.02	0.14	0.28	0.34	0.45	0.55	1.00	
10. Contractual ambiguities	−0.04	0.02	0.02	0.13	0.07	0.51	0.48	0.36	0.49	1.00

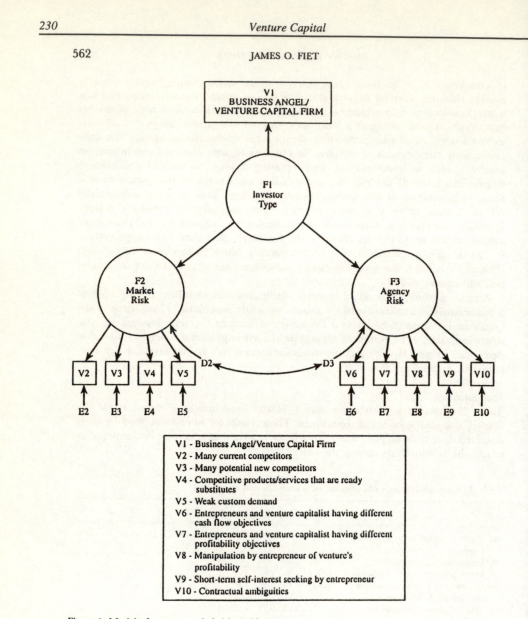

Figure 1. Model of venture capital risk avoidance

The purpose of the model in Figure 1 was to develop statistically significant tests of the hypotheses and to evaluate the impact of measurement error on the results. The 'E's represent errors in measurement for a particular indicator variable. The 'D's are disturbance terms and represent errors in measurement for the endogenous constructs. Because investor type is dichotomously coded (as a zero when it represents business angels and as a one when it represents venture capital firms), it is assumed to be unaffected by measurement error, and thus does not have an 'E1' acting upon it. The curved, double-headed arrow between the 'D's represents the partial correlation between market risk and agency risk and is a measure of the possible extent to which investors do not specialize in either market or agency risk.

There are four ways to verify that the measurement of the constructs is statistically significant. First, the value for the chi-square statistic for the overall model had to exceed the standard cutoff value of 0.05. The other three fit indicators are the Bentler–Bonett Normed Fit Index, the Bentler–Bonett Non-Normed Fit Index, and the Comparative Fit Index. For a model to fit the data, each of the last three indicators had to be greater than 0.95. As indicated in Appendices VI and VII, these criteria were satisfied for both the market and agency risk constructs.

Before the model in Figure 1 could be tested it had to be assessed for multicollinearity among the construct indicators, which was done using a null modelling procedure. All of the construct indicators in the model were freed to covary. Table III contains the results of the null model test. If there were multicollinearity, the null model would not fit the data, which is what occurred in the initial stages of the analysis. To correct the lack of fit, it was assumed that the net effect of all the unknown influences on the hypothesized relationships (or in the case of the null model, the relationships among the construct indicators) could be isolated and reduced by correlating the errors in measurement of the indicator variables, or 'E's. (Refer to an extensive discussion of this fitting technique in Bollen, 1989.) Identifying the errors to be correlated was accom-

Table III. Null model of venture capital risk avoidance

Indicator / question	Standardized coefficient	P Value
Venture capital firm/business angle (Q5)	1.00	Not applicable
Many current competitors (Q12)	0.780	<0.0001
Many potential new competitors (Q13)	0.757	<0.0001
Competitive products/services that are ready substitutes (Q14)	0.682	<0.0001
Weak customer demand for product/service (Q15)	0.391	<0.0001
Entrepreneurs and venture capitalist having different cash flow objectives (Q20)	0.820	<0.0001
Entrepreneurs and venture capitalist having different profitability objectives (Q21)	0.880	<0.0001
Manipulation of profitability (Q25)	0.568	<0.0001
Short-term self-interest seeking by entrepreneur (Q25)	0.484	<0.0001
Contractual ambiguities (Q26)	0.5555	<0.0001
Overall chi-square for null model	28.993	
Degrees of freedom	24.000	
Probability value for chi-square	0.2204	
Bentler–Bonett Normed Fit Index	0.9650	
Bentler–Bonett Non-Normed Fit Index	0.9888	
Comparative Fit Index	0.9940	

564   JAMES O. FIET

plished through the systematic use of the Lagranian multiplier test (Bentler, 1989; Bollen, 1989; Fiet, 1995). Thus, to fit the null model to the data, the errors were correlated. Their correlation produced the model in Table III. The correlated error terms are available from the author.

RESULTS

After fitting the null model, the hypothesized relationships indicated in Figure 1 were added to the null model. The results are contained in Table IV. It also contains the disturbance terms, D2 and D3, for the two endogenous constructs. The reliabilities of the construct indicators are available from the author.

Statistical Analysis

Hypothesis 1 was tested by examining the relationship between F1 (investor type) and F2 (market risk) in Figure 1. Given that venture capital firms were coded as one, to reject the null hypothesis that the mean difference scores for investor type and market risk are equal, the sign of the coefficient indicating the direction of the relationship had to be positive and the p value had to be less than 0.05. The following is the structural equation for market risk:

$$\text{market risk} = F2 = (0.127)(F2) + 0.992(D2) \tag{1}$$

Both conditions held. The standardized difference in the means between investor type, coded as 1, and market risk was 0.127 and the p value for that coefficient was 0.0359. Thus, at a significance level of 0.05, the alternative hypothesis was accepted. Venture capital firms are likely to view market risk as more important than agency risk.

Hypothesis 2 was tested by examining the relationship between F1 (investor type) and F3 (agency risk) in Figure 1. Given that business angels were coded as zero, to reject the null hypothesis that the means are equal, the sign of the coefficient indicating the direction of the relationship had to be negative and statistically significant ($p < 0.05$). The following is the structural equation for agency risk:

$$\text{agency risk} = F3 = (-0.167)(F1) + 0.986(D) \tag{2}$$

Table IV. Results

Relationships being evaluated	Mean difference scores	P value
Investor type and market risk	0.127	0.0359
Investor type and agency risk	−0.167	0.0077
Agency risk and its disturbance term, D3	0.986	< 0.001
Market risk and its disturbance term, D2	0.992	< 0.0001
D3 and D2	0.174	< 0.001

Again, both conditions held. The standardized difference in the means between investor type, coded as zero, and agency risk was -0.167 and the p value for that coefficient was 0.0077. Thus, the null hypothesis that the means were equal was rejected. The business angels in the sample are more likely to view agency risk as more important than market risk.

Hypothesis 3 was tested by comparing equations (1) and (2). Given that venture capital firms were coded as one, to reject the null hypothesis that venture capital firm investors viewed agency risk as being of equal importance or more important than market risk, the mean difference score between investor type and market risk had to be positive and significant while the mean difference score between investor type had to be negative and significant. All of these conditions held. Thus at a p value less than 0.05, market risk is viewed as more important by venture capital firm investors than business angels.

Hypothesis 4 is the obverse of hypothesis 3. Thus, agency risk is viewed as more important by business angels than by venture capital firm investors ($p < 0.05$).

As indicated by the existence of measurement error, the model is not completely reliable. It is also apparent by the correlation between D3 and D2 that some venture capitalists view both market risk and agency risk as being important. Despite the unknown effects of measurement error upon the modelled relationships, which may result from misspecification, the relationships that were tested in the four hypotheses could only have occurred by chance at a p value less than 0.05.

The Follow-up Interviews
This research buttressed its statistical findings with *ex post*, face-to-face interviews with both types of investors – 21 with venture capital firms and 23 with business angels. The purpose of these interviews was to review the subject's responses to items on the survey to determine the reasoning behind each response. These interviews were supportive of the statistical findings and provided a richer understanding of their comparative risk assessment processes.

Venture capital firms. The following comments by venture capital firms were supportive of their concern for evaluating market risk. One said: 'We hire industry specialists to assess market risk.' Another said: '. . . to control losses due to market risk, we consult with customers of the business, people who have worked with the firm's management, and industry, market and technical experts.' A third venture capital firm investor summarized the practices of his firm with this comment:

> 'Venture capital firms manage risk by trying to identify potential issues and risks prior to the investment and doing sufficient due diligence to be comfortable that the risk is controllable. Our risk is controlled by a broad set of management procedures and in the end can only be minimized but can never be removed.'

A statement that could have been made by many venture capital firm investors was the following: 'My ability to control market risk is because I understand [my] market.'

566   JAMES O. FIET

The following comment provided collateral evidence that venture capital firms consider agency risk to be a less important factor than market risk: 'We always bet on Joe, not the market. However, *markets are most important – more important than people. Agency risk is difficult to distinguish from competency.*'

Several comments suggested that venture capital firms could control agency risk more effectively *ex post* than *ex ante*. One affirmed, '. . . *thirty to fifty per cent of managers are replaced, usually during the last part of three years* [which provides some evidence that agency issues are temporary provided they are anticipated in the contract]. There is an inclination to make management changes early.' Another counselled, 'Don't worry about the equity split. Sooner or later it will be Friday afternoon and more money will be needed for payroll. It is easy to renegotiate with the entrepreneur on Friday afternoon.'

Business angels. The following comments by business angels were supportive of their concern for evaluating agency risk. One said: 'Agency risk is much higher than market risk. There are a hell of a lot of unethical people out there – I would not have been so trusting . . . *You want to do business with people who you can shake hands with and they'll just go out and do what they say.*'

Being more concerned for agency risk than market risk was a common theme among business angels. One said: '*Agency risk is more serious than market threats. If you have "good people", you can go into a highly competitive market.*' Another said: 'I can not stress enough how important it is to "feel" comfortable about an investment and particularly the entrepreneur. I've learned to listen carefully to my intuition when it appears to be in conflict with the intellectual, particularly when evaluating people in a proposed deal.'

DISCUSSION

This research compared risk avoidance strategies employed by business angels and venture capital firm investors. It found that differences in their strategies for evaluating risk lead them to hold predictably different views of the dangers of market and agency risk. Venture capital firm investors attach more importance to market risk than agency risk. They are less concerned with agency risk because they have learned how to protect themselves from it using stringent boilerplate contractual provisions. Boilerplate allows them to perfunctorily replace an entrepreneur who under-performs, is guilty of malfeasance or who is found to be incompetent. They are able to economize on the cost of writing complex, contingent-claims contracts by using boilerplate. This boilerplate strategy effectively protects venture capital investors from market risk because they attach more importance to it in their screening process.

In the present study, there was statistically significant evidence that the following four types of market risk information were viewed by venture capital firm investors as being more important than agency risk information: (1) current competitors, (2) potential new competitors, (3) products or services that were ready substitutes, and (4) customer demand. They can be very selective in choosing which entrepreneurs they will fund because their information channels provide them with as many as a thousand deals a year to evaluate.

In contrast, business angels utilize a different strategy to avoid risk. They report that they are frustrated because they do not have access to a comparable number of deals, in many cases, only a handful of them a year. One consequence of a limited access to deals could be that business angels possess insufficient comparative data to evaluate market risk. Recognizing this lack of information about market risk, this research found that they attach more importance to agency risk because they believe that if they can find the right entrepreneur, they can rely upon him or her to limit their losses due to adverse market conditions. Thus, the business angel strategy for avoiding risk is to substitute reliance upon a competent and trustworthy entrepreneur for their own competence in limiting losses due to market risk. Compared with venture capital firm investors, business angels place much more importance upon screening entrepreneurs than deals for market risk.

The present study found that there was statistically significant evidence that the following five types of agency risk information were viewed by business angels as being more important than market risk information: (1) differences in cash flow objectives, (2) differences in profitability objectives, (3) evidence of manipulation of profitability, (4) evidence of short-term self-interest seeking, and (5) evidence of contractual ambiguity.

This research also noted that differences in the importance that each of these venture capitalists attach to risk can exist because risk-reducing information is characteristically specific information. They tend to selectively acquire information about different types of risk because no one can evaluate all of it. Specializing in the acquisition of one type of risk-reducing information minimizes its cost through the development of economies of scale. Thus, it was not surprising that one finding was that not only do venture capital firms specialize more in market risk than agency risk, but they did so more than business angels. While business angels were found to specialize more in agency risk than market risk and did so more than venture capital firm investors.

Another finding of this research is that venture capitalists manifest broad avoidance strategies for particular types of risk, strategies that could not have been detected using previously utilized research methodologies. Because these patterns do not seem to be directly related to what they do, previous efforts to document the steps in the venture capital decision process never would have been able to uncover them. Moreover, instead of utilizing covariance structure modelling, most venture capital and entrepreneurship researchers have relied upon regression/correlation techniques that depend upon variables being measurable (Jacobson, 1992). However, to measure a variable, it must first be observable, which is not true of either market risk or agency risk. This bias is unfortunate because the identification of these strategies is the first step in the development of a theory of venture capital market segmentation.

To reinforce what has been suggested here, we must know much more about possible substitution strategies that could be employed by venture capitalists to compensate for their own deficiencies. If we do not examine the possibilities for and effects of resource substitution, we are likely to have an incomplete understanding of the factors that drive market segmentation.

This research has some practical implications for entrepreneurs searching for financial backing. If they knew, for example, that venture capital markets were

568 JAMES O. FIET

segmented based on investor strategies for avoiding particular types of risk, they could use this information to match their own deal's risk profile with the most promising providers of capital. An entrepreneur who could convince an investor of his or her competence, intentions, and integrity would probably be able to use this advantage more effectively among business angels than among venture capital firms. An entrepreneur with a technical or market advantage would probably find a more receptive investor audience among venture capital firms.

APPENDIX I

Evolution of Market Risk Indicators

Original indicators from literature	Changed indicators after pre-testing	Final indicators after factor analysis
Technical obsolescence	Technical obsolescence	Dropped out. Non significant
Numerous competitors	**Many current competitors**	Stayed in model. Significant
Potential new competitors	**Many potential new competitors**	Stayed in model. Significant
Substitute products/ services	**Competitive products/ services that are ready substitutes**	Stayed in model. Significant
Weak customer demand	Unchanged after pre-testing	Stayed in model. Significant
Market attractiveness	Unattractiveness of industry	Dropped out. Non significant
	Few buyers*	Dropped out. Non significant

The bold indicators are those that stayed in model after pre-testing and factor analysis.
*'Few buyers' was added as a result of pre-testing. 'Few buyers' would increase their power and the level of rivalry among sellers for market share (Porter, 1980). It dropped out of the model after factor analysis.

APPENDIX II

Evolution of Agency Risk Indicators

Indicators from literature	Indicators after pre-testing	Final indicators after factor analysis
Potential dishonesty	Dishonest entrepreneurs	Dropped out. Non significant
Information asymmetry	**Entrepreneurs and venture capitalist having different cash flow objectives***	Stayed in model. Significant
Great distance	**Entrepreneurs and venture capitalist having different profitability objectives***	Stayed in model. Significant
Numerous ventures to monitor	Many entrepreneurs to monitor	Dropped out. Non significant

© Blackwell Publishers Ltd 1995

RISK AVOIDANCE STRATEGIES 569

Self-interest seeking	**Short-term self-interest seeking**	Stayed in model. Significant
Shirking	**Manipulation of profitability****	Stayed in model. Significant
Game playing	**Contractual ambiguities*****	Stayed in model. Significant

The bold indicators are those that stayed in model after pre-testing and factor analysis.

*Both differing profitability and cash flow objectives are derived directly from the definition of agency risk, namely, separate and possibly divergent interests.

**Manipulation of profitability would be a manifestation of more than simple self-interest seeking. It would indicate self-interest seeking with guile, or opportunism.

***Contractual ambiguities allow for ineffective monitoring and increase the potential returns from self-interest seeking with guile.

APPENDIX III

Survey Questions for Market Risk

When they invest, venture capitalists (both individual investors and firms) nearly always run the risk of losing some of their principal. The risks that venture capitalists face seem to fall into two categories: (1) market risks and (2) agency risks. **MARKET RISKS** are due to unforseen competitive conditions. **AGENCY RISKS** are caused by the separate and possibly divergent interests of investors and entrepreneurs. Agency risks may result from entrepreneurs acting in bad faith, holding conflicting objectives, and the like. One of the purposes of this study is to get your views about these two types of risk. The questions on this page relate to **MARKET RISKS**. For each question, how do you view the following statement?

"IF THIS PROBLEM IS NOT TAKEN CARE OF, IT COULD CAUSE A VENTURE THAT I INVEST IN TO LOSE MONEY." (Refers to questions 11 thru 18)

> STRONGLY DISAGREE **means** problem is completely manageable
> MILDLY DISAGREE **means** problem is largely manageable
> NO OPINION **means** neither agree nor disagree
> MILDLY AGREE **means** problem will cause venture to lose money
> STRONGLY AGREE **means** problem could result in bankruptcy

Your view of the seriousness of the **MARKET RISK** (Circle your answer)				

	STRONGLY DISAGREE	MILDLY DISAGREE	NO OPINION	MILDLY AGREE	STRONGLY AGREE
11. Technical obsolescence	STRONGLY DISAGREE	MILDLY DISAGREE	NO OPINION	MILDLY AGREE	STRONGLY AGREE
12. Many current competitors	STRONGLY DISAGREE	MILDLY DISAGREE	NO OPINION	MILDLY AGREE	STRONGLY AGREE
13. Many potential new competitors	STRONGLY DISAGREE	MILDLY DISAGREE	NO OPINION	MILDLY AGREE	STRONGLY AGREE

570   JAMES O. FIET

14. Competitive
    products/services
    that are ready
    substitutes   STRONGLY   MILDLY   NO   MILDLY STRONGLY
                           DISAGREE   DISAGREE OPINION   AGREE   AGREE

15. Weak customer
    demand for
    product/service   STRONGLY   MILDLY   NO   MILDLY STRONGLY
                           DISAGREE   DISAGREE OPINION   AGREE   AGREE

16. Unattractiveness
    of industry   STRONGLY   MILDLY   NO   MILDLY STRONGLY
                           DISAGREE   DISAGREE OPINION   AGREE   AGREE

17. Few buyers   STRONGLY   MILDLY   NO   MILDLY STRONGLY
                           DISAGREE   DISAGREE OPINION   AGREE   AGREE

18. Other Market Risk
    (Specify) ————
    —————————— STRONGLY   MILDLY   NO   MILDLY STRONGLY
                           DISAGREE   DISAGREE OPINION   AGREE   AGREE

APPENDIX IV

Survey Questions for Agency Risk
The questions on this page relate to **AGENCY RISK**. For each question, please tell us
how you view the following statement? (Recall that agency risks result from entrepreneurs
acting in bad faith, holding conflicting objectives, and the like.)

**"IF THIS PROBLEM IS NOT TAKEN CARE OF, IT COULD CAUSE A
VENTURE THAT I INVEST IN TO LOSE MONEY." (Refers to questions 19
thru 26)**

          STRONGLY DISAGREE **means** problem is completely manageable
          MILDLY DISAGREE **means** problem is largely manageable
          NO OPINION **means** neither agree nor disagree
          MILDLY AGREE **means** problem will cause venture to lose money
          STRONGLY AGREE **means** problem could result in bankruptcy

          ┌───┐
          │   Your view of the seriousness of the **AGENCY RISK**   │
          │   (Circle your answer)   │

19. Dishonest
    entrepreneurs   STRONGLY   MILDLY   NO   MILDLY STRONGLY
                           DISAGREE   DISAGREE OPINION   AGREE   AGREE

20. Entrepreneurs and
    venture capitalist
    having different cash
    flow objectives   STRONGLY   MILDLY   NO   MILDLY STRONGLY
                           DISAGREE   DISAGREE OPINION   AGREE   AGREE

RISK AVOIDANCE STRATEGIES   571

21. Entrepreneurs and
    venture capitalists
    having different
    objectives for
    profitability   STRONGLY   MILDLY   NO   MILDLY STRONGLY
                             DISAGREE DISAGREE OPINION   AGREE   AGREE

22. Short-term self-
    interest seeking
    by entrepreneur   STRONGLY   MILDLY   NO   MILDLY STRONGLY
                             DISAGREE DISAGREE OPINION   AGREE   AGREE

23. Many
    entrepreneurs
    to be monitored   STRONGLY   MILDLY   NO   MILDLY STRONGLY
                             DISAGREE DISAGREE OPINION   AGREE   AGREE

24. Not performing
    agree to
    responsibilities   STRONGLY   MILDLY   NO   MILDLY STRONGLY
                             DISAGREE DISAGREE OPINION   AGREE   AGREE

25. Manipulation by
    entrepreneur of
    venture's
    profitability   STRONGLY   MILDLY   NO   MILDLY STRONGLY
                             DISAGREE DISAGREE OPINION   AGREE   AGREE

26. Contractual
    ambiguities   STRONGLY   MILDLY   NO   MILDLY STRONGLY
                             DISAGREE DISAGREE OPINION   AGREE   AGREE

APPENDIX V

Factor Model for Market Risk

Indicator / question	Standardized coefficient	P Value
Many current competitors (Q12)	0.794	< 0.0001
Many potential new competitors (Q13)	0.767	< 0.0001
Competitive products/services that are ready substitutes (Q14)	0.665	< 0.0001
Weak customer demand for product/service (Q15)	0.361	< 0.0001

Overall chi-square for confirmatory factor model	0.058
Degrees of freedom	1.000
Probability value for chi-square	0.810
Bentler-Bonett Normed Fit Inex	1.000
Bentler-Bonett Non-Normed Fit Index	1.020
Comparative Fit Index	1.000

572   JAMES O. FIET

APPENDIX VI

Factor Model for Agency Risk

Indicator / question	Standardized coefficient	P Value
Entrepreneurs and venture capitalist having different cash flow objectives (Q20)	0.829	< 0.0001
Entrepreneurs and venture capitalist having different profitability objectives (Q21)	0.863	< 0.0001
Manipulation of profitability	0.723	< 0.0001
Short-term self-interest seeking by entrepreneur	0,579	< 0.0001
Contractual ambiguities (Q26)	0.556	< 0.0001

Overall chi-square for confirmatory factor model	1.502
Degrees of freedom	2.000
Probability value for chi-square	0.473
Bentler–Bonett Normed Fit Index	1.005
Bentler–Bonett Non-Normed Fit Index	1.005
Comparative Fit Index	1.000

NOTE

[1] This data collection procedure has previously been reported in Fiet (1995). For clarity, it is reported again here.

REFERENCES

ALCHIAN, A. A. and DEMSETZ, H. (1972). 'Production, information costs, and economic organization'. *American Economic Review*, **62**, 777–95.

BAIN, J. S. (1956). *Barriers to New Competition*. Cambridge, Mass.: Harvard University Press.

BARNEY, J. B. (1986). 'Strategic factor markets: expectations, luck, and business strategy'. *Management Science*, **32**, 10, 1231–41.

BARNEY, J. B. and OUCHI, W. G. (1986). *Organizational Economics*. San Francisco: Jossey-Bass.

BARNEY, J. B., BUSENITZ, L., FIET, J. O. and MOESEL, D. (1989). 'The structure of venture capital governance: an organizational economic analysis of relations between venture capital firms and new ventures'. *Best Papers Proceedings* of Academy of Management, Washington.

BENTLER, P. M. (1989). *EQS – Structural Equations Program Manual*. Los Angeles: BMPD, Inc.

BOLLEN, K. A. (1989). *Structural Equations with Latent Variables*. New York: John Wiley & Sons.

BYGRAVE, W. D. (1988). 'The structure of investment networks of venture capital firms'. *Journal of Business Venturing*, **3**, 137–57.

BYGRAVE, W. D. and TIMMONS, J. A. (1992). *Venture Capital at the Crossroads*. Cambridge, Mass.: Harvard Business School Press.

DAFT, R. L. and LENGEL, R. H. (1986). 'Organizational information requirements, media richness and structural design'. *Management Science*, **32**, 5, 554–71.

Day, G. S. (1986). *Analysis for Strategic Market Decisions*. St Paul: West Publishing Company.

Dillman, D. A. (1978). *Mail and Telephone Surveys: The Total Design Method*. New York: John Wiley & Sons.

Driscoll, F. R. (1974). 'Venture capital: the risk–reward business'. IEE International Convention.

Dubin, R. (1978). *Theory Building*. New York: Free Press.

Eisenhardt, K. M. (1989). 'Agency theory: an assessment and review'. *Academy of Management Review*, **14**, 1, 57–74.

Fama, E. F. (1970). 'Efficient capital markets: a review of theory and empirical work'. *Journal of Finance*, **25**, 383–417.

Fiet, J. O. (1991a). 'Managing investments in specific information: a comparison of business angels and venture capital firms'. Unpublished doctoral dissertation, Texas A&M University.

Fiet, J. O. (1991b). 'Venture capital risk assessment: an empirical test comparing business angels and venture capital firms'. *Best Papers Proceedings* of Academy of Management, Miami.

Fiet, J. O. (1995). 'Reliance upon informants in the venture capital industry'. *Journal of Business Venturing*, **10**, 3, 195–223.

Gaston, R. J. (1989). *Finding Private Venture Capital for Your Firm*. New York: John Wiley & Sons.

Gaston, R. J. and Bell, S. (1985). 'Informal risk capital investment in the sunbelt region'. US Small Business Administration, Office of Advocacy, Washington, DC.

Gorman, M. and Sahlman, W. A. (1989). 'What do venture capitalists do?'. *Journal of Business Venturing*, **4**, 231–48.

Gupta, A. K. and Sapienza, H. J. (1992). 'Determinants of venture capital firms' preferences regarding the industry diversity and geographic scope of their investments'. *Journal of Business Venturing*, **7**, 347–62.

Haar, N. E., Starr, J. and MacMillan, I. C. (1988). 'Informal risk capital investors: investment patterns on the East Coast of the U.S.A.'. *Journal of Business Venturing*, **3**, 11–29.

Hall, H. J. (1989). 'Venture capitalist decision making and the entrepreneur: an exploratory investigation'. Unpublished doctoral dissertation, University of Georgia, Athens.

Hall, J. and Hofer, C. W. (1993). 'Venture capitalists' decision criteria in new venture evaluation'. *Journal of Business Venturing*, **8**, 25–42.

Hayek, F. A. (1945). 'The use of knowledge in society'. *American Economic Review*, **35**, 519–30.

Hirshleifer, J. (1970). *Investments, Interest, and Capital*. Englewood Cliffs, NJ: Prentice Hall.

Jacobson, R. (1992). 'The "Austrian" school of strategy'. *Academy of Management Review*, **17**, 4, 782–807.

Jensen, M. and Meckling, W. H. (1978). 'Theory of the firm: managerial behavior, agency costs, and ownership structure'. *Journal of Financial Economics*, **3**, 305–60.

Klein, B., Crawford, R. G. and Alchian, A. A. (1978). 'Vertical integration, appropriate rents and the competitive contracting process'. *Journal of Law and Economics*, **21**, 297–326.

McGee, J. S. (1988). *Industrial Organization*. Englewood Cliffs, NJ: Prentice Hall.

Porter, M. E. (1980). *Competitive Strategy*. New York: Free Press.

Rea, R. H. (1989). 'Factors affecting success and failure of seed capital/start-up negotiations'. *Journal of Business Venturing*, **4**, 149–58.

Rumelt, R. (1988). 'Competitive marketing strategy. Panel discussion'. ORSA/TIMS Marketing Science Conference, Seattle, WA.

Scherer, F. M. (1980). *Industrial Market Structure and Economic Performance*, 2nd edn. Boston, Mass.: Houghton Mifflin Company.

574 JAMES O. FIET

SCHUMPETER, J. A. (1936). *The Theory of Economic Development: An Inquiry Into Profits, Capital, Credit, Interest and the Business Cycle*. Cambridge, Mass.: Harvard University Press.

SILVER, A. D. (1985) *Venture Capital: The Complete Guide for Investors*. New York: John Wiley & Sons.

STIGLER, G. J. (1961). 'Economics of information'. *Journal of Political Economy*, **69**, 213–25.

SULLIVAN, M. K. (1990). 'Segmenting the informal investment market: a benefit-based typology of informal investors'. Unpublished doctoral dissertation, University of Tennessee.

TIMMONS, J. A. and SAPIENZA, H. A. (1992). 'Venture capital: the decade ahead'. In Sexton, D. L. and Kasarda, J. D. (Eds), *The State of the Art of Entrepreneurship*. Cambridge, Mass.: Balinger, 85–108.

TYEBJEE, T. T. and BRUNO, A. V. (1984). 'A model of venture capital investment activity'. *Management Science*, **30**, 1051–66.

WELLS, W. A. (1974). 'Venture capital decision making'. Unpublished doctoral dissertation. Carnegie Mellon University, Pittsburg.

WETZEL, W. E. (1981). 'Informal risk capital in New England'. In Vesper, K. (Ed.), *Frontiers of Entrepreneurship Research*. Wellesley: Babson College.

WETZEL, W. E. (1983). 'Angels and informal risk capital'. *Sloan Management Review*, **24**, 4, 23–34.

WETZEL, W. E. (1986). 'Informal risk capital: knowns and unknowns'. In Sexton, D. L. and Smilor, R. W. (Eds), *The Art and Science of Entrepreneurship*. Cambridge, Mass.: Balinger.

WETZEL, W. E. (1987). 'The informal venture capital market: aspects of scale and market efficiency'. *Journal of Business Venturing*, **2**, 299–313.

WILLIAMSON, O. E. (1975). *Markets and Hierarchies*. New York: Free Press.

WILLIAMSON, O. E. (1985). *The Economic Institutions of Capitalism*. New York: Free Press.

Part III
Venture Capital Monitoring

[12]

VENTURE CAPITALISTS' INVOLVEMENT IN THEIR INVESTMENTS: EXTENT AND PERFORMANCE

IAN C. MACMILLAN and
DAVID M. KULOW
University of Pennsylvania

ROUBINA KHOYLIAN
Venture Economics, Inc.

EXECUTIVE SUMMARY

Venture capitalists responded to a questionnaire that asked them to identify their degree of involvement in a number of activities for a funded venture as well as other characteristics of the venture, including its performance. The three-page questionnaire was distributed to a sample of 350 venture capitalists during December 1986 and February 1987. In all, 62 questionnaires (18%) were completed and returned.

The results indicated that venture capitalists were involved most—compared to the entrepreneur—in the financial aspects of the venture. The activity that had the highest degree of involvement was serving as a sounding board to the entrepreneur. The lowest degree of involvement occurred in those activities concerning the ongoing operations. Factor analysis on involvement patterns in the venture activities identified four distinct areas of involvement: development and operations, management selection, personnel management, and financial participation.

The venture capitalists indicated that if they could change their degree of involvement, overall they would have done so only slightly. It was evident, however, that they would have increased their involvement in those activities requiring a minimal time commitment, such as formulating business strategy or marketing plans, or serving as a sounding board to the entrepreneur. It was evident that they would have decreased their involvement in activities that required substantial time commitment, such as developing production or service techniques, selecting vendors and equipment, or soliciting customers or distributors.

Perhaps the most important result was the identification of three distinct levels of involvement adopted by venture capitalists: 1) Laissez Faire involvement, in which the venture capitalists exhibited limited involvement; 2) Moderate involvement, in which venture capitalists exhibited moderate involvement; and 3) Close Tracker involvement, in which venture capitalists exhibited more involvement than the entrepreneur in a majority of the identified activities. Because tests regarding the venture firms, the products or services in relation to the market, and management team characteristics did not significantly explain why the three distinct types of venture capitalist involvement emerged, it appears that venture capitalists exhibited different involvement levels solely because they elected to do so. Tests also indicated that the difference in the performance level of the ventures among the three groups was statistically insignificant.

Journal of Business Venturing 4, 27–47
© 1988 Elsevier Science Publishing Co., Inc. 655 Avenue of the Americas, New York, NY 10010

0883–9026/88/$3.50

28   I.C. MACMILLAN, D.M. KULOW AND R. KHOYLIAN

Regression analyses indicated that for each of the three types of involvement, involvement in various activities had different correlations with performance. Among Laissez Faire involvement ventures, developing the professional support group had a positive correlation with venture performance. Among Moderate involvement ventures, monitoring operations had a positive correlation with venture performance while involvement at the strategic level and in searching for management candidates exhibited negative correlations. Finally, among Close Tracker involvement ventures, negotiating employment terms with management had a positive correlation with performance, while searching for management candidates exhibited a negative correlation. It is interesting that searching for management candidates in both the Moderate and Close Tracker ventures had a negative correlation with venture performance.

These results are important because they show that depending on the involvement types selected by venture capitalists, different involvement strategies in the various activities should be more suitable. If venture capitalists recognize this they can adopt more appropriate strategies, which may lead to more successful ventures.

INTRODUCTION

A study by Gorman and Sahlman (1986) indicates that venture capitalists do not spend an inordinate amount of time directly involved with the management of their portfolio companies, intervening only cursorily in the day to day operations of those companies. According to their study the amount of involvement depends on whether the venture capitalist is a lead/early stage or a non-lead/late stage investor. A typical early stage investment receives an average of approximately two hours of direct attention per week from its lead venture capitalist while a late-stage investment receives approximately three-quarters of an hour per week from a non-lead investor. Lead investors visit their companies approximately one and a half times per month and stay for approximately five hours per visit. A non-lead investor involved at the early stage visits half as often and stays for approximately two-thirds as long. Because lead investing venture capitalists play more active roles in their portfolio companies, this study focuses solely on lead investor involvement in their selected ventures.

Several studies have indicated that, in addition to providing capital, venture capitalists perform many other roles in their portfolio companies (Gorman and Sahlman 1986; Timmons and Bygrave 1986; Timmons 1985; Davis and Stetson 1987). However, none of these studies has empirically examined how the venture capitalists' involvement correlates with the venture performance. This study attempts to identify any correlations between venture capitalist involvement with venture performance.

METHODOLOGY

Some of the ways that venture capitalists are directly involved in the venture are: 1) assistance in finding and selecting key management team personnel; 2) solicitation of essential suppliers and customers; 3) strategic planning; 4) assistance in obtaining additional financing; 5) operational planning; and 6) replacement of management personnel when appropriate. The questionnaire was designed to consider the venture capitalists' involvement that had been identified in these earlier studies. Venture capitalists were asked to indicate, for a specific venture, the extent of their involvement in each one of 20 activities, as well as the organization level of the venture capitalist representatives that intervened. In addition, the venture capitalists were asked to respond to several questions regarding the selected venture, including the venture capital firm's characteristics and the venture's product or service in relation to its market. Finally, the venture capitalists were asked to evaluate the performance of the venture on which they reported. A sample of the questionnaire is provided in the Appendix.

TABLE 1 Profile of Respondents

	Mean	Standard Deviation	Maximum	Minimum
Amount of capital under management (millions)	$93.5	$89.8	$400.0	$1.5
Years typical investments are held	5.60	1.23	10.00	3.00
Years firm has been in venture capital business	10.95	6.82	26.00	2.00
Number of senior-level professionals at firm	4.54	2.46	12.00	1.00
Number of mid-level professionals at firm	2.83	2.86	12.00	0.00

The targeted venture capitalists were selected from a combination of data bases from the Sol C. Snider Entrepreneurial Center of the Wharton School and Venture Economics, Inc.

Statistics of Venture Capital Firms Responding

The responding firms represented a broad cross section of industries and varied substantially in their amount of capital under management, typical investment longevity, experience, and number of employed professionals. Table 1 provides the data regarding these criteria.

First, the venture capital firms managed an aggregate total of $5.4 billion of venture capital funds, representing over 20% of the total funds for the industry as of year end 1986. The firm with the most capital under management had $400.0 million while the firm with the least managed capital had only $1.5 million. Respondents reported that the average number of years that typical investments were held was 5.6 years, while the average venture capital experience of their firms was 11.0 years. Sixty percent of the responding firms had been in the venture capital business less than 10 years; only six of the responding firms possessed over 20 years of experience. Finally, the responding firms had a mean number of mid-level to senior level professionals of approximately eight and the mean ratio of senior level to lower level professionals within the firms was 1.60 to 1.00.

Statistics on Type of Venture Reported

The ventures in the completed questionnaires also exhibited broad geographic dispersion. California, the Midatlantic states, and the Northeast were the most frequently invested locations with 19, 16, and 12 venture investments.

In addition to broad geographic dispersion, we were primarily interested in ventures that occurred in three popular, but very different, industries for new ventures: computers and related products, medical and health care, and specialty retailing. The responses were heavily weighted towards involvement in the computers and related products industry, which totalled 41 of the 62 sample ventures. This result is not surprising given that approximately 70% of all ventures occur in the high technology category (*Venture Capital Journal* 1984). Eleven reported ventures were in medical and health care and seven in specialty retailing.

30   I.C. MACMILLAN, D.M. KULOW AND R. KHOYLIAN

TABLE 2   Characteristics of Venture Reported

	Mean	Standard Deviation
Product/service in relation to market		
Innovation demonstrated by product/service	3.87	1.03
Clear market acceptance of product service	3.47	1.13
Prospects for insulation from competition	3.14	0.97
Benefits of patents, secrets and production methods	3.14	1.26
Market competition at end of second year	3.02	0.85
Anticipated market competition at entry	3.02	0.86
Management team characteristics		
Knowledge of product service	4.19	0.78
Capacity for sustained effort	3.94	0.93
Knowledge of market for product service	3.83	1.03
Degree of experience within market for product service	3.69	1.03
Degree of previous leadership experience	3.35	1.09

Most venture investments were in products rather than services (44 product ventures versus 18 service ventures). Forty-seven investments were made at the introductory stage, versus 12 and 3 in the growth and mature/decline stages, respectively. This bias toward earlier stage investment in the ventures is consistent with the findings of Timmons and Bygrave (1986), which showed that venture capitalists' investments in highly innovative technological ventures are made at early stages of development by a ratio of 2 : 1.

Statistics on Characteristics of Venture Reported

The respondents were asked to identify characteristics of the ventures regarding the product or service in relation to the market and the management team. Previous research has indicated that these criteria are important to the success of a venture.

Table 2 indicates that the mean response to each question regarding the product or service in relation to the market was at least average, which was represented by a value of three. The degree of innovation demonstrated by the product/service was significantly above average. Clear market acceptance and prospects for insulation from competition, both identified by Macmillan, Zemann and SubbaNarasimha (1986) as important criteria to a venture, were slightly higher than average. The level of competition, identified by Roure and Maidique (1986) as a key predictor of success, at entry and after two years, was average.

For each question regarding management team characteristics, Table 2 indicates that the venture capitalists generally thought that management was above average, which was represented by a value of three. Both knowledge of product or service and capacity for sustained effort established by MacMillan, Siegel and SubbaNarasimha as important criteria to venture capitalists, were significantly above average. Also significantly above average was management's knowledge of the market for the product or service.

We asked the respondents to rate the performance of the venture, compared to their expectations on four performance criteria, performance being rated on a 1 to 5 scale. A rating of 1 represented performance as being far below expectations, a rating of 3 represented achieving expectations, and a rating of 5 represented far above expectations. Respondents

TABLE 3 Performance of Ventures

	Mean	Standard Deviation
Market share	2.66	0.86
Return on investment	2.50	0.92
Sales volume	2.49	1.07
Net profits	2.26	0.93

were requested to present the ventures' success based on four criteria (sales volume, market share, net profits, and return on investment) in order to avoid arguments regarding which criteria are appropriate in assessing venture performance. The results in Table 3 indicate that the reported ventures achieved below venture capitalist expectations on every one of these four evaluation criteria. Since venture capital firms do not have a high proportion of very successful ventures, these generally mediocre results, for all four criteria, indicate that there was not a bias toward reporting only successful ventures.

Venture Capitalist Involvement

In evaluating the extent to which venture capitalists participated in the activities of the ventures, the respondents were asked to identify, for 20 selected activities:

1. Their degree of involvement (in terms of their contribution to the activity compared to the contribution of the venture team),
2. The venture stage during which involvement occurred.
3. The degree they would change their involvement if they could, and
4. The professional level within the venture capital firm from which involvement occurred.

The stage during which involvement in the activities occurred was used as a control. Four stage criteria were included: seed stage, start up stage, growth stage, and later stage. There was little variance by stage for any of the 20 activities.

Similar results were obtained when controlled for the professional level within the firm at which involvement occurred: mid-level/associate only, mid-level/associate mostly, equal amounts, senior level/partner mostly, senior level/partner only. For all 20 activities, the average involvement was mostly at the senior-level/partner level. This finding supports Gorman and Sahlman's (1986) results that, within a venture capital firm, senior members are the professionals primarily involved in the post-funding management of the venture, and suggests that the mid-level professionals are generally more involved in the pre-funding process. Interviews we have held with venture capitalists support this suggestion.

Of the six most substantial involvement activities, serving as a sounding board to the entrepreneur team had the highest rating for involvement in the ventures (Table 4). This result supports Timmons' (1987) suggestion that one of the most important contributions of a venture capitalist is to act as an advisor. Gorman and Sahlman also suggest that serving as the entrepreneur's confidant is important.

Four of the next five most involved activities are financially oriented: obtaining alternative sources of equity financing, interfacing with the investor group, monitoring financial performance and obtaining alternative sources of debt financing. The high degree of involvement in the financial aspects of the venture is not surprising, and supports research

32   I.C. MACMILLAN. D.M. KULOW AND R. KHOYLIAN

TABLE 4   Activities With Most Venture Capitalist Involvement

	Mean	Standard Deviation
Serving as sounding board to entrepreneur team	3.77	1.19
Obtaining alternative sources of equity financing	3.63	1.23
Interfacing with investor group	3.62	1.14
Monitoring financial performance	3.18	0.88
Monitoring operating performance	2.82	0.98
Obtaining alternative sources of debt financing	2.70	1.58

conducted by Gorman and Sahlman. In their study, helping to obtain additional financing was ranked first in terms of importance to the venture and was performed in 75.0% of the ventures in their sample.

From Table 5 it is evident that the activities in which the venture capitalists demonstrated the least involvement were in the strategic or operations functional areas. This result suggests that either the venture capitalists did not feel that involvement in these activities was important or that due to the continual nature of the involvement in these activities, the venture capitalists may not have been able to devote substantial time to them.

Because of the similarities in those activities in which the venture capitalists were involved the most and the least, we conducted a rotated orthogonal factor analysis to identify any patterns of involvement. Table 6 displays the results of this analysis and identifies four distinct involvement factors.

The first factor loaded on several activities that entailed involvement in development and operations. As a group, involvement in these activities demonstrated the lowest mean involvement score. It appears that the low involvement resulted because these activities require a substantial amount of hands-on participation. performed on a continual basis. Gorman and Sahlman found that venture capitalists spend approximately two hours of direct attention per week in early stage investments. This limited amount of time per investment does not allow for a substantial amount of venture capitalist involvement in activities that require substantial and continual involvement.

The second factor loaded on activities that entail involvement in the management team selection, which includes searching for candidates, interviewing and selecting management, and negotiating employment terms. Involvement in these activities may require a substantial amount of time, but not on a continual basis.

TABLE 5   Activities With Least Venture Capitalist Involvement

	Mean	Standard Deviation
Selecting vendors and equipment	0.60	0.95
Developing production or service techiques	0.71	0.98
Developing actual product or service	0.72	0.83
Soliciting customers or distributors	0.94	0.94
Testing or evaluating marketing plan	1.64	1.13
Formulating marketing plans	1.85	1.19

TABLE 6　Rotated Orthogonal Factor Analysis for Participation in Venture Activities

	Factor 1 Dev. Oper.	Factor 2 Management Selection	Factor 3 Personnel Management	Factor 4 Financial
Selecting vendors and equipment	85	11	−1	4
Developing production or service techniques	83	26	−11	9
Developing actual product or service	79	18	−11	5
Soliciting customers or distributors	77	16	32	1
Formulating marketing plans	74	15	31	21
Testing or evaluating marketing plans	70	−32	15	18
Interviewing and selecting management team	16	89	24	22
Searching for candidates of management team	11	89	15	9
Negotiating employment terms with candidates	19	86	20	22
Motivating personnel	−9	21	88	−2
Serving as sounding board to entrepreneur team	9	7	77	16
Managing crises and problems	21	38	69	16
Obtaining alternative sources of debt financing	4	20	−7	86
Obtaining alternative sources of equity financing	10	43	25	68
Monitoring financial performance	30	1	39	66
Eigenvalues	3.89	3.00	2.43	1.90

The third factor represents activities that involve dealing with the personnel of the venture. The three activities included in this factor, serving as a sounding board to the entrepreneurial team, motivating personnel, and managing crises and problems, implicitly entail continual involvement throughout the venture, but not necessarily a substantial amount of time commitment.

The last factor represents activities of a financial nature. As a group this factor exhibited the highest mean score. This result may have occurred because these activities are best suited to the expertise of the venture capitalists and/or because involvement in these activities does not require substantial or continual involvement.

Finally we asked venture capitalists to indicate whether they would have liked to change their degree of involvement for each venture activity. Overall the venture capitalists would change their degree of involvement only slightly. The aggregate mean for the 20 activities over the entire sample was 3.12 on a scale where a value of 3 represented the same degree of involvement as actually occurred. Table 7 displays those activities in which the venture capitalists would have most liked to increase their degree of involvement.

The activities in which the venture capitalists would like to have decreased their degree of involvement are presented in Table 8. All these activities call for involvement in ongoing

34   I.C. MACMILLAN, D.M. KULOW AND R. KHOYLIAN

TABLE 7 Activities in Which Venture Capitalists Would Most Like to Have Increased Their Involvement*

	Mean	Standard Deviation
Formulating business strategy	3.38	0.70
Formulating marketing plan	3.33	0.61
Serving as sounding board to entrepreneurial team	3.28	0.59
Replacing management personnel	3.26	0.72
Monitoring operating performance	3.24	0.60
Interviewing and selecting management team	3.24	0.66

*A score of more than 3 indicates that the respondent would liked to have been more involved in the activity.

operations, which would require a significant time commitment from the venture capitalists. By contrast, those activities in which venture capitalists would have preferred to increase their involvement would not require continuous attention.

Inspection of Tables 4 through 8 indicates that in general venture capitalists in the sample had the following "regrets" regarding their level of involvement in specific activities:

1. None of the venture capitalists regretted their level of involvement in any of those activities in which they were highly involved. Furthermore, although they had considerable involvement in serving as a sounding board and in monitoring operating performance, they would have preferred even more involvement.
2. Although the venture capitalists had little involvement in selecting vendors and equipment, in developing either the production techniques or the actual product itself, and in soliciting customers and distributors, they would have preferred even less involvement.
3. The venture capitalists had little involvement in formulating the marketing plan, but they generally wished that they had been more involved. Possibly they identify this activity as important to the venture success and feel that more involvement in this activity would have contributed to a more successful venture.

TABLE 8 Activities in Which Venture Capitalists Would Like to Have Decreased their Involvement*

	Mean	Standard Deviation
Developing production or service techniques	2.86	0.58
Selecting vendors and equipment	2.88	0.57
Developing actual product or service	2.88	0.60
Soliciting customers or distributors	2.89	0.49
Negotiating employment terms with employees	2.93	0.31

*A score of less than 3 indicates that the respondent would have preferred to be less involved in the activity.

CLUSTER ANALYSIS

Given the variety of venture capital firms in the sample and the variety of investments made, it seemed appropriate to perform a cluster analysis based on the degree of involvement in the activities. This cluster analysis was done using the SAS Fastclus procedure. The number of clusters where the cubic clustering criterion showed a change in slope was 3 so the three-cluster solution was selected.

The results of the cluster analysis are reported in Table 9. What is remarkable about these results is that the patterns of involvement fall into three very clear groups based entirely on the degree of involvement the venture capitalists chose to undertake. First is a group of venture capitalists who exhibited very limited involvement compared to their peers—a group we called the Laissez Faire group. Second is a group that exhibited moderate involvement which we called the Moderates group. Finally, there is a group that consistently and systematically exhibited more involvement, in virtually every activity, than their peers—a group we called the Close Trackers. The Close Trackers are *very* involved in their investments. Note that the mean scores for nearly all the activities are 3 or more, which means that these venture capitalists felt that they participated at least as much as the entrepreneurial team.

To determine whether there was an underlying reason why clusters based almost entirely on degree of involvement emerged, we analyzed the means of the general venture and firm characteristics for the three clusters. Table 10 displays the statistics for these characteristics. Our tests indicated that there were no significant differences among the cluster means for any of the characteristics. Thus, based on the data collected in this study, there appears to be no evidence that the three clusters of venture capitalist involvement type resulted from any factor other than that the venture capitalists elected to be that type. In support of this contention was the finding that no significant difference emerged among the three clusters concerning the venture capitalists' regrets, i.e., that they would have liked to change their degree of involvement in an activity, for any of the involvement activities.

We then examined the performances of the ventures within each cluster to determine whether ventures funded by one type of venture capitalist performed better than the others. It was evident that there were no significant performance differences among ventures in the three clusters. In particular, the Close Tracker group's investments were no more or less successful, on any of the performance criteria, than the other groups, so it appears that this is not a situation in which the Close Trackers were venture capitalists who were closely managing ventures in trouble while the Laissez Faire groups were venture capitalists who were leaving their highly successful ventures alone. We were also concerned that the lack of performance differences among the clusters might have been due to different performance expectations among the venture capitalists. For instance, if a Laissez Faire had low expectations for a venture that consequently was unsuccessful while a Close Tracker had high expectations for a venture that consequently was successful, their responses regarding venture performance might have been similar. However, given the insignificant differences among the clusters' venture firm characteristics and given that venture capitalists in general only fund ventures they expect to be successful, we do not feel that variability in expectations among the clusters caused venture performance evaluations to be similar.

In addition we analyzed the frequency distributions within each cluster, to examine the possibility of a bimodal distribution of the performance criteria. We were particularly concerned with the performance of the Close Trackers, where venture capitalists might have become significantly involved because: 1) the venture was performing extremely poorly, or 2) they added substantial value thus causing the venture to be highly successful. None of the three groups exhibited bimodal distribution for any of the performance criteria.

36   I.C. MACMILLAN, D.M. KULOW AND R. KHOYLIAN

TABLE 9   Cluster Results

	Cluster 1 Laissez faire N = 18		Cluster 2 Moderately involved N = 27		Cluster 3 Close trackers N = 17	
	Mean	SD	Mean	SD	Mean	SD
1. Searching for candidates of management team	0.94	0.94	2.70	1.27	4.06	1.20
2. Interviewing and selecting management team	0.78	0.81	2.78	0.75	4.29	1.26
3. Negotiating terms with management candidates	0.72	0.89	2.56	0.97	4.59	1.23
4. Interfacing with investor group	2.82	0.95	3.56	0.80	4.53	1.18
5. Developing professional support group	1.11	1.08	2.22**	1.20	2.60	1.64
6. Obtaining alternative sources of debt financing	2.22*	1.66	2.33	1.34	3.87	1.30
7. Obtaining alternative sources of equity	2.53	1.18	3.73	0.78	3.86	0.96
8. Formulating initial business strategy	1.83	0.92	2.81	0.88	3.44	1.03
9.	0.81**	0.68	1.12	1.05		
10. Developing production or service techniques	0.22	0.54	0.59	0.69	1.42	1.33
11. Selecting vendors and equipment	0.23	0.55	0.59***	0.57	1.00	1.50
12. Formulating marketing plans	1.00	0.91	1.81	0.68	2.88	1.41
13. Testing or evaluating marketing plans	1.33*	1.24	1.63**	0.79	2.00	1.42
14.	1.00	0.68	1.47	1.18		
15. Monitoring financial performance	2.72*	0.89	3.11	0.64	3.76	0.90
16. Monitoring operating performance	2.16	0.71	2.81	0.78	3.53	1.07
17. Serving as sounding board to mgmt. team	3.17*	1.34	3.77	0.91	4.41	1.12
18. Motivating personnel	1.39	1.19	2.19***	1.10	2.76	1.09
19. Replacing management personnel (if any)	0.94	1.09	3.30***	0.95	3.47	1.74
20. Managing crises and problems	1.44	0.86	3.03***	0.81	3.47	1.01

*All means significantly different for groups 1 and 2 at 0.05 levels except those thus indicated.
**All means significantly different for groups 2 and 3 at 0.05 level except those thus indicated.

TABLE 10 Characteristics for Ventures Reported per Cluster

	Cluster 1 Laissez faire N = 18		Cluster 2 Moderates N = 27		Cluster 3 Close trackers N = 17	
	Mean	SD	Mean	SD	Mean	SD
Product/service						
Innovation demonstrated by product/service	3.67	1.03	4.00	1.00	3.88	1.11
Clear market acceptance of product/service	3.41	1.12	3.50	1.10	3.47	1.23
Insulation from competition	2.72	0.96	3.26	0.86	3.41	1.06
Benefits of patents, secrets and production methods	2.83	1.38	3.33	1.18	3.18	1.29
Market competition at end of second year	3.07	1.00	3.04	0.82	2.93	0.80
Market competition at entry	3.00	0.97	3.07	0.87	2.94	0.75
Management						
Knowledge of product/service	4.22	0.81	4.04	0.85	4.41	0.62
Capacity for sustained effort	4.06	0.94	4.00	0.73	3.88	1.22
Knowledge of market	4.11	1.02	3.59	0.89	3.94	1.20
Experience within market	4.11	0.90	3.37*	0.93	3.76	1.20
Previous leadership experience	3.67	1.03	3.15	0.91	3.35	1.37
Venture capital firm						
Amount of capital under management (millions)	$59.85	$74.88	$119.31*	$101.20	$87.07	$74.16
Years typical investments are held	5.31	1.30	5.81	1.23	5.53	1.19
Years firm has been in venture capital business	9.29	5.40	12.44	7.64	10.24	6.58
Senior-level professionals	4.06	2.84	4.62	2.12	4.93	2.66
Mid-level professionals	2.69	3.11	2.56	2.73	3.46	2.90
Distance of firm from venture	3.00	1.19	2.89	1.15	3.12	1.32
Performance						
Market share	2.75	0.86	2.77	0.86	2.41	0.87
Return on investment	2.43	1.01	2.60	1.08	2.41	1.18
Sales volume	2.62	0.96	2.50	1.03	2.35	0.70
Net profits	2.33	0.98	2.15	0.78	2.35	1.11

*Means are significantly different from cluster 1 at 0.05 level.

This set of results from our data indicates something very interesting. It is clear that from the point of view of investment performance, there is little point in discussing whether venture capitalists in general should be more heavily or less heavily involved in their investments—those that get heavily involved feel that they do as well, or as badly, as those that take a hands off approach. A more relevant issue in need of examination is the opportunity cost of the heavier involvement.

REGRESSION ANALYSIS

The next step was to regress the involvement variables on venture performance variables for each cluster. First, we ran regressions on the performance variables using the four

38 I.C. MACMILLAN, D.M. KULOW AND R. KHOYLIAN

TABLE 11 Regression Analyses on Performance for Various Groups

	Sales	Market Share	Profits	ROI
Close Tracker group				
Searching for candidates of management team	−0.22	−0.44[a]	−0.67[b]	−0.57[a]
Negotiating employment terms with candidates	+0.33[a]	+0.41[a]	+0.71[b]	+0.76[b]
Adjusted r^2	0.16	0.27[a]	0.53[b]	0.46[b]
Moderate group				
Formulating business strategy	−0.37[a]	−0.34[b]	0.04	−0.56[b]
Monitoring operations	+0.47[a]	+0.37[c]	+0.42[a]	+0.53[b]
Searching for candidates of management team	−0.14	−0.11	−0.25[a]	−0.43[b]
Adjusted r^2	0.17[c]	0.17[c]	0.34[b]	0.54[d]
Laissez Faire group				
Developing professional support group	+0.76[d]	+0.77[d]	+0.73[d]	+0.76[d]
Soliciting customers and distributors	−0.72[b]	−0.59[b]	−0.56[a]	−0.36[c]
Managing crises and problems	−0.67[b]	−0.52[b]	−0.66[a]	−0.71[b]
Adjusted r^2	0.69[b]	0.74[c]	0.62[b]	0.69[b]

[a] $P < 0.05$.
[b] $P < 0.01$.
[c] $P < 0.1$ (reported only where $P < 0.05$ for other regressions).
[d] $P < 0.001$.

identified factors of involvement, but the results indicated that these factors had no significant correlation with performance. These results could have been due to the loss of variance caused by factoring the involvement variables or because involvement in different activities within a factor had opposite associations with performance. Therefore we performed regressions on the performance variables using involvement in specific activities as the independent variables. Earlier, an inspection of the correlation matrix had revealed a potential problem with multicollinearity among the involvement variables, so we ran stepwise regressions to identify the specific activities for inclusion as independent variables in the regression analysis. Given the small sample sizes of the clusters, we were also interested in selecting the most parsimonious set of explanatory variables.

Table 11 reports the results of the final regression analyses, for each of the three clusters. Each will be discussed in turn, but before presenting the results of the analysis, a general observation is appropriate. Cases where venture capitalist involvement in an activity is not significantly associated with performance should not be taken to imply that such involvement has no effect or association—at this stage the research is too exploratory to reach such conclusions. Furthermore, where significant relations are identified, a negative beta for a particular type of involvement does not mean that involvement should be discontinued, nor does a positive beta mean that a major increase in effort on that particular activity is required. Rather, we suggest that those interventions that *do* reveal significant correlations with performance should be given careful consideration. After all, venture capitalists have always felt very time constrained, so any indication that certain types of involvement might be increased or decreased is worthy of considerable attention. In particular, when there are both negative and positive betas in a regression, redeploying involvement from the negative beta activity to the positive beta activity might lead to significant benefits at no additional effort.

One must be sensitive about inferring cause and effect relationships from the positive or negative correlations between involvement in specific activities and venture performance. We suggest possible explanations regarding the identified relationships, based on our data and subsequent interviews we have held with venture capitalists, but do not imply that they are the only explanations.

Close Tracker Group (17 respondents = 27%)

The Close Tracker group had generally consistent betas across all performance measures, moderate and highly significant r^2 values for the profitability measures, and modest but significant r^2 values for the sales volume measures.

Surprisingly, it appears that excessive involvement in the search for venture management by Close Trackers is associated with performance problems. Note from Table 9 that the *average* level of involvement for this group in the search for candidates of the management team is 4.06, indicating that *on average* the respondents felt they spent much more time than the entrepreneurs searching for management. Clearly, those venture capitalists who scored *higher than the average* must have come close to monopolizing the process, implying that the entrepreneur was hardly involved. We suggest that because the entrepreneur was little involved in the search process, lack of compatibility between the entrepreneur and the candidates may be an explanatory factor for the negative association with venture performance. Managers with first class credentials may have been identified, but then a high degree of incompatibility emerged with the entrepreneur, which may have consequently led to friction and performance problems. Several venture capitalists who were interviewed intimated that the compatibility issue was most relevant when the manager searched for was at the Chief Executive Officer or Chief Operating Officer levels. It was implied that compatibility may have been affected by the entrepreneur's resistance to sharing control or responsibility.

Another possible explanation for the negative correlation between venture performance and Close Tracker involvement in searching for management could be because the venture is already performing poorly. Because of the poor performance the venture capitalists may have wanted to either replace management or bring in additional management, possibly due to lack of confidence in the existing management. In the questionnaire one of the activities for involvement was replacing management personnel. However, involvement in this activity did not demonstrate any significant correlation with any measure of performance for the Close Tracker ventures. In fact, replacing management personnel had no significant correlation with any of the performance criteria for any of the three identified clusters. Therefore, it does not appear that a phenomenon was occurring in which venture performance was poor, leading to search for new management candidates.

Particularly interesting is the strong positive correlation, for *all* measures of performance, between performance and the negotiation of employment terms with the venture management. Venture capitalists, with their experience in establishing compensation structures, could have negotiated compensation incentives (i.e., stock options and bonuses) and corresponding performance evaluation criteria. These compensation structures may have significantly motivated the venture management to maximize the venture's performance. It is interesting to note that in general the venture capitalists identified negotiation of employment terms as one activity in which they would liked to have decreased their involvement. Clearly they did not recognize the importance of their involvement in this activity.

It appears that those venture capitalists who elect to become highly involved in their venture investments could do well by taking a less dominating role in the search for management

40   I.C. MACMILLAN, D.M. KULOW AND R. KHOYLIAN

and by transferring this effort to taking a more aggressive role in negotiating the compensation structures and performance requirements of compatible managers once they are found.

Moderate Group (27 respondents = 44%)

r^2 results for the moderate group were best for the profitability measures, in which beta coefficients were generally significant. Although the betas for the sales volume measures were not significant, the signs of the coefficients for the volume measures were generally consistent with those of the profitability measures.

There were two classes of activity that yielded consistently negative betas: involvement in strategy development and search for members of the management. Moreover, there were consistently positive betas for monitoring of operations, suggesting that the moderately involved venture capitalists could benefit their ventures by trading off some of the time devoted to "big picture" issues, specifically executive search and strategy development, for time devoted to the more concrete activity of assessing ongoing operations. Their moderate levels of involvement presumably allow them to be sufficiently knowledgeable about the business to make monitoring of operations a very worthwhile activity.

The consistency with which there are negative associations between the search for management candidates and the performance of the venture, on all performance measures and for both the Moderates and the Close Tracker investors, calls for a major reassessment of how these two types of venture capitalists structure their involvement. The negative correlation with performance of excessive involvement in the management team search, by both Moderates and by Close Trackers was surprising, since the prior studies we have cited have identified helping to select key management team members as a major value-added contribution of the venture capitalist. Venture capitalists add value during the search process because of their broad range of contacts and resources and there appears to be no reason why venture capitalists should not use such resources and contacts to identify candidates. However, as we suggested, the success of the venture is critically dependent on the ability of the entrepreneur and management to work cohesively as a team. So the venture capitalist should not totally dominate the process, but should ensure that the entrepreneur also participates extensively in the search, so that *compatible*, as well as competent, managers are found.

Laissez Faire Group (18 respondents = 29%)

The results for the Laissez Faire group, reported in Table 11, are perhaps the best set of results, in terms of consistency across *all* performance variables. r^2 values are in the range of 0.6 to 0.7, and all beta coefficients are highly significant. What is particularly gratifying is that similar results are obtained for *several* dependent variables, which increases our confidence in these results.

The message from this set of results for those venture capitalists who adopt a laissez faire style in a venture appears to be—stick to it! Whether profits or sales volume are sought, it seems that it is an ineffective practice to maintain a generally hands off attitude and then, with little experience concerning the details of the venture, to intervene in the process by attempting to solve crises and problems or to solicit distributors and customers. Even if poor performance precipitated the high level of these types of interventions, it is clear that involvement in this activity did not turn the situation around.

It appears that the most constructive role for laissez faire venture capitalists is to deploy their limited attention to building strong professional support groups for the venture—a useful, and easily achievable, strategic contribution that can be accomplished with relatively little effort. This result supports the contention by Davis and Stetson (1987) that one of the most important value-added contributions of a venture capitalist is to develop the right support group for the venture. By building a strong professional support group to assist in the venture, the venture capitalists are to more effectively maintain their laissez faire style.

In general, the regression results indicate that at least some of the regrets that venture capitalists had regarding their level of involvement in specific activities were justified. Clearly those Laissez Faire investors who wished that they had been less involved in soliciting customers and distributors were correct, since their involvement in that activity had a negative correlation with performance. Similarly, the Moderates who regretted not spending more of their effort on monitoring operating performance were correct, since their involvement in that activity had a positive correlation with performance.

Although this study was limited in scope, its findings provide insights into the venture capital interventions in their investments. In particular, it identified three distinct involvement strategies that appear to be deliberately selected by venture capitalists—high, moderate, and hands-off involvement. It appears that each involvement strategy is about equally effective; the mean performance was similar for all three. What may have to be taken into account is the opportunity cost associated with the higher levels of involvement. The three different involvement strategies appear to call for somewhat different efforts when it comes to specific interventions. Those investors who practice higher levels of involvement could possibly benefit by avoiding an overly dominating role in executive searches. Those that elect to maintain a laissez faire attitude could benefit by building the strongest professional support groups for the enterprise.

Clearly the results raise several new questions that should be answered by further research. Why are there different associations between involvement in venture activities and venture performance among the three identified venture capitalist involvement types? What are the specific cause and effect relationships between involvement in specific activities and venture performance? What should the optimal involvement level be for each type of involvement strategy? Can there be a systematic involvment strategy for each type of involvement strategy? For highly successful ventures what is the value of venture capitalist involvement?

REFERENCES

Davis, Thomas J. Jr. and Stetson, Charles P. Jr. 1987. Creating successful venture-backed companies. *Pratt's Guide to Venture Capital Sources, Eleventh Edition*. Wellesley Hills, MA: Venture Economics, Inc., pp. 123–129.

Gorman, Michael and Sahlman, William A. 1986. What do venture capitalists do? *Frontiers of Entrepreneurship Research 1986*, Wellesley, MA: Babson College, pp. 414–436.

MacMillan, Ian C. and SubbaNarasimha, P.N. 1986. Characteristics distinguishing funded from unfunded business plans evaluated by venture capitalists. *Frontiers of Entrepreneurship Research 1986*, Wellesley, MA: Babson College, pp. 404–413.

MacMillan, Ian C., Zemann, Lauriann and SubbaNarisimha, P.N. Spring 1987. Criteria Distinguishing Successful from Unsuccessful Ventures in the Venture Screening Process. *Journal of Business Venturing* 2:123–138.

MacMillan, Ian C., Siegel, Robin and SubbaNarisimha, P.N. Winter 1985. Criteria Used by Venture Capitalists to Evaluate New Venture Proposals. *Journal of Business Venturing* 1:119–128.

Roure, Juan B. and Maidique, Modesto A. Fall 1986. Linking prefunding factors and high technology venture success: An exploratory study. *Journal of Business Venturing* 2:295–306.

Timmons, Jeffry A. 1987. Venture capital: More than money? *Pratt's Guide to Venture Capital Sources, Eleventh Edition*. Wellesley Hills, MA: Venture Economics, Inc., pp. 47–51.

Timmons, Jeffry A. and Bygrave, William D. Spring 1986. Venture capital's role in financing innovation for economic growth. *Journal of Business Venturing* 2:161–176.

Venture Capital Journal. May 1984, Wellesley, MA: Capital Publishing Co., p. 8.

42   I.C. MACMILLAN, D.M. KULOW AND R. KHOYLIAN

APPENDIX

Industry in Which Venture Occurred? _____

I. For the following activities that occurred during the venture please
indicate the amount of participation that your firm had in the activity.

	0 No participation at all by your firm	1 Much less than entrepreneur team	2 Less than entrepreneur team	3 As much participation as entrepreneur team
1. Searching for candidates of management team?	0	1	2	3
2. Interviewing and selecting management team?	0	1	2	3
3. Negotiating employment terms with candidates?	0	1	2	3
4. Interfacing with investor group?	0	1	2	3
5. Developing professional support group?	0	1	2	3
6. Obtaining alternative sources of debt financing?	0	1	2	3
7. Obtaining alternative sources of equity financing?	0	1	2	3
8. Formulating business strategy?	0	1	2	3
9. Developing actual product or service?	0	1	2	3
10. Developing production or service techniques?	0	1	2	3
11. Selecting vendors and equipment?	0	1	2	3
12. Formulating marketing plans?	0	1	2	3
13. Testing or evaluating marketing plans?	0	1	2	3
14. Soliciting customers or distributors?	0	1	2	3
15. Monitoring financial performance?	0	1	2	3
16. Monitoring operating performance?	0	1	2	3
17. Serving as sounding board to entrepreneur team?	0	1	2	3
18. Motivating personnel?	0	1	2	3
19. Replacing management personnel?	0	1	2	3
20. Managing crises and problems?	0	1	2	3

VENTURE CAPITALISTS' INVESTMENT INVOLVEMENT **43**

4 More than entrepreneur team	5 Much more than entrepreneur team	6 All by your firm; none by entrepreneur team	II. Please indicate during which stage(s) the participation occurred, if any.			
			1 Seed stage	2 Start up stage	3 Growth stage	4 Later stage
4	5	6	1	2	3	4
4	5	6	1	2	3	4
4	5	6	1	2	3	4
4	5	6	1	2	3	4
4	5	6	1	2	3	4
4	5	6	1	2	3	4
4	5	6	1	2	3	4
4	5	6	1	2	3	4
4	5	6	1	2	3	4
4	5	6	1	2	3	4
4	5	6	1	2	3	4
4	5	6	1	2	3	4
4	5	6	1	2	3	4
4	5	6	1	2	3	4
4	5	6	1	2	3	4
4	5	6	1	2	3	4
4	5	6	1	2	3	4
4	5	6	1	2	3	4
4	5	6	1	2	3	4
4	5	6	1	2	3	4
4	5	6	1	2	3	4

44   I.C. MACMILLAN, D.M. KULOW AND R. KHOYLIAN

III. If you could change the amount that your firm had participated in each
activity during the venture, how would the new amount of participation compare?

	1 Much less	2 Less	3 The same amount
1. Searching for candidates, of management team?	1	2	3
2. Interviewing and selecting management team?	1	2	3
3. Negotiating employment terms with candidates?	1	2	3
4. Interfacing with investor group?	1	2	3
5. Developing professional support group?	1	2	3
6. Obtaining alternative sources of debt financing?	1	2	3
7. Obtaining alternative sources of equity financing?	1	2	3
8. Formulating business strategy?	1	2	3
9. Developing actual product or service?	1	2	3
10. Developing production or service technique?	1	2	3
11. Selecting vendors and equipment?	1	2	3
12. Formulating marketing plans?	1	2	3
13. Testing or evaluating marketing plans	1	2	3
14. Soliciting customers or distributors?	1	2	3
15. Monitoring financial performance?	1	2	3
16. Monitoring operating performance?	1	2	3
17. Serving as souunding board to entrepreneur team?	1	2	3
18. Motivating personnel?	1	2	3
19. Replacing management personnel?	1	2	3
20. Managing crises and problems?	1	2	3

VENTURE CAPITALISTS' INVESTMENT INVOLVEMENT **45**

IV. Please indicate at what level within your firm the original participation occurred, if any.

4 More	5 Much more	1 Mid-level/ associate only	2 Mid-level/ associate mostly	3 Equal amounts	4 Senior-level/ partner mostly	5 Senior-level/ partner only
4	5	1	2	3	4	5
4	5	1	2	3	4	5
4	5	1	2	3	4	5
4	5	1	2	3	4	5
4	5	1	2	3	4	5
4	5	1	2	3	4	5
4	5	1	2	3	4	5
4	5	1	2	3	4	5
4	5	1	2	3	4	5
4	5	1	2	3	4	5
4	5	1	2	3	4	5
4	5	1	2	3	4	5
1	2	3	4	5		
4	5	1	2	3	4	5
4	5	1	2	3	4	5
4	5	1	2	3	4	5
4	5	1	2	3	4	5
4	5	1	2	3	4	5
4	5	1	2	3	4	5
4	5	1	2	3	4	5

46   I.C. MACMILLAN, D.M. KULOW AND R. KHOYLIAN

Regarding the venture please answer the following questions.

Performance of venture	1 Far below expectations	2 Below expectations	3 Achieved the expectations	4 Above expectations	5 Far above expectations
21. Sales volume?	1	2	3	4	5
22. Market share (of served market)?	1	2	3	4	5
23. Net profits?	1	2	3	4	5
24. Return on investment?	1	2	3	4	5

25. Date of initial investment? _____; Amount? _____

26. Date of subsequent investments, if any? _____; Amount? _____

_____; Amount? _____

_____; Amount? _____

_____; Amount? _____

27. Location of venture? _____

28. Distance from the venture?
    (a)   within 15 minutes.
    (b)   15 minutes to one hour.
    (c)   one hour to two hours.
    (d)   two hours to four hours.
    (e)   over four hours.

29. Was the venture for a product or service? _____

30. Stage of market development of the product or service category at the initial investment?
    (a)   Introductory Stage.
    (b)   Growth Stage.
    (c)   Mature or Decline Stage.

Product/service and market	1 Far below average	2 Below average	3 Average	4 Above average	5 Far above average
31. Benefit to venture of patents, trade secrets, and production methods?	1	2	3	4	5
32. Prospects for insulation from competition?	1	2	3	4	5
33. Degree of innovation demonstrated by product or service?	1	2	3	4	5
34. Degree that product or service had clear market acceptance?	1	2	3	4	5
35. Anticipated competition in served market at entry?	1	2	3	4	5
36. Degree of competition at end of second year?	1	2	3	4	5

Management team characteristics	1 Far below average	2 Below average	3 Average	4 Above average	5 Far above average
37. Knowledge of product or service?	1	2	3	4	5
38. Knowledge of market for product or service?	1	2	3	4	5
39. Degree of experience within market of product or service?	1	2	3	4	5
40. Degree of previous leadership experience?	1	2	3	4	5
41. Capacity for sustained effort?	1	2	3	4	5

Please answer the following questions regarding your firm.

42. Number of years that your firm has been in venture capital business? ⎯⎯⎯⎯⎯⎯
43. Amount of capital under management? ⎯⎯⎯⎯⎯⎯⎯
44. Number of partners within firm? ⎯⎯⎯⎯⎯⎯⎯ Number of associates? ⎯⎯⎯⎯⎯⎯⎯
45. Number of years your firm holds a typical investment? ⎯⎯⎯⎯⎯⎯⎯
46. Your name? ⎯⎯⎯⎯⎯⎯⎯⎯⎯⎯⎯⎯⎯⎯⎯⎯⎯⎯⎯⎯⎯⎯⎯⎯⎯
47. Title within firm? ⎯⎯⎯⎯⎯⎯⎯⎯⎯⎯⎯⎯⎯⎯⎯⎯⎯⎯⎯⎯⎯⎯⎯⎯

THE JOURNAL OF FINANCE • VOL. L, NO. 1 • MARCH 1995

Venture Capitalists and the Oversight of Private Firms

JOSH LERNER*

ABSTRACT

This article examines the representation of venture capitalists on the boards of private firms in their portfolios. If venture capitalists are intensive monitors of managers, their involvement as directors should be more intense when the need for oversight is greater. I show that venture capitalists' representation on the board increases around the time of chief executive officer turnover, while the number of other outsiders remains constant. I also show that distance to the firm is an important determinant of the board membership of venture capitalists, as might be anticipated if the oversight of local firms is less costly than more distant businesses.

FINANCIAL INTERMEDIARIES SUCH AS banks and venture capital organizations are increasingly understood to play a role distinct from that of other capital providers. Because they gain a detailed knowledge of the firms that they finance, these inside investors can provide financing to young businesses that otherwise would not receive external funds. (Bhattacharya and Thakor (1993) and Barry (1994) review the theoretical literature.) Many of the specific institutional features of these financial intermediaries are shaped by the need to provide monitoring and to limit the opportunistic behavior that this type of inside access can engender (see Rajan (1992) and Admati and Pfleiderer (1994)).

These theoretical insights have spurred empirical research into the relationships between inside investors and the firms in their portfolios. Several studies have examined the ties between banks and the firms that they finance.[1] Reflecting the difficulty of data collection, relatively little attention

* Harvard University. George Baker, Carliss Baldwin, Richard Caves, Joetta Forsyth, Stuart Gilson, Paul Gompers, Zvi Griliches (my dissertation chair), Lisa Meulbroek, Edward Rice, Richard Ruback, William Sahlman, Andrei Shleifer, Erik Sirri, René Stulz (the editor), Howard Stevenson, Eli Talmor, Peter Tufano, Michael Vetsuypens, Karen Wruck, and two anonymous referees made helpful comments. Jesse Reyes of Venture Economics, Mark Edwards of Recombinant Capital, and Mark Dibner of the North Carolina Biotechnology Center provided data; Michael Fogarty and Neil Bania of Case Western Reserve University provided computational support. Wendy Wood helped with data coding. Financial support was provided by the Consortium on Competitiveness and Cooperation, the Center for Science and International Affairs, Kennedy School of Government, Harvard University, and the Division of Research, Harvard Business School. Any errors and omissions are my own.

[1] A series of studies, beginning with James (1987), document that the presence of bank loans is a favorable signal to other capital providers. Hoshi, Kashyap, and Scharfstein (1990) and Petersen and Rajan (1994) show that relationships with banks enable firms to receive financing at times when other businesses cannot. Kaplan and Minton (1994) suggest that bank-affiliated directors are appointed to the boards of Japanese firms that encounter financial difficulties.

has been devoted to the role of venture capital organizations. This is unfortunate, as venture capitalists finance firms with few tangible assets that banks —even in countries where they can hold equity in firms—find difficult to finance. Venture capitalists are understood to provide intensive oversight of the firms in their portfolios. Their involvement includes service on the boards of firms in their portfolios, frequent informal visits, meetings with customers and suppliers, and active involvement in key personnel and strategic decisions.[2]

This article examines the role of venture capitalists as monitors of private firms using evidence from boards of directors. I examine whether venture capitalists' representation on the boards of the private firms in their portfolios is greater when the need for oversight is larger. This approach is suggested by Fama and Jensen (1983) and Williamson (1983), who hypothesize that the composition of the board should be shaped by the need for oversight. These authors argue that the board will bear greater responsibility for oversight—and consequently that outsiders should have greater representation—when the danger of managerial deviations from value maximization is high. If venture capitalists are especially important providers of managerial oversight, their representation on boards should be more extensive at times when the need for oversight is greater.

I examine changes in board membership around the time that a firm's chief executive officer (CEO) is replaced, an approach suggested by Hermalin and Weisbach's (1988) study of outside directors of public firms. The replacement of the top manager at an entrepreneurial firm is likely to coincide with an organizational crisis and to heighten the need for monitoring. I find that an average of 1.75 venture capitalists are added to the board between financing rounds when the firm's CEO is replaced in the interval; between other rounds, 0.24 venture directors are added. No differences are found in the addition of other outside directors.

Venture capitalists' oversight of new firms involves substantial costs. The transaction costs associated with frequent visits and intensive involvement are likely to be reduced if the venture capitalist is proximate to the firms in his portfolio. Consistent with these suggestions, I find that geographic proximity is an important determinant of venture board membership: organizations with offices within 5 miles of the firm's headquarters are twice as likely to be board members as those more than 500 miles distant. Over half the firms in the sample have a venture director with an office within 60 miles of their headquarters. This has important implications due to the uneven

---

[2] Gorman and Sahlman (1989) report that the average lead venture capitalist visits each company in his portfolio nineteen times annually. Empirical work on this topic includes Barry et al.'s (1990) documentation that venture capitalists have a substantial representation on the boards of private firms, that their lengthier tenure on the board is associated with reduced underpricing of IPOs, and that venture involvement continues well after the firm goes public. Gompers (1994) argues that venture capitalists adjust the size and timing of venture investments to address agency problems. Much of our knowledge, however, stems from clinical studies and surveys (reviewed in Sahlman (1990)).

regional distribution of venture capitalists. Petersen and Rajan (1993) demonstrate that the concentration of bank credit can lead to highly different financing patterns across markets. The presence or absence of venture capitalists may likewise lead to significant differences in the availability and pricing of venture capital across regions.

This article differs from other work on venture capital in its focus on a single industry, biotechnology. My approach allows me to use a variety of industry-specific information sources. Through these data sources, I can more thoroughly analyze the behavior of firms that ultimately went public and include in my sample many firms that were acquired or terminated before going public. I compare board membership in this sample with the interindustry population of venture-backed initial public offerings (IPOs) assembled by Barry *et al.* (1990) and find few differences.

The organization of the article is as follows. In Section I, I discuss the sample that I employ. In Section II, I present the empirical analysis. Section III concludes the article.

I. The Sample

I base this analysis on the database of venture capital financings assembled by Venture Economics. I introduce the Venture Economics database in the companion article to this one (Lerner (1994)). Because this database has only recently become available to researchers,[3] in this Section I discuss the completeness and accuracy of the sample that I employ.

The database identifies 307 biotechnology firms that received venture capital as privately held entities between 1978 and 1989. (While the database contains earlier records, data collection was not a primary focus prior to mid-1977). From the original sample, I drop thirteen foreign firms that were funded by U.S. capital providers (who may face different regulatory, tax, or institutional environments), four buy-outs or divisional "spin-outs" involving private capital providers, three duplicative entries of the same firm under different names (I find name changes in *Capital Changes Reporter* (Commerce Clearing House (1992)), *Directory of Obsolete Securities* (Financial Stock Guide Service (1992)), *Documentation for Companies Database* (North Carolina Biotechnology Center (NCBC) (1990b)), *Predicasts F & S Index of Corporate Change* (Predicasts, Inc. (1992)), and other sources), and sixteen firms that received venture capital only after going public.

To assess the completeness of the remaining 271 firms, I identify firms missing from the sample. I search for U.S. biotechnology firms that received

---

[3] Venture Economics has focused on collecting data on venture investments since 1977. Researchers' access to this data was very restricted prior to the firm's purchase by Securities Data Company (SDC) in 1991. Venture Economics did, however, publish the names of investors in firms that went public in their *Venture Capital Journal*. Barry *et al.* (1990) and Megginson and Weiss (1991) use this information (and, in the former article, cross-tabulations of these records). Much of the Venture Economics data are now publicly available as the SDC Venture Intelligence Database.

venture capital as privately held firms but are not in the Venture Economics sample. I use Securities and Exchange Commission (SEC) filings,[4] the records of Recombinant Capital (1991, 1992), a San Francisco-based firm specializing in collecting information on the biotechnology industry from SEC filings and state filings, several industry directories (Corporate Technology Information Services (1992), Mega-Type Publishing (1992), NCBC (1990b), and Oryx Press (1992)) that list privately held firms and provide information about their financing sources, press releases in Mead Data Central's (1988) NEXIS/ALLNEWS and LEXIS/PATENT/GENBIO files, and contacts with venture capitalists and biotechnology firms. These efforts lead to the identification of an additional 37 U.S. biotechnology firms that received venture capital as privately held entities between 1978 and 1989.[5]

I assess the significance of the 37 omitted firms using three measures. First, I use a U.S. Department of Commerce, Patent and Trademark Office (1990) compilation of all biotechnology patent awards from January 1978 through June 1989. Patenting is extremely important in biotechnology and is the focus of virtually every small biotechnology firm. Of the entire number of patents awarded to venture-backed biotechnology firms in this period, the Venture Economics sample accounts for over 98 percent. Second, the NCBC (1990a) compiles an "Actions" database of events in the biotechnology industry (including regulatory approvals, product introductions, and ownership changes) from press releases and specialized trade journals. Firms in the Venture Economics sample account for over 95 percent of the entries about venture-backed firms between November 1978 (the inception of the database) and December 1989. Finally, using data from Venture Economics, Recombinant Capital, SDC's Corporate New Issues database, SEC filings, and press releases, I determine (or, in a few cases, estimate) the total amount of external financing received by venture-backed firms. The Venture Economics sample accounts for over 91 percent of the financing raised by these firms between 1978 and 1989. Taken together, the results suggest that the omitted firms are less significant than the ones included.

I correct the information on these firms' financing rounds as follows:

- *Firms included in the Recombinant Capital database.* I compare the Venture Economics records to those of Recombinant Capital. If they are

[4] I identify IPOs and acquisitions of biotechnology firms through *Capital Changes Reporter* (Commerce Clearing House (1992)), *Directory of Obsolete Securities* (Financial Stock Guide Service (1992)), *Going Public: The IPO Reporter* (Howard and Company (1992)), *Documentation for Actions Database* (NCBC (1990a)), and *BioScan: The Worldwide Biotech Industry Reporting Service* (Oryx Press (1992)).

[5] As of 1989, Venture Economics (1989) had gathered information on approximately 65 percent of funds formed between 1970 and 1987. Because firms are usually financed by multiple venture funds, the comprehensiveness of their information on venture-backed firms is considerably higher than their coverage of funds. When Venture Economics obtains information on the same company from several sources, their staff attempts to reconcile any inconsistencies. If they are unable to resolve conflicts, their tendency is to err on the side of inclusiveness. This is part of the reason for the inclusion of multiple records for a single venture round discussed below.

identical, I consider the Venture Economics records as corroborated.[6] If they conflict, and SEC filings are available, I use these to resolve the conflict. If they conflict, and SEC filings are not available, I rely on company and venture capitalist contacts. If I cannot make any contacts, I use the Venture Economics data.

- *Firms not included in the Recombinant Capital database, but with SEC filings.* I compare the Venture Economics records to the SEC filings. If they conflict, I use the SEC filings.
- *Firms not included in the Recombinant Capital database without SEC filings.* I rely on company and venture capitalist contacts to corroborate the Venture Economics data. If I am unable to make any contacts, I use the Venture Economics data.

Table I summarizes the final sample, disaggregated by year and round of investment. The table presents the number of financing rounds, as well as the cumulative and average size of these transactions. (All size figures are in millions of 1989 dollars.) Observations are concentrated in the latter half of the sample. While no trend appears in the size of transactions over time, the greater size of later financing rounds is apparent (Sahlman (1990)).

I compare the Venture Economics dataset to the corrected information, omitting the cases where I am unable to obtain any corroboration of the Venture Economics records. For each firm, I compute the ratio of the reported to the actual size and number of private financings. I find that the reporting of the amount of external financing provided is unbiased, with the ratio of total funds recorded in the Venture Economics database to the actual amount being 1.04. The number of venture rounds, however, is overstated: the database reports 28 percent more rounds than actually occurred. I disaggregate the data to determine whether the bias in the number of rounds varies in a systemic manner. I divide rounds by the age of the firm and the date at the time of the venture round. I find that the spurious rounds are most frequent in older firms and in chronologically earlier records. This may be due to a single round being recorded as two or more rounds when all the cash is not disbursed simultaneously, whether by accident or design, or when the various sources of information aggregated by Venture Economics differ. Both problems are likely to be more severe in later rounds, which typically have more investors.

I find information about the boards of these firms in several locations. IPO prospectuses report board members at the time of the offering, and in many cases indicate former board members in the "Certain Transactions" and "Principal and Selling Shareholders" sections. When these listings do not mention former directors, I check the firm's original and amended articles of incorporation, which are usually reproduced in its S-1 registration statement.

[6] I do not include as external financing rounds situations where founders contributed a small amount of funds (typically under $20,000) in exchange for common stock, or bridge loans by venture capital providers in the six months prior to the IPO, due immediately after the offering. These entries are relatively infrequent in the Venture Economics dataset.

306   *The Journal of Finance*

Table I

The Corrected Financings Sample

The table presents the number of financing rounds of private biotechnology firms in the corrected Venture Economics sample, the total dollars disbursed, and the average size[a] of each round (in millions of 1989 dollars). The sample consists of 653 financing rounds of 271 biotechnology firms between 1978 and 1989. Financing rounds are segmented by year and by round number.

Panel A. Financings Segmented by Year			
Year	Number of Rounds	Aggregate Size (1989 $ Millions)	Average Size (1989 $ Millions)
1978	7	17.23	2.46
1979	8	54.43	6.80
1980	16	123.45	7.72
1981	41	140.88	3.61
1982	46	195.17	4.34
1983	62	227.88	3.80
1984	46	142.84	3.32
1985	55	149.14	3.04
1986	79	269.94	3.70
1987	102	359.98	3.79
1988	102	307.30	3.23
1989	89	336.46	4.31

Panel B. Financings Segmented by Round Number			
Financing Round	Number of Rounds	Aggregate Size (1989 $ Millions)	Average Size (1989 $ Millions)
First round	270	527.10	2.11
Second round	186	689.31	3.94
Third round	113	651.02	6.14
Later round	84	457.28	5.94

[a] Because I cannot determine the size of some financing rounds, the aggregate size does not equal in all cases the product of the number of rounds and the average round size.

Information is often available about the boards of private firms that are acquired by public firms or file for an abortive IPO in the acquirers' proxy, 10-K, or 10-Q statements, or in the (ultimately withdrawn) registration statements. In addition, in the fall of 1990 I gathered the material on these firms in the files of the North Carolina Biotechnology Center. The NCBC has solicited information from public and private firms on an annual basis. Their files include promotional material (used to produce an industry directory) and surveys conducted for the U.S. Office of Technology Assessment. These materials detail both the firms' managements and their boards.

The IPO prospectuses provide biographies of directors. Other sources, however, often only list directors' names. I identify directors using *Pratt's Guide to Venture Capital Sources* (Venture Economics (1992)), biographical material in other prospectuses (many individuals serve on more than one board), general business directories (*Who's Who in Finance and Industry*

(Marquis Who's Who (1993)), *Register of Corporations, Directors, and Executives* (Standard and Poor Corporation (1993)), and *BioPeople* (BioVenture View (1993))). I supplement these sources with information from the *Documentation for Actions Database* (NCBC (1990a); a compilation of trade magazine stories) and Mead Data Central's databases.

Panel A of Table II presents the distribution of board members by round of investment. I use each case where I know the board members at the time of the investment or within three months of the investment date. Following Baysinger and Butler (1985), I divide directors into quasi insiders, outsiders, and insiders. Quasi insiders are those parties who do not work directly for the firm, but who have an ongoing relationship with the concern. I count affiliated academics who hold full-time teaching or clinical positions as quasi insiders rather than insiders, even if they hold an official title in the firm and draw substantial compensation. Outside directors include investors and disinterested outsiders. I include in this category representatives of corporations who have invested in or financed research at the firm.[7] I distinguish between venture capitalists and other outsiders.[8]

The number of board members increases in each round, from a mean of four in the first round to just under six in the fourth and later rounds. In the fourth and later rounds, venture capitalists control a mean of 2.12 board seats. This sample corresponds closely to the inter-industry population of 433 venture-backed IPOs of Barry *et al.* (1990). In their mean firm, venture capitalists control two out of six board seats. I present the distribution of the directors in more detail in Panel B. In this table, I use only one observation of each firm: the directors at the time of the last round of venture financing in the sample period.

II. Empirical Analysis

A. Board Membership and CEO Turnover

I examine changes in board composition around the time of turnover of these firms' CEOs. I expect that the need for monitoring will be greater in these cases. As with public firms (Weisbach (1988)), the replacement of the CEO frequently occurs when the firm is encountering difficulties. In addition,

---

[7] A number of corporations, rather than investing directly in smaller firms, channel their funds through a corporate venture capital subsidiary. In these cases, a corporate venture capitalist may sit on the board. I count these officials as other outsiders rather than as venture capitalists. I repeat the analysis in Section II.*A*, recording these individuals as venture capitalists. Neither the magnitude nor the significance of the results changes markedly.

[8] I define venture capitalists as individuals who are general partners or associates at partnerships focusing on venture capital investments (i.e., equity or equity-linked securities with active participation by the fund managers in the management or oversight of the firms). I count these individuals as venture capitalists, even if they officially work for the firm. (Most partnership agreements between general and limited partners require that salaries be paid out of the management fee and not by the fund. Venture capitalists can get around this restriction by being paid by a firm in their portfolio.) I only include venture organizations that are either unaffiliated with any other organization or else affiliated with a financial institution.

Table II

The Board Membership of Private Biotechnology Firms

The sample consists of 653 financing rounds of 271 biotechnology firms between 1978 and 1989; I present the board membership by round for each of the 362 rounds where membership can be determined. Venture Capitalists are defined as individuals who are general partners or associates at venture capital organizations that are either unaffiliated with any other organization or else affiliated with a financial institution. I count full-time affiliates of a venture capital organization as venture capitalists, even if they work for a venture-backed firm. Other Outsiders include corporate investors, other investors (individuals who (i), either alone or in a partnership, held a five percent stake in the organization at some time, (ii) never were an officer of the firm, and (iii) never were an affiliate of a company which signed a collaborative arrangement with the firm or of a venture investor), and individuals that do not have another relationship with the firm. Insiders are either senior (the chief executive officer, president, and chairman of the board) or junior managers employed directly by the firm. Quasi Insiders are those parties who do not work directly for the firm, but who have an ongoing relationship with the concern. Panel B reports the professional affiliation of board members at the time of the last financing round in the sample.

	Panel A. Board Membership by Round Number			
	Mean Number of Board Members			
Financing Round	Venture Capitalists	Other Outsiders	Insiders	Quasi Insiders
First round	1.40	0.86	1.28	0.52
Second round	1.87	0.86	1.40	0.56
Third round	2.09	1.02	1.61	0.67
Later round	2.12	1.27	1.73	0.54

Panel B. Professional Affiliation of Board Members at Time of Last Financing Round (%)	
Outside directors	
Venture capitalist	36.2
Corporate partner	6.4
Other investor	3.1
Executive with other health care or biotechnology firm	3.5
Retired health care or high-technology executive	3.6
Academic without firm affiliation	0.9
Lawyer, consultant, or investment banker without firm affiliation	1.4
Other or unidentified	5.1
Inside directors	
Senior manager	20.3
Junior manager	7.1
Quasi-inside directors	
Academic affiliated with the firm	8.9
Lawyer affiliated with the firm	0.5
Investment or commerical banker affiliated with the firm	1.0
Former manager of the firm	0.6
Relative or other	1.3

since the uncertainty about the new CEO's ability is likely to be high, his activity may be more intensively monitored.[9]

I only identify as cases of CEO turnover instances where the firm's top executive was replaced. I wish to avoid instances that may generate a spurious correlation between the addition of board members and CEO turnover; e.g., cases where neither a CEO has been hired nor a complete board assembled when the firm begins operations. I consequently do not include instances when a venture capitalist who originally held the title of "chairman and CEO" relinquishes the second title. I similarly eliminate cases where a firm run by an "acting CEO" or by one or more vice presidents hires a full-time chief.

I identify cases of CEO turnover using the sources described above. I identify 40 cases of CEO turnover meeting my criteria. Few of these changes are retirements: the median age of the exiting CEOs at the time of the last financing round in which they are in office is 40. (The median age of the CEOs holding office at the time of the last financing round in the sample is 43.) Only one replaced CEO is between the ages of 64 and 66 at the time of his exit, the criterion used by Weisbach (1988) to identify CEO retirements.

Table III summarizes the changes in board membership between venture rounds. I first examine the 180 second or later venture rounds where I know the board membership at the time of the current and previous financing round and there was no CEO turnover in this interval. (I also include cases where I have an observation of board members up to three months after the financing.) There is a slight increase in the representation of each class of board member.

I then examine the 40 rounds in the sample where I know the board membership at the time of the current and previous financing and where there was CEO turnover in this interval.[10] In these rounds, the representation of each class of board member increases at a greater rate than between rounds without CEO turnover. The increase in insiders and quasi insiders is not surprising, as in some cases the departing CEO will remain a board member, whether he continues as a lower level employee or becomes an ex-employee (who are classified as quasi insiders). By far the largest increase (1.75) is in the number of venture directors. I test whether the change in the number of directors is the same in rounds with and without CEO turnover. I use *t*-tests and Wilcoxon tests. Because in each case an *F*-test rejects the

---

[9] Robert Kunze (1990) of Hambrecht and Quist notes that the replacement of the CEO "is the *single most critical development* in the life of a baby company. The time spent hiring the new chief executive officer, the shock to the organization when the changeover takes place, the lack of direction in the interim, the quality of the new person hired, and the speed with which he or she seizes command, all impact heavily on the health and potential of the company. In the best of circumstances replacing a chief executive officer is a wrenching experience and companies can easily fail at this juncture."

[10] I examine whether the 40 rounds coinciding with CEO replacements differ from the other 180: e.g., if they tend disproportionately to be early venture rounds. I find that the distribution of rounds with and without CEO turnover are virtually identical.

Table III

The Changes in Board Membership between Financing Rounds

The sample consists of 220 second or later financing rounds where the board membership at the time of the current and previous round can be determined. Panel A indicates the change in board membership since the last financing round, divided by whether chief executive officer (CEO) turnover occurred. Venture Capitalists are defined as individuals who are general partners or associates at venture capital organizations that are either unaffiliated with any other organization or else affiliated with a financial institution. I count full-time affiliates of a venture capital organization as venture capitalists, even if they work for a venture-backed firm. Other Outsiders include corporate investors, other investors (individuals who (i), either alone or in a partnership, held a 5 percent stake in the organization at some time, (ii) never were an officer of the firm, and (iii) never were an affiliate of a company that signed a collaborative arrangement with the firm or of a venture investor), and individuals that do not have another relationship with the firm. Insiders are managers employed directly by the firm. Quasi Insiders are those parties who do not work directly for the firm, but who have an ongoing relationship with the concern. Panel B presents *p*-values from *t*-tests and non-parametric Wilcoxon tests of whether the change in board membership differs in rounds with CEO turnover. The *t*-tests do not assume that the two distributions have the same variance.

Panel A. Changes in Board Membership between Financing Rounds				
	Mean Change in the Number of Board Members Since the Last Financing Round			
	Venture Capitalists	Other Outsiders	Insiders	Quasi Insiders
180 rounds without CEO turnover	+0.24	+0.28	+0.10	+0.06
40 rounds with CEO turnover	+1.75	+0.33	+0.23	+0.25

Panel B. Tests of Equality of Changes in Board Membership between Financing Rounds				
	p-Value, Test of Null Hypothesis of No Difference between CEO Turnover Rounds and Other Rounds			
	Venture Capitalists	Other Outsiders	Insiders	Quasi Insiders
p-value, *t*-test	0.000	0.750	0.339	0.140
p-value, Wilcoxon test	0.000	0.519	0.094	0.297

equality of variances, I do not assume in the *t*-tests that the distributions have the same variance. I employ non-parametric Wilcoxon tests, because the change in the number of board members is an ordinal number. Panel B presents the *p*-values from these tests. The increase in the representation of venture board members is significantly larger when there is CEO turnover. The differences in the changes of other directors are insignificant.

I then examine these patterns econometrically. Following Hermalin and Weisbach (1988), I employ a Poisson specification and examine the number of new directors. (In these regressions, a goodness-of-fit test cannot reject the Poisson specification.) I run two separate regressions, using as dependent variables the number of new directors who are venture capitalists and other outsiders. I use all 216 second and later venture rounds where I know both the board membership and funds provided at the time of the current and previous rounds. As independent variables, I use a dummy variable indicating if there was CEO turnover between the current and previous venture round (with 1.0 indicating such a change) and two control variables. The first controls for the difference between the funds provided in the current and previous venture round (expressed in millions of 1989 dollars). An increase in funding may lead to the involvement of new investors, who may be offered a board seat. The second controls for the number of directors who have exited the board since the previous round. As Hermalin and Weisbach note, if firms routinely fill vacated board seats, a regression without such a control may be biased.

As Panel A of Table IV reports, the coefficient of the CEO turnover variable in the venture capitalist regression, 1.88, is highly significant. At the mean of the other independent variables, the exit of the CEO increases the number of new venture directors from 0.25 to 1.59. This coefficient in the other outsider regression is of the opposite sign and insignificant. In Panel B, I compare the

Table IV

Poisson Regression Analysis of the Addition of Board Members between Financing Rounds

The sample consists of 216 second or later financing rounds where the board membership at the time of and the amount invested in the current and previous round can be determined. In Panel A, I estimate separate regressions using the number of new directors who are venture capitalists and other outsiders as the dependent variable. Independent variables include a dummy indicating if there was chief executive officer (CEO) turnover between the previous and current round, the difference in the amount invested in the current and previous round (expressed in millions of 1989 dollars), and the number of board members who departed the board between the previous and current round. Absolute t-statistics are in brackets. In Panel B, I test whether the coefficients of the CEO turnover variable in the two regressions are equal.

Panel A. Poisson Regression Analysis of the Addition of Board Members between Financing Rounds

	Dependent Variable: Number of New Board Members who are ...	
	Venture Capitalists	Other Outsiders
CEO turnover	1.88 [8.86]	−0.04 [0.13]
Change in dollars invested	0.02 [0.89]	−0.06 [2.28]
Number of departing board members	0.15 [2.06]	0.19 [1.41]
Constant	−1.43 [8.94]	−1.13 [8.00]
Log likelihood	−175.29	−157.20
χ^2-statistic	112.50	7.56
p-Value	0.000	0.056
Number of observations	216	216

Panel B. Test of the Equality of Coefficients in the Venture Capitalist and Other Outsider Regressions

p-Value, χ^2-test of null hypothesis that CEO turnover coefficients are equal	0.000

coefficients of the CEO turnover variable in the venture capitalist and other outsider regressions. The table presents the p-value from the χ^2 test of the null hypothesis of no difference. I reject the null hypothesis at the one percent level of confidence. This difference is robust to modifications of these regressions. For instance, I add an independent variable that controls for the time between the current and previous venture round and create separate independent variables for each class of director who leaves the board. I also use the number of new investors as an independent variable instead of the increase in the funds provided.

Hermalin and Weisbach (1988) propose an alternative explanation for the addition of outside directors around a CEO succession. They suggest that corporate insiders who are passed over for the top position leave after a new CEO is selected. The firm—facing a shortage of qualified insiders—then fills the board seats with outsiders. This explanation is unlikely to apply here. Managers who depart private firms voluntarily often must pay a heavy financial penalty: selling their shares back to the firm at the same discounted price that they originally paid (typically a small fraction of the current value). Consequently, voluntary departures of senior executives from private venture-backed firms are infrequent.

B. Board Membership and Geographic Proximity

I also examine the distance between venture capitalists and the private firms on whose boards they sit. The cost of providing oversight is likely to be sensitive to the distance between the venture capitalist and the firm in which he invests. If the provision of oversight is a significant and costly role for venture capitalists, then proximity should be an important determinant of which venture investors serve on the board.

I first examine the geographic proximity of venture directors. To compute this measure, I use the zip codes in which the firm has its headquarters and the venture capital organization has its office nearest the firm. To determine the former, I use the specialized industry directories cited above and the records of Venture Economics. The latter information is available for each venture organization in several sources (Clay (1991), National Register Publishing Company (1992), Venture Economics (1988, 1992)). If possible, I use the edition of *Pratt's Guide* published in the year of the firm's final financing round in the sample. (*Pratt's* information is gathered through a survey of venture organizations conducted in January of the year of publication.) Since the Venture Economics database lists the name of the fund, I must determine the associated venture organization. The name of the venture organization is often obvious. (For instance, Mayfield, VII, L.P., is managed by the Mayfield Fund.) In other cases, I must use an unpublished Venture Economics database to identify the venture organization. To compute the distance between the zip codes, I employ a computer program developed by the Center for Regional Economic Issues at Case Western Reserve University. The program computes the mileage between the center of pairs of zip codes.

Venture Capitalists and the Oversight of Private Firms 313

Panel A of Table V presents the distance from each firm's headquarters to its most proximate, furthest, and median venture director at the time of the last venture round in the sample. The results suggest that for the majority of the firms, the nearest venture director is quite close. More than half the firms have a venture director with an office within 60 miles of their headquarters. Twenty-five percent of the firms have a venture director within seven miles. Panel B examines the probability that a venture investor is a director at the time of the final round in the sample. The probability that a venture investor with an office within five miles of the firm serves as a director is 47 percent; for a venture capitalist whose nearest office is more than 500 miles away, the probability is 22 percent. An F-test examines whether these probabilities are equal. I reject the null hypothesis of no difference at the one percent confidence level.

To correct for other determinants of board membership, I estimate a probit regression. I use as observations each venture investor in the firm as of the last round in the sample. I use as the dependent variable a dummy indicating whether a representative of the venture organization served on the firm's board at the time of the last round in the sample (with 1.0 denoting a board member). I use as independent variables the distance from the investor's nearest office to the firm's headquarters (in thousands of miles) and several control variables. A venture organization with a larger equity stake in a firm should be more likely to be a director, as it has more at risk. I determine the stake that venture organizations hold in firms through the Venture Economics database, as well as information from Recombinant Capital and SEC filings. Larger and older venture capitalists may be more likely to serve as board members: experienced venture capitalists may either be more effective monitors or may more effectively certify the firm to potential investors. To determine the age and size of the venture organization, I use *Pratt's Guide* and several other sources (Clay (1991), National Register Publishing Company (1992), and Venture Economics (1988, 1992)). I express the age of each venture organization in years; size is the ratio of the capital committed to the venture organization at the time of the investment to the total pool of venture capital. I employ a ratio because the size of the venture pool changes dramatically over this period. I run separate regressions using venture capitalist age and size as control variables because these two measures are highly correlated.

I present the results in Panel C of Table V. The coefficient for distance is highly significant in explaining the service of venture capitalists on boards, even after controlling for ownership and experience. Since I cannot always compute the venture organization's stake, I omit this variable in the third and fourth regressions. The results are robust to the use of the larger sample.[11]

---

[11] In unreported regressions, I employ the logarithm of distance as an independent variable, which proves to have even more explanatory power.

Table V

The Relationship between Proximity and Board Membership for Venture Investors

I first present the distance (in miles) between the headquarters of the firm and the nearest office of each venture capitalist that served as a board member at the time of the last venture round in the sample. The sample consists of 700 pairs of venture capital organizations and private biotechnology firms. Panel B presents the relationship between probability of a venture investor serving as a board member and its distance to the firm, and the *p*-value from an *F*-test of this pattern. Panel C presents a probit regression analysis of the relationship between venture investor proximity and board membership. The dependent variable is a dummy indicating whether a representative of the venture organization served on the board at the time of the last venture round in the sample. (1.0 denotes a director.) Independent variables include the distance from the venture organization's nearest office to the headquarters of the firm (in thousands of miles), the fraction of the firm's equity held by the venture organization, the age of the venture organization (in years), and its size (the ratio of its committed capital to the total venture capital pool). I calculate all variables at the time of the last venture round in the sample. Absolute *t*-statistics are in brackets.

Panel A. Proximity of Venture Capitalist Directors

		Distance from Venture Capitalist's Nearest Office to Firm Headquarters (in Miles)		
	Mean	First Quartile	Median	Third Quartile
Nearest venture director	359	7	59	418
Median distance venture director	584	32	287	965
Furthest venture director	993	73	419	1951

Table V—*Continued*

Panel B. Relationship between Proximity of Venture Investor and Probability of Board Membership

	Distance from Venture Capitalist's Nearest Office to Firm Headquarters (in Miles)			
	<5	5–50	50–500	<500
Probability of joining board (%)	46.7	30.7	34.9	21.8
p-Value, *F*-test of null hypothesis of no relationship				0.000

Panel C. Regression Analysis of Board Membership

	Dependent Variable: Venture Investor Served on Board			
	Using Venture Capitalist Age and Stake	Using Venture Capitalist Size and Stake	Using Venture Capitalist Age	Using Venture Capitalist Size
Venture office to firm (000 miles)	−0.18 [3.72]	−0.20 [4.04]	−0.16 [4.16]	−0.20 [4.71]
Stake held by venture organization	−4.21 [6.96]	4.19 [6.61]		
Age of venture organization (years)	0.01 [1.54]		0.01 [2.18]	
Organization's share of total venture pool		18.64 [2.17]		18.62 [2.77]
Constant	−0.86 [7.33]	−0.87 [7.57]	−0.51 [5.80]	−0.48 [6.07]
Log likelihood	−319.48	−297.36	−413.19	−384.85
χ^2-statistic	82.68	85.58	27.12	35.66
p-Value	0.000	0.000	0.000	0.000
Number of observations	580	548	700	661

III. Conclusion

This article examines the role of venture capitalists as directors of private venture-backed firms. I examine whether the representation of venture capitalists increases around the time of CEO turnover, as might be expected if these individuals were intensively monitoring managers. I find that unlike other outside directors, the representation of venture capitalists increases around such events. I also examine the geographic proximity of venture directors. Since the provision of oversight is costly, venture capitalists should seek to minimize this cost by overseeing local firms. I find that firms are likely to have a nearby director and that proximity is an important determinant of board membership. These findings complement earlier empirical studies of how venture capitalists address agency problems, as well as analyses of the ties between banks and the firms to which they lend.

The results of this analysis suggest several avenues for future investigation. The first of these is the impact of venture capitalists' involvement in firms after going public. Barry *et al.* (1990) and Lin and Smith (1994) document the continuing role of venture capitalists as directors and shareholders in the years after going public. In some cases, venture capitalists terminate their relationships with the firm quickly; but, in a significant number of instances, venture capitalists retain a board seat even after distributing their holdings to the limited partners of their funds. If venture capitalists are specialized providers of oversight, it might be expected that these firms will be less prone to agency problems.[12]

A second avenue for empirical analysis is suggested by the results concerning the importance of geographic proximity of venture capitalists. Regions differ dramatically in their concentration of venture capitalists (Florida and Smith (1993)). Akin to Petersen and Rajan's (1993) finding of differences across credit markets with different degrees of lending concentration, firms located in regions where venture capital is relatively scarce may face different price schedules for or availability of this form of financing.

---

[12] An alternative possibility is that a relationship between firm success and venture involvement exists, but that this pattern is driven by reverse causality. Venture capitalists may choose to remain on the boards of successful companies, whether out of the belief that board membership highlights their past accomplishments to outsiders or else out of hubris.

REFERENCES

Admati, A. R., and P. Pfleiderer, 1994, Robust financial contracting and the role of venture capitalists, *Journal of Finance* 49, 371–402.

Barry, C. B., 1994, New directions in research on venture capital finance, *Financial Management* 23 3–15.

———, C. J. Muscarella, J. W. Peavy III, and M. R. Vetsuypens, 1990, The role of venture capital in the creation of public companies: Evidence from the going-public process, *Journal of Financial Economics* 27, 447–471.

Baysinger, B. D., and H. N. Butler, 1985, Corporate governance and the board of directors: Performance effects of changes in board composition, *Journal of Law, Economics and Organization* 1, 101–124.

Venture Capitalists and the Oversight of Private Firms 317

Bhattacharya, S., and A. Thakor, 1993, Contemporary banking theory, *Journal of Financial Intermediation* 3, 2–50.

BioVenture View, 1993, *BioPeople* (BioVenture, San Francisco).

Clay, L., 1991, *The Venture Capital Report Guide to Venture Capital in Europe* (Pitman, London).

Commerce Clearing House, 1992, *Capital Changes Reporter* (Commerce Clearing House, Chicago).

Corporate Technology Information Services, 1992, *Corporate Technology Directory* (CorpTech, Woburn, Mass.).

Fama, E. F., and M. C. Jensen, 1983, Separation of ownership and control, *Journal of Law and Economics* 26, 301–325.

Financial Stock Guide Service, 1992, *Directory of Obsolete Securities* (Financial Information, Inc., Jersey City, N.J.).

Florida, R., and D. F. Smith, 1993, Venture capital formation, investment, and regional industrialization, *Annals of the Association of American Geographers* 83, 434–451.

Gompers, P. A., 1994, Optimal investment, monitoring, and the staging of venture capital, Working paper, University of Chicago.

Gorman, M., and W. A. Sahlman, 1989, What do venture capitalists do?, *Journal of Business Venturing* 4, 231–248.

Hermalin, B. E., and M. S. Weisbach, 1988, The determinants of board composition, *Rand Journal of Economics* 19, 589–606.

Hoshi, T., A. Kashyap, and D. Scharfstein, 1990, The role of banks in reducing the costs of financial distress in Japan, *Journal of Financial Economics* 45, 33–60.

Howard and Company, 1992, *Going Public: The IPO Reporter* (Howard, Philadelphia).

James, C., 1987, Some evidence on the uniqueness of bank loans, *Journal of Financial Economics* 19, 217–235.

Kaplan, S. N., and B. A. Minton, 1994, Appointments of outsiders to Japanese boards: Determinants and implications for managers, *Journal of Financial Economics* 36, 225–258.

Kunze, R. J., 1990, *Nothing Ventured: The Perils and Payoffs of the Great American Venture Capital Game* (HarperBusiness, New York).

Lerner, J., 1994, Venture capitalists and the decision to go public, *Journal of Financial Economics* 35, 293–316.

Lin, T., and R. Smith, 1994, The unwinding of venture investments: Insider selling during equity IPOs, Working paper, Arizona State University.

Marquis Who's Who, 1993, *Who's Who in Finance and Industry* (Marquis, Chicago).

Mead Data Central, 1988, *Reference Manual for the LEXIS/NEXIS Services* (Mead, Dayton, Oh.).

Mega-Type Publishing, 1992, *Genetic Engineering and Biotechnology-Related Firms—Worldwide Directory* (Mega-Type, Princeton Junction, N.J.).

Megginson, W. L., and K. A. Weiss, 1991, Venture capital certification in initial public offerings, *Journal of Finance* 46, 879–903.

National Register Publishing Company, 1992, *Corporate Finance Sourcebook* (National, Wilmette, Ill.).

North Carolina Biotechnology Center, Biotechnology Information Division (NCBC), 1990a, *Documentation for Actions Database* (NCBC, Research Triangle Park, N.C.).

———, 1990b, *Documentation for Companies Database* (NCBC, Research Triangle Park, N.C.).

Oryx Press, 1992, *BioScan: The Worldwide Biotech Industry Reporting Service* (Oryx Press, Phoenix, Ariz.).

Petersen, M. A., and R. G. Rajan, 1993, The effect of credit market competition on firm-creditor relationships, Working paper, University of Chicago.

———, 1994, The benefits of lending relationships: Evidence from small business data, *Journal of Finance* 49, 3–37.

Predicasts, Inc., 1992, *Predicasts F & S Index of Corporate Change* (Predicasts, Inc., Cleveland, Oh.).

Rajan, R. G., 1992, Insiders and outsiders: The choice between informed and arm's-length debt, *Journal of Finance* 47, 1367–1399.

Recombinant Capital, 1991, *Valuation Histories for Private Biotechnology Companies* (Recombinant Capital, San Francisco).

————, 1992, *Valuation Histories for Public and Acquired Biotechnology Companies* (Recombinant Capital, San Francisco).

Sahlman, W. A., 1990, The structure and governance of venture-capital organizations, *Journal of Financial Economics* 27, 473–521.

Standard and Poor Corporation, 1993, *Standard and Poor's Register of Corporations, Directors and Executives* (Standard and Poor, New York).

U.S. Department of Commerce, Patent and Trademark Office, 1990, *Technology Profile Report: Genetic Engineering, 1 / 1963–6 / 1989* (USPTO, Washington, D.C.).

Venture Economics, 1988, *Guide to European Venture Capital Sources* (Venture Economics, London).

————, 1989, *Venture Capital Performance* (Venture Economics, Needham, Mass.).

————, 1992, *Pratt's Guide to Venture Capital Sources* (Venture Economics, New York).

Weisbach, M. S., 1988, Outside directors and CEO turnover, *Journal of Financial Economics* 20, 431–460.

Williamson, O. E., 1983, Organization form, residual claimants, and corporate control, *Journal of Law and Economics* 26, 351–366.

[14]

THE JOURNAL OF FINANCE • VOL. L, NO. 5 • DECEMBER 1995

Optimal Investment, Monitoring, and the Staging of Venture Capital

PAUL A. GOMPERS*

ABSTRACT

This paper examines the structure of staged venture capital investments when agency and monitoring costs exist. Expected agency costs increase as assets become less tangible, growth options increase, and asset specificity rises. Data from a random sample of 794 venture capital-backed firms support the predictions. Venture capitalists concentrate investments in early stage and high technology companies where informational asymmetries are highest. Decreases in industry ratios of tangible assets to total assets, higher market-to-book ratios, and greater R&D intensities lead to more frequent monitoring. Venture capitalists periodically gather information and maintain the option to discontinue funding projects with little probability of going public.

THE ASYMMETRIC INFORMATION ASSOCIATED with startup companies makes project governance extremely important. During the screening process, venture capitalists review business plans of young companies and design contracts with entrepreneurs that minimize potential agency costs. Sahlman's extensive field research (1990) describes venture capital in terms of the control mechanisms employed to manage these agency costs. Three control mechanisms are common to nearly all venture capital financing: 1) the use of convertible securities; 2) syndication of investment; and 3) the staging of capital infusions. The first two control mechanisms are examined by Gompers (1993a, 1993b) and Lerner (1994a). This paper examines factors affecting the structure of periodic investment by venture capitalists. The evidence indicates that the staging of capital infusions allows venture capitalists to gather information and monitor the progress of firms, maintaining the option to periodically abandon projects.

Sahlman notes that staged capital infusions are the most potent control mechanism a venture capitalist can employ. Prospects for the firm are peri-

---

* Graduate School of Business Administration, Harvard University. I would like to thank Eli Berman, Robert Dammon, Joanne Dushay, Steve Kaplan, Tarun Khanna, Josh Lerner, Andrew Metrick, Mitch Petersen, Jim Poterba, Raghu Rajan, Richard Ruback, Bill Sahlman, Andrei Shleifer, Jeremy Stein, René Stulz, Rob Vishny, Luigi Zingales, two anonymous referees, and seminar participants at the 1994 Western Finance Association meetings, the Financial Decision and Control Workshop at the Harvard Business School, the Federal Reserve Bank of Chicago, the University of Illinois, and the University of Chicago for helpful comments and suggestions. Phil Hamilton provided invaluable assistance in collecting the Venture Economics data. Chris Allen provided technical assistance with COMPUSTAT. Any errors or omissions are my own. This research was funded by the Division of Research at the Graduate School of Business Administration, Harvard University and the Center for Research on Securities Prices, University of Chicago.

odically reevaluated. The shorter the duration of an individual round of financing, the more frequently the venture capitalist monitors the entrepreneur's progress and the greater the need to gather information. The role of staged capital infusion is analogous to that of debt in highly leveraged transactions, keeping the owner/manager on a "tight leash" and reducing potential losses from bad decisions. While the duration of a particular round is one potential metric for the intensity of monitoring, the size of each investment, total financing provided, and number of financing rounds are also important measures of the staged investment structure.

This paper develops predictions from agency theory that shed light on factors affecting the duration and size of venture capital investments. Venture capitalists weigh potential agency and monitoring costs when determining how frequently they should reevaluate projects and supply capital. Venture capitalists are concerned that entrepreneurs' private benefits from certain investments or strategies may not be perfectly correlated with shareholders' monetary return. Because monitoring is costly and cannot be performed continuously, the venture capitalist will periodically check the project's status and preserve the option to abandon. The duration of funding and hence the intensity of monitoring should be negatively related to expected agency costs. Agency costs increase as the tangibility of assets declines, the share of growth options in firm value rises, and asset specificity grows.

Agency theory predicts that the information generated by venture capitalists is valuable. Models of venture capital have emphasized the role of information production.[1] Chan (1983) develops a model in which venture capitalists improve allocational efficiency by overcoming asymmetric information. Admati and Pfleiderer (1994) derive robust financial contracts when lead venture capitalists are better informed than other investors. They demonstrate that a contract in which the lead venture capitalist maintains a constant fraction of the firm's equity is the only form of financing that is robust to small changes in possible outcomes.

This paper utilizes a unique data set to test the agency and monitoring cost predictions. A random sample of 794 venture capital-financed companies provides a detailed picture of the structure of venture capital investments and the distribution of outcomes for venture-backed projects (e.g., initial public offering (IPO), merger, bankruptcy, etc.). The results confirm the predictions of agency theory. Venture capitalists concentrate investments in early stage companies and high technology industries where informational asymmetries are significant and monitoring is valuable. Venture capitalists monitor the firm's progress and if they learn negative information about future returns, the project should be cut off from new financing. Firms that go public (these firms yield the highest return for venture capitalists on average) receive more total

---

[1] Amit, Glosten, and Muller (1990) present an alternative model in which venture capitalists cannot generate information and separate high ability entrepreneurs from low ability entrepreneurs. In this case, adverse selection leads only low ability entrepreneurs to accept venture capital financing.

financing and a greater number of rounds than other firms (those that go bankrupt or are acquired). I also find that early stage firms receive significantly less money per round. Increases in asset tangibility increase financing duration and reduce monitoring intensity. As the role of future investment opportunities in firm value increases (higher market-to-book ratios), duration declines. Similarly, higher R&D intensities lead to shorter funding durations.

The paper also provides evidence about the relationship between investment and liquidity in the venture capital market. In periods when venture capitalists are able to raise more capital for new investments, they invest more money per round and more frequently in the firms they finance. Greater commitments to new venture capital funds may measure entry of new, inexperienced venture capitalists or free cash flow agency costs.

The paper is organized as follows. Section I presents predictions about factors that should affect the structure of staged capital infusions. The data set is described in Section II, and trends in venture capital investing are discussed. Factors affecting the staging of venture capital investments are analyzed in Section III. Section IV examines alternative explanations. Section V concludes the paper.

I. Factors Affecting the Structure of Staged Venture Capital Investments

A. Agency and Monitoring Costs

Venture capitalists claim that the information they generate and the services they provide for portfolio companies are as important as the capital infused. Many entrepreneurs believe that venture capitalists provide little more than money. If the monitoring provided by venture capitalists is valuable, certain predictions can be made about the structure of staged capital infusions.

If monitoring and information gathering are important, venture capitalists should invest in firms in which asymmetric information is likely to be a problem. The value of oversight will be greater for these firms. Early stage companies have short or no histories to examine and are difficult to evaluate. Similarly, firms in industries with significant growth opportunities and high R&D intensities are likely to require close monitoring. A significant fraction of venture investment should therefore be directed toward early stage and high technology companies.

Total venture financing and the number of financing rounds should also be higher for successful projects than for failures if venture capitalists use information in investment decisions. Venture capitalists monitor a firm's progress and discontinue funding the project if they learn negative information about future prospects. In Venture Economics' (1988) review of returns on venture capital investments, venture capital-backed companies that eventually did initial public offerings yielded the highest return for venture investors, an average 59.5 percent per year (7.1 times invested capital returned over 4.2 years). Acquisitions offered average returns of only 15.4 percent per year (1.7

times invested capital returned over 3.7 years) while liquidations lost 80 percent of their value over 4.1 years. Firms going public should, therefore, receive greater total funding and more rounds of financing than firms that are acquired or liquidated.

The positive relationship between going public and level of investment is not obvious unless venture capitalists use information during the investment process. If venture capitalists only provide capital, firms that go public might quickly turn profitable and would need *less* venture capital financing and fewer rounds than companies that are acquired or liquidated.

If asymmetric information and agency costs do not exist, the structure of financing is irrelevant. As Hart (1991) points out, if entrepreneurs pursue shareholder value maximizing strategies, financing is simple. Venture capitalists would give entrepreneurs all the money they need and entrepreneurs would decide whether to continue the project based on their information. In the case of startups, entrepreneurs would derive stopping rules that maximized shareholder value using methods described in Roberts and Weitzman (1981) and Weitzman, Newey, and Rabin (1981). Based on their private information, they would decide whether to continue the project or not.

The private benefits from managing the firms they create, however, may not always be perfectly correlated with shareholders' monetary returns. Entrepreneurs may have incentives to continue running projects they know have negative net present value (NPV). Similarly, entrepreneurs may invest in projects that have high personal benefits but low monetary returns for investors. If venture capitalists could costlessly monitor the firm, they would monitor and infuse cash continuously. If the firm's expected NPV fell below the stopping point, the venture capitalist would halt funding of the project.

In practice, venture capitalists incur costs when they monitor and infuse capital. Monitoring costs include the opportunity cost of generating reports for both the venture capitalist and entrepreneur. If venture capitalists need to "kick the tires" of the plant, read reports, and take time away from other activities, these costs can be substantial. Contracting costs and the lost time and resources of the entrepreneur must be imputed as well. Each time capital is infused, contracts are written and negotiated, lawyers are paid, and other associated costs are incurred. These costs mean that funding will occur in discrete stages.

Even though venture capitalists periodically "check up" on entrepreneurs between capital infusions, entrepreneurs still have private information about the projects they manage. Gorman and Sahlman (1989) indicate that between financing rounds, the lead venture capitalist visits the entrepreneur once a month on average and spends four to five hours at the facility during each visit. Non-lead venture capitalists typically visit the firm once a quarter for an average of two to three hours. Venture capitalists also receive monthly financial reports. Gorman and Sahlman show, however, that venture capitalists do not usually become involved in the day-to-day management of the firm. Major review of progress, due diligence, and the decision to continue funding are

Investment, Monitoring, and the Staging of Venture Capital   1465

generally done at the time of refinancing. Venture capitalists are concerned that between evaluations, entrepreneurs might behave opportunistically.

Two well-known companies illustrate how venture capitalists use staged investment to periodically evaluate a firm's progress. Apple Computer received three rounds of venture capital financing. In the first round, venture capitalists invested $518,000 in January 1978 at a price of $0.09 per share. The company was doing well by the second round of venture financing in September 1978. Venture investors committed an additional $704,000 at a price of $0.28 per share, reflecting the progress the firm had made. A final venture capital infusion of $2,331,000 was made in December 1980 at $0.97 per share. At each stage, the increasing price per share and the growing investment reflected resolution of uncertainty concerning Apple's prospects.

Federal Express represents a second example of how venture capitalists use staged capital infusions to monitor the firm. Federal Express also received three rounds of venture capital financing, but the firm's prospects developed in a much different manner. The first venture financing round occurred in September 1973 when $12.25 million was invested at a price of $204.17 per share. The firm's performance was well below expectations and a second venture financing round was necessary in March 1974. $6.4 million was invested at $7.34 per share and reflected the poor performance of the company. Performance continued to deteriorate and a third round of financing was needed in September 1974. At this stage, the venture capital investors intervened extensively in the strategy of the company. The $3.88 million investment was priced at $0.63 per share. Ultimately, performance improved and Federal Express went public in 1978 at $6 per share, but the staged investment of the venture capitalist allowed the venture investors to intervene and price subsequent rounds so they could earn a fair rate of return.

Two related types of agency costs exist in entrepreneurial firms. First, entrepreneurs might invest in strategies, research, or projects that have high personal returns but low expected monetary payoffs to shareholders. For example, a biotechnology company founder may choose to invest in a certain type of research that bring him/her great recognition in the scientific community but provides less return for the venture capitalist than other projects. Similarly, because entrepreneurs' equity stakes are essentially call options,[2] they have incentives to pursue high variance strategies like rushing a product to market when further testing may be warranted.

Second, if the entrepreneur possesses private information and chooses to continue investing in a negative NPV project, the entrepreneur is undertaking inefficient continuation. For example, managers may receive initial results from market trials indicating little demand for a new product, but entrepre-

---

[2] The entrepreneurs' equity stakes are almost always junior to the preferred equity position of venture capital investors. The seniority of the venture capitalists' stake makes the entrepreneur's payoff analogous to levered equity, hence it is also equivalent to a call option. Similarly, if the firm is doing poorly and the option is "out of the money," entrepreneurs may have incentives to increase risk substantially.

neurs may want to keep the company going because they receive significant private benefits from managing their own firm.

The nature of the firm's assets may have important implications for expected agency costs and the structure of staged venture capital investments. The capital structure literature motivates a search for those factors. Much of this literature (see Harris and Raviv (1991)) has emphasized the role of agency costs in determining leverage. Asset characteristics that increase expected agency costs of debt reduce leverage and make monitoring more valuable. Therefore, factors reducing leverage should shorten funding duration in venture capital transactions.

Williamson (1988) argues that leverage should be positively related to the liquidation value of assets. Higher liquidation values imply that default is less costly. Liquidation value is positively related to the tangibility of assets because tangible assets (e.g., machines and plants) are on average easier to sell and receive a higher fraction of their book value than do intangible assets like patents or copyrights. In empirical research on capital structure, many researchers including Titman and Wessels (1988), Friend and Lang (1988), and Rajan and Zingales (1995) use the ratio of tangible assets to total assets as a measure liquidation value. All find that use of debt increases with asset tangibility.

In the context of staged venture capital investments, intangible assets would be associated with greater agency costs. As assets become more tangible, venture capitalists can recover more of their investment in liquidation, and expected losses due to inefficient continuation are reduced. This reduces the need to monitor tightly and should increase funding duration.

Shleifer and Vishny (1992) extend Williamson's model by examining how asset specificity might affect liquidation value and debt levels. They show that firms with assets that are highly industry- and firm-specific would use less debt because asset specificity significantly reduces liquidation value. Firms that have high R&D intensities likely generate assets that are very firm- and industry-specific. Bradley, Jarrell, and Kim (1984) and Titman and Wessels (1988) use the ratio of R&D to sales to measure uniqueness of assets in investigating the use of debt. Both find a negative relationship between leverage and R&D intensity. Similarly, Barclay and Smith (1993) use the ratio of R&D to firm value to explore debt maturity.

Asset specificity would also influence the structure of staged venture capital investments. Industries with high levels of R&D intensity would be subject to greater discretionary investment by the entrepreneur and increase risks associated with firm- and industry-specific assets. These factors increase expected agency costs and shorten funding durations.

Finally, Myers (1977) argues that firms whose value is largely dependent upon investment in future growth options would make less use of debt because the owner/manager can undertake investment strategies that are particularly detrimental to bondholders. Myers suggests that a firm's market-to-book ratio may be related to the fraction of firm value that is comprised of future growth opportunities. Empirical results support this prediction. Rajan and Zingales (1995) find a negative relationship between firm market-to-book ratios and leverage. Similarly, Barclay and Smith (1995) find that debt maturity declines with a firm's market-to-book ratio.

Entrepreneurs have more discretion to invest in personally beneficial strategies at shareholders' expense in industries where firm value is largely dependent upon future growth opportunities. Firms with high market-to-book ratios are more susceptible to these agency costs, thus increasing the value of monitoring and reducing funding duration.

Why can other financial intermediaries (e.g., banks) not do the same sort of monitoring? First, because regulations limit banks' ability to hold shares, they cannot use equity to fund projects.[3] Asset substitution becomes a problem if banks provide debt financing for very high risk projects. Though several papers focus on monitoring by banks (James (1987), Petersen and Rajan (1994, 1995), Hoshi, Kashyap, and Scharfstein (1991)), banks may not have the necessary skills to evaluate projects with few collateralizable assets and significant ex ante uncertainty. In addition, Petersen and Rajan (1995) argue that banks in competitive markets will be unable to finance high-risk projects because they are unable to extract rents in subsequent transactions with the company. Taking an equity position in the firm allows ex post settling up, guaranteeing that the venture capitalist benefits if the firm does well.

In addition, because the probability of failure is so high, venture capitalists need a substantial fraction of the firm's equity in order to make a fair return on their portfolio of investments. Even if banks were to make loans to high-risk firms, required interest payments would be extraordinarily high, creating severe liquidity problems that would limit a firm's growth and exacerbate risk-shifting problems. Finally, venture capital funds' high-powered compensation schemes examined by Gompers and Lerner (1995) give venture capitalists incentives to monitor firms more closely because their individual compensation is closely linked to the funds' returns.

B. Venture Capital, Liquidity, and Investment

The growth of inflows to new venture capital funds may also have effects on the structure of investment. During the past twenty years, the venture capital industry has gone through several fund raising cycles. Figure 1 shows the amount of capital committed to new venture capital funds. During periods of low fundraising, venture capitalists might be liquidity constrained. Liquidity constraints and their effects on investment have been examined in several contexts (Fazzari, Hubbard, and Petersen (1988); Hoshi, Kashyap, and Scharfstein (1991); Petersen and Rajan (1994)). Venture capitalists would like to make more and bigger investments (which are positive NPV), but they are unable to raise enough money to invest in all of these projects. If constraints restrict investment, greater commitments to new funds lead venture capitalists to invest more money per round and to invest more often.

---

[3] Banks and their affiliates in other countries do venture capital-like financing (Sahlman (1992)), but their ability to hold equity is critical.

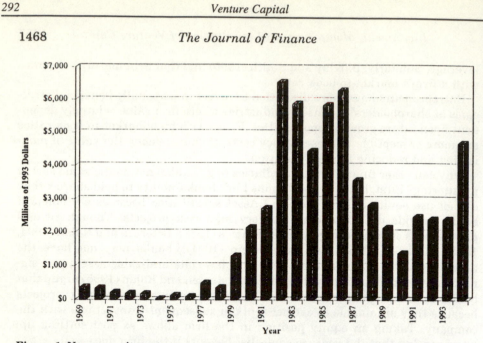

Figure 1. New commitments to venture capital funds in constant 1993 dollars.

Free cash flow theory (Jensen (1986)) also predicts that increases in commitments to venture capital funds would lead to larger investments and shorter time between investments. Venture capitalists would try to put the increased level of commitments to use. Free cash flow agency costs have been documented by Blanchard, Lopez de Silanes, and Shleifer (1994), who provide evidence that cash windfalls adversely affect companies' investment behavior. Law suit winners seem to invest in bad projects rather than give cash to shareholders. If free cash flow problems affect venture capitalists, more frequent and larger investment implies venture capitalists may be overinvesting.

Similarly, growth of the venture capital pool may measure entry by inexperienced venture capitalists. These new entrants may overinvest and may not monitor companies as effectively as experienced venture capitalists. As in the case of free cash flow agency costs, the increase in investment is excessive.

II. Sample Description

A. *Individual Firm Financing Information*

A random sample[4] of 794 firms that received venture capital financing between January 1961 and July 1992 was gathered from the Venture Econom-

---

[4] The random sample was generated as follows: At the time the data were collected, approximately 7000 firms were contained in the Venture Economics database. Each firm is given a number from 1 to 7000 by Venture Economics. 800 unique random numbers were generated from 1 to 7000 in a spreadsheet. These 800 numbers were used as firm reference numbers. Six firms were eliminated from the final sample because their data were suspect. The six firms had venture financing dates that were more than ten years apart. Apparently, for each of these six entries two firms with the same name had been venture financed and their records merged.

ics' Venture Intelligence Database, which collects funding information on venture capital-backed firms. The firms were included in the sample if their first round of venture capital financing occurred before January 1, 1990. This ensured that I had data for at least the first thirty months of the companies' existence. Data collected included: 1) name of the company; 2) date founded; 3) present status; 4) total amount of venture capital funding to date; 5) dates of individual fundings; 6) amount of capital committed in each stage; 7) identity of venture capital investors; 8) type of financing (e.g., seed, start-up, etc.); 9) industry code; and 10) date of IPO, if relevant.

The current status of each firm was verified with Lexis/Nexis databases. COMPANY and NEWS databases were searched for all records concerning the firms. If no news stories or legal filings were found, the firm was assumed to be private. The data are limited in several respects. First, I do not know how well each company is doing at each round of financing. Second, the data do not have information on other types of financing that the firms receive.

B. Venture Capital Funds Information

I utilize a database of venture capital funds compiled by Venture Economics' Investors Services Group to collect annual information on total venture capital funds under management, new capital commitments to the industry, and the amount of venture capital invested. The Venture Economics' database includes over two thousand venture capital funds, Small Business Investment Companies (SBICs), and related organizations and is used in preparation of directories such as their annual volume *Venture Capital Performance*. This database is compiled from information provided by venture capitalists and institutional investors.

C. Industry and Macroeconomic Data

Because accounting data for private firms is unavailable, I collect annual SIC industry averages from COMPUSTAT for each firm that received venture capital financing to control for industry effects. If the four digit Standard Industrial Classification (SIC) group had fewer than four companies, the three digit industry was used. Similarly, if the three digit group had fewer than four companies, I collected the two digit SIC group averages. Variables were collected to calculate various measures of asset tangibility (the ratio of tangible assets to total assets), growth opportunities (market value of equity to book value), and research intensity (either the ratio of R&D expenditures to total assets or R&D expenditures to sales). The data were matched by date and industry to each firm and each round of financing. The inflation rate and real return on Treasury bills and common stocks were collected for each month from 1961 to 1992 from Ibbotson Associates.

D. Summary Information and Statistics

Table I provides summary information on the dates and amounts of total venture capital financing for the 794 firms. These 794 firms received 2143

Table I

**Time Series of Random Sample from the
Venture Economics Database**

The sample is 794 randomly selected companies from the set of firms that received their first
venture capital investment prior to January 1, 1990. The table shows the number of rounds, total
amount invested, and the number of new firms in each year in the sample of random firms.
Amount of known investment is in thousands of dollars.

Year	Rounds of Venture Capital Financing	Amount of Venture Capital Investment (Thousands of Dollars)	Number of New Firms Receiving Venture Capital
1961	1	280	1
1962	1	200	1
1968	1	250	1
1969	3	2,135	2
1970	6	1,911	4
1971	8	2,257	4
1972	4	2,470	1
1973	9	19,436	6
1974	9	16,384	1
1975	14	10,775	9
1976	17	18,174	9
1977	23	9,064	12
1978	35	17,733	24
1979	44	64,788	30
1980	55	34,392	30
1981	77	113,794	50
1982	126	179,965	64
1983	170	380,648	82
1984	208	518,408	84
1985	179	517,447	66
1986	204	484,405	95
1987	219	434,966	60
1988	225	594,322	85
1989	234	418,940	67
1990	142	157,786	0
1991	109	142,878	0
1992	16	42,771	0

individual rounds of venture capital financing and represent roughly 15 percent of all venture capital over this period.[5] The coverage of the data seems to
be better for the latter half of the sample period. This may reflect increasing
completeness of the Venture Economics database over time. During the 1970s
venture capital investing was modest in size. The number of rounds per year,
the number of new firms financed, and total venture investment show a
dramatic rise after the liberalization of ERISA's "prudent man" rule in 1979,
which eased pension fund restrictions on investments in venture capital.

---

[5] My sample represents slightly more than 15 percent because certain data on financing
amounts were missing.

Investment, Monitoring, and the Staging of Venture Capital 1471

Table II
Percentage of Investment by Industry and Stage of Development in Each Year

Data are 2143 financing rounds for a random sample of 794 venture capital-backed firms. Panel A shows the industry composition of venture investments in the sample through time. Industry classifications are reported by Venture Economics. Panel B shows how the stage of firm development for venture investments varies in the sample. Early stage investments are seed, startup, early, first, and other early stage investments. Late stage financing is second, third, or bridge stage investments. All values are in percent.

	1975	1976	1977	1978	1979	1980	1981	1982	1983	1984	1985	1986	1987	1988	1989
Panel A: Percentage of Rounds Invested by Industry															
Communications	28.6	23.5	18.2	8.6	18.2	11.1	13.3	12.9	14.9	13.3	12.4	12.3	11.9	12.0	11.5
Computers	0.0	0.0	0.0	2.9	2.3	3.7	4.0	8.9	10.1	10.1	6.2	3.9	4.6	4.4	1.3
Computer related	0.0	5.9	4.5	11.4	15.9	11.1	13.3	21.8	19.6	16.1	17.5	14.2	14.2	11.1	15.8
Computer software	7.1	0.0	0.0	0.0	0.0	0.0	6.7	10.5	13.7	9.6	14.7	13.2	11.4	9.3	11.1
Electronic components	0.0	0.0	4.5	0.0	2.3	5.6	2.7	0.8	3.6	3.2	4.5	3.4	4.6	3.6	3.0
Other electronics	28.6	35.3	4.5	2.9	4.5	11.1	10.7	8.9	3.6	7.8	6.8	4.4	4.1	4.9	5.6
Biotechnology	7.1	0.0	0.0	2.9	6.8	3.7	2.7	5.6	3.6	3.7	1.1	4.4	5.0	6.7	6.4
Medical/health	0.0	0.0	9.1	20.0	4.5	9.3	2.7	6.5	10.1	11.0	16.4	13.2	14.6	15.6	12.0
Energy	14.3	0.0	31.8	5.7	6.8	7.4	4.0	3.2	3.0	0.0	0.6	1.5	0.5	1.3	0.9
Consumer products	0.0	11.8	4.5	17.1	13.6	18.5	10.7	4.8	6.0	11.9	9.6	9.3	11.4	15.1	13.7
Industrial products	7.1	17.6	4.5	14.3	9.1	9.3	17.3	9.7	4.2	6.0	4.0	7.8	7.8	9.8	8.5
Transportation	0.0	0.0	18.2	0.0	4.5	0.0	1.3	2.4	0.6	0.9	0.6	2.0	0.9	1.8	0.0
Other	7.1	5.9	0.0	14.3	11.4	9.3	10.7	4.0	7.1	6.4	5.6	10.3	9.1	4.4	10.3
Panel B: Percentage of Rounds Invested by Stage of Development															
Early stage	69.2	92.9	85.7	63.3	70.6	66.7	52.3	59.5	54.9	55.3	47.7	43.1	39.7	40.0	34.5
Late stage	30.8	7.1	14.3	36.7	29.4	33.3	47.7	40.5	45.1	44.7	52.3	56.9	60.3	60.0	65.5

Table II looks at the distribution of investments across various industries by the percentage of rounds invested. Industry trends can be discerned. Computer firms received significant amounts of financing from 1982 to 1984, but investment subsequently declined. After the oil embargoes of the 1970s, energy related investments were popular; these declined substantially after the early 1980s when domestic exploration declined. On the other hand, medical and health related firms have been receiving increasing attention from venture capitalists.

What is evident from the industry results, however, is the focus on high technology firms (e.g., communication, computers, electronics, biotechnology, and medical/health). The percentage of venture capital invested is high technology firms never falls below 70 percent of annual investments. For firms in the sample, the average *industry* ratio of R&D to sales is 3.43 percent (median 3.82 percent). The average for all COMPUSTAT industries during the time period 1972–1992 was 1.30 percent (median 2.66 percent). Asymmetric information and agency costs are a major concern in R&D intensive firms which may require specialized knowledge to monitor. Industry investment composition suggests that venture capitalists specialize in industries in which monitoring and information evaluation are important.

Table II also examines the distribution of investment by stage.[6] The table documents the relative decline in early stage financing and the growing importance of later stage investments. This trend reflects the effects of a maturing industry. While the venture capital industry was growing rapidly in the early 1980s, more investment went to early stage companies. As the industry matured, the investment mix reflected previous investments. Early stage investments in the mid-1980s became late stage investments in the late 1980s. Even with the decline, a substantial fraction of investment is in early stage companies where monitoring is important.

The distribution of outcomes for firms that received venture capital financing is examined in Table III. Firms can go public (IPO), undergo a merger or acquisition, file for bankruptcy, or remain private as of July 31, 1992. For purposes of Table III, I classify only those firms that had not received a venture capital infusion since January 1, 1988 as venture-backed firms that remain private. Other firms may yet receive another venture capital investment or may achieve some other exit (e.g., IPO, merger, etc.) While this measure is imprecise, and it is impossible to be certain of the eventual status of all projects, the present classification gives some indication of relative outcomes. Such a determination is critical if research is to determine how investment structure affects a firm's success.

Table III shows that in the entire sample 22.5 percent of the firms go public, 23.8 percent merge or are acquired, 15.6 percent are liquidated or go bankrupt, and 38.1 percent remain private. In transportation, biotechnology, and medical/health, the proportion of firms that go public is quite high. This may reflect either the relative success of companies in this industry or their need for large capital infusions which an IPO provides. In electronic components, industrial products, and other (services), the proportion of IPOs is quite low and many more firms remain private. These results may understate the proportion of liquidations, however. First, some of the acquisitions/mergers may be distressed firms that provide little more than physical assets to their acquirer.[7] The return to the venture capitalist from these firms would be very low. Similarly, a number of the firms classified as private may have been liquidated, but I was unable to locate any record of the event. Firms without any debt would have no need to file for bankruptcy.

Funding statistics by industry and outcome are presented in Table IV. Average total funding received, number of rounds, and age at first funding show considerable variability across industries. High technology ventures receive more rounds and greater total financing than low technology ventures.

---

[6] Rounds are classified as early stage if the investment is seed, startup, or early stage. The investment is classified as late stage if it is expansion, second, third, or bridge financing.

[7] Initial public offerings and acquisitions may also be viewed as one large financing round. Examining the amount of venture capital invested, classifying firms by outcome, is still important for understanding the venture capitalists' return.

Investment, Monitoring, and the Staging of Venture Capital   1473

Table III

Outcomes for 794 Venture Capital-Backed Firms by Industry

The number of firms that had performed an initial public offering, merged, went bankrupt, or remained private as of July 31, 1992. The first column is firms that went public. The second column is all firms that were acquired or merged with another company. The third column is all firms that filed for bankruptcy. The fourth column is all firms that are still private and have not received venture capital financing since January 1, 1988. Percentage of outcome classification for each industry are in parentheses.

Industry	IPOs	Mergers/ Acquisitions	Liquidations/ Bankruptcies	Private
Communications	17	17	9	26
	(24.6)	(24.6)	(13.0)	(37.7)
Computers	5	7	9	4
	(20.0)	(28.0)	(36.0)	(16.0)
Computer related	20	19	15	15
	(29.0)	(27.5)	(21.7)	(21.7)
Computer software	11	9	11	20
	(21.6)	(17.6)	(21.6)	(39.2)
Electronic components	2	6	0	9
	(11.8)	(35.3)	(0.0)	(52.9)
Other electronics	6	9	6	9
	(20.0)	(30.0)	(20.0)	(30.0)
Biotechnology	9	5	2	2
	(50.0)	(27.8)	(11.1)	(11.1)
Medical/health	17	17	12	10
	(30.4)	(30.4)	(21.4)	(17.9)
Energy	4	3	2	11
	(20.0)	(15.0)	(10.0)	(55.0)
Consumer products	19	10	6	33
	(27.9)	(14.7)	(8.8)	(48.5)
Industrial products	4	20	6	27
	(7.0)	(35.1)	(10.5)	(47.4)
Transportation	5	2	1	4
	(41.7)	(16.7)	(8.3)	(33.3)
Other	8	10	9	45
	(11.1)	(13.9)	(12.5)	(62.5)
Total	127	134	88	215
	(22.5)	(23.8)	(15.6)	(38.1)

The four industries with the highest total funding per firm are communications, computers, computer related, and biotechnology. Four of the five industries with lowest total funding per firm are energy, industrial products, transportation, and other (primarily services). Age at first funding does not seem to follow any clear pattern even though one might think that high technology companies need access to venture capital soon after incorporation. Biotechnology, electronic components, and medical/health companies are relatively young. Firms in computers, consumer products, and transportation are substantially older on average. Most firms are not startup; they are typically well over one year old when they receive their first venture capital infusion. These firms received other funding (personal, "angel," or bank financing) before receiving venture capital.

Table IV also stratifies funding data by outcome. Examining the structure of funding by outcome can determine whether venture capitalists periodically evaluate a firm's prospects. The total amount and number of rounds of financing are greater for the sample of IPO firms than for either the entire sample or the subsamples that go bankrupt or are acquired/merged. The data indicate that venture capitalists stage capital infusions to gather information and monitor the progress of firms they finance. New information is useful in determining whether or not the venture capitalist should continue financing

Table IV

Number of Investments, Age at First Funding, and Total Funding Received by Industry and Outcome

The sample is 794 venture capital-backed firms randomly selected from the Venture Economics database. The number of rounds, age at first funding, and total venture capital financing (in constant 1992 dollars) are tabulated for various industries and various outcomes. Firms can either go public in an IPO, go bankrupt, or be acquired. Average total funding is in thousands of dollars. Average age at first funding is in years. Median values are in parentheses.

Industry	Number of Rounds				Age at First Funding			
	Full	IPO	Bankrupt	Acquired	Full	IPO	Bankrupt	Acquired
Communications	2.78	3.41	2.44	2.47	3.46	3.29	2.56	5.11
	(2)	(2)	(2)	(2)	(0.92)	(1.34)	(1.87)	(1.34)
Computers	3.89	4.60	4.33	3.42	4.19	1.11	2.75	2.30
	(3)	(6)	(4)	(3)	(1.33)	(0.17)	(1.84)	(1.29)
Computer related	3.66	4.0	3.47	3.32	4.29	3.74	4.10	4.10
	(3)	(4)	(2)	(3)	(1.88)	(1.67)	(2.75)	(2.75)
Computer software	2.99	2.91	2.00	3.22	3.59	3.83	4.30	4.30
	(3)	(2)	(1)	(3)	(1.92)	(3.67)	(2.59)	(2.59)
Electronic components	3.27	4.00	na	3.50	0.86	0.53	na	0.77
	(2)	(4)		(3.5)	(0.00)	(0.53)		(0)
Other electronics	3.21	2.50	3.50	2.78	3.45	2.54	5.67	5.46
	(2)	(2)	(2.5)	(2)	(2.38)	(3.17)	(3)	(3.92)
Biotechnology	3.69	3.56	4.00	4.60	1.21	0.89	0.37	2.08
	(4)	(3)	(4)	(4)	(0.71)	(0.50)	(0.37)	(2)
Medical/health	2.98	3.94	1.91	2.53	1.97	2.30	0.58	1.59
	(2)	(3)	(1)	(2)	(1.00)	(1.41)	(0.12)	(0.71)
Energy	1.91	2.25	2.00	1.67	2.85	7.01	2.13	2.00
	(1)	(2)	(2)	(1)	(2.00)	(5.17)	(2.13)	(2)
Consumer products	2.14	2.16	2.33	1.20	5.90	7.63	0.98	17.92
	(1)	(2)	(2)	(1)	(1.67)	(4.41)	(0.75)	(17.35)
Industrial products	2.09	3.75	2.17	1.65	3.79	5.94	18.97	4.66
	(1)	(2)	(1.5)	(1)	(2.25)	(6.38)	(10.46)	(2.46)
Transportation	1.93	2.00	2.00	2.50	6.33	15.84	na	9.09
	(2)	(2)	(2)	(2.5)	(5.67)	(5.27)		(9.09)
Other	1.60	1.63	1.78	1.80	5.83	12.48	1.00	10.11
	(1)	(1)	(1)	(1)	(2.25)	(3.17)	(0.46)	(5.96)

Investment, Monitoring, and the Staging of Venture Capital 1475

Table IV—Continued

Industry	Total Funding (Thousands of Dollars)				Number of Firms			
	Full	IPO	Bankrupt	Acquired	Full	IPO	Bankrupt	Acquired
Communications	7,402	7,017	2,841	4,693	98	17	9	17
	(3,300)	(4,260)	(2,000)	(1,447)				
Computers	16,162	20,483	15,507	5,363	27	5	9	7
	(7,750)	(20,483)	(6,000)	(2,492)				
Computer related	8,062	13,386	7,432	4,965	90	20	15	19
	(4,050)	(8,766)	(5,000)	(4,323)				
Computer software	4,537	7,584	2,978	6,108	77	11	11	9
	(2,092)	(3,463)	(1,500)	(1,604)				
Electronic components	10,479	12,425	na	6,914	22	2	0	6
	(3,484)	(12,425)		(2,483)				
Other electronics	5,228	6,371	6,777	3,160	41	6	6	9
	(4,000)	(6,330)	(1,637)	(1,875)				
Biotechnology	8,562	12,716	7,659	8,066	29	9	2	5
	(5,500)	(10,957)	(5,716)	(12,000)				
Medical/health	5,680	10,246	2,853	3,736	90	17	12	17
	(3,000)	(3,645)	(1,236)	(3,400)				
Energy	3,086	3,918	4,698	1,963	22	4	2	3
	(899)	(2,434)	(4,698)	(850)				
Consumer products	6,551	11,161	2,654	5,694	103	19	6	10
	(2,237)	(5,473)	(1,259)	(958)				
Industrial products	2,982	9,855	3,149	2,274	89	4	6	20
	(1,500)	(7,875)	(1,881)	(1,200)				
Transportation	4,983	6,468	4,000	5,875	15	5	1	2
	(3,252)	(2,500)	(4,000)	(5,875)				
Other	4,526	12,889	2,810	8,738	96	8	9	10
	(1,968)	(8,000)	(1,664)	(4,277)				

the project. Promising firms receive new financing while others either are liquidated or find a corporate acquirer to manage the assets of the firm.

III. The Structure of Staged Investment

A. The Duration and Size of Financing Rounds

The analysis in this section classifies each financing according to the company's stage of development at the time of financing as reported by Venture Economics (e.g., seed, startup, first stage, etc.) This information is self-reported by venture capital firms. There are no clear divisions between the definitions of each stage, so divisions should be seen as relative measures of firm development rather than absolute measures. To overcome some of the potential reporting biases in the regression results, I group various stages into either early rounds, middle rounds, or late rounds. I

Table V

Duration, Amount of Investment, and Cash Utilization by Stage of Development

The sample is 794 venture capital-backed firms randomly selected from the Venture Economics database. Investment type is self-reported stage of development for venture capital-backed firms at time of investment. Median values are in parentheses. Time to next funding is the duration (in years) from one reported financing round to the next. Amount of funding is the average size of a given type of financing round (in thousands of 1992 dollars). Cash utilization is the rate at which the firm is using cash between rounds of financing (in thousands of 1992 dollars per year).

Type of Funding	Time to Next Funding	Amount of Funding (Thousands of Dollars)	Cash Utilization (Thousands of Dollars per Year)	Number
Seed	1.63	921	565	122
	(1.17)	(290)	(248)	
Startup	1.21	2,387	1,987	129
	(1)	(1,098)	(1,098)	
Early stage	1.03	1,054	1,023	114
	(0.83)	(750)	(904)	
First stage	1.08	1,928	1,785	288
	(0.92)	(1,000)	(1,087)	
Other early	1.08	2,182	2,020	221
	(0.75)	(1,200)	(1,600)	
Expansion	1.26	2,343	1,860	377
	(0.88)	(1,000)	(1,136)	
Second stage	1.01	2,507	2,482	351
	(0.83)	(1,350)	(1,627)	
Third stage	0.86	2,784	3,237	181
	(0.75)	(1,200)	(1,600)	
Bridge	0.97	2,702	2,785	454
	(0.83)	(1,500)	(1,807)	

classify all seed and startup investments as early rounds. These investments are usually made in very young companies. First stage and early stage investments are classified as middle rounds because even though the firms are still relatively young, they are further developed than seed or startup companies. Finally, second, third, expansion, or bridge stage funding is considered to be late stage financing.

Table V summarizes average duration, amount of venture capital funding, and the rate at which the firm uses cash during that particular round (in dollars per year) for various types of investment. In general, the duration of financing declines for later stage companies and the average amount of financing per round generally rises. Venture capitalists may know more about later stage firms and may therefore be willing to invest more money and for longer periods of time. Later stage companies would be associated with lower agency costs. Similarly, the rate of cash utilization rises for later stage firms. Cash utilization rates for later rounds might be higher because the need for invest-

Investment, Monitoring, and the Staging of Venture Capital 1477

ment in plant and working capital accelerates as the scale of the project expands.[8]

Regression results in Table VI present a clearer picture of the factors affecting venture capital staging patterns. The regressions include dummy variables to control for early and middle stage financing using the Venture Economics classifications for type of investment.[9] The regressions also include industry accounting variables to control for the nature of the firm's assets and investment opportunities. Because private firm balance sheet data is unavailable, industry averages from COMPUSTAT should be viewed as instruments for the private firms' true values. To the extent that any of the coefficients on the industry variables are significant, significance levels for firms' true values are probably even higher.

From the previous discussion, firms that are subject to greater agency costs should be monitored more often, and funding durations should be shorter. The ratio of tangible assets to total assets for the industry should be related to the liquidation value of the firm. The coefficient on the ratio of tangible assets to total assets should be positive in regressions for the duration of financing rounds. Tangible assets lower expected agency costs of inefficient continuation. The market-to-book ratio should rise as the fraction of growth options in firm value rises. Because potential agency costs associated with investment behavior rise with growth options, the coefficient on the market-to-book ratio should be negative. I also include two measures of research and development intensity, R&D expenditure to sales and R&D expenditure to total assets. R&D intensive firms are likely to accumulate physical and intellectual capital that is very industry- and firm-specific. As asset specificity increases, so do expected losses in liquidation. Therefore, coefficients on R&D measures should be negative in the duration regressions.

I also include firm age when it receives venture financing. Older firms may have more information available for venture capitalists to evaluate. Therefore, holding stage of development and all else constant, informational asymmetries are smaller and the funding duration should be longer (i.e., the coefficient on age should be positive in the duration regressions).

Finally, I measure the effects of venture capital market growth on financing using the amount of money (in constant 1992 dollars) raised by venture capital funds in the year before the financing of the firm. If venture capitalists cannot make all the investments they would like because they have insufficient capital, more liquidity should decrease the duration of financing (firms receive follow-on funding sooner) and increase the amount of funding per round.

---

[8] A second possibility is that only poorly performing firms receive later rounds of financing (profitable firms generate their own cash). The higher cash utilization rate indicates a selection bias caused by selecting poor performers. Evidence from the sample of 127 firms going public indicates that the selection bias is not a problem. Successful firms have *higher* cash utilization rates.

[9] The results are unchanged if firm development is measured by using round number (e.g., first investment, second investment, etc.) instead of dummies for early, middle, and late stage firms.

The dependent variable in Panel A is the duration of a particular venture financing round, the time in years from one particular financing to the next. The estimation of regressions with duration data introduces certain methodological issues. First, the data is right censored: we only observe the duration of financing when a subsequent financing occurs. A subsequent financing might not be observed for two reasons: firms may be in the middle of an

Table VI

Regressions for Duration and Funding Amount per Round Controlling for Firm and Industry Factors

The sample is 2143 funding rounds for 794 venture capital-backed firms for the period 1961 to 1992. The dependent variables are the time in years from funding date to the next funding date and the logarithm of the round's funding amount in thousands of 1992 dollars. Independent variables include a dummy variable that equals 1 if the funding round is either seed or startup (early stage) and a dummy variable that equals 1 if the round is either early, first, or other early (middle stage). Liquidity in the venture capital industry is controlled using new capital commitments to venture capital partnerships in the previous year in constant 1992 dollars. Tangibility of assets is measured by the average ratio of tangible assets to total assets for company's in the firm's industry. Market-to-book is the average industry ratio of market value of equity to book value of equity. Research and development intensity is proxied by the average industry ratios of R&D to sales or R&D to assets. The age of the venture capital-backed firm is months from incorporation to financing date. Panel A are maximum-likelihood estimates for Weibull distribution duration models. Panel B estimates are ordinary least squares. t-statistics for coefficients are in parentheses.

	Panel A: Regressions for Duration of Financing Round					
	Dependent Variable: Duration of Financing Round					
Independent Variables	(1)	(2)	(3)	(4)	(5)	(6)
Constant	−0.030	0.361	0.407	0.417	0.070	0.082
	(−0.19)	(2.50)	(2.86)	(2.93)	(0.39)	(0.42)
Investment was in an early stage firm?	0.051	0.040	0.037	0.047	0.036	0.031
	(0.63)	(0.49)	(0.44)	(0.56)	(0.44)	(0.38)
Investment was in a middle stage firm?	−0.054	−0.058	−0.103	−0.094	−0.102	−0.106
	(−0.93)	(−1.00)	(−1.72)	(−1.55)	(−1.71)	(−1.75)
Capital committed to new venture funds in previous year	−0.60 × E-04	−0.56 × E-04	−0.52 × E-04	−0.55 × E-04	−0.54 × E-04	−0.56 × E-04
	(−4.97)	(−4.56)	(−4.10)	(−4.41)	(−4.22)	(−4.36)
Industry ratio of tangible assets to total assets	0.405				0.400	0.398
	(4.01)				(3.84)	(3.23)
Industry market-to-book ratio		−0.047			0.000	−0.019
		(−1.87)			(0.00)	(−0.41)
Industry ratio of R&D expense to sales			−3.390		−2.268	
			(−2.52)		(−1.79)	
Industry ratio of R&D expense to total assets				−0.795		−0.194
				(−2.69)		(−1.67)
Age of the firm at time of venture financing round	0.016	0.016	0.016	0.017	0.016	0.017
	(3.58)	(3.68)	(3.49)	(3.56)	(3.52)	(3.60)
Logarithm of the amount of venture financing this round	0.011	0.012	0.016	0.011	0.010	0.009
	(0.71)	(0.73)	(0.68)	(0.65)	(0.59)	(0.52)
Pseudo-R^2	0.045	0.037	0.045	0.046	0.053	0.051
Model χ^2	56.00	42.25	48.64	49.47	62.74	60.38

Investment, Monitoring, and the Staging of Venture Capital 1479

Table VI—Continued

Panel B: Regressions for Size of Each Financing Round

Independent Variables	Dependent Variable: Logarithm of the Financing Amount in the Round					
	(1)	(2)	(3)	(4)	(5)	(6)
Constant	6.580	6.756	6.902	6.929	6.379	6.108
	(38.00)	(39.02)	(46.39)	(46.27)	(26.97)	(22.39)
Investment was in an early stage firm?	−0.635	−0.608	−0.703	−0.703	−0.748	−0.760
	(−4.14)	(−4.22)	(−4.83)	(−4.83)	(−5.14)	(−5.23)
Investment was in a middle stage firm?	−0.224	−0.216	−0.308	−0.309	−0.314	−0.328
	(−2.29)	(−2.20)	(−3.06)	(−3.06)	(−3.13)	(−3.26)
Capital committed to new venture funds in previous year	0.0001	0.0001	0.0001	0.0001	0.0001	0.0001
	(3.94)	(4.21)	(3.91)	(3.98)	(3.10)	(3.08)
Industry ratio of tangible assets to total assets	0.352				0.612	0.810
	(2.23)				(3.64)	(4.16)
Industry market-to-book ratio		−0.051			0.041	0.084
		(−0.64)			(0.49)	(1.03)
Industry ratio of R&D expense to sales			1.578		3.618	
			(0.72)		(1.56)	
Industry ratio of R&D expense to total assets				−0.099		1.372
				(−0.21)		(2.43)
Age of the firm at time of venture financing round	−0.019	−0.019	−0.014	−0.014	−0.014	−0.014
	(−2.58)	(−2.58)	(−1.82)	(−1.86)	(−1.90)	(−1.89)
R^2	0.031	0.028	0.039	0.031	0.041	0.044
F-statistic	9.33	8.40	8.50	8.40	8.03	8.55

ongoing financing round or firms might not receive another investment because they went bankrupt, went public, or were acquired. Models of unemployment (Lancaster (1979, 1985)) deal with similar censoring. I utilize duration data techniques used in unemployment estimation, surveyed in Kiefer (1988).

A firm is assumed to have a certain probability of receiving financing in each period. The instantaneous probability of receiving financing is called the hazard rate, $h(t)$. $h(t)$ is defined as:

$$h(t) = \frac{\text{Probability of receiving funding between } t \text{ and } t + \Delta t}{\text{Probability of receiving funding after } t} \quad (1)$$

To estimate the duration model, assumptions about the distribution of the hazard rate must be made. The two most common distributions used in duration models are the Weibull and exponential distributions. The Weibull distribution offers two advantages. First, the time dependency of the hazard rate can be estimated. Second, the likelihood function for the Weibull model can be easily modified to allow for censored data. Other distributional assumptions (e.g., exponential or normal) were estimated and did not affect the qualitative results, although the Weibull model gave better fit. The model estimated in Tables VI and VIII is:

$$h(t) = h_0(t)e^{\beta_0 + \beta_1 X_1 + \cdots + \beta_K X_K} \qquad h_0(t) = t^{1/(\sigma-1)} \qquad (2)$$

where $h_0(t)$ is the baseline hazard function.

Coefficients β_0, β_1, $\cdots$ are estimated via maximum likelihood estimators. These coefficients yield estimates of the probability that the firm receives financing in a particular month given values of the independent variables (including time from last investment). The resulting estimates from the Weibull regressions can be presented in multiple ways. Table VI and Table VIII present the model in log expected time parameterization, i.e., for given values of the independent variables, the model gives the logarithm of the expected time to refinancing. The interpretation of coefficients is straightforward, positive coefficients imply longer financing duration on average. Conversely, negative coefficients imply shorter expected durations.

The results of Table VI are generally consistent with the implications of an informational and agency cost explanation for staged venture capital infusions. In Panel A, financing duration declines with decreases in the industry ratio of tangible assets to total assets, increases in the market-to-book ratio, and greater R&D intensity. The coefficients are significant between the seven and one percent confidence levels. These factors are associated with greater agency costs of investment and liquidation and therefore lead to tighter monitoring.

The age of the venture-backed firm at the time of financing is positively and significantly related to financing duration. More information may be available for venture capitalists to evaluate older projects. One might also expect that larger financing rounds lead to longer funding duration. That is not the case. None of the coefficients on amount of venture financing are significant. The results indicate that industry- and firm-specific factors are important in determining the financing duration independent of the investment size.

Finally, in regressions (5) and (6), I include all industry accounting variables together to determine which of the asset measures are relatively more important. The ratio of tangible assets to total assets remains the most significant variable. Market-to-book drops out completely. Higher R&D intensities still reduce funding duration, but size and significance of the coefficients are reduced when the other asset measures are included. The results indicate that tangible assets may be particularly important in lowering expected agency costs.

Panel B examines factors affecting the size of the venture round. The dependent variable is the logarithm of the size of the financing round, in thousands of 1992 dollars. The ratio of tangible assets to total assets has the greatest effect on the amount of financing. Increases in tangibility increase the amount of financing per round. More R&D intensive industries also appear to receive more financing per round controlling for tangibility.

Panel A also shows that the duration of early and middle stage financings are not significantly different from late stage financings. The stage of development does, however, affect the amount of financing per round. Results from regressions in Panel B show that average early stage investments are between $1.30 and $2.03 million smaller than comparable late stage investments. Similarly, middle stage investments are on average $0.70 to $1.21 million smaller than late stage investments. The increasing size of investment per round reflects the growing scale of a firm. Greater investment is needed to expand the firm.

The duration of financing and the amount of funding per round is also sensitive to the growth in the venture capital industry. Greater commitments of capital to new venture funds reduces duration of financing and increases financing amount per round. A one standard deviation increase in new commitments to venture capital funds decreases funding duration by two months and increases the average funding by almost $700,000.

If venture capitalists are capital rationed, larger cash commitments allow venture capitalists to invest more often in positive NPV projects and with larger cash infusions. If venture capitalists are susceptible to free cash flow agency costs, they might waste the extra cash by investing more, and more often, in bad projects. Similarly, the growth in new and inexperienced fund managers during the mid-1980s could have led to a deterioration in investment quality and monitoring. Sahlman and Stevenson's (1987) case study of the computer disk drive industry shows that venture capital investment in certain industries during the early and middle 1980s might have been excessive. This period coincides with the dramatic increase in commitments to venture capital funds and might indicate that either free cash flow agency costs or venture capitalist inexperience is a more likely explanation for the investment sensitivity to fundraising during this period of rapid entry.

B. Total Venture Financing and Number of Rounds

Data on total venture capital invested and the number of rounds provide another measure of monitoring intensity. Table VII presents results for both variables. Included in the regressions are three dummy variables for the outcome of venture financing: a dummy variable that equals one if the firm went public, another dummy variable that equals one if the firm was liquidated or filed for bankruptcy, and a third dummy variable that takes the value one for all firms that are acquired or merge with another company. Coefficients on these dummies provide information about the impact of monitoring for projects of varying success.

The dependent variable in Panel A is the logarithm of the total amount of venture financing that the firm received. The results show that firms that go public receive between $3.36 and $5.67 million more venture capital financing than firms that remain private. There is no difference in the total funding for those firms that are acquired and those that are liquidated compared to firms that remain private. Even controlling for the number of financing rounds, firms that eventually go public receive more total financing.

The results in Panel B for the number of financing rounds confirm these results. Because the dependent variable is non-negative and ordinal, I estimate Poisson regressions for the number of rounds received. Firms that go public receive more financing rounds than those that remain private, while firms that are acquired or go bankrupt do not receive more rounds on average than those that remain private.

Table VII

Regression for Total Venture Capital Funding and Number of Rounds of Financing

The sample is 794 venture capital-backed firms for the period 1961 to 1992. The dependent variables are the total venture capital funding that the firm received in thousands of 1992 dollars and the number of distinct rounds of venture financing. Independent variables include a dummy variable that equals 1 if the firm completed an initial public offering, a dummy variable that equals 1 if the firm filed for bankruptcy, and a dummy variable that equals 1 if the firm was acquired by or merged with another company. Tangibility of assets is measured by the average ratio of tangible assets to total assets for companies in the firm's industry. Market-to-book is the average industry ratio of market value of equity to book value of equity. Research and development intensity is proxied by the average industry ratios of R&D to sales or R&D to assets. Estimates in Panel A are from ordinary least squares regressions. Estimates for equations in Panel B are from Poisson regressions. t-statistics for regression coefficients are in parentheses.

Panel A: Regressions for Total Funding

Independent Variables	Dependent Variable: Logarithm of Total Venture Financing Received					
	(1)	(2)	(3)	(4)	(5)	(6)
Constant	11.017	7.075	7.290	7.427	4.714	4.771
	(12.38)	(38.22)	(67.40)	(68.38)	(4.41)	(4.47)
Firm exited via an IPO?	1.043	1.018	0.882	0.905	0.664	0.666
	(6.18)	(6.01)	(4.88)	(4.96)	(4.31)	(4.32)
Firm went bankrupt or was liquidated?	−0.023	−0.024	−0.102	−0.047	−0.085	−0.077
	(−0.11)	(−0.12)	(−0.49)	(−0.22)	(−0.48)	(−0.44)
Firm exited via merger or acquisition?	−0.125	−0.129	−0.003	−0.009	0.124	0.123
	(−0.76)	(−0.78)	(−0.02)	(−0.05)	(0.84)	(0.83)
Industry ratio of tangible assets to total assets	−3.660				1.118	1.036
	(−3.90)				(1.12)	(1.04)
Industry market-to-book ratio		0.311			0.402	0.420
		(2.90)			(3.52)	(3.69)
Industry ratio of R&D expense to sales			13.033		3.600	
			(4.02)		(1.24)	
Industry ratio of R&D expense to total assets				5.709		2.540
				(1.95)		(1.02)
Number of rounds of venture financing received					0.396	0.399
					(15.19)	(15.43)
R^2	0.073	0.064	0.067	0.048	0.337	0.336
F-statistic	13.40	11.60	11.05	7.82	44.37	44.26

Investment, Monitoring, and the Staging of Venture Capital   1483

Table VII—*Continued*

Panel B: Poisson regressions for number of rounds

Independent Variables	Dependent Variable: Number of Financing Rounds Received			
	(1)	(2)	(3)	(4)
Constant	2.904	0.945	0.796	0.888
	(10.51)	(13.88)	(18.82)	(21.55)
Firm exited via an IPO?	0.255	0.239	0.186	0.203
	(4.35)	(4.06)	(2.91)	(3.18)
Firm went bankrupt or was liquidated?	0.054	0.052	0.017	0.052
	(0.71)	(0.68)	(0.23)	(0.68)
Firm exited via merger or acquisition?	0.027	−0.006	−0.010	−0.004
	(0.43)	(−0.09)	(−0.16)	(−0.06)
Industry ratio of tangible assets to total assets	−2.054			
	(−6.96)			
Industry market-to-book ratio		0.021		
		(0.54)		
Industry ratio of R&D expense to sales			7.416	
			(6.25)	
Industry ratio of R&D expense to total assets				2.907
				(2.73)
Pseudo-R^2	0.020	0.006	0.019	0.007
Model χ^2	60.25	18.55	50.07	18.81

A plausible explanation for these results is that venture capitalists gather information about the potential profitability of projects over time. If venture capitalists receive favorable information about the firm and it has the potential to go public, the venture capitalist continues to fund the project. If the project is viable but has little potential to go public, the venture capitalist quickly searches for a corporate buyer. Firms that have little potential are liquidated.

Industry factors appear to have an important impact on total funding received. Panel A shows that firms in industries with more tangible assets receive less total financing. Firms in industries with high market-to-book ratios receive more total financing. Similarly, R&D intensive industries receive significantly greater amounts of financing.

The most important factor influencing total venture financing is the number of financing rounds the firm has received. In fact, when the number of financing rounds is included in regressions with industry variables, tangibility of assets and R&D intensity are no longer significant. The coefficient on industry market-to-book ratio is unchanged, however. Even controlling for the number of financing rounds, firms in industries with high market-to-book ratios receive more total venture funding. If market-to-book measures the potential profitability of investment and growth opportunities, investment should be relatively higher in industries that have more growth opportunities. Similarly, firms in high market-to-book industries may have less access to debt financing and may therefore rely more on venture capital.

Panel B shows that tangibility of assets and R&D intensity do indeed work through the number of financing rounds. Firms in industries with a greater fraction of tangible assets receive fewer rounds of venture financing. Similarly, firms in R&D intensive industries receive more rounds of financing.

Overall, the evidence suggests that venture capitalists are concerned about the lack of entrepreneurial incentive to terminate projects when it becomes clear that projects will fail. Venture capitalists minimize agency costs by infusing capital more often. As asset tangibility and liquidation value increase, venture capitalists can recover more of their money if liquidation occurs, and the need to monitor declines. By gathering information, venture capitalists determine whether projects are likely to succeed and continue funding only those that have high potential.

IV. Alternative Explanations

While the results from Section III are consistent with predictions from agency theory, alternative explanations may explain the results. Cost of monitoring may affect investment structure through the efficacy of interim monitoring. Tangible assets may be easy to monitor without formal evaluation. A venture capitalist can tell if a machine is still bolted to the floor. If costs of monitoring are very low, the venture capitalist may choose to have long financing rounds to avoid costs of writing new contracts. At the same time, venture capitalists could monitor the firm more often between capital infusions. Easier interim monitoring would reduce expected agency costs between financing rounds and, hence, increase funding duration.

Both monitoring and agency costs are important. Conversations with practitioners, however, indicate that they normally make continuation decisions when a new financing round occurs. Venture capitalists evaluate a firm based upon performance progress, not whether a machine is still bolted down. Future work should examine the importance of monitoring costs in determining investment structure and the frequency of monitoring.

The relation between funding duration and the nature of firm assets may also be driven by differences between high technology and low technology firms. High technology firms may naturally pass through more milestones. Because industry measures like the ratio of tangible assets to total assets, market-to-book, and R&D intensity are highly correlated with high technology and low technology status, shorter funding duration may be correlated with these measures. The coefficients in Table VI would measure the amount of information revealed over time and the number of benchmarks used to evaluate the firm. The more information that is revealed, the more often the project is reevaluated.

If the alternative of technology-driven milestones is true, then coefficients on asset measures would be driven by the difference between high technology and low technology industries. If we rerun the duration regressions within technology groups, the effect of asset tangibility, industry market-to-book ratios, and R&D intensities should be much less important. Table VIII presents Weibull distribution maximum likelihood estimates for each technology cohort. In Panel A, the sample is high technology firms which include communications, computers, computer related, software, electronic components, other electronics, biotechnology, and medical equipment companies. The sample in Panel B is low technology firms, which include medical services, energy, consumer products, industrial products, transportation, and other (primarily services) companies.

The coefficients on industry asset measures are surprisingly similar for the high technology and low technology cohorts and both have estimates that are close to the estimates for the entire sample. It is impossible to reject the hypothesis that the coefficients for the tangibility of assets, market-to-book ratio, and the R&D intensity are equal across types of industries. The similarity of the coefficients shows that the relation between duration and asset measures is consistent within industrial classifications as well. In unreported regressions, finer industry divisions had no qualitative effect on the coefficients.

The one major difference between the two groups is the effect of firm age. The age of the firm receiving financing does not have an effect on the financing duration for high technology firms but has a significantly positive effect in the low technology cohort. Firm age may be more important in measuring potential asymmetric information for low technology firms but may have only a small impact on asymmetric information for high technology companies.

While alternative explanations may help explain some of the results, conversations with venture capitalists indicate that they are concerned about the entrepreneur's continuation decisions and strategy choices. Results in Section III are consistent with venture capitalists' stated concern that entrepreneurs have private information about future viability of the firm, that they always want to continue, and that entrepreneurs may want to enrich their reputation through activities at investors' expense.

V. Conclusion

Corporate control is a fundamental concern of investors. If individuals knew all potential outcomes, state-contingent contracts would be able to solve any potential agency cost. But such complete knowledge does not exist, and investors must minimize potential agency costs. Mechanisms in financial contracts between venture capitalists and entrepreneurs directly account for potential agency costs and private information associated with high-risk, high-return projects.

This paper has demonstrated that the staging of venture capital investments can be understood in an agency and monitoring framework. Results from a sample of venture capital-backed companies are consistent with the predictions presented. Venture capitalists are concerned that entrepreneurs with private information and large private benefits will not want to liquidate a project even if they have information that the project has a negative net

The Journal of Finance

present value for shareholders. Entrepreneurs may also pursue strategies that enrich their reputation at shareholders' expense. Agency costs increase with declining asset tangibility, increasing growth options, and greater asset specificity. Venture capitalists monitor entrepreneurs with increasing frequency as expected agency costs rise.

Table VIII

Regressions for Duration Controlling for Firm and Industry Factors with the Sample Split into High Technology and Low Technology Companies

The sample is 2143 funding rounds for 794 venture capital-backed firms for the period 1961 to 1992. The dependent variable is the time in years from funding date to the next funding date. Independent variables include a dummy variable that equals 1 if the funding round is either seed or startup (early stage) and a dummy variable that equals 1 if the round is either early, first, or other early (middle stage). Liquidity in the venture capital industry is controlled using new capital commitments to venture capital partnerships in the previous year in constant 1992 dollars. Tangibility of assets is measured by the average ratio of tangible assets to total assets for company's in the firm's industry. Market-to-book is the average industry ratio of market value of equity to book value of equity. Research and development intensity is proxied by the average industry ratios of R&D to sales or R&D to assets. The age of the venture capital-backed firm is months from incorporation to financing date. All regressions are maximum-likelihood estimates for Weibull distribution duration models. t-statistics for coefficients are in parentheses.

Panel A: Regressions for Duration of Financing Round for High Technology Industries

Independent Variables	Dependent Variable: Duration of Financing Round					
	(1)	(2)	(3)	(4)	(5)	(6)
Constant	−0.036	0.464	0.542	0.549	0.022	−0.056
	(−0.17)	(2.56)	(2.99)	(3.03)	(0.09)	(−0.22)
Investment was in an early stage firm?	0.066	0.065	0.042	0.046	0.036	0.029
	(0.68)	(0.66)	(0.42)	(0.45)	(0.36)	(0.30)
Investment was in a middle stage firm?	−0.022	−0.009	−0.085	−0.084	−0.101	−0.109
	(−0.32)	(−0.13)	(−1.15)	(−1.14)	(−1.38)	(−1.48)
Capital committed to new venture funds in previous year	−0.63 × E-04	−0.59 × E-04	−0.54 × E-04	−0.57 × E-04	−0.59 × E-04	−0.61 × E-04
	(−4.50)	(−4.01)	(−3.59)	(−3.82)	(−3.81)	(−3.93)
Industry ratio of tangible assets to total assets	0.514				0.553	0.633
	(3.47)				(3.60)	(3.55)
Industry market-to-book ratio		−0.059			0.037	−0.003
		(−0.66)			(0.39)	(−0.03)
Industry ratio of R&D expense to sales			−2.418		−0.986	
			(−1.83)		(−0.51)	
Industry ratio of R&D expense to total assets				−0.541		−0.315
				(−1.88)		(−1.68)
Age of the firm at time of venture financing round	−0.001	−0.001	−0.005	−0.005	−0.006	−0.005
	(−0.17)	(−0.09)	(−0.70)	(−0.70)	(−0.74)	(−0.64)
Logarithm of the amount of venture financing this round	0.001	0.003	−0.002	−0.002	−0.004	−0.005
	(0.07)	(0.13)	(−0.08)	(−0.08)	(−0.21)	(−0.22)
Pseudo-R^2	0.036	0.029	0.032	0.032	0.041	0.040
Model χ^2	31.07	20.75	21.85	21.99	33.63	33.81

Investment, Monitoring, and the Staging of Venture Capital 1487

Table VIII—*Continued*

Panel B: Regressions for Duration of Financing Round for Low Technology Industries

Independent Variables	Dependent Variable: Duration of Financing Round					
	(1)	(2)	(3)	(4)	(5)	(6)
Constant	−0.078	0.399	0.382	0.400	0.130	0.208
	(−0.29)	(1.50)	(1.54)	(1.62)	(0.45)	(0.62)
Investment was in an early	−0.050	−0.095	−0.087	−0.068	−0.093	−0.098
stage firm?	(−0.35)	(−0.66)	(−0.61)	(−0.48)	(−0.65)	(−0.69)
Investment was in a middle	−0.148	−0.194	−0.210	−0.179	−0.196	−0.195
stage firm?	(−1.45)	(−1.88)	(−2.03)	(−1.72)	(−1.89)	(−1.88)
Capital committed to new venture	−0.43	−0.38	−0.37	−0.40	−0.38	−0.38
funds in previous year	× E-04	× E-04	× E-04	× E-04	× E-04	× E-04
	(−1.86)	(−1.89)	(−1.68)	(−1.72)	(−1.68)	(−1.62)
Industry ratio of tangible assets	0.433				0.393	0.337
to total assets	(2.90)				(2.55)	(2.17)
Industry market-to-book ratio		−0.076			−0.053	−0.078
		(−1.41)			(−0.91)	(−1.43)
Industry ratio of R&D expense			−4.270		−2.006	
to sales			(−2.18)		(−1.89)	
Industry ratio of R&D expense				−1.067		−0.388
to total assets				(−2.41)		(−1.66)
Age of the firm at time of	0.026	0.028	0.030	0.031	0.029	0.030
venture financing round	(4.07)	(4.34)	(4.44)	(4.54)	(4.34)	(4.41)
Logarithm of the amount	0.022	0.018	0.017	0.014	0.019	0.017
of venture financing this round	(0.79)	(0.63)	(0.61)	(0.50)	(0.66)	(0.59)
Pseudo-R^2	0.086	0.075	0.088	0.091	0.100	0.100
Model χ^2	39.27	33.29	39.38	40.34	46.19	45.82

The evidence indicates that venture capitalists use their industry knowledge and monitoring skills to finance projects with significant uncertainty. Venture capitalists concentrate investment in early-stage companies and high technology industries. Results also demonstrate that the duration of financing is related to the nature of the firm's assets. Higher industry ratios of tangible assets to total assets, lower market-to-book ratios, and lower R&D intensities are associated with longer funding duration. Firms that go public have received significantly more financing and a greater number of rounds than have firms that are acquired or liquidated.

This paper raises several interesting questions for future research. Because large firms also engage in projects that compete with investments by venture capitalists, comparing the structure and timing of investment of large corporations with those of venture capitalists might shed light on the comparative advantage of each. What implications does the structure of venture capital investment have on the future performance of new business and established firms? Can the structure of investment increase the probability that an entrepreneurial project ends up like Apple Computer, Genentech, or Microsoft? Cross-sectional and time series effects of firm- and industry-specific factors on

1488   *The Journal of Finance*

the outcome of investment (e.g., IPO, merger, bankruptcy, or remaining private) need to be examined.

The effect of growth in the venture capital industry on investment should be investigated further. Do free cash flow costs, liquidity constraints, or the entry of inexperienced venture capitalists better describe venture capitalists' response to changes in capital commitments to new funds through the 1980s? Does the fund raising ability of the venture capitalist affect only the size of the investment or does it lead to softer benchmarks as well?

The data in this paper is limited because it examines only venture capital equity financing. Most venture capital-backed firms receive some financing before they tap venture capital. What are these sources and how significant are they? "Angels," wealthy individuals that invest in entrepreneurial ventures, are one source. Family and friends are also major contributors. Bank lending may be important in certain industries, but very high risk companies might not have access to debt financing. Future work should examine appropriate sources of capital for new firms and how those sources change as the firm evolves. Determining the relationship among sources of capital for startup enterprises would be pivotal in understanding the genesis of new firms.

REFERENCES

Admati, A. R., and P. Pfleiderer, 1994, Robust financial contracting and the role for venture capitalists, *Journal of Finance* 49, 371–402.

Amit, R., L. Glosten, and E. Muller, 1990, Entrepreneurial ability, venture investments, and risk sharing. *Management Science* 36, 1232–1245.

Barclay, M. J., and C. W. Smith, Jr., 1995, The maturity structure of corporate debt, *Journal of Finance* 50, 609–631.

Blanchard, O., F. Lopez de Silanes, and A. Shleifer, 1994, What do firms do with cash windfalls?, *Journal of Financial Economics* 36, 337–360.

Bradley, M., G. Jarrell, and E. H. Kim, 1984, On the existence of an optimal capital structure: Theory and evidence, *Journal of Finance* 39, 857–878.

Chan, Y., 1983, On the positive role of financial intermediation in allocation of venture capital in a market with imperfect information, *Journal of Finance* 38, 1543–1568.

Fazzari, S., R. G., Hubbard, and B. Petersen, 1988, Investment and finance reconsidered, *Brookings Papers on Economic Activity*, 141–195.

Friend, I., and L. Lang, 1988, An empirical test of the impact of managerial self-interest on corporate capital structure, *Journal of Finance* 43, 271–281.

Gompers, P., 1993a, Syndication, hold-out problems, and venture capital, Working paper, University of Chicago.

Gompers, P., 1993b, Incentives, screening, and venture capital: A role for convertible debt, Working paper, University of Chicago.

Gompers, P., and J. Lerner, 1995, An analysis of compensation in the US venture partnership, Working paper, University of Chicago and Harvard University.

Gorman, M., and W. Sahlman, 1989, What do venture capitalists do?, *Journal of Business Venturing* 4, 231–248.

Harris, M., and A. Raviv, 1991, The theory of capital structure, *Journal of Finance* 46, 297–356.

Hart, O., 1991, Theories of optimal capital structure: A principal-agent perspective, Working paper, Harvard University.

Hoshi, T., A. Kashyap, and D. Scharfstein, 1991, Corporate structure, liquidity, and investment, *Quarterly Journal of Economics* 106, 33–60.

Investment, Monitoring, and the Staging of Venture Capital 1489

James, C., 1987, Some evidence on the uniqueness of bank loans: A comparison of bank borrowing, private placements, and public offerings, *Journal of Financial Economics* 19, 217–235.

Jensen, M., and W. Meckling, 1976, Theory of the firm: Managerial behavior, agency costs, and ownership structure, *Journal of Financial Economics* 3, 5–50.

Jensen, M., 1986, Agency cost of free cash flow, corporate finance and takeovers, *AER Papers and Proceedings* 76, 323–329.

Kiefer, N., 1988, Economic duration data and hazard functions, *Journal of Economic Literature* 26, 646–679.

Lancaster, T., 1979, Econometric methods for the duration of unemployment, *Econometrica* 47, 939–956.

Lancaster, T., 1985, Generalized residuals and heterogeneous duration models: With applications to the Weibull model, *Journal of Econometrics* 28, 155–169.

Lerner, J., 1994a, The syndication of venture capital investments, *Financial Management* 23, 16–27.

Lerner, J., 1994b, Venture capital and the oversight of privately-held firms, *Journal of Financial Economics* 35, 293–316.

Myers, S., 1977, Determinants of corporate borrowing, *Journal of Financial Economics* 5, 147–175.

Petersen, M., and R. Rajan, 1994, The benefits of firm-creditor relationships: A study of small business financings, *Journal of Finance* 49, 3–35.

Petersen, M., and R. Rajan, 1995, The effect of credit market competition on lending relationships, *Quarterly Journal of Economics* 110, 407–444.

Pindyck, R., 1991, Irreversibility, uncertainty, and investment, *Journal of Economic Literature* 29, 1110–1148.

Rajan, R., and L. Zingales, 1995, What do we know about capital structure? Some evidence form international data, *Journal of Finance*, forthcoming.

Roberts, K., and M. Weitzman, 1981, Funding criteria for research, development, and exploration projects, *Econometrica* 49, 1261–1288.

Sahlman, W., 1990, The structure and governance of venture capital organizations, *Journal of Financial Economics* 27, 473–524.

Sahlman, W., 1992, Insights from the venture capital industry, Working paper, Harvard University.

Sahlman, W., and H. Stevenson, 1987, Capital Market Myopia, Harvard Business School Case.

Shleifer, A., and R. Vishny, 1992, Liquidation value and debt capacity: A market equilibrium approach, *Journal of Finance* 47, 1343–1366.

Titman, S., and R. Wessels, 1988, The determinants of capital structure, *Journal of Finance* 43, 1–19.

Weitzman, M, W. Newey, and M. Rabin, 1981, Sequential R&D strategy for synfuels, *Bell Journal of Economics* 12, 574–590.

Williamson, O., 1988, Corporate finance and corporate governance, *Journal of Finance* 43, 567–591.

[15]

Journal of Management Studies 28:6 November 1991
0022–2380 $3.50

UK VENTURE CAPITAL FUNDS AND THE FUNDING OF NEW TECHNOLOGY-BASED BUSINESSES: PROCESS AND RELATIONSHIPS*

R. C. SWEETING

Manchester School of Management, UMIST

ABSTRACT

Through the 1980s the UK venture capital industry, with its perceived focus on risky and innovative businesses, has experienced substantial growth in terms of the number of funds, amounts invested and number of individual investments. In this article, the Tyebjee and Bruno (1984) venture capital deal creation model which was originated in the US has been used to explore the process of venture capital provision and the development of relationships between venture capital funds and operating business managements. An empirical study of how UK-based venture capital funds operate has been undertaken. The findings generally corroborated the model in a UK context. It was also observed that while venture capitalists actively worked to nurture good relationships with operating business managements they were prepared to act decisively and proactively to protect their investments when they saw them being threatened fundamentally. There was also some evidence which suggested a slackening of interest in innovative, technology-based businesses, particularly those in their early stages of development. Further work is needed to identify if there are conceptual problems with the provision of venture capital to these types of businesses or implementation problems which are tractable.

BACKGROUND

During the 1980s there was a major growth in both the number of venture capital funds and the investments which they made (Bannock, 1987). In a review of venture capital by the Bank of England in 1982 this expansion was anticipated and it was noted that this would happen if for no other reason than there had been very successful growth and returns from venture capital investment in industry in the USA. Lorenz, in 1985, attributed the unprecedented level of venture activity to a realization that in the UK a major shift was needed, away from mature industries that were in decline. Increasing numbers of new technology initiatives were being spawned in independent, start-up businesses. Financial institutions recognized that these needed to be

Address for reprints: R. C. Sweeting, Manchester School of Management, UMIST, PO Box 88, Manchester, M60 1QD.

supported financially and managerially in order not only to survive but to grow. Venture capital with its basic concept of offering funding (normally including an equity element) and the supply of managerial assistance was conceived as a possible route to achieving this. This means of funding became particularly appealing to managements of new technology-based businesses (NTBBs) because it was made available to ventures that were considered to be more speculative and risky than investments in general, that risk being rewarded in principle with potentially much greater than average returns.

An important watershed has now been reached in the UK venture capital industry. Many of the investments made by venture capitalists in the earlier part of the 1980s have reached the stage of realization or have been realized. The industry is therefore undergoing a period of reassessment and re-evaluation that will have a significant impact on what types of businesses are being funded (*Independent*, 1990), the ways in which those investments are assessed and how relationships between operating businesses and venture funds are developed. It is the process of venture capital investment, the experience once investments have been made, and the implications for the reappraisal of the UK venture capital industry that are examined in this article.

Observations of venture capital investment activity, with particular reference to investments in NTBBs, have been made in a sample of UK funds. The following aspects have been focused upon: the sourcing of deals; their screening and evaluation; the development of relationships between managements of venture funds and operating businesses once deals have been made. A model of venture fund investment activity originated by Tyebjee and Bruno (1984), based upon US experience, has been used as a framework around which to associate data. The US venture capital industry has been longer established than that in the UK (see, for example, Bank of England, 1982) and, at present, there is little academic research data available on venture fund activity in the UK.

A PROCESSUAL MODEL OF VENTURE FUND ACTIVITY

Table I outlines the main stages of the Tyebjee and Bruno (1984) processual model of venture fund activity. The model incorporates refinements based on their survey data collected from 87 venture capital funds and comments received from managers in a further seven funds, all based in the US. It was as a result of their final validation exercise that Tyebjee and Bruno made an important point:

The diversity of the responses, both in content and style, demonstrates the heterogeneity in practices of different venture capital firms. This heterogeneity cautions against too rigid a specification in any model describing venture capital management.

The authors commented that over-elaboration of models probably only served to make them relevant to individual funds. Nonetheless, the model

Table I. A processual model of US venture capital fund activity*

STAGE	FEATURES
I. Deal origination	Most deals are referred by third parties
	Referrals by other venture capitalists are often invitations to join syndicates
	Venture capitalists are rarely proactive in searching out deals
II. Deal screening	Most frequently-used screening criteria are: technology and/or market; stage of financing
III. Deal evaluation	Decision to invest based upon expected return compared with level of risk. Factors considered include:
	Market attractiveness Product differentiation Management team capabilities Protection of business from uncontrollable factors, *e.g.* competition, product obsolescence
IV. Deal structuring	Venture capital funds use a wide range of approaches. An aim can be to help motivate managers to perform
	Price can be determined by: quality of opportunity; past experience with similar realized deals and so on
V. Post-investment activities	Venture funds provide management guidance and business contacts
	Representative(s) of the venture funds normally sit on boards of operating businesses; they assist with development of business strategy
	Venture fund representatives can act as 'sounding boards' for operating business management

*Based upon the model developed by Tyebjee and Bruno (1984)

does act as a useful framework around which to marshal observations of venture capital fund activity and this is its main function in this article. It is suggested that while there may be cultural differences between the US and UK, many venture capital practices and techniques may be transportable.

GENERAL COMMENTS ON THE PROCESS

Deal Origination

Tyebjee and Bruno (1984) commented, based on their observations which were made in the period early to mid-1980s, that proactive behaviour by venture capitalists in seeking out deals[1] was not a widely adopted means of deal origination. The most popular approach was to wait passively for deal proposals to be put to them.

604   R. C. SWEETING

Deal Screening

The assessment of deal proposals requires a wide range of skills and experience. Because individual funds will probably have limited staff with the necessary attributes to undertake analyses and authority to make decisions, then it may be expected that the number of investments made by any one fund will be so constrained. Gorman and Sahlman (1989) surveyed 49 US venture capital funds and found that the median number of partners per firm was four (range 1–15) and each managed a median number of eight (range 4–20) investments.

Due to the limited amounts of 'hard' data that are available and the apparent inappropriateness of over-sophisticated analytical techniques, assessments may involve much 'soft' data and subjectivity. As a consequence of this, considerable mutual trust and good informal information exchange between staff in the individual venture funds will be required.[2] Therefore, it may be expected that the compactness of individual funds will be an advantage as this will enable informal processes to operate more effectively. There may also be a desire not to proliferate 'small' investments when the time involved in assessment and monitoring these may be as great as for 'large' ones (see Tyebjee and Bruno, 1984).

Deal Evaluation

Studies in the US have generally cited market, technology/product and management factors as the ones about which venture capitalists are most concerned in business proposal evaluations. They need to be comforted and assured about these. Market acceptability, proprietorial position, the shape of current and near term competition have been the subject of close scrutiny (see, for example, Macmillan *et al.*, 1987; Macmillan *et al.*, 1989; Roure and Maidique, 1986). Managerial capabilities, drive and openness to recognizing and recruiting management personnel where there are any deficiencies are also key considerations (see, for example, Bruno and Tyebjee, 1985; Macmillan *et al.*, 1989; Macmillan *et al.*, 1985). The analogies between these factors and those seen in evaluations of new product proposals have been noted and commented upon (Tyebjee and Bruno, 1984). This reflects the general concerns of those who have responsibility and accountability for the allocation of resources to business venture activities which are surrounded by intense uncertainties.

After proposals to venture capitalists have passed through initial screening procedures, then the interpersonal skills which the management team possess can be important in determining whether or not a deal is completed. Rea (1989) reported, *inter alia*, the following factors amongst those influencing a sample US venture capitalist to decline particular deals: 'Chief Executive Officer too abrasive', 'people (in the management team) thought too much of themselves' and the management team 'too self-confident'.

Deal Structuring

Tyebjee and Bruno (1984) did not examine in detail the structuring of deals. However, they did comment that the capital asset pricing model had limited applicability and that what venture managers effectively do is strive to achieve a position where 'potentially higher returns offset the greater risks'. Gorman and Sahlman (1989) characterized the position when deals are actually made as follows:

> Venture-backed companies are thinly staffed and thinly capitalized by design. Venture capitalists, for their part, generally seek to provide their entrepreneurs with only the minimum of cash required. They tend to dole out discrete amounts closely matched to the attainment of clear milestones, enabling them to limit damage by refusing additional financing if the company is unsuccessful in the early stages. Meanwhile, entrepreneurs, because they are motivated to retain for themselves as much as they can of their business's value, are loathe to incur any upfront expenditure that might conceivably be avoided. Selling too much of the company at the earliest stages amounts to an expensive mortgage on the future wealth against which the entrepreneur has wagered his or her career. Thus both venture capitalists and entrepreneurs willingly conspire to impose stringent limits on the resiliency of their enterprise.

This lack of resilience may have significant implications. Particularly in the case of early-stage, new technology-based businesses, it may induce failure through over constraining their adaptability, flexibility and scope for entrepreneurism.

Post Investment Activities
Once an investment has been made, then it is in the interests of both operating business managers and venture capitalists to do everything possible to ensure that 'their' operating businesses succeed – they effectively become active 'collaborators' (Tyebjee and Bruno, 1984). Involvement may take place across the whole spectrum of managerial activity, from strategic planning to operational matters. Rosenstein (1988) has shown that venture capitalists in the US can be vigorous and influential board members and play a significant part in shaping operating business strategies. They also act as very useful 'sounding boards' for ideas generated by operating business managers (Macmillan *et al.*, 1989).

Mainly because of time constraints, venture capitalists tend not to become over-involved in day-to-day operations unless major problems arise (see, for example, Gorman and Sahlman, 1989; Macmillan *et al.*, 1989). The assistance most frequently given by venture capitalists observed by Gorman and Sahlman (1989) included help in raising additional funds and strategic analysis and help in management recruiting. The latter is an important activity because these researchers found weakness in senior management to be the most frequently-cited reason given by venture capitalists for operating business failure. Paradoxically, a more intense level of involvement by venture capitalists does not necessarily mean that operating businesses will necessarily perform any better than where there is only a limited involvement (Macmillan *et al.*, 1989).

606   R. C. SWEETING

THE UK VENTURE MARKET IN GENERAL

Given that a main focus of this article is to examine the experience of UK venture funds, it is appropriate to present a short review of some of the features of the UK venture capital industry:

(1) There has been rapid overall growth in both the number of venture capital funds and the investments made by UK venture capitalists during the 1980s. Bannock (1987) reported data, from a number of sources, that between 1981 and 1986 the funds invested by UK-based venture capital organizations had increased from £195m to £671m. In more recent years, commitments to venture capital funds have continued to grow. A review of the UK venture capital industry in 1990 (*Independent*, 1990), quoting Venture Economics sources, reported £1.76bn committed to independent UK venture capital funds in 1989 compared with £739m in 1988. Between the end of the 1970s and 1990 the membership of the British Venture Capital Association, (BVCA), a representaive group of the UK venture capital industry, has grown from 40 founding members to 120 full members.

(2) Behind this growth in the industry there have been significant changes in the types of investments which have been made by particular funds. The increase in investment between 1988 and 1989 was mainly accounted for by a small number of very large funds aiming to invest in later-stage funding, for example, management buy-outs, not early-stage business funding (*Independent*, 1990). Towards the end of the 1980s, BVCA (1989) data disclosed a move away from both start-up and technology business-related investments (see table II).

While there is insufficient data to identify a clear trend, this shift is disturbing. The term venture capital itself has connotations of investment in risky, new businesses which are often based in new technology (Bank of England, 1982). However, as Eadie (1990) commented:

> In the early and mid Eighties, high-tech was deemed a sexy area of investment for (UK) venture capitalists keen to be at the leading edge of the enterprise culture (then emerging in the UK). In the Nineties, the community has largely retreated from that edge, its enthusiasm tempered by underperformance of investments.

Table II. Start-up and technology related venture capital investments

Feature	1988 (%)	1987 (%)
Start-up business investments (as a percentage of total)	5	8
Technology related businesses (as a percentage of total)	9	16

Source: BVCA, 1989

There is some evidence, therefore, that there is already a change in attitude towards investment in NTBBs, particularly in their early stages of development, by the venture capitalist community. There appears to be a move towards investments in more mature businesses operating with more established technologies. This is not to say that early-stage, new technology businesses have been totally abandoned. Eadie (1990) went on to observe:

Despite changes in attitude to newer technology businesses, there are still a number of specialist players providing venture capital finance.

RESEARCH STUDY

A research study has been undertaken, aimed at examining the operation of small number of UK venture capital funds and how their relationships with operating businesses were developed. Of particular interest was the way in which they identified, made and managed investments in early-stage NTBBs. Primary research data was obtained by means of face-to-face semi-structured interviews with senior managers in the sample funds.

Secondary data were collected from published statistics, the technical press, venture fund reports and publications by intermediaries, such as accountants. In the presentation of data from the study and its discussion, reference to specific funds has been avoided in order to preserve confidentiality undertakings which were given to research participants.

Three venture capital funds were selected from the British Venture Capital Association Directory of 1987 and letters were written, outlining the purpose of the research, to the contact names, all of them senior managers. The letter requested co-operation and undertook to maintain confidentiality. The three funds were selected at random from those in the directory which indicated a willingness to offer venture capital to new technology-based businesses. All funds which were approached agreed to co-operate with the study.

The study sample was increased subsequently, in early 1988, by the inclusion of one further UK fund whose co-operation was obtained through contacts made in the earlier stages of the study. Details of the sample funds are shown in table III.

The sample was limited in size in order to enable an in-depth examination of the nature of the investment process to be made and how relationships developed over time. While general conclusions for venture funds as a whole cannot be drawn, the data do provide insights into the way that a particular set of funds which invested in risky NTBBs was constituted and operated. As well as being informative in itself, this work may also guide more extensive, further studies. Moreover, in the course of the research, fund managers made comments in the light of their general experience, knowledge of the venture capital market and new technology business deals in general. It should be noted that their experience could be quite broad because of the extensive use

608   R. C. SWEETING

Table III. Features of the study sample venture capital funds

| Feature | Fund | | | |
	1	2	3	4
Preferred areas of investment	Technology and service businesses	Technology and service businesses	None preferred	Technology businesses
Capital invested	£20M–£25M	£5M–£10M	£95M–£100M	£30M–£35M
Involved in syndication	Yes	Yes	Yes	Yes
Representation on board of directors	Normally yes	Normally yes	Normally yes	Normally yes
Typical periods to realization	3–5 years	3–7 years	3–7 years	3–7 years
Number of investments in portfolio	20–25	15–20	150–155	55–60

of syndication of deals between venture funds not just in the UK but internationally.

RESULTS FROM THE RESEARCH STUDY

General

The funds in the study sample drew their financial backing from a wide range of sources. All had support from financial institutions which normally included banks and/or pension funds. Other sources included universities, local authorities and companies. These money providers all sought the specialist investment making and interactive management expertise offered by the venture capital funds and the potentially higher than average return on their investments.

(a) The general philosophies of the funds were expressed in terms of: wanting to invest in growth businesses; willingness to work closely with operating businesses; availability of a wide range of helpful business contacts; willingness to be patient for several years with their investment before requiring realization, and so on. All the funds outlined, in differing degrees of detail, the characteristics of the businesses which they would examine in the process of deciding whether or not to make an investment. Prominence was given to the need, on the part of fund managers, to be able to make assessments of: the quality and ability of the management team; the proposed or actual markets in terms of growth and competition; proprietary positions of products and their profitability, and so on. One fund did not specify the content of business plans to be submitted to them, while the remainder did this in reasonable detail.

(b) Initially, none of the funds in the sample excluded the possibility of investing in new technology businesses. Two of them specifically stated that this was a particular area where investments were sought. All managers interviewed expressed an interest and experience in making investments in new technology-based businesses. However, towards the end of the field research, in early 1989, the situation in one of the funds had changed. The poor results from investments in new technology-based businesses were such that the parent organization of the venture fund decided that it was not inclined to make these types of investment in future. One other fund, while not specifically excluding these types of business investments, was more hesitant in making them.

(c) Only one fund in the sample did not set a lower limit on the amount at which it would create a deal. The others set lower limits, typically in the range of £100K to £300K, below which they would not normally make deals. There was, therefore, some evidence in support of the so called 'funding gap'.[3] However, the actual *total* amounts of venture capital funds obtained by *individual* operating businesses could be considerably higher than these statements might suggest. This was because several venture funds could contribute to a single operating business via a syndicate. It was not unusual for syndicates of four or more funds to become involved with *one* operating business.

(d) All the funds expressed an interest in making investments in operating businesses at both start-up and the early stages of corporate development. No exclusive preference for either of these was expressed in principle.

(e) All the funds stated that it was part of their funding policy to become involved actively with operating businesses once investments had been made. They all reserved the right to appoint a nominee (most often one of their own staff members) as a director onto the board of operating businesses. The funds were also able to call on the services of experienced businessmen known to them to act on their behalf as representatives on boards of operating businesses.

(f) All the funds believed that once a deal had been made they could make valuable general management contributions to the operating businesses by assisting with, for example, strategy formulation, executive recruitment, commercial contacts and so on.

VENTURE CAPITAL FUND ACTIVITY

Deal Origination

Requests for funding originated from a number of sources. The range of these is shown in table IV. The preferred sources of requests for the different funds are described in table V.

One senior fund manager commented that many entrepreneurs seemed to know very little about venture capital provision. It appeared to him that many approaches by entrepreneurs were *ad hoc* and resulted from random

Table IV. Sources of requests for funding made to sample venture funds

(A)	Passive	Incidence amongst funds*
	Sources:	
	Direct from entrepreneurs who were not previously known to the fund	4
	Via intermediaries, *e.g.* accountants	4
	Via parent organizations	1
	Via existing portfolio businesses	3
(B)	Proactive	
	Search for entrepreneurs/business combinations through contacts with consultants, industry, universities *etc.*	3
	Putting together managements and business ventures	3
(C)	Syndication	
	Responding to requests to join investment syndicates and originating such syndicates	4

*Each fund normally had more than one source

selection from venture capital fund directories. In his experience, where the approaches were totally 'out of the blue', it was highly unlikely that they would be successful in gaining funds. Generally, the source of the request for funding was a conditioning factor in the manner in which it was subsequently processed by venture funds.

The findings in examples (A) and (B) in table V suggest a move away, in some funds, from a mainly passive stance of awaiting deal approaches to be submitted (Tyebjee and Bruno, 1984) to one where a much more proactive approach was adopted with venture capitalists going out and putting together the ingredients of deals.

Deal Screening

A feature of the screening of requests was the very short time that was initially made available for each proposal. This reflected, in part, the volume of requests which each senior manager was required to handle (see 'deal evaluation' section, below). Ten to 15 minutes per proposal was the time typically mentioned by these managers for initially screening each proposal. If proposals passed this brief review, then they were subjected to a more detailed 'desk review'.

The task of the first brief screening was normally undertaken by one of the senior fund managers. These people were normally very familiar with the criteria necessary to be fulfilled if a request was to be successful and were key players in the investment appraisal process. There was a need, therefore, for proposals to make an immediate impact – but in what areas? The research revealed that requests for funding had to indicate that the entrepreneurs had

Table V. Preferred sources of request for funding (order of description not related to funds in table III)

(A)	The fund managers preferred to search out investments proactively. This involved:
	Examination of markets that were fragmented but had good prospects. This could result in the identification of a company involved in a desired market with a relevant technology but poorly managed and/or underfunded. Subsequently, the fund could arrange for the introduction of a new management team and/or injection of necessary new funds.
	The fund was also involved with creating new businesses 'on the back' of existing operating businesses which were already in the fund portfolio.
	Managers in the fund believed that by being proactive it was possible to get a lower deal price than by operating in the open market and passively awaiting requests to come to them.
(B)	The fund managers believed that deals which originated from industrial contacts, as a consequence of fund managers going out and 'ferreting' around, performed best. Therefore, fund managers actively involved themselves in talking to industry and university groups. This resulted in entrepreneurs feeling that they knew about the fund managers and the fund before they made a formal request for funding. Fund managers believed that this enabled a good relationship to be built up between themselves and entrepreneurs at an early stage. Approximately 70 per cent of approaches for funding resulted from this proactive style.
(C)	The fund managers preferred approaches through respected and previously used intermediaries. Fund managers found that the intermediaries had done a considerable amount of preliminary 'filtering' work and this saved them effort and enabled them to make better use of their limited time.
(D)	The fund managers preferred entry into deals by syndication and were prepared to join or to initiate syndicates. Presumably because of this known interest in syndication, many approaches for funding were therefore by invitations from other venture funds to join in syndicates. The fund limited its risk by joining syndicates and also by restricting the individual amounts of investments that it was prepared to make.

a sound knowledge of target markets where there were good prospects of higher than average returns. The products and/or services on offer normally had to be 'protected' in some way, possibly through being based upon proprietary technology.

Operating business managements needed to demonstrate that they could probably capture substantial shares of established markets or, alternatively, strong positions in growing markets. One fund wanted to ascertain that it was planned by the entrepreneurs that the products would gain entry to US markets. As a general prerequisite, most funds wanted to see good export possibilities for products and/or services. Thus the main screening criteria reported in the Tyebjee and Bruno (1984) and other, subsequent, US studies (for example, Macmillan *et al.*, 1985) were corroborated.

The requests for funding were supported by *initial* business plans which were examined in detail during the 'desk' review stage of the bid assessment.

This work could involve in-house research staff and/or external consultants. All the venture funds, except one, set out in reasonable detail in their publicity material the issues to be addressed and questions to be answered in business plans submitted to them. One of the funds deliberately avoided prescribing the detailed form and/or content of business plans, leaving it to the discretion of the entrepreneurs to decide what to include. In this case, senior fund managers preferred to see the untutored efforts of the entrepreneurs but recognized that assistance from intermediaries might be sought and given. It would also be reasonable to expect that many operating business managers had 'shopped around' venture funds for themselves and had obtained their brochures and so would be familiar with what was generally expected in a proposal.

At the initial screening stage, the venture funds put different emphases upon the composition of the operating business' management teams. One fund placed considerable emphasis on there being a good range of skills – marketing, technical, finance and so on. At the other extreme, one fund was not over-concerned with the total composition of management team at the screening stage. It believed that a good business, based on sound product/market concepts, with protected proprietary technology, could attract relevant good management in whatever areas they were needed.

Deal Evaluations
Once requests for funding had passed through the early selection and desk review processes then the management teams of the successful operating businesses were, in all cases, invited to make a presentation of their business plans to the venture fund managers. Normally, at least two members of the venture fund were present when these presentations were made, in order that they could compare and contrast their views after the meeting. It was at these meetings that important impressions were established by both parties on whether or not they could subsequently work together, should a funding deal be agreed.

There could be a substantial attrition rate between requests for funding being received, personal presentations being made and further, more detailed analyses being undertaken by the venture funds. For example, one fund manager spoke of receiving approximately 600 requests for funding in the year prior to the interview. After initial review about 300 of these were discarded. A 'desk review' in more detail was undertaken on the remainder, resulting in about 250 of these being discarded. Venture fund staff went on to carry out further research on the remaining bids and interviewed the management teams. As a result of these interviews, and further analyses and investigations, about 10 requests were finally successful. In another fund, the statistics were: of every 50 requests received, meetings with about 10 management teams were arranged; of these, discussions and meetings continued with three or four teams, resulting in about one successful deal being made. The overall statistics, therefore, on this limited information, suggest that one bid in 50 or 60 is ultimately successful in terms of a deal being made. Also, that the attrition rate after the first meeting with the management team is very high. It should be noted that the rejection need not necessarily be one-sided, because the operating business management may themselves decide not to proceed with their request (see, also, Bruno and Tyebjee, 1985).

The only general feature to emerge from interviews with venture capitalists on the conduct of initial meetings with management teams was that detailed analysis and discussion of financial statements in the business plans was not given a high priority. 'Bean counting', as one chartered accountant, senior venture fund manager, commented 'was of secondary importance'. The management team had to convince the venture capitalists of their grasp of the 'business' – markets, technology, production and so on. At the same time the venture capitalists were observing how the team worked together. There was generally no consistency in the format of the presentation as between individual cases and as between venture funds. One senior venture manager commented: 'It is not a very scientific process', and another: 'We are looking for the nuances of the deal to come out during the course of our chat – we are looking for knowledge, drive and the ability to make a money spinner out of the business'. These are similar features to those looked for by US venture capitalists (Macmillan *et al.*, 1985).

All this is not to say that the financial history and projections and other quantitative data were completely disregarded at these early meetings. One senior fund manager commented that he was trying to establish that 'they [the fund managers] could *believe* the figures'. This fund, along with all the others, did its own research and analyses of the figures but was looking to see how convincing the team were in presenting and substantiating their own data.

Senior fund managers were interested to see that the teams fully understood the problems of underfunding in new technology growth businesses and had allowed adequately for sufficient resources to finance potentially heavy expenditure on, for example, research and development and marketing. At the same time, they wanted to see that there was a product(s) in view in the near term that could be sold to provide a good return. In this context, a senior fund manager commented: 'We look to see that the business will have a good cash flow. If it is high tech, we want to see that the business *will* get a product on the road!'.

There was uniformity across the sample of the venture funds in the *mechanics* of their in-depth evaluation of funding requests. For example, they all checked the quantitative data for consistency with assumptions and calculations. All the funds sought advice and data independently on costs, sales volumes, mixes and prices and so on. These data were collected from a wide range of sources including consultants and contacts the funds had with actual and/or potential supplier and customer organizations. Two of the funds had links with specialist technology consultants. In one of these cases the consultancy carried out detailed analyses of all proposals of a high technology nature that were put to the fund, after they had passed the initial, 'coarse' screening stage.

The networks (see Jarillo, 1989) available to the venture capitalists were, therefore, important enabling systems. These networks existed amongst other venture capitalists, customers and users, university and research establishments, financial institutions, and so on. Contacts with consultants working in marketing, technology, production and so on were frequently used as sounding boards for information produced by management teams. Without well-developed network access, venture funds would have been considerably more exposed to the dense uncertainties surrounding the business ventures which they were evaluating. The networks provided them with a rich source of relevant information and analysis.

The funds had differing perspectives during their in-depth evaluations. For example, one fund commented that they sought 'a full understanding of the threats to the success of the business' and employed their in-house research department to identify these and make assessments upon them. Another fund commented that it deliberately put in a 'negative bias' to eliminate weak proposals. There was a general view that business plans should not be taken at face value and that it was incumbent on funds not only to search out their own data on businesses (which may or may not corroborate those in the business plans) but also to undertake their own analyses in the form that their own experience might dictate was the most appropriate (once again this could diverge from those used in the plans). These exercises were certainly not aimed at 'catching out' the operating business management teams but rather the application of a thorough and professional approach.

Deal Structuring

Deal structuring was not a particular focus for examination in this study. Information on it was obtained, *inter alia*, in the interviews with senior venture fund managers and is commented upon here to give continuity to the process of activity followed by the funds.

The deals, when they were eventually made between venture capitalists (either acting independently or in syndicates) and operating businesses were customized to meet the needs and aims of *all* parties and were generally based on compromise. As one senior venture fund manager commented: 'Deals are usually arrived at at the extremes of greed of all parties'. A bargain was usually struck 'between an equally unwilling buyer and seller!'.

The deals could be typically characterized as follows:

A customized financial package to suit the funding needs of the particular business and prevent, as far as possible, underfunding problems.

The value placed on the operating business involved many subjective evaluations. Normally, at least two senior venture fund managers were involved in agreeing the deal value.

The way that the operating business could received its money was either in a lump sum or on some incremental basis triggered when targets were reached. In the latter case, in theory, funds would only be released if some predetermined milestone/performance targets were achieved by the operating business. Two of the funds positively declined to become involved in these types of deal. This was mainly because they recognized that predetermined plans would almost certainly not be met due to the high degree of uncertainty surrounding new technology businesses. One of the fund managers commented that 'renegotiating' the release of funds was found to lead, in many cases, to a 'souring of relationships', which was counterproductive to the overall management of the investment.

Post Investment Activities

Once a deal had been made between the venture capitalist(s) and operating business then it was in the interests of all parties to ensure that 'the relationship' worked.

Normally, the venture capitalists included an option in their deal agreements to appoint a member of their staff, or another representative, to the board of directors of the operating business. It was not unusual for the venture capitalists to arrange for the appointment of an experienced business person to be chairman of the board. All the venture funds were involved in the development of strategy for the operating businesses in their portfolios. During the interviews with fund managers, one commented that his fund had been known to change operating business managements where it was found that they could or would not take a strategic view. This approach is similar to those observed in US studies (see, for example, Rosenstein, 1988).

The people who were appointed by the venture capital funds to boards of directors of operating businesses frequently faced difficulties with conflicts of interests. The venture fund nominees were an important means of communication – funds to operating businesses and *vice versa*. They helped to translate and interpret much of the informal information that supplemented what were in many cases only basic formal management reports. The latter reports normally contained, *inter alia*, profit and loss accounts, balance sheets, cash flow statements, and so on. In undertaking their monitoring role the venture fund representatives had to retain their objectivity yet at the same time be helpful and co-operative towards operating business managements. Two of the senior venture fund managers commented they had to be careful that their representatives did 'not go native' and become too biased towards the operating businesses and so compromise their positions with respect to the funds.

The venture funds in the study had differing views as to what extent they should become involved in managerial and systems development in operating businesses. Normally, venture funds required a qualified accountant to be employed in the operating businesses once a deal had been made. Also, one of the leading accounting firms was normally appointed as auditor. The senior fund managers were concerned to establish a hallmark for the financial statements that operating businesses produced. Audited figures were important in any subsequent realization of their investment via the sale of shares or the business itself.

Senior venture fund managers commented that it was, in their view, the accountants in the businesses who were primarily responsible for development of systems to ensure that transactions were recorded accurately, analysed and incorporated properly in financial reporting statements. They observed that it was not always the case that cost management systems were given a high priority for development in operating businesses. The ability of the senior venture fund managers themselves to get changes introduced into operating businesses, once funding had been given, was limited. They did not want to insist on all requirements in deal agreements if the benefit from these cost too much in terms of damaging any working relationships that had been developed. One senior venture manager commented: 'We only have two controls: a feather and a hammer – and you only get to use the hammer once'.

616   R. C. SWEETING

Another described the relationship between the fund managers and operating businesses as 'a hovering hands approach'.

Early identification of problems in operating businesses was a key issue to the senior venture fund managers. As noted earlier, two of the funds in the sample, as a matter of routine, called on the assistance of specialist consulting firms that were familiar with identifying and managing the problems that can arise in NTBBs, to help in this process. The funds had developed a close working relationship with these consulting firms who were aware of the styles, requirements and objectives of the respective funds. One senior venture manager commented that he realized that the founders of operating businesses were in a very lonely position and that he actively tried to provide operating business managers with sources of assistance: 'We know a lot of people who can help and our aim is to sort out problems while they are still capable of solution'.

VENTURE CAPITAL FUND ACTIVITY AND LEARNING FROM EXPERIENCE

As might be anticipated with any portfolio of businesses, the performance of individual investments was mixed. For example, one senior fund manager made the following classification of the investments in his fund:

	(%)
'Winners'	13
'Gone bust'	9
'Suffering from under-funding'	13
'Living dead'	4
'Question marks'	61

The venture fund manager's terminology has been used. These assessments are subjective and not clearly defined – apart from 'gone bust'. An interesting figure to note is the large number of businesses where it was not practicable to hazard a guess at the outcome (the 'question marks'). In another fund, the senior manager who was interviewed commented that in his fund's portfolio, only one business investment had 'gone bad' – and that had been because the venture fund had not been able to act swiftly enough 'to change the management'. It was a feature of the venture funds that they were prepared to induce management changes, if necessary, in operating businesses. One senior venture fund manager commented: 'Technology is not a problem – people are'.

The process of assessing operating business out-turns with a view to adjusting procedures for searching out potential investments, screening, evaluation, and so on, was extremely difficult to achieve in any systematic and objective way, and this was recognized by venture fund managers. Attempts to do so were made. The fact is that a considerable folklore can build up about investment appraisal processes. Some observers suggest that certain funds are 'successful', however defined, and therefore have some 'winning formula' – but is this *really* so?

There was, in general, a rapid divergence between operating business budgets and other plans and what unfolded in reality once investments had been made. This was widely expected and therefore when it happened it created little surprise. Surprises were reduced by the close involvement of venture capitalists, through their representatives, in the operating businesses. The process of monitoring and appraisal was generally not done in a scientific or detailed way – it relied largely on the individual senior venture fund manager's judgement. This judgement base was largely built around an individual's experience of *actually* making deals and living with those decisions. There was a high degree of informality in the way much of the information from operating businesses was received and assessed.

Historical data on deals were also collected. One venture capital fund created a 'deal flow' list in which it tracked all deals which passed through the initial vetting procedures. It included, therefore, deals which it accepted *and* those it ultimately rejected and tracked *all* the out-turns. In this way venture fund management were able to reassess their procedures.

A REVISED MODEL

Within the scope of the field research, the summarized Tyebjee and Bruno (1984) model, in table I, was substantially corroborated by the evidence found in four UK venture capital funds. However, it should be noted that it was not a particular focus of this study to examine deal structuring. Also, our understanding of the post-investment phase, especially the development of relationships between venture capitalists and operating business managers will be widened and deepened by further, complementary studies within operating businesses, by undertaking interviews with their managers.

The main difference observed between contemporary UK and early 1980s[4] US venture capitalist activity was in the area of deal orgination. UK venture capitalists were found to be more proactive in putting deals together and searching out potential deals than their US counterparts in the early 1980s. In an effort to find if this was a more general phenomenon, the researcher had an opportunity to interview two US venture capitalists towards the end of the field research in 1989. One of these was in a US associate of one of the sample UK funds and the other was in a separate fund that specialized in investments in NTBBs. They both commented that, in their view, proactivity in deal creation by venture fund staff was now a more frequently adopted approach in the US than it had been in the early 1980s. This may, in part, reflect the reported poor performance of NTBBs and a feeling that the venture capitalists themselves should become more closely involved in putting together and shaping the embryonic stages of these types of businesses in which they planned to invest. Also, as one of the senior venture capital managers in the main study commented, by adopting this proactive approach they were able to be involved with the entrepreneurs at a much earlier stage and so were well placed to get to know and understand them and their businesses. Subsequently they were in a better position to put together a deal. Moreover, if a venture capitalist is approached with a deal so may be several others. This, coupled with syndication, and the general discourse between venture capitalists, may contribute to reduced competition between venture capitalists and the development of consensus views on particular deal opportunities. Consequently perceived 'better' deals may become overpriced as a number of venture capitalists with common interests strive to become involved. Alternatively, deals perceived as 'marginal' and/or 'too risky' may never receive funding. Many early stage NTBB proposals may now be falling into this latter category. This does not mean to say that all venture capitalists necessarily follow a common process in handling deal opportunities.

The range of experience reported by the UK venture capitalists supports Tyebjee and Bruno's (1984) conclusion, following their model validation exercise, that there is considerable heterogeneity in practice between different funds. This is not altogether surprising given the range of influences affecting individual funds, the form and shape of their backing, experience with individual portfolio investments, skills and experience of their staff, and so on. The finding counsels against outlining any detailed form of practice. Indeed it is this variability between funds and their individual flexibility which probably gives them one of their greatest strengths to handle the uncertainties which surround them.

CONCLUDING COMMENTS

UK and US venture capitalists appear to share many similar concerns and adopt comparable practices in the assessment and monitoring of investments. In particular, they attempted to assess, *inter alia*, whether or not: the operating business entrepreneurs had as good a knowledge as could reasonably be expected of target markets; the products/services could achieve a strong market position while at the same time making above-average returns; there was some measure of proprietorial protection for the products/services, at least for such a period as to enable good returns on effort and expense to be recouped by the business, and so on. These criteria were embedded in the work of Tyebjee and Bruno (1984) and other subsequent US work (see, for example, Macmillan *et al.*, 1985; Rea, 1989; Roure and Maidique, 1986). However, an important dimension, which figured more prominently in this UK study than in the US work, was an interest on the part of UK venture capitalists to see that the entrepreneurs planned to capture export market share (especially US market share, as was cited by one fund). This difference may be because US businesses do not see exports as crucial. Certainly there was a perceived need amongst the UK venture capitalists interviewed to see that operating businesses planned to become 'world players'.

There was a general consensus amongst the sample UK venture capitalists that an assessment of the operating business management team capabilities should be made early in the assessment process and elaborated upon as the proposal passed through the screening and evaluation stages. This was consistent with observations in the similar studies in the US (for example, Macmillan *et al.*, 1985). However, it was noted amongst the UK venture capitalists that there was a preparedness to proceed with discussions to make a deal where weaknesses in the management team were recognized but the business concept was otherwise sound – good product/market, proprietorial market position, good returns, and so on. This was associated with venture capitalists who tended to be proactive in their style and had a belief that they could attract good managers to the businesses in which they chose to invest. The sample was too small to give any statistical underpinning to this view, but it is worthy of wider research if only because a proactive style seems to be on the increase amongst venture capitalists. There is already some evidence to suggest that venture capitalists are active in shaping operating business strategy once they have made investments and in reshaping their management teams (see, for example, Rosenstein, 1988).

All this is not to underrate the crucial importance of having in place at the outset a capable management team to make the operating business a success. Research has shown that weak operating business senior management is a dominant cause of failure (Gorman and Sahlman, 1989). It is also in the venture capitalists' interests to seek out operating businesses with managements who possess congruity of management style and interests with those of the venture capitalists. This should enable the synergistic effects betwen the two groups to flourish at an early, critical stage of business development. To seek out and recruit management in order to make good any deficiencies in operating businesses is probably too time consuming for venture capitalists, whose time is in short supply. Also the disruption to the operating business may damage developing relationships.

Not surprisingly, venture capitalists in this study, as well as establishing the professional competencies of members of the management team were seeking to establish whether or not they could simply 'get along with' team members and trust them. The benefits of this mutual understanding and trust were evident even before a deal was made. It facilitated decision-making in an environment where much of the information was 'soft' and many of the assessments were made in unscientific and informal ways (see Macintosh, 1985, for a general discussion of these information handling issues and Rock, 1987, for a venture capitalist's perception of them). The use of networks helped venture capitalists feel their way through the dense uncertainties which surrounded the assessments of proposals received from NTBBs, particularly those in their early stages of development (see Jarillo, 1989 and Littler and Sweeting, 1989 for a general discussion of the use of new technology business networks). These networks included other venture capitalists, suppliers, customers, competitors, and so on.

Once deals have been made, both operating business and venture capital fund managements perceived themselves as working in collaboration. This was consistent with Tyebjee and Bruno's (1984) finding. But does the involvement of venture capitalists really improve matters in an operating business? The suggestion from this research was that venture capitalists can, either directly from their own organization, or their access to networks, bring a wide range of expertise and assistance to the aid of operating business managements. Work in the US (Macmillan *et al.*, 1989) has identified three broad categories of level of involvement by venture capital funds in operating

620   R. C. SWEETING

businesses – limited, moderate and high ('close tracker'). Surprisingly, statistical tests on field study data from 62 venture capital funds suggested that there was no significant difference in operating business performance between these three different levels of involvement. Moreover, certain activities, namely searching for management candidates in the case of moderate and 'close tracker' funds, had a negative correlation with operating business performance. Notwithstanding this, there is a view held by UK venture capitalists that their involvement does improve matters. Nash (1988), the managing director of a leading UK venture fund which invests in NTBBs and who was the 1988 chairman of the British Venture Capital Association, commented:

> If a good relationship is established between the venture capitalist and the company in which he invests, then the evidence is that the company will achieve a higher valuation than is typical for a company without venture capital involvement.

All the venture capital funds in the UK sample wanted not only a relatively close relationship with operating business managements but also an open one. They recognized that many of the signals from the operating businesses that needed to be picked up in the monitoring process and subsequently translated and understood, did not flow through formal means such as profit and loss accounts and balance sheets. The venture capitalists needed to sensitize themselves to the gossip and innuendo of the operating businesses, having first given themselves access to it. This was a time-consuming process but paid dividends by allowing venture capitalists to become aware of and involved with operating business problems early, while they were still capable of solution. Similar behaviour has been observed in US studies (see, for example, Gorman and Sahlman, 1989; Macmillan *et al.*, 1989). The UK venture capitalists were prepared to act decisively and proactively when they saw their investment being threatened fundamentally. Their US counterparts have been observed to act in much the same way (Gorman and Sahlman, 1989; Macmillan *et al.*, 1989; Rosenstein, 1988), this despite the almost inevitable consequences of destroying any 'special relationship' that might have hitherto been cultivated.

A focus of the work reported in this article was the funding of NTBBs in their early stages of development, mainly when their needs are for start-up funding. There was some evidence, both from the interviews with venture capitalist practitioners and industry statistics, to demonstrate a decline of interest in these types of investments. More extensive research is required to identify if this is in fact a trend. If this is the case, then work is needed to identify whether there are conceptual problems with the provision of venture capital funds to these types of operating businesses, or whether there are implementation problems which are tractable. There must be concern, if for no other reason than venture capital has hitherto been perceived as an appropriate and available type of funding for these types of businesses.

UK VENTURE CAPITAL FUNDING 621

NOTES

*The author is very grateful for the helpful comments received from anonymous referees on an earlier draft of this article.

[1] This proactive behaviour might take the form of searching out operating businesses in areas of technology and/or markets which interested them and/or putting together management teams and business opportunities.

[2] For a discussion of how these processes operate in these types of environment see, for example, Macintosh (1985).

[3] An expression in general use in the UK for the problem of obtaining relatively small (£200K or less) capital sums for funding purposes from financial institutions. For a discussion of this and related problems in the electronics sector see NEDO (1986).

[4] This was the base period for many of the observations incorporated in the Tyebjee and Bruno (1984) model of venture capitalist activity.

REFERENCES

BANK OF ENGLAND (1982). 'Venture capital'. *Bank of England Quarterly Bulletin*, December, 511–13.

BANNOCK, G. (1987). *Britain in the 1980s: Enterprise Reborn?*'. London: Investors in Industry.

BRUNO, A. V. and TYEBJEE, T. T. (1985). 'The entrepreneur's search for capital'. *Journal of Business Venturing*, 1, 61–74.

BVCA (1989). 'Report on investment activity – 1988'. London: British Venture Capital Association.

EADIE, A. (1990). 'Specialist tactics in pursuit of the sexy sector.' *Independent*, London, 14 March, 26.

GORMAN, M. and SAHLMAN, W. A. (1989). 'What do venture capitalists do?'. *Journal of Business Venturing*, 4, 231–48.

INDEPENDENT (1990). 'Venture capital survey'. *Independent*, London, 14 March, 23.

JARILLO, J. C. (1989). 'Entrepreneurship and growth: the strategic use of external resources'. *Journal of Business Venturing*, 4, 133–47.

LITTLER, D. A. and SWEETING, R. C. (1989). 'Management accounting: the challenge of technological innovation – management accounting in technological businesses'. London: Chartered Institute of Management Accountants.

LORENZ, T. (1985). *Venture Capital Today*. Cambridge: Woodhead Faulkner.

MACINTOSH, N. B. (1985). *The Social Software of Accounting and Information Systems*. Chichester: John Wiley.

MACMILLAN, I. C., KULOW, D. M. and KHOYLIAN, R. (1989). 'Venture capitalists' involvement in their investments: extent and performance'. *Journal of Business Venturing*, 4, 27–47.

MACMILLAN, I. C., SIEGEL, R. and SUBBA NARASIMHA, P. N. (1985). 'Criteria used by venture capitalist to evaluate new venture proposals'. *Journal of Business Venturing*, 1, 119–28.

MACMILLAN, I. C., ZEMANN, L. and SUBBA NARASIMHA, P. N. (1987). 'Criteria distinguishing successful from unsuccessful ventures in the venture screening process'. *Journal of Business Venturing*, 2, 123–37.

NASH, J. (1988). 'From small beginnings'. *International Chartered Accountants Review*, 65–8.

622   R. C. SWEETING

NEDO (1986). *Finance for Growth*. London: National Economic Development Office.
REA, R. H. (1989). 'Factors affecting success and failure of seed capital/start-up negotiations'. *Journal of Business Venturing*, **4**, 149–58.
ROCK, A. (1987). 'Strategy vs tactics from a venture capitalist'. *Harvard Business Review*, November–December, 63–7.
ROSENSTEIN, J. (1988). 'The board and strategy: venture capital and high technology' *Journal of Business Venturing*, **3**, 159–70.
ROURE, J. B. and MAIDIQUE, M. A. (1986). 'Linking prefunding factors and high technology venture success: an exploratory study'. *Journal of Business Venturing*, **1**, 295–306.
TYEBJEE, T. T. and BRUNO, A. V. (1984). 'A model of venture capitalist investment activity'. *Management Science*, **30**, 9, 1051–66.

[16]

Accounting and Business Research, Vol. 25. No. 99. pp. 186–196, 1995

Post Investment Demand for Accounting Information by Venture Capitalists

Falconer Mitchell, Gavin C. Reid and Nicholas G. Terry*

Abstract—The key concepts of principal-agent analysis are utilised to investigate influences on venture capitalists' accounting information requirements as used in their dealings with investees. The findings are based on structured interviews held with 20 leading venture capitalists, managing funds which together comprise over three quarters of all UK venture capital funds. The results confirm that a number of the key concepts of principal-agent analysis are mirrored in the financial communication process between venture capital investors and their investees. They reveal the venture capitalists' appreciation of the dangers of moral hazard and information asymmetry. It is shown that, as a consequence, their information demands are designed to provide safeguards through bonding arrangements. These establish and define an information flow which can be utilised as the basis for frequent and regular monitoring of the investee.

Introduction

This paper explores the venture capitalist's demand for accounting information. Within a principal-agent framework, it examines, through data gathered by direct interviews, the information requirements of this increasingly important specialist investor. The data provide a unique opportunity to study the methods used to meet the needs of these sophisticated users of investees' accounting information.

The focus of the paper is on the individual practices of investors in obtaining and processing information as a basis for investment decisions. It is in the tradition of research that attempts to directly investigate investor behaviour. For example, in the UK, studies by Lee and Tweedie (1981), Arnold and Moizer (1984) and Day (1986) have respectively utilised interview, questionnaire and process tracing methods to gather data on institutional investors' perceptions of the relative importance of accounting information, the types and mechanics of the information analyses that they undertake, their comprehension of financial information and their views on how information provision could be improved. This research has, in general, confirmed the high degree of importance accorded to the financial statements provided in interim and annual shareholder reports, both as confirmation of previous estimates and as inputs to future financial forecasts.

While the above studies emphasise stock market investments, this study examines the demand for accounting information by institutional investors in a less restrictive context. It is concerned particularly with the accounting portions of the information flows to venture capitalist investors (VCIs) from their investee firms. This provides the opportunity to investigate the institutional investor's demands for information in a situation where their demand for information can directly influence supply. The VCIs can negotiate their own terms of access to financial information as part of the investment deal struck with the individual investee.[1] Information provision in itself can therefore be variable; but it can also extend considerably

*The authors are, respectively, professor of management accounting. University of Edinburgh; professor of economics and director of CRIEFF, University of St Andrews; and senior lecturer in finance, University of Edinburgh.
The research upon which this paper is based was funded by the Esmée-Fairbairn Trust. the Carnegie Trust and the Centre for Financial Markets Research, University of Edinburgh. The authors are grateful for the comments of participants at the Scottish Economics Society's Conference, April 1994, and the British Accounting Association's Scottish Conference, September 1994, where earlier versions of the paper were presented. The authors are grateful for the comments of two anonymous referees, which have materially improved the final form of this paper. We remain responsible for any errors of omission or commission that this paper may yet contain.
Correspondence should be addressed to Professor Falconer Mitchell, Department of Accounting and Business Method, University of Edinburgh, William Robertson Building. 50 George Square, Edinburgh EH8 9JY.

[1] According to the VCI interviewees in this study, their formal rights to accounting information are enshrined in the subscription agreement which provides the legal basis of the investment relationship. While interviewees were willing to discuss the nature and implications of this subscription agreement, there was extreme reluctance to provide examples on grounds, first, of confidentiality to clients and, second, on commercial grounds because the subscription agreement is a key source of their competitive advantage. Data gathered in this study were therefore restricted to the oral information provided to the researchers in interviews.

Table 1
Total Venture Capital
Investment, 1985–1993

Year	Value £m
1985	325
1986	46
1987	1,029
1988	1,394
1989	1,647
1990	1,394
1991	989
1992	1,434
1993	1,422

Source: British Venture Capital
Association (BVCA).

investor will expect to earn an adequate investment return within a few years through one of a variety of exit routes, such as stock market flotation, sale to a trade buyer or sale to management. While the US has been the major location for the development of venture capital, over the last decade the growth in venture capital funds in the UK has been dramatic (see Table 1). Growth of funds invested grew rapidly from £325m in 1985 to a peak of £1,647m in 1989. After a slight falling away of investment since then, it has recovered well. Indeed, in the UK, most of the leading financial institutions have created venture capital funds (cf. BVCA Handbook) and a range of autonomous organisations have also emerged. It is also interesting to note that many of the staff managing these funds have trained as professional accountants (Venture Economics, 1986). Their demands for accounting information can therefore be expected to reflect a high level of expertise. Indeed, previous studies have indicated that accounting information is a key component of any decision to commit funds (Tybjee and Bruno, 1984; MacMillan et al., 1987). It is therefore likely to be an important aspect of the ongoing assessment by VCIs of investment outcomes.

beyond that contained in conventional shareholder reports. In this less regulated situation, examination of the practices developed by UK VCIs in obtaining and using accounting information will provide additional and novel insights into the information needs of the institutional investor.[2] This paper explores the pattern of demand for accounting information by the VCI and examines how these demands may be influenced by the nature of the relationship between the two parties to the investment, viewed from a principal-agent (or simply 'agency') perspective.

It proceeds by providing background information on venture capital investment and principal-agent analysis. The sample is then considered and its relation to the population of VCIs in the UK. The results are then presented under the headings of accounting information flows, information asymmetry and moral hazard safeguards. The paper ends with a detailed discussion of results, and a brief conclusion.

A number of researchers have shown that the post investment relations between VCIs and investees can be close and constructive with the VCI giving advice, utilising business contacts and facilitating finance, in addition to monitoring performance in a variety of ways (Gorman and Sahlman, 1989; MacMillan et al., 1989). Studies have shown that venture capitalists do vary in their interaction with investees, altering the extent of their involvement in response to their perception of the need for assistance (MacMillan et al., 1989; Sweeting, 1991).

While differences in the VCI/investee relationship and in the extent of contact between them are apparent, the reasons for these variations have not been so deeply explored. One approach to the study of external investor-investee relations that has stimulated increasing interest and provided a basis for analysing small firms has already shown promise (Eisenhardt, 1989; Sapienza, 1989) and it has recently been suggested that the VCI/investee relationship would be amenable to this type of analysis (Harrison and Mason, 1992; Mitchell et al., 1992).

Venture capital investment

Venture capital involves the provision of equity finance to firms that are typically small in size, are unquoted and provide an opportunity for 'gain through growth potential', contingent on acquiring finance to permit new investment. Normally, the

Principal-agent analysis

An applied version of principal-agent analysis has been adopted to provide a framework for the investor/investee relationship in this study of accounting information used by VCIs. In a principal-agent relationship, one party (the agent) acts on behalf of another party (the principal). The agent is not fully supervised, and has a measure of

---

[2] It must, however, be borne in mind that there are significant differences in the nature of established stock market and venture capital investments. The latter will typically involve smaller firms and possibly more novel products or services. Their risk levels and the information needs of investors might therefore be considered greater. Thus, the evidence of this study may also reflect partly the impact of increased risk on the institutional investors' demand for information. However, the existence of portfolios of investments and the larger equity stakes normally held by the management team may be viewed to some extent as risk limiting factors.

independence, which he may be tempted to exploit to avoid risk and to shirk on effort. The principal therefore tries to construct a contract that will give the agent an incentive to share risk efficiently and to optimise his effort (Reid, 1987).

The use of the principal-agent model in accounting research was initiated by the likes of Baiman (1982) and consolidated in textbook treatments such as Strong and Walker (1987). Applied principal-agent analysis has been used on the client-VCI relationship by Sahlman (1990). Here, we take the analysis one step further down the tier of superior-subordinate relations, and look at the VCI's relation to the investee. Since the work of Chan, Siegel and Thakor (1990) it has been established that the VCI can be treated as a risk-neutral principal, with the investee as a risk-averse agent. Much further work has since been accomplished along these lines (e.g., Gompers and Lerner, 1994; Admati and Pfleiderer, 1994). A special interest has also emerged in explicit modelling of information and communication, especially as regards its control implications (e.g., Gordon, Loeb and Stark, 1990; and Cohen, Loeb and Stark, 1992).

Despite this flourishing of theoretical work, the empirical character of the VCI/investee relationship is still very poorly understood. This cannot be resolved by the use of secondary source data: it requires paying deliberate attention to the details of real contracting practices. The purpose of this study is to provide exactly such detail, and to explore its practical implications for risk-sharing and incentive alignment.

At the post investment stage a principal-agent (or 'agency') relationship exists between the VCI and the investee. The VCI assumes the role of principal and the investee firm's directors the role of agent. Their relationship places the principal in a position where the problem of *moral hazard* has to be addressed. The directors of the investee firm, acting in self-interest and having relinquished full ownership of the firm (perhaps subsequently retaining only a minority share), are motivated to consume perquisites ('perks') and to limit effort. They will obtain 100% of the benefit from these acts but will bear only a proportion (based on their remaining ownership stake) of their cost. The principal may therefore, through the subscription agreement or by other less formal means, attempt to establish arrangements to attenuate the effects of this moral hazard. These can take the form of *bonding* or *bond posting* whereby the principal imposes penalties on the investees if certain levels of performance are not met and establishes performance boundaries (e.g., gearing ratio standards) and decision autonomy limits (asset disposals) for the agent.

More positively, *incentives* may be provided through the reward package set for the agent (e.g., performance linked pay). Moreover, the principal may attempt to influence the agent by *monitoring* the effectiveness of his/her performance. Performance measurement (or monitoring) will also be needed to operationalise bonding and the incentivated reward structure. For a principal such as a VCI, monitoring by direct ·observation of the agent's actions is impractical and therefore requires a flow of information. This is usually focused on the outcomes or results of the agent's actions.

The use of such information to assess and motivate the agent suffers from two disadvantages. First, it is difficult for a principal to identify to what extent any outcome is due to good fortune rather than the agent's effort and ability. Second, the agent possesses a greater familiarity with business operations than the principal, as well as having control over the generation of information. There is an imbalance or *asymmetry* of information. Given the pursuit of self-interest the agent may misrepresent performance or provide information selectively in order to make outcomes appear more favourable. Again, the principal may react by establishing disclosure rules and a syntax to govern the information flows.

The agency theory model is thus heavily dependent on information flows between agent and principal. Accounting, which provides financial measurements of inputs and outcomes, constitutes an integral part of this flow. It certainly is an important influence on those ex ante expectations that drive investment decisions. Equally, it appears logical that accounting information would be used in the ex post assessment of performance. In addition, it may help to limit the effects of moral hazard by providing a basis for bonding and for monitoring the agent. The problem of information asymmetry is, however, one which is not simply solved by information per se, but by consideration of the agent's control over the accounting systems of the firm.

This study examines how VCIs, as principals, establish and use accounting information flows from their investee firms, as agents. It does this within a principal-agent (or agency) theory framework, utilising the above concepts. It is therefore primarily concerned with monitoring behaviour. Within this context the views of these investors on moral hazard and information asymmetry are also investigated.

The sample

The study involved gathering data from 20 VCIs, adopting a methodology that has several precedents in the development of user oriented research in accounting (e.g., Day, 1986; Mitchell et al., 1989). The sample frame was given by the alphabetic listing of venture capital funds in the *Venture Capital Report* (fourth edition), which

Table 2
Main Characteristics of Sample and Population

	(1) Sample values n = 20	(2) Population values n = 38
	(Mean values with standard deviations in brackets)	
VCFUND (£m)	67.3	72.9
	(60.2)	(93.9)
AVERG (£m)	0.98	0.78
	(1.12)	(0.65)
MINEQ	6.1	6.3
	(8.2)	(6.7)
MAXEQ	57.6	56.7
	(19.6)	(18.2)
FREQIN	15.5	11.4
	(6.1)	(2.2)
EMPLOY	26.6	14.0
	(37.7)	(16.6)
TIMESCALE	5.0	7.9
	(1.2)	(2.3)
NEWINV	15.4	10.2
	(20.8)	(10.4)
VCEXEC	7.0	6.5
	(6.2)	(4.3)
TFUNVAL (£m)	38.8	32.6
	(18.6)	(17.2)

Notes:
(a) **Definitions of variables**
  VCFUND   venture capital funds under management (£m)
  AVERG   average value of investments made (£m)
  MINEQ   minimum equity stake taken (%)
  MAXEQ   maximum equity stake taken (%)
  FREQIN   number of involvements per annum with investee
  TIMESCALE
               timescale for investment (in years)
  EMPLOY   total number of employees
  NEWINV   number of new investments made each year
  VCEXEC   total number of full-time venture capital executives
  TFUNVAL total value of funds invested at valuation (£m)
(b) **Sampling frame** based on listing of 47 funds in Cary (1989) *Venture Capital Report: Guide to Venture Capital in the UK*, 4th edition. Sample values in column (1) are based on a random sample of 20 from this listing, with values obtained during interviews. Population values in column (2) are based on 5th edition of same work (1991), computed for 38 remaining funds from original sampling frame.

provides a comprehensive listing of active venture capital investors in the UK. A simple random sample of 20 was selected, and the selected venture capitalists were approached by pre-letter and subsequently by telephone. If it was not possible to conclude an interview, the next name on the list was selected. The original sample frame had 47 funds in it, and the sample selected, 20. Table 2 lists the main characteristics of the population and sample, giving mean values for each characteristic, with the standard deviation in brackets.

There is a general similarity between the characteristics of the sample of funds and the population of funds. For example, venture capital funds under management are £67.3m and £72.9m in the sample and population, respectively. Further, the total value of funds invested is £38.8m and £32.6m in the sample and population respectively. There is one notable exception to this, the total number of employees. This has a high sample standard deviation (37.6) mainly because two firms had 106 and 150 employees respectively. With them excluded, the mean and standard deviations of employees in the sample are 13.8 and 9.5 respectively, which are similar to the population values. Thus while a useful feature of our sample is that it includes the two largest players in the UK venture capital market, in a sense, being the largest, they are not typical. Subject to this caveat, the sample appears to give a good representative picture of the UK venture capital industry.

A useful device for providing a sense of what the sample is like is to present a statistical picture of the typical, average, or modal VCI in the sample. This generalises the presentation of data in Table 2. This information is based on 'basic data sheets' that VCIs were requested to complete at the time of interview. By business type VCIs were: banking (35%); independents (40%); public sector (10%); subsidiaries (10%); and investment managers (5%). Thus in the sample the typical VCI is an independent. It had no industry preference (avoiding the cynically named 'bleeding edge' of technology) and a slight geographical preference for the UK. It had been in existence for six years. About 550 proposals were received each year, of which some 165 (30%) were reviewed, leading to 15 new investment involvements (3%). Typically, it took about 15 weeks from proposal to the completion of investment.

In terms of size, the typical VCI of the sample had 27 employees and seven venture capital executives. It had about £67m funds under management, and £24m available to invest. Total funds invested at cost were £45m and at valuation £67m. The smallest and largest investments that would normally be contemplated were £0.3m and £4.1m respectively. In practice, the smallest investment made was £0.4m. The average investment size was £1m. By type of investment, the breakdown was: start-up (11%); development (45%); buyout (40%); other (4%). Thus the typical VCI involvement was in development capital provision, with the 'pure' form of VC investment accounting for 4% or less. The minimum and maximum equity stakes contemplated were 6% and 57% respectively. Typically, management/monitoring fees were charged, as were directors' fees. The desired timescale for investment was five years. By preferred exit route the breakdown was: management repurchase (5%); trade sale (47%); market listing/flotation (19%); other (28%). Thus the typical preferred exit route was a trade sale. The breakdown by type of investment was: sole (35%); lead (33%); consortium (31%). Thus, sole investment was slightly the preferred investment involvement.

In terms of monitoring, the average frequency of reporting was 15 times per year in the sample. Representation on the board had frequencies: always (35%); almost always (20%); sometimes (30%). Typically, the VCI always required representation on the board of directors. The required internal rate of return for investee involvement ('hurdle rate') was 32%. In 30% of

investment involvements the equity stake could be bought back.

These summary statistics have been provided to give the reader a background feeling for the VCIs examined below. The analysis itself is largely qualitative; and how the qualitative data were gathered is explained below.

A structured interview—concerning VCIs' use of and views on their investees' accounting information, utilising the information aspects of principal-agent theory as discussed above—was conducted with each subject. The main headings of the interview agenda were: types of information, asymmetries of information, sharing and trading information, information selection, information error, and costs of information. Interviews were conducted between June 1992 and September 1993. Two researchers were involved in each interview, one as interviewer and one as recorder. Interviews varied in duration from one and a half to two and a half hours. As well as the interview material, accounting data, financial PR, brochures, etc., were also collected. A site visit and tour were common, as was an introduction to key personnel.

The interviewees' firms accounted for over three-quarters of UK venture capital finance provision. Based on available biographies, interviewees (who were nominated by their firms) had, in general, considerable (typically 12 years) experience in the venture capital industry and often a familiarity with accounting methods (e.g., a professional accounting qualification and/or qualifications in finance, economics and business). Amongst the full-time executives of each VC fund almost inevitably there was an accountant, though s/he was not always nominated as the interviewee for the study.

Accounting information flows

Types of Information

Despite the existence of a variety of contacts and information sources in investee firms (e.g., client meetings, board membership), accounting information was a universal requirement of the VCIs. Indeed, one said that: 'We won't invest in a company unless they have a good accounting system.' Four respondents remarked on the value of receiving the annual audited accounting report, and in the main, the accounting information VCIs requested and obtained was of a fairly conventional composition. Central to the information flow were the three core financial statements: balance sheet; profit and loss account; and cash flow statement. The importance of the cash flow statement for assessing an investee's performance was particularly emphasised by over half of the interviewees.

Although these three financial statements are all a required part of the content of the annual shareholders report, the actual form of disclosure to the VCI extended significantly beyond statutory requirements in six distinct ways:

1. The frequency of their provision was considerably increased from the statutory one of once or (in the case of interim reports) twice a year. Twelve VCIs obtained them monthly and five at least monthly. They were actively used to monitor investees' performance over these short time periods. For the most part they were, in fact, the key components of the investee firms' management accounting package, and were therefore readily available for distribution to the VCI. The other three VCIs also utilised the management accounting information of their clients but did not specify exactly the time period requirement for its provision.

2. As a part of the management accounting package these statements were expressed in a much more detailed form than those provided to shareholders. For example, the profit and loss account would disclose the components of cost of sales, identify all overheads, and possibly show profitability segmented by product line and by corporate division.

3. In one quarter of the cases it was specifically mentioned that these financial results were assessed within the context of the firm's budgeted performance. In many cases this provided a direct link to the forecasts on which investment decisions were made. Variance from budget provided an important 'attention directing' signal to the VCI.

4. In a small number of cases (two) it was indicated that all of this information had to be provided within a strict time limit from the end of the reporting period.

5. The supplementation of the financial information by a qualitative explanatory summary of performance by the management team was specified by a significant minority (six) of VCIs.

6. Further types of information were highlighted by several VCIs as being an important part of information disclosure by investees. These comprised: capacity utilisation levels (one investee); further non-financial measures of performance (one); capital expenditure analysis (two); order book position (two); and the auditors' management letter (one). Whilst important, these additions merely modify, but do not challenge, the primacy accorded to the conventional accounting reports.

Variability of Information Requirements

The degree of detail, content and frequency of information all represented sources of possible variation in the nature of information required and received by VCIs. They were specifically asked whether their information flow varied over time (longitudinally) or at a point in time (cross-sectionally) for investees in their portfolios. Table 3 summarises their responses.

Over a third of the VCIs had fixed requirements for information provision. They did not permit variation from them for any reason. In four cases the inability of the investee to produce information up to the standard normally expected was the main way in which information flow was constrained. Such investees were typically small, start-up businesses. However, the capabilities of investees to generate a good quality of financial information did develop over time. One VCI suggested that, as investees developed their skills in information provision, information overload could become problematic, saying: 'Information varies by firm capability—sometimes it's too detailed and sophisticated.' Deviations from the expected performance levels by the investee also prompted changes in the requests for information provided. Two VCIs increased the requirement for information when the investee's performance dipped below target. They considered tighter monitoring was necessary in such circumstances. On the other hand, two VCIs reduced their information demands when performance was better than expected. Direct comments by VCIs on each of these responses to negative and positive variations were: 'Yes, there can be fundamental change if there are problems, for example, with customers or new projects', and, 'As it gets better and the more we feel comfortable, the less we want to stress them in this area.'

The maturity of investees' projects also influenced the need for information for seven of the VCIs. This was evident in two contrasting ways. Three venture capitalists accepted that less information would be available on new investees, particularly when they were small and at, or near, start-up. These VCIs appeared to appreciate that other factors might require priority. One said: 'I expect very little when they start out. I like to get the cash book balanced. Often I don't even get that and I don't press for it too much. I think it's a waste of time. They're working to build a business. As they develop, accounting information becomes more important.' The other four VCIs were of the opinion that information flows could be reduced over time as the client became established. An exception to this would be if re-financing were required, where the control aspect would be expected to be more significant once more. This aside, more information was required in the early years where investors had less familiarity with investees and there was more risk associated with the investments. However, for one of the four, the lighter information burden on more mature investees was due to a more liberal policy on information provision having been adopted when drawing up subscription agreements in previous years. A tightening of information requirements

Table 3
Information Variation

	n^*
No variation in information provision	7 firms
Variation caused by investee's inability to provide required information	4 firms
Variation caused by changing circumstances of investee (e.g. new projects, poor performance)	4 firms
Variation by maturity of investee's projects	7 firms

Note: *Two venture capitali ts indicated two influencing factors.

since then had resulted in more recent investees being required to provide more information.

Information Cost

Only two investors indicated that cost was a critical factor in influencing their information gathering activities. Both had found it impractical to access all the information that they would ideally have liked, and were prepared to compromise on cost grounds. For example, one VCI would have liked to take comprehensive soundings from all its customers on investee performance but restricted this to the 'occasional one or two'.

All the others did not consider cost to be a serious constraint on obtaining relevant information. The typical views of these VCIs are reflected in the following statements:

'... very important to get information and if it does cost more so be it. There is no greater crime than to report back "don't know".'

'... we are conscious of the cost of information but this does not deter us from getting it if we need it'.

'I'm not ever aware of having used cost as a basis for not getting information.'

Several VCIs argued that the cost of information provision was mainly borne by the investee, and in that sense was not an investor's problem. Whilst it was true that investees were required to provide the information asked of them by investors, many VCIs observed that the costs had already been borne in meeting the information demands which any normal firm would find being generated routinely by the investees' own senior management. The incremental (i.e. marginal) cost of providing the data to investors was therefore negligible.

The costs to the venture capitalist of processing the information provided by investees was only raised as an important issue by two investors. They were trying to avoid 'information overload'. If it were threatened, they required curtailment of the information supplied:

'Processing it is the problem. You can only absorb so much data and information. We occasionally shout "stop!".'

'We like to think we don't ask for information we can't process. It is important to home in on one of the key variables. We are not into information overload.'

Information asymmetry

Investee Informational Advantage

All VCIs accepted that their investees had some informational advantage over them. Indeed, several remarked that the absence of such advantage would be good reason for not investing in the managerial team concerned. In other words, part of the gain to be obtained from entering into a contract with the investee was in sharing this expertise. Investees were expected to be experts in the type of business that they ran.

The nature of the informational advantage was perceived as having different aspects to it. Central was the sectoral technical expertise and the operational knowledge of the specific firm management was inevitably assumed to possess. Their more direct exposure to the business situation and their participation in day-to-day decision-making typically imbued them with a unique knowledge of their firm's current affairs and prospects. Being positioned at the 'sharp end' ensured that they certainly obtained information on problems *before* the VCI (one respondent). Another VCI attributed the inevitability of informational advantage in part at least to the existence of a portfolio of investments which all required attention by him. The size and diversity of the portfolio precluded the development of a particularly detailed familiarity (matching that of management) with any of them.

Investors (five) held that investees may attempt to hide operational problems or delay reporting bad news, even though this information was needed by VCIs at the earliest opportunity. It was emphasised that a VCI did consider it an obligation of investees to 'put all their cards on the table from the start', with one suggesting that 'if we suspected we weren't getting full answers we wouldn't continue the relationship'. In addition to investees hiding problems, another VCI suggested that those with a particularly good performance might mask it to allow the management team to achieve a preferable exit deal by changing backers. It is difficult to judge how serious a comment this was, as there is not yet an active secondary market in venture capital investments in the UK. Therefore it would be difficult for management to operationalise this without raising the suspicions of the existing backers.

Three factors were also cited as *limiting* the adverse effects of management's informational advantage. First, the nature of the investee's line of business could be kept simple (one respondent) with complex businesses such as biotechnology and microelectronics being excluded. In fact only four out of the 20 VCIs expressed an exclusive preference for high technology involvements. Second, the relationships established were based on trust. 'We buy integrity not information' was how one venture capitalist expressed this idea. Another said, 'We have faith in the people. If we didn't, we shouldn't have invested.' Third, a congruence in the interests of both venture capitalist and investee was considered to exist, centred on the substantial ownership of shares in the firm by both parties. Therefore the personal attachment of management to the company and the cost of perquisite consumption ('perks') would be greater than normally found in the stock market context. The investee's informational advantage was also thought to be limited by the tendency of VCIs to have development-stage and sectoral specialisations.

Selective Information

Most investors (17) considered their investees to be selective in the information they provided. The three who did not thought that their rigorous selection procedures limited adverse selection. This ensured that only those who would be 'open with us' were chosen for investment. All of the others accepted that full disclosure did not occur. One remarked that they have 'a rational motivation to misrepresent' and another that they 'give you what you want to hear'. Most (11 respondents) felt that an optimistic bias did tend to pervade reported information. In particular, aspects of poor performance, a deterioration in the market, or a decline in customer relations, were not fully communicated, and only reported when it became unavoidable.

Information Conformity with Reality

We have seen that monitoring may be hampered by the deliberate manipulation of information by the investee. It is also possible that monitoring is handicapped by the intrinsic inability of accounting information to reflect the reality of performance. Seventeen investors considered that this was an additional problem affecting the usefulness of the accounting information provided to them by investees.

The most prominent contributory factor was the time lag with which accounting statements reflected reality. This was not merely associated with the delay in producing financial statements. Several VCIs mentioned that an accrual accounting based profit figure could indicate an apparent level of success at the time of reporting which was not matched by corresponding cash generation. Thus conflicting signals of reality were often conveyed by the information. There was also some appreciation that performance could not be properly assessed from accounts in the short run. As one VCI remarked: 'In the first two years we don't really know how the client [investee] is doing.' Others suggested that monthly information has to be accumulated in order to allow trends to become apparent.

Other less classifiable problems of matching information with reality included the following. In one case the investee's accounting information was used to translate physical product reality into financial terms. This obscured the fact that the investee's firm was not actually selling the product for which they were financed. It was also noted that errors could be made in the construction of management accounts and these could mislead investors. Moreover, accounting reports may not include vital contextual information on the market situation that may affect an investee's performance (e.g., a tripling of a competitor's capacity output).

Serious problems or 'disasters' were often not adequately represented in accounts. Indeed two VCIs noted that they had needed to 'send someone in' in these circumstances to find out what was happening. Finally, one VCI reported that accounting policy changes by an investee created an inconsistency in translating events into reported information, which had the potential to result in misleading assessments of their progress.

Moral hazard safeguards

Vetting Investees' Accounting Systems

All but one of the VCIs vetted their clients' systems. The one VCI who did not was in the process of developing a means of so doing. Seven VCIs observed that their vetting tended to be done as a one-off exercise at the time of making the investment. This was done to ensure that a reasonable information flow would be forthcoming in the post-investment period and also to ensure that management were able to control and make decisions on an informed basis. The vetting tended to cover key business systems (e.g., sales, credit control and product costing). Where deficiencies were identified changes were required as a condition of investment. To illustrate, in one case, a VCI imposed basic cash control systems on many of his small investees.

In some cases vetting was not done directly by the investor. Five of the venture capitalists, at least on some occasions, hired firms of professional accountants to produce formal reports (incorporating recommendations for improvement) on the investees' accounting systems. A further five consulted the investees' auditors. As one VCI put it, by depending on the auditors' familiarity with financial systems he could 'get comfort that the information which is produced will be reliable and accurate'.

Investee Audit

The statutory audit of investee companies was of considerable interest to the venture capitalist. All but one VCI claimed to have an impact on the audit process. The nature of any influence exerted varied. It could be both direct and indirect. Most commonly it took the form of participating in the selection of the auditor.[3] Six venture capitalists imposed their choice of audit firm, often as a condition of investment. The change to a 'large respectable' auditor (usually one of the Big Six), was what they required of the investee.

However, the VCI's influence extended beyond auditor selection in a number of ways. One venture capitalist met with the appointed auditor at an early stage to 'let them know we are investors and that we are relying on their report'.[4] Another discussed the investee's accounting policies with the auditor, and had influenced them in one case by having the levels of provision raised to ensure 'there would be no skeletons in the cupboard to hinder improvement when recession ends'. The results of the audit were also of interest, with six of the venture capitalists monitoring the auditors' feedback through membership of the investee audit committee and by scrutiny of the management letter.

Direct Access to the Investee's Accounting System

There was an almost even split amongst the VCIs sampled on this issue. Eleven had no direct access to their investees' accounting systems. However, several of these venture capitalists made the point that they could request any accounting information they wished, and one mentioned that he could instigate a third party investigation. Another with no direct access did use the client's auditor as a surrogate source of information. Again, the requirement to trust the investee was mentioned by one of the venture capitalists. Of the nine venture capitalists claiming direct access to investees' accounting systems, three achieved this through directorships, while one stated that such access was a condition in the subscription agreement. The others gave no specific justification for their right of access.

Discussion of results

This study prompts the following observations on the use of accounting information by institutional investors of the venture capital variety. In this investment sector the absence of stock market (and arguably 'efficient') prices for shares precludes the use of both technical and beta analysis. The investor has to rely on fundamental analysis. Fortunately, this is facilitated by the absence of stock market-like restrictions on information access. This allows VCIs to effect a more liberal expression of their information needs.

It was clear from the results of the study that accounting information is a key requirement of this type of investor. Superficially their information demands are centred on the same three financial statements as those conventionally provided to stock market shareholders. However, there was considerable evidence that their information needs extended well beyond those generated by traditional external financial accounting methods. Although conventional accounting statements remained the centrepiece of the accounting information flow, they had to be provided more *regularly* (typically monthly) and in a *more detailed form* (as per the management accounts). Moreover they usually had to be set in the context of agreed budgets and narrative explanations, and were subject to regular query. The monitoring behaviour of these sophisticated information users revealed a keenness to maintain as current a financial information flow as possible.

This greater intensity of scrutiny of investee performance was important in motivating the agent to act in accordance with the principal's objectives. It also ensured that the investor was well placed to react promptly to any deviations from plan. In the absence of a stock market the VCI is unable to effect an exit in the short term. As a result of this 'lock-in' effect, the VCI's main reaction to difficulties experienced by the investee has to be constructive. Thus VCIs can bring to bear their financing expertise, can utilise their

---

[3] This does indicate a greater than normal shareholder involvement in the appointment of the auditor. In practice, it is common for the appointment and the re-appointment of the auditor to be simply approved by shareholders at an AGM on the basis of a nomination by the company directors.

[4] The nature of the auditors' liability to shareholders has long been a contentious issue (Gwilliam, 1987). This type of behaviour could be construed as an attempt to establish a relationship which could facilitate litigation by the VCI in the event of business failure. In effect, it may be viewed as another means of confronting the problem of moral hazard.

network of business contacts and in extremis can exercise their powers to replace management.

Their main concern appeared to be to ensure losses were disclosed promptly, and that difficulties were thereby contained, rather than being allowed to intensify because they were unidentified. The avoidance of operational 'disasters' (the occasional outcome of extreme downside risk), which could seriously affect the value of the investment, appeared to be a primary concern underlying VCIs' monitoring behaviour. They were certainly keen to identify perquisite consumption ('perks') by their agents, but their perception of the main threat of moral hazard was that it lay mainly in the investee's ability to delay the disclosure of serious problems that could threaten their firm's survival. While procrastination could bring short-term benefit to the agent (e.g., in terms of continued remuneration, avoidance of loss of face and the opportunity autonomously to 'turn things round'), it did heighten the risk of ultimately experiencing a substantial loss.

The *existence* of moral hazard is a common problem across different situations. It is intrinsic to risk-sharing situations with information asymmetry. However, the *response* to moral hazard (generally governed by its severity) varies across investor-investee involvements. Among the VCIs interviewed there was little experience with start-up and early-stage investment where proactive policies are common. The emphasis rather was on development capital and buyouts. These differ mainly by adverse selection (a pre-contract problem of information asymmetry and risk classification) rather than moral hazard (with its post-contract problems of efficient risk sharing and effort elicitation). The paper gives an account of variations to be found in practice in the treatment of moral hazard problems through monitoring policies.

While the nature of the financial information flow provided by investees was generally similar, there was evidence to suggest that variations were allowed. These permitted variations to be rewards for good performance or recognition of a sound track record. In such cases a reduction in reporting frequency was permitted, although no VCI would allow information to be received at less than quarterly intervals. This pattern of behaviour indicated that for investees who were perceived by VCIs to be in a relatively low risk category, a more conventional approach to information provision was often deemed acceptable, taking the stock exchange disclosure protocol as a benchmark. This behaviour is as would be predicted for VCIs subject to moral hazard of the sort described above.

The constructive role of VCIs extended to their proactive influence in the development of management accounting systems in investee firms. For example, they were prepared to design some of their clients' systems and would buy-in consultancy expertise to improve their investees' situation. The emphasis on budgeting and cash flow analysis reinforces VCIs' prime concern for the viability of their investees' enterprises. Their contractual involvements can therefore guarantee that no less than the basic level of information necessary for operational effectiveness is available to the investee firm's management. Indeed, this is probably one of the more beneficial consequences of venture capital involvement.

Our study shows that information asymmetry was ubiquitous in investor-investee relations in the UK venture capital industry. This was generally recognised and was considered particularly serious if it delayed the identification of deteriorating situations. These were the particular province of proactive or interventionist actions by VCIs. Even the high degree of information access accorded to VCIs did not completely remove this problem. Indeed, in some situations, it was felt that conventional accounting methods could compound the difficulties of a crisis situation because of their susceptibility to 'managerial masking' of the real, current financial position of the investee. While there was no suggestion that the comprehension of the information provided constituted a significant barrier to communication between the two parties, masking or selection of information could degrade its quality and volume.

Conclusions

The results presented above confirm that a number of the key concepts of principal-agent analysis are mirrored in the financial communication process between VCIs and their investees. They reveal VCIs' appreciation of the dangers of *moral hazard*, against which some safeguard is sought, through their *bonding* arrangements, to establish a sound supply of accounting information. This contributes to their *monitoring* of investees' performance, which is typically maintained on a regular short-term basis. A concern with *information asymmetry* is also evident in their doubts about the completeness and reliability of this information, particularly because of its managerial origins.

However, in a context in which the VCI has the power to influence information supply fairly directly, there has been no pressure applied to firms to make them diverge from conventional accounting procedures. Traditional financial statements remain at the centre of the reporting process. A marked increase in the frequency of their provision, and the incorporation of considerable management accounting detail in their construction, appear to be the main differences from the regulated accounting supply. These findings tend to confirm the preoccupation of institutions with the short-term performance of investments. This occurs even when the option of a short-term decision to sell is not commonly available and it therefore suggests that close monitoring is indeed viewed by the VCI as a means of combating moral hazard.

Further, these findings suggest that VCIs, in their role as institutional investors who use accounting information, do not represent a radical force for change in financial reporting. This lack of desire for change in the substance of accounting procedures is probably unconnected with the perceived relevance or otherwise of information flowing to them, for user studies show that institutional investors as a class are enthusiastic users of financial statements. Thus their apparent acceptance of the status quo should simply be regarded as indicating a substantial degree of satisfaction with conventional financial statements. VCIs are certainly practised in their use, and this facility with them undoubtedly enhances the quality of investors' attempts to monitor, to the end of uncovering (and, if need be, rectifying) the consequences of moral hazard.

References

Admati, Anat R. and Pfleiderer, Paul (1994), 'Robust Financial Contracting and the Role of Venture Capitalists', *Journal of Finance*, 49(2).

Arnold, J. and Moizer, P. (1984), 'A Survey of the Methods Used by UK Investment Analysts to Appraise Investments in Ordinary Shares', *Accounting and Business Research*, Summer.

Baiman, S. (1982), 'Agency Research in Managerial Accounting: A Survey', *Journal of Accounting*, 1.

BVCA (1994), *Directory* (London: Jeffrey Pellin).

Cary, L. (1989), *The Venture Capital Report Guide to Venture Capital in Europe*, 4th edition (Venture Capital Report).

Chan, Y.-S., Siegel, D. and Thakor, A. V. (1990), 'Learning, Corporate Control and Performance Requirements in Venture Capital Contracts', *International Economic Review*, 31.

Cohen, S. I., Loeb, M. P. and Stark, A. W. (1992), 'Separating Controllable Performance from Non-Controllable Performance: The Case of Optimal Procurement Contracting', *Management Accounting Research*, 3.

Day, J. F. S. (1986), 'The Use of Annual Reports by UK Investment Analysts', *Accounting and Business Research*, Autumn.

Eisenhardt, K. M. (1989), 'Agency Theory: An Assessment and Review', *Academy of Management Review*, Vol. 14, No. 1.

Gompers, P. and Lerner, J. (1994), 'An Analysis of Compensation in the US Venture Capital Partnership', forthcoming *Journal of Political Economy*.

Gordon, L. A., Loeb, M. P. and Stark, A. W. (1990), 'Capital Budgeting and the Value of Information', *Management Accounting Research*, 1.

Gorman, M. and Sahlman, W. A. (1989), 'What Do Venture Capitalists Do?', *Journal of Business Venturing*, No. 4.

Gwilliam, D. (1987), 'A Survey of Auditing Research', *Research Studies in Accounting Series* (ICAEW/Prentice-Hall).

Harrison, R. and Mason, C. (1992), 'The Roles of Investors in Entrepreneurial Companies: A Comparison of Informal Investors and Venture Capitalists', Venture Capital Research Project: Working Paper No. 5 (University of Southampton).

Lee, T. A. and Tweedie, D. P. (1981), *The Institutional Investor and Financial Information* (Institute of Chartered Accountants in England and Wales).

Macmillan, I. C., Kulow, D. M. and Khoylian, R. (1989), 'Venture Capitalist's Involvement in their Investments: Extent and Performance', *Journal of Business Venturing*, No. 4, 1989.

Macmillan, I. C., Siegel, R. and Subba Narasimha, P. N. (1987), 'Criteria Used by Venture Capitalists to Evaluate New Venture Proposals', *Journal of Business Venturing*, No. 1.

Mitchell, F., Reid, G. C. and Terry, N. (1992), 'Some Agency Aspects of Venture Capital Investment Behaviour', Centre for Financial Markets Research Working Paper (University of Edinburgh).

Mitchell, F., Sams, I. and White, P. (1989), 'Institutional Investors and Industrial Relations Data: An Empirical Survey', *Industrial Relations Journal*, Summer.

Reid, G. C. (1987), *Theories of Industrial Organization* (Oxford: Basil Blackwell).

Sahlman, W. A. (1990), 'The Structure and Governance of Venture Capital Organizations', *Journal of Financial Economics*, 27.

Sapienza, H. J. (1989), 'Variations in Venture Capitalist–Entrepreneur Relations: Antecedents and Consequences', University of Maryland Working Paper.

Strong, Norman and Walker, M. (1987), *Information and Capital Markets* (Oxford: Basil Blackwell).

Sweeting, R. C. (1991), 'Early-Stage New Technology-Based Businesses: Interactions with Venture Capitalists and the Development of Accounting Techniques and Procedures', *British Accounting Review*, Vol. 23, No. 1.

Tybjee, T. T. and Bruno, A. V. (1984), 'A Model of Venture Capitalist Investment Activity', *Management Science*, 30 September.

Venture Economics (1986), 'Human Resources of the UK Venture Capital Industry', *UK Venture Capital Journal*, March.

[17]

THE "LIVING DEAD" PHENOMENON IN VENTURE CAPITAL INVESTMENTS

JOHN C. RUHNKA
University of Tennessee

HOWARD D. FELDMAN
THOMAS J. DEAN
University of Colorado—Boulder

EXECUTIVE SUMMARY

"Living dead" investments represent the middle ground of venture capital investing outcomes, lying between "winners" that produce adequate multiples of return on investment and "losers" that result in loss of invested funds. Living dead investments are typically mid- to later-stage ventures that are economically self-sustaining, but that fail to achieve levels of sales growth or profitability necessary to produce attractive final rates of return or exit opportunities for their venture capital investors. This article reports the results of a survey of 80 U.S. venture capital firms that investigated the living dead phenomenon and strategies used by venture capital investors to deal with living dead companies.

Venture capital managers reported that living dead conditions were usually caused by deficiencies in investee management, particularly in responding to market conditions, as well as markets that were too small or two slow growing, missed opportunities, and unanticipated competition. The timeframe of this phenomenon is typically after product development and initial sales have been achieved and during the "rollout" stage of pushing for rapid growth and market share. The key characteristic of living dead companies in the eyes of their investors is their very poor prospects for producing a successful exit for their investors, usually because of more limited growth than originally anticipated or inadequate profitability. Although the rate of return boundaries for living dead companies were wide, ranging from a rate of return (ROR) of 0% on the low side to 10% on the high side, most were described by venture capital managers as economically self-sustaining in the near term, and a number of living dead companies had reached $5 M to $15 M in revenues. Thus the concept of a "living dead investment" is specific to the context of venture capital-backed investing, and represents primarily a failure of investor expectations as distinct from an economic failure of the venture. Overall, the 80 venture capital firms projected that 20.6% of their investments would end up as "living dead" companies by the point of final distribution.

When living dead situations occur, venture capital managers use a number of strategies to

Address correspondence to Dr. John C. Ruhnka, 24 Field Way, Cambridge CB1 4RW, England.

The authors wish to acknowledge the valuable assistance of Graduate Research Assistant Kevin Jerome in the data collection phase of this study.

Journal of Business Venturing 7, 137–155
© 1992 Elsevier Science Publishing Co., Inc., 655 Avenue of the Americas, New York, NY 10010

0883-9026/92/$5.00

137

138   J.C. RUHNKA ET AL.

*attempt to turnaround these companies or to achieve an exit. The most-often-used strategy was to
attempt to sell or merge the company, but usually only after one or more preliminary steps to turnaround
the company had been attempted first, including replacing investee management, "repositioning" the
product, and making revisions to the venture opportunity strategy. Firms that projected lower percentages of living dead investments at distribution, as well as firms using high rate-of-return targets
for their portfolios, were slightly more likely to use active intervention strategies to turnaround or
liquidate living dead investments than firms that expected higher percentages of living dead companies
at distribution or firms that used lower rate-of-return targets. Overall, venture capital managers were
able to achieve a successful turnaround or exit in only 55.9% of living dead situations, and these
results were unrelated to the age of the venture capital firms, their size, or the relative availability
of investor personnel for monitoring investees. This result, in conjunction with the high number of
causal factors identified for living dead situations that involved adverse market factors, suggests that
successful or unsuccessful outcomes with living dead investments may be largely determined by the
underlying causation of the living dead problems, and whether or not these causal factors are controllable by the venture capital investors. Inadequate investee management and internal operational
problems can potentially be remedied by venture capital investors, whereas markets that are too small
or too slow-growing, or severe industry oversupply conditions are largely outside of their control.*

INTRODUCTION

In recent years, venture capital-backed companies that have become "winners" for their
investors, such as Compaq Computer, Lotus Development, and Federal Express, have received the lion's share of attention from the business press. Researchers that have investigated
causal factors in the performance of venture capital investments, on the other hand, have
tended to focus on investment failures and the causation for these failures. Examples include
Hill and Hlavacek (1977), Bruno et al. (1986), Bruno and Leidecker (1987), and MacMillan
et al. (1987). Gorman and Sahlman (1989), for example, argue that "failure is at the very
least endemic to the venture capital process, an expected commonplace event; in some cases,
the process itself may even promote failure." As yet little attention has been paid to the
critical middle ground of venture capital investments, "living dead" companies, that were
once expected to become winners but that stall out in revenue growth and profitability in
the later stages of their development.

Living dead investments are of critical concern to venture capital investors, for most
are mid- or later-stage ventures that have successfully survived the perils of start-up, which
were once expected to produce a high-multiple return on investment. Additionally, living
dead companies impose heavy costs in time and management resources on their venture
capital investors in attempts to "turnaround" or liquidate these investments, whether or not
these efforts succeed. Most importantly, the failure of living dead companies to achieve
projected sales growth or strong profitability means that chances for a high-multiple exit,
or in some cases any exit at all, diminish radically. Finally, the sub-par ROR on living dead
investments acts as a continuing drag on compounding portfolio ROR, reducing the chances
of their investors achieving attractive final ROR the longer these companies remain in their
portfolios.

METHODOLOGY

Interviews with eight managing partners from six venture capital firms in the Denver-Boulder
area were used to identify a variety of definitions and boundaries surrounding the living
dead phenomenon, potential causal factors in living dead companies, and strategies used to

TABLE 1 Representativeness of Sample of 80 VC Firms

Aggregate investments	Sample of 80 VC firms	1988 U.S. VC Industry,% of total firms
	% of total firms	
0–$10 million	5.41	32.68
$10–24 million	8.11	22.09
$25–49 million	10.81	18.31
$50–74 million	17.57	9.23
$75–99 million	8.11	4.24
$100–199 million	25.68	8.62
Over $200 million	24.32	4.84

Source: *Venture Capital Journal*, March 1989.

deal with such investments. This information was used to design a four-page questionnaire that was mailed to 320 venture capital firms listed in the 1988 Directory of the National Venture Capital Association. Telephone follow-up enabled completed questionnaires to be obtained for 80 U.S. venture capital firms representing a response rate of 25%.

Table 1 shows the distribution of our sample of 80 venture capital firms by aggregate funds under management compared with the U.S. venture capital industry in 1988 as reported in the *Venture Capital Journal*. This indicates that our 80-firm sample significantly under-represented smaller firms ($0–24 million funds), was a fairly good fit with the venture capital industry in mid-sized firms ($25 million to $99 million under management), and overrepresented firms with over $100 million in funds. In fact, our sample contained one-half of all U.S. venture capital firms with $100 million or more in funds under management.

VENTURE CAPITAL FIRM DEMOGRAPHICS

We first examined the demographics of our sample of venture capital firms as to the size and age of the firms, numbers of monitoring personnel, the percent of their deals in which they were lead investor, aggregate funds under management, and the size of their portfolios. Table 2 shows the mean figures for our sample.

TABLE 2 Demographics of Sample of VC Firms

	Mean	SD	Range	N
Age of firm in years	10.9	7.9	2–44	76
Number of monitoring personnel	6.2	4.5	2–30	77
% of deals in which lead investor	55.6%	25.4	2–100%	76
Funds under management (millions)	$147.2	162.3	2–700	74
Number of portfolios	2.6	7.8	1–12	65

Investments	Average	Median		N
Age of all portfolios	5.1 yrs	5.0 yrs		65
Size of portfolios (millions)	$37.2	$25		63
Number of companies per portfolio	22.4	20		65

140   J.C. RUHNKA ET AL.

Size and Age of the Firms

For the purpose of examining the relationship of the size and age of our venture capital firms with other variables, we used four size categories ("smaller" firms $0–$25 million in investments; "mid-sized firms" $26–$100 million; "large firms" $101–$300 million; and "very large firms" of over $300 million in investments) and six age categories. This grouping of our sample of 80 firms produced the following distributions (Table 3).

TABLE 3   Size and Age Distributions of Our Sample

Size of firm	N	% of our sample	Age of firm	N	% of our sample
$0–$25 million	10	13.51	0–4 yrs	7	9.2
$26–$100 million	27	36.49	5–9 yrs	40	52.6
$101–$300 million	24	32.43	10–14 yrs	6	7.9
Over $300 million	13	17.57	15–19 yrs	6	7.9
			20–24 yrs	12	15.8
			25+ yrs	5	6.6

Relationship of size to age

Size of VC firm	Av. no. years in operation
$0–$25 million	5.3 yrs
$26–$100 million	9.8 yrs
$101–$300 million	14.8 yrs
over $300 million	12.9 yrs

Investing Strategies, Portfolio Distributions, and Rate of Return Targets

Based on the responses from our preliminary interviews, and a search of the literature, venture capital firms were asked to select from one of three choices to characterize the portfolio strategy they were presently using: (1) "invest primarily in early-stage deals;" (2) "invest in more, smaller, early-stage deals and fewer, but larger, mid- and later-stage deals;" and (3)"invest mostly in safer mid- and later-stage deals." Table 4 shows these primary investment strategies by size an age of the firms. It can be seen that smaller firms reported a strategy of investing primarily in early-stage deals and less in mid- and later-stage deals than did the larger firms. These differences in portfolio strategies were less noticeable when the firms were differentiated by age.

The venture capital firms were also asked to estimate the percentage of their investments made in early-stage (seed and start-up), middle-stage, and later-stage deals, as well as the percentage of funds invested in companies in each stage of development. Table 5 displays these data.

It can be seen that as a percentage of total numbers of investments, the firms invested in 52.1% early-stage, 25.8% middle-stage, and 23.3% later-stage companies. The larger and older firms invested in smaller percentages of early-stage investments and a larger percentage of later-stage investments than did smaller and younger firms.

We next asked the venture capital firms to indicate the target rate of return that they expected for their portfolios at distribution, expressed in annual compound ROR (Table 6). An analysis of variance procedure indicated that the variance relationship between the size of the venture capital (VC) firm and target ROR was not significant (p = 0.66). The

TABLE 4   Primary Portfolio Strategy by Size and Age of VC Firms (%)

	Early stage	Early & mid	Mid & later
Size of firm			
$0–$25 million	60	20	20
$26–$100 million	52	20	28
$101–$300 million	50	41	9
Over $300 million	31	23	46
Age of firm			
0–4 yrs	57	14	29
5–9 yrs	53	23.5	23.5
10–14 yrs	33	50	17
15–19 yrs	50	33	17
20–24 yrs	42	33	25
25+ yrs	40	20	40
All firms	47.2	29.1	23.6

correlation between age of the firm and expected target ROR ($r = -0.142$, $p = 0.124$) was also not significant, but indicated a negative correlation, i.e., it appears that younger firms had slightly higher final ROR expectations on average than did the older firms.

VC Firm Staffing

We examined the staffing of our sample of VC firms in order to test the hypothesis that the relative availability or scarcity of personnel with responsibility for monitoring the perfor-

TABLE 5   Stage of Development of Investments by Size and Age of VC Firms

	Seed/start-up % Inv / % Funds	Middle-stage % Inv / % Funds	Later-stage % Inv / % Funds
Size of firms[a]			
$0–$25 million	77.0 / 66.4	18.9 / 8.3	9.3 / 14.2
$26–$100 million	59.6 / 51.2	25.7 / 29.3	14.7 / 19.5
$101–$300 million	51.6 / 43.0	25.8 / 27.9	22.6 / 29.1
Over $300 million	28.2 / 23.1	24.4 / 20.2	47.3 / 56.6
Age of firm[a]			
0–4 yrs	66.1 / 60.4	27.0 / 30.3	12.5 / 15.8
5–9 yrs	50.6 / 40.9	25.8 / 24.2	24.6 / 31.7
10–14 yrs	63.8 / 48.8	21.2 / 26.2	15.0 / 25.0
15–19 yrs	47.3 / 42.7	25.8 / 27.2	26.8 / 30.2
20–24 yrs	57.7 / 50.4	25.9 / 23.8	16.4 / 25.8
25+ yrs	40.2 / 29.2	25.0 / 31.0	34.8 / 39.8
All firms	52.1 / 43.8	25.8 / 25.6	23.3 / 29.8

[a] $N = 65$. Some of respondents' estimated distributions did not total to 100%.

142   J.C. RUHNKA ET AL.

TABLE 6   Target ROR on VC Portfolios Expected at Distribution

	Mean target ROR (%)
Size of firm	
$0–$25 million	27.1
$26–$100 million	28.9
$101–$300 million	31.3
over $300 million	26.1
Age of firm	
0–4 yrs	34.2
5–9 yrs	27.1
10–14 yrs	38.7
15–19 yrs	29.2
20–24 yrs	27.3
25+ yrs	29.2
All firms	29.1

mance of portfolio investments might influence the strategies used for dealing with living dead investments, and the successful or unsuccessful outcomes achieved with these companies. Table 7 shows the percentage of deals in which each firm indicated it was "lead investor," and the number of portfolio investments for each VC staffer with responsibility for monitoring investees. It can be seen that the lead investor role did not differ significantly by size or age of the firms. Analysis of variance indicated that VC firm size was not a factor in the number of investees per monitoring personnel ($p = 0.115$), but newer firms (0–9 years in business) had significantly fewer investments per monitoring staffer than did older firms ($p = 0.000$).

TABLE 7   Percentage of Investments in Which "Lead" Investor and Number of Investments per Monitoring Personnel

	% of deals in which "lead" investor (%)	Mean no. investments per monitor
Size of firm		
$0–$25 million	51	5.8
$26–$100 million	58	8.8
$101–$300 million	53	10.7
over $300 million	66	10.0
Age of firm		
0–4 yrs	56	5.5
5–9 yrs	55	7.8
10–14 yrs	44	10.0
15–19 yrs	60	17.5
20–24 yrs	60	11.7
25+ yrs	44	11.7
All firms	55.6	9.0

TABLE 8 Percentages of "Winners," "Living Dead," and "Losers" Projected at Distribution

	"Winners"	"Living dead"	"Losers"
Size of firm			
$0–$25 million	65.8	19.7	15.0
$26–$100 million	59.9	19.3	19.8
$101–$300 million	39.0	21.6	33.1
over $300 million	68.4	21.2	10.4
Age of firm			
0–4 yrs	83.2	9.5	7.3
5–9 yrs	56.9	21.7	20.7
10–14 yrs	33.8	18.8	47.5
15–19 yrs	50.2	26.2	23.7
20–24 yrs	55.6	23.5	20.9
25 + yrs	48	34	18
All firms	55.2	20.6	20.6

Respondents' estimated distributions did not total to 100% in some cases.

PORTFOLIO DISTRIBUTIONS OF LIVING DEAD INVESTMENTS

Because of the difficulties in obtaining ROR data for completed investments of private VC firms and associated confidentiality and comparability issues, and the fact that the average age of the portfolios of our firms was 5.1 years or only at about the halfway point to final distribution, the firms were asked to project the final results of their present portfolio investments at the point of distribution. Since the VC managers we interviewed were comfortable with distinctions between "winners," "living dead", and "losers" for classifying investments, we asked each firm in our sample to project the percentages of "winners," "living dead," and "losers" in their existing portfolios at the point of final distribution. These results, representing 3,418 separate investments, are displayed in Table 8 by both the size and age of the responding firms.

Overall, our sample projected 55.2% "winners," 20.6% "living dead," and 20.6% "losers" among their investments at distribution. There was a negative relationship between the age of the firms and the percentage of winners projected at distribution (r = −0.393, p = 0.001), i.e., younger firms expected a slightly larger percentage of winners and smaller percentages of living dead deals and losers than did the older firms. The higher projections of winners by the younger firms in our sample must be viewed with caution due to the longer average length of time remaining until harvest with the investment of younger firms, as well as their lack of long-term experience compared with the older firms.

Since we did not specify the ROR boundaries to be used for classifying winners, living dead, and losers, our distributions of portfolio outcomes are not directly comparable with prior ROR analyses of distributed portfolios such as those by Huntsman and Hoban (1980) or Dehudy et al. (1981). The firms in our sample may have differed slightly in the ROR boundaries they used between "winners" and "living dead." The 80 firms reported a significant range of lower and upper annual ROR boundaries for "living dead" investments, with a median of 0% annual ROR on the low side to a 10% annual ROR on the high side. Thus, undoubtedly, some winners may have been characterized as living dead deals, or vice versa, if another VC firm was making the distinctions, although we would expect these differences at the margins to cancel out due to the large number of firms involved.

Venture Capital

144 J.C. RUHNKA ET AL.

TABLE 9 Percentage of "Winners," "Living Dead," and "Losers" Projected at Distribution and Reported Investment Strategy of VC Firms

Investment strategy used	"Winners"	"Living dead"	"Losers"
Invest primarily in early-stage deals	53.9	24.5	19.0
More early-stage deals + fewer, larger, mid- to later-stage deals	47.7	18.8	28.2
Invest mostly in safer mid- and later-stage deals	69.8	16.1	14.1

The performance of VC investments may also be expected to vary between firms depending upon when the bulk of their investments were made. Bygrave et al. (1989) reported that VC funds started in 1978–79 were performing at more than 30% annual ROR, whereas funds started in 1980–84 were performing at less than 10% annual ROR due to the large influx of new venture funds in that period and the lower valuations received by investors.

We next examined the relationship of the projected distributions of winners, living dead, and losers by the firms with their reported primary portfolio strategies, and Table 9 displays the results.

As expected, winners predominated regardless of the investment strategy used. However, none of the correlations was statistically significant. Intuitively, it appears that firms characterizing their portfolio strategy as "investing primarily in safe mid- and later-stage deals" anticipated higher percentages of winners and smaller percentages of living dead and losers at distribution than did firms that reported they invested primarily in early-stage deals, or firms that invested in "mixed" portfolios consisting of more, smaller, early-stage deals combined with fewer and larger mid- and later-stage deals.

CHARACTERISTICS OF LIVING DEAD INVESTMENTS

VC managers were asked to identify the key characteristics of their "living dead" investments. This was an open-ended question and the 165 responses were grouped into mutually exclusive categories using content analysis techniques (Table 10).

This grouping of responses reveals that the most-often-mentioned characteristic of a "living dead" company was the very poor chances for a successful exit by its investors.

TABLE 10 Major Charcteristics of Living Dead Investments

	Number	% of total
Poor exit potential	39	24
Self-sustaining	33	20
Limited growth potential	31	19
Inadequate profitability	31	19
Operational/management problems	12	7
Miscellaneous factors	19	12
Total	165	100

Without opportunities for an exit, VC investments are almost totally illiquid, and for all intents and purposes are equivalent to a loss of investment for their investors. This fear of poor chances for a successful exit in turn appears to be the result of two other key characteristics of living dead companies that tied for third place: limited growth potential and inadequate profitability.

Substantial growth potential and adequate profitability are both important preconditions to a successful high-multiple exit by VC investors. For a harvest via an initial public offering (IPO), a minimum of $15 million or more in annual revenues is usually required, along with substantial profitability. Accordingly, when a VC-backed company stalls in its growth to "IPO-sized" revenues, this damages its investors' chances for an exit via an IPO, irrespective of the profitability of the venture, although perhaps not their chances for a lower-multiple harvest via a sale or merger with a larger established company, or a leveraged buy-out by investee management or others. A lack of adequate profitability, on the other hand, can damage investors' chances for an exit via an IPO, sale, merger, or leveraged buy-out, irrespective of the size of the venture, and often indicates serious competitive or management deficits.

It is perhaps surprising that the second-most-mentioned characteristic for living dead companies was "self-sustaining," since in most small business development paradigms a new venture that develops to the point of becoming economically self-sustaining is viewed as an economic "success." In the context of VC investing, by contrast, an investment is not deemed a "success" unless its VC investors, within an investment horizon of 8 to 12 years, can liquidate their investment at an ROR that adequately rewards the risks incurred and the holding period for the investment. The 80 VC firms in our sample reported a mean portfolio target ROR of 29.1% compounded annually. Thus over a holding period of 10 years, an investment would have to grow almost 13 times in value to achieve the average target ROR used by these firms.

Thus, we conclude that the concept of a "living dead" investment is *unique* to the context of VC investing in high-growth-potential companies, and represents a *failure of investor expectations* as distinct from an economic failure of the venture. The characteristics reported for living dead investments indicated that most such companies were still "living," and a number of respondents reported that living dead companies often reached $5 to $15 million in revenues, but still will not achieve the high growth and profitability required for high investment multiples at exit. The difference between "winners" and "living dead" investments was expressed by one venture capitalist in agency theory terms as follows. Whereas "winners" are fulfilling both their debt and equity contract expectations, "living dead" investments are generally maintaining a positive cash flow and meeting their debt contracts, but are not generating enough revenue growth or profitability to fulfill their investors' expectations, or their equity contracts.

Other characteristics less often identified for living dead companies involved operational and management problems. These included factors such as "technology leapfrogged," business plan goals not met, and inadequate investee management. Several VC managers observed that "living dead" status was not always viewed as a disaster by investee founders. Some founders may be secretly relieved that their company is not going to grow so large that technologically focused founders will have to be supplanted by market or financially oriented managers. Finally, 12% of the characteristics identified for living dead investments were miscellaneous factors including: additional cash infusion needed, shrinking market, and negative cash flows. This indicates that not all living dead companies are able to remain self-sustaining for very long.

146   J.C. RUHNKA ET AL.

TABLE 11   The Onset of the Living Dead Phenomenon in VC Investments

Stage	Frequency	%
Seed	0	0
Start-up	2	2.5
1st stage	12	15.4
Rollout	38	48.7
Mezzanine	25	32.0

TIMEFRAME OF THE LIVING DEAD PHENOMENON

The fact that VC managers described most living dead investments as self-sustaining suggests that the stage-wise development of living dead ventures has typically progressed to the point where sufficient revenues and cash flows are being generated to keep the enterprise alive for at least the near term. Early stage (seed stage and start-up stage), and first and second round investment failures are usually "write-offs" in the first two or three years of existence due to fundamental problems with the venture opportunity that cannot be fixed, such as a failure to achieve cost-effective production, or the realization that a commercially viable market does not exist.

VC managers were asked to indicate on a "stage of development" timeline the point at which their investments usually slipped into living dead status. The timeline had six points: (1) seed; (2) start-up; (3) first stage; (4) rollout; (5) mezzanine; and (6) exit stage. The mean point of "living dead" onset on this timeline was 3.95 and the median was 4.00, indicating that the living dead phenomenon usually occurs *after* the stage when product development has been completed and initial sales achieved, and in the "rollout" stage of ramping-up production and pushing for rapid sales growth and market share. Table 11 indicates that "living dead" investments are a mid- to later-stage developmental phenomenon that usually occur when a company attempts to push for rapid revenue growth and market share necessary to produce high-multiple returns for its VC investors.

CAUSATION

We asked VC managers to rate the importance of a number of factors derived from a literature search of causes of failure in VC-backed investments in the *causation* of living dead investments, distinguishing between high-tech and non-high-tech ventures. The five-point Likert scale used ranged from (1) "no importance" to (5) "most important," and the mean scores for each factor have been ranked in their order of importance (Table 12).

A rating of 4 or more indicated "very important" to "most important," and "management weaknesses" with a rating of 4.2 for high-tech companies and 4.5 for non-high-tech companies was identified by the VC firms as the most important causal factor in most living dead investments. VC managers reported that this often took the form of investee management paying insufficient attention to competitive demands of the marketplace, or improperly positioning the product or market strategy to respond to competitive shifts that had occurred since the venture got underway. The next four most important causal factors, carrying rankings of "some importance" to "very important," all dealt with market and competitive factors. This result suggests that living dead situations often occur when new ventures fully enter the marketplace and either the market is too small or too slow growing, or else the

TABLE 12 Causal Factors in High-Tech and Non-High-Tech Living Dead Investments

Causal factors	High-tech[a]	Rank	Non-high-tech[a]	Rank
Management weaknesses	4.2	1	4.5	1
Absolute size of market too small	3.8	2	3.9	2
Market growth too slow	3.8	3	3.3	3
Investee missed market opportunity	3.4	4	3.1	4
Unforeseen competition arises	3.2	5	3.1	5
Technology obsolete	2.8	6	2.0	10
Follow-on funding unavailable	2.8	7	2.9	6
Divergence in goals among VC investors	2.7	8	2.7	8
Investee undercapitalized	2.6	9	2.9	7
Material costs escalate	2.2	10	2.4	9

[a] 1 = no importance; 2 = little importance; 3 = some importance; 4 = very important; 5 = most important.

venture does not have sufficient competitive advantages to achieve rapid growth or adequate profitability in this environment. It is also noteworthy that factors such as "technology obsoleted," "material costs escalate," and "investee undercapitalized" were generally not perceived to be critical in causing living dead situations for VC-backed companies. Thus, in the perception of VC investors, the key causes of living dead situations were inadequate investee management and adverse market and competitive conditions.

STRATEGIES FOR DEALING WITH LIVING DEAD INVESTMENTS

In our interviews with Denver-Boulder VC managers we identified seven different actions that these firms reported having used to respond to living dead situations. In our questionnaire, VC managers were asked to estimate how often they used each of these seven actions in dealing with their living dead companies on a geometric scale ranging from 1 (used in only 0–5% of their living dead cases) to 5 (used in 75–100% of their living dead cases). Table 13 displays these strategies for dealing with living dead companies by the size of responding VC firms, and Table 14 displays the strategies used by age of the firms.

It can be seen that the most-often-used strategy (used in more than 75% of living dead situations) was an attempt to sell or merge the company—typically to a larger company with

TABLE 13 Strategies Used for Dealing with Living Dead Investments by Size of VC Firms

Strategy used	Average rating[a] by size category				
	0–25M	26–100M	101–300M	300M +	All firms
Sell or merge investee	4.6	4.5	4.8	4.6	4.6
Replace management	3.6	3.7	3.8	3.7	3.7
VC decision-making	3.6	3.6	3.6	3.2	3.5
Reposition product	4.0	3.2	3.4	3.5	3.4
Let company go sideways	2.7	2.4	2.6	2.3	2.5
Fund follow-on product	2.9	2.3	2.4	2.0	2.3
Force a cash-out	1.5	1.8	2.1	2.2	1.9

[a] Key: 1 = used in 0–5% of cases; 2 = used in 5–25% of cases; 3 = used in 25–50% of cases; 4 = used in 50–75% of cases; 5 = used in 75–100% of cases.

148 J.C. RUHNKA ET AL.

TABLE 14 Strategies Used for Dealing with Living Dead Investments by Age of VC Firms

Strategy used	Average rating[a] by age category					
	0–4	5–9	10–14	15–19	20–24	25+
Sell or merge investee	4.2	4.7	5.0	4.3	4.7	4.8
Replace management	4.2	3.7	3.6	2.7	3.8	4.4
VC decision-making	4.0	3.5	4.4	3.2	3.2	4.0
Reposition product	3.3	3.6	3.6	3.2	3.2	3.2
Let company go sideways	1.3	2.6	3.0	2.4	2.5	2.2
Fund follow-on product	2.3	2.5	2.6	2.2	1.7	2.0
Force a cash-out	1.0	2.0	1.0	2.2	2.1	2.4

[a]**Key:** 1 = used in 0–5% of cases; 2 = used in 5–25% of cases; 3 = used in 25–50% of cases; 4 = used in 50–75% of cases; 5 = used in 75–100% of cases.

a related product line or technology. The next three most-often-used strategies (replacing investee management, active investor involvement in investee decision-making, and "repositioning" the product), were attempted in 50% or more of living dead situations. Whereas none of the relationships between size or age of the VC firms and strategies used was statistically significant, firms over four years of age appeared to be a little more willing to let their living dead go sideways, i.e., to let them hang on with no further infusions of capital, to replace management a bit less often, and to more frequently try to sell or merge their living dead companies than younger firms.

We also asked VC firms if they used a sequence of actions in trying to turnaround or liquidate their living dead investments, and, if so, what sequence was usually followed. Table 15 shows these responses.

It can be seen that while attempting to sell or merge a living dead investment was the most-often-used strategy (constituting 35% of all actions attempted), it typically was used only *after* one or more other steps to turnaround the company had been tried first, such as replacing investee management or repositioning the product. Whereas 33.8% of the re-

TABLE 15 Sequence of Actions Used with Living Dead Investments

Action	% of firms using the step			
	Step 1	Step 2	Step 3	% of all steps
Try to sell/merge investee	5.2	11.7	18.1	35.1
Replace investee management	15.6	7.8	6.5	29.9
Reposition product	6.5	10.4	1.3	18.1
Identify the problem	11.7	1.3	0	13.0
Develop a new strategy	2.6	5.2	1.3	9.1
VC firm decision-making	3.9	2.6	2.6	9.1
Improve P&L or cashflow	6.5	0	0	6.5
Liquidate investee	0	0	5.2	5.2
Seek strategic alliance	0	3.9	1.3	5.2
Push internal buy-out	0	1.3	1.3	2.6
Create consensus with Board	1.3	1.3	0	2.6
Firms reporting no fixed sequence used				33.8

TABLE 16 Correlation between Strategies Used and VC Monitoring Personnel

	Correlation with monitoring personnel per investee	
Strategy used	Correlation	Significance
Sell or merge investee	−0.013	p = 0.149
Replace management	−0.027	p = 0.416
VC decision-making	0.355	p = 0.002
Reposition product	0.054	p = 0.337
Let go sideways	−0.137	p = 0.140
Fund follow-on product	0.042	p = 0.378
Force a cash-out	0.101	p = 0.220

spondents indicated that they did not use a fixed sequence of actions to deal with living dead investments, 27% of the responding firms used a sequence of actions that first changed investee management and then attempted to sell or merge the investee. It is perhaps surprising that few VC firms indicated that they became actively involved in day-to-day investee decision-making for their living dead companies (only 9.1% of the total actions used), perhaps due to a scarcity of investor personnel with the requisite managerial skills and time to devote to these companies, or an assessment that such active involvement in the day-to-day decision-making of investees was not often successful.

We also examined the data for correlations between the strategies used by VC firms for dealing with living dead situations and their investments per monitoring personnel, in order to test the hypothesis that firms with *more* monitoring resources per investee were more likely to use active intervention strategies, such as becoming actively involved in investee decision-making, or attempting to "reposition" a product, than firms with *fewer* monitoring resources. We hypothesized that this latter group was more likely to use actions not requiring as much day-to-day involvement, such as selling or merging the company, or if that failed, letting the company drift sideways to see if conditions would improve. Table 16 shows the correlations between the strategies used with living dead investments and the number of investments per investor personnel with monitoring responsibilities.

It can be seen that firms with more monitoring personnel per investee were more likely to become actively involved in day-to-day decision making for their living dead investees (r = 0.355, p = 0.002) and were also slightly less apt to choose sell or merge as a strategy, or to let a living dead investee drift sideways, strategies that require less investor involvement, although these latter two strategies did not show significant relationships. We also checked the relationship between the primary portfolio strategy reported by the firms (investing primarily in early-stage deals, investing in "mixed" portfolios of early- and later-stage deals, or investing mostly in safer later-stage deals) and the monitoring personnel per investee, but found no significant correlations. Firms that reported that they invested primarily in early-stage deals had an average of 0.15 monitor per investment, firms using a "mixed" investing strategy had 0.18 monitor per investment, and firms investing primarily in later-stage deals had 0.16 monitor per investment (p = .843). Thus the intensity of monitoring resources used by the firms seems unrelated to their primary portfolio strategies—some firms used more monitoring personnel per investment irrespective of whether they invested primarily in more-volatile early-stage deals or in safer later-stage deals. This result appears to contradict the hypothesis of Gorman and Sahlman (1989) that VC firms tend to follow one of two basic strategies in managing their investments: either they closely manage a few, mostly

150   J.C. RUHNKA ET AL.

TABLE 17   Correlation between Strategies Used and Target ROR

	Correlation with target ROR for portfolios	
Strategy used	Correlation	Significance
Sell or merge investee	−0.014	p = 0.452
Replace management	0.04	p = 0.376
VC decision-making	0.13	p = 0.143
Reposition product	−0.179	p = 0.073
Let go sideways	−0.263	p = 0.016
Fund follow-on product	−0.201	p = 0.06
Force a cash-out	−0.029	p = 0.408

early-stage investments, or else they loosely manage a large stable of investments made in most cases after the company is well on its feet.

It might also be hypothesized that investors with higher portfolio ROR targets, and thus higher overall expectations for their investees, would be less likely to embark on lengthy steps to turnaround a company or to reposition a product, or to let a living dead investment simply drift sideways, and would take actions to quickly sell, merge, or liquidate a living dead company so that it would not drag down the compounding of portfolio returns. Table 17 shows the correlations between the strategies used for living dead investments and the reported portfolio ROR targets of the VC firms.

It appears that the higher the target ROR used by a VC firm, the less likely it was to let its living dead investees drift sideways (r = −0.263), to fund a follow-on product (r = −0.201), or to attempt to reposition a product (r = −0.179), all of which actions take considerable time to produce a cure—if they succeed at all.

Finally, we examined the relationship between the strategies used for dealing with living dead investments and the distributions of winners, living dead, and losers in the final portfolio outcomes projected by the firms. We hypothesized that firms that projected higher percentages of living dead investments at distribution might be slightly more tolerant of living dead situations and would use less-active interventions to turnaround or liquidate their living dead investments than firms that expected smaller percentages of living dead outcomes (Table 18). Whereas most of the relationships were not statistically significant, firms that

TABLE 18   Correlation between Strategies Used and Percentage of Living Dead Investees Expected at Distribution

	Correlation with % living dead expected at distribution	
Strategy used	Correlation	Significance
Sell or merge investee	0.022	p = 0.435
Replace management	−0.076	p = 0.284
VC decision-making	−0.22	p = 0.052
Reposition product	0.042	p = 0.382
Let go sideways	0.289	p = 0.018
Fund follow-on product	0.160	p = 0.129
Force a cash-out	0.111	p = 0.214

TABLE 19   Outcomes Achieved with Living Dead Investments by Size of VC Firms

Outcome	Average % of living dead outcomes by size category				
	0–25M	26–100M	101–300M	300+	All firms
Able to sell or merge	18.4	37.7	35.5	37.5	33.3
Write it off	34.9	23.6	23.3	28.1	26.7
Let company go sideways	18.4	19.5	17.5	15.1	18.1
Replacing mgmt. worked	10.1	13.8	14.8	14.3	13.6
Able to reposition product	5.9	8.2	7.2	7.1	7.4
Able to force cash-out	8.0	0.6	2.5	0	2.9
No exit achieved	4.2	0	0.4	3.3	1.2
Successful outcomes	42.4	59.1	60.0	56.2	55.9
Unsuccessful outcomes	57.5	40.9	40.0	43.9	44.1

projected *higher* percentages of living dead outcomes at distribution were more likely to let a living dead company "go sideways" to see if the situation improved (r = 0.289, p = 0.018). Firms that expected a *smaller* percentage of living dead outcomes at distribution, on the other hand, were somewhat more likely to become actively involved in decision-making for their living dead investments than firms that expected more living dead outcomes (r = −0.22).

SUCCESSFUL AND UNSUCCESSFUL OUTCOMES WITH LIVING DEAD INVESTMENTS

VC firms were given a list of seven different successful and unsuccessful outcomes for living dead investments and asked to indicate to what extent these various outcomes had resulted with their living dead companies. The specific outcomes and aggregate successful and unsuccessful outcomes are displayed by the size of the firms in Table 19 and by the age of the firms in Table 20. Overall, the firms in our sample were able to achieve successful outcomes with only 55.9% of their living dead companies (replacing management worked; able to reposition the product; or able to sell or merge the company). Whereas the percentage of successful and unsuccessful outcomes appears to differ by the size and age of the VC firms, we found no statistically significant differences in outcomes achieved with living dead investments based on either of these variables.

We also examined the relationship of the number of VC monitoring personnel per investment of the firms with the successful and unsuccessful outcomes achieved with their living dead investments and with the distributions of winners, living dead, and losers projected at distribution (Tables 21 and 22). Table 21 indicates that the relative intensity of VC monitoring personnel per investment did not influence successful or unsuccessful outcomes achieved with living dead investments, whereas Table 22 indicates a weakly significant positive correlation between the intensity of monitoring personnel and the percentage of winners projected at distribution, and a negative correlation with the percentage of living dead and losers projected at distribution. Thus whereas the firms with relatively more monitoring resources projected slightly fewer living dead investments at distribution than did firms with fewer monitoring resources, having more monitoring personnel per investee did not produce more successful turnarounds or exits with living dead investments.

152 J.C. RUHNKA ET AL.

TABLE 20 Outcomes Achieved with Living Dead Investments by Age of VC Firms

Outcome	Average % of living dead outcomes by age category					
	0–4	5–9	10–14	15–19	20–24	25+
Able to sell or merge	31.2	34.3	25.7	32.7	31.1	45.7
Write it off	32.6	25.7	33.3	22.7	30.7	17.3
Let company go sideways	6.4	21.5	20	16	16.3	9.0
Replacing mgmt. worked	20.6	9.5	12.3	20.3	20.0	24.7
Able to reposition product	9.0	8.8	5.7	5.0	6.3	0
Able to force cash-out	0	4.0	1.7	1.0	0	3.0
No exit achieved	0	1.4	1.7	0.7	0	0
Successful outcomes	60.8	54.3	45.3	59.0	57.4	73.3
Unsuccessful outcomes	39.0	45.8	55.0	39.3	42.6	36.3

TABLE 21 Effect of Number of VC Monitoring Personnel on Successful and Unsuccessful Outcomes Achieved with Living Dead Investments

	Correlation of outcome with monitoring personnel per investee	
	Correlation	Significance
Able to sell or merge	−0.087	p = 0.269
Write it off	0.027	p = 0.426
Go sideways	0.013	p = 0.465
Replacing mgmt. worked	0.163	p = 0.131
Able to reposition product	0.155	p = 0.144
Able to force cash-out	0.118	p = 0.215
No exit achieved	−0.025	p = 0.436
Successful outcomes	−0.052	p = 0.351
Unsuccessful outcomes	−0.008	p = 0.477

TABLE 22 Correlation between Projected Portfolio Outcomes and VC Monitoring Personnel per Investee

	Correlation with monitoring personnel per investee	
Projected outcome	Correlation	Significance
Winners	0.220	p = 0.058
Living dead	−0.231	p = 0.050
Losers	−0.264	p = 0.031

DISCUSSION AND CONCLUSIONS

Our survey of the experience and actions of 80 VC firms with living dead investments helps to better understand this phenomenon along several important dimensions.

Portfolio Distributions of Living Dead Companies

The portfolio outcomes for 3,418 individual investments by our 80-firm sample, projected at distribution, was 55.2% "winners," 20.6% "living dead," and 20.6% "losers." Newer firms expected a slightly higher percentage of winners and a smaller percentage of losers on average than did older firms. Since the newer firms in our sample had slightly more monitoring personnel per investee on average than did the older and larger firms, newer firms may have believed that more intensive screening of investments or more active "positioning" of their investees would produce more eventual winners. Firms that characterized their portfolio strategy as "investing primarily in safe mid- and later-stage deals" projected a higher percentage of winners and smaller percentages of living dead and losers at distribution, as might be expected, than did firms that reported they invested primarily in early-stage deals, or firms that invested in "mixed" portfolios consisting of more, smaller, early-stage deals combined with fewer and larger investments in mid- and later-stage deals.

Characteristics of Living Dead Investments

The characteristic most often identified for living dead investments keyed on the very poor chances for a successful exit by their VC investors. This poor exit potential was usually coupled with two other key characteristics of living dead investments: more limited growth potential than originally anticipated, and inadequate profitability. Since it was reported that some living dead companies had achieved sales of $5 million to $15 million, and most were described as "self-sustaining" (a mark of economic "success" in small business development paradigms), we concluded that the "living dead" phenomenon is *unique to the context of VC-backed companies* and represents primarily a failure of *investor expectations* rather than a financial failure of the company.

Timeframe and Causation

VC firms reported that their investees usually began to slip into living dead status after the stage when product development had been completed and initial sales achieved, and the "rollout" stage of ramping-up production and pushing for rapid sales growth and significant market share was underway. Thus the "living dead" phenomenon is typically a mid- to later-stage developmental phenomenon that appears when a VC-backed company attempts to push for the rapid revenue growth and profitability necessary to produce high-multiple returns for its investors. The highest-ranking cause of living dead situations in both high-tech and non-high-tech companies was management weaknesses. However, the next four most highly ranked causal factors all dealt with adverse market factors such as: the absolute size of the market was too small, market growth was too slow, the investee missed the market opportunity, and unforeseen competition. The key point is that these external market and competitive factors that cause many living dead situations are largely beyond the control of the VC investors to remedy.

154   J.C. RUHNKA ET AL.

Strategies Used with Living Dead Investments

The strategy most often used by VC firms in living dead situations was an attempt to sell or merge the company (used in more than 75% of the cases), but typically only after one or more other actions to fix the problem had been attempted first, such as replacing investee management or attempting to "reposition" the product. Replacing investee management, active investor involvement in investee decision-making, and attempting to reposition the product were also attempted in 50% or more of living dead situations. While 33.8% of the VC managers indicated that they did not use a fixed sequence of steps to deal with living dead investments, 27% of the firms used a sequence of actions that first changed investee management to attempt to turnaround the company, and then attempted to sell or merge the investee.

We found that VC firms with more monitoring personnel per investee were more likely than firms with fewer monitoring resources per investee to become involved in day-to-day decision making for their living dead investees, and were also slightly less apt to choose a sell or merge strategy, or to let a living dead company drift sideways. The higher the target portfolio ROR used by a VC firm, the less likely it was to use turnaround strategies that required a significant length of time to work, such as letting companies drift sideways, or attempting to reposition a product, or to fund a follow-on product.

Firms that projected high percentages of living dead investments at distribution generally used fewer active interventions to turnaround or to exit living dead investments and were more likely to let living dead investees drift sideways than firms that projected a smaller percentage of living dead outcomes. By contrast, firms that expected fewer living dead outcomes in their portfolios used active intervention strategies for their living dead companies more often.

Success and Failure with Living Dead Situations

Overall the VC firms in our sample were able to achieve "successful" outcomes with only 55.9% of their living dead investments. Successful outcomes included selling or merging the company (achieved in 33.3% of the cases), and situations in which replacement investee management achieved a turnaround (13.6% of the cases). The most prevalent unsuccessful outcomes were to write off the investment (26.7% of the cases) or to simply let the company drift sideways (18.1% of the cases). We found no statistically significant differences in successful turnarounds or exits achieved with living dead investments based on either VC firm size or age, nor did having comparatively more monitoring personnel per investee significantly improve successful outcomes in living dead situations. Older and more experienced VC firms, as well as firms with comparatively more monitoring resources per investment, were no more successful at fixing living dead problems than smaller or less-experienced firms, or firms with comparatively fewer monitoring resources. This result suggests that successful or unsuccessful outcomes with living dead investments are largely determined by the underlying causation of the specific living dead problems. Internal management and operational problems that are under the control of VC investors can potentially be fixed, but living dead problems caused by too small or too slow markets, industry oversupply, or cut-throat competition are largely outside the control or influence of VC investors.

LIMITATIONS OF THE STUDY AND DIRECTIONS FOR FURTHER RESEARCH

Our sample of 80 VC firms significantly underrepresented smaller firms as compared with the total U.S. VC industry, which may have slightly biased several of our findings, such as the aggregate distributions of winners, living dead, and losers projected at distribution. The smallest firms in our sample projected slightly more winners than did firms in the $26–$100 M and $101–$300 M size categories. Smaller firms also used slightly higher target ROR for their portfolios on average than did the larger firms. Thus, the projected portfolio outcomes for our 80-firm sample may show a slightly less favorable distribution of winners, living dead, and losers among VC investments than if more smaller firms had been included. In general, however, the strategies used by VC firms for dealing with living dead situations and the outcomes achieved with these investments did not vary significantly by the size or the age of the firms.

A more significant limitation of the findings is that strategies for dealing with living dead investments, and successful and unsuccessful results achieved, were not examined on a case-specific basis. It may be assumed that the underlying cause of a living dead situation will influence the choice and sequence of remedial strategies attempted in that specific case. For example, a number of VC managers pointed out that living dead companies did not survive for long in rapidly changing and highly competitive high-tech markets. In this environment, the competition is often too quick to allow much time to get a flawed product or marketing strategy back on track. Under these conditions, strategies for "turnaround" would be extremely limited, and most VC managers would probably elect to try to quickly sell or merge the company, or failing that, to liquidate it. More durable or forgiving concepts in less competitive markets, on the other hand, allow more leeway for changing management or attempting to reposition a product, or simply letting a company drift sideways to see if the market or profitability improves.

Finally, as suggested earlier, the chances for a successful turnaround or exit in a living dead situation may be largely determined by whether or not the underlying causes of the living dead problems are susceptible to control by the VC investors. Inadequate management teams and defective financial control systems can potentially be replaced or fixed, but markets that are too small or too slow growing, and the emergency of unforeseen competitors, are largely outside the control of even experienced VC managers.

REFERENCES

Bruno, A., Leidecker, J., and Harder, J. 1986. Patterns of failure among Silicon Valley high technology firms. In J.A. Hornaday, F. Tarpley, Jr., J.A. Timmons, and K.H. Vesper, eds., *Frontiers of Entrepreneurship Research*. Wellesley, MA: Babson Center for Entrepreneurial Studies, pp. 677–693.

Bruno, A., and Leidecker, J. 1987. A Comparative Study of New Venture Failure: 1960 vs. 1980. In J.A. Hornaday, F. Tarpley, Jr., J.A. Timmons, and K.H. Vesper, eds., *Frontiers of Entrepreneurship Research*. Wellesley, MA: Babson Center for Entrepreneurial Studies, pp. 375–388.

Bygrave, W., Fast, N., Khoylian, R., and Vincent L. March 1989. Early rates of return of 131 venture capital funds started 1978–1984. *Journal of Business Venturing* 4(2):93–106.

Dehudy, T., Fast, N.D., and Pratt, S.E. 1981. *Venture Economics*, Wellesley MA.

Gorman, M., and Sahlman, W. July 1989. What do venture capitalists do? *Journal of Business Venturing* 4(4):231–248.

Hill, R., and Hlavacek, J.D. Summer 1977. Learning from failure. *California Management Review*, 19(4):5–16.

Hunstman, B., and Hoban, J.P. 1980. Investment in new enterprise: Some empirical observations on risk, return, and market structure. *Financial Management* 9:44–51.

MacMillan, I., Zemann, L., and Narasimha, P.S. 1987. Criteria distinguishing successful from unsuccessful ventures in the venture screening process. *Journal of Business Venturing* 2:123–137.

Part IV
Investment Realization and Performance

[18]

THE JOURNAL OF FINANCE • VOL. XLVI, NO. 3 • JULY 1991

Venture Capitalist Certification in Initial Public Offerings

WILLIAM L. MEGGINSON and KATHLEEN A. WEISS*

ABSTRACT

This paper provides support for the certification role of venture capitalists in initial public offerings. Consistent with the certification hypothesis, a comparison of venture capital backed IPOs with a control sample of nonventure capital backed IPOs from 1983 through 1987 matched as closely as possible by industry and offering size indicates that venture capital backing results in significantly lower initial returns and gross spreads. In effect, the presence of venture capitalists in the issuing firms serves to lower the total costs of going public and to maximize the net proceeds to the offering firm. In addition, we document that venture capitalists retain a significant portion of their holdings in the firm after the IPO.

THE ABILITY OF THIRD-PARTY specialists to certify the value of securities issued by relatively unknown firms in capital markets that are characterized by asymmetric information between corporate insiders and public investors has attracted much academic interest in recent years. Several authors, including James (1990), Blackwell, Marr, and Spivey (1990), and Barry, Muscarella, Peavy, and Vetsuypens (1991) have developed and tested models based at least in part on the formal certification hypothesis presented in Booth and Smith (1986). A related body of work, represented by DeAngelo (1981), Beatty and Ritter (1986), Titman and Trueman (1986), Johnson and Miller (1988), Carter (1990), Simon (1990), and Carter and Manaster (1990) has examined how investment bankers and auditors help resolve the asymmetric information inherent in the initial public offering (IPO) process.

In this paper we examine whether the presence of venture capitalists, as investors in a firm going public, can certify that the offering price of the issue reflects all available and relevant inside information. We hypothesize that venture capitalists can perform this function; that it will be an economically

*The University of Georgia, Department of Banking and Finance, School of Business Administration, Athens; and The University of Michigan, School of Business Administration, Ann Arbor; respectively. We are grateful to Mike Barclay, David Blackwell, Michael Bradley, Susan Chaplinsky, Harry DeAngelo, Cliff Holderness (discussant), E. Han Kim, Laura Kodres, Ron Masulis, Jeff Netter, Annette Poulsen, Bill Sahlman, H. Nejat Seyhun, Dennis Sheehan, and seminar participants at Harvard University, the University of Oregon, and Purdue University for their comments and recommendations. We also acknowledge the data collection assistance provided by Rick Mull, Eric Van Houwelingen, and So Han Lee. Financial support for this project was provided by the Center for Entrepreneurial Studies at New York University, the University of Michigan Summer Research Program, and the University of Georgia Research Foundation.

valuable function; and that the certification provided by venture capitalists will be both a partial subsititute for and a complement to the certification provided by prestigious auditors and investment bankers. We employ a matched pairs methodology where a sample of venture capital (VC) backed IPOs is matched by industry and offering size with a qualitatively equivalent set of non-VC backed IPOs, to focus as clearly as possible on the question of whether venture capital certification occurs and is valuable. Our results strongly indicate that the presence of venture capitalists in offering firms maximizes the fraction of the proceeds of the IPO, net of underpricing and direct costs, which accrues to the issuing firm.

Specifically, we document that VC backing reduces the mean and median degree of IPO underpricing and that such backing significantly reduces the underwriting spread charged by the investment banker handling the issue. Further support for the venture capitalist certification hypothesis is provided by our finding that VC backed issuers are able to attract more prestigious auditors and underwriters than non-VC backed issuers. In addition, VC backed issuers also elicit greater interest from institutional investors during the IPO and are able to go public at a younger age than other firms. Finally, the credibility of venture capitalists' information is enhanced by the fact that they are major shareholders prior to the IPO and retain significant portions of their holdings after the offer.

This study is organized as follows. In Section I, a general model of venture capital certification is provided. The sample selection criteria and descriptive statistics are presented in Section II. In Section III, the comparison of underwriter and auditor quality and the level of institutional shareholdings between VC and non-VC backed firms is examined. Empirical tests of the certification hypothesis are presented in Section IV. The pre- and post-IPO ownership structure of venture capitalists in the issuing firm is documented in Section V. Section VI concludes the study.

I. Certification by Venture Capitalists

Third party certification has value whenever securities are being issued in capital markets where insiders of the issuing firm and outside investors have different information sets concerning the value of the offering firm. Corporate insiders have an incentive to conceal (or at least delay the revelation of) adverse information because doing so will allow them to sell securities at a higher price. Rational outside investors understand these incentives and will only offer a low average price for the securities offered unless they can be credibly assured that the offering price already reflects all relevant private information. This informationally induced standoff can lead to market failure of the type described by Akerlof (1970) unless the information asymmetry can be reduced.

Although Allen and Faulhaber (1989), Grinblatt and Huang (1989), and Welch (1989), have presented signalling models which predict that corporate insiders can unilaterally convey their private information, there are several factors which make first-party statements and actions suspect. For one thing, Gale and Stiglitz (1989) show that IPO signalling models break down when insiders are allowed to sell equity more than once. More fundamentally, insiders have everything to gain and very little to lose from signalling falsely at the time of an IPO. They sell securities only infrequently and thus would only be "punished" far in the future if at all. Their gain, however, would be immediate and possibly quite large. While disclosure regulation will surely discourage flagrant lying and material omissions [see Tinic (1988)], it is unlikely to be completely effective in forcing disclosure of all relevant information. Therefore, in the absence of effective signalling mechanisms in IPOs, outside investors are likely to be convinced that accurate information disclosure has occurred only if a third party, with reputational capital at stake, has asserted such and will be adversely and materially affected if that assertion proves false.

Specifically, for third-party certification to be believable for outside investors, three tests must be met. First, the certifying agent must have reputational capital at stake which would be forfeited by certifying as fairly priced an issue which was actually over-valued. Second, the value of the agent's reputational capital must be greater than the largest possible one-time wealth transfer or side payment which could be obtained by certifying falsely. Third, it must be costly for the issuing firm to purchase the services of (lease the reputational capital of) the certifying agent, and this cost must be an increasing function of the scope and potential importance of the information asymmetry regarding intrinsic firm value.

There are strong a priori reasons to believe that all three of these tests are met by venture capitalists and that the certification they can provide will have value in an IPO. First, as the *Venture Capital Journal* (VCJ) (1988) makes clear, many of the more established venture capitalists bring companies in their portfolio to market on an ongoing basis as well as participating, over time, in a stream of direct equity investments in entrepreneurial firms. In our sample, 53 venture capitalists bring more than five firms public from 1983 to 1987. Venture capitalists, therefore, have a very strong incentive to establish a trustworthy reputation in order to retain access to the IPO market on favorable terms. Furthermore, the greater a venture capital fund's perceived access to the IPO market the more attractive it will be to entrepreneurs, thus assuring a continuing deal flow. Finally, a reputation for competence and honesty will allow venture capitalists to establish enduring relationships with pension fund managers and other institutional investors who are vitally important as investors in venture capital funds and as purchasers of shares in IPOs.

Support for the second criterion, that the value of venture capitalists' reputational capital must exceed the maximum possible benefit from certifying falsely, is provided by Sahlman (1990). He documents that (1) successful venture capitalists are able to achieve very high returns on relatively modest capital outlays; (2) these returns are directly related to the age and historical performance of the VC fund, as well as to the size of its investment portfolio;

882   *The Journal of Finance*

(3) successful VC fund managers are able to establish profitable "follow-on" funds and are also able to achieve an enhanced deal flow from entrepreneurs; and (4) the VC fund manager market is a relatively small, tight-knit, and efficient labor market where individual performance is constantly monitored and valued. Therefore, the investment in reputational capital by venture capitalists allows them to remain competitive in the venture capital industry as well as the capital markets.

In addition to venture capitalists' investment in reputational capital, they also are large shareholders in the issuing firm. One way in which they might profit from false certification and take advantage of the high price is to sell shares in the IPO. Retention by venture capitalists of their holdings after the offer, therefore, can act as a bonding mechanism for credible certification.

The final criterion for third-parity certification to be successful or economically valuable is that the services of the certifying agent must be costly for the issuing firm to obtain and the cost structure must be such that a separating equilibrium is achieved between high and low information quality firms. Venture capitalists certainly appear to meet this test since the bundle of services they provide—including financial capital, managerial and technical expertise, enhanced access to other financial specialists as well as certification when the firm ultimately goes public—is both very costly and very difficult to obtain. For example, Morris (1987), Gartner (1988), and Sahlman (1990) all demonstrate that venture capitalists expect to earn a compound annual return of from 25 to over 50 percent (depending upon the stage of the investment) on their investments in private companies. Therefore, entrepreneurs typically hand over large holdings of equity in exchange for relatively small cash infusions.

Nor is this the only cost of VC investment for entrepreneurs. In addition to very high required rates of return, venture capitalists invariably structure their investments in such a way that most of the business and financial risk is shifted to the entrepreneur. As described in Golder (1987), Testa (1987), and Sahlman (1988, 1990), venture capitalists employ rather draconian features in their capital investments, including (1) the use of staged investment under which the venture capitalist retains the right to cancel (cease funding) an entrepreneur's venture; (2) the use of convertible preferred stock as an investment vehicle, which gives the venture capitalist both a claim senior to that of the entrepreneur and an enforceable nexus of security covenants;[1] and (3) the retention by the venture capitalist of the option to replace the entrepreneur as manager unless key investment objectives are met.

The cost and stringency of VC investment, as well as the sheer difficulty in obtaining it (venture capitalists typically fund less than one percent of all the proposals they receive), implies that only those firms which would benefit most from the services venture capitalists provide will be willing and able to accept such participation. While the role of venture capitalists in the firm is

---

[1]Megginson and Mull (1991) find that 41.9% of the VC backed firms have convertible preferred stock in their capital structure compared to 12.6% of non-VC backed firms.

obviously not limited to their activity at the IPO, one of the services that entrepreneurial firms purchase with VC funding is easier access to capital markets and the ability of venture capitalists to reduce asymmetrical information in the offering process. Logic suggests that growth options which are characterized by both greater information asymmetry and uncertainty are more likely to be associated with new entrepreneurial firms than with older, more established companies. Therefore, the certification function of venture capitalists should be most attractive to relatively young, rapidly growing, research and development-intensive companies. This being the case, we expect such firms to make greater use of VC than do other firms.[2]

The model of VC certification in IPOs developed above yields three testable hypotheses. First, since the ongoing nature of venture capitalists involved with firms going public builds relationships with all participants in the offering process, VC backed IPOs should have higher quality underwriters and auditors as well as a larger institutional following than comparable non-VC backed firms. Second, the ability of venture capitalists to reduce the information asymmetry associated with a firm involved in the offering process should result in a reduction of both the underpricing associated with the issue as well as the costs of underwriter, legal, auditor, and other miscellaneous expenses. If venture capitalists are able to convey credible information about the firm, the compensation to investors, underwriters, and auditors will be reduced since their cost of acquiring information about the company (personally certifying the issue) will be lowered. Finally, an additional bonding mechanism that ensures that venture capitalists' certification is credible is the level of their capital investment in the firm both before and after the offer. Venture capitalists who retain significant holdings in the firm give up the opportunity to profit from false certification. Therefore, we hypothesize that venture capitalists will not be selling a large portion of their shares in the IPO.

II. Sample Selection Criteria

In order to test the certification role of venture capitalists in the IPO market, we match a sample of 320 VC backed firms with 320 non-VC backed firms in the same industry as closely as possible by offering size.

The universe of 2,644 firm commitment IPOs issued from January 1983 through September 1987 from which the matched sample is constructed is obtained from Investment Dealer's Digest Corporate Database (IDD). After eliminating financial institutions, S&Ls, reverse LBOs, and firms whose first day trading price is unavailable from *Standard and Poor's Daily Stock Price Record: Over-the-Counter*, the remaining sample consists of 1,833 offers.[3]

---

[2]Mull (1990) documents that venture capitalists do in fact concentrate their investments in rapidly growing industries and VC backed firms are able to grow faster, use less debt, and invest significantly more in R&D than do non-VC backed firms.

[3]This sample excludes, by definition, closed-end funds since they trade either on the NYSE or the AMEX.

Initially, 390 VC backed offers issued from January 1983 through September 1987 were identified in the *Venture Capital Journal* which reports IPOs of VC backed firms with offering amounts of $3 million or more and offer prices of at least $5. In order to be included in our sample, the VC backed firm must be contained in the screened IDD sample and must also have an offering prospectus available from Bechtel Information Service. Furthermore, any VC backed firm that is either misclassified as having venture capital participation from the prospectus or has other confounding events at the time of the IPO, such as an acquisition, is also eliminated.[4]

Given that venture capital activity and the level of returns on the first trading day (see Ritter (1984)) tends to be clustered by industry, we match the sample of VC backed firms as closely as possible by offering amount to non-VC backed firms in the same three-digit SIC classification.[5] The final sample consists of 320 VC backed and 320 non-VC backed firms.[6] Table I documents the concentration of VC backed IPOs in certain industries. The majority of the sample falls within 11 separate industries with a large concentration in the high technology area. In addition, as shown in Table II, there are no apparent differences in the number of offerings in each year between VC backed and non-VC backed firms.

Table III reports the differences in offering and firm characteristics for VC versus non-VC backed IPOs using a standard t-test as well as a van der Waerden nonparametric test. Even though firms within the same industry are matched as closely as possible on the offering amount, VC backed IPOs, on average, have higher offering amounts ($19.7 million versus $13.2 million) and offer prices ($11.18 versus $10.16) than non-VC backed IPOs. In fact, the majority of IPOs with the largest offering amounts in specific industries tend to be VC backed firms.

A comparison of the preceding year's revenue of the VC sample and the control sample indicates that the sample is well matched in terms of operating revenues. VC backed IPOs have $37.1 million in revenue reported for the previous year while non-VC backed offers have a slightly higher revenue of

---

[4] We define an inside shareholder (listed in the prospectus) as a venture capitalist if (1) the prospectus notes define him as such or (2) the shareholder is clearly a company and has the word "venture," "capital" or "investment company" in its title.

[5] In our matching criteria, we attempted to follow the same offering characteristics as the *Venture Capital Journal* (price $\geq$ $5 and amount offered $\geq$ $3 million). Due to the large concentration of VC backed firms in the Office, Computing & Accounting Machines industry as well as the Electronic Components & Accessories industry, we included 18 non-VC backed IPOs that had either prices less than $5 or offering amounts less than $3 million. If we exclude these smaller firms from the control sample our results do not change.

[6] As a sensitivity test to the choice of control sample selection, we compared the results using the matched sample to the results utilizing all of the 496 non-VC backed firms that are in the same industries as the VC backed sample and met the *Venture Capital Journal* criteria. Our results using the sample of all non-VC backed firms in the same industries do not materially differ. This screen, however, tends to overrepresent some industries which have a low percentage of VC backed firms but a large number of IPOs and underrepresents the industries mentioned in the previous footnote.

Table I

SIC Classification For Venture Capital and Non-Venture Capital Backed IPOs

SIC classification and percentage of the total sample in each industry for the matched sample of 320 VC backed and 320 non-VC backed IPOs issued from January 1983 through September 1987 as identified from Investment Dealer's Digest Corporate Database and the *Venture Capital Journal*.

SIC Code	Classification	Number of IPOs	Percentage of IPOs
283	Drugs	30	4.7%
357	Office, Computing & Accounting Machines	154	24.1%
366	Communication Equipment	30	4.7%
367	Electronic Components & Accessories	48	7.5%
382	Measuring & Controlling Instruments	12	1.9%
384	Surgical, Medical & Dental Instruments & Supplies	26	4.0%
581	Eating and Drinking Places	14	2.2%
599	Retail Stores Not Elsewhere Classified	10	1.6%
737	Computer and Data Processing Services	70	10.9%
739	Miscellaneous Business Services (Biotech and Pharmaceutical Engineering)	52	8.1%
808	Outpatient Care Facilities	10	1.6%
	Other	184	28.7%
	TOTAL	640	100.0%

Table II

Number of VC Backed and Non-VC Backed IPOs By Year

Year	Venture Capital Backed	Non-Venture Capital Backed
1983	104 (32.5%)	137 (42.8%)
1984	47 (14.7%)	42 (13.1%)
1985	36 (11.2%)	44 (13.8%)
1986	78 (24.4%)	58 (18.1%)
1987	55 (17.2%)	39 (12.2%)
TOTAL	320	320

Table III

Tests of Differences in Sample Descriptive Statistics for VC Backed and Non-VC Backed IPOs[a]

Tests of differences in offering characteristics using a difference in means test and a van der Waerden normal scores test for the sample of 320 VC backed and 320 non-VC backed IPOs matched as closely as possible by industry and offering size. Source: Investment Dealer's Digest Corporate Database and the offering prospectus.

Variable	Venture Capital Backed	Non-Venture Capital Backed	Difference in Means t-stat	van der Waerden Z score
Amount offered	$19.7m [15.0m]	$13.2m [9.2m]	5.20*	6.38*
Offering price	$11.18 [10.50]	$10.16 [10.00]	2.83*	3.41*
Preceding year's revenue	$37.1m [16.2m]	$39.4m [13.0m]	−0.33	1.49
Book value of assets	$23.9m [12.9m]	$27.2m [7.6m]	−0.76	3.90*
Growth in EPS per year	76.8% [61.1%]	65.5% [42.1%]	1.28	0.98
Total debt as a percentage of the book value of assets	31.3% [16.0%]	31.9% [21.5%]	−0.11	−2.61*
Book value of common equity as a percentage of the book value of assets	41.7% [44.8%]	28.1% [34.2%]	3.02*	3.70*
Years from incorporation date to offer date	8.6 yrs [5.3]	12.2 yrs [8.1]	−3.70*	−2.30**

[a]Medians in brackets.
*Significant at the 0.01 level.
**Significant at the 0.05 level.

$39.4 million. This difference is insignificant using either a *t*-test or the van der Waerden test. The average book value of assets is insignificantly different between VC backed firms ($23.9 million) and non-VC backed IPOs ($27.2 million). The median, however, is larger for VC backed issues.

The mean and median yearly growth in earnings per share does not significantly differ between the two samples, with VC backed firms having a somewhat higher average growth rate in earnings per share (EPS) of 76.8% than non-VC backed offers with an average of 65.5%. In addition, the average proportion of the book value of debt as a percentage of the book value of equity is not significantly different (31.3% for VC backed firms versus 31.9% for non-VC backed firms). The median level of debt, however, is significantly higher for non-VC firms. Furthermore, VC backed firms have a significantly higher ratio of the book value of common equity to the book value of assets than non-VC firms (41.7% versus 28.1%) under both tests.

Muscarella and Vetsuypens (1989) document a statistically significant negative relationship between the age of the firm and the corresponding initial return. They attribute their findings to the higher amount of publicly available information associated with older firms. In our sample, VC backed firms are younger in age than their non-VC backed counterparts. The average number of years from the incorporation date to the offer date is 8.6 years for VC backed IPOs and 12.2 years for non-VC IPOs, and these differences are significant under both tests. The difference in ages between the two samples supports the role of venture capitalists in reducing information asymmetry. Venture capital participation and the associated certification allow the firm to go to the public market sooner than non-VC backed companies.[7]

III. Underwriters, Auditors, and Institutional Holdings

As the firm approaches the public offering for the first time, it has the task of hiring underwriters and auditors to manage the issue as well as to certify the information in the prospectus. After the preliminary prospectus is filed with the SEC, the management of the firm travels with the underwriter on a "road show" to provide information as well as to generate interest with institutional investors for the IPO. In general, searching for underwriters and auditors is both costly and time-consuming for firms wishing to go public. For the VC backed firms, however, it is likely that the venture capitalist has been involved with other IPOs in the past and will have built relationships with underwriters, auditors, and institutional shareholders. Furthermore, each of these participants can infer information concerning the IPO from their prior experience with the venture capitalist. Because venture capitalists have reputational capital at stake in both their ability to maintain access to the public capital markets and to attract entrepreneurial firms for investment in the future, they have an incentive to reveal information truthfully about the new issue. This being the case, VC backed firms should attract higher quality underwriters and auditors since it both lowers these participants' cost of due diligence and protects their own reputational capital. The venture capitalists' association with high quality underwriters, in turn, will increase their ability to place the issue with institutional managers.

A. *Frequency of Underwriter Use By Venture Capitalists*

An assumption of the certification role of venture capitalists is that they build valuable relationships with underwriters that would be forfeited if they certified falsely. Table IV shows that many of the venture capitalists in the sample are frequent participants in the IPO market. As mentioned previously, 53 of the venture capitalists in our sample bring five or more issues to

---

[7]Admittedly, the differences in the financial and operating characteristics at the time of the IPO between the two samples cannot be solely attributed to the presence of venture capitalists. From the information publicly available about the control firms, we are unable to determine if the non-VC backed companies attempted to obtain venture capital financing and were turned down or simply did not need that type of capital.

Table IV
Frequency of Board Participation, Percentage of Issues That the Venture Capitalist is the Lead and Underwriter Selection for Venture Capitalists Who Brought 8 or More Issues to Market

Number of issues brought to market from 1983 to 1987 for the venture capitalist, percentage of those issues for which the venture capitalist was the lead and the most frequent underwriters used by the venture capitalist.

Venture Capitalist	Number of Issues Brought to Market	Percentage of issues the VC is on the Board of Directors	Percentage of issues the VC is the lead[a]	Most Frequent Underwriters[b]
Kleiner, Perkins, Caufield & Byers	22	50%	27%	Robertson, Colman (9) Morgan Stanley (7)
Hambrecht & Quist Venture Partners	21	67%	38%	Hambrecht & Quist (14)
Citicorp Venture Capital	15	40%	40%	Alex. Brown (4)
Mayfield Funds	15	80%	33%	Robertson, Colman (9)
TR Berkeley Funds	14	0%	7%	Robertson, Colman (6) Alex. Brown (5)
Venrock Associates	14	86%	21%	Robertson, Colman (5) Morgan Stanley (6)
Greylock Partners	13	77%	23%	Hambrecht & Quist (8) Morgan Stanley (5)
Merrill, Pickard, Anderson & Eyre	13	39%	0%	Morgan Stanley (6) Robertson, Colman (5)
Oak Investment Partners	13	69%	23%	Alex. Brown (7)
Advent Funds	11	82%	73%	L. F. Rothschild (3)
TA Associates	11	55%	45%	L. F. Rothschild (3)
Bessemer Venture Partners	10	70%	40%	Robertson, Coleman (3) L. F. Rothschild (3)

Table IV—Continued

Venture Capitalist	Number of Issues Brought to Market	Percentage of issues the VC is on the Board of Directors	Percentage of issues the VC is the lead[a]	Most Frequent Underwriters[b]
JH Whitney & Co.	10	80%	30%	Alex. Brown (5), Morgan Stanley (5)
New Enterprise Associates	10	90%	20%	Alex. Brown (5), Robertson, Colman (5)
Continental Illinois Venture Corp	9	22%	22%	Alex. Brown (3)
Charles River Partnership	9	44%	44%	Hambrecht & Quist (3), Robertson, Colman (3)
Sequoia Capital	9	67%	0%	Hambrecht & Quist (4)
Norwest Growth Fund	8	63%	38%	Alex. Brown (2)
Technology Venture Investors	8	100%	62%	Alex. Brown (4)
Venad Funds	8	100%	50%	Robertson, Colman (4)

[a] Lead is defined as the venture capitalist with the largest stake in the issuing firm.
[b] Only the two most frequent underwriters are included in this category. For venture capitalists that have only one underwriter listed, it was not possible to make a distinction for the second most frequent investment banker. There are 31 additional venture capitalists that are involved in at least 5 offerings.

market over the time period from 1983 to 1987. Furthermore, many venture capitalists, such as Kleiner, Perkins, Caufield, and Byers, are involved in more than 10 issues during these 5 years. In many cases, the venture capitalist uses the same underwriter for more than one issue.[8] Out of the 15 IPOs issued with Mayfield Fund as one of the venture capitalists, nine are underwritten by Robertson, Coleman.

Also documented in Table IV is the board participation of venture capitalists in the offering firm. The more active venture capitalists frequently have seats on the board of directors as well as acting as lead venture capitalists.[9] Given their active participation in the operations of the issuing firm, venture capitalists are likely to influence the choice of underwriter as well as reduce the amount of information asymmetry regarding the firm by certifying the value of the issue to the underwriter.

B. Underwriter and Auditor Quality

We measure the quality of each underwriter as the percentage of the total dollar amount brought to market of all 2,644 offers ($70.3 billion) classified as IPOs in Investment Dealers' Digest Corporate Database from January 1983 through September 1987. If the issuing firm has more than one lead underwriter indicated in the IDD database, the average of the lead underwriters' market share is used as the measure of quality. In measuring the quality of the underwriter we are assuming that the greater the average market share of the lead underwriters, the higher is the quality.[10]

Table V presents the results on underwriter and auditor quality. On average, VC backed firms go public with underwriters who have a significantly greater percentage of the IPO market than do underwriters of non-VC backed firms (4.4% versus 3.0%). Furthermore, underwriters in VC backed firms are also involved in more offers (62) than underwriters in non-VC backed firms (53). These results indicate that VC backed firms are under-

---

[8]Note that many of the firms in the VC backed sample have both a syndicate of venture capitalists involved in the company as well as an underwriting syndicate involved in the offering. For this reason, there is some double counting in the number of issues brought to market by each venture capitalist as well as in the frequency of underwriting.

[9]We define the venture capitalist as the lead if he holds the largest stake of all venture capitalists in the issuing firm.

[10]Simon (1990) also uses this method in computing underwriter reputation. A comparison of our method using the market share of the underwriter as a measure of quality and the rankings calculated by Carter and Manaster (1990) is presented in Appendix A. We choose to use our method for two reasons. First, the Carter and Manaster sample ends in the year this sample begins. If we were to use the Carter and Manaster rankings, we would be assuming that the reputational capital of investment bankers does not change over time. However, this may not be the case as evidenced by the results of Beatty and Ritter (1986) and the recent decline of some firms in the investment banking community, most notably Drexel Burnham Lambert. Second, using the market share of the underwriter rather than a ranking results in cardinal rather than ordinal values. A comparison of our measure of quality with those of Carter and Manaster results in a high degree of positive correlation between the two.

Table V

Tests of Differences in Mean Institutional Holdings, Average Market Share of Lead Underwriters and Auditor Quality for VC Backed and Non-VC Backed IPOs[a]

Tests of differences in institutional holdings from *Spectrum 3: Institutional Holdings* at the end of the first quarter following the offer date, the lead underwriters' market share and auditor quality for the sample of 320 VC backed and 320 non-VC backed IPOs matched by industry and size using a difference in means test and a van der Waerden normal scores test. The market share of each lead underwriter is computed using the full 2,644 IPOs in the IDD sample from 1983 to 1987. The total dollar amount of IPOs that are brought to market over the time period for each lead underwriter is divided by the total dollar amount of all IPOs issued ($70.3 billion). The market shares of all lead underwriters for a particular IPO are then averaged. The differences in the frequency of use of Big Eight auditors is tested using a chi-square test.

Variable	Venture Capital Backed	Non-Venture Capital Backed	Difference in Means *t*-stat	van der Waerden Z-score
Average market share of lead underwriters	4.4% [3.4%]	3.0% [0.8%]	4.30*	6.02*
Average number of IPOs brought to market by lead underwriter	62 [60]	53 [38]	2.56*	2.98*
				Chi-Square 19.89*
Number of IPOs using a big eight auditor	267 (83%)	219 (64%)		
Average institutional holdings as a percentage of the amount offered for the quarter-end following the offer date	42.3% [39.5%]	22.2% [14.3%]	9.02*	9.35*
Average number of institutional managers	10.2 [8.0]	5.4 [4.0]	8.09*	8.72*

[a] Percentage of firms in parentheses. Medians in brackets.
*Significant at the 0.01 level.

written by higher quality underwriters than their non-VC backed counterparts.

In a similar fashion, we hypothesize that venture capitalists are able to attract higher quality auditors by reducing the asymmetry of information between the issuing firm and the auditor. In this case, auditor quality is measured by whether or not the firm uses a "Big Eight" accounting firm.[11] Eighty-three percent of VC backed firms and 64% of the non-VC backed firms use Big Eight auditors at the IPO indicating that VC backed IPOs are able to attract higher quality auditors than non-VC backed firms.

---

[11] The Big Eight accounting firms are: Arthur Andersen, Arthur Young, Coopers & Lybrand, Deloitte Haskins & Sells, Ernst & Whinney, Peat Marwick Main & Co., Price Waterhouse, and Touche Ross & Co. Mergers within this group after 1987 reduced the Big Eight to the "Big Six."

C. The Level of Institutional Holdings

In addition to attracting higher quality auditors and underwriters in the IPO, we hypothesize that the presence of venture capitalists and the quality of the investment banker will be used to elicit institutional interest. If both venture capitalists and underwriters certify the offer price, then the cost of acquiring information by institutional shareholders will decline. This being the case, we expect VC backed firms to have higher fractions of their shares held by institutions than non-VC backed companies.

Data on institutional holdings are available on a quarterly basis and are collected from *Spectrum 3: 13(f) Institutional Stock Holdings Survey* which reports the number of shares held by institutional managers who control $100 million or more in equity. As shown in Table V, the average percentage of IPOs held by institutions at the end of the first quarter of the offer is significantly higher for VC backed IPOs than for non-VC backed IPOs using both a differences in means test and the van der Waerden normal scores test. Institutions hold, on average, 42.3% of the offer in VC backed firms as compared to 22.2% of the amount offered in non-VC backed firms. In addition, the average number of institutional managers who hold shares in the VC backed firm is 10.2 compared to 5.4 for non-VC backed firms.[12]

In summary, our results indicate that VC backed firms have higher quality underwriters and auditors as well as a larger institutional following than do non-VC backed offers. We attribute these findings to the ability of venture capitalists to certify the quality of the firm by their historical investment in reputational capital, as well as to their capacity to build and maintain relationships with underwriters, auditors, and institutional managers through their ongoing involvement in other IPOs.

IV. Tests of Venture Capitalist Certification

Two testable implications of the certification hypothesis as it pertains to venture capitalists are that the level of underpricing and the amount of compensation to underwriters (and others) will be less for VC backed firms than non-VC backed firms. If venture capitalists are able to reduce the information asymmetry between both potential investors and underwriters, the level of compensation to these participants for acquiring information will be lowered. This being the case, initial returns and gross spreads for VC backed firms should be lower than for non-VC backed IPOs.

---

[12] In order to measure the relative influence of VC participation and the size of both the offer and firm on institutional investment, Tobit regressions are run using the percentage of institutional holdings as the dependent variable and a dummy variable for whether the firm was VC backed, the log of amount offered, and the book value of assets as independent variables. Each of the three independent variables is positively related to institutional holdings and significant at the 1% level. These results indicate that institutional holdings are related to whether or not the firm has VC backing as well as the size of the offering amount and the assets of the firm.

A. Differences in Initial Returns, Underwriter Compensation, and the Costs of Going Public

Table VI provides evidence in support of the hypothesis that VC backed IPOs have lower initial returns, gross spreads, and miscellaneous offering expenses than non-VC backed offers. Initial returns are calculated as the first closing or bid price recorded in *Standard and Poor's Daily Stock Price Record: Over-the-Counter* minus the offer price divided by the offer price. Underwriter compensation is defined as the gross spread as a percentage of the offer price. Miscellaneous offering expenses include such expenditures as auditor, legal, printing, and registration fees and are also measured as a percentage of the offer price.

Consistent with the certification hypothesis, as indicated by the results in Panel A of Table VI, the average intitial return for VC backed IPOs is 7.1% compared to 11.9% for the matched sample of non-VC backed IPOs, and the difference in initial returns is statistically significant under both tests. A comparison of the number of issues that have positive returns yields no apparent differences between the control sample and the VC backed IPOs. On average, 61.2% of VC backed firms and 60.3% of non-VC backed issues experience positive returns on the first trading day.

The significant difference in first trading day returns using a matched sample contrasts with the results found in the study by Barry et al. (1991) which finds no significant differences in underpricing for VC backed IPOs versus a sample of non-VC backed firms offered from 1983 through 1987 that are announced in *The Wall Street Journal*. In order to compare our findings with theirs, we construct a control sample of all non-VC backed IPOs from IDD that have offering amounts of $3 million or more and offer prices of at least $5. This control sample results in 991 firms.[13] Using all IPOs that meet the *VCJ* criteria as a control sample replicates as closely as possible the non-VC sample of Barry et al. In Panel B of Table VI, we find comparable insignificant differences in initial returns to VC backed (7.1%) and non-VC backed firms (7.6%). We attribute the differences in initial returns between our sample and theirs to their construction of the non-VC backed sample and corresponding lack of an adequate industry control. While we cannot determine the number of firms in the Barry et al. sample that are in industries without venture capital participation, approximately 50% of the non-VC firms that replicate their study which meet the *VCJ* criteria are in industries with no venture capital participation whatsoever.

Also presented in Table VI is the average compensation, or gross spread, as a percentage of the offer price, paid to underwriters by the matched sample of

---

[13]While the number of firms in our control sample is identical to the number of firms in Barry et al., the average offer size for our non-VC control sample is smaller at $16 million with a median of $9.4 million. As in the Barry et al. study, however, the difference in means for offering amount between VC backed issues and the full sample of non-VC backed IPOs is insignificant.

Table VI

Tests of Differences in Initial Returns and Offering Expenses for VC Backed and Non-VC Backed IPOs

Tests of differences in initial return using a difference in means test and a van der Waerden normal scores test for (1) the sample of all (991) non-VC IPOs with offer prices > = \$5 and amount offered > = \$3 million and the 320 VC backed firms and (2) for the matched sample of 320 VC backed and 320 non-VC backed issues matched by industry and offering size. Also presented are differences in offering expenses and total proceeds (excluding overallotment). Initial returns are defined as the first trading day close or bid price recorded in *Standard and Poor's Daily Stock Price Record: Over the Counter* minus the offer price divided by the offer price.

	Venture Capital Backed	Non-Venture Captial Backed	Difference in Means t-stat	van der Waerden Z Score
Panel A: Comparison of the Matched Sample of VC Backed and Non-VC Backed IPOs				
Number of firms	320	320		
Mean initial return	7.1%	11.9%	− 3.62*	− 1.87**
	[2.5%]	[3.6%]		
Percentage of IPOs with positive initial returns	61.2%	60.3%		
Average gross spread as as a percentage of the offer price	7.4%	8.2%	− 7.82*	− 6.14*
	[7.1%]	[7.3%]		
Average of miscellaneous offering expenses as a percentage of the offer price[a]	3.6%	4.3%	− 3.50*	− 3.11*
	[3.0%]	[3.6%]		
Ratio of net proceeds to the offering amount[b]	0.89	0.87	7.28*	6.44*
	[0.90]	[0.88]		
Ratio of net proceeds to the first trading day amount[b,c]	0.84	0.80	4.97*	4.02*
	[0.86]	[0.83]		
Panel B: Comparison of VC Backed IPOs and All Non-VC Backed Firms with Price ≥ \$5 and Amount Offered ≥ \$3 million				
Number of firms	320	991		
Mean initial return	7.1%	7.6%	− 0.52	− 0.86
	[2.5%]	[1.6%]		

[a]Miscellaneous offering expenses include such expenditures as auditor, legal, printing, and registration fees.
[b]Net proceeds is defined as the offering amount minus underwriter fees and miscellaneous offering expenses.
[c]The first trading day amount is calculated as the number of shares offered multiplied by the first trading day price.
*Significant at the 0.01 level.
**Significant at the 0.05 level.

VC backed and non-VC backed firms. The gross spread consists of underwriting, selling, and managing fees. Inherent in the gross spread is the cost of due diligence as well as the potential probability of subsequent liability due to material omissions in the prospectus (Tinic (1988)). The presence of venture capitalists lowers the underwriter compensation, for example, by lowering the underwriters' cost of due diligence. The process of acquiring information about the firm as part of the due diligence process will be easier if the venture capitalist has a reputation for having fairly represented information to the underwriter about firms in prior IPOs. Furthermore, venture capitalists may be more efficient in disseminating information than owners in a non-VC backed firm because unlike other firms issuing equity for the first time, they have prior experience in going public. As hypothesized, the compensation paid to the underwriter as a percentage of the offer price is significantly lower for VC backed firms (7.4%) than for non-VC backed IPOs (8.2%).

The percentage of miscellaneous offering expenses paid as auditor, legal, printing, and registration fees is related to the level of underwriter compensation in VC and non-VC backed firms. Using a similar argument as that for underwriter compensation, we expect that continuing relationships of venture capitalists with other participants such as auditors and attorneys will also lower the expenses of obtaining legal counsel, auditing services, and printing. As expected, the average of miscellaneous expenses as a percentage of the offer price is significantly lower for VC backed firms (3.6%) than non-VC backed firms (4.3%).

Given that the level of initial returns and the expenses associated with the offering are less for VC than for non-VC backed offers, the implication is that the net proceeds (the amount offered excluding the overallotment option minus the underwriter compensation and miscellaneous offering expenses) to the firm should be higher for firms with venture capital participation. In other words, the total costs of going public should be lower for VC backed issues than for their non-VC backed counterparts. Ritter (1987) has defined the costs of going public as both the direct offering expenses and the underpricing associated with the IPO. In order to measure the percentage of the offering amount that the firm is able to keep, we calculate two ratios: (1) the ratio of the net proceeds to the offering amount which measures the percentage of the offer that the firm retains after offering expenses and (2) the ratio of the net proceeds to the first trading day amount which incorporates the total effect of both underpricing and offering expenses on the proceeds to the issuing firm. (The first trading day amount is calculated as the number of shares offered multiplied by the closing or bid price on the first trading day.) Using the ratio of the net proceeds to the amount offered, VC backed firms, on average are able to keep 89% of the amount offered after all offering expenses compared to non-VC backed firms which retain 87%. The ratio of the net proceeds to the first trading day amount, which measures the total costs of going public, is higher for VC backed firms (84%) than for non-VC backed IPOs (80%). Both of these ratios are significantly different using the *t*-test and the van der Waerden test. In other words, after taking into effect both the direct (offering expenses) and indirect (underpricing) costs of going public, non-VC backed firms are able to retain a higher proportion of the total issue.

B. OLS Regression Analysis

Tests of the certification hypothesis as it applies to initial returns and gross spreads using a regression analysis are presented in Tables VII and VIII. We examine the relationship of both initial returns and gross spreads to the following variables:

(1) *A dummy variable for whether or not the issue is VC backed (TYPE)*. The level of initial returns should be lower for VC backed issues (TYPE = 1) than for non-VC backed offers (TYPE = 0). In addition, we hypothesize that the presence of venture capitalists certifies the issue and lowers the cost of due diligence. Therefore, there should be a negative relationship between the dummy variable and both initial returns and gross spreads.

(2) *The natural log of the amount offered (LOGAMT)*. Ritter (1984) has documented a significant relationship between the size of the offering and initial returns. Since VC backed firms tend to be larger in terms of offering amount, controlling for size allows us to measure the relative influence of VC backing. If the presence of venture capitalists lowers initial returns, then the coefficient on this variable should be insignificant and negative. Furthermore, Ritter (1987) has documented

Table VII

OLS Regressions of Initial Returns (R_1) against Whether or Not the Issue is VC Backed (TYPE), the Log of the Amount Offered (LOGAMT), the Average Market Share of the Lead Underwriters (MKTSHR), and the Age of the Firm (AGE) for the Matched Sample of 320 VC Backed and 320 Non-VC Backed IPOs during the Period 1983–1987[a]

$$R_1 = \alpha_0 + \alpha_1 TYPE + \alpha_2 LOGAMT + \alpha_3 MKTSHR + \alpha_4 AGE + e_i^b$$

Regression	α_0	α_1	α_2	α_3	α_4	R^2	F-Statistic	Significance of F-Test
(1)	0.137	−0.045	−0.008			0.018	5.7	0.0036
	(5.81*)	(−2.95)*	(−0.84)					
(2)	0.116	−0.412	0.012	−0.847		0.044	9.7	0.0001
	(4.86)*	(−2.76)*	(1.19)	(−4.18)*				
(3)	0.141	−0.052	0.011	−0.722	−0.002	0.059	9.4	0.0001
	(5.66)*	(−3.37)*	(1.03)	(−3.55)*	(−3.00)*			

[a] t-Statistics are given in parentheses.
[b] R_1 = percentage return from the offer price to the first trading day price,
TYPE = dummy variable for whether the IPO is VC backed (VC backed = 1, non-VC backed = 0),
LOGAMT = log of offering amount (excluding the overallotment option) in millions,
MKTSHR = average market share of all lead underwriters for a particular IPO defined as the percentage of all IPOs brought to market by each underwriter from 1983–1987 for the full sample of 2,644 IPOs, and
AGE = age of the firm in years from incorporation date to offer date.
*Significant at the 0.01 level.

Table VIII

OLS Regressions of Gross Spreads (GRSPD) against Whether or Not the Issue is VC Backed (TYPE), the Log Of the Amount Offered (LOGAMT), the Average Market Share of the Lead Underwriters (MKTSHR), and the Age of the Firm (AGE) for the Matched Sample of 320 VC Backed and 320 Non-VC Backed IPOs during the Period 1983–1987[a]

$$GRSPD = \alpha_0 + \alpha_1 TYPE + \alpha_2 LOGAMT + \alpha_3 MKTSHR + \alpha_4 AGE + e_i^{b}$$

Regression	α_0	α_1	α_2	α_3	α_4	R^2	F-Statistic	Significance of F-Test
(1)	0.106 (109.53)*	−0.003 (−4.31)*	−0.011 (−28.48)*			0.600	474.9	0.0001
(2)	0.105 (108.94)*	−0.002 (−4.09)*	−0.010 (−22.99)*	−0.052 (−6.35)*		0.622	349.7	0.0001
(3)	0.106 (108.40)*	−0.003 (−5.39)*	−0.010 (−22.69)*	−0.045 (−5.60)*	−0.0001 (−6.20)*	0.649	277.4	0.0001

[a] *t*-Statistics are given in parentheses.
[b] GRSPD = gross spread paid to the underwriter as a percentage of the offer price,
TYPE = dummy variable for whether the IPO is VC backed (VC backed = 1, non-VC backed = 0),
LOGAMT = log of offering amount (excluding the overallotment option) in millions,
MKTSHR = average market share of all lead underwriters for a particular IPO defined as the percentage of all IPOs brought to market by each underwriter from 1983–1987 for the full sample of 2,644 IPOs, and
AGE = age of the firm in years from incorporation date to offer date.
*Significant at the 0.01 level.

economies of scale in the costs of going public. If this is the case, underwriter compensation should be negatively related to the size of the offer.

(3) *The average market share of the lead underwriters (MKTSHR)*. We include the market share of the underwriter in order to separate the effect of venture capital backing from the quality of the underwriter. In addition to the certification provided by venture capitalists, we expect that underwriters will also certify the issue. As in previous studies by Johnson and Miller (1988), Carter and Manaster (1990), and Simon (1990), we expect the market share of the underwriter, as a proxy for quality, to be negatively related to initial returns. In terms of the gross spread, we include the market share of the underwriter to control for the size of the underwriting firm.

(4) *The age of the firm (AGE)*. Age is included in the regression equations as a control for the degree of information asymmetry. Similar to Muscarella and Vetsuypens (1989) we expect a negative relationship between initial returns and gross spreads. This implies that older firms have a lower degree of information asymmetry than do younger firms. Furthermore, if the age of the firm is positively correlated with information asymmetry, the cost of due diligence will decline. Therefore,

there should also be a negative relationship between the age of the firm and the gross spread.

B.1. OLS Regression Results for Initial Returns

The results in Table VII using the matched sample strongly support the certification role of venture capitalists in lowering initial returns. In all equations, the coefficient of TYPE is negative and statistically significant indicating that the presence of venture capitalists lowers initial returns in IPOs. Furthermore, the variable LOGAMT is insignificant. The market share of the underwriter (MKTSHR) as a proxy for underwriter quality is negative and significant at conventional levels. This result is consistent with the literature on underwriter certification and is complementary to those found in Simon (1990). As in Muscarella and Vetsuypens, the age of the firm is significant and negatively related to initial returns even though VC backed firms tend to be younger than their non-VC backed counterparts.[14]

In other words, the presence of venture capitalists significantly lowers initial returns after controlling for the size of the issue as well as for the certification provided by the quality of the underwriter.

B.2. OLS Regression Results for Gross Spreads

We measure the influence of VC backing on the compensation paid to the underwriter using the same independent variables as the OLS regression equation on initial returns. Table VIII presents the results of the regression of gross spread on TYPE, LOGAMT, MKTSHR, and AGE. The gross spread is defined as the underwriter compensation as a percentage of the offer price. The coefficients on all variables are significant at conventional levels and negatively related to the gross spread. In other words, VC backing lowers the cost of underwriting the issue. As in Ritter (1987), there are economies of scale in going public with larger offering sizes having a lower percentage gross spread. The market share of the underwriter is also negatively related to the gross spreads and implies that, in our sample, higher quality underwriters charge lower gross spreads. Finally, the older the firm, and hence the lower the information asymmetry, the lower is the underwriter compensation.

---

[14] In order to compare our results for initial returns, we estimate the OLS equations using our proxy of 991 non-VC backed firms for the Barry et al. (1990) sample as a control sample. (*t*-statistics in parentheses)

$$\text{Initial Return} = 0.066 + - 0.004 \text{ TYPE} + 0.013 \text{ LOGAMT} + - 0.572 \text{ MKTSHR}$$
$$(4.87) \quad (-0.45) \quad\quad (2.17) \quad\quad\quad (-5.09)$$

The results indicate an insignificant relationship between whether or not the firm is VC backed and initial returns. Furthermore, LOGAMT is insignificant and negative. The quality of the underwriter lowers initial returns as the coefficient on MKTSHR is negative and significant. Using the sample of all non-VC backed firms, regardless of industry, results in initial returns being inversely related to the quality of the underwriter and to the amount offered but unassociated with the presence of venture capitalists. The regression equation with age as an independent variable is not presented since the number of years from incorporation to the offer date is not available for all IPOs in the sample.

The results of the two previous sections indicate that the presence of venture capitalists in an issuing firm certifies the offer to both investors and underwriters, which lowers the two most important components of the costs of going public: (1) underpricing and (2) underwriter compensation.

V. Pre- and Post-IPO Holdings of Venture Capitalists

The credibility of venture capitalists in certifying an IPO is conveyed both through their investment in reputational capital and by their financial holdings in the firm. This section examines the extent of insider holdings and sales at the time of the IPO by documenting the change in ownership structure associated with venture capitalists. The certification hypothesis predicts that venture capitalists will retain substantial holdings in the firm as a bonding mechanism for credible certification. In order to examine the selling behavior of venture capitalists at the time of the initial public offering, Table IX presents the pre- and post-offering characteristics of venture capitalist shareholdings.

A. Pre-Offering Venture Capital Characteristics

As a hedge against risk, the majority of VC backed firms have a venture capitalist syndicate with more than one venture capitalist as a shareholder of the firm prior to going public. As shown in Table IX, Panel A, the average holding by venture capitalists in a VC backed firm is 36.6%. Twenty-eight percent of the offers, or 89 IPOs, have venture capitalists owning 50% or more of the equity of the firm prior to going public. These pre-offering holdings of venture capitalists indicate a substantial equity position in the issuing firm prior to the offer.

B. Post-Offering Venture Capital Characteristics

Panel B of Table IX presents the post-offering holdings of venture capitalists. The results indicate that venture capitalists retain a majority of their holdings after the IPO. Less than half (43.3%) of VC backed IPOs have venture capitalists selling *any* of their shares in the offering. Furthermore, only three VC backed IPOs have venture capitalists selling 100% of their total shares in the offering. The mean percentage of venture capitalist holdings sold at the IPO is 8.0%. On average, 6.9% of the offering amount is composed of venture capitalists' sales.

In order to compare the selling by venture capitalists with the sales by other insiders of the firm, we examine the percentage of the amount offered that is composed of secondary shares. Secondary shares are shares sold by insiders of the firm. Of the 181 VC backed IPOs that have secondary shares as part of the offering, on average, 39.6% of secondary sales are composed of venture capitalists' shares. The remaining secondary shares are sold by other inside shareholders.

Also shown in Panel B of Table IX, venture capitalists suffer a dilution of their holdings after the offer. The decline in the percentage of equity held by

Table IX

Pre- and Post-Offering Characteristics of VC Holdings[a]

	All VC IPOs (N = 320)
Panel A: Pre-Offering Characteristics	
Average percentage of equity owned by all venture capitalists prior to the offer	36.6% [36.3%]
Number of IPOs where venture capitalists own 50% or more of the shares prior to the offer	89 (28%)
Panel B: Post-Offering Characteristics	
Number of firms which have venture capitalists selling at the IPO	139 (43.3%)
Number of venture capitalists who sell 100% of their holdings	3 (0.9%)
Average percentage of venture capitalists' holdings sold at the IPO	8.0% [0.0%]
Average percentage of the amount offered that is composed of venture capitalists' shares	6.9% [0.0%]
Average percentage of secondary shares sold by venture capitalists (only for the 181 VC backed IPOs with secondary shares)	39.6% [33.8%]
Average percentage of the firm held by venture capitalists after the offer	26.3% [25.9%]
Number of IPOs where venture capitalists own 50% or more of the shares after the offer	27 (8.4%)

[a]Medians in brackets. Percentage of firms in parentheses.

venture capitalists is due to both the sales of VC shares at the IPO and the issuance of additional primary shares to the public. The fraction of equity held by venture capitalists in the issuing firm drops from 36.6% prior to the offering to 26.3% after the firm goes public. Furthermore, prior to the IPO, 28% of VC backed IPOs have venture capitalists owning 50% or more of the shares, but the number and fraction of VC backed IPOs with venture capitalists owning 50% or more after the offer falls to 27 or 8.4%. These results indicate that while a large number of venture capitalists give up voting control of the firm, the majority retain a significant portion of their holdings in the issuing firm. The large post-offering holdings of venture capitalists can be used as an additional sign of credibility at the time of the offer since venture capitalists forego the opportunity to profit directly from false certification.

VI. Conclusions

This paper provides support for the certification role of venture capitalists in bringing new issues to market by examining the impact of venture capitalists on the pricing and subsequent ownership structure of IPOs. The presence of venture capitalists in the offering firm certifies the quality of the issue through their investment in financial and reputational capital. A comparison of VC backed IPOs and a control sample of non-VC backed offers from 1983–1987, matched by industry and offering size, indicates that VC backed firms are significantly younger, have greater median book values of assets, and a larger percentage of equity in the capital structure than their non-VC backed counterparts.

One assumption inherent in the certification hypothesis is the degree of repeat business venture capitalists have with the offering participants. Our results indicate that larger venture capitalists tend to use the same underwriters with great frequency. In addition, VC backed firms are able to attract higher quality underwriters and auditors as well as a larger institutional following than non-VC backed IPOs.

By reducing the asymmetry of information between the issuing firm and investors and financial specialists such as underwriters and auditors, venture capitalists are able to lower the costs of going public. We find evidence of significantly lower underpricing and underwriter compensation, holding offering size, underwriter quality, and firm age constant for VC backed IPOs than for non-VC backed firms. Evidence on subsequent ownership structure of VC backed IPOs indicates that venture capitalists are not using the IPO as an opportunity to cash out of their holdings and realize a return on investment. Indeed, a majority of venture capitalists do not sell *any* of their holdings at the offer date.

Appendix A
Comparison of the Top Underwriters by Dollar Amount Market Share to the Carter and Manaster (1990) Ranking

Underwriter	Market Share[a]	Carter and Manaster Rankings
Merrill Lynch Capital Markets	22.3%	9.0
Lehman Brothers	17.9	8.0
Saloman Brothers	15.4	9.0
Goldman, Sachs and Co.	14.7	9.0
First Boston Corp.	13.9	9.0
E. F. Hutton	11.2	8.0
Morgan Stanley	9.4	9.0
Drexel Burnham Lambert	8.9	7.0
Prudential Bache Securities	7.9	8.0
Alex. Brown and Sons	7.4	7.5
Dean Witter Reynolds	6.8	8.0
Bear, Stearns and Co.	6.1	8.0
Kidder Peabody and Co., Inc.	5.6	8.0
Paine Webber	4.6	7.5
Lazard Freres and Co.	4.4	8.0
Smith Barney, Harris Upham and Co.	3.7	8.0
A. G. Edwards	3.5	6.5
Donaldson, Lufkin and Jenrette	3.4	7.0
L. F. Rothschild Unterberg	2.9	8.0
Hambrecht and Quist	2.8	6.0

[a]These rankings are based on the dollar amount ($70.3 billion) of all 2,644 offers classified as IPOs by Investment Dealers' Digest Corporate Database.

REFERENCES

Akerlof, George, 1970, The market for lemons: Quality, uncertainty and the market mechanism, *Quarterly Journal of Economics* 84, 488-500.

Allen, Franklin and Gerald Faulhaber, 1989, Signaling by underpricing in the IPO market, *Journal of Financial Economics* 23, 303-323.

Barry, Christopher, Chris Muscarella, John Peavy, and Michael Vetsuypens, 1991, The role of venture capital in the creation of public companies: Evidence from the going public process, *Journal of Financial Economics*, Forthcoming.

Blackwell, David, Wayne Marr, and Michael Spivey, 1990, Shelf registration and the reduced due diligence argument: Implications of the underwriter certification and the implicit insurance hypothesis, *Journal of Financial and Quantitative Analysis* 25, 245-259.

Beatty, Randolph and Jay Ritter, 1986, Investment banking, reputation and the underpricing of initial public offerings, *Journal of Financial Economics* 15, 213-232.

Booth, James and Richard Smith, 1986, Capital raising, underwriting and the certification hypothesis, *Journal of Financial Economics* 15, 261-281.

Carter, Richard, 1990, Underwriter reputation and repetitive public offerings, Working paper, Iowa State University.

——— and Steven Manaster, 1990, Initial public offerings and underwriter reputation, *Journal of Finance* 45, 1045-1067.

DeAngelo, Linda, 1981, Auditor independence, 'low balling,' and disclosure regulation, *Journal of Accounting and Economics* 3, 113-127.

Gale, Ian and Joseph Stiglitz, 1989, The informational content of initial public offerings, *Journal of Finance* 44, 469-477.

Gartner, William, 1988, Venture capital, in Dennis Logue, ed.: *Handbook of Modern Finance* (Warren, Gorham and Lamont, New York).

Golder, Stanley, 1987, Structuring the financing, in Stanley Pratt and Jane Morris, ed.: *Pratt's Guide to Venture Capital* (Venture Economics, Inc., Wellesley Hills, MA), pp. 52-59.

Grinblatt, Mark and Chuan Yang Huang, 1989, Signalling and the pricing of new issues, *Journal of Finance* 44, 383-420.

James, Christopher, 1990, Relationship specific assets and the pricing of underwriter services, Working paper, University of Florida.

Johnson, James and Robert Miller, 1988, Investment banking prestige and the underpricing of initial public offerings, *Financial Management* 17, 19-29.

Megginson, William and Rick Mull, 1991, Financial characteristics and financing decisions of venture capital backed firms, Working paper, University of Georgia.

Morris, Jane, 1987, The pricing of a venture capital investment, in Stanley Pratt and Jane Morris, ed.: *Pratt's Guide to Venture Capital* (Venture Economics, Inc., Wellesley MA), pp. 55-61.

Mull, Rick, 1990, Towards a positive theory of venture capital, Unpublished dissertation, University of Georgia.

Muscarella, Christopher and Michael Vetsuypens, 1989, Initial public offerings and information asymmetry, Working Paper, Southern Methodist University.

Ritter, Jay, 1984, The 'hot issue' market of 1980, *Journal of Business* 57, 215-241.

———, 1987, The costs of going public, *Journal of Financial Economics* 19, 269-281.

Sahlman, William, 1988, Aspects of financial contracting in venture capital, *Journal of Applied Corporate Finance* 1, 23-36.

———, 1990, Venture capital: A model of project governance, Working paper, Harvard University.

Simon, Carol, 1990, The role of reputation in the market for initial public offerings, Working Paper, University of Chicago.

Testa, Richard, 1987, The legal process of venture capital investment, in Stanley Pratt and Jane Morris, eds.: *Pratt's Guide to Venture Capital Sources* Eleventh Edition, (Wellesley Hills, MA: Venture Economics). pp. 66-77.

Tinic, Seha, 1988, Anatomy of initial public offerings of common stock, *Journal of Finance* 43, 789–822.

Titman, Sheridan and Brett Trueman, 1986, Information quality and the valuation of new issues, *Journal of Accounting and Economics*, 8, 159–172.

Venture Capital Journal, 1988, Exiting: New patterns in the 1980s (Venture Economics, Inc., Needham, MA), August, pp. 12–16.

Welch, Ivo, 1989, Seasoned offerings, imitation costs, and the underpricing of initial public offerings, *Journal of Finance* 44, 421–449.

[19]

MANAGERIAL AND DECISION ECONOMICS, VOL. 16 593–606 (1995)

Venture Capitalist Participation and the Post-issue Operating Performance of IPO Firms

Bharat A. Jain

School of Business and Economics, Towson State University, Towson, MD, USA

and

Omesh Kini

Goizueta Business School, Emory University, Atlanta, GA, USA

Previous studies have identified the value-added potential of venture capitalist monitoring in the initial public offering (IPO) market. We test this proposition by comparing the post-issue operating performance of venture capitalist-backed IPOs with a matched sample of non-venture capitalist-backed IPOs. We find that venture capitalist-backed IPO firms exhibit relatively superior post-issue operating performance compared to non-venture capital-backed IPO firms. Further, the market appears to recognize the value of monitoring by venture capitalists as reflected in the higher valuations at the time of the IPO. Finally, we find that proxies for the quality of venture capitalist monitoring are positively related to post-issue operating performance.

The role of venture capitalists in the creation of public companies has recently attracted considerable attention among academics and practitioners. Fueling this interest has been the widely publicized successes of numerous venture capital-backed new issues, including firms such as Apple Computer, Intel, Federal Express, Lotus Development, Microsoft, Genentech, etc. Why are venture capitalists so successful in nurturing new issues? Sahlman (1990) suggests that the venture capital industry has evolved operating procedures and contracting practices that are well adapted to environments characterized by uncertainty and information asymmetries between principal and agents. Prior research suggests that venture capitalists are actively involved in the management of firms they finance and often take membership on the board of directors along with concentrated equity positions, thereby, retaining significant ownership and economic rights (see Sahlman, 1990; Barry *et al.*, 1990; Megginson and Weiss, 1991). Venture capitalists usually specialize in particular industries and use their knowledge and contacts to help the company recruit key employees, develop supplier and customer relations, and assist in production and operations (Warne, 1988). Gladstone (1989) suggests that some venture capitalists maintain consulting staff that participate in the management of portfolio companies. Thus, venture capitalists are typically active investors who try to add value to their portfolio companies through ongoing longer-term involvement with continuing business development (*Venture Capital Journal*, March 1987).

The above discussion suggests that venture capitalists may be able to provide valuable services in the form of third-party monitoring similar to the role played by leveraged-buyout (LBO) specialists and large block stockholders. Jensen (1989) suggests that these type of 'active investors' have a potential to play important roles in monitoring and reorganization of companies in which they participate. Studies by Kaplan (1989), Muscarella and Vetsuypens (1990) and Smith (1990 find evidence of significant performance improvements in corporations that go private through MBOs or LBOs. However, as Barry, Muscarella, Peavy, and Vetsuypens (1990) (henceforth BMPV) point out, venture capitalists, unlike LBO specialists, usually invest in young, high-risk entrepreneurial companies with unpredictable cash flows and future prospects. Their investment in such high risk ventures is consistent with their claims that they invest in industries in which their expertise and ability to monitor and guide are most in demand.

This study examines whether venture capitalist participation leads to superior post-issue operating performance of initial public offerings (IPOs). Venture capitalists invest in privately held companies about whom there is little or no publicly available information. Since venture capitalists fund only a small fraction of firms they evaluate, presumably they have developed an effective screening procedure that allows them to identify superior future performers. Thus, when a venture capitalist-backed firm decides to go public, it generally has been adequately screened and financed, has a carefully selected management team and board of directors in place, is endowed with a promising product in a well-defined market, and has the benefit of vendor and market contacts. If the above activities/benefits of venture capitalist participation provides value additivity, we would expect venture capitalist-backed IPO firms to out-perform similar non-venture capitalist-backed firms in the post-IPO period.

We examine the post-issue operating performance relative to the pre-IPO year of a sample of venture capitalist-backed IPO firms with a closely matched sample of non-venture capitalist-backed IPO firms using a matched-pairs methodology. In addition to comparing the post-issue operating performance of these two groups of IPO issuers, we examine whether the market recognizes the value-added potential of venture capitalist participation and monitoring. Finally, we examine whether proxies for quality of venture capitalist monitoring are related to post-issue operating performance.

The rest of this paper is organized as follows. In the next section a model of venture capitalist monitoring is provided. In the third section we present a description of our data and discuss our methodology. A discussion of the empirical results comparing the operating performance as well as market expectations of future perfor-

mance of venture capitalist-backed and non-venture capitalist-backed IPO firms is provided in the fourth section. The relation between quality of venture capitalist monitoring and operating performance is explored in the fifth section. Finally, we present our conclusion.

VENTURE CAPITALIST MONITORING

Venture capitalists (henceforth VCs) tend to focus on a relatively narrow set of industries, where the potential for value additivity as a result of their expertise and monitoring is the greatest. This section attempts to identify potential reasons why monitoring by VCs is likely to be more effective than self-monitoring by entrepreneurs when the company is private and market monitoring when it goes public. Sahlman (1990) suggests that VC contracts are designed to provide staged financing at different points, which preserves the right to abandon the project at any time during the life of the venture. The staged financing allows the VCs to terminate their involvement and cut their losses if the expected net present value of the project falls below expectations. It also prevents the management from investing in non-value-maximizing activities and reduces the free cash flow problem. Further, VCs design compensation schemes which are directly linked to value creation and retain the option of replacing the entrepreneurs as managers unless certain key objectives are met.

Sahlman (1990) states that the stringent contractual provisions between entrepreneurs and VCs addresses three fundamental problems. The first is the sorting problem which involves matching the best VC firm with the best entrepreneurial firm. The restrictive contractual provisions ensure that only entrepreneurs who foresee significant benefits of VC participation and are confident of their ability to execute the conditions laid down by the VCs will agree to their participation. By the same token, only the best VC firms with a track record of success will be able to get entrepreneurs to agree to the highly restrictive contracts. The second problem addressed by the contractual provisions is the classical agency problem since VC participation ensures that managers do not indulge in non-value-maximizing activities. The third problem addressed is operational, which involves attempts to minimize the present value of the operating costs. All three issues are directly linked to value creation and the extent of VC value additivity depends on their effectiveness in monitoring and control responsibilities.

Although it is clear that VCs in their own self-interest would closely monitor the company when it is still private, the rationale for post-IPO monitoring is less obvious. Since the IPO provides a convenient exit strategy, VCs have incentives to work intensely to ensure growth as well as window-dress the company prior to the issue. Alternatively, they could time their offering to coincide with market peaks to achieve inflated valuations. At the IPO, they could divest their holdings and redeploy their skills in other private firms in early stages of growth where their marginal productivity is higher. However, there are several reasons why VCs are unlikely to the window-dress/time their issues and exit at the IPO. First, the market recognizes the incentives for VCs to window-dress and exit at the IPO and accounts for it in the offering price particularly if significant VC equity is put up for sale at the IPO. Second, VCs in their own best interests usually continue to maintain significant equity positions in the post-IPO firm.[1] The *Venture Capital Journal* (March 1983) reports that contrary to the widely held belief that VCs realize the bulk of their gains in the IPO of the portfolio company, they in fact achieve most of their profits by holding positions in the aftermarket. VCs realize that emerging companies will generally experience their major growth subsequent to going public. The experienced VC will maintain a stock position through the rapid growth phase, taking profits over time or in a seasoned offering. The existing empirical evidence is consistent with VCs continuing to hold significant ownership and board positions in the post-IPO firm. BMPV (1990) report that VCs, on average, hold 34% of the equity prior to the IPO and, on average, sell 6.60% of their pre-IPO shares. In addition, 58% of VCs in their sample did not sell any shares at the IPO. Further, VCs continue to maintain a significant post-issue presence on the board of directors. Megginson and Weiss (1991) also document strong evidence of continued VC involvement in their projects after the IPO. Thus, significant equity stake in the post-IPO firm ensures monitoring by VCs.

Another important contributory factor for continued post-IPO monitoring by VCs is their reputation capital at stake. VCs often have to bring other partners on board and form syndicates to participate in certain deals. Sahlman (1990) points out that the VC industry is a small tight-knit community where individual performance is closely monitored. Successful fund-managers are able to establish profitable follow up funds more easily. Further, VCs deal in several IPOs and need to frequently collaborate with investment bankers and auditors who are also extremely conscious of their reputation capital at stake. We find that a small number of VCs frequently reappear in our sample. VCs, by virtue of their success in taking companies public, become well known among issuers, underwriters, and investors in the IPO market. Their past success becomes a strong selling point as they negotiate VC contracts with issuers or raise funds from investors. Thus, the long-term continual involvement in the IPO market provides VCs with incentives to maintain their reputation by carefully screening their investments and subsequently monitoring their performance in the aftermarket. VCs who deviate by managing issues which consistently fail in the aftermarket will find it difficult to find investors to form syndicates or reputable investment bankers/auditors willing to take their company public.

Hence, stringent contractual arrangements, significant equity stake in the post-IPO firm, and reputation capital effects ensure that the benefits of monitoring and other services provided by VCs do not end at the IPO. If the screening/selection process by VCs identify the best entrepreneurs and their continued monitoring and expertise create value, we would expect VC-backed issuers to outperform non-VC-backed issuers in the post-IPO period. On the other hand, if the monitoring services and other activities are not value enhancing or create other conflicts, the performance of VC-backed firms would be no different or even worse than similar non-VC-backed firms.

In a recent study involving 682 IPOs, Jain and Kini (1994) find that issuers, on average, demonstrate a decline in operating performance relative to their pre-IPO levels. Further, there is no sign of a turnaround over a five-year period subsequent to going public. They speculate that the post-issue decline in performance can be attributed to (1) increased agency conflicts as a result of diluted ownership, (2) window-dressing of accounting numbers by managers prior to the issue, and (3) issuers timing their offering to coincide with periods of unusually good performance which are not subsequently sustained. However, for the reasons outlined earlier in this section, VCs have minimal incentives to window-dress or time their issue, and their presence reduces the agency problem. Despite this, VC-backed firms may exhibit declines in post-issue performance. Jensen (1993) suggests that often competitors rush to simultaneoulsy implement new, highly productive technology which can lead to overinvestment in the industry, thereby causing a decline in performance. Sahlman and Stevenson (1985) analyze the Winchester disk drive industry where VCs had invested $400 million and IPOs contributed an additional $800 million between 1977 and 1984. As a result of this overinvestment, they note that the market value of twelve VC-backed hard disk manufacturers declined from $5.4 billion in mid-1983 to $1.4 billion at the end of 1984. Thus, because of the overinvestment problem in high technology and growth industries, VC-backed issuers may also exhibit declines in performance relative to their pre-IPO levels. However, the proposition that VC provide value-added services would be validated if their post-issue operating performance is relatively superior to similar non-VC-backed issuers. We examine this issue in the remaining section.

DATA DESCRIPTION AND METHODOLOGY

A sample of firm commitment IPOs are collected for the period 1976–88 from the following two sources: (1) *Going Public: The IPO Reporter* and (2) *Investment Dealers Digest's Five-year Directory of Corporate Financing*. The sample was constructed by imposing the following selection criteria: (1) the offer price is at least $5.00, (2) all issues raise more than $3 million at the IPO, (3) unit issues, reverse LBOs, IPOs of closed-end mutual funds, and real estate investment trusts are excluded from the data set, (4) financial institutions and S&Ls, are also excluded from the sample, and (5) each firm is required to have financial data available on the Compustat tapes for the fiscal year prior to the IPO.[2]

Next, we identify, 177 VC-backed issues meeting the above-mentioned selection criteria from the *Venture Capital Journal*, which reports IPOs of VC-backed firms with offering amounts of at least $3 million and offering price of at least $5.00.[3] Since VCs tend to specialize by industry, we follow the Megginson and Weiss (1991) matched-pair methodology to construct a matching sample of non-VC-backed IPOs. Thus, VC-backed firms are matched as closely as possible by offering amount to non-VC-backed firms in the same three-digit SIC classification. The final sample consists of 136 VC-backed and 136 non-VC-backed IPOs.[4,5] Table 1 presents the industry distribution of the VC- and non-VC-backed IPOs. Consistent with the belief that venture capitalists specialize by industry, we find that the sample is heavily represented by issues from the office computing and accounting machines industry and the computer and data processing services industry.

To measure the operating performance of the VC- and non-VC-backed IPO issuers, two cash flows related performance measures are employed. The first measure is the operating return on assets, which is operating income (before depreciation and taxes) divided by total assets (Compustat data item 13 divided by data item 6). The operating income equals net sales less cost of goods sold and selling, general and administrative expenses before depreciation, depletion and amortization. The second measure of operating performance is operating cash flows deflated by total assets (Compustat data item 13 less data item 128 deflated by data item 6).[6] The operating cash flows equals operating income minus capital expenditures. The measures of operating performance employed in this paper have been widely used in the financial economics literature (see Kaplan, 1989; Smith, 1990; Jain and Kini, 1994 as examples). The change in operating performance is measured as the median change in either of our two operating performance measures. For example, [Operating return on assets$_i$ (t) – Operating return on assets$_i$ (-1)] represents the increase in operating return on assets for firm i measured over a time-window starting the year prior to the IPO to t fiscal years after the IPO.[7,8] Since VCs tend to focus on risky, high-growth companies, any differences in performance can be attributed to increase in sales, capital expenditures, or discretionary expenditures. To address this issue, we also compare the post-IPO growth

Table 1. Industry Classification for VC-backed and Matched Non-VC-backed IPOs

SIC	Classification	Number of IPOs	Percentage of IPOs
283	Drugs	14	5.14
355	Special Industry Machinery	6	2.20
357	Office, Computing & Acct. Machine	46	16.91
366	Communication Equipment	20	7.35
367	Electronic Components & Accessories	26	9.55
381	Search, Det, Nav, Guide, Aero Systems	4	1.47
382	Measuring and Controlling Instruments	22	8.08
384	Surgical, Medical and Dental Instruments	6	2.20
481	Telephone & Communications	4	1.47
504	Commercial Equipment & Supply	4	1.47
573	Radio, TV and Music Stores	10	3.67
737	Computers and Data Processing Services	48	17.64
806	Hospitals	8	2.94
870	Engr, Acc, Res, & Mgmt Services	4	1.47
873	Research, Development and Testing Svcs	6	2.20
	Others	44	16.17
	Total	272	100.00

in sales (Compustat data item 12), capital expenditures (Compustat data item 128) and discretionary expenditures for VC- and non-VC-backed companies. The expense items employed in computing discretionary expenditures include capital expenditures (Compustat data item 128), R&D expenses (Compustat data item 46), and advertising expenses (Compustat data item 45). All reported significance tests are based on the two-tailed Wilcoxon signed-rank tests.[9]

OPERATING PERFORMANCE OF VC-BACKED AND NON-VC-BACKED IPOS

In this section, we explore the differences between VC-backed and a matched sample of non-VC-backed IPOs. First, we compare the differences in offering characteristics. We then compare the post-issue operating performance of the two groups relative to the year prior to the IPO (Year − 1). We conduct cross-sectional regression analysis to determine if differences in performance exist after controlling for other determinants of post-issue performance. We also examine whether the market recognizes the value-added potential of VC participation.

Characteristics of VC-backed and Non-VC-backed IPOs

In Table 2, the differences in offering and firm characteristics of the VC-backed and non-VC-backed IPOs are reported. Consistent with Megginson and Weiss (1991), we find that VC-backed IPOs have higher median IPO offering size and offer price in comparison to non-VC-backed IPOs. For instance, the median offer size of VC-backed issues is $14.80 million versus $11.60 million for the non-VC-backed issues with the difference significant at the 0.05 level. The median offer price for VC-backed issues is $12.12 versus $11.12 for the non-VC-backed issues with the difference also significant at the 0.05 level. However, the VC-backed and non-VC-backed IPO firms are closely matched on the basis of pre-offering measures of sales and total assets. For instance, the median sales in year − 1 is $15.08 million for the VC firms versus $14.22 million for the non-VC firms and the difference is insignificant. The median total assets in year − 1 for the VC firms is $12.75 versus $9.59 million for the non-VC firms and the difference is again insignificant. Thus, VC-backed firms are similar to non-VC-backed firms in terms of pre-offering sales and total assets though their IPO offering size is significantly higher.[10]

A comparison of the median levels of the oper-

Table 2. Summary Statistics of VC-backed and Non-VC-backed IPOs

Description	VC-backed	Non-VC-backed	Wilcoxon's Z
Median size of issue ($ million)	14.80	11.60	2.33[b]
Median price ($)	12.12	11.12	2.06[b]
Median initial return (%)	3.77	0.00	2.35[b]
Median sales (year − 1) ($m)	15.08	14.22	0.12
Median total assets (Year − 1) ($m)	12.75	9.59	1.36
Median alpha (%)	74.69	73.29	1.75[c]
Median operating return on assets (year − 1) (%)	18.12	23.13	−2.70[a]
Median operating cash flows/assets (year − 1) (%)	8.13	11.60	−3.00[a]
Median capital exp/assets (year − 1) (%)	10.07	7.14	3.41
Median discretionary exp/assets (year − 1) (%)	26.62	17.93	3.13[a]
Median discretionary exp/sales (year − 1) (%)	17.85	12.56	3.57[a]

Characteristics of 136 VC-backed IPOs compared with those of a matched sample of 136 non-VC-backed IPOs issued between 1977 and 1988. The IPOs have a price of at least $5.00 and are firm commitment offerings. In addition, all these IPOs have data available on the Compustat Annual and Research Tapes for the fiscal year prior to the IPO. The initial return is defined as the difference in the first CRSP listed aftermarket price and the offering price as a proportion of the offering price. Alpha is the fraction of the firm retained by the original owners and is computed on the assumption that overallotment options, if any, are not exercised. Operating return on assets equals operating income before depreciation as a percentage of total assets. Operating cash flows are defined as operating income less capital expenditures. Discretionary expenses include capital expenditures, R&D expenses, and advertising expenses. Year − 1 is the fiscal year preceding the year during which the firm goes public. The test for differences between the two groups is performed using the Wilcoxon two-sample signed-rank test.
[a] Significant at 0.01 level.
[b] Significant at 0.05 level.
[c] Significant at 0.10 level.

ating performance measures in the year prior to the IPO reveals that VC-backed firms have significantly lower operating return on assets (18.12% versus 23.13%) and operating cash flows over assets (8.13% versus 11.60%) in comparison to non-VC-backed IPOs. The VC-backed firms, however, have significantly higher capital expenditures deflated by assets (10.07% versus 7.14%) compared to the non-VC-backed firms. One interpretation of these results is that monitoring by venture captialists deters management from cutbacks in capital expenditures or other attempts to window-dress the accounting numbers prior to going public in the hope of securing higher than justified valuations. For instance, managers can attempt to pump up pre-IPO performance measures by deferring expenses, borrowing income from future periods, or cutting back on discretionary expenditures. Further support for this conjecture is provided by examining the differences in discretionary expenditure between the two groups prior to the IPO. The VC-backed firms have significantly higher pre-IPO median levels of discretionary expenditures deflated by total assets (25.62% versus 17.93%) and discretionary expenditure deflated by sales (17.85% versus 12.56%) compared to non-VC-backed firms. Since lower profit margins and higher discretionary expenditures characterize the early growth phase of the industry life cycle, the above results seem to indicate that VC-backed issuers are able to go public at an earlier phase in their growth cycle than would be otherwise possible.

Comparison of Operating Performance of VC-backed and non-VC-backed IPOs

In Table 3, comparisons of the post-issue operating performance of the VC-backed and a matched sample of non-VC-backed firms relative to the

Table 3. Comparison of the Post-issue Operating Performance of VC-backed and a Matched Sample of Non-VC-backed IPOs

Measure of operating performance	Years relative to completion of IPO											
	−1 to 0			−1 to +1			−1 to +2			−1 to +3		
	VC-backed IPOs	Non-VC-backed IPOs	Z	VC-backed IPOs	Non-VC-backed IPOs	Z	VC-backed IPOs	Non-VC-backed IPOs	Z	VC-backed IPOs	Non-VC-backed IPOs	Z
Panel A: Operating return on assets												
Median change (%)	−4.23[a]	−4.44[a]	−1.84[b]	−7.36[c]	−9.49[a]	−1.91[b]	−7.39[b]	−14.36[a]	−2.18[b]	−4.66	−13.43[a]	−1.68[c]
Number of observations	130	131		123	121		115	111		110	102	
Panel B: operating cash flows/total assets												
Median change (%)	−2.80[b]	−5.07[a]	−2.16[b]	−6.81[a]	−11.63[a]	−2.70[a]	−7.27[a]	−11.48[b]	−2.42[b]	−5.51[a]	−8.20[a]	−1.71[c]
Number of observations	133	126		126	117		119	107		114	99	
Panel C: Sales growth												
Median percentage change	51.58[a]	38.61[a]	−2.55[a]	126.87[a]	70.97[a]	−2.83[a]	177.36[a]	113.66[a]	−2.75[a]	219.95[a]	141.48[a]	−2.85[a]
Number of observations	135	131		128	123		122	112		116	105	
Panel D: Capital expenditure growth												
Median change (%)	90.12[a]	115.71[a]	1.18	146.86[a]	166.89[a]	0.75	201.09[a]	139.01[a]	−0.21	172.45[a]	200.64[a]	0.03
Number of observations	133	128		126	120		119	109		113	102	

Table values are for the median change/growth rates expressed as a percentage for VC-backed and a matched sample of non-VC-backed IPOs issued during the period 1976 through 1988. Operating return on assets equals operating income before depreciation as a percentage of total assets. Operating cash flows are defined as operating income less capital expenditures. Sales growth equals the growth in net sales. Year −1 is the fiscal year preceding the year during which the firm goes public. The test for difference between the two groups is based on Wilcoxon's two sample-signed rank test.

[a] Significant at 0.01 level.
[b] Significant at 0.05 level.
[c] Significant at 0.10 level.

pre-IPO fiscal year are provided. In panel A, the median change in operating returns on assets for the VC and non-VC group are reported. The evidence suggests that while the operating return on assets decline for both groups relative to their pre-IPO levels, the decline is significantly higher for the non-VC-backed IPOs. For instance, the change in operating return on assets for the years 0, $+1+2$ and $+3$ relative to year -1 are -4.23%, -7.36%, -7.39% and -4.66% for the VC group and -4.44%, -9.49%, -14.36% and -13.43% for the non-VC group. Further, in each post-issue year relative to year -1, the VC group demonstrates relatively superior performance in terms of the operating return on assets compared to the non-VC group, with the differences significant at the 0.10, 0.10, 0.05, and 0.10 levels respectively.

In panel B of Table 3, the median change in post-issue operating cash flows deflated by assets for the VC-backed and non-VC backed IPOs are compared. Once again, the VC-backed issuers demonstrate significantly superior operating performance relative to the non-VC-backed issuers in each post-issue year. It is also clear that the VC-backed issuers display significantly lower levels of decline relative to the pre-IPO year compared to the non-VC group. For instance, the decline in operating cash flows over assets for year $+3$ relative to year -1 is significantly lower for the VC group (-5.51% versus -8.20%) compared to the non-VC group. A similar pattern is evident for all the other post-issue years considered.

In panel C, the median post-issue sales growth for the VC-backed and non-VC-backed IPOs are compared. The VC-backed firms exhibit significantly higher increase in sales in each post-issue year relative to the pre-IPO year. For instance, the increase in sales in year $+3$ relative to year -1 for the VC group is 219.95% compared to an increase of 141.48% for the non $-$ VC-backed group, with the difference significant at the 0.01 level. The results are consistent with the conjecture that VCs are able to bring issues to the market in the early phase of the growth cycle and are able to select candidate firms with good sales growth prospects.

One possible explanation for the relatively superior performance of VC-backed firms is that they cut back on capital expenditures after the initial offering, which may lead to higher margins at least in the short run. To investigate this issue, we compare the growth in capital expenditures for the two groups in panel D. The results suggest that while both VC-backed and non-VC-backed IPOs increase their post-issue capital expenditures relative to the pre-IPO year, there is no difference between the two groups. Thus, there is no evidence to suggest that the relatively superior performance of VC-backed IPOs is the result of cutbacks in capital expenditures.

In summary, while both VC-backed and non-VC-backed issuers exhibit a decline in performance relative to their pre-IPO levels, the VC group demonstrates relatively superior operating performance compared to the non-VC group. This result is robust to both the specific performance metric as well as the time-window over which performance change is measured.

Cross-sectional Regression Analysis

It is possible that the relatively superior performance of VC-backed IPOs documented above can be attributed to other factors such as IPO offer size, management ownership retention, changes in discretionary expenditures, etc. To address this issue, cross-sectional regression analysis examining whether the change in operating performance is related to venture capital participation after controlling for these other factors is presented in Table 4. The change in operating performance is measured over the following two time-windows; (1) between year -1 and $+1$, and (2) between year -1 and the average of years $+1$ to $+3$.[11]

The independent variables include the natural logarithm of IPO offer amount ($LSIZE$), fraction of the firm retained by entrepreneurs after the IPO ($ALPHA$), venture capital participation (VC), and changes in discretionary expenditures ($DISCR$).[12] $DALPHA$ is a dummy variable taking on the value 1 if the management ownership retention is above the median level and 0 otherwise. The variable VC is a dummy variable taking on the value 1 if there is VC participation and 0 otherwise. Jain and Kini (1994) find $DALPHA$ and $LSIZE$ to be significant explanatory variables in explaining post-issue operating performance of IPOs. They interpret the positive relation between post-issue operating performance and $DALPHA$

Table 4. Cross-sectional Regression Analysis

Dependent variable	Intercept	DALPHA	LSIZE	DISCR	VC	R^2	F-value	N
Panel A: Operating return on assets								
Change in operating return on assets from year −1 to year +1	−36.14 (−8.15)[a]	5.10 (1.89)[c]	6.73 (4.47)[a]	−0.39 (−4.27)[a]	5.67 (2.10)[b]	17.52	13.79	241
Change in operating return on assets from year −1 to average of year +1 to +3	−37.91 (−7.99)[a]	5.50 (1.89)[c]	6.83 (4.23)[a]	−0.38 (−3.85)[a]	4.80 (1.65)[c]	17.42	11.86	206
Panel B: Operating cash flows/total assets								
Change in operating cash flows/total assets from year −1 to +1	−38.51 (−8.76)[a]	7.10 (2.66)[a]	6.60 (4.44)[a]	−1.02 (−10.77)[a]	6.83 (2.56)[a]	40.70	42.01	239
Change in operating cash flows/total assets from year −1 to average of years +1 to +3	−38.03 (−7.97)[a]	6.22 (2.14)[b]	6.66 (4.13)[a]	−0.91 (−9.01)[a]	6.06 (2.08)[b]	36.37	30.15	204

Cross-sectional regression analysis of changes in operating performance of a sample of 136 VC-backed and a matched sample of non-VC-backed IPOs is reported. The variable *DALPHA* is a dummy variable taking on the value 1 if the fraction of the firm retained by entrepreneurs (alpha) is above the median and 0 otherwise. The variable alpha is computed on the assumption that overallotment options, if any, are not exercised. The variable *LSIZE* represents the logarithm of the IPO offer amount. The variable *DISCR* represents the change in discretionary expenditures (sum of capital expenditures, advertising, and R&D) over total assets in year −1. The change in discretionary expenditures is measured contemporaneously with the change in operating performance. The variable *VC* is a dummy variable which when equal to 1 indicates venture capital participation and is zero otherwise. The independent variables are the operating return on assets and operating cash flows deflated by total assets. The change in operating performance is measured from years +1 and the average of years +1 to +3 relative to year −1. The *t*-statistics for each parameter are reported in parentheses and the significance levels are also indicated. All reported significance levels are based on two-tailed Wilcoxon's signed-rank test. Year −1 is the fiscal year preceding the year during which the firm goes public.

[a] Significant at the 0.01 level.
[b] Significant at the 0.05 level.
[c] Significant at the 0.10 level.

as evidence consistent with the Jensen and Meckling (1976) agency hypothesis and the Leland and Pyle (1944) signalling hypothesis. Holthausen and Larcker (1993) find a significant positive relation between changes in discretionary expenditures and post-issue operating performance changes of reverse LBOs, a special class of IPOs. They argue that this result implies that the decline in operating performance of reverse LBOs cannot be explained by increased discretionary expenditures. Consistent with these studies, we include *DALPHA* and *DISCR* as independent variables in the cross-sectional regression analysis in an attempt to isolate the effect of VC participation after controlling for other factors affecting performance. If venture capitalists provide value-added monitoring and control services, we would expect a positive and significant coefficient associated with the variable *VC*.

The results in Table 4 suggest that changes in operating performance are significantly positively related to *VC* and *LSIZE* and negatively related to *DISCR*. The coefficient associated with the

variable *DALPHA* is positive and generally significant. In panel A, the results with operating return on assets as the performance measure is reported. The coefficient associated with the variable *VC* is consistently positive and significant, suggesting that venture capital participation leads to improved performance after controlling for other potential determinants of post-issue operating performance. The coefficient of the changes in discretionary expenditure variable is negative and significant, which suggests that the increase in discretionary expenditures is associated with a decline in operating return on assets. Apparently managers spend too much on discretionary expenditures leading to overinvestment and a subsequent decline in operating performance. These results are consistent with Jensen's (1993) conjecture that simultaneous adoption of technological innovation can lead to excess capacity and reduced margins.

The results in panel B with operating cash flows over assets are essentially similar to those reported in panel A. The coefficient associated with the variable *VC* is consistently positive and significant in all regressions. Thus, the results in Table 4 suggest that VC-backed firms provide relatively superior operating performance compared to non-VC firms even after controlling for other potential determinants of post-issue performance.

Does the Market Recognize the Value of Venture Capitalist Montioring?

While our evidence is indicative of the value of VC participation in the IPO market, an interesting question which arises is whether the market recognizes this value-added potential. To address this question, we examine whether the market has higher expectations of future earnings performance from VC-backed firms relative to non-VC-backed firms. VCs usually claim that they help firms go public at higher price/earnings (P/E) ratios. To test the validity of this conjecture, in Table 5 we compare the median levels of the market-to-book ratio and the P/E ratio for the VC-backed and non-VC-backed IPO firms for several post-issue years.[13]

In panel A of Table 5 the median market-to-book ratio of VC-backed and non-VC-backed IPO firms are compared for years 0 to +3. The evidence suggests that VC-backed IPO firms have higher median market-to-book ratio compared to the non-VC-backed IPO firms in each post-issue year. The difference is significant every year starting year 0 until year +2. In panel B, the P/E ratio of the two groups are compared. Initially, the median P/E ratio of the VC-backed group is significantly higher than the non-VC-backed

group. For instance, in year 0, the median P/E ratio of the VC group is 18.92 while that of the non-VC-backed group is 13.86, with the difference significant at the 0.01 level. A similar pattern is observed in years +1 and +2. In year +3, however, there is no difference in the P/E ratio of the two groups.

Thus, the results suggest that the market recognizes the value of venture capitalist monitoring which is reflected in the higher levels of market-to-book ratios and P/E ratios at the time of the offering. The results also seem to support the contention of venture capitalists that they are able to take issuers public at higher P/E ratios. However, as the IPO firms season, the differences in the market-to-book ratios and P/E ratios between the two groups disappear. We believe that there are at least two potential reasons for these measures to converge for the VC-backed and non-VC-backed groups. First, as the IPO firms season and their growth phase levels off, the VCs tend to divest their holdings and redeploy their resources in other growing private companies. The levelling of growth prospects and the reduction in monitoring as a result of the departure of the VCs is recognized by the market and manifested in the form of lower market-to-book and P/E ratios. Second, as the firm seasons, the information asymmetry is reduced and capital market monitoring takes over, thereby, reducing the incremental value of additional monitoring by VCs. Since these two explanations are not mutually exclusive it is difficult to pinpoint which of the two is the primary factor affecting market assessments.

Table 5. Market Expectations of Operating Performance

Description	Year 0			Year +1			Year +2			Year +3		
	VC	Non-VC	Z	VC	Non-VC	Z	VC	Non-VC	Z	VC	Non-VC	Z
Market to book	3.09	2.71	1.75[c]	2.47	1.97	1.96[b]	2.18	2.07	0.52	1.88	1.59	1.05
	(133)	(134)		(129)	(124)		(123)	(113)		(116)	(105)	
Price/earnings	18.93	13.86	1.63	18.29	12.71	2.62[a]	15.76	12.79	2.31[b]	12.50	13.13	0.73
(P/E) ratio	(133)	(131)		(128)	(124)		(127)	(112)		(113)	(104)	

The median levels of the market-to-book ratio and the price/earnings (P/E) ratio for each post-issue IPO year are reported for VC-backed and a matched sample of non-VC-backed IPOs. Fiscal year 0 represents the first post-IPO fiscal year. The Wilcoxon two sample signed-rank test is used to test for differences in the median levels between the VC- and non-VC-backed IPOs.
[a] Significant at the 0.01 level.
[b] Significant at the 0.05 level.
[b] Significant at the 0.10 level.

QUALITY OF MONITORING AND OPERATING PERFORMANCE

Even among venture capitalists there is likely to be wide variation in the quality and effectiveness of monitoring services provided by them. In this section, we attempt to identify factors which proxy for the quality of venture capitalists monitoring and test the association between quality of monitoring and operating performance. Our investigation is similar in spirit to BMPV (1990), who examine the relation between proxies for monitoring quality and the underpricing at the IPO. They document a negative relation between underpricing and several proxies for monitoring quality such as number of venture capitalists involved, length of service on the board of directors, age of venture capitalists, etc. Jain and Kini (1994), however, find no relation between post-issue operating performance and initial underpricing. Further, Michaely and Shaw (1994) find no relation between long-run investment performances and initial underpricing. Thus, examining the relation between VC monitoring quality and post-issue operating performance instead of underpricing is a more appropriate and direct test of the value of VC participation in the IPO market.

We examine the relation between post-issue operating performance and three proxies for the quality of VC monitoring. The data sources for these proxies include the *Venture Capital Journal* and *Pratt's Guide to Venture Capital Sources*. Our first proxy of monitoring quality is the number of VCs with equity positions in the firm before the IPO (NVC). The presence of larger number of VCs suggests that the issuer has convinced several informed investors that its future prospects are good. Further, the lead venture capitalist has greater incentives to monitor the firm carefully since its reputation capital is at stake and failure could mean diminished ability to establish subsequent deals. Hence, we would expect a positive relation between post-issue operating performance and the number of venture capitalists.

Another proxy for monitoring quality employed is the length of time between the induction of the first VC on the board of directors and the IPO (BD). The longer the service on the board of directors, the greater the ability to monitor and influence actions taken by the firm. Consequently, a positive relation between operating performance and length of service on the board is expected. However, as BMPV (1990) point out, extended board service can also indicate that the issuer is a marginal company that needs extensive preparation before it can go public. The third proxy of monitoring quality that we examine is the number of VCs on the board of directors at the time of the IPO (NBD). Larger numbers of VC board members imply enhanced ability to control and execute their agenda. Hence, a positive relation is expected.

We estimate separate cross-sectional regressions for each proxy of monitoring quality. As the above variables are all proxies for monitoring quality and tend to be correlated, each time that we estimate a cross-sectional regression, we only include one of these proxies of monitoring quality as an independent variable. In line with our analysis in Table 4, we include *LSIZE*, *DALPHA*, and *DISCR* as control variables in all regressions and these variables are as defined earlier. The results are reported for both operating return on assets and operating cash flows over assets. Further, as before, we report regression results with performance changes measured over: (1) the period -1 to $+1$ and (2) the period -1 to the average of $+1$ to $+3$. The results of the cross-sectional regression analysis is reported in Table 6.

In panel A, the results with the number of VCs with equity positions prior to the IPO are reported. With both measures of performance and every time-window considered, the coefficient associated with the variable *NVC* is positive and significant. Thus, larger numbers of VCs with pre-IPO equity positions increase effectiveness of monitoring leading to improved performance. In panel B, the relation between operating performance measures and the number of VC board members is examined. As expected, the coefficient of the variable is positive in each regression. However, the relation is significant only for the operating return on assets measured over the period -1 to $+1$. In panel C, the relation between operating performance and duration of board service is examined. The results suggest that there is no relation between duration of board service and operating performance. As argued earlier, this result is not unexpected as longer duration of board service may indicate greater ability to monitor but also indicate that the issuer is a marginal company.

Table 6.   Monitoring Quality and Post-issue Operating Performance.

Variables	OPRA (−1 to +1)	AVOPRA (−1 to Avg of +1 to +3)	OCFA (−1 to +1)	AVOCFA (−1 to Avg +1 to +3)
Panel A: Number of venture capitalists (*NVC*)				
Intercept	−25.77 (−3.46)[a]	−28.14 (−3.45)[a]	−26.98 (−3.72)[a]	−29.42 (−3.72)[a]
DALPHA	5.32 (1.32)	2.49 (0.55)	5.80 (1.49)	2.98 (0.69)
LSIZE	3.25 (1.22)	3.37 (1.16)	3.34 (1.30)	3.86 (1.38)
DISCR	−0.34 (−2.64)[a]	−0.46 (−3.24)	−1.14 (−8.02)[a]	−1.12 (−7.61)[a]
NVC	0.95 (2.11)[b]	1.24 (2.44)[b]	0.75 (1.70)[c]	1.14 (2.32)[b]
F	5.61	6.38	20.38	18.64
R²	17.90	22.31	44.42	45.87
Panel B: Board participation by venture capitalists (*NBD*)				
Intercept	−28.90 (−3.82)[a]	−32.29 (−3.85)[a]	−29.17 (−3.96)[a]	−32.74 (−4.01)[a]
DALPHA	6.72 (1.67)[c]	5.21 (1.15)	6.95 (1.78)[c]	5.52 (1.26)
LSIZE	3.86 (1.48)	4.94 (1.72)[c]	4.02 (1.58)	5.59 (2.01)[b]
DISCR	−0.31 (−2.33)[b]	−0.41 (−2.74)[a]	−1.13 (−7.73)[a]	−1.09 (−7.01)[a]
NBD	3.62 (1.92)[c]	3.03 (1.36)	2.22 (1.22)	1.86 (0.87)
F	5.33	5.12	19.53	16.44
R²	17.31	18.89	43.61	43.05
Panel C: Duration of VC participation on board of directors (*BD*)				
Intercept	−20.49 (−2.24)[b]	−25.21 (−2.48)[b]	−22.20 (−2.55)[a]	−27.46 (−2.83)[a]
DALPHA	6.86 (1.44)	4.81 (0.91)	6.77 (1.49)	5.02 (1.01)
LSIZE	3.36 (1.19)	4.58 (1.40)	3.47 (1.21)	5.32 (1.70)[c]
DISCR	−0.37 (−2.51)[a]	−0.44 (−2.64)[a]	−1.17 (−7.03)[a]	−1.09 (−6.25)[a]
BD	−0.06 (−0.99)	−0.02 (−0.23)	−0.07 (−1.07)	−0.02 (−0.25)
F	2.91	2.96	13.40	11.62
R²	12.59	14.71	40.12	40.60

Cross-sectional regression analysis of changes in operating performance of a sample of 136 VC-backed IPOs is reported. *OPRA* is defined as the change in operating return in assets from year −1 to +1 while *AVOPRA* is measured as the change in operating return on assets from year −1 to average of years +1 to +3. *OCFA* is the change in operating cash flows deflated by assets from year −1 to year +1 while *AVOCFA* is the change in operating cash flows over assets from year −1 to average of years +1 to +3. *ALPHA* is the fraction of the firm retained by entrepreneurs which is computed based on the assumption that overallotment options, if any, are not exercised. The variable *DALPHA* is a dummy variable taking on the value 1 if the level is above the median and 0 otherwise. The variable *LSIZE* represents the logarithm of the IPO offer amount. The variable *DISCR* represents the change in discretionary expenditures (sum of capital expenditures, advertising, and R & D) over total assets in year −1. The change in discretionary expenditures is measured contemporaneously with the change in operating performance. The variable *NVC* represents the number of venture capitalists with equity positions in the company prior to the IPO. The variable *BD* represents the time between the first venture capitalist joining the board of directors to the IPO. The variable *NBD* represents the number of venture capitalists serving on the board of directors at the time of the IPO. The independent variables are the operating return on assets and operating cash flows deflated by total assets. The change in operating performance is measured from years +1 and the average of years +1 to +3 relative to year −1. The *t*-statistics for each parameter are reported in parentheses. All reported significance levels are based on the Wilcoxon's two-tailed signed-rank tests. Year −1 is the fiscal year preceding the year during which the firm goes public
[a] Significant at the 0.01 level.
[b] Significant at the 0.05 level.
[c] Significant at the 0.10 level.

Thus, our results suggest that variations in the quality of monitoring affect post-issue operating performance. Further, the number of VCs with equity position in the pre-IPO firm best captures variations in the quality of monitoring and is positively related to the post-issue operating performance.

CONCLUSIONS

This paper examines the link between VC participation and the post-issue operating performance of initial public offerings. Earlier studies have observed that VCs specialize their investments in firms requiring intensive monitoring services.

Consistent with the conjecture that VCs also provide post-issue value-added monitoring services, we find that VC-backed IPOs exhibit relatively superior post-issue operating performance compared to a control sample of non-VC-backed IPOs matched as closely as possible to industry and offering size. Further, cross-sectional regression analyses reveal that the VC-backed firms continue to demonstrate relatively superior operating performance after controlling for other determinants of post-issue operating performance.

We find evidence to suggest that the capital markets recognize the value-added potential of VC monitoring. The VC-backed issuers initially have significantly higher levels of market-to-book ratio and price/earnings ratio compared to the non-VC-backed issuers. Subsequently, the difference between the two groups of IPO issuers disappears. One explanation for this result is that the monitoring services of VCs are most valuable during the early stages of the issuers transition to a public corporation. Subsequently, as the VCs exit and market monitoring takes over, the incremental value-added potential of VC monitoring declines.

Overall, our results provide additional evidence of the important role VCs play in bringing new issues to the market and guiding them through the initial years as a public company. Our study has implications both for managers of issuing firms and investors in the IPO market. Managers of issuing firms, especially those in risky and growing market segments with uncertain future prospects, should seek VC participation. The involvement of VCs speeds up the process of development and allows the company to go public earlier than it would be otherwise possible. The companies also go public at higher valuations than would be possible otherwise, providing issuers with additional capital at the IPO. Further, in the initial stages of a public corporation, VC monitoring adds value as evidenced by improved corporate performance. From the investors' point of view, VC participation signals quality. This should lead to increased interest in VC-backed IPOs compared to similar non-VC-backed issues.

NOTES

1. VCs may, however, have incentives to time the IPO by going public when equity values are high even if they do not themselves sell equity at the initial offering. Taking companies public when equity values are high minimizes the dilution of VCs' ownership stake. Lerner (1994) finds evidence of VCs timing their IPOs in a study involving 136 VC-backed IPO firms in the biotechnology industry.

2. To avoid the problem of survivorship bias, there are no requirements that these firms have post-IPO financial data on Compustat for all years studied in this paper. As a result, the number of firms in the sample varies for different time-windows under consideration.

3. Constraining the offering size to $3 million in 1976 dollars marginally reduces the sample size but does not qualitatively change any of our results.

4. The number of VC-backed IPOs is reduced from 177 to 136 due to the following reasons: (1) no three-digit SIC matches are available and (2) in some industries the number of VC-backed firms in the initial sample is larger than the number of non-VC-backed IPOs. For instance, in SIC code 357, there are 44 VC-backed firms in comparison to 23 non-VC-backed firms and in SIC code 367, there are 16 VC-backed firms in comparison to 13 non-VC-backed firms.

5. We repeat the analysis using the full sample of 177 VC-backed and 505 non-VC-backed IPOs that meet our sample selection criteria and compare the performance of the two groups based on both raw and industry-adjusted operating performance measures. The results are qualitatively similar to those reported in the paper. However, we believe that the matched-pairs methodology allows us to focus more closely on the question of the effect of VC participation on performance.

6. All results are replicated by deflating the two measures of operating performance by net sales (Compustat data item 12) rather than total assets. The results are qualitatively similar. For purposes of brevity, they are not reported here but are available upon request from the authors.

7. Prior studies examining operating performance changes typically employ median measures. As examples, see Kaplan (1989), Smith (1990), Muscarella and Vetsuypens (1990), and Degeorge and Zeckhauser (1993). As a robustness check, we repeat the analysis using means for the non-skewed measures. We arrive at similar conclusions using means rather than medians.

8. By employing change in levels, an attempt is being made to measure the improvement in the firm's operating performance during the first few post-IPO years. Typically in assessing a firm's value, investors in addition to levels are also interested in the improvement in operating performance. Earlier studies by Kaplan (1989), Smith (1990) and Degeorge and Zeckhauser (1993) also use change in levels to measure operating performance improvement.

9. Since we are in most cases interested in whether VC-backed firms outperform non-VC-backed firms,

606   B. A. JAIN AND O. KINI

using a two-tailed test understates the significance of the results.
10. The frequency distribution by year for the VC-backed and non-VC-backed IPO firms is also very similar.
11. Regressions using several other time-windows over which performance changes are measured are also estimated. The results are qualitatively similar to those reported in Table 4.
12. Changes in discretionary expenditures are measured contemporaneously with the change in operating performance.
13. The market-to-book ratio is defined as the ratio of market value of equity to the book value of equity (Compustat data item 24 × data item 25)/(data item 60). The price/earnings ratio is defined as the price divided by earnings per share (Compustat data item 24/data item 58).

REFERENCES

C. B. Barry, C. J. Muscarella, J. W. Peavy and M. R. Vetsuypens (1990). The role of venture capital in the creation of public companies. *Journal of Financial Economics*, **27**, 447–71.

F. Degeorge and R. Zeckhauser (1993). The reverse LBO decision and firm performance: theory and evidence. *Journal of Finance*, **48**, 1323–48.

D. Gladstone (1989). *Venture Capital Investing*, Englewood Cliffs, NJ: Prentice Hall.

R. W. Holthausen and D. F. Larcker (1993). The financial performance of reverse leveraged buyouts. *Journal of Financial Economics*, forthcoming.

R. G. Ibbotson (1975). Price performance of common stock issues. *Journal of Financial Economics*, **2**, 235–72.

B. A Jain and O. Kini (1994). The post-issue operating performance of IPO firms. *Journal of Finance*, **49**, 1699–1726.

M. C. Jensen and W. Meckling (1976). Theory of the firm: managerial behavior, agency costs and ownership structure. *Journal of Financial Economics*, **3**, 306–60.

M. C. Jensen (1993). The modern industrial revolution, exit and control systems. *Journal of Finance*, **48**, 831–80.

S. Kaplan (1989). The effect of management buyouts on operating performance and value. *Journal of Financial Economics*, **24**, 217–54.

H. E. Leland and D. Pyle (1977). Information asymmetries, financial structure, and financial intermediation. *Journal of Finance*, **32**, 371–87.

J. Lerner (1994). Venture capitalists and the decision to go public. *Journal of Financial Economics*, **35**, 293–316.

W. Megginson and K. Weiss (1991). The certification role of venture capitalists in bringing new issues to the market. *Journal of Finance*, **46**, 879–903.

R. Michaely and W. H. Shaw (1994). Asymmetric information, adverse selection and the pricing of initial public offerings. *Review of Financial Studies*, forthcoming.

C. J. Muscarella and M. R. Vetsuypens (1990). Efficiency and organizational structure: A study of reverse LBOs. *Journal of Finance*, **45**, 1389–1413.

W. A. Sahlman (1990). The structure and governance of venture-capital organization. *Journal of Financial Economics*, **27**, 473–521.

W. A. Sahlman and H. H. Stevenson (1985). Capital market myopia. *Journal of Business Venturing*, **1**, 7–30.

A. Smith (199). Corporate ownership structure and performance: The case of management buyouts. *Journal of Financial Economics*, **27**, 143–64.

K. Warne (1988). Risk and industry characteristics of venture capital investments. Washington University of St Louis, working paper.

[20]

The *Second* 'Equity Gap': Exit Problems for Seed and Early Stage Venture Capitalists and Their Investee Companies

by Gordon Murray

Tʜᴇ ᴀʟʟᴇɢᴇᴅ ᴇxɪsᴛᴇɴᴄᴇ ᴏғ ᴀɴ 'equity gap' facing new and small enterprises is well documented in official reports (MacMillan 1931, Bolton 1971, Wilson 1979 and NEDO 1986). The absence, or limited use (Keasey and Watson, 1992), of long-term risk finance, i.e. equity, and the consequent excessive reliance by small firms on short-term debt increases their vulnerability particularly in times of high interest rates (Cowling *et al* 1991) and/or other demands on gross revenues. The rise in mortality rates among small and medium-sized enterprises during the recent recession in the UK (individual and corporate insolvencies in England and Wales rose by 83 per cent and 45 per cent respectively from 1990 to 1991, DTI 1992 and continued to rise in 1992) has lead to calls from industry pressure groups, including the Confederation of British Industry (1993) for a greater contribution from external providers of long-term equity in the total funding of small firms[1]. This debate has been engaged during a period when the relationship between clearing banks and SME owners and their trade associations had been sufficiently hostile for the Government to initiate a Treasury/Bank of England enquiry into the behaviour of banks towards SME financing. The Director General of the Office of Fair Trading subsequently reported (*Financial Times*, 28th June, 1991) that there was no evidence that the banks had abused an oligopolistic market position.

New technology-based firms (NTBFs) are particularly vulnerable to shortages of adequate finance in their formative periods (Kay, 1992; Oakley, 1984). The frequent absence of substantial collateral other than intellectual property rights, coupled with the commercial and technical risks associated with novel and unproven technologies (Van Glinow & Mohrman, 1990) make these firms unattractive to risk-adverse providers of debt finance (Binks *et al*, 1992).

Moore (1993), in a UK small firm survey, segregated 89 small high-technology companies in a series of in-depth, face-to-face interviews. Further questions were specifically asked on seed capital and start-up finance in a subsequent follow-up, telephone survey. Personal finance was of 'overwhelming importance' on start-up for 44 per cent of the small, high-technology companies interviewed. 'Star' companies, which had demonstrated the most rapid rise in

employment growth, were particularly reliant (56 per cent) on their own sources of funds. In contrast, while 69 per cent of the sample had considered bank finance as a source of initial financing, the survey showed that only 7 per cent of the 42 companies re-interviewed had received bank loans on start-up. This compared to 10 per cent of firms which had received venture capital finance. Moore's findings on the relative unimportance of bank debt on start-up corroborates the US experience of NTBFs (Roberts, 1991).

The potential of NTBFs and their initially parlous financial resources would suggest that they are suitable condidates for the more speculative finance of venture capitalists rather than bank debt. However, in a 1990 survey (Murray, 1991) of twenty-two of the UK's leading[2] venture capitalists, commissioned by the British Venture Capital Association, respondents were asked their opinion of the single biggest failure of the UK venture capital industry in its first decade

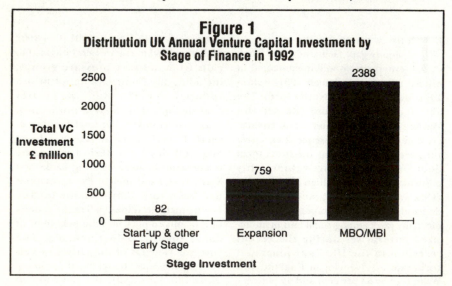

Figure 1
Distribution UK Annual Venture Capital Investment by Stage of Finance in 1992

(1980–90) of activity. Almost unanimously, respondents cited the limited support given by the industry to funding new, entrepreneurial companies, particularly in the field of technology. There was a consensus that the UK industry had rapidly moved from providing *primary capital* for new ventures to the less risky and more profitable *replacement capital* activities of development finance, management buy-outs and buy-ins, and secondary financing.

While respondents bemoaned the lack

firms, was almost universally regarded as incapable of realising acceptable investment returns when returns compensate for illiquidity and firm-specific risk. Murray and Lott, 1992 found that venture capitalists required an annualised Internal Rate of Return of 57 per cent and 52 per cent on seed capital and start-up investments in NTBFs, respectively. A corroboration of the general unattractiveness of early stage investment to the majority of venture capitalists can be found in the Autumn 1992 survey of the UK venture capital

Table 1
European and UK 'Early Stage' Venture Capital Statistics 1984–1992

Year	European Venture Capital Industry				British Venture Capital Industry	
	Seed Capital		Start-ups		Start-ups	
	£ million[1]	% Total	£ million[1]	% Total	£ million	% Total
1984	n.a.	n.a.	n.a.	n.a.	24.7	17.8
1985	24.4	2.9	188.3	22.5	31.6	11.7
1986[2]	7.7	0.5	236.0	16.9	57.9	15.1
1987	20.9	1.1	216.7	11.0	75.0	8.0
1988	6.5	0.3	296.3	12.3	70.0	5.4
1989	27.1	0.9	268.1	9.0	86.0	6.1
1990	22.9	0.7	237.5	7.7	76.0	6.9
1991	32.2	1.0	191.5	5.9	35.0	3.5
1992	19.9	0.6	185.1	5.3	43.0	3.0

Sources: EVCA Yearbooks 1987–93, BVCA Reports on Investment Activity 1984–92.
[1] Figures converted ECU to £ Sterling at rates specified in EVCA Yearbooks.
[2] 1986 figures taken from 1988 EVCA Yearbook.
[3] While there have been definitional changes over time to BVCA annual statistics, they do not obscure the underlying trend. EVCA figures, which in 1993 include 17 European countries, should be viewed as approximations, particularly in the earlier years.

of 'true venturing' (the term "classic venture capital" is also used in the US by Bygrave and Timmons, 1992) within the maturing UK venture capital industry, they observed that early stage investment, particularly in new technology-based

industry by accountants Levy Gee. 134 investing organisations were asked to rank their preferred stage of investment. Development capital and MBOs ranked first and second by choice. Out of a total of nine investment categories, start-up

62 | *International Small Business Journal 12, 4*

finance was placed seventh and seed capital ranked last.

Industry statistics from the European Venture Capital Association[3] and the British Venture Capital Association similarly indicate the venture capital industry's diminishing involvement with 'early stage' finance. Since the two 'vintage' years of extraordinary venture capital activity in 1988/89, early stage investment in all enterprises, including both NTBFs and non-technology-based firms has declined both in nominal values and relative importance to other, later stage investments.

Venture capitalists in Murray's 1990 survey did not question the economic importance of the new, entrepreneurial firm. Indeed, respondents saw the increasing status of entrepreneurs in the UK throughout the 1980s as one of the most important factors promoting the growth of the venture capital industry, and its political influence. Venture capitalists' intuitive acknowledgement of the economic importance of NTBFs is supported by several academic studies (for example, Monck *et al*, 1988; Rothwell, 1989; ACOST, 1990) which indicate the key contribution made by NTBFs in the UK to R&D efficiency, economic growth and employment.

While Venture capitalists may see the role of NTBFs as important to the economy, observers have questioned the role that the industry plays in supporting new and young firms (Murray and Lott, 1992). One conclusion of the ACOST study (p35) into barriers to growth in smaller UK firms reflected a general consensus which was also held by the managers of early stage, technology funds: *"In short, the contribution of the venture capital industry to overcoming barriers to growth in smaller firms remains limited."*

Focus of the Research — The 'Complementarity' of Early Stage and Development Capital Activity

Given the apparent unattractiveness[4] for the majority of UK venture capitalists of providing small amounts of early stage finance, the present research was concerned to view this situation from the perspective of those few funds[5] that have specialised in the apparently heroic area of early stage investment activity. Early stage funds are, by definition, primarily concerned with NTFB investment. Given the high investment performance targets cited, returns of this order are only likely to be widely feasible for successful firms in rapidly growing, technology markets.

Specifically, the research focus concentrated on the issue of the 'realisation' or 'exit'. This is either the outright sale of an early stage fund's investment in an investee company to a third party or the refinancing of that business for further growth with new investors, primarily development capitalists, being invited to participate ('syndicate') with the original investor in the continued funding of the portfolio company. In looking at the options available to the early stage venture capitalists, this paper particularly explores their relationship with development capitalists or other new financial partners in arranging the follow-on finance required to support the future growth of the investee firms in the seed capitalists' portfolios.

It is hypothesised that there exists the opportunity for a *'complementarity'* between early stage venture capitalists and later stage, development capitalists which will, in theory at least, allow for reciprocal and mutually advantageous co-operation. Later stage venture capitalists reject approximately 95 per cent

(Bannock, 1991; Dixon, 1991) of all investee applicants. A number of these applicants may well have potentially attractive proposals but be at too early a stage for the involvement of the development capitalist. These latter investors typically prefer making equity investments of £0.5 million upwards to management teams with an assessable track record. In addition, most development capitalists are not organised to provide the intensive 'hands-on' support, and often elementary business advice, required by the inexperienced technology entrepreneur (Gorman and Sahlman, 1989; Flynn, 1991).

Unlike their development capitalist counterparts, early stage venture capitalists usually command very modest investment resources. Three-quarters of the twelve early stage firms sampled had funds of under £10 million. In contrast, the largest thirty investors members of the British Venture Capital Association each commanded funds of over £100 million in 1992. A recent review of the European Seed Capital Fund Scheme found that the average size of fund of the original twenty-one seed capital organisations was 1.7 million Ecu. — a sum which the authors considered unsustainably small (Murray and Francis, 1992). While organised to give the intensive, 'hands-on' support necessary to nurture a very young company, few early stage investors have the financial resources to fund the successive stages of follow-on finance required by a successful and rapidly growing young company.

Thus, there would appear to be the potential for a symbiotic relationship. Early stage investors could nurture new and young companies (some of which would be redirected to the early stage investor by the development capitalist) up until the stage where the investee company needs financing beyond the resources of the original equity investors. At this stage, the early stage investor would either syndicate with, or sell its interest outright to, one or a number of development capitalists. These latter investors would take the company through successive rounds of further finance until the company was ready for a market listing or trade sale. Such a putative relationship would, at least in theory, be to the advantage of the early stage investor by allowing the firm to realise its investments in an orderly manner or to continue as a minority shareholder in the subsequent development of the investee firms. The development capitalist would have access to early stage deal flow. It would also be in receipt of greater information on the new and now operational investment than if it had invested 'cold' in a previously unknown company thereby reducing information asymmetries.

Thus, early and later stage development capitalists could each appear to benefit from a relationship characterised both by redirected/exchanged deal flow and joint investment. The existence of a reciprocal relationship would, it is argued, be seen most clearly at the time when an early stage venture capitalist sought to realise his investment either outright through a sale, or partially by inviting a new investor(s) to share, through syndication, a major part of the future financing burden. A number of early stage, UK venture capitalists were approached to explore empirically their experience of attracting further finance for their portfolio companies from development capitalists.

The Survey

In order to identify the population of early stage UK venture capital investors, two data sets were initially used — the British Venture Capital Association's 'Directory 1991' and KPMG's 1992 published list of sources of UK venture capital funds. The former document lists 121 full BVCA members, i.e. active venture capitalists, and categorises individual firms by size of funds available, and 'investment preferences' including the sectors, stages of investment, and minimum scale of financing considered. KPMG similarly lists 197 sources which includes BVCA members and a range of other equity providers from the public, private and corporate sectors. These sources contract to 128 and 94 funders if the minimum investment threshold is reduced to <£250,000 and <£100,000, respectively. The two data sets were cross-referenced with a list of 'UK's Leading Venture Capital Funds' given in the Venture Capital survey supplement of the Financial Times of the 25th September, 1992 in order to ensure all relevant venture capital firms were identified.

The data sets were not segregated by the indicated preferred size of investments. This classification was deemed unreliable. Many BVCA members, for example, note in the Directory that they will do start-ups and other small-scale financings but, in practice, rarely undertake such investments[6]. Rather, early stage 'specialists' were defined by the author as:

"Those specialist organisations managing dedicated funds which invest at seed, start-up and/or early stages but do not engage in management buy-outs or buy-ins, replacement equity or rescue finance."

Using these criteria, thirteen companies were identified. The requirement that the investors were specialist early stage investors and did not take part in later-stage, development finance activities was a particularly strong discriminating variable. Another three UK organisations were included in the final respondent list as they were known to operate seed capital funds because of their membership of the European Seed Capital Fund (ESCF) Scheme, an initiative of the Enterprise Directorate General (DGXXIII) of the Commission of the European Communities[7].

Only twelve of the sixteen companies were eventually interviewed. One company declined to participate in the research while arrangements for two other interviews could not be concluded within the tight, research deadline[8]. A further company, while cited on the KPMG list, was no longer in business. The interviews, which were undertaken with the chief executive of the organisation (excluding three cases where another partner or investment executive responsible for seed capital was interviewed) comprised of an extended, semi-structured, telephone discussion around a questionnaire format. The questionnaire was sent to all respondents prior to the interview. The telephone interviews took, on average, twenty minutes to complete.

Survey Findings

While 81 per cent of the identified population was interviewed, the small numbers associated with the survey severely limit the use of statistical evaluation.

(i) Size and Purpose of the Fund.

Three of the twelve funds were 'open', i.e. neither the size of fund nor the period of investment was fixed. Resources were called down from their backers when required. Two such funds were among the largest interviewed with investment resources substantially in excess of £10 million. Of the nine organisations with fixed-term[9], early stage funds, the three largest funds averaged £15.5 million (range £11.5–21m). With the average fund size (including two open funds) was £9.5 million. If the two smallest funds in this latter category, each of £1.6 million fund size, are removed, the average for commercial funds rises to £13.6 million (range £5–21m). The relative smallness of publicly supported, regional funds was also evidenced in the cited 1992

Table 2
Minimum Viable Size of a Commercial Seed Captial Fund

Estimated Minimum Size of a Commercial Seed/ Start-up Fund	Frequency (n=10)	Average Existing Size of Seed/Start-up Funds making Estimate
£5 million or less	5	£2.3 million range £1.1–5.0m
£>5–20 million	5	£11.6 range £1.62[1]–21m
No Estimate Given	2	

[1]This figure was an outlier with the other four fund sizes averaging £15.8 million, range £11.5–21 million.

---

the exception of one fund at £5 million, the remaining five funds were tiny in relation to later stage funds averaging £1.41 million (range £0.5–1.6m).

Five investors also had a regional, social/development role, which constrained purely economic investment criteria. They were numbered among the smallest funds with the organisations (including one open fund) having average funding of £1.45 million (range £0.5–2m). These funds were all predominantly public financed and their remit of encouraging economic development was restricted to a geographic area. Their modest size is in contrast to those funds only espousing strict, commercial goals, i.e. maximising net return on capital to investors, where

appraisal of the ESCF scheme. Thirteen of the twenty-one ESCF funds surveyed also had a publicly supported, regional development role. The average size of these funds, at ECU 1.35 million, was 74 per cent smaller than the privately financed, commercial funds in the scheme.

(ii) Minimum Necessary Size of Early
    Stage Fund
Respondents were asked for their views as to the minimum size[10] that a seed/start-up fund would need to reach in order to achieve commercial viability, i.e. the ability to operate over the life of the fund without subsidies or other 'soft' assistance. A considerable variety of minimum sizes was suggested.

Overall, the most popular estimate of the minimum size for a commercial, early stage fund was £5 million, being mentioned by five respondents. The four largest respondents were at variance with their smaller colleagues. Their estimates averaging £10.5 million (range £5–17.5 million). In contrast, those organisations which estimated a minimum fund size of £5 million or less were, without exception, small funds. Their relatively modest estimates possibly reflected the limited, new investment opportunities which they had experienced in their locations.

While there was agreement among respondents that early stage funds were undercapitalised and thus lacked fee income[11], the fact that 82 per cent of respondents gave estimates under of £10

investment executive (Murray, 1991). Those organisations arguing for funds in excess of £10 million were primarily viewing the extra resources as being available for follow-on investment within their existing portfolios rather than allowing a material increase in the number of firms in the existing portfolio.

The question of the minimum size of a fund hinges on definitional issues. A fund which does not intend to provide follow-on finance preferring to exit by the sale of its interest to a later stage investor may be viable at under £10 million. However, those funds suggesting a larger minimum figure were also the more established firms. Their arguably greater experience of the difficulties of realising an attractive exit value from immature and unproven investee companies may well have

Table 3
Sources of Follow-on Finance for Seed Capitalists

Proposed Sources of Additional Funds for Follow-on Investment	Weighted Ranking	Frequency (n=12)
Venture (Development) Capitalists	1st	10
Corporate Investors	=2nd	5
In-house Finance	=2nd	5
Private Investors	4th	3
Banks (loans)	5th	1

million suggest that early stage funds are frequently constrained by exogenous factors, particularly the supply of attractive new investment opportunities. The small number of executive staff also affects the size of the existing portfolio. On average, the funds had three or less full-time investment managers. A hands-on investment style (also termed "close tracker" by MacMillan *et al*, 1989) generally limits the number of portfolio companies to approximately five per

influenced their appreciation of the necessity of also being the source of follow-on finance.

(iii) Means of Providing for Additional Investee (Follow-on) Finance

The respondents were asked how they had, or intended to provide, additional finance to meet the needs of their investee companies given the limitations of their own funds. They were requested to rank the three most common sources of further funds.

Development capital was the most frequently mentioned source. It was the first preferred option of five investors and the second choice of another five respondents. Corporate investors and in-house financing were each mentioned by five organisations. When in-house financing was mentioned, it was the most preferred source of additional finance. All early stage investors attempted to attract corporate investors. However, the respondents recognised that corporate interest normally required technologies to be at an advanced stage of commercial readiness or application. In-house financing was employed when organisations had direct access to separate funds within the parent investor organisation for later stage investments. With one exception, in-house funding was not the preferred option of the larger (>£5 million) funds which preferred to seek outside, investment partners.

Three smaller funds mentioned the possibility of obtaining additional finance from high net worth, private individuals — commonly termed 'Business Angels'. Although such individuals have been shown by Wetzel (1983) to be an important source of informal risk capital in the USA, with the exception of Harrison and Mason's work (1991), there has been little study of their role in the financing of UK entrepreneurs. Harrison and Mason indicated that business angels are generally observed to operate locally (within 100 miles of their base), and, given the small amounts of finance available (usually in the range of £10,000 per investment), concentrate on early stage deals. It is therefore consistent that they were only mentioned by the smaller, more parochial, early stage investors. Even in the uncommon event that

business angels syndicate among themselves for larger deal financing, they are unlikely to be a material source of funds for early stage investors seeking development capital scale (i.e. >£250,000) further investment.

The limited role perceived by the funds for bank finance is a likely reflection of the inappropriateness of debt at the highly speculative stages of a new NTBF venture.

(iv) Perceived Problem of Raising Follow-on Finance

In the previous question, the respondents were asked for both actual and intended sources of additional funds for their portfolio companies. For more recently established funds with less than five years' history, their stated intentions had not yet been tested. Accordingly, in order to understand the confidence they had in obtaining future funds, all respondents were asked to rate, on a scale of 1 to 5, their assessment of the dificulty of this task.

Two of the three organisations, which envisaged having no problems with future fund raising, were among the very largest funds with substantial, technology-based portfolios. They both had a track

Table 4
Problems with Future Fund-raising for Seed Capitalists

Rating of Problem of Raising Future Finance	Frequency (n=11)
1 (no problem)	3
2	0
3	2
4	5
5 (Major problem)	1

record of successful investment realisations. The third fund was associated with a major metropolitan authority and had preferential access to additional, internal funds.

However, the most frequent response rating was four. Eight of the eleven organisations answering this question therefore perceived some clear difficulty in attracting future funds. Thus, the intentions cited above (in Section 4iii) appear to be qualified with some significant concern as to whether additional finance will be forthcoming for the future growth of their investee companies.

(v) Balance of Power between Existing and New Funders

In order to assess the experience of early stage investors when new investors had been approached to support a portfolio company's future development, the respondents were asked for their opinion as to the fairness of the resulting refinancing arrangement. They were restricted to three general descriptions of the outcomes, i.e. "to your benefit/equal benefit/to the new investors' benefit". Only two organisations, both aggressively commercial and larger investors, argued that, on average, the negotiations had been concluded to their benefit. Their negotiating strength could also be a function of the attractiveness of the individual companies for which they were seeking additional finace.

Four of the eleven respondents saw the transactions as being equitable to the interests of both parties. However, the remaining five organisations, i.e. nearly half the sample, believe that the outcomes which had been negotiated were clearly to the advantage of the new, better financed, later stage investors. The

majority of these new investors were development capitalists. Unless the original investor's share holding is revalued at a premium when significantly larger amounts of additional money are put into the investee company as equity, the original investor's share holding and authority is considerably diluted.

In answering this question, several respondents made use of a vivid and colourful vocabulary to describe this unequal distribution of power. For all but a minority of highly attractive investments, the bargaining power was perceived by the respondents as being heavily skewed in favour of the new investor. Development capitalists are experienced and professional negotiators. They recognise that the early stage venture capitalist has bery few alternatives when an investment needs a substantial tranche of additional funds. In addition, most investors are proscribed in their articles from investing more than ten per cent of their total fund in a single investment. This compounds the potential weakness of a modestly resourced, early stage venture capitalist with an investment in a rapidly growing but cash hungry, portfolio firm. Paradoxically, it is the very companies which the early stage investor wishes to target, i.e. rapidly growing and potentially internationally successful NTBFs, that are most likely to increase the venture capitalists' vulnerability. Such potential 'stars' may well require several stages of follow-on investment before they become cash generative.

The imbalance in power is evidenced in the financial structure resulting from the negotiation. The finance constrained, original investor will see his equity holding diluted as additional share holders' capital is injected into the

Venture Capital   *421*

The Second 'Equity Gap': Exit Problems for Seed & Early Stage Venture Capitalists and their Investee Companies | **69**

investee. Substantial investment for the purpose of commercial manufacture and market development will result in the original investor becoming a minority shareholder. This may not prevent the original fund continuing to be the 'lead investor' with primary responsibility for the investee company. Only three respondents saw the new investor(s) as usually assuming this role. These three funds were among the smallest in the sample. Two further funds saw 'joint leads' as the usual modus operandi. The continued influence of the initial investor is to be expected as it is that fund which is likely to have the specialist skills to manage the company and to understand its technology and marketplace. This need for the new investors to keep the early stage investor 'on board' financially (and, more importantly, fully committed to the eventual success of the investee company) will mean that it would be counter-productive for the refinancing terms to be perceived as penal by the original investor.

A small majority (6:4) usually arranged follow-on finance from among a limited number of development capitalists syndicate partners (rarely more than five) in seeking further finance for investee companies. Three of the four who, conversely, preferred a wide choice in selecting new investors were strongly commercial organisations although three other commercial organisations also preferred a closer relationship to a smaller group of favoured, development capitalists. The view of those early stage investors preferring no 'special relationship' was best put by one respondent who stated that it was in his best interest to be "promiscuous".

Two of the respondents had each received a contribution to their original fund from (different) development capitalists. The original logic of these contributions was to explore the concept of complementarity. Both funds had received deal flow from the development capitalists. While one of the sample funds had gained further investment from its sponsor to refinance an investee company, the other respondent had put up four separate proposals for follow-on financing. In each case, the development capitalist sponsor had declined to invest follow-on finance.

(vi) Intended Exit Routes from Early Stage Investments

For those fund seeking a new investor(s) in a portfolio company, their intention is to manage the timing of their final exit from the company until such times as the organisation can be sold at a price which mets their projected capital gain or return on capital[12] objective for the investment. The time scale over which the early stage fund will be involved in the investee company is, at seven to ten years, well in excess of double the investment horizon of the development capitalist (Bannock, 1991). The preferred time period for the development capitalist is 3–5 years[13]. If the investment is held longer than planned for in the original financial structure of the deal without a commensurate increase in exit price, the return on capital can be significantly eroded[14].

In practice, the arrangement of follow-on financing by syndication appears to be a less common occurrence for a seed capitalist than a full realisation, i.e. exit, from the investee company by sale to a third party. The respondents were asked to rate the three most important exist routes which they had used or were intending to use.

Table 5		
Planned Exit Routes for Seed Capitalists		
Planned/Actual Exit Route	Weighted Ranking	Number (n=12)
Trade Sale	1st	11
Buy Back	2nd	5
Initial Public Offering	3rd	4
Sale to Dev. Capitalist	4th	3

A trade sale to a corporate buyer dominated the ambitions of the respondents. Nine of the eleven early stage venture capitalists choosing a trade sale put it as their first choice. The only organisations not citing this route was a large and specialist venture capitalist operating in life science technologies. This organisation preferred, and had the international resources, to take successful investments to a public listing in the UK or the USA. Given the depressed state of the UK market for small company stocks during the present recession, one-third of the twelve respondents also made the unprompted observation that a flotation was not a realistic alternative at the present time. While four respondents put IPOs as their second preferred choice, they observed that it was more 'in hope than in expectation' for the foreseeable future[15].

Respondents also saw the sale of an investee to a corporate buyer, which was interested in the potential of externally sourced new technologies, products and/or processes, as having several advantages. A corporate buyer could frequently be identified early in the investment cycle; could pay an attractive price for a proven technology; the sale realised cash[16]; and the negotiation did

not raise the conflicts involved in dealing with a development capitalist.

'Buy back' is the situation whereby the entrepreneur who has been financed by the venture capitalist is offered the opportunity to repurchase the shares held by the latter. It is not an attractive route for an organisation seeking capital gains of 'ten times plus' as the entrepreneur rarely has the funds, or the desire, to pay a high valuation for the stock he or she does not control. The respondents citing this route were exclusively the small funds including the two respondents who still saw themselves as strictly commercial operations. The social/development funds particularly favoured using this exit route. One such respondent noted that, if the local entrepreneur was not given this option, it would be much harder to attract any deals. This observation confirms studies (see Keasey and Watson, 1992; Bannock, 1991; Small Business Research Trust, 1990) which indicate that independence is the main motive for small firm owners in creating their own business and that, in consequence, small firm owners are often hostile to allowing third party, equity participation.

For the larger commercial funds and for development capitalists, the most likely use of this mechanism is where an investment was seen as unlikely to succeed in achieving the level of returns originally projected. (Such disappointing investments are frequently referred to as 'the living dead'.) The repurchase of shares by the entrepreneur removes the firm from the venture capitalists's portfolio and realises cash. However, the capital gain is likely to be severely limited. In short, it is a route more associated by venture capitalists with commercial failure than success.

Venture Capital   *423*

The Second 'Equity Gap': Exit Problems for Seed & Early Stage Venture Capitalists and their Investee Companies | **71**

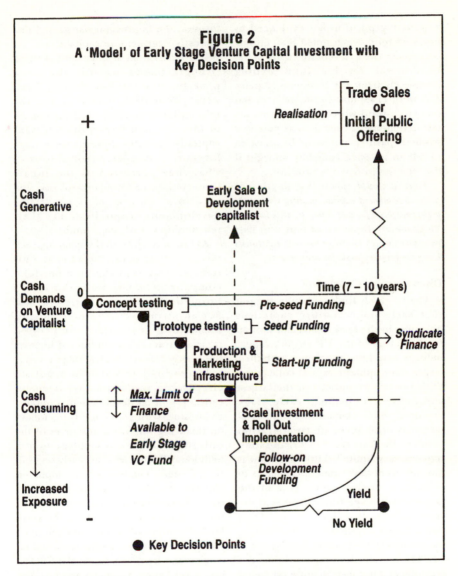

Figure 2
A 'Model' of Early Stage Venture Capital Investment with Key Decision Points

Given the comments made earlier, it is noteworthy that only three of the twelve respondents had used, or planned to use, development capitalists as a means of exit. Two of these respondents were social/development funds in less favoured areas where the absence of a strong industry base restricted trade sale opportunities. (However, this limitation also similarly reduces the attraction of the portfolio companies to a development capitalist.) The weakness of their negotiating position was evidenced by one seed fund which noted that, on one occasion, a sale to a venture capitalist was conditional on his fund exiting completely from the investee company. The third exeeption to the majority was one large fund which more commonly saw development capitalists as potential syndicate partners but would be prepared to sell an investee company outright if the offer was sufficiently attractive.

Thus, it would appear that, despite later stage, development capitalists being seen as the preferred option for additional finance for early stage investors' portfolio companies, early stage investors do not envisage venture capitalists being the primary route for investee exists.

Discussion and Conclusion

The research findings would suggest that early stage venture capitalists operating in the seed capital and start-up funding areas of the UK venture capital industry have little in common with their larger development capital colleagues. With the few exceptions of the largest and most established, early stage investors, which remain in a numerical minority, the level of co-operation between the two types of organisation remains very limited. Little deal flow is directed from development capitalists to early stage organisations. One of the largest, early stage funds expressed the view that the deal flow directed from development capitalists, while existing, was essentially irrelevant to his business.

When investee companies within the portfolio of early stage venture capitalists need additional finance beyond the resources of their early stage investor, the funds are more likely to seek a trade partner or buyer. On the occasions where a development capitalist partner is prepared to co-invest with the original

investor, the impression was gained that the early stage venture capitalists see the benefit of such an arrangement as being strongly biased towards the more powerful, new investor. Smaller funds were particularly likely to see the relationship as primarily to the advantage of the new, and larger, development capitalist investor. Several early stage investors were openly cynical towards what they perceived as the innate conservatism, i.e. avoidance of risk, and rapacious nature of later stage, development capitalists in their relationship to early stage funds.

As can be seen from the diagram, each successive stage of investment by an early stage venture capitalist in a portfolio company increases both the fund's financial exposure and, therefore, risk. For an attractive investee company, demanding significant and often repeated tranches of additional finance, the poorly resourced early stage investor is increasingly less able to negotiate effectively a syndication arrangement with a potential development capitalist co-investor. With scarce funds for follow-on financing within the resources of the early stage fund, it may well have to seek additional financing at an early stage in the investee's commercial development. However, for the development capitalist, the investee company may well still be at too premature a stage in both the small level of funds needed and in the investee's ability to demonstrate a sufficiently robust, commercial track record. As the CEO of one development capitalist argued, later stage funds are not primarily concerned with investing for growth. Rather, they invest in change, primarily through new ownership, in established and frequently mature businesses.

Thus, the investee company financed

by an early stage fund may well face *two* 'equity gaps', i.e. the insufficient provision of long-term, external equity sources to finance the creation and development of the young, growing business. The first 'gap' is experienced in trying to obtain the initial funds to create the enterprise. The second 'gap' occurs when attempting to attract sufficient, additional funds for substantial development and expansion to full commercial operation after the initial funding from its early stage investor has been exhausted.

The realisation that established venture capitalists rarely represent a source of follow-on finance for early stage investee companies has obliged seed and start-up funds to reconsider their funding strategies. A number of the most commercially aggressive funds are considering the opportunities for a major increase in the funds at their disposal. An expansion of funds to, say, £20+ million would allow them to retain the ability to finance successive stages of follow-on finance up until the stage when the investee company was ready for for an exit by trade sale or flotation. For technologies requiring substantial increases in finance for successive development stages, e.g. computer hardware manufacture or bio-genetically derived drugs, major syndication and/or an initial public offering may still be necessary but a substantial fund allows the early stage investor to retain a material stock interest.

It is perhaps indicative of the reappraisal of the logic and feasibility of early stage venture capital that the popularity of the term 'seed capital' is rapidly diminishing. Several respondents noted that this term is invariably associated with small, very risky and frequently unsuccessful investment. Accordingly, a number of firms, including members of the European Seed Capital Fund Network, have elected to use the term, 'early stage venture capital', as a more accurate alternative.

Despite the current reappraisal of the activities by early stage investors, this segment of venture capital activity continues to remain the 'Cinderella' of the UK and European industries when appraised by the number of operating funds or the finance at their disposal. The UK Chancellor of the Exchequer in his 1992 Budget speech argued that there was little need for additional financial support for start-up firms given the existence of a well-established venture capital industry in the UK. A number of early stage venture capitalists and their investee companies might have cause to disagree with this contention.

Acknowledgement

This research was funded jointly by the Department of Trade and Industry, the Anglo-German Foundation and the Bundesministerium Fur Forschung Und Technologie, whose support is gratefully acknowledged. The findings were first presented at the Anglo-German Seed Capital Workshop, Oxford, September 1992.

Notes

[1] It would be dangerous to assume that the limited availability of equity was the sole or major reason for firm failures during this period. No evidence of causality was offered by the CBI.

[2] The 'leading' venture capitalists were selected by the Council of the BVCA. The sample was strongly biased towards large, well established, development capitalists.

[3] Unlike the BVCA annual statistics, EVCA's Yearbook separates out seed capital from

start-up investment by country.

4 Only 21 of the 113 full members of the BVCA in 1992/93 Directory list a minimum investment threshold of under £100,000, i.e. the sums of finance most commonly associated with the initial investment in a new, start-up enterprise. A number of venture capitalists are prepared to finance larger start-up investments but they are a minority within the BVCA membership.

5 The terms 'fund' and 'investor' are both used interchangeably to describe a venture capital organisation with a dedicated sum of money for investment in client companies (investees).

6 This statement was not formally tested. However, in discussions with several dozen BVCA members held by the author, there was a very strong consensus that investment guidelines relating to start-up interest noted within the BVCA Directory do not necessarily reflect investors' practices.

7 A report on the first three years of the ESCF scheme in the EC's member states has been prepared for DGXXIII by Murray and Francis (1992).

8 This research material was first presented at an Anglo/German Seed Capital Workshop at Oxford Science Park on 30th September 1992.

9 Most funds managed by independent, venture capitalists on behalf of their investors are for a fixed, ten year term.

10 Where a range of funding sizes was given, the midpoint value was taken and rounded up to the nearest million.

11 For the majority of independent venture capitalists, operating costs are financed from a fixed fee on the monies raised in the fund. This fee is usually in the range of 2–4 per cent p.a. for early stage funds.

12 The evaluation technique of Internal Rate of Return, despite its technical shortcomings, is universally used within the industry (Dixon, 1991; Lorenz 1989).

13 Bannock (1991, p10) suggests 1–3 years for later stage financings. This period in late 1992 is considered excessively optimistic. Twelve years is also considered excessive of seed investments.

14 The severity of the present recession in the

UK is acting as a significant brake on the selling of unquoted firms as well as reducing the value of the firms *per se*. This is likely to have a major effect on the final investment performance of a number of fixed term, venture capital funds.

15 The announced termination of the UK's Unlisted Securities Market in 1996 (*Financial Times*, 1st December, 1992, p20) supports respondents' pessimism.

16 Most trade sales are conditional on warranties covering potential liabilities to the purchaser. This is likely to involve a third party retention of a percentage of the purchase price thereby reducing immediate cash payments.

References

Bannock, G. (1991), *Venture Capital and the Equity Gap*, London, National Westminster Bank.

Binks, M. R., Ennew, C. T., and Reed, G. V. (1992), 'Information Asymmetries and the Provision of Finance to Small Firms', *International Small Business Journal*, 11, 1.

Bolton, J. E. (1971), *Small Firms*, Report of the Committee of Enquiry on Small Firms, Cmnd. 4811, London, HMSO.

Brealey, R., and Myers, S. (1984), *Principles of Corporate Finance*, (2nd Ed.), London, McGraw Hill.

British Venture Capital Association (1984–92), *Annual Reports on Investment Activity*, London, BVCA.

Butchart, R. L. (1987), 'A New Definition of the High-technology Industries', *Economic Trends*, 400, February, pp82–88.

Bygrave, W. D., and Timmons, J. A. (1992), *Venture Capital at the Crossroads*, Boston MA, Harvard Business School Press.

Cabinet Advisory Council on Science and Technology (ACOST) (1990), *The Enterprise Challenge: Overcoming Barriers to Growth in Small Firms*, London.

Confederation of British Industry (1993), *Finance for Growth: Meeting the Needs of Small and Medium Enterprises*, London, CBI.

Cowling, M., Samuels, J., and Sugden, R. (1991), *Small Firms and Clearing Banks*, Report for the Association of British Chambers of Commerce, London.

Department of Trade and Industry, The Insolvency Service (1992), *Insolvency: General Annual Report for the Year 1991*, London, HMSO.

Dixon, R. (1991), 'Venture Capital and the Appraisal of Investments', *Omega*, 19, 5, pp333–344.

European Venture Capital Association (1987–92), *EVCA Yearbook: Venture Capital in Europe*, Brussels, KPMG/EVCA.

Flynn, D. M. (1991), 'The Critical Relationship Between Venture Capitalists and Entrepreneurs: Planning, Decision Making and Control', *Small Business Economics*, 3, pp185–196.

Gorman, M., and Sahlman, W. A. (1989), 'What Do Venture Capitalists Do?', *Journal of Business Venturing*, 4, pp231–248.

Harrison, R. T., and Mason, C. M. (1991), 'Informal Investment Networks: A Case Study from the UK', *Entrepreneurship and Regional Development*, 3, pp269–279.

KPMG Peat Marwick (1992), *A Directory of Sources of Venture Capital Under £250,000*, HMSO, London.

Kay, J. (1992), 'Innovation in Corporate Strategy'. In Bowen, A., and Ricketts (eds.), *Stimulating Innovation in Industry*, NEDO, London.

Keasey, K., and Watson, R. (1992), *Investment and Financing Decisions and the Performance of Small Firms*, National Westminster Bank, London.

Levy Gee (1992), *The United Kingdom Venture Capital Database*, Levy Gee Chartered Accountants, London.

Lorenz, T. (1989), *Venture Capital Today* (2nd Ed.), Woodhead-Faulkner, London.

MacMillan, I. C., Siegal, R., and Subba Narishima, P. N. (1989), 'Criteria Used by Venture Capitalists to Evaluate New Business Proposals', *Journal of Business Venturing*, 1,1, pp126–141.

MacMillan, H. (1931), *Report of the Committee on Finance and Industry*, Cmnd. 3897, HMSO: London.

Monck, C. S. P., Porter, R. B., Quintas, P., Storey, D. J., and Wynarczyk, P. (1988), *Science Parks and the Growth of High-technology Firms*, Croom Helm and Peat Marwick McLintock, London.

Moore, B. (1993), *Financial Constraints to the Growth and Development of Small, High-technology Firms*, Small Business Research Centre, Cambridge University, England.

Murray, G. C. (1991), *Change and Maturity in the UK Venture Capital Industry, 1991–95*, BVCA, London.

Murray, G. C., and Francis, D. (1992), *The European Seed Capital Fund Scheme: A Review of the First Three Years*, DGXXIII, Commission of the European Communities, Brussels.

Murray, G. C., and Lott, J. (1994 forthcoming), 'Have UK Venture Capitalists a Bias Against Investment in New Technology-based Firms?', *Research Policy*.

National Economic Development Office (1992), 'Draft Report on the Financing of Biotechnology in the UK', London.

National Economic Development Office (1986), *External Capital for Small Firms. A Review of Recent Developments*. Committee on Finance for Industry, London.

National Venture Capital Association

(1992), 'Annual Report 1991', Venture Economics Inc., Arlington VA.

Oakley, R. (1984), *High-technology Firms*, Francis Pinter, London.

Organisation of Economic Co-operation and Development (1992), Industrial Policy in OECD Countries: Annual Review, OECD, Paris.

Pavitt, K., Robinson, M., and Townsend, J. (1988), 'A Fresh Look at the Size Distribution of Innovating Firms'. In Arcangeli, F., David, P., and Dosi, G. (eds.), *The Diffusion of New Technologies: Modern Patterns in Introducing and Adopting Innovations*, Oxford University Press, London.

Poindexter, J. B. (1976), 'The Efficiency of Financial Markets: The Venture Capital Case', unpublished doctoral dissertation, New York University, New York Bulletin, 30(1), Feb., pp78–83.

Roberts, E. B. (1991), *Entrepreneurs in High-Technology*, Oxford University Press, New York.

Rothwell, R. (1989), 'Small Firms, Innovation and Industrial Change', *Small Business Economics*, 1, pp51–64.

Small Business Research Trust (1990), *Quarterly Survey of Small Firms in Britain*, 6, 2.

Van Glinow, M. A., and Mohrman, S. A. (1990), Managing Complexity in High-technology Organisations, Oxford.

Wells, W. A. (1974), 'Venture Capital Decision Making', unpublished doctoral dissertation, Carnegie Mellon University, Pittsburgh.

Wetzel, W. E. (1983), 'Angels and Informal Risk Capital', *Sloan Management Review*, 24, Summer, pp23–34.

Wilson, H. (1979), *The Financing of Small Firms*, Interim Report of the Committee to Review the Functioning of Financial Institutions, Cmnd. 7503, HMSO: London.

[21]

1042-2587-94-182$1.50
Copyright 1994 by
Baylor University

Harvesting and the Longevity of Management Buy-outs and Buy-ins: A Four-Country Study

Mike Wright
Ken Robbie
Yves Romanet
Steve Thompson
Robert Joachimsson
Johan Bruining
Artur Herst

The last decade has seen the development of a buy-out market in Europe, both building on techniques used initially in the US and developing new ones specific to individual countries (Wright, Thompson, & Robbie, 1992). The backgrounds to improvements arising from buy-outs can be seen in consideration of both agency cost theory and entrepreneurship theory (Bull, 1989). The latter may have particular relevance to smaller buy-outs where management teams typically have majority equity stakes. While much attention has focused on large transactions, many US and especially European buy-outs are relatively small. Indeed, in the UK, the second most developed buy-out market after the US, some 92% of transactions are completed for purchase prices of less than the approximate equivalent of $20 million.

As buy-out markets have developed, both in Europe and the US, key attention has focused upon the longevity of such structures and the means and timing of harvesting investments by the parties concerned. Considerable debate has arisen concerning the length of time over which buy-outs retain their initial structure, with there being conflicting views as to whether buy-outs are long-term or short-term phenomena (Jensen, 1989; Rappaport, 1990). Recent evidence from the US (Kaplan, 1991) and from Europe (reviewed and extended below) shows that the short term–long term debate is somewhat simplistic since buy-outs are very much heterogeneous organizations.

Buy-outs and buy-ins involve a fusion of the different objectives of managers, financiers, and the companies themselves. In essence, a buy-out involves incumbent managers in acquiring a significant equity stake whilst a buy-in involves external managers, as individuals with institutional support, acquiring control of the company. A major aspect concerns the long-term plans of managers and financiers for the company and how both parties can realize their investment in a manner that is optimum for each of themselves, which in turn may have implications for the optimum life-cycle of the company itself. Although, these issues may well have been addressed at the time of the buy-out, significant actual and potential conflicts of interest may remain and be increased by financial and acquisition market conditions that are considerably different from those foreseen at the time of the buy-out and that significantly affect the ability of the parties concerned to effect a harvest at the time and by the means initially envisaged. Moreover, different conditions prevailing in buy-out markets in individual countries may have important influences on the timing and form of harvest.

This situation raises important questions concerning harvesting which are of direct relevance to the new owner-managers, venture capitalists, bankers, professional advisers, and indeed policy makers. The longevity of this form of organization is of considerable importance. If buy-outs represent a form of organization in which management has greater incentives to perform than hitherto and in which institutions exert considerable influence, then there are clear issues for each of these parties as to whether the resultant gains are sustained over long periods or are merely transitory; these also may provide an explanation as to why some buy-out structures last a long time and others do not. In analysing these issues, the paper draws on a number of perspectives. In addition to issues concerning the objectives and the behavior of managers who become owner-managers, the discussion is also founded on interrelated developments in the finance and economics literatures. Buy-outs and buy-ins rely heavily on particular types of financing institutions and control devices to enable this organization form to be created, which may be in contrast to the creation of many new entrepreneurial ventures. Such institutions have their own individual perspectives on the longevity of buy-outs and buy-ins because of their time-horizons regarding the harvesting of investments, and they utilize a range of control devices to help ensure that their investment objectives are met. Economic factors, at both macro and micro levels, also influence both the nature and timing of the meeting of such objectives.

The purpose of this paper is to test hypotheses relating to the factors that influence the nature and timing of the harvesting of investments in management buy-outs and buy-ins, and the control devices and processes used by institutions in seeking to ensure that harvesting is achieved in a timely fashion. These issues are addressed in a four-country study involving buy-out markets in the UK, France, Holland, and Sweden in order to enable hypotheses concerning the influence of differing environments and states of development of buy-out markets to be examined.

BUY-OUT LONGEVITY

The classic buy-out candidate is often viewed as being in a mature sector with stable cash flow and modest investment requirements, but market trend analyses show the existence of a wide range of buy-out types (Chiplin, Wright, & Robbie, 1992) either in terms of sectors, control mechanisms, or financing structures. In the US, where attention has focused primarily on very large debt-financed transactions, venture capital has nevertheless also played an important role in the buy-out market (Malone, 1989). This is even more true of European markets (Wright, Thompson, & Robbie, 1992). These observations suggest both the need to adopt a contingency perspective in analysing the link between governance structures, longevity, and performance, and that there may be good reasons why some buy-outs last a long time and some do not. In general terms, a contingent model of the buy-out control process can be elaborated as shown in Figure 1. The need is to ensure an appropriate match between the buy-out's governance structure and the relevant contingent factors so that the life-cycle of the bought-out company can move into the next stage at the appropriate time. In order to test the various elements of this model a number of hypotheses are generated from the following discussion.

Evidence shows that the control structures in buy-outs embrace mechanistic aspects to do with meeting interest payments, requirements to keep within debt covenants, board representation, levels of managerial equity stakes contingent upon performance, and regular detailed reports and meetings (Wright, Thompson, & Robbie, 1992; Green & Berry, 1991). The overall governance of buy-outs thus involves a combination of both structural mechanisms and a process by which adaptation to changing circumstances occurs. These structures mirror similar ones identified for venture capitalist investments generally by Sweeting (1991) and MacMillan, Kulow, and Khoylian (1989), but which also link with organizations specifically focused on buy-outs (Sahlman, 1990). Examination of the buy-out process suggests that for each individual transaction the interests of the three parties—management, institutions and the company itself—must be satisfied before a buy-out can be completed (Wright, Thompson, Chiplin, & Robbie, 1991).

The influence of managers may be particularly important where the initiative for a buy-out is taken by management who perceive an opportunity. There is, of course, a lack of consensus as to what constitutes an entrepreneur. There is further discussion as to whether management in buy-outs are actually becoming entrepreneurs (Bull, 1989; Wright, Thompson, & Robbie, 1992), although Kelly, Pitts, and Shin (1986) provide

Figure 1
General Contingent Model of the Buy-out Control Process.

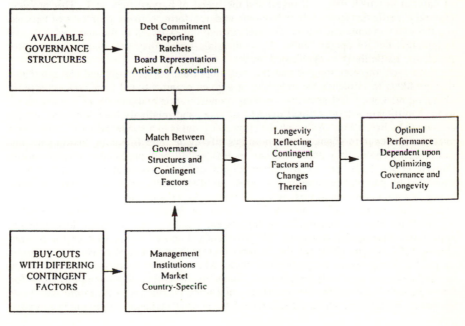

some preliminary tests. It is beyond the scope of this paper to enter into this debate. For the purpose of this paper the term owner-manager is used to signify that in a buy-out, managers become significant, if not majority, owners of the business where they were previously only salaried employees, and that a buy-in introduces new equity-owning managers. Where management have highly specific non-transferable skills they may have little option to remain with the firm into the long term and evidence from buy-outs suggests widespread long-term commitment to the firm (Wright & Coyne, 1985). By the same token, outside purchasers may be dissuaded from acquiring such a company where incumbent managers are reluctant to accept them. The extent to which managers may wish to continue to pursue a career as owner-managers rather than exiting through becoming managerial employees again or through retirement also affects longevity. Ronstadt (1986), in a study of entrepreneurs in general, found that career exit rates are much lower than venture exit rates but that entrepreneurs who start their entrepreneurial careers relatively late are more likely to have short entrepreneurial careers. Differences in the motivations of buy-out managers (e.g. reacting to a one-off opportunity versus proactive recognition of a chance to implement one's own growth strategy (Wright, Thompson, & Robbie, 1992, p. 60)) may be an important element in their decision to continue as owner-managers. Moreover, to the extent that it may be an important behavioral trait that managers buying out or buying in became owner-managers by acquiring rather than creating a business, continuation of such a position after they have sold out from their original investment may depend on the availability of new investment opportunities and in turn on the role of funding institutions in identifying such possibilities.

The buy-out markets in the four countries examined here involve a variety of institutional participants, ranging from local clearing banks through various venture capitalists to large specialist debt and equity institutions providing closed-end funds (Wright & Robbie, 1991). Requirements for institutions to provide returns to shareholders in the short term, such as in respect of closed-end funds, will influence the type of buy-out in which they will invest and the speed of harvest they seek. This problem may raise particular issues where buy-outs underperform, causing problems of harvesting through conventional routes. Differences may be expected in the approach of institutions that do not operate under this constraint, which may provoke serious control problems, particularly in syndicated deals.

Life-cycle theories suggest that the most important company-related characteristics that are likely to influence the longevity of a given organizational form concern rapidly changing markets, a fast-growing company, concentrating markets where it is necessary to have sufficiently large critical mass to survive, and relatively high levels of merger activity (Mueller, 1988). Although the classic buy-out is in a stable industry, unforeseen events may occur to change the appropriate life-cycle, and financing instruments are available to enable buy-outs to occur in less stable and predictable circumstances (Wright et al., 1991, ch. 8). Moreover, divestiture and privatization which had been frustrated by parental constraints may grow rapidly initially after the transfer of ownership but soon come up against new constraints. As a result, they may need to exit, in order to survive to enable growth to be achieved or develop (Green & Berry, 1991).

Such pre-buy-out constraints on investment policies, new product development, appropriate managerial structures, etc. frequently imposed by private sector parents (Jones, 1992; Singh, 1990) and the arguably greater degree of such constraints imposed on public sector divisions, particularly those whose parents were being prepared for privatization, are now well documented. Financing structures may attempt to allow for future growth but considerable uncertainty and underestimation of its extent may pose problems. In addition, where a division has been constrained and lost ground in a rapidly growing market it may be difficult to catch up, indicating that exit to become part of a larger group is warranted.

Individual country contexts may also be expected to influence both financing structures and longevity. Clearly, the relative development of stock markets influences the extent to which an IPO is a feasible and attractive option for harvesting. In addition, outside the UK context, the market for corporate control and corporate governance generally places less emphasis on complete ownership transfer and greater weight on investor influence in the running of a business (Franks & Mayer, 1990).

This section has indicated a number of issues concerning the nature, timing and control processes involved in harvesting management buy-out and buy-in investments. It also suggests that differences in forms in which buy-outs are harvested may be expected both within and between buy-out markets. The discussion suggests the following hypotheses:

H1: The governance structure in a buy-out will attempt to match both structural mechanisms and processes of control to the contingent factors facing each transaction, which will include an initial expectation of the timing and nature of harvesting.

H2a: Within a given market, larger buy-outs and those where managers have ratchet incentives will have a higher propensity to be harvested than smaller buy-outs where managers have major equity holdings.

H2b: Buy-outs that experience the greatest pre-buy-out constraints and the greatest post-buy-out catching-up problems, notably those that had been constrained as part of the public sector or within diverse groups, may also need to exit earlier.

H3: The relative importance and nature of the parties to a buy-out—that is, principally management and financing institutions—will influence the control process and timing of harvesting. To the extent that these factors differ both within and between buy-out markets in different countries, then differences in the timing and form of exit may be expected.

H4: The preferred form of harvesting will vary between countries and also in the same country over time, depending upon the state of development of buy-out, stock and corporate assets markets, and economic conditions that affect the feasibility of harvesting types and their timing.

H5a: Requirements for institutions to provide returns to shareholders within fixed time periods, such as in respect of closed-end funds, will influence the speed of harvest they seek and the nature of control they use. Such funders will need to adopt special approaches to harvesting buy-outs that underperform.

H5b: Transactions involving syndicated financing will involve control and exiting problems where the funders have differing harvesting horizons and objectives.

H6: Management's objectives for the buy-out or buy-in, their longer-term career plans, and the availability of new investment opportunities will influence the timing and form of exit and whether they remain with the firm after the institution has harvested its investment.

DATA AND METHODOLOGY

The data presented in this paper are drawn from the authors' database of over 6,000 European management and employee buy-outs. In order to compile the database several sources were used: a six-month survey of all known financing institutions and the major accounting participants in the UK buy-out market; a systematic search of on-line text databases and financial news services covering Europe; a systematic search of annual reports of major firms based in the UK; monitoring of the London *Gazette;* and a search of other specialist financial press and other specialist publications across Europe. In order to examine the length of time that buy-outs survive in this form, analysis was carried out using data derived from a representative sample of 158 buy-outs completed in the period from mid-1983 to the beginning of 1986, where it was possible to monitor subsequent harvesting or other forms of exists through CMBOR's regular monitoring of financial institutions and public sources of information (see Wright, Thompson, & Robbie, 1992 for a detailed description of the sample). The sampling frame for the survey was the database of UK buy-outs compiled by the authors, which through a systematic six-month survey of financing institutions, press reports, and company annual reports effectively provides the population of UK buy-outs. No significant differences were found between the demographic characteristics of the sample and the population of buy-outs contained on the CMBOR database. For purposes of the analysis that follows, harvesting is identified as involving four types: sale to a third party; IPO (stock market flotation); secondary buy-out/buy-in; and receivership.

In the four countries face-to-face interviews were held with senior representatives of the major financing institutions, selected to provide a cross-section of perspectives on buy-out exit. Interviews in the four countries were conducted on the basis of a common checklist of questions developed through discussions between the researchers in each country; copies are available from the authors. The interviews generally lasted at least two hours.

CHARACTERISTICS AND TRENDS

The four markets examined in this paper, UK, France, Holland, and Sweden, may all be characterized as displaying several of the necessary conditions for buy-out development: a need to effect ownership transfer, though not necessarily for the same reason; a relatively or absolutely important venture capital industry; and a legal framework that facilitated such transactions (see Wright, Thompson, & Robbie, 1992, for a detailed outline of the framework). The trends in the number and value of deals completed in the four markets are shown in Tables 1 and 2, respectively.

Table 1

Buy-out and Buy-in Numbers in UK, France, Holland, Sweden

Year	UK	France	Holland	Sweden
1980–86	1576	150	145	57
1987	434	50	30	18
1988	486	100	32	23
1989	521	130	45	32
1990	594	150	37	40
1991	565	120	57	19
Total	4176	700	346	189

CMBOR

Table 2

Buy-out and Buy-in Values in UK, France, Holland, Sweden (£m)

Year	UK	France	Holland	Sweden
1989	7501	850	211	785
1990	3110	1755	90	780
1991	2829	1578	340	486

Source: CMBOR

Except for Holland, peak levels of buy-out volume occurred in 1990. Whilst the UK market has seen a sharp decline from the peak level of 1989, only Sweden shows a similar shift. The dominance of the UK market is emphasized when values are deflated by GDP, with the value of the UK market (at 0.55% of GDP) being twice that of France and Holland.

In addition to differences in the volume and value of buy-outs between countries there are also marked differences in sources of deals (Table 3). Buy-outs arising on succession in family businesses account for the highest share of the market in France, followed by the UK. Divestment buy-outs are most prominent in the Dutch and Swedish markets and lowest in France, especially domestic sell-offs. Receivership buy-outs are most important in the UK, whilst buy-outs of quoted companies account for the highest share of the market in Sweden.

Hypothesis 3 drew attention to the potential importance of differences in stock markets and markets in corporate assets. A general indication of harvesting opportunities is provided by the sizes of stock markets and acquisitions markets in each country. The UK has by far the largest and most active stock and takeover markets. The French markets have become considerably more active in recent years, but the capitalization of

Table 3

Sources of Buy-outs and Buy-ins, 1989–91

Source	UK (%)	France (%)	Holland (%)	Sweden (%)
Receivership	10.7	3.0	0.0	1.3
Domestic Divestment	42.6	24.0	57.8	62.4
Foreign Divestment	7.1	12.9	24.4	7.5
Privatization	3.0	2.1	1.1	2.5
Family Succession	32.2	52.8	16.7	6.3
Stock Market	4.4	5.2	0.0	20.0
Total	100.0	100.0	100.0	100.0
Sample Size	1,648	233	90	80

Source: CMBOR

the domestic Dutch stock market is twice as large as that in France when deflated by GDP. There are also marked differences in the nature of takeovers in the four countries. Franks and Mayer (1990), in comparing the UK and France, note the lower level of hostile takeovers, greater levels of protection for employees and managers, higher levels of restrictions on voting rights of shareholders and mutual cross-shareholdings between corporations, extensive acquisitions of minority equity stakes, and the key role played by the "noyau dur" of shareholders in France compared to the UK. In Sweden, the takeover market has been particularly active in respect of smaller firms and quoted companies (Cooke, 1988).

HARVESTING OF BUY-OUTS AND BUY-INS—QUANTITATIVE EVIDENCE

The analysis in this section focuses principally on the UK where quantitative information on harvests is most accessible and aims to shed light on Hypotheses 2, 4, and 5a.

UK

The majority of UK buy-outs and buy-ins completed in the period from 1981 to 1991 have yet to be harvested. Only a little over a quarter (25.6%) of buy-outs and buy-ins have been harvested by means of either IPO, trade sale, secondary buy-out/buy-in, or receivership (Table 4).

The most common form of harvest for buy-outs has been trade sale, followed by receivership. The newness of the buy-outs and buy-ins completed towards the end of the period partly accounts for their lower rate of being harvested, but economic conditions

Table 4

UK MBO and Private MBI Exits (at end of June 1992)

Year of MBO/ MBI	Float*		Trade Sale		MBO/MBI		Receivership		No Exit**		Total	
	No.	%	No.	%	No.	%	No.	%	No.	%	No.	%
1981	18	12.3	25	17.1	4	2.7	14	9.6	85	58.3	146	100.0
1982	23	9.5	38	15.8	5	2.1	16	6.6	159	66.0	241	100.0
1983	26	10.7	38	15.6	5	2.1	18	7.4	156	64.2	243	100.0
1984	19	7.9	50	20.7	6	2.5	18	7.4	149	61.5	242	100.0
1985	24	8.4	40	14.0	7	2.5	23	8.0	192	67.1	286	100.0
1986	22	6.5	48	14.1	7	2.1	21	6.2	242	71.1	340	100.0
1987	16	4.1	57	14.6	7	1.8	42	10.7	269	68.8	391	100.0
1988	9	2.0	40	8.7	2	0.4	64	13.9	345	75.0	460	100.0
1989	3	0.6	20	4.1	2	0.4	66	13.4	401	81.5	492	100.0
1990	1	0.2	9	1.5	1	0.2	48	8.3	522	89.8	581	100.0
1991	2	0.4	3	0.5	0	0.0	12	2.2	540	96.9	557	100.0

* Includes USM, Third & OTC markets, reverse-ins and floats which were subsequently subject to trade sale, etc.

** Includes Refinancing

Source: CMBOR/BDCL/Touche Ross

of a less buoyant economy and corporate assets market in particular have also had an effect. The already relatively high failure rate of transactions completed at the time of the buy-out market peak in 1988 and 1989 is notable. Further analysis of this overall pattern of harvesting which looks at whether the transaction was financed by a closed-end fund (which typically has a specified life) or not reveals the following. For the period from 1985 (when closed-end buy-out funds first appeared in the UK) to 1991, 37.6% of buy-outs and buy-ins funded by closed-end funds had been harvested by June 1992 compared with 26.5% of buy-outs and buy-ins funded from other sources.

Marked differences occur in the proportions of buy-outs of different sizes that have been harvested (Table 5). To the end of June 1992, a sixth (16.2%) of buy-outs completed for a purchase price below £10 million in the period from 1981 to 1990 had been harvested by means of an IPO, trade sale, or secondary buy-out/buy-in. In contrast, well in excess of a third (35.3%) of larger buy-outs completed in this period, those with a transaction value of £10 million (about $20 million) or more had pursued one of these methods. Harvesting rates amongst larger buy-outs completed from 1988 onwards show a marked falling off in comparison to earlier deals, reflecting stock market conditions and the fall in the mergers and acquisitions market.

Monitoring of harvests by differing sources of the original deal shows that buy-outs that were previously part of the public sector and those that were originally divestments

Table 5

Exits of Buy-outs Completed Between 1981 & 1990 at end of June 1992

	Original Transaction Value					
	Less than £10m			£10m and Over		
Year of MBO	Exit by Flotation, Trade Sale Secondary MBO/MBI		All Buy-outs in Category	Exit by Flotation, Trade Sale Secondary MBO/MBI		All Buy-outs in Category
	No.	% of all MBOs		No.	% of all MBOs	
1981	42	29.8	141	2	100	2
1982	59	25.4	232	5	100	5
1983	59	26.0	227	6	75	8
1984	71	30.7	231	4	66.7	6
1985	51	21.0	243	18	90.0	20
1986	58	19.6	296	13	68.4	19
1987	55	17.4	316	18	64.3	28
1988	32	9.8	327	12	25.0	48
1989	14	4.4	316	4	7.0	57
1990	7	1.6	436	3	6.3	48
Total	448	16.2	2,765	85	35.3	241

z-Test of differences between total percentages existing in the two size categories in the period yields z = 7.37 (significant at 1% level).

Source: CMBOR/BDCL/Touche Ross

from non-UK parents record by far the highest propensity to be harvested by means of an IPO, trade sale, or secondary buy-out/buy-in (Table 6). Buy-outs from receivership are more likely to fail than buy-outs from other sources. Buy-outs of quoted companies show the third highest propensity to be harvested, but this is little different from the overall exit rate.

The cumulative extent of harvesting over a seven-year period post buy-out of a representative sample of 158 buy-outs completed in 1983-1986 surveyed by CMBOR, details of which were outlined earlier, shows that the proportion of buy-outs that have not been harvested declines steadily over time. Seven years after buy-out some 40% of the sample had exited. The greatest increase in harvesting occurred in years three to five after buy-out. In year two, only 6% had exited, by year three, 14% had, and by the end of year five some 29% had either floated, been sold to a third party, been the subject of a secondary buy-out, or had failed. The principal indication from this evidence is that most buy-outs last a long time and a minority do not. Dividing the sample into size categories as defined by their original transaction value shows that the smallest buy-outs have a substantially higher propensity to remain as buy-outs within a seven-year period than do larger transactions. After seven years, 64.4% of the buy-outs completed for an initial purchase price below £1 million, 57.9% of those with an initial purchase price of £1-5 million, and 42.1% of those with an initial purchase price above £5 million had *not* been harvested. Actual harvesting patterns of the sample were also compared with their initial intentions as expressed in the survey questionnaire. Of the 86 buy-outs in the sample expressing an intended exit route (54.4% of the sample), only a fifth (17 buy-outs) had by June 1992 been harvested in this manner. The most notable differences between intentions and actual exit concerned the low level of harvesting through secondary market floatation and the high level of trade sale.

Table 6

Exit by Source of Buy-outs Completed before end of 1990

Source	Number Exiting*	Total Buy-outs	Exit Total %
Divestment (UK parent)	266	1562	17.0
Divestment (overseas parent)	93	293	31.7
Private/Family	103	622	16.6
Privatization	45	140	32.1
Receivership	23	168	13.7
Going Private	6	30	20.0
Total	536	2815	19.0

z-tests Total v. Divestment (overseas parent) $z = 5.20*$
       Total v. Privatisation: $z = 3.97*$
       Total v. Receivership: $z = 1.71$
       Total v. Private: $z = 1.41$
       Total v. Going Private: $z = 0.14$
       Total v. Divestment (UK parent) $z = 0.0$
*: Significant at 1% level

*: By means of flotation, trade sale or secondary buy-out/buy-in.

Source: CMBOR/BDCL/Touche Ross

France

In France harvesting rates have generally been well below those seen in the UK because investors have generally seen buy-outs as a longer term investment. IPOs have always been rare as a form of harvest, the only significant examples involving Fonderies Waeles, Le Creuset (IPO on the London USM), and Biopat. However, in June of 1991 the venture capital firm IDI came to the market four years after it was privatized in a FF 1.6 billion management buy-out. For the most part, harvest has involved a trade sale and it is not unusual for sale to involve only a part of the equity, thus bringing in an industrial partner to enable growth to occur, or enabling institutions to exit from the deal.

From the beginning of 1991 some notable problem cases involving restructuring and failure amongst French buy-outs and buy-ins can be identified (Wright & Desbrieres, 1992) and recent cases have also involved the sale of partial equity stakes in buy-outs with long-term prospects but where the combination of initial high gearing and the recession has meant that necessary investment levels cannot be met.

Holland

Available information suggests that of the 346 buy-outs and buy-ins estimated to have been completed in Holland between 1980 and 1991 almost a sixth (52 cases) were harvested initially through an IPO, trade sale, or failure. The largest single form of harvest has been trade sale, with some 26 being recorded, followed by IPOs (14) and bankruptcy (9). Of the IPOs, ten occurred before the stock market crash in 1987, with only four Dutch buy-outs coming to market since then.

Sweden

The pattern of Swedish buy-out harvests has fluctuated over the last five years and in contrast to the UK picture does not display a rising trend in the late 1980s and early 1990s. The most common form of harvest has been trade sale, with some 21 out of a total of 33 exits identified in the period from 1986 to 1991. Only two exits by IPO have occurred, the latest being in 1988; the remaining ten exits have been through receivership.

INVESTOR AND MANAGERIAL PERSPECTIVES ON HARVESTING

The interviews conducted in the four countries with financing institutions and managers of buy-outs sought to identify commonalities and differences in attitudes, mechanisms, and processes concerning harvest. The analysis in this section aims to shed light on Hypotheses 1, 3, 4, and 5 by highlighting behavior on each aspect in the four countries.

Preferences for Different Forms of Harvesting

The rankings of the various forms of preferred harvesting method by country to emerge from our interviews with *institutions* are shown in Table 7 and shed light on Hypothesis 4.

A key attraction of trade sale across all four countries is the ability to achieve actual realization of cash. Partial sale was less favored than full because institutions essentially lose control of further exit. Similarly, trade buyers will also usually want control. An

Table 7

Harvesting Preferences By Institutions

UK	FRANCE	HOLLAND	SWEDEN
TRADE SALE	TRADE SALE (FULL) TRADE SALE (PARTIAL)	TRADE SALE	IPO
IPO	SECONDARY MBO	SALE TO OTHER INVESTORS	TRADE SALE
REFINANCING/ SECONDARY MBO	PRIVATE SALE TO NEW INVESTORS	SHARE REPURCHASE	SALE TO FINANCIAL INVESTOR
SHARE PURCHASE	REFINANCING	PRIVATE SALE THROUGH THIRD MARKET	REFINANCING
	IPO	IPO	IPO/SALE AFTER BUILDING-UP GROUP THROUGH ACQUISITIONS

IPO in the short term involves only partial harvest by both institutions and management. In such cases, the investors must decide very carefully how long they will remain with the company since they no longer have the advantages of being insiders. In France, partial sales may typically involve management retaining an equity stake, in order to maintain their motivation, whilst institutions exit. In the UK, the extent of one institution buying out another as a harvest form has hitherto been limited. This situation is less true in the other countries in the study. Differences in fee structures for restructurings and similar forms of harvest between the countries covered in the study, with the UK fees reportedly being less attractive, were noted as important influences on the relevant extent of such activities.

In the recessionary conditions of the early 1990s many institutions across the four countries report the delaying of harvests by trade sale because of the general absence of buyers. Where buyers can be found at what appear to be reasonable prices for firms within a distinctive competence, it is becoming common practice to include ''no embarrassment mechanisms'' to allow the venture capitalists to share in future gains within an agreed period.

Whilst, in principle, IPO is the most preferred form of harvesting in Sweden, it is not particularly common. Indeed, recent changes in taxation regulations (Joachimsson, 1991) have meant that the Swedish OTC market is no longer a viable harvest route. Other difficulties in Sweden in the general takeover market, which have meant that few trade buyers are available, have led to the development of a strategy to use a buy-out as a core company around which to build a group of significant size through subsequent acquisition. Once such a group has been assembled, harvesting through IPO or trade sale may be more feasible.

Preferred harvesting form may not be independent of size. IPO may be impractical for small companies, even in the absence of market constraints, and larger potential trade purchases may be less interested in acquiring the smaller companies. In Holland, for example, the more likely form of harvest for smaller buy-outs is share repurchase by management, whilst the existence of participating dividends in the financing structure of UK buy-outs may put pressure on management to refinance or buy-out the institution. Problems with the liquidity of secondary tier stock markets in France and the UK, in particular, pose difficulties in floating smaller buy-outs. In the UK, a minimum market capitalization of £25 million is now considered necessary before an IPO can occur. A particular issue identified in the UK is the investment behavior of pension funds and insurance companies who currently tend to trade only in good companies with market capitalizations in excess of £100 million, thus further limiting harvest possibilities in smaller buy-outs. However, there are some strong views within the industry that in the recessionary conditions of the early 1990s, pension funds are over-committed to equities (*Financial Times*, 11.2.92, p. 8.)

The recessionary conditions of the early 1990s may seriously limit the ability of funds to harvest in the time scale they need. Funds may have flexibility in that they can ask investors for an extension to the fund of up to two years, or alternatively (at least in theory) investments could be returned in specie. One possibility for increasing the liquidity of closed-end funds is to develop a secondary market whereby a new fund would buy the investments of limited life funds at lower cost or net realizable value, (NRV). Any appreciations in the investments after being acquired by the new fund would be shared between the previous investors and the new ones on the basis of an agreed formula.

Harvesting Perspectives at Time of Buy-out

A common theme from all four countries was that it was unusual to specify precisely a form and type of harvest at the time of the deal, but it has become more common for some consideration to at least be given to harvest to ensure that management and investors have the same fundamental perspectives. In closed-end funds it is particularly important to consider harvest, but even where ratchets based on harvesting are set initially, changing conditions may advance (as in the late 1980s) or retard (as in the early 1990s) actual harvest. If there were exceptions to this view they were in respect of smaller buy-outs including hand-ons (transmissions) of family firms, which were considered in general to have less need for harvest. This point was especially prevalent in France where, as seen in Table 3, this form constitutes the highest share of any of the four markets. In Holland, it is now considered that there is essentially little difference between actual and expected harvests, even though harvests are taking longer than was the case in the late 1980s. Rather, many buy-outs completed in the conditions of the mid-1980s were harvested two to three years sooner than had been anticipated.

Harvesting Control Mechanisms

Hypothesis 1 distinguished control mechanisms and control processes. One of the most controversial harvest control mechanisms is the equity ratchet, whereby as noted earlier, management's equity stake can rise (or possibly fall) if they meet (or fail to meet) harvest targets within a given period of time (Thompson & Wright, 1991). Amongst the four countries studied, ratchets have been most common in the UK, although there has recently been a sharp waning in enthusiasm amongst institutions. Whilst it is still the case that it may be necessary to use a ratchet to enable a deal to be completed, the problems of disputes over the crystallization and renegotiation have encouraged institutions to avoid them where possible. Whilst the highly buoyant markets of the late 1980s caused problems with ratchets being triggered early, the recessionary conditions of the early 1990s frequently mean harvest is delayed and call for further negotiation. In some cases, specific cash bonuses were paid to managers if valuation levels were achieved. In France, they are not common because management stakes are generally high given the predominance of smaller buy-outs and the requirements of the RES legislation (see Heuze, 1991, and Wright & Desbrieres, 1992, for details).

In Holland and Sweden, the existence of many buy-outs that are effectively investor-led buy-outs suggests less emphasis on this mechanism, and management equity stakes are usually considered large enough to provide adequate motivation. In Sweden, in cases where ratchets might be used, concern was expressed over the lock-up problem whereby management might try to block an early harvest by trade sale because the value of their ratchet is not as great as it is likely to be in two to three years.

Emphasis now appears to be switching to the redemption of financial instruments and the use of participating dividends. These are mechanisms whereby, as profits increase institutions are available to participate in them by having the right to an increased dividend (see Wright & Coyne, 1985, for further details). In so doing, pressure is put on management to harvest the investment through sale to a third party or IPO or find some means of paying off the shares. Other institutions are also shifting preferences to sweet equity and options for management.

Harvesting Control Processes

The importance of controlling for harvest through various processes reflects the difficulties in using formal mechanisms when it is necessary to take account of the interests of the various participants in the buy-out and changing circumstances, thus indicating that the governance structure in a buy-out needs to be more subtle and flexible than a simple attempt at matching at the time of the buy-out. Across the four countries, board representation was seen to play an important part in steering the company towards harvest. However, there was some distinction between the countries on the roles played by management in determining the nature and timing of harvest, as suggested by Hypothesis 3. In the UK and France, where management have majority equity stakes in most buy-outs, it was seen as essential to obtain the agreement of management before harvest was possible. Even if management do not have a majority stake, their important role, together with that of their advisers in creating the buy-out, still meant that their views were of crucial importance. Hence, for example, it was reported that some IPOs of buy-outs in the UK in the early 1990s could have been trade sales but management would not cooperate. In Holland and Sweden, it was reported as more common for investors to lead the deal and to be majority owners and thus have greater control over the harvest process. This European position may be somewhat in contrast to that typically found in the US.

Harvesting control processes in syndications may be particularly difficult, as put forward in Hypothesis 5b, and may lead to attempts to avoid large syndications (as particularly observed in Sweden) or for various syndicates to develop between institutions with common objectives (as in Holland and the UK). In Sweden the delay in decision making that can occur where each syndicate member has to consult his or her board has tended to lead to agreements for the syndicate leader to be able to *act* as a majority shareholder. The objectives of the minority participants may be protected by rules agreeing to let members exit from the deal if they wish after a minimum specified period of time has passed. In the UK, difficulties in control have been a contributory factor in reducing the size of syndicates.

Harvesting Problem Cases—Refinancing "Living Dead" and "Good Rump"

Hypothesis 5a drew attention to the potential problems facing closed-end funds in particular, which need to achieve specific harvesting targets. The recessionary conditions of the early 1990s have brought into sharp focus the problem of having to deal with investments that seriously underperform.

It is possible, in fact, to identify two problem cases. "Living Dead" investments may be written down to a very low but realistic valuation so that it then does not matter significantly whether harvest occurs or not. However, such investments still risk involving a disproportionate amount of management time. Moreover, it may be difficult for the venture capitalist to implement change in such companies until a pressure point, which cannot be relieved by other funding sources, arises. More recently, active efforts may be made either to solicit an offer, which may be to sell for a nominal sum to a trade buyer or, more likely, to persuade management to buy them. A further issue arises in respect of the role of management in such cases in large and small deals. In small buy-outs, management may own the vast majority of the equity and a very small group of managers may carry out the major functions, thus making it difficult to remove underperforming management or enforce a trade sale. In larger buy-outs, no single manager may be indispensable. When sales do occur, because the possibility for a turnaround may still exist and lead to significant gains on a nominal purchase price, institutions may include "non embarrassment clauses" to participate in future gains.

The second category, "Good Rump," is distinguishable from the first in that these firms are viewed as capable of being turned around, but the effects of restructuring have yet to be seen. Such cases may be underperforming because of general sectoral problems. In both cases the nature of the restructuring to be undertaken in order to turn the business around may be problematical and be heavily influenced by whether the institutions are controlling shareholders or not.

In Sweden, underperformance is likely to lead to a considerable increase in monitoring by the funding institution, including increased frequency of meetings and reporting. However, institutions in Sweden tend to be very cautious about changing management, unless underperformance is clearly their fault. In the UK, if institutions are controlling shareholders, making changes is theoretically straightforward. However, because of the importance of management to the business, great care is needed in taking action. Institutions report that the principal strategy is to produce a consensus on necessary action but it may be difficult to argue with UK managers over asset disposals or deferrals of capital expenditure programs. A problem of refinancing is that it may be difficult to agree with other parties what form it should take and it may cause problems in the continued motivation of managers who, if they remain, have had their equity stakes greatly diluted. This problem was also noted in France in particular. In syndicated investments, restructuring may be delayed or take a particular direction because of differences in the attitudes of syndicate members. In the UK, if management are seriously at fault and it is possible to enforce change, a management buy-in of a buy-out may be an option, especially if managers are available who match the requirements of the problem company. Occasionally such a route may also be used in Holland.

Management After Harvest

As suggested in Hypothesis 6, if management are a key element in the buy-out, their longer term objectives and behavior are crucial to both the timing of harvest and what happens thereafter. In an IPO, management, for obvious reasons, invariably stay with the firm for a reasonable period. In trade sales the patterns are more mixed. Typically management may be locked into the new parent on the basis of, say, a one year service contract. Management may not wish to be contracted beyond this stage, at least initially, because of the uncertainty as to how the new owners will behave. Moreover, it may be difficult to motivate such individuals as employees now that they have high levels of personal wealth. A few managers may choose the point of the trade sale to retire from the company, although not necessarily from their business career. Some managers in the team may not be required when the buy-out becomes part of a new parent.

Across the four countries, very few managers have exited from their companies, especially outside the UK. In the UK, three core activities for ex-buy-out managers have been identified. First, a small number may be used to lead new buy-ins. However, there is some concern expressed that the second deal does not work as well as the first, partly for motivational reasons and partly because the buy-out manager is less familiar with the new situation. If buy-out managers are to be used in such instances it is necessary to identify which members of the team are capable to lead a buy-in. Some members of the buy-out team may be good function directors but be unsuitable to lead a buy-in. Some managers with specialist finance and marketing functions (less so production) may be placed in buy-outs and buy-ins where there are skills gaps. A second role for exiting buy-out managers is in undertaking the due diligence requirements in new deals, in preference to accountants, since the buy-out manager may have more commercial experience and hence produce higher quality work at lower cost. A third role is for ex-buy-out managers to become board representatives where the managers of the venture capitalist do not have the requisite skills for making a positive contribution to the monitoring of a buy-out investment. There appears to be as yet little active attempt to seek to place owner-managers exiting from buy-outs in non-executive roles or in buy-ins in Sweden and Holland.

CONCLUSIONS

This study has examined issues concerning the longevity of buy-outs in four European countries with developed buy-out markets. In this section, the principal findings are summarized and suggestions for further research are made.

Summary of Findings

● European buy-out markets differ considerably, both from that in the US and between European countries, according to how well developed and favorable the necessary conditions for market growth are at a given point in time. The opportunities for completing buy-out transactions also vary between countries according to differences in ownership and industrial structures. Practitioners need to be aware of these differences and their implications for buy-out opportunities. The four countries examined here represent the most developed European markets, with divestments providing greatest buy-out opportunities in the UK, Holland, and Sweden, but family succession in France. In the UK, buy-outs of companies in receivership and buy-ins are also significant parts of the market.

● Figure 1 and Hypothesis 1 suggested that the governance structure in a buy-out will attempt to match the mechanisms and processes of control to a given situation. The evidence presented here provides some support for this hypothesis but also indicates that the process is more subtle and flexible. It was clear that formal mechanisms may be problematical and inflexible and that in monitoring investee companies a process that permits flexibility and adaptability is key to steering companies towards an appropriate harvest. Although a perspective on an initial harvesting intention may be taken on buy-out, these routes are not commonly achieved. The evidence is, though, that it is important to give some consideration to eventual harvest at the time of the deal to provide a frame of reference for future discussions and reduce the possibility for potential conflicts between entrepreneurs and investors. In addition, there is a need for continual monitoring of the nature and form of harvest within the overall process of governance of buy-outs.

● Hypotheses 2a and 2b concerned differing harvesting expectations according to the size and source of a buy-out or buy-in and the quantitative evidence provides support for both hypotheses. Across the four countries harvest rates are greater for larger deals, buy-outs from the public sector, and particularly those buy-outs that were divestments from non-domestic groups.

● Hypothesis 3 focused on the relative importance of the different parties to a buy-out. In France and the UK, in particular, management have a key role to play in the timing and form of harvest; even in Holland and Sweden, where management and investor buy-outs tend to be more common, the views of management concerning harvest seriously need to be taken into account.

● Hypothesis 4 suggested that important differences between buy-out markets need to be appreciated in respect of both expected time scale to harvest and the form that exit is likely to take. In all four countries most buy-outs have not exited, although a quarter have in the UK and a sixth have in Holland. The UK is the most developed buy-out market and has the most harvesting activity. Since the late 1980s, sales to third parties have replaced flotations as the most common form of exit, although more recently receiverships have come to prominence. In Holland and Sweden, despite a high level of interest in flotations, trade sale is also the most common exit route. In France, partial sales, often involving institutions selling either to other institutions or to industrial partners, are an important addition to the straightforward trade sale. In adverse economic conditions, investors need to be alert to different harvest possibilities such as secondary buy-outs and buy-ins, buy-backs, partial sales, and restructurings as an alternative to the more conventional trade sales and floats. The importance and feasibility of these alternative mechanisms, however, vary between countries, with possibilities being greatest in the UK and less so in France, Sweden, and Holland.

● Hypothesis 5a focused on harvesting needs of closed-end funds. Notwithstanding the finding that buy-outs financed by closed-end funds are harvested at a greater rate than other buy-outs, the finding that most buy-outs in which these funds have invested have yet to exit has major implications for closed-end specialist buy-out funds who need to realise their investments to achieve returns to investors. Hypothesis 5a also raised the problem of harvesting buy-outs and buy-ins that had underperformed. The evidence presented here in terms of problem buy-outs shows that an important distinction needs to be made between ''living dead'' and ''good rump'' which has implications for the nature and feasibility of harvesting.

● Hypothesis 5b noted the potential difficulties with syndicated financings. Problems in managing for harvest in larger deals were shown to arise due to different perspectives by syndicate members and these have been accentuated in the UK in particular by extensive use of harvest-dependent ratchet mechanisms. This suggests a need to choose syndicate partners carefully and to simplify incentive mechanisms for management.

● Hypothesis 6 raised issues concerning the influence of owner-managers' objectives and follow-on possibilities in influencing the timing and form of harvesting. The evidence presented here indicates that very few managers have exited from their companies even when the institution has harvested its investment, especially outside the UK in France, Holland, and Sweden. Very few owner-managers from buy-outs and buy-ins have become owner-managers in subsequent firms, and financial institutions have yet to develop a systematic strategy towards utilizing those managers who have achieved a successful harvest in new investments in buy-ins or to complete buy-outs where there are gaps in the team. There is some evidence though that funders are wary about using former owner-managers from harvested buy-outs to lead new buy-ins because of concerns about their possession of the appropriate skills, although they may be used in various specialist roles such as undertaking due diligence and non-executive directorships.

Suggestions for Further Research

The findings of this study suggest a number of possible areas for future research. The evidence of different harvesting patterns between different sizes and initial sources of buy-outs in the UK in particular suggests the need for a comparative analysis in the US buy-out market where evidence to date on longevity has focused principally on larger transactions. Relatively little is as yet known about the objectives and behavior of owner-managers in buy-outs. Further research on this aspect, in addition to addressing broader issues concerning the nature of entrepreneurs in buy-outs, might usefully examine the extent to which management consider themselves as one-off owner-managers or whether an initial buy-out or buy-in provokes a desire to repeat the experience in another firm. A related question is to explore the scope for and mechanisms by which financing institutions might identify and screen what might be called "second time owner managers."

REFERENCES

Bull, I. (1989). Management performance in leveraged buy-outs: An empirical analysis. *Journal of Business Venturing, 3*(2), 263-278.

Chiplin, B., Wright, M., & Robbie, K. (1992). *UK management buy-outs in 1992—Annual review from CMBOR.* Nottingham: CMBOR.

Cooke, T. (1988). *International mergers and acquisitions.* Oxford: Blackwell.

Ennew, C., Robbie, K., Wright, M., & Thompson, S. (1992). Entrepreneurial characteristics of buy-in managers and the link with post buy-in performance. Paper presented at the Babson Entrepreneurship Conference, INSEAD, Fontainebleau, July 1992.

Franks, J., & Mayer, C. (1990). Capital markets and corporate control: A study of France, Germany and the UK. *Economic Policy, 10,* (April), 191-231.

Green, S., & Berry, D. (1991). *Cultural structural and strategic change in management buy-outs.* London: MacMillan.

Heuze, C. (1991). Management buy-outs in France. In M. Wright (Ed.), *Economist guide to buy-outs* (6th ed.). London: Economist Publications.

Jensen, M. C. (1989). Eclipse of the public corporation. *Harvard Business Review,* Sept/Oct., 61-74.

Joachimsson, R. (1991). Management buy-outs in Sweden. In M. Wright (Ed.), *Economist guide to buy-outs* (6th ed.). London: Economist Publications.

Jones, C. S. (1992). Accounting and organisational change: An empirical study of management buy-outs. *Accounting, Organisations and Society, 17*(2), 151-168.

Kaplan, S. (1991). The staying power of leveraged buyouts. *Journal of Financial Economics, 29,* 287-313.

Kelly, J. M., Pitts, R. A., & Shin, B. (1986). Entrepreneurship by leveraged buy-out: Some preliminary hypotheses. In R. Ronstadt, J. A. Hornaday, R. Peterson and K. H. Vesger (Eds.), *Frontiers of entrepreneurship research*, pp. 281-292. Wellesley, MA: Babson College.

Malone, S. (1989) Characteristics of smaller company leveraged buy-outs. *Journal of Business Venturing,* 4(3), 349-359.

MacMillan, I., Kulow, D., & Khoylian, R. (1989). Venture capitalists' involvement in their investments: Extent and performance. *Journal of Business Venturing,* 4(1), 27-47.

Mueller, D. (1988). The corporate life-cycle. In S. Thompson & M. Wright (Eds.), *Internal organisation, efficiency and profit*, ch. 3. Oxford: Philip Allan.

Rappaport, A. (1990). The staying power of the public corporation. *Harvard Business Review,* Jan/Feb., 96-104.

Robbie, K., Wright, M. & Thompson, S. (1992). Management buy-ins in the UK. *Omega, 20*(4), 445-456.

Ronstadt, R. (1986). Exit, stage left: Why entrepreneurs end their entrepreneurial careers before retirement. *Journal of Business Venturing, 1*(3), 323-338.

Sahlman, W. (1990). The structure and governance of venture capital organisations. *Journal of Financial Economics, 27*(2), 473-524.

Singh, H. (1990). Management buy-outs and shareholder value. *Strategic Management Journal, 11*(5), 111-129.

Sweeting, R. (1991). Early-stage new technology-based business: Interactions with venture capitalists and the development of accounting techniques and procedures. *British Accounting Review, 23,* 3-21.

Thompson, S., & Wright, M. (Eds.). (1988). *Internal organisation, efficiency and profit*. Oxford: Philip Allan.

Thompson, S., & Wright, M. (1991). UK management buy-outs: Debt, equity and agency cost implications. *Managerial and Decision Economics, 12*(1), 15-26.

Thompson, S., Wright, M., & Robbie, K. (1990). Management buy-outs and privatisation: Ownership structure and incentive issues. *Fiscal Studies, 11*(3), 71-88.

Wright, M., & Coyne, J. (1985). *Management buy-outs*. Beckenham: Croom-Helm.

Wright, M., & Desbrieres, P. (1992). Buy-outs in France. *Acquisitions Monthly Buy-out Supplement,* October, 102-104.

Wright, M., & Robbie, K. (1991). Trends in United Kingdom and European buy-outs. In J. Grierson & P. Jenkins (Eds.), *The European buy-out directory*. London: Pitman.

Wright, M., Thompson, S., & Robbie, K. (1992). Venture capital and management-led leveraged buy-outs: European evidence. *Journal of Business Venturing, 7*(1), 47-71.

Wright, M., Thompson, S., Chiplin, B., & Robbie, K. (1991). *Buy-ins and buy-outs: New strategies in corporate management*. London: Graham & Trotman.

Wright, M. (Ed.). (1991). *Economist guide to buy-outs* (6th ed.). London: Economist Publications.

Mike Wright is Professor of Financial Studies at the University of Nottingham.

Ken Robbie is a research fellow at the University of Nottingham.

Yves Romanet is Professor of Finance at Ecole Superieure de Commerce, Lyon.

Steve Thompson is Professor of Managerial Economics at the University of Nottingham.

Robert Joachimsson is Senior Lecturer in Management at the University of Uppsala.

Johan Bruining is Associate Professor of Industrial Organization at Erasmus University.

Artur Herst is Professor of Finance at the University of Limburg, Holland.

Thanks to Frank Hoy, Christine Ennew, Tom Lamb, Chris Ward, Angela Haygarth, Bill Bygrave and participants at the EFER Conference on Harvesting, IPOS and Trade Sales, London, December 1992 for comments on an earlier draft. Financial support for CMBOR from Touche Ross Corporate Finance and Barclays Development Capital Limited is gratefully acknowledged. The research assistance of Marcel Bonnet and Kunle Ajayi is also acknowledged.

[22]

EARLY RATES OF

RETURN OF 131

VENTURE CAPITAL FUNDS

STARTED 1978–1984

WILLIAM BYGRAVE
Babson College

NORMAN FAST, ROUBINA KHOYLIAN,
LINDA VINCENT, and WILLIAM YUE
Venture Economics

EXECUTIVE SUMMARY

The organized venture capital industry is now more than 40 years old. In the last decade, the pool of venture capital has increased almost tenfold to a current total of about $30 billion. Despite its comparative maturity, there has been no systematic tracking of the financial performance of the industry. An extensive search of the scholarly literature found that published information on rates of return was skimpy and not very reliable.

In response to the need for valid and reliable industrywide rates of return, Venture Economics launched a data base in 1985 that records the rates of return of venture capital funds quarterly. For the period 1970–1984, there are 131 different funds in the data base. For the period 1970–1978, the data base covers 15% of all new capital committed to private funds; for the period 1981–1982, it covers 50%. Venture Economics adds funds to the data base on an ongoing basis.

Preliminary analysis of the compound annual rates of return for the period 1978–1985 shows that funds started in 1978–1979 performed magnificently, with returns well in excess of the oft-quoted industry expectation of 25–30%. Funds started in the later part of the period did not perform nearly as well.

However, it is much too early to make any predictions about the final rates of return of the funds because the oldest fund for which the rates are presented in this paper was 7 years old and the youngest was 15 months. Because they will have a life of at least 10 years, these funds have a long way to go before their portfolios are fully harvested and their final rates of return are known.

The implications of the work reported in this paper will be derived from the following fact: The rates of return of venture capital are being recorded in a systematic way for the first time in the history of the organized industry. It is now possible to study the performance of venture capital with valid and reliable data. We expect that those studies will cover a range of applications from pragmatic analyses such as the performance of investment portfolios to theoretical questions such as the efficiency of the market in allocating venture capital.

Address correspondence to: Dr. William Bygrave, Babson College, Center for Entrepreneurial Studies, 222 Tomasso Hall, Babson Park (Wellesley), MA 02157-0901.

Journal of Business Venturing 4, 93–105

94   W. BYGRAVE ET AL.

INTRODUCTION

At the end of 1987, venture capital firms in the United States managed approximately $29.0 billion of funds (*Venture Capital Journal*, April 1988). The money in the pool of venture capital came primarily from pension funds, insurance companies, corporations, wealthy individuals, overseas investors, endowment funds, and foundations. Since the easing of the ERISA "prudent man" rule at the end of the 1970s, pension funds have grown increasingly prominent as a source of venture capital. In fact, it was estimated that 39% of all new capital flowing into venture capital funds in 1987 was from pension funds.

In general, institutional portfolio managers have an abundance of information on rates of return when they invest in stocks, bonds and debt instruments. When they invest in venture capital partnerships, however, they have a dearth of reliable information on rates of return.[1] As one pension fund manager at a major institution remarked, "Depending on whose numbers we believe, we should have as little as 5% or as much as 50% of our portfolio in venture capital partnerships."

While there is a dearth of reliable numbers, there is no shortage of anecdotal accounts and hearsay. Stevenson, Muzyka, and Timmons (1986) reported that some pension fund managers were hoping for 75% returns on long-term funds. That, according to Stevenson et al., was a very optimistic expectation in light of the excellent 25% annual returns on venture capital that were experienced at the end of the 1970s. Stevenson et al. noted that if the 1985 pool of venture capital grew at an annual rate of 75% per annum, it would represent 13% of the total equity of the Fortune 1,000 firms in 7 years.

Have the excellent returns that venture capital earned in the late 1970s continued in the 1980s, or have there been changes in the environment that have affected the rates of return? For example, the flow of new money into the pool of venture capital dried up to a mere trickle by the mid-1970s after the advent of the Tax Reform Act of 1969 (e.g., Bygrave and Timmons 1985). A common complaint by entrepreneurs at that time was that there was not enough venture capital available. There were too many potential deals and not enough money to invest in them. It was an investor's market. After the 1978 Steiger amendment, which restored the favorable tax treatment of capital gains, the floodgates opened quickly, and the United States was awash with venture capital. The situation of the mid-1970s was rather suddenly reversed, and, according to some observers, there was too much capital chasing too few good deals (Bancroft 1988). What effect did that have on the rates of return?

Brophy (1986) noted that although the period 1978–1984 saw a strong surge of funding enter the venture capital business, there had been no analysis of the performance results of this investment and no evaluation of the benefits accruing to the investors. The research that underlies this paper attempts to respond to the need for systematic evaluation of the performance of venture capital funds. The performance criterion for a venture capital partnership is its rate of return (IRR), computed at the end of each calendar year.

LITERATURE SURVEY

Historical Data

Probably the most famous venture capital backed startup of all time is Digital Equipment Corporation (DEC). It seems as if everyone knows about American Research and Devel-

---

[1]Throughout this paper, unless we specifically state otherwise, we use the terms rate of return and IRR for a venture capital fund's compound annual rate of return over a period that starts with the date of its first takedown of capital from its investors and ends on the date specified.

TABLE 1 Venture Capital: Annualized Rates of Return (Published Information)

Percent (period)	Firms (Reference)
14% (1946–1988)	American Research and Development (Rotch 1968)
17% (1967–1974)	Bessemer (Poindexter 1976)
15% (few years through 1972)	Hambrecht & Quist (Poindexter 1976)
11%	14 public VCs (primarily SBICs) (Faucett 1971)
12% (1961–1973)	29 public VCs (mainly SBICs) (Poindexter 1976)
13%	59 VCs managing 1/3 VC pool (Poindexter 1976)
23%	Gross. 110 actual investments in portfolio companies (Hoban 1976)
27% (1974–1979)	11 public VCs (Martin and Petty 1983)
16% (1959–1985)	Public VCs (Ibbotson and Brinson 1987)

opment's (ARD) investment in DEC. It is part of the folklore of the industry, and deservedly so. Even if the amount invested varies from $60,000 to $67,000, and the amount returned in about 12 years varies from $500,000,000 to $600,000,000 depending on who recounts the tale (e.g., Kozmetsky et al. 1984; Wells 1974), the rate of return of 130% or thereabouts is the stuff of which legends are made. But what is the reality? Even with as spectacular an investment as DEC in its portfolio, ARD's rate of return for the 20 years 1946–1966 was only 14% according to Rotch (1968). True, in 1966, its investment in DEC had yet to come to full fruition, but it was blossoming very nicely. By the late 1970s, after DEC had been harvested and ARD had become part of Textron, ARD's rate of return fell into the single digits (Gevirtz 1985).

Since so many of the venture capital firms are private, data on rates of return are hard to find. Two of the most respected private venture capital firms are Bessemer Securities and Hambrecht and Quist. According to Poindexter (1976), Bessemer reported a 17% rate of return for the period 1967–1974, and Hambrecht and Quist a 15% rate of return over several years through 1972.

Table 1 presents a summary of published scholarly research on rates of return of venture capital. Most studies of venture capital returns have used small samples of publicly held firms, primarily small business investment companies (SBICs). A study of 14 public venture capital firms found the rate of return to be 11% on average (Faucett 1971). Hoban (1976) constructed a portfolio composed of 110 actual venture capital investments in 50 different companies made by four different venture capital firms during the period 1960–1968. The four venture capital firms consisted of a publicly held SBIC, a private partnership, a private corporation owned by a wealthy family, and a subsidiary of a large bank holding company. He found the gross (before management fees and income taxes) rate of return of the portfolio to be 22.9% for the period through the end of 1975. If Hoban's rate of return is adjusted for the typical annual management free of 3%, the rate of return is about 19.9%.

Poindexter (1976) gathered data from 29 publicly held firms consisting of 26 SBICs and three corporations investing in venture capital. The geometric mean of annual rate of return for the 29 firms over the period 1961–1973 was 11.6%. That rate compared with the 7.1% percent rate of return for Standard and Poor's 500 over the same period. The rates of return for Poindexter's sample of venture capital firms varied considerably with the calendar period over which it was computed. For example, it was 10.7% for the period 1961–1966, 31% for 1967–1971, and 1.2% for 1972–1973.

Martin and Petty (1983) analyzed the performance of eleven publicly traded venture

96   W. BYGRAVE ET AL.

capital firms, of which all but two were in Poindexter's sample. They computed the rate of
return on the publicly traded stock for each of the 6 years in the period 1974–1979, and
they found the average rate of return over this period to be 27%. Unfortunately, Martin and
Petty's rate of return on publicly traded stock is not the actual rate of return on the firm's
venture capital investments, and the two should not be compared because there may be little
or no relationship between their values at any one time. For example, Arthur D. Little,
former chairman of Narragansett Capital Corporation, which was in both Poindexter's and
Martin and Petty's samples, recently stated that in the mid-1970s, Narragansett's share price
fell to 80% below the value of the assets in its portfolio (Wayne 1988).

A study by First Chicago Investment Advisors (Ibbotson and Brinson 1987) used a
methodology similar to Martin and Petty's (1983) to study the rates of return of public
venture capital companies from 1959 through 1985. The compound annual rate of return
over the 26-year period was 16%.

It is not easy to get the data that are needed to calculate the actual rates of return of
venture capital investments— not even for publicly held funds such as Poindexter's sample
of 29. In fact, Poindexter commented that it was an arduous task. To get the actual rate of
return, it is necessary to dig into the financial statements published in annual reports and
10Ks to get operating expenses, interest expenses, income dividends, capital gains dividends,
net assets, long-term debt, and net worth. Those numbers must be adjusted to allow for any
additional public offerings and stock splits. The reliability of the net-asset figure may be
questionable because most of its value resides in a fund's portfolio, for which the value is
only an estimate, because most of the companies in it are private.

Poindexter (1976) surveyed 270 venture capital firms that managed the bulk of the
domestic venture capital pool. He estimated that the respondents who supplied rate of return
data managed one-third of the domestic pool of venture capital. They were asked to estimate
their firms' rates of return since inception. The mean of the estimated rates of return of the
59 firms was 13.3%, with a range from 35% to −40%.

METHODOLOGY

Venture capital partnerships are composed of limited partners and general partners. The
limited partners provide the money; the general partners provide the management. Venture
capitalists in one venture capital firm may be general partners in more than one partnership
that is under the management umbrella of that firm. Some of the older venture capital firms
manage half a dozen or so partnerships. In return for managing the partnership, the general
partners receive an annual management fee and a share of any profit that the partnership
makes. The general partners' annual management fee is usually 2–3% of the paid-in-capital,
and the general partners' share of the profit is usually 20%, with the other 80% going to
the limited partners. Partnerships generally have a 10-year defined term, which can often
be extended.

When a new partnership is formed, the money that the limited partner commits to the
partnership is paid in several installments (or what are called takedowns) over the first 2 or
3 years. The general partners send reports and financial statements to the limited partners,
usually quarterly. From those financial statements, a limited partner can calculate its share
of the book value of the partnership (or what is called the residual value). The residual value
consists of any uninvested capital and the partnership's share of the estimated value of
portfolio companies in which the partnership has invested. When a company in the partnership's portfolio goes public, the limited partner may receive its share of the stock in that

company (called a disbursement), although the venture capital company often holds the stock for a period before distributing it. This disbursement is usually valued by the partnership at the price per share of the public offering. When the stock carries restrictions on its sale, its price is often discounted by 20–30%. In addition to stock, there may be other disbursements, such as cash dividends.

Traditionally, venture capital partnerships do not disseminate information from which it is possible to determine their performance, specifically their rates of return. As Boylan observed (1982), the venture capital industry is shrouded in secrecy. However, limited partners have information on takedowns, disbursements, and residuals from which the IRRs can be computed.

Data Sets

In 1985, Venture Economics launched an effort to collect data from institutions that invest in venture capital funds. Participating institutional investors allowed us access to their records to collect data from which IRRs could be calculated.[2] In some cases, we were allowed to go through actual transactions and quarterly financial reports, and thereby compile our own data sets; in other cases, we were given data sets that the limited partners had compiled. Those data formed the beginning of Venture Economics' rates of return data base. Venture Economics updates each fund's records quarterly and adds funds to the data base on an ongoing basis.

There were over 200 venture capital partnerships in the data sets collected from the institutions. Some partnerships appeared in more than one institution's portfolio, and others were started during 1985 and were of no use for our analysis. After duplicates and 1985 partnerships were removed from the data sets, 140 different partnerships with starting dates from 1971 to 1984 remained in the data base that was used for the analysis that follows. The bulk of them were started after 1977. The partnerships in that sample comprised approximately 15% of all new venture capital committed to private funds for the period 1971–1978, 43% for 1979–1980, and 50% for 1981–1982.

Computations of IRRs

The algorithm for computing the IRRs is fairly simple in principle. The residuals, the disbursements, and the takedowns are each reduced to their present value on the date of the first takedown. A disbursement of D dollars has a present value of $D/(1 + IRR/100)^t$, where IRR is the internal rate of return, and t is the time in years from the date of the first takedown to the date of the disbursement. The present values of a takedown of T dollars and a residual of R dollars are computed in the same way. Then, by iteration, the value of the IRR is computed at the end of each calendar quarter by finding its value when the present value of the takedowns equals the present value of all the disbursements plus the present value of the residual.

Limitations

In practice, computing the IRRs was not quite so simple. The data had limitations, which will be discussed next. However, it should be stressed that although the data were not perfect,

---

[2]The names of the institutions and the individual venture capital partnerships are confidential.

we believe they were the most extensive and reliable that ever had been used to calculate the rates of return of venture capital funds.

First, some institutions recorded the actual dates of the transactions, while others recorded them at the end of the month in which they occurred. Transactions were computed as if they occurred on the last day of the month in order to put them all on the same basis.

Second, although it is easy to construct an algorithm that computes the limited partner's share of a residual, it is difficult to compute it reliably without knowing the intricate details of the partnership agreement, specifically how and when the general partner's share of the profit is recognized. In principle, the general partner does not get any share of the profit until the limited partner has received back all that money that it has paid into the fund. After that, the profit is split, usually on a 20/80 basis. Once the residual plus distributions exceeds the sum of the takedowns, the fund is making a profit on paper. Most funds then recognize the unrealized profit that is locked up in the residual. After that point is reached, the general partner holds back its anticipated share of future profits from subsequent disbursements to the limited partners.

A third limitation of the data was missing residuals. Where a residual was missing, it was estimated from the last known value adjusted for any disbursements or takedowns in the investing period.

A fourth limitation was the reliability of the valuation of the residuals. Most funds have a valuation committee that estimates the value of its portfolio of investments in companies that have no publicly traded stock. Thus, the value of the residual is a somewhat subjective judgment made by each fund's valuation committee. This problem is mitigated to some extent because there were 131 different funds, and there was no reason to believe that there was any overall bias, either high or low, by valuation committees.

RESULTS

IRRs were computed at the end of each calendar year, starting when a fund was 1 year old and continuing through the last year for which the residual was known. They were computed for every fund in each of the institution's portfolios. When the same fund appeared in more than one portfolio, it was used to check the reliability of the different data sets. In the analysis of the performance of the funds, however, it was included only once.

The IRRs of the funds by calendar year for the period 1979–1985 are shown in Figure 1 for all funds started from the beginning of 1978 through the end of 1984. It shows that the mean IRR of all funds peaked in 1980 at about 32%. In general, it shows a decline in the IRRs from 1980 through 1985, apart from a peak of about 29% in 1983. By the end of 1985, the mean IRR was less than 10%.

The information presented in Figure 1 must be viewed with caution because it agglomerates the IRRs of all funds in a given year regardless of the age of the funds. To do so is potentially misleading because it is expected that as funds grow older, their portfolio companies move closer to being harvested (e.g., initial public offerings, mergers, etc.) or have actually been harvested. Thus, it is likely that the IRR of a fund will increase with age, all other things being equal. Of course, all other things are not equal. One important "other thing" is the calendar date, which can have a major effect on IRRs. For example, as Figure 1 shows, IRRs peaked in 1983. Thus, there are three temporal factors that have to be separated: 1) the year a fund was started, 2) its age, and 3) calendar date.

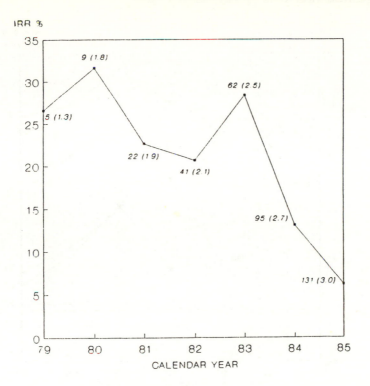

Labels are Number of Funds and Their Mean Age (Years)

FIGURE 1   IRRs of funds by calendar year: all funds grouped together.

Calendar Date

The funds were grouped according to the year in which they were begun.[3] The IRRs of each group of funds by calendar year are presented in Figure 2. The right-hand margin gives the number of funds in each group. The 1978–1979 group, which comprised nine funds, performed spectacularly, with an average rate of return of about 40%. Funds formed after 1979 did not perform as well. For example, at the end of 1985, the average rates of return of funds started in 1981, 1982, 1983, and 1984 were all lower than 10%, with the 1984 funds' average IRR being slightly negative.

ANOVAs were performed at each calendar year, 1981–1985, to see if the differences among the IRRs for the funds grouped according to their starting dates were significant. Those differences were significant ($p < 0.002$) for each of the years 1981, 1982, 1983, 1984, and 1985.

Age of Funds

We next examined the effect of age on the rates of return. The IRRs of the funds grouped according to their starting dates were plotted against the age of the funds, as shown in Figure

---

[3]The years 1978 and 1979 were grouped together to increase the number of funds in that set.

100 W. BYGRAVE ET AL.

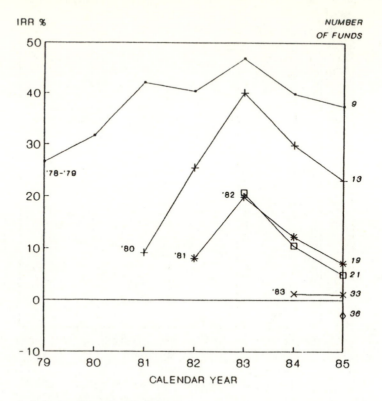

Labels Are Years Funds Started

FIGURE 2 IRRs of funds by calendar year grouped by year fund started.

3. The plot shows that at any given age, the earlier a fund was started, the higher its rate of return (with the exception of the 1981 and 1982 funds at an age of 1 year). The peaks for each group of funds (age 4 for 1978–1979 funds, age 3 for 1980 funds, age 2 for 1981 funds, and age 1 for 1982 funds) occurred in calendar year 1983.

ANOVAs were performed at each level to see if the differences among the IRRs for the funds grouped according to their starting dates were significant. Those differences were significant ($p < 0.002$) for 2-, 3-, 4-, and 5-year-old funds.

Frequency Distribution of IRRs

The frequency distribution of each of the groups of 3- and 5-year-old funds is shown in Figure 4. It shows that the median of the distribution is higher for the older funds than the younger ones (25% versus 13%).[4] As we stated earlier, that is what was expected.

---

[4]The frequency distributions should be viewed with caution because they are not controlled for the starting date of the funds. For example, the starting date of 3-year-old funds could be any year from 1978 to 1982.

EARLY RATES OF RETURN OF 131 VENTURE FUNDS   **101**

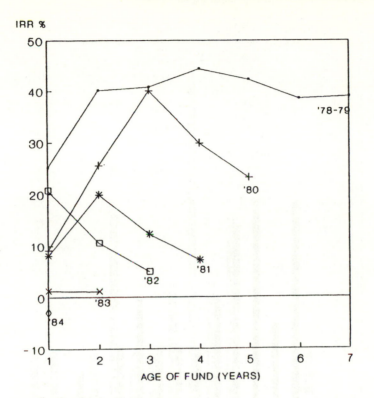

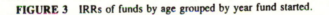

Labels Are Years Funds Started

FIGURE 3   IRRs of funds by age grouped by year fund started.

DISCUSSION

Before we discuss the significance of our findings, it is important to stress that none of the partnerships had run their full course. The funds in our data set were limited partnerships with a 10-year life. As many observers of the industry have noted, the lemons in a venture capital fund's portfolio drop in 2–3 years, whereas the plums sometimes take 7 or so years to ripen (e.g., Timmons et al. 1985). Venture capital partnerships are long-term rather than short-term investments. During the 10-year life of a partnership, many changes occur in the environment (e.g., "hot" or "cold" IPO markets) that have dramatic short-term effects on the rates of return. In the long term, the final rate of return of a fund is less sensitive to those short-term market conditions. Hence, it is important not to draw premature conclusions about the rates of return that the funds may finally achieve. With that in mind, we will first consider our findings about the returns, then we will compare our results with those of other researchers.

Performance of Funds Started 1978–1984

One trend is unmistakable: When funds are compared at the same age, those started toward the end of the 1978–1984 period were not performing nearly as well as ones started toward

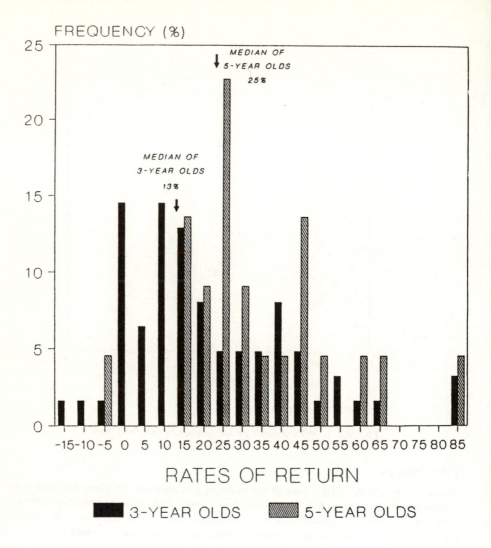

RATES OF RETURN

■ 3-YEAR OLDS ▨ 5-YEAR OLDS

Funds Started 1978 through 1982

FIGURE 4 Distribution of IRRs: all 3- and 5-year-old funds.

the beginning. For example, when the funds started in 1978–1979 were 3 years old, their compound annual return was about 40%; when the funds started in 1982 were 3 years old, their return was less than 10%. That finding must be treated with caution because we are comparing two 3-year periods when the environments were quite different. Nevertheless, our findings appear to substantiate a trend that is being discussed more and more in the industry: Rates of return of venture capital funds have, in general, been declining in recent years. For example, at the National Venture Capital Association annual meeting in May 1987, William Hambrecht, one of the leaders of the venture capital industry, commented that what is happening in the industry today is "Economics 101." He said that he expected winners and losers among venture capital funds (Hambrecht, 1987).

What has been happening in the industry that might explain the decline in the rates of return? From the early 1970s through 1977, venture capital was relatively scarce. It was likely that there was a pent-up supply of companies and entrepreneurs that merited venture capital but had not yet been able to get it. Once venture capital became relatively abundant beginning in 1978, existing venture capital partnerships, together with those started in 1978 and 1979, were able to take the pick of the crop of the companies that were seeking venture capital. Hence, venture capital funds started in 1978–1979 should have performed particularly well. Indeed, that happened. As McClane (1988), a general partner of TA Associates, said about the performance of its investments made at the end of the 1970s compared to those made after 1983, "It used to be hard not to make money. It is definitely not as easy [to make money] now."

As the supply of venture capital became increasingly plentiful, more and more venture capital funds were started. For example, 2 new and follow-on partnerships were formed in 1977, 13 in 1978, 14 in 1979, 22 in 1980, 37 in 1981, 54 in 1982, and 87 in 1983. The money committed to those partnerships was $20 million in 1977, $216 million in 1978, $170 million in 1979, $661 million in 1980, $866 million in 1981, $1423 million in 1982, and $3400 million in 1983 (*Venture Capital Journal* October 1982, January 1984). With so many newly formed partnerships and so much money, in the short term there was a shortage of experienced venture capitalists, and there was more competition for good deals in which to invest. According to a 1984 study of 267 venture capital firms by the Joint Economic Committee (U.S. Congress 1985), "Most fund managers reported that the recent increase in venture capital availability reduced the quality of their decision-making and significantly increased the competition for deals within the venture capital community."

Comparison with Findings of Other Researchers

Published information seems to indicate that the overall rates of return of venture capital have usually been below 20% for most of the 40 or so years since the birth of the industry. As Poindexter (1976) observed, however, there have been short-run booms, such as the ones that occurred in 1961, 1967–1969, and 1972, when the rates of return sometimes were more than 30%. He wrote, "These boomlets affect the portfolios of most firms by allowing early liquidation of maturing private investments in the most favorable market for venture capitalists, the 'hot' new issues market." There can be little doubt that 1979–1983 was one of those boom periods. The initial public offerings market, which was virtually dormant from 1973 through 1978, came to life in 1980 and reached a peak in 1983, which was probably the "hottest" new issues market ever. Two of the many possible examples include the following: Stratus went public in 1983 at almost 200 times annualized earnings, and

104   W. BYGRAVE ET AL.

Sevin-Rosen's $2.1 million of venture capital invested in Lotus was worth $70 million at the public offering in 1983. As Figure 2 shows, the average rate of return of the 1978–1979 vintage of funds peaked above 45% in 1983 and led to an air of euphoria throughout the venture capital industry.

At 5 years of age, the median rate of return of funds started in the period 1978–1980 was 25%, and the mean was 31% (Figure 4). Those were the funds that profited most from the hot IPO market of the early 1980s. Some funds were performing magnificently: Three had rates of return above 60%, and one of those was above 80%. We are struck by the similarity between the shape of the frequency distribution of the IRRs of the 22 funds in Figure 4 and that predicted by Stevenson, Muzyka, and Timmons (1986) in their Monte Carlo simulation of the performance of 100 funds. However, it is too soon for us to draw any conclusions about their model because the funds in our sample were limited partnerships with 5 more years remaining in their lives.

CONCLUDING COMMENTS

Our data set included about 50% of the new capital committed to private funds in the period 1979–1980. Therefore, it is probable that the performance of our sample closely represents the performance of the industry as a whole. Hence, it is reasonable to conclude that overall returns on venture capital have been declining since 1983. What does that mean for the industry? According to the *Venture Capital Journal* (May 1987), "Levels of investment activity have been reduced since the excesses of 1983 and investment is continuing on a more cautious basis. Many funds are concentrating on building value in their current portfolios and are careful not to over-extend their human resources."

The growth of the industry has been more stable in the 5 years since the IPO frenzy of 1983. Venture capitalists are taking a longer-term perspective with their investments. Instead of aiming for a relatively early IPO to finance the growth of portfolio companies, venture capitalists "have got to be able to nurse their companies through all the rounds (of capital), not just the first one or two. That means assigning more money per investment and more responsibility in financial planning," according to Boury (1988) of Warburg, Pincus Ventures.

Bancroft (1987), a widely respected veteran of the venture capital industry, believes that venture capital firms have oversold their ability to produce extraordinary results. High-technology investments cannot be relied upon to produce continuous opportunities. He said that the industry will have to turn in new directions in an effort to secure moderate returns in exchange for extraordinary returns that are so difficult to attain. He saw LBOs and "beat up" public companies as two avenues to pursue.

As a final comment, despite the decline in the rates of return, the pool of venture capital continues to swell. Inflows of capital in 1987 were the second highest ever. We think this is because long-term investors of the sort that invest in venture capital know that over almost the entire history of the industry, returns on venture capital funds have, on average, out-performed those on the S&P 500 stocks by a margin of at least 50% and sometimes by more than 100%. The period since 1983 during which the S&P 500 stocks have equalled or out-performed venture capital is an anomaly, because in comparison with their historical performance, S&P 500 stocks have performed exceptionally well. Because much of the pool of venture capital is composed of funds that are less than 5 years old, it is too soon to make a prognosis about their final rate of return at the end of their 10-year lives. We should keep in mind, however, that it might take only one sustained "hot" new issue market to make a dramatic increase in their rates of return.

REFERENCES

Bancroft, P. May 1987. Quoted in *Venture Capital Journal*, p. 1.

Bancroft, P. March 1988, Quoted in "Too much money, too few deals," *Forbes*, p. 144.

Boury, N. March 1988. Quoted in "Where venture capital is investing now." *High Technology Business*, pp. 19–25.

Boylan, M. January 1982. What we know and don't know about venture capital. American Economic Association Meetings, December 28, 1981. National Economist Club.

Brophy, D.J. 1986. Venture capital research. In D.L. Sexton and R.W. Smilor, eds., *The Art and Science of Entrepreneurship*. Cambridge, MA: Ballinger.

Bygrave, W.D. and Timmons, J.A. 1985. An empirical model for the flows of venture capital. In J.A. Hornaday, E.B. Shils, J.A. Timmons, and K.H. Vesper, eds., *Frontiers of Entrepreneurship Research*. Wellesley, MA: Babson College, pp. 105–125.

Faucett, R.B. 1971. *The Management of Venture Capital Investment Companies*. Masters thesis, MIT.

Gevirtz, D. 1985. *The New Entrepreneurs: Innovation in American Business*. New York: Penguin Books.

Hambrecht, W. May 1987. Quoted in *Venture Capital Journal*, p. 2.

Hoban, J.P. 1976. *Characteristics of Venture Capital Investing*. PhD. diss., University of Utah.

Ibbotson, R.G. and Brinson, G.P. 1987. *Investment Markets*. New York: McGraw-Hill. pp. 99–100.

Kozmetsky, G., Gill, M.D. Jr., and Smilor, R.W. 1984. *Financing and Managing Fast-Growth Companies: The Venture Capital Process*. Lexington, MA: Lexington Books.

Martin, J.P. and Petty, W.P. 1983. An analysis of the performance of publicly traded venture capital companies. *Journal of Financial and Quantitative Analysis* 18(3):401–410.

McLane, P.A. March 1988. Quoted in "Too much money, too few deals." *Forbes*, p. 144.

Poindexter, J.B. 1976. *The Efficiency of Financial Markets: The Venture Capital Case*. Ph.D. diss., New York University.

Rotch, W. September–October 1968. The pattern of success in venture capital financing. *Financial Analysis Journal* 24:141–147.

Stevenson, H.H., Muzyka, D.F., and Timmons, J.A. 1986. Venture capital in a new era: A simulation of the impact of changes in investment patterns. In R. Ronstadt, J.A. Hornaday, R. Peterson, and K.H. Vesper, eds., *Frontiers of Entrepreneurship Research*. Wellesley, MA: Babson College, pp. 380–384.

Timmons, J.A., Smollen, L.S., and Dingee, A.L.M. 1985. *New Venture Creation*. Homewood, IL: Richard D. Irwin, Inc., pp. 79–80.

U.S. Congress. 1985 Joint Economic Committee. Venture capital and innovation. Washington, D.C.: U.S. Government Printing Office.

Venture Capital Journal, October 1982, January 1984.

Venture Capital Journal, April 1988.

Wayne, L. January 1988. Management's tale. *New York Times Magazine*, p. 42.

Wells, W.A. 1974. *Venture Capital Decision-Making*. Ph.D. diss., Carnegie-Mellon University.

Part V
Alternative Sources of Venture Capital: Informal Venture Capitalists, Corporate Venture Capital and Relationship Banking

[23]

ENTREPRENEURSHIP & REGIONAL DEVELOPMENT, 7 (1995), 85–94

Angels: personal investors in the venture capital market

JOHN FREEAR, JEFFREY E. SOHL† and
WILLIAM E. WETZEL, Jr
Center for Venture Research, Whittemore School of Business and
Economics, University of New Hampshire, Durham, NH 03824, USA

The role of private investors in the equity financing of new technology-based ventures is examined. The research studies the venture capital market from a demand and supply perspective and delineates the role of the private investor with that of the more visible venture capital funds. The entrepreneur's perceptions of raising venture capital are also examined. The research suggests that the private investor is the most common source of seed and start-up financing, especially if the round of financing is less than US$500 000. While private investors are harder to find than their venture capital fund counterparts, it appears to take less time to close a deal with private investors and the financing is less expensive than financing from venture capital funds. Both private investors and venture capital funds add value to their investments through the establishment of working relationships with the ventures they finance, and entrepreneurs perceive these working relationships to be a productive component of the deal.

Keywords: private investors; venture capital; technology-based ventures; entrepreneurs

1. Introduction

Evidence is mounting that the late 1970s marked the end of an era in US economy – the so-called industrial economy – and the beginning of a new era – the entrepreneurial economy (Birch 1987, 1988; Huey 1994). In 1979, output of the Fortune 500 peaked at 58% of GNP, up from 37% in 1954. Employment reached 16 million and political economists foresaw a new industrial state dominated by large firms (Hale 1992). Between 1979 and 1993, Fortune 500 payrolls fell by over 25% to US$11.5m. In 1993 total employment among the 500 fell for the ninth straight year, from 11 802 133 to 11 546 647, while median employment dropped 5.3% to 10 136 (Huey 1994). Simultaneously, largely invisible entrepreneurial ventures created over 20 million new jobs (Hale 1992).

Today the restructuring of America is well under way. More and more of the nation's work is being done by entrepreneurs and the fast, focused, flexible ventures they lead. As the Fortune 500 continue to 'build down', entrepreneurs and their investors are leading the US out of recession. Despite the compelling evidence of their job-generating power, today's entrepreneurs face a daunting task in their search for equity financing, the fuel for the engine that creates jobs and moves technology from the laboratory to the marketplace. Founder's capital, sweat equity and bootstrap financing alone cannot provide the necessary equity for the most promising technology-based ventures.

During the late 1980s and early 1990s, most entrepreneurs came up empty in their search for venture capital. Seed and start-up financing by professional venture capital funds, the best-known source of venture financing, virtually disappeared (Bygrave and Timmons 1992). However, even in the best of financial times, venture capital funds are

†Author for correspondence.

not the place to look for early-stage financing. Entrepreneurs have been knocking on the wrong doors in their search for funds.

Research on early-stage investing has identified the informal venture capital market as the major source of equity financing for entrepreneurial ventures (Wetzel 1983). This informal venture capital market consists of a diverse set of high net worth individuals (business angels) who invest a portion of their assets in high risk, high return entrepreneurial ventures. Like most of the ventures they bankroll, these private investors are a nearly invisible segment of the venture capital markets. There are no directories of business angels and no public records of their investment transactions. Research has, however, clearly established the importance of the informal market in the United States and Canada (Freear *et al.* 1994; Gaston 1989a; Haar *et al.* 1988; Riding and Short 1987). More recent research has extended the findings on the US informal venture market to the UK (Harrison and Mason 1993; Mason and Harrison 1992) and Sweden (Landstrom 1992, 1993).

In an attempt to add to the knowledge base of the informal investor market, this paper examines the venture capital market for new technology-based firms. The research views this market from both a demand and supply perspective and attempts to delineate the role of the private investor with respect to the more visible venture capital funds. The research also focuses on the entrepreneur's perceptions of raising venture capital.

2.   Venture capital markets

A sense of the scale and structure of demand and supply in the venture capital markets provides a useful background for an examination of the role of angels in these markets.

2.1   *Demand for venture capital*

Venture investors look for opportunities to back entrepreneurial companies that offer the prospect of long-term capital gains substantial enough to justify the risks and lack of short-term liquidity inherent in venture investing. There are no hard data on the number of these high potential start-ups and high growth private companies or their annual capital requirements. Educated guesses place the number of private companies growing faster than 20% per year at about 500 000. David Birch's research indicates that 4% of US firms account for 70% of all job growth (Birch *et al.* 1993). The 1993 INC. 500 fastest growing private companies are obvious examples (INC 1993). The number of start-ups with attractive capital gains potential for investors is estimated to be 50 000 per year, less than 5% of total annual business start-ups. The equity financing requirements of these high growth and start-up ventures is somewhere in the neighbourhood of US$60 billion per year. Sixty billion dollars per year of high risk, patient, value-added capital is one measure of the capital formation challenge confronting the US economy.

2.2   *Supply of venture capital*

There are two primary sources of venture financing for entrepreneurs – one visible and one invisible. The visible venture capital market is composed of over 500 venture capital funds that manage about US$35 billion. In the early nineties, venture capital funds were investing between US$2 and US$3 billion annually in entrepreneurial ventures. Considering the demand for this capital, US$3 billion per year represents a significant shortfall in the capital requirements of high growth entrepreneurial ventures. Compounding this capital gap is the fact that venture capital funds bankroll less than 2000 companies per year and two thirds of these financings are for ventures already in their portfolios. A typical round of financing from a venture capital fund is a later-stage deal in excess of US$1m.

The invisible venture capital market is the oldest and the largest segment of the US venture capital market. It is made up of over two million individuals with a net worth in excess of US$1m, excluding personal residences. The majority of these individuals are self-made millionaires (first-generation money) – individuals with substantial business and entrepreneurial experience (Postma and Sullivan 1990; Gaston and Bell 1988). While estimates of the scale of this informal venture capital market vary considerably (Aram 1987; Gaston 1989b; Gaston and Bell 1986; Ou 1987) conservative estimates suggest that about 250 000 angels invest approximately US$10 billion every year in about 30 000 ventures.

For ventures with competent, committed management and a convincing business plan, the odds of raising angel financing are much higher than the odds of raising capital from venture capital funds. A typical angel deal is an early-stage round in the US$100 000 to US$500 000 range, raised from six or eight investors. These co-investors usually are trusted friends and business associates. Find one angel and you have found five or ten.

3. The data

The data used in the present study of the financing of new, technology-based firms (NTBFs) were collected from 284 companies founded in New England between 1975 and 1986. The 284 companies represent 27% of 1073 firms in CorpTech's Corporate Technology database (CorpTech 1986). The data were collected and analysed in two stages.

In the first stage, financial histories were collected from the 284 NTBFs. Financial histories included the year of each round of financing, the source, the amount and the stage of the financing. One hundred and seven firms (38%) were launched and grew using only founder's capital, sweat equity and bootstrap financing. The other 177 firms (62%) raised US$671 million in 445 rounds of equity financing (Freear and Wetzel 1990).

In the second stage, entrepreneurs who had raised equity capital were asked about the process of raising funds and the characteristics of their investors, particularly individual investors (business angels) and venture capital funds. Data included methods employed for locating investors, the length of the search process, perceptions of investors' required rates of return, expected holding periods, relationships between investors and the management of the firm and entrepreneurs' perceptions of the value of these investor relationships (Freear *et al.* 1990).

In drawing inferences from the data, it is important to note two points. First, the data were collected from ventures that were founded during a period of rapid growth in the capital under management by venture capital funds. Second, most of these venture funds were invested in NTBFs. Therefore, the relative size of the capital invested in NTBFs by private investors and venture capital funds should not be extrapolated to the population of all ventures that obtained capital from these two sources.

4.   Financial history

The financial histories of the technology-based firms in the sample provide insights for today's entrepreneurs. To highlight what appear to be the most compelling implications of the data, angel financing is contrasted with financing provided by venture capital funds. The data provide valuable insights when segmented by the size and the stage of the investment during the early life of a venture.

Sources of equity financing included private individuals (business angels), venture capital funds, non-financial corporations, public stock offerings and other general sources. Of the 177 firms that raised outside equity, 124 firms (70%) raised one or more rounds from private individuals (excluding members of the founding management team and their relatives). Ninety firms (51%) raised one or more rounds from venture capital funds. Fewer than 40 firms raised funds from any other single source. Of the 445 rounds of financing, Table 1 indicates that angels provided 177 rounds (40%) and venture capital funds provided 173 rounds (39%). The remaining three sources collectively accounted for 95 rounds (21%).

The sample firms raised US$76m from angels and almost five times that amount, US$370 million, from venture capital funds. When the data for angel and venture capital funds are segmented by the size of a round of financing (Table 1), the distinctive role of angels in smaller deals is apparent. For the 213 rounds under US$1m, angels accounted for 56% of the dollars and 75% (160) of the rounds, compared to 44% of the dollars and 25% (53) of the rounds for venture capital funds. An examination of rounds under US$1m reveals a boundary area between angel financing and financing by venture capital funds in the neighbourhood of US$500 000. Angels provided 93% of the rounds involving less than US$250 000 and 75% of the rounds between US$250 000 and US$500 000. In rounds under US$500 000, angels were dominant in terms of dollars as well as rounds, providing a total of US$23m compared to US$6m from venture capital funds, a ratio of 4:1. Thirty per cent of angel dollars, as opposed to 2% of the dollars from venture capital funds, were invested in rounds under US$500 000.

In financings over US$500 000 the role of angels diminishes rapidly. Between US$500 000 and US$1m, angels accounted for 33% of the rounds and for rounds over US$1m only 14%. As the size of a round of financing increases, angels are replaced by venture capital funds as the dominant players.

When investments are segmented by the stage of the financing, a second distinguishing characteristic of angel financing is evident. The stages investigated include seed, start-up, first, second, third and bridge financing (Morris *et al.* 1990). In total dollars, angels were the largest single source of seed financing, accounting for US$12m (48%) of the US$26m invested in seed capital deals (Table 2). Their role declined sharply at the start-up stage, accounting for US$29m (20%) of start-up investments. At the first

Table 1.   Rounds invested in NTBFs.

Size of round (US$)	Private individuals		Venture capital funds		Total
<250 000	102	58%	8	5%	110
250 000–499 999	43	24%	14	8%	57
500 000–999 999	15	8%	31	18%	46
≥1 000 000	17	10%	120	69%	137
Total	177	100%	173	100%	350

and second stages, angels accounted for only 8% of the capital raised. By the third stage, angels provided only 2% of the dollars raised.

Venture capital funds provided almost as much seed capital as angels, US$11m compared to US$12m (Table 2). At the start-up stage, venture capital funds were the largest single source of capital, providing 45% of the US$144m invested in start-ups, compared to 20% from angels and 19% from public stock offerings. Venture capital funds were the dominant source of first, second and third stage financing, accounting for 69, 58 and 52% of the total capital, respectively.

The central role of angels in early-stage financing becomes more apparent when rounds, rather than dollars, are used as the measure of activity. As indicated in Table 3, angels provided 52 rounds of seed financing, representing 83% of the 63 seed deals. Angels also provided more rounds of start-up financing than venture capital funds, 55 compared to 38.

At the seed stage, the evidence suggests that most entrepreneurs should seek funds from angels, especially when the financing is under US$300 000. At the seed stage, angels invested more funds, in more rounds, for more firms than any other single source. In a very real sense, angels are 'seeding' ventures that will require larger rounds of follow-on financing as well as ventures that never raise equity from other sources. The median round of angel seed financing was US$100 000–$199 000. The median round of seed financing from venture capital funds was US$400 000–US$499 000.

At the start-up stage the business angel continues to be an important player, especially when the capital required is under US$500 000. Angels provided 42 rounds of start-up financing under US$500 000. Only two start-up rounds under US$500 000 were raised from venture capital funds. For rounds above US$500 000 the angels are replaced by the venture capital funds as the dominant source of funding. The median round of start-up financing from angels was US$100 000–US$199 000, compared to a median start-up round of US$1m–US$2m from venture capital funds.

Table 2.   Dollars invested in NTBFs (US$million).

Stage	Private individuals	Venture capital funds	Other	Total
Seed	12	11	3	26
Start-up	29	63	52	144
First stage	13	118	39	170
Second stage	15	111	65	191
Third stage	2	59	46	107
Bridge	5	8	20	33
Total	76	370	225	671

Table 3.   Rounds invested in NTBFs.

Stage	Private individuals		Venture capital funds		Total
Seed	52	29%	11	6%	63
Start-up	55	31%	38	22%	93
First stage	29	16%	56	32%	85
Second stage	26	15%	46	27%	72
Third stage	10	6%	19	11%	29
Bridge	5	3%	3	2%	8
Total	177	100%	173	100%	350

Angels clearly are more active in seed and start-up financing than venture capital funds. Fifty-four per cent of angel dollars and 60% of angel deals were invested at the seed or start-up stage as compared to 20% of the dollars and 28% of the deals from venture capital funds. Early-stage financing entails both greater risks and longer holding periods than later-stage financing. In their venture deals, angels exhibit less risk-aversion and more patience than their professional counterparts. Avery and Elliehausen (1986) provided insights into the risk and liquidity attitudes of high income households. Compared to all US families, high income households displayed a significantly higher propensity to assume above-average financial risks in order to earn above-average returns. High income families also displayed a significantly higher propensity to tie up funds for long periods of time in order to earn substantial returns.

In later-stage financing, the size of the round is the characteristic that distinguishes angels from venture capital funds. The size of the rounds provided by these two sources drifts further apart as the stage of the financing advances. For angels, the median size of the round of first stage financing was US$200–US$299 (thousand), and for second and third stage financing the median size (in thousands) was US$100–US$199. In contrast, for venture capital funds, the median size of the round of first and second stage financing (in millions) was US$1–US$2 and for third stage financing the median size (in millions) was US$2–US$3. Given the investment criteria of venture capital funds, this pattern is not surprising. Firms that can support expectations of a public stock offering or acquisition by a larger firm within five years typically require multiple rounds of financing in excess of US$1m.

The financial histories of the technology-based firms in the sample contain two fundamental lessons for today's entrepreneurs. Angels are the primary sourse of funds when the size of the deal is under US$1m and angels typically invest earlier in the life of a technology-based firm than other sources of outside equity capital. These findings suggest that angels and venture capital funds play complementary roles in the financing of NTBFs. Angels are deciding which entrepreneurial ventures merit the equity financing and, in turn, are providing the market for the venture capital funds.

5.   Raising venture capital

The second stage in this research was the collection of data describing entrepreneurs' perceptions of the process of finding investors and raising funds, investors' expected rates of return, expected holding periods and the nature and value of working relationships between entrepreneurs and investors. This stage in the study also focused on differences between angel financing and financing by venture capital funds. Seventy-four firms, 69% of the 177 firms that raised outside equity capital, participated in Stage 2 of the study.

5.1   *The search for investors*

Entrepreneurs were asked who was most helpful in locating investors. Since the names and addresses of venture capital funds are readily available, this question dealt only with finding individual investors. Sources of leads included friends, business associates, other entrepreneurs, attorneys, accountants, commercial and investment bankers, customers/suppliers and paid advertising.

Entrepreneurs reported significant differences in the effectiveness of sources of prospective investors. Eighty-three per cent of the entrepreneurs found friends and business associates helpful. The next most helpful source was other entrepreneurs (31%). The ratings of the remaining sources ranged from 26% for attorneys to 2% for paid advertising.

To test for significant differences between angels and venture capital funds in the time it takes to raise equity capital, entrepreneurs were asked how long it took to secure financing from the two sources. The fund-raising process was divided into two stages: the elapsed time between the decision to raise funds and the first meeting with an angel or managing partner of a venture capital fund, and the elapsed time between the first meeting and the receipt of funds.

In Stage 1, the median elapsed time was 1 month to find and meet the first angel and 1.75 months to find and meet the first managing partner of a venture capital fund. This result seems counterintuitive, given the relative obscurity of angels. Although venture capital funds are easier to find, it appears to require more persistence to arrange an appointment with a managing partner than with an angel. An alternative explanation for the shorter period of time to meet an angel is that for private investors self-selection by entrepreneurs may play a significant role. This type of pre-screening may in turn hasten the time needed for the entrepreneur to secure a face to face meeting with a potential private investor.

A more significant difference was reported in the elapsed time between the first meeting and the receipt of funds. The median elapsed time was 2.5 months for private investors and 4.5 months for venture capital funds. The shorter deliberation time ('due diligence') for angel deals may be due to the smaller number of people involved in the decision process or to the fact that angels tend to invest in fields with which they are familiar.

5.2 The cost of venture capital

Significant differences existed in entrepreneurs' perceptions of the rates of return required by angels and venture capital funds. Median returns expected by angels were 32.5% per annum compared to 40% for venture capital funds. This difference is also counterintuitive, given the propensity of angels to invest more often than venture capital funds in high risk seed and start-up deals. One explanation may be a factor unique to angel financing.

In addition to competitive financial rewards, individual investors often consider the non-financial characteristics of their investments and thus part of their return is in the form of psychic income. Previous research (Wetzel 1983) indicates that 50% of angel investors reported that they accept lower returns or assume higher risks when the ventures they back are expected to create jobs in their communities, commercialize socially useful technology (such as medical, energy-saving or environmental technology), assist women entrepreneurs or entrepreneurs from ethnic minority groups. The most influential non-financial factor was the satisfaction derived from assisting an entrepreneur build a successful business. Entrepreneurs sensitive to the match between the characteristics of their ventures and the personal tastes of angels should be able to raise funds on terms that are attractive to both parties. While the explanation may depend on the specific investment, entrepreneurs perceive angel financing to be less expensive than financing by venture capital funds. Although differences exist in the required return, both angel and venture capital fund investors are perceived to have similar exit horizons. The median holding period expectation for angels was 4.75 years and 5 years for venture capital funds.

5.3   Value-added investors

Both angels and venture capital funds invest their know-how as well as their capital in the ventures they finance (Ehrlich *et al.* 1994; Harrison and Mason 1992). Entrepreneurs reported that 80% of angel investors and 81% of venture capital funds maintained a working relationship with their firms. For both groups, the most common form of this working relationship was representation on the board of directors. Although not as prevalent as board representation, a majority of the private investors and venture capital funds also served as consultants to the entrepreneurial venture. In addition, individual investors participated in ways not open to venture capital funds, with nearly one-quarter of the private individuals working in a full or part-time capacity for the firms in which they had invested.

In addition to capital, entrepreneurs recognize a significant value-added component in their investor relationships. Table 4 summarizes the evaluation by entrepreneurs of the quality of this value-added component. Almost three-quarters of the entrepreneurs who had a working relationship with their private investors consider this relationship to be productive. Similar results were found for venture capital funds, with nearly 80% of the entrepreneurs rating the relationship as productive. Thus, both angels and venture capital funds add a significant value to their equity investments through productive working relationships with the firms they bankroll.

6.   Conclusions

The invisible angel segment of the venture capital markets appears to play a central role in maintaining the vitality of the US entrepreneurial economy. It appears that for new technology-based ventures angels are the most common source of seed and start-up financing, especially if the round of financing is less than US$500 000. Despite the fact that there are no directories of business angels, entrepreneurs report that it takes less time to find and close a deal with angels than with venture capital funds and the financing is perceived to be less expensive. The value angels place on the non-financial characteristics of the ventures they back is a distinguishing feature of the angel segment of the venture capital market in the US. Both angels and venture capital funds add value to their investments through the establishment of working relationships with the ventures they

Table 4.   Quality of the working relationship.

	Angels (%)	Venture capital funds (%)
Very productive	44	39
Moderately productive	30	39
Neutral	22	13
Moderately counterproductive	4	8
Very counterproductive	0	2

finance, and entrepreneurs perceive these working relationships to be a productive component of the deal.

The history of business in the United States is the history of equity financing. For entrepreneurs, raising equity is arduous. Multiple rejections are part of the process. However, business history and the stock market pay tribute to the entrepreneurs who stuck it out. The vital role played by business angels is slowly being recognized, but their know-how and their capital are still largely untapped entrepreneurial resources. Entrepreneurs who understand the distinctive roles of angels and venture capital funds can save time and increase the odds of raising capital from the right source at the right time.

Acknowledgement

The authors wish to thank Gerald Sweeney, Colin Mason and an anonymous reviewer for their helpful comments during the revision process.

References

Aram, J. D. 1987, *Informal Risk Capital in the Eastern Great Lakes Region* (Washington: Office of Advocacy, US Small Business Administration).
Avery, R. B. and Elliehausen, G. E. 1986, Financial characteristics of high income families, *Federal Reserve Bulletin*, 72: 163–177.
Birch, D. L. 1987. The atomization of America (Boston: Cognetics), 21.
Birch, D. L. 1988, The hidden economy, *The Wall Street Journal*. 10 June 1988, p. 23R.
Birch, D., Haggerty, A., Parsons, W. and Rossel, C. 1993, *Entrepreneurial Hot Spots* (Boston: Cognetics), p. 4.
Bygrave, W. D. and Timmons, J. A. 1992, *Venture Capital at the Crossroads* (Boston: Harvard Business School Press).
CorpTech 1986, Corporate Technology Information Services, Woburn, MA.
Ehrlich, S., De Noble, A., Moore, T. and Weaver, R. 1994, After the cash arrives: a comparative study of venture capital and private investor involvement in entrepreneurial firms, *Journal of Business Venturing*, 9: 67–82.
Freear, J. and Wetzel, W. E., Jr 1990, Who bankrolls high-tech entrepreneurs?, *Journal of Business Venturing*, 5: 77–89.
Freear, J., Sohl, J. E. and Wetzel, W. E., Jr 1990, Raising venture capital: entrepreneurs' views of the process. In Churchill, N., Bygrave, W., Hornaday, J., Muzyka, D., Vesper, K. and Wetzel, W. (eds) *Frontiers of Entrepreneurial Research* (Wellesley: Babson College).
Freear, J., Sohl, J. E. and Wetzel, W. E., Jr 1994, Angels and non-angels: are there differences?, *Journal of Business Venturing*, 9: 109–123.
Gaston, R. J. 1989a, *Finding Private Venture Capital for Your Firm: A Complete Guide* (New York: Wiley).
Gaston, R. J. 1989b, The scale of informal capital markets, *Small Business Economics*, 1: 223–230.
Gaston, R. J. and Bell, S. E. 1986, *Informal Risk Capital Investment in the Sunbelt Region* (Washington: Office of Advocacy, US Small Business Administration).
Gaston, R. J. and Bell, S. E. 1988, *The Informal Supply of Capital* (Washington: Office of Economic Research, US Small Business Administration).
Haar, N. E., Starr, J. and MacMillan, I. C. 1988, Informal risk capital investors: investment patterns on the east coast of the USA, *Journal of Business Venturing*, 3: 11–29.
Hale, D. 1992, For new jobs, help small business, *The Wall Street Journal*, 10 August 1992, B10.
Harrison, R. and Mason, C. 1992, The roles of investors in entrepreneurial companies: a comparison of informal investors and venture capitalists. In Churchill, N., Birley, S., Bygrave, W., Muzyka, D., Wahlbin, C. and Wetzel, W. (eds) *Frontiers of Entrepreneurship Research* (Wellesley: Babson College).
Harrison, R. and Mason, C. 1993, Finance for the growing business: the role of informal investment, *National Westminster Quarterly Review*, May, 17–29.
Huey, J. 1994, Working up to the new economy, *Fortune*, 27 June 1994, pp. 36–46.
INC 1992, October.
Landstrom, H. 1992, The relationship between private investors and small firms: an agency theory approach, *Entrepreneurship and Regional Development*, 4: 199–223.

Landstrom, H. 1993, Informal risk capital in Sweden and some international comparisons, *Journal of Business Venturing*, 8: 525–540.

Mason, C. M. and Harrison, R. T. 1992, The supply of equity finance in the UK: a strategy for closing the equity gap, *Entrepreneurship and Regional Development*, 4: 357–380.

Morris, J. K., Isenstein, S. and Knowles, A. (eds) 1990, *Pratt's Guide to Venture Capital Sources* (Needham: Venture Economics), pp. 2–3.

Ou, C. 1987, 'Holdings of privately-held business by American families: findings from the 1983 Consumer Finance Survey', unpublished manuscript, Office of Economic Research, US Small Business Administration, Washington, DC.

Postma, P. D. and Sullivan, M. K. 1990, 'Informal risk capital in the Knoxville region', Unpublished report, University of Tennessee.

Riding, A. and Short, D. 1987, Some investor and entrepreneur perspectives on the informal market for risk capital, *Journal of Small Business and Entrepreneurship*, 5: 19–30.

Teitelbaum, R. S. 1994, Hats off! It was a heck of a year, *Fortune*, 18 April, 1994, p. 210.

Wetzel, W. E. Jr 1983, Angels and informal risk capital, *Sloan Management Review*, 24: 23–34.

[24]

AFTER THE CASH ARRIVES:

A COMPARATIVE STUDY

OF VENTURE CAPITAL

AND PRIVATE INVESTOR

INVOLVEMENT IN

ENTREPRENEURIAL FIRMS

SANFORD B. EHRLICH and ALEX F. DE NOBLE
San Diego State University

TRACY MOORE
Dataquick Information Systems

RICHARD R. WEAVER
Classic Cars Inc.

EXECUTIVE SUMMARY

Equity investments in entrepreneurial firms continue to grow in number and dollar amount from both venture capital and private investment sources. Increasingly, these two sources of capital play an important role in the development of new and existing entrepreneurial ventures. Due to the sometimes hurried attempt to turn their dream into reality, entrepreneurs may fail to consider similarities and differences in the value-added benefits supplied by venture capital firms (VCs) and private investors (PIs).

Accordingly, the purpose of this study was to determine how initial relationships are established and maintained between entrepreneurs and their primary investors. Specifically, we asked entrepreneurs to assess characteristics of the relationship with their primary investor. We then contrasted the results between entrepreneurial firms that had received venture capital funding versus private investor funding. Differences were examined along the following lines:

- *Levels of investor involvement in entrepreneurial firms*
- *Reporting and operational controls placed on the firm*
- *Types of expertise sought by the entrepreneur*

Address correspondence to Professor Sanford B. Ehrlich, Department of Management, San Diego State University, San Diego, CA 92182-0096.

Journal of Business Venturing 9, 67–82
© 1994 Elsevier Science Inc., 655 Avenue of the Americas, New York, NY 10010

0883-9026/94/$6.00

68   S.B. EHRLICH ET AL.

METHOD AND SAMPLE

We began by developing a survey instrument around the above issues and distributing it to a group of entrepreneurs whose firms are located in Southern California. In total, 70 entrepreneurs responded to the questionnaire, of which 47 were included in this study since they had received primary funding from either a VC or a PI. Over 80% of the firms in this sample consisted of high-technology companies operating in the computer, electronics, biotechnology, semiconductor, and medical device industries. Other firms included in the sample were from industries such as film production, pollution control, equipment manufacturing, and material processing.

The 47 entrepreneurs in the sample averaged 13.4 years of experience in their respective industries and were running companies generating annual revenues ranging from $1 million to over $5 million.

RESEARCH FINDINGS

Levels of Investor Involvement in Entrepreneurial Firms

This study found that entrepreneurs perceive that both venture capitalists (VCs) and private investors (PIs) are involved in similar sets of activities, such as interfacing with the investor group, obtaining alternative sources of equity financing, monitoring financial and operating performance, serving as a sounding board to the entrepreneurial team, and formulating business strategy. In evaluating changes in investor involvement, entrepreneurs receiving financing from VCs and PIs reported that greater participation would be welcomed in obtaining alternative sources of debt and equity financing. Additionally, entrepreneurs receiving PI financing desired more investor involvement in activities such as managing crises and problems, serving as a sounding board, and developing professional support groups.

Reporting and Operational Controls

Entrepreneurs indicated that they had more difficulty in achieving performance targets set by venture capital firms. While VCs set higher performance standards for their investments, they do provide more frequent, detailed feedback than PIs when the firm is not achieving these standards. This form of help may be needed when the firm is experiencing problems. Since PIs may be involved in more outside activities, they may not have the flexibility or time to monitor their investments closely.

The more formalized approach of a VC may be needed by entrepreneurs with a strong technical or scientific background and limited managerial experience. VCs appear to be more likely to aid the entrepreneur in establishing appropriate managerial systems and controls. However, experienced managers may feel that the time spent in generating frequent reports takes away time dedicated to other activities and thus they may enjoy the greater flexibility provided by a PI.

Types of Expertise Sought by the Entrepreneur

This study found that entrepreneurs seek expertise through their investors generally in the areas of staffing and financial management. However, VCs provide assistance in selecting the venture's management team significantly more often than PIs. These findings suggest that entrepreneurs with strong managerial experience may prefer PIs because they are less likely to alter the makeup of the team that they have assembled. However, entrepreneurs with technical backgrounds may find that a venture capital firm provides valuable help in accessing and attracting top management personnel with relevant experience.

CONCLUSION

These preliminary results indicate that there are important distinctions between VCs and PIs in terms of the value-added benefits they bring to entrepreneurial firms. Thus, in searching for capital, an overzealous founder may find that the long-term costs can far exceed the short-term benefits if there is a mismatch in expectations between the relevant parties. Who the entrepreneur gets his/her money from is just as important as how much capital is obtained initially. The right match can yield a synergistic relationship that will propel the firm to higher levels of excellence. Further studies on this critical relationship between the entrepreneur and the primary investor are needed to increase our level of understanding of the dynamics involved. This initial survey has set the framework for more in-depth research examining how particular relationships with primary investors facilitate or inhibit the growth and development of entrepreneurial start-ups.

INTRODUCTION

Equity investments in entrepreneurial firms by venture capitalists (VCs) and private investors (PIs) play an important role in the development of new and existing entrepreneurial ventures. From the entrepreneur's perspective, in addition to capital, a primary investor may provide a wide array of benefits to a venture, such as networking and operating expertise, involvement in operations, management and personnel recruitment, or financial and strategic management. These skills constitute a set of value-added benefits that may evolve through interactions between entrepreneurs and their primary investors.

Most recent research explores the relationship between entrepreneurs and their primary investors by examining a VC's level of involvement in start-up ventures and their perceptions of the benefits of such interactions (Gorman and Sahlman 1989; MacMillan et al. 1988; Rosenstein 1988; Bygrave 1987). To date, little emphasis has been placed on examining this relationship from the entrepreneur's perspective (Rosenstein et al. 1990, 1989) and even less work has been done that addresses the value-added benefits provided by PIs. Due to the sometimes hurried attempt to turn their dream into reality, entrepreneurs may fail to consider the post-financing ramifications of choosing between a venture capital firm and a private investor. It is reasonable to expect that there may be dissimilarities between VCs and PIs in terms of their post-financing contribution based upon their motivation for investment, areas of expertise, and competing time commitments. Consequently, the purpose of this study is to provide insights concerning potential differences in value-added benefits between these two sources of financing.

BACKGROUND

Similarities and Differences Between VCs and PIs

In a review of literature, two primary similarities were found between VCs and PIs. First, both types of investors prefer to fund ventures with potential for high capital appreciation in markets or technologies in which they have experience or familiarity (Sullivan 1991; Tyebjee and Bruno 1984). Second, both VCs and PIs desire to liquidate their investments in a five to ten-year time period (Sullivan 1991; Wetzel 1985; Tyebjee and Bruno 1984).

Differences between VCs and PIs include the stage and size of the investment, geographic location of the firm, and motivation for investment. Freear and Wetzel (1990), in their study of the financing of new technology-based ventures, concluded that PIs were more likely to provide funding in the seed and start-up stages, especially if the financing requirements were less than $500,000. As the size of the round increased in excess of $500,000, VCs played a more dominant role. In subsequent stages of financing, the size of the round more clearly distinguished between private investor and venture capital participation. Thus, for PIs involved in first-, second-, or third-stage financing, these authors

70   S.B. EHRLICH ET AL.

found that investments ranged from $100,000–$300,000. However, for VCs participating in similar stages, the size of the investment ranged from $1–3 million.

With respect to geographic location, PIs have a propensity to seek ventures that are usually within 50 miles of their home. VCs, to the contrary, place less emphasis on geographic proximity but do seek ventures in major metropolitan areas where networking with other VCs and service providers is possible (Florida and Kenney 1988; Wetzel 1985; Tyebjee and Bruno 1984). As implied by Wetzel (1985), PIs tend to choose ventures close to home so that they might derive "psychic income" from the growth of a new venture. Moreover, the private investor may seek to help a friend or family member (Sullivan 1991) or to derive nonpecuniary rewards from assisting other entrepreneurs in the creation and growth of their ventures (Wetzel 1985).

The above research findings depict some of the similarities and differences between VCs and PIs at the pre-investment stage. Research conducted at the post-investment stage has provided an understanding of the types of involvement activities that occur between entrepreneurs and VCs (Sullivan 1991; Rosenstein et al. 1990, 1989; Gorman and Sahlman 1989; Sapienza and Timmons 1989; MacMillan et al. 1988; Rosenstein 1988). However, little knowledge is available on how entrepreneurs perceive the value-added benefits that accrue from involvement with PIs.

Levels of Involvement in Entrepreneurial Firms

Investor involvement activities depicted at the post-investment stage have been examined in the aforementioned studies by focusing on the dyadic relationship that evolves between the entrepreneur and a venture capital investor. First, the predominant methodology employed in these studies has been to collect survey or interview data from VCs about specific companies within their investment portfolios (Gorman and Sahlman 1989; MacMillan et al. 1988; Rosenstein 1988). Second, using a similar methodology, another research focus has been to collect data from entrepreneurs about their VCs' involvement activities (Rosenstein et al. 1990, 1989). Third, by making the entrepreneur–VC dyad as the unit of analysis, Sapienza and Timmons (1989) collected data from both parties to evaluate VC–entrepreneur relations and VC effectiveness.

VCs' Perceptions of the Entrepreneur–VC Relationship

Studies examining the relationship between entrepreneurs and VCs, as viewed from the VCs' perspective, have focused on the following areas: degree of involvement of VCs in portfolio companies, the relationship between stage of investment and degree of involvement, identification of high and low investor–involvement activities, and the relationship between investor involvement activities and firm performance. Gorman and Sahlman (1989) and MacMillan et al. (1988) created survey instruments to assess the degree of involvement of VCs in their portfolio companies. In analyzing responses from 62 VCs, MacMillan et al. (1988) identified the following three different involvement categories from a cluster analysis: low (laissez-faire), moderate, and high (close-tracker) involvement groups. In examining the link between these investor–involvement classifications and self-reports regarding venture performance, MacMillan et al. (1988) did not find any significant differences. For those VCs that did maintain higher levels of involvement, the predominant activities were serving as a sounding board and assisting in financially related issues. VCs tended to be least involved in strategic or operations functional areas.

VENTURE CAPITAL VS. PRIVATE INVESTOR INVOLVEMENT 71

Gorman and Sahlman (1989) used a mail survey to study 49 VCs' relations with their portfolio companies. In dividing the sample by stage of investment, Gorman and Sahlman found the VCs with early-stage investments spend about two hours per week in direct contact with their portfolio companies. Although this appears to be a minimal level of contact, it is ten times greater than the time that VCs spent with late-stage investments. Activities performed by VCs generally fell into the categories of building the investor group, reviewing and helping to formulate business strategy, and filling in the management team.

Rosenstein (1988) conducted loosely structured interviews with six Dallas-based venture capital partnerships and two major small business investment companies. The focus of his research was on investor involvement in the management of portfolio companies through board participation. Rosenstein (1988) found that VCs employed two different approaches in dealing with entrepreneurial companies. Immediately after making investments, one group of VCs replaced the founding entrepreneur team with experienced professional managers from larger companies. Other VCs followed a different strategy of nurturing and working with the existing management team to develop their general management skills. In either case, VCs (through board participation) placed a great deal of pressure on the management team to achieve high results consistent with the business plan. Accordingly, most VCs take a highly active role in the management of their portfolio companies through participating on the board, accessing additional expertise, and influencing strategic directions.

Entrepreneurs' Perceptions of the Entrepreneur–VC Relationship

In examining VC involvement from the entrepreneur's perspective, two studies by Rosenstein et al. (1990, 1989) adapted MacMillan et al.'s (1988) survey instrument. In the first study conducted by Rosenstein et al. (1989), 162 CEOs were surveyed concerning the extent and usefulness of VC involvement on the firms' boards of directors. The CEOs indicated that the five most important areas of VC involvement were serving as a sounding board to the management team, interfacing with the investor group, monitoring financial and operating performance, and recruitment/replacement of the CEO. They found that in areas such as negotiating employment terms, locating sources of debt financing, providing contacts with key vendors and customers, and evaluating product/market opportunities, CEOs indicated that VC involvement was higher and more useful in the early rather than the later stages in the firm's lifecycle. This study identified gaps between effort and usefulness (where CEOs perceived that VCs' efforts were greater than their usefulness) in three specific areas: monitoring operating performance, monitoring financial performance and formulating marketing plans.

In a follow-up study, 98 CEOs from their first sample responded to telephone interviews about involvement of top-20 VCs on their boards of directors (Rosenstein et al. 1990). They classified the 98 companies into 3 categories: (1) those where the lead investor was a top-20 venture capital firm, (2) those where either the lead investor or another investor was from the top-20, and (3) those where there was no representation of the top-20 on the board. With respect to activities of involvement, their findings paralleled earlier work by Rosenstein (1988) and MacMillan et al. (1988). CEOs found that activities of highest involvement included serving as a sounding board, interfacing with investor groups, and monitoring financial performance, respectively. When top-20 VCs are involved with a portfolio company, they are more likely to be involved in the recruitment and replacement of a CEO. In cases where a top-20 VC is not involved, investors are more likely to provide assistance on short-term crisis problems.

72   S.B. EHRLICH ET AL.

Joint Perceptions of the Entrepreneur–VC Dyad

Sapienza and Timmons (1989) collected survey data from 51 VC–entrepreneur dyads. The objective of their study was to determine the importance that entrepreneurs and VCs place on various roles assumed by VCs in ventures they fund and to discern what factors influence the importance of these roles. Entrepreneurs and VCs responded to items concerning the types of roles that VCs assumed in their portfolio companies. From the perspective of both VCs and entrepreneurs, the following three sets of roles varied in their level of importance. High importance roles were serving as a sounding board and business consultant. Moderately important roles included coach/mentor, financier, and friend/confidant. Roles with low importance included management recruiter, industry contact, and professional contact.

Clearly, the existing research on investor involvement in corporate governance has focused on the VC as the primary investor. Thus, to gain more insight into these issues from a broader perspective, additional research that addresses differences in levels of involvement between VCs and PIs is necessary. As opposed to VCs who typically act in a fiduciary capacity and must in turn report to an entire pool of third-party investors, PIs manage their own funds and may bring a different set of expectations to their relationship with entrepreneurs. Therefore, it is reasonable to assume that VCs and PIs take different approaches in managing their investments. Accordingly, the following exploratory research questions were developed:

Q1: In what areas do entrepreneurs perceive that primary investors are most and least involved in the operations of the new venture?

Q2: Do VC-funded entrepreneurs differ from VCs in reporting about levels of investor involvement?

Q3: a) Do VC-funded entrepreneurs differ from PI-funded entrepreneurs with respect to perceptions of investor involvement?

Q3: b) To what extent do VC- and PI-funded entrepreneurs desire a change in the level of involvement of their primary investor?

Q4: Do VC-funded entrepreneurs differ from PI-funded entrepreneurs with respect to perceptions of types of functional controls, frequency of reporting requirements, and the characteristics of performance targets imposed by primary investors?

Q5: Do VC-funded entrepreneurs differ from PI-funded entrepreneurs with respect to the types of expertise sought from their primary investors?

METHOD

Sample

To create a pool of potential respondents, entrepreneurs were identified from their participation in the San Diego Technology and Financial Forum or their inclusion in the Business Link database (Dataquick Information Network 1991). Of 142 potential respondents, 70 (49%) entrepreneurs agreed to complete the survey. The final sample consisted of 47 entrepreneurs who received funding from a venture capital firm or a private investor and were considered suitable for this study. The remaining 23 entrepreneurs obtained alternative sources of financing and therefore were excluded from further analysis. With respect to stage of financing, approximately 68% of entrepreneurs received funds from PIs in the seed or start-up phases. In contrast, among entrepreneurs receiving venture funding, only

48% provided seed or start-up financing. These results are similar to the breakdowns reported by Freear and Wetzel (1990) in their study of the financing of new technology-based ventures.

Over 80% of the firms in this final sample consisted of high-technology companies operating in the computer, electronic, biotechnology, semiconductor, and medical device industries. Other firms included in the sample were from industries such as film production, pollution control, equipment manufacturing, and material processing. Twenty-five entrepreneurs received funding from a venture capital firm, and 22 received funding from a private investor. Additionally, in excess of 80% of the entrepreneurs had been associated with their primary investors for fewer than five years, and over 85% of these primary investors held equity positions of 50% or less.

On average, entrepreneurs possessed 13.4 years of experience in their respective industries, had worked with their management teams for a period of 5.8 years, employed 90 people, and produced seven products. Additionally, 45.7% of these entrepreneurs were founders or co-founders of past ventures and of these founders, 76.2% indicated that their past ventures were still in existence. With respect to revenues, 59% of the firms had sales exceeding $1 million. When asked about their firms' projected sales and net profits, over 50% of the entrepreneurs indicated that sales were below their expectations, and 67% reported that net profits were below their expectations. However, more than two-thirds of the entrepreneurs indicated that their firms had met or exceeded market share expectations.

Survey Instrument

The survey instrument was designed to obtain information on different types of investor involvement activities. It consisted of the following measures:

Levels of Investor Involvement

Twenty items adapted from MacMillan et al.'s (1988) instrument were altered to determine the entrepreneurs' perceptions (as opposed to VCs' perceptions) about the amount of participation that their primary investors have in different activities. Examples of activities included searching for candidates of the management team, obtaining alternative sources of equity or debt financing, selecting vendors and equipment, and formulating marketing plans. A seven-point Likert scale ranging from "no participation at all by the investors" to "all participation by the investor" (no involvement by the entrepreneur) was used.[1] Moreover, the entrepreneurs were asked on a five-point Likert scale whether they would like their investors to be "much less" to "much more" involved in each of these sets of activities. The mid-point of this scale corresponds to a desire for no change in the level of investor participation.

Measures of Reporting and Operational Controls

Involvement activities related to the use of managerial controls were measured with several additional items. To assess the level of control imposed upon the entrepreneur by the primary investor, entrepreneurs were asked if reports are required on sales, profitability, costs, capital expenditures, personnel, and accounts receivable. If their primary investors required reports, the entrepreneurs were then asked whether these reports needed to be provided on a weekly, monthly, quarterly, semi-annual, or annual basis. Finally, the entrepreneurs were asked what

---

[1] MacMillan, et al. (1988) factor-analyzed this set of activities and formed four composite measures. In this current study, however, reliabilities on these four measures were unacceptably low; therefore, individual items were used.

74   S.B. EHRLICH ET AL.

types of actions the primary investor would typically take in the event of problems with the firm's performance. Actions included working with the firm on-site or via telephone calls, holding meetings to address the problem, or requiring additional reports. A five-point Likert scale ranging from "rarely" to "constantly" was used to measure the frequency of these activities.

A second set of items covered performance targets set by the investors. A five-point Likert scale was utilized to measure the perceived clarity of these performance targets. Responses ranged from "targets are very unclear" to "targets are very clear." Another item queried the entrepreneurs about the level of difficulty in attaining these performance targets. Entrepreneurs responded to a six-point Likert scale that varied from "very easy to attain" to "impossible to attain." Finally, to address the frequency of performance feedback provided to the entrepreneur by the investor, a six-point Likert scale was constructed that varied from "never" to "several times daily."

Measures of Expertise Sought from Primary Investors

Items were designed to assess whether or not entrepreneurs sought access to the following forms of expertise from their primary investors: operations, management selection, personnel management, and financial management. Response options ranged from "very little" to "very much" on a five-point Likert scale.

RESEARCH FINDINGS

Types and Levels of Investor Involvement

To examine research questions 1–2, mean values obtained for investor involvement activities from this sample were rank-ordered and compared to rankings reported in MacMillan et al. (1988). Such a comparison illustrates a significant similarity in the rankings between the samples employed in each study. As shown in the upper portion of Table 1, the top five activities where entrepreneurs report greatest involvement from their VCs match MacMillan et al.'s (1988) results and are consistent with reports of private investor involvement for four out of five activities. However, the rankings created from the entrepreneurs' perspective of VC activities differ in several respects from the VCs' self-reports in the MacMillan et al. (1988) study. For example, the greatest discrepancy occurs with the activity of serving as a sounding board to the entrepreneur team. VCs perceived that they were most involved in this particular activity, while entrepreneurs reported that VC involvement in this activity ranked fourth overall. But, the close agreement in the grouping of activities from both studies at the extremes of the ranks indicates that this discrepancy may be of little importance. This is not the case when examining the differential level of involvement between the two studies. In comparing the adjusted mean values, it appears that the entrepreneurs in this sample perceive that primary investors tend to be less involved overall in company activities than VCs reported in the MacMillan et al. (1988) study.

The lower portion of Table 1 depicts activities in which investors are least involved with their ventures. The results obtained from this study show agreement between the perceptions of entrepreneurs who received VC and private investor financing. In comparing these results to those obtained by MacMillan et al. (1988), four activities: developing production or service techniques, selecting vendors and equipment, developing actual products or services, and testing or evaluating marketing plans, were ranked similarly across the two samples.

TABLE 1 Rankings Among Mean Scores for Investor Involvement Activities as Compared to MacMillan et al.'s (1988) Study of Venture Capitalist Involvement[a]

	VC-funded Entrepreneurs	PI-funded Entrepreneurs	MacMillan et al. (1988) VCs
Activities of greatest involvement			
Interface with investor group	2.41 (1)	1.74 (1)	3.62 (3)
Obtain alternative equity financing	2.30 (2)	1.16 (6)	3.63 (2)
Monitor financial performance	2.13 (3)	1.67 (2)	3.18 (4)
Serve as sounding board to entrepreneur team	1.96 (4)	1.58 (3)	3.77 (1)
Monitor operating performance	1.67 (5)	1.21 (5)	2.82 (5)
Formulate business strategy	1.50 (6)	1.26 (4)	—
Activities of least involvement			
Develop production or service techniques	.04 (20)	.16 (18.5)	.71 (19)
Select vendors and equipment	.08 (19)	.16 (18.5)	.60 (20)
Develop actual product or service	.42 (18)	.37 (17)	.72 (18)
Testing or evaluating marketing plans	.46 (17)	.37 (17)	1.64 (16)
Replace management personnel	.59 (16)	.39 (15)	—
Develop professional support group	.63 (15)	.37 (17)	—

[a] The upper and lower quartiles of the 20 investor involvement activities were compared across VCs, PIs, and VCs from the MacMillan et al. (1988) study. Mean values from this study (on a 1–7 Likert scale) were adjusted to correspond to the 0–6 Likert scale used in the MacMillan et al. (1988) study. Numbers in parentheses correspond to ranks within investor groups. To obtain maximum overlap between these samples, it was necessary to generate a list of more than five activities for greatest and least involvement.

In addressing research questions 3a and 3b, one-way analysis of variance (ANOVA) was utilized to locate significant differences between entrepreneurs' perceptions of: (1) VC and private investor levels of participation, and (2) desired changes in the level of investor participation in various managerial activities. As shown in Panel A of Table 2, "obtaining alternative equity financing" was the only activity in which entrepreneurs perceived that VCs were significantly more involved than PIs (F = 11.5; $p < .010$).

Additionally, Panel B of Table 2 presents the results of a paired t-test analysis where mean values for changes in participation were compared to a scale value of 3, corresponding to a desire for "the same amount" of involvement. In the MacMillan et al. (1988) study, VCs were interpreted as desiring greater involvement in an activity when scale values exceeded 3. The approach used here is more conservative in that we only focused on mean scores that were statistically greater than 3. Additionally, one-way ANOVA was used to test for significant differences between desired changes in participation across VCs and PIs. From a statistical perspective, there is no significant demand for diminished involvement from either VCs or private investors in any area of participation. Both entrepreneur subsamples indicate a desire for greater involvement by their primary investor in obtaining alternative debt and equity financing. In addition, PI-funded entrepreneurs express a desire for increased investor involvement in five other areas: developing professional support groups, soliciting customers and distributors, monitoring financial performance, serving as a sounding board, and managing crises and problems. In two of these five activities, monitoring financial performance and serving as a sounding board to the entrepreneurial team, the level of change desired by PI-funded enterprises was significantly greater than that desired by VC-funded firms. In each case, the mean response for VC-funded entrepreneurs indicated no desire for change while PI-funded entrepreneurs desired significantly greater participation.

76   S.B. EHRLICH ET AL.

TABLE 2   One-way ANOVA Comparing Amount of Participation by Investor Type

	Mean Values							
	Panel A Level of Participation[a]				Panel B Change in Participation[b]			
Areas of Participation	VC	PI	df	F	VC	PI	df	F
Search for management team	2.38	2.05	1,41	.75	3.00	3.21	1,40	.80
Interview/select management team	2.46	2.00	1,41	1.52	3.04	2.95	1,40	.18
Negotiate employment term	1.75	1.79	1,41	.01	2.78	3.05	1,40	2.36
Interface with investor group	3.41	2.74	1,39	2.85	3.36	3.37	1,39	.00
Develop professional support group	1.63	1.37	1,41	1.43	3.24	3.42**	1,38	.88
Obtain alternative debt financing	2.14	2.63	1,38	1.12	3.70**	3.74***	1,37	.02
Obtain alternative equity financing	3.30	2.16	1,40	11.54**	3.52*	3.84***	1,38	1.21
Formulate business strategy	2.50	2.26	1,41	.59	3.05	3.16	1,39	.23
Develop actual product/ service	1.42	1.37	1,41	.03	2.86	2.95	1,39	.18
Develop production/ service	1.04	1.16	1,40	.99	2.95	3.05	1,38	.24
Select vendors/equipment	1.08	1.16	1,41	.38	2.82	2.95	1,39	.65
Formulate marketing plans	1.96	1.79	1,41	.31	2.95	3.16	1,39	.65
Test/evaluate market plans	1.46	1.37	1,41	.17	3.09	3.26	1,39	.76
Solicit customers/ distributors	1.54	1.53	1,41	.00	3.14	3.47*	1,39	2.12
Monitor financial performance	3.13	2.67	1,40	2.13	2.82	3.28*	1,38	8.94**
Monitor operating performance	2.67	2.21	1,41	1.87	2.91	3.21	1,39	3.29
Serve as sounding board	2.96	2.58	1,41	1.50	3.24	3.79***	1,38	4.27*
Motivate personnel	1.75	1.83	1,40	.08	3.14	3.26	1,38	.23
Replace management personnel	1.59	1.39	1,38	.49	2.75	3.11	1,36	3.86
Manage crises and problems	1.83	1.79	1,41	.02	2.90	3.32**	1,38	3.57

[a]Seven-point scale: 1 = no participation at all by investor(s) to 7 = all by the investor(s), none by you.
[b]Five-point scale: 1 = much less to 5 = much more desired investor involvement. Means ᶜ⁻ᵉ indicate that desired change in participation is significantly different from a value of 3 (corresponding to "no desired change in level of involvement") as determined from a paired t-test analysis.
*$p < .05$.
**$p < .01$.
***$p < .001$.

To further investigate research question 3a, entrepreneurs were asked to indicate how often their investors responded to problems by using methods such as working with the firm on-site, holding meetings, making telephone calls, and requiring additional reports. As seen in Table 3, the form of involvement used most often by both types of investors was help via telephone calls. Moreover, VCs were significantly more involved in this activity than PIs (F

TABLE 3 One-way ANOVA Comparing the Frequency of Investor Involvement by Investor Type[a]

	Mean Values			
Type of Involvement	VC	PI	df	F
Works with firm on-site	1.68	1.68	1,42	.00
Holds meetings	2.12	1.70	1,43	1.97
Works with firm via telephone	3.32	2.30	1,43	11.39[b]
Requires additional reports	1.72	1.90	1,42	.40

[a]Five-point scale: 1 = rarely; 5 = constantly.
[b]$p < .010$.

$= 11.39$; $p < .010$). Finally, the results indicate that the method of involvement used least by both investor types was working with the firm on-site.

Reporting and Operational Controls

To investigate research question 4, a chi-square test was utilized to determine differences in the controls placed on entrepreneurs by their investors. This analysis assessed whether VCs or PIs required more information in the form of reporting controls such as operational controls, financial controls, management controls, or production controls. In Table 4, the results of these chi-square tests are presented.

As displayed in Table 4, entrepreneurs reported that all VCs require sales. and profitability controls. Cost controls were required by 20 out of 23 VCs. In each of these cases, the results indicate that PIs are less likely to require these types of controls than VCs. To assess whether or not there were differences in the frequency of reporting requirements by investor types, a one-way ANOVA was employed. The results of this analysis are displayed in Table 5. As shown in this table, VCs required reports on a more frequent basis than PIs in the areas of sales, profitability, and accounts receivables.

Finally, to determine whether or not there were any differences in the clarity of performance targets, what difficulty there was in attaining these performance targets, and the frequency of feedback by investor types, a one-way ANOVA was employed on these measures. The results of this analysis are displayed in Table 6.

For the above results on clarity and frequency of performance targets, there were no significant differences between investor types. From the data, it appears that entrepreneurs

TABLE 4 Results of 2X2 Crosstabulations Comparing Primary Investor (VC/PI) to Functional Controls Required (Yes/No)

		Yes/No		
Areas	N	VC	PI	X^2
Sales	46	24/0	16/6	5.32[b]
Profitability	46	24/0	17/5	4.00[a]
Cost controls	45	20/3	9/13	8.50[b]
Capital expenditures	45	21/2	14/8	3.51
Personnel	45	16/7	8/14	3.74
Accounts receivables	45	19/4	13/9	1.99

[a]$p < .05$.
[b]$p < .01$.

78   S.B. EHRLICH ET AL.

TABLE 5   One-way ANOVA Comparing the Frequency of Reporting Requirements by Investor Type[a]

Areas	Mean Values			
	VC	PI	df	F
Sales	2.21	2.94	1,38	8.47**
Profitability	2.21	2.88	1,39	7.43**
Cost controls	2.40	2.67	1,27	.63
Capital expenditures	2.85	2.93	1,32	.04
Personnel	2.81	3.00	1,22	.15
Accounts receivables	2.37	3.08	1,30	4.25*

[a] Five-point scale: 1 = weekly; 2 = monthly; 3 = monthly; 3 = quarterly; 4 = semi-annually; 5 = annually.
*$p < .05$.
**$p < .010$.

may have more difficulty attaining performance targets set by VCs than those set by PIs (F = 2.88; $p < .10$).

Types of Expertise Sought by the Entrepreneur

Research question 5 was assessed using a one-way ANOVA. Table 7 presents ANOVA results comparing expertise sought from the entrepreneurs by investor type. In the areas of operations and personnel management, the magnitude of the mean values indicates the entrepreneurs sought little help from both VCs and PIs in the areas of firm operations and personnel management. These results also indicate that the most important type of help that both types of investors can provide is in the area of financial management. The only significant result between entrepreneurs' perceptions of VCs and PIs occurred with respect to management selection (F = 9.9; $p < .010$). It appears that entrepreneurs seek expertise from VCs on management selection to a much greater extent than those entrepreneurs involved with PIs.

DISCUSSION

Several implications can be drawn from an analysis of the results of this study. These implications are relevant for choices that entrepreneurs must make in seeking a source of capital.

TABLE 6   One-way ANOVA Comparing Performance Targets and Feedback by Investor Type

Targets and Feedback	Mean Values			
	VC	PI	df	F
Clarity of targets[a]	2.96	2.59	1,44	.71
Difficulty to attain targets[b]	3.83	3.11	1,40	2.88[d]
Frequency of feedback[c]	3.00	2.91	1,44	.19

[a] Five-point scale: 1 = no targets were set; 5 = targets are very clear.
[b] Five-point scale: 1 = no targets were set; 5 = targets impossibly difficult to attain.
[c] Five-point scale: 1 = never; 5 = several times daily.
[d] $p < .10$.

TABLE 7 One-way ANOVA Comparing Expertise Sought by Entrepreneur by Investor Type[a]

Areas of Expertise	Mean Values			
	VC	PI	df	F
Operations	1.44	1.50	1,45	.05
Management selection	2.88	1.82	1,45	9.91[b]
Personnel management	1.52	1.45	1,45	.08
Financial	3.12	3.00	1,45	.10

[a] Five-point scale: 1 = very little; 5 = very much.
[b] $p < .010$.

Types and Levels of Investor Involvement

The results of this study are consistent with prior research conducted from both the VCs' and entrepreneurs' perspective (Rosenstein et al. 1990, 1989; Gorman and Sahlman 1989; Sapienza and Timmons 1989; MacMillan et al. 1988). Specifically, this study found that entrepreneurs perceive that their primary investors are actively involved in similar sets of activities, such as obtaining alternative sources of equity financing, monitoring financial and operating performance, and serving as a sounding board to the entrepreneurial team. However, across all activities, entrepreneurs in this study reported lower levels of involvement by their primary investors than the levels of involvement reported by VCs in the MacMillan et al. (1988) study.

In using a more conservative approach than MacMillan et al. (1988) to examine desired changes in investor involvement, our results showed that entrepreneurs funded by VCs and PIs wanted increased involvement in obtaining alternative sources of debt and equity financing. This result is considerably different from MacMillan et al. (1988) and Rosenstein (1988) studies where VCs desired to be involved with entrepreneurs in activities such as formulating business strategies and marketing plans, monitoring operating performance, and selecting and replacing management personnel. Thus, our results suggest that VC-funded entrepreneurs are relatively content with their investors' levels of involvement and might not welcome any increased involvement in the areas identified by MacMillan et al. (1988).

In contrast, PI-funded entrepreneurs desired increased involvement in areas such as managing crises and problems, monitoring financial performance, developing a professional support group, soliciting customers and distributors, and serving as a sounding board. Given similar levels of perceived involvement by both VCs and PIs, these results may indicate that PI-funded entrepreneurs are dissatisfied with the level and type of participation by their primary investors.

Reporting and Operational Controls

The responses of entrepreneurs in this study support prior assertions by Rosenstein (1988) that venture capital firms set higher performance standards for their investments. Additionally, this study found that VCs provide more frequent, detailed feedback when the firm is not achieving these standards as compared to firms funded by PIs. Although this form of help is certainly needed when the firm is experiencing problems, entrepreneurs perceive that PIs offer little assistance in this area. Since PIs may be more involved in other activities, they may not have the time or flexibility to closely monitor their investments.

80   S.B. EHRLICH ET AL.

Entrepreneurs with a strong technical or scientific background and limited managerial experience may desire the more formalized approach of a venture capital firm since that firm will aid the entrepreneur in establishing appropriate managerial systems and controls. Experienced managers may feel that the time spent in generating frequent reports takes away from time dedicated to other activities and thus they may enjoy the greater flexibility provided by a private investor.

Types of Expertise Sought by the Entrepreneur

A quality management team is often cited as a critical prerequisite for a new venture start-up. It is reasonable to expect that entrepreneurs would seek advice from their investors in locating and attracting key management personnel to their firms. Consistent with this expectation, this study finds that entrepreneurs seek financial and staffing expertise from their primary investors. In the area of staffing, VC-funded entrepreneurs sought significantly greater assistance than PI-funded entrepreneurs. PI-funded entrepreneurs may seek staffing assistance less often because they have an established management team or realize that PIs are less inclined to alter the make-up of their existing management team. However, entrepreneurs with technical backgrounds who need to assemble a management team should seek funding from a venture capital firm that does provide assistance in accessing and attracting top management personnel (Rosenstein 1988). Thus, entrepreneurs who have solidified their management teams may be more inclined to receive funding from PIs. Alternatively, VCs may be less likely to fund ventures when they are unable to influence the composition of the management team.

Directions for Future Research

This exploratory research has yielded some preliminary insights into the nature of relationships that evolve between entrepreneurs and their primary investors. Particular emphasis was placed on differentiating between VC- and PI-funded ventures, from the entrepreneur's perspective. However, in future research, there is a need for more studies that collect joint data on both the entrepreneur–VC and the entrepreneur–PI dyad, using the approach developed by Sapienza and Timmons (1989). Moreover, Sullivan's (1991) research underscores the need for further studies that differentiate among private investor types, particularly with respect to prior entrepreneurial experience. Other variables relevant to understanding the nature of this important relationship include the stage of development of the venture, stage of financing, size of the round, and competitive conditions triggering the need for more or less involvement.

CONCLUSION

Our findings support a popular stereotype that venture capital firms are more likely to place stringent controls on an entrepreneurial venture than PIs. Moreover, venture capital firms require entrepreneurs to report to them on a more frequent basis and supply a higher amount of verbal feedback. Although we might expect that entrepreneurs receiving capital from PIs would be comfortable with fewer reporting requirements, our results suggest that these entrepreneurs desire greater involvement from their PIs, especially with regard to financial expertise.

Also, entrepreneurs receiving funds from venture capital firms appear to be more likely to gain access to additional rounds of equity at critical stages in their development. Thus, the

VENTURE CAPITAL VS. PRIVATE INVESTOR INVOLVEMENT 81

decision to seek capital from a venture capital firm or a private investor may hinge upon the need to locate future sources of funds. Initial decisions to accept funds from PIs may result in fewer opportunities to access subsequent capital in the long run.

Clearly, these preliminary results indicate that there are important distinctions between VCs and PIs in terms of the value-added benefits they bring to entrepreneurial firms. Thus, in searching for capital, an overzealous founder may find that the long-term costs far exceed the short-term benefits if there is a mismatch in expectations between the relevant parties. Who the entrepreneur gets his/her money from is just as important as the amount of capital obtained initially. The right match can yield a synergistic relationship that propels the firm to higher levels of excellence. Further studies on this critical relationship between the entrepreneur and the primary investor are needed to increase our level of understanding of the dynamics involved. This initial survey has set the framework for more in-depth empirical studies examining how particular relationships with primary investors facilitate or inhibit the growth and development of entrepreneurial start-ups.

The authors would like to thank the Entrepreneurial Management Center at San Diego State University for their support of this research project. Also, thanks to Ian MacMillan and to two anonymous reviewers for their helpful comments during the revision process.

REFERENCES

Byers, B.H. 1985. Relationship between venture capitalist and entrepreneur. In S.E. Pratt and J.K. Morris, eds., *Pratt's Guide to Venture Capital Sources.* Wellesley Hills, MA: Venture Economics, Inc. 11:116–118.

Bygrave, W.D. 1987. Syndicated investments by venture capital firms: A networking perspective. *Journal of Business Venturing* 2:139–154.

Dataquick Information Network. 1991. *Business Link.* On-line database in conjunction with Trinet Incorporated, San Diego, CA.

Florida, R.L., and Kenney, M. 1988. Venture capital and high technology entrepreneurship. *Journal of Business Venturing* 4:301–319.

Freear, J., and Wetzel, W.E. 1990. Who bankrolls high-tech entrepreneurs? *Journal of Business Venturing* 5:77–89.

Gorman, M., and Sahlman, W.A. 1989. What do venture capitalists do? *Journal of Business Venturing* 4:231–248.

MacMillan, I.C., Kulow, D.M., and Khoylian, R. 1988. Venture capitalists' involvement in their investments: Extent and performance. *Journal of Business Venturing* 4:27–47.

Rosenstein, J., Bruno, A.V., Bygrave, W.D., and Taylor, N.T. 1990. How much do CEOs value the advice of venture capitalists on their boards? In W. Bygrave, N. Churchill, J. Hornaday, D. Muzyka, K. Vesper, and W. Wetzel, eds., *Frontiers of Entrepreneurship Research.* Babson College, Wellesley, MA: Center for Entrepreneurial Studies, pp. 238–249.

Rosenstein, J., Bruno, A.V., Bygrave, W.D., and Taylor, N.T. 1989. Do venture capitalists on boards of portfolio companies add value besides money? In R.H. Brockhaus, N.C. Churchill, J. Katz, B.A. Kirchhoff, K.H. Vesper, and W.E. Wetzel, eds., *Frontiers of Entrepreneurship Research.* Babson College, Wellesley, MA: Center for Entrepreneurial Studies, pp. 216–229.

Rosenstein, J. 1988. The board and strategy: Venture capital and high technology. *Journal of Business Venturing* 3:159–170.

Sapienza, H.J., and Timmons, J.A. 1989. The role of venture capitalists in new ventures: What determines their importance? *Academy of Management Proceedings,* pp. 74–78.

82   S.B. EHRLICH ET AL.

Sullivan, M.K. 1991. Entrepreneurs as informal investors: Are there distinguishing characteristics? In
     N.C. Churchill, W.D. Bygrave, J.G. Covin, D.L. Sexton, D.P. Slevin, K.H. Vesper, and W.E.
     Wetzel, eds., *Frontiers of Entrepreneurship Research*. Babson College, Wellesley, MA: Center
     for Entrepreneurial Studies, pp. 456–468.

Tyebjee, T.T., and Bruno, A.V. 1984. A model of venture capitalist investment activity. *Management
     Science* 30(9):1051–1066.

Wetzel, W.E., Jr. 1985. Informal investors—when and where to look. In S.E. Pratt and J.K. Morris, eds.,
     Pratt's Guide to Venture Capital Sources. Wellesley Hills, MA: Venture Economics, Inc.
     11:91–96.

[25]

CORPORATE VENTURE
CAPITAL: STRATEGIES
FOR SUCCESS

HOLLISTER B. SYKES
New York University

EXECUTIVE SUMMARY

Currently, about 80 major companies have venture capital programs that were started for strategic reasons—to help foster new business development. Yet the results have been mixed. Some companies consider their programs successful. Others have doubts. Others have quit.

To explore causes for this disparity of results, survey data were gathered from 31 major corporations through questionnaires and follow-up interviews. Only strategic investment programs, where the motivating purpose is to assist corporate new business development, were covered. Programs conducted solely for financial return were excluded. Data on two modes of venture capital investment were obtained: venture capital investment (VCI) directly in new ventures and investment in venture capital limited partnerships (VCLPs) managed by private venture capital firms.

Corporations were asked to rate, on a five-level scale, the overall contribution (added value) of their programs in meeting their strategic objectives. In the survey, eight factors were probed to determine their possible effect on the strategic value rating. Four of these factors appear to have a significant influence on strategic value: choice of primary strategic objective, type and frequency of communications with the ventures or VCLPs, return on portfolio investment, and mode of investment (VCI vs. VCLP).

Objectives that produce a mutually supportive environment, such as formation of corporate/venture business relationships, are more likely to lead to success. Objectives that induce a potential conflict of interest between the corporations and the venture, such as venture acquisition, may lead to a nonproductive environment and failure of the relationship.

Modes of communication that involve direct and frequent contact between the corporation and the venture regarding areas of special or mutual interest produce the highest strategic value. Of questionable value are routine reports and attendance at venture board meetings.

Reported return on investment for those programs that had been in operation for five or more

Address correspondence to Professor Hollister B. Sykes, Graduate School of Business Administration, New York University, 100 Trinity Place, New York, NY 10006.

Journal of Business Venturing 5, 37–47

0883-9026/90/$3.50

38   H. B. SYKES

years averaged 14 to 15%. Portfolio ROI% was positively related to strategic value in the case of investment in VCLPs, but no significant relationship was found in the case of VCI investments.

Comparison of the strategic value of direct vs. VCLP investment showed opinion predominantly in favor of direct investment if only one strategy were chosen. However, as the interviews brought out, the two programs can serve somewhat different purposes and be complementary to one another. The most effective combination is one in which the VCLP investments provide contacts with the venture capital community and "deal flow" *and the direct investments* enhance specific business relationships *such as marketing or research agreements.*

The implication of these results for corporate investors is that program strategic success can be significantly enhanced by a proactive approach involving frequent interaction with the ventures or venture capital firms regarding specific issues of mutual interest. One of the most effective channels for interaction is through the formation of business relationships ("strategic partnerships" in current parlance). Financial returns will probably be acceptable and additive to any strategic returns.

INTRODUCTION

The sole investment objective of the private venture capitalist is return on capital. On the other hand, the primary objective of most corporate venture capital programs is strategic. The impact of possible capital gains on total corporate results is viewed as minor compared with the potential for development of new business.

In the 1960s a number of major U.S. corporations began to experiment with venture capital as a supplement to internal new business development activities. Direct venture capital investment (VCI) programs were started at Dow, DuPont, Exxon, Ford, General Electric, Grace, Hercules, Singer, and Union Carbide, among others. The strategic objectives of these programs were to provide a "window" on potential new business growth areas and to provide a source of potential acquisitions for entry into these new areas.

The "window" concept appeals because history demonstrates that major new business growth areas have evolved from new products originally developed by innovative small companies. Melberg and Fast (1980) and Klein (1987) recommend venture capital investment as a way to provide early insight into the potential for a new business market or technology. However, venture capital investment as a means to acquire independent new ventures often hasn't worked out. Hardymon et al. (1983) note that the venture capital opportunities available to a corporation are restricted by a number of factors that diminish the chance of strategic success.

One difficulty with the "window" concept noted by Hardymon et al. (1983) and Rind (1981) is that corporate exposure to a venture's proprietary technical or marketing information can be a legal problem. As a solution Rind recommended investment in venture capital limited partnerships (VCLPs) in order to insulate the corporation from direct exposure.

In a formal research study of corporate venture capital, Siegel et al. (1988) concluded that the best *financial performance* is obtained when the corporate venture capital group has nearly independent autonomy and a committed source of funds. However, these attributes did not appear to differentiate *strategic performance*, except possibly in a negative direction when the primary strategic objective was acquisition.

Over 100 major U.S. corporations have, at one time or another, tried venture capital investment as an aid to new business development. Since 1980, the number of corporate programs has increased threefold. However, as many as one quarter of the companies who have tried such investing have since stopped, and a number of others have questioned the value of the activity. Those continuing investment are trying new approaches to improve results. A few consider their programs to be very successful.

This range of experience could result from random distribution, but it seems probable that certain management approaches work better than others. From prior experience and talks with personnel at a number of companies with active venture capital programs, we assembled a list of eight factors, one or more of which were believed to affect program success:

1. Choice of primary strategic objective
2. Type and frequency of contact between the corporation and the ventures or venture capital limited partnerships (VCLPs)
3. Mode of investment (direct VCI vs. investment in one or more VCLPs)
4. Portfolio financial return
5. Corporate venture capital manager experience and compensation
6. Organizational position of the primary corporate contact
7. Source of direct (VCI) investment opportunities
8. Number of corporate investors in the same VCLP

By use of a questionnaire, these eight factors were probed to determine their possible effect on the perceived strategic value of the venture capital programs. To measure strategic value, the corporate personnel were asked to rate, on a five-level scale, the overall contribution (added value) of their programs toward meeting the corporate new business development (strategic) objective.

Based solely on statistical measures, the first four factors had the most significant effect on strategic value. The results related to these factors will be reviewed in some depth, followed by a brief commentary on findings related to the other factors. Results are reported on two levels: statistical analysis of data obtained from questionnaires sent to each corporation and interpretive comments based on interviews with the corporations.

STUDY SCOPE

Venture capital investment as used herein is defined as the purchase of non-publicly traded equity in an *independently* managed start-up or growth company. Therefore, this study does not include internally developed and managed corporate ventures. Also, this study is concerned with only "strategic" venture capital investments—those undertaken for the primary purpose of assisting corporate new business development. Investment programs managed strictly for financial return, such as corporate pension fund investments or the investments of GE's former GEVENCO affiliate, are not part of this study.

Two generic modes of strategic corporate venture capital investment are followed: investments managed through an independent venture capital limited partnership (VCLP) and direct venture capital investment (VCI) in individual ventures. Data on both modes were obtained and analyzed in this study and will be referred to by the abbreviations VCI and VCLP.

DATA BASE

Eighty-six corporations known to have venture capital investment programs were asked to respond to a questionnaire covering their objectives and investment management practices. Thirty-three provided data for the questionnaire. Two of these responses fell outside the scope of this study, leaving 31 usable for analysis. The data were supplemented through personal or telephone follow-up interviews.

40   H. B. SYKES

TABLE 1   Investment Profile for Companies in the Study

Median per company	VCI group	VCLP group
Time since first investment, years	4	4
Number of investments, total	4	6.5
Investment rate, $M/year	2.3	4.9

Of the 31 companies, 25 had made investments in venture capital limited partnerships and 26 had made direct investments in individual ventures. Twenty companies had made both kinds of investments. This provided an opportunity to compare the two modes of investment for relative strategic value.

The fractional (38%) response rate raises the question of nonrespondent bias. To check this we called all of the nonrespondent companies and determined that 21 (24%) did not have adequate records to respond because of limited programs or because their programs had been abandoned and 11 (13%) had a corporate policy against replying to such inquiries. Only 21 (24%) would not respond at all. We attribute this to work priorities rather than any reluctance to reveal their program results. Consequently, we estimate that about 60% of those companies that could have provided useful data were sampled and that the data are reasonably representative.

Annual revenues for all but two companies in our sample were in excess of $1 billion. All were industrial or communications companies. The median investment profile for those corporations making VCI and VCLP investments is summarized in Table 1.

PROGRAM STRATEGIC VALUE RATING

The major dependent variable in this study is a five-level rating $(-1, 0, +1, +2, +3)$ by the corporate respondents which measured their perception of the overall strategic value of the program to their corporation. Only 36 to 40% of the companies rated program value at the highest level of $+2$ or $+3$. Twenty to 24% said the program was of nil (0) to negative (-1) overall strategic value. The distribution of the value ratings is depicted in Figure 1.

Because the perceived strategic value rating (referred to as "VALU") is a qualitative and personal judgment, personal bias of the respondents could affect the answers. To test for bias, the VALU data were sorted into two groups. The "a" group included those respondents employed by or directly responsible for the VC program. All other respondents were included in the "b" group. A chi-squared test indicated that correlation of VALU with the group type was not significant ($p > .5$ for the VCI data and $p > .2$ for the VCLP data). However, the "a" group comprised 70 to 80% of the respondents. If there was bias among this group, we believe it reasonable to assume that it affected the absolute rather than relative valuations.

PRIMARY STRATEGIC OBJECTIVE VS. VALUE

Venture capital investment is a strategy that has been recommended (Melberg and Fast 1980; Klein 1987; Rind 1981) to meet various corporate new business development objectives. A list of possible strategic objectives, drawn from our prior discussions with corporate venture

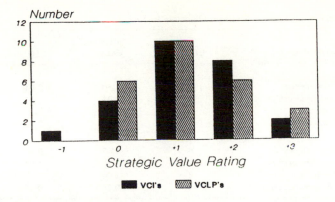

FIGURE 1 Distribution of value ratings.

capital groups, was provided in the questionnaire. Respondents were asked to rank them in order of their program priority. Table 2 lists the strategic objectives and the mean of the priority rankings for each investment mode (VCI vs. VCLP).

Identification of new business opportunities (the "window" objective) and development of business relationships ranked at the top of the list. Typical business relationships include agreements under which the corporation markets products developed by the venture or the venture conducts research in its area of specialization for the corporation.

Our primary interest was to determine whether choice of primary objective resulted in significant differences in rated strategic value of the overall program. For instance, Hardymon et al. (1983) had questioned the efficacy of venture capital–related acquisitions. To test this, the objective ranked #1 by each respondent was compared with their program strategic value ranking (VALU). Table 3 lists the mean of the VALU rankings for each group of companies that cited the same first-priority objective.

In the VCI group, the acquisition objective yielded the lowest mean VALU rating. Of the five companies who listed acquisition as their primary objective, the two with the most experience (investing for five or more years) gave their programs the lowest VALU ratings. Their overall program valuations were − 1 and 0, both lower than the five-company mean. In the VCLP group, the acquisition objective also scored a low mean value. To test the

TABLE 2 Strategic Objective Rankings

	Mean priority ranking	
Strategic objective	VCIs	VCLPs
Identify new opportunities	2.0	2.9
Develop business relationships	2.4	2.7
Find potential acquisitions	3.3	3.8
Learn how to do venture capital	—	4.0
Change corporate culture	4.2	—
Assist spin-outs from the corporation	4.7	4.7

42   H. B. SYKES

TABLE 3   Relation of Primary Strategic Objective to VALU

Primary strategic objective	Count	Mean VALU	SD	TSp*
VCI group				
Identify new opportunities	10	1.60	0.84	.021
Develop business relationships	9	1.33	1.00	.054
Change corporate culture	1	1.00	—	—
Find potential acquisitions	5	0.40	0.89	base
VCLP group				
Identify new opportunities	6	1.67	0.82	.054
Develop business relationships	12	1.50	1.00	.056
Find potential acquisitions	2	1.00	0	base
Learn how to do venture capital	4	0.25	0.50	.041

*Significance of mean VALU differences tested by two-sample *t* tests of each mean relative to the "base" mean VALU.

significance of differences in VALU rankings for the objectives, two-sample *t* tests were performed and are listed in the column headed "TSp".[1]

The numerical results were directionally supported by our interviews with the company representatives. Several commented that initiating venture capital investments with the intention of using them as an option for future acquisition induces a negative environment. The better entrepreneurs and venture capitalists don't want to lose the option of taking the venture public at some point.

COMMUNICATIONS VS. STRATEGIC VALUE

Achievement of any of the *strategic* objectives would, of course, depend on effective communication between the corporate managers and the venture or VCLP managers. The questionnaire provided a list of types of contact, drawn from previous interviews, and asked the frequency of each. To compare type and frequency of communication with VALU, the companies were grouped into three samples according to VALU rating. The first sample, the "failures," includes programs with VALU ratings of −1 and 0. The second, or middle sample includes all data from programs with a VALU rating of 1. The third sample, the "successes," includes programs with VALUs of 2 and 3. The mean frequencies of each type of communication for the "failure" and "success" samples were compared for significance by a two-sample *t* test.

Table 4 summarizes the types of communication examined and the two-sample significance for the "failure"/"success" pair, referred to by the abbreviation "TSp."

Data on frequency and type of VCI contact showed significant two-sample VALU differences in only two instances: corporate requests for expert advice from the ventures and meetings with the ventures regarding business relationships. However, this significance was not confirmed by Pearson correlation of the complete spectrum of frequency data because of wide scatter of data in the middle group (VALUs of 1). Routine contacts and commu-

[1]The relationship between pairs of continuous variables was tested for significance by two-sample *t* tests of means. Because of the small sample size, significance tests were calculated assuming samples with separate variances. All significance figures are reported as one-tailed probabilities that the null hypothesis is true. Two-sample probabilities are indicated by the abbreviation "TSp."

TABLE 4 Relation of Frequency of Communication to VALU

Type of communication	"Failures"			"Successes"			
	n	Mean	SD	n	Mean	SD	TSp
VCI group							
Corporate requests for expert advice from a venture	3	0	0	6	5.00	4.10	.020
Corporate meetings with ventures regarding business relationships	4	0.25	0.50	6	8.33	6.71	.020
Periodic reports by ventures on their activities	4	7.00	3.83	6	9.50	3.89	.175
Investment opportunities submitted by the ventures to the corporation	2	2.50	3.54	5	103	272	.186
Board meetings attended by corporate representatives	5	4.40	4.51	8	6.13	3.80	.249
Venture requests for expert advice from the corporation	4	3.25	4.57	6	5.17	3.43	.253
VCLP group							
Corporate requests for meetings with the VCLP managers	4	0.25	0.50	7	2.43	1.40	.004
Investment referrals from VCLPs	3	2.33	0.58	8	27.1	31.4	.032
Corporate/venture contacts initiated by the corporation	4	0.75	0.96	7	6.14	6.79	.043
VCLP requests for advice from the corporation	3	2.67	2.31	8	13.6	15.3	.044
Corporate/venture contacts initiated by the VCLP	3	1.00	1.00	7	21.0	35.1	.093
VCLP routine reports on venture activities	3	4.33	1.53	7	3.20	1.10	.169
VCLP routine reports on deals seen	3	5.00	6.24	6	6.40	4.59	.377
Corporate requests for investment advice from VCLPs	4	2.25	2.06	8	3.13	3.27	.293

nication, such as periodic reports by the ventures on their activities and attendance at board meetings, were of intermediate or questionable value by both statistical methods.

The VCLP data provided a more definitive confirmation of the VCI results. Direct communications between the corporation and the ventures or VCLP regarding items of special interest (such as investment referrals) were of significant value. Periodic routine reports were of questionable value. Moreover, the significance of the VCLP two-sample differences shown in Table 4 was confirmed by Pearson correlations using the complete spectrum of data.

Formation of Business Relationships

Communication between the corporation and individual ventures concerning some activity of mutual interest would be expected to be more meaningful than routine meetings or standardized information exchange. As demonstrated by the communication data, such interaction is likely to result from the formation of business relationships such as research contracts or marketing arrangements. Data on the number of business relationships formed in the course of each program were obtained and compared with the strategic value rating.

In Table 5, the corporate programs are grouped in ranges according to the number of business relationships entered. Mean program VALU ratings are listed for each group.

44 H. B. SYKES

TABLE 5 VALU vs. Number of Business Relationships

Number of business relationships entered	Mean VALU	Count	SD	Mean VALU significance TSp*	TSp*
VCI group					
0	0	6	0.6	base	.003
1–2	1.2	5	0.4	.003	base
3–4	1.4	7	0.5	.001	—
4+	2.0	5	0.7	.001	.035
VCLP group					
0	0.7	10	0.5	base	.065
1–2	1.3	6	0.8	.065	base
3–4	1.5	2	0.7	.195	—
4+	2.5	4	0.6	.005	.016

*Significance of mean VALU differences tested by two-sample t tests of each mean relative to the "base" mean VALU.

For both types of programs, two-sample t tests indicate a significant relationship between the perceived strategic program value and the number of business relationships entered. Pearson correlations of VALU vs. number of business relationships entered confirmed these results ($R = .60, p = .001$ for the VCI group; $R = .75, p = .001$ for the VCLP group). To test whether time was a factor, Pearson correlations were also run on VALU vs. the number of relationships entered *per year*. For the VCI group, $R = .4$ and $p = .03$; for the VCLP group, $R = .8, p = .006$.

Our interviews supported the statistical findings. Respondents stressed that communication between the venture and those corporate units having a specific strategic interest is necessary for an effective relationship. Also, there were some strong opinions that the most valuable communication was at direct working relationship meetings with individuals in the ventures, rather than at board meetings.

A number of company representatives said they would not make an equity investment in a new venture unless there was some kind of business relationship involved. One said, we will "continue to invest only in companies where we have a contractual business relationship," and "an operating division must sponsor and take responsibility."

A representative of one of the companies expressed doubts that "pure" equity investments (meaning without concurrent business relationships) would yield insights that couldn't as well be obtained through a business relationship.

Contacts with the Investment Community

A good "deal flow" is considered necessary to provide a wide choice for investment. The VCLP data indicated that there was significant value in the investment referrals to the corporation by the VCLP managers. In the VCI survey we collected data on the sources of investment referrals. Venture capitalists were the most frequent sources (an average of 27% vs. the next highest referral source, corporate personnel, at 20%).

Contacts with the investment community, primarily venture capitalists, are developed through VCLP investments and coinvestments with the VCLPs in individual ventures. Effective working relationships are built over time, usually by coinvesting. For example, we found a significant (Pearson $p = .038$) relationship between the percentage of referrals from venture capitalists and the number of years the VCI program had been in operation. The average percentage of referrals from this source was 42% for those programs with terms of five years or more, versus an average of 22% for those programs in operation for less than five years.

STRATEGIC VALUE OF VCI VS. VCLP INVESTMENT

An obvious issue is whether one mode of investment is more effective than the other. And, is it useful to have both types of programs? During interviews each respondent was asked to compare the relative *strategic* value of direct investment in ventures vs. investment in limited partnerships. From the 20 companies that had both types of programs, we obtained 17 responses. Of these, 10 favored direct VC investments (VCIs), six were neutral, and one favored VCLP investments.

Although qualitative opinion was predominantly in favor of direct investment, given only one choice, the respondents noted that the two programs can serve somewhat different purposes and be complementary to one another. This distinction was most evident from the comments of those individuals in companies that had been active for many years in both types of programs. In their opinion, the most effective strategy is a combination of both modes of investment. The VCLP investments *provide contacts with the venture capital community and "deal flow;"* and the direct investments *enhance specific business relationships*. Investment first in VCLPs provides a useful learning experience, although it should not be the primary objective.

RETURN ON INVESTMENT VS. STRATEGIC VALUE

Unlike independent venture capital funds, most corporations do not make venture capital investments primarily for investment return. Those few who have done so generally set up the venture capital program as a more autonomous operation, which in several cases (GE, Grace, and Inco) has eventually resulted in spin-out of the activity as an independent fund, often including other institutional investors as limited partners. (Data from these companies were eliminated from our data base.)

Strategic value ratings were compared with reported ROI% to determine whether there was a significant relationship. A positive relationship to rated VALU was found in the case of the VCLP programs (Pearson $R = .53, p = .02$), but was less significant for the VCI programs ($R = .36, p = .12$). These results could mean that higher financial returns increase strategic value *or* that the strategic value ratings were biased by the level of ROI% achieved.

Although return on investment is not a primary corporate objective, it seems logical that if a venture cannot survive commercially, it is a poor prospect as a "window" on opportunity. More critically, it would be a poor candidate for a business relationship. The spokesman for one corporation stated that they have a policy of investing only in those ventures in which venture capitalists have already invested. He considered this an important test of economic viability.

Our ROI data showed no correlation with the number of years the VCI or VCLP programs had been in operation, which would indicate no experience effect. However, factors other than experience are involved, for example the methods of evaluating portfolios before there are earnings or public trading of the shares and the time it takes for failures to show up.

46 H. B. SYKES

In assessing average financial results of the venture capital programs, we excluded data from those programs that had been in operation for four years or less. The averaged annual ROI for the nine VCI programs that had been in operation for five years or more was 15%. Four reported returns of 10% or less, and four reported returns of more than 20%. The average ROI for 11 VCLP programs was similar, at 14%. Five reported returns of 10% or less, and four reported returns of more than 20%.

On balance it can be concluded that strategic investment programs for the past few years have had a positive financial effect. So the strategic benefits, if any, did not come at an average net cost to the companies.

OTHER FACTORS

The primary *source of investment opportunities* for direct investment was referrals from venture capitalists. As noted previously, the percentage of referrals from venture capitalists increased significantly with the term of the venture program. However, we found no significant correlation between program strategic value and the dominant source of referrals.

Neither the *term of the program* nor the years of *venture capital experience* of the corporate program managers showed a significant correlation with strategic value. However, there was a very significant correlation (Pearson $p = .006$) between the term (years) of the program and the number of corporate venture capital program personnel who left each year to join private venture capital firms.

The *primary contact person* between the corporation and a venture, after the investment has been made, can be from several organizational locations, e.g., the venture capital program group, R&D department, or line operating divisions. We found no significant strategic value associated with these three locations or the *position level* of the contact person. However, a spokesman for one of the highest-rated programs expressed the opinion that, to satisfy the "window" objective, the primary contact should be a high-level person with broad contacts throughout the corporation and credibility with both top and operating management.

In the last few years *"focused"* VCLPs, dedicated to serving the specific business area interests of a sole corporate investor, have made an appearance. This is almost like having a direct investment portfolio, except independently managed. Our data were too sparse to compare this mode of investment with investment in the more common VCLPs which have multiple investors (limited partners). Only two companies in our survey were sole investors in at least one VCLP in addition to being one of three or more investors in other VCLPs. Both companies reported that the sole investor relationship was more strategically effective.

MANAGEMENT IMPLICATIONS

Several implications for management can be derived from the results of the statistical analysis supplemented by the interview comments. One failure mode of corporate venture capital may be pursuit of the wrong objective. Objectives that produce a potential conflict of interest between the corporation and the venture can lead to a nonproductive environment and failure of the relationship. Objectives that produce a mutually supportive environment can lead to success.

Corporate conflict of interest objectives include:

- A unilateral corporate desire for acquisition
- Expectation of strategic information input in exchange for equity investment only

Mutually supportive objectives include:

- Investment for the primary purpose of building a viable, independent company (the venture capitalist's objective)
- Establishment of mutually beneficial business relationships, such as marketing agreements
- Corporate assistance to the venture in areas of the corporation's expertise in return for a window on emerging technologies and markets

The working relationship between the corporation, the venture, and the venture capital community will be improved by emphasis on organizational and management strategies that:

- communicate awareness of each other's specific needs and interests between the individuals concerned,
- balance the needs of one party with the motivation to fill those needs by the other party, and
- build long-term relationships.

Corporations should continue to employ venture capital investment as one mode of remaining alert to new opportunities for business development in areas that relate to or could be extensions of their existing business. Use of venture capital to explore entirely new, unrelated business areas also may be of value, but development of effective communication channels and implementation of follow-on strategies will be more difficult because it will be more difficult to find areas for mutually beneficial business relationships.

REFERENCES

Hardymon, G. F., DeNino, M. J., and Salter, M. S. May–June 1983. When corporate venture capital doesn't work. *Harvard Business Review* 114:120.

Klein L. E., Winter 1987. How a venture capital initiative can help the corporate 'intrapreneur': A case study. *Business Development Review* 1(4):22–27.

Melberg, R. S., and Fast, N. D. 1980. Identifying new business opportunities. *SRI International, Business Intelligence Program*. Guidelines No. 1053, November.

Rind, K. W. 1981. The role of venture capital in corporate development. *Strategic Management Journal* 2:169–180.

Siegel, R., Siegel, E., and MacMillan, I. C. Summer 1988. Corporate venture capitalists: Autonomy, obstacles, and performance. *Journal of Business Venturing* 3(3):233–247.

Name Index